PROPERTY LAW AND PRACTICE

PROPERTY LAW AND PRACTICE

Clare Harris

and

Anne Rodell

CLP

Published by

The University of Law,
2 Bunhill Row, London EC1Y 8HQ

British Library Cataloguing-in-Publication Data

A catalogue record for this book is available from the British Library.

ISBN: 978 1 80502 172 8

Typeset by Style Photosetting Ltd, Mayfield, East Sussex

Tables and index by Moira Greenhalgh, Arnside, Cumbria

Preface

This book is intended as an introduction to property law and practice for those studying on the Legal Practice Course. It is hoped, however, that it will also be of use to others wanting an introduction to property practice and procedure. Its approach is essentially practical, and it does not pretend to contain a detailed analysis of the underlying law. Some background law is included, but it is assumed that readers will have the basic knowledge of land law and contract on which an understanding of property law and practice depends.

We should both like to acknowledge the debt we owe to Neil Duckworth, co-author of previous editions of this book, whose support and advice to students and colleagues alike was unfailing. He is much missed.

Thanks also to all our colleagues and students at The University of Law for their assistance, some of it unwitting.

The law is generally stated as at 1 May 2025.

Clare Harris
Birmingham

Anne Rodell
Guildford

Acknowledgements

The Standard Conditions of Sale and the Standard Commercial Property Conditions are reproduced for educational purposes only by kind permission of the Solicitors' Law Stationery Society Limited and The Law Society of England and Wales.

We also acknowledge with thanks the kind permission of The Law Society to reproduce the following:

- the Law Society Conveyancing Protocol;
- the Law Society's formulae for exchanging contracts by telephone, fax or telex;
- the Law Society's code for completion by post;
- the form of undertaking to discharge building society mortgage.

Contents

Table of Cases

Table of Statutes

Bill

International legislation

Table of Statutory Instruments, Codes, Rules, Conditions and Guidance

Glossary of Terms

Absolute title	This is the best of the four classes of title that Land Registry can give to land.
Abstract of title	A summary of the title deeds and documents which prove title to unregistered land. Nowadays an epitome of title is normally used.
Acknowledgement and undertaking	A confirmation contained in a deed that the person named has the right to see a document not in their possession and a promise that the person who has possession of that document will keep it safe.
Additional rent	A sum payable under a lease (eg, service charge payments) which is to be treated as rent, giving the landlord the same remedies as if it were rent.
Adverse possession	The occupation of land without the permission of the owner. In certain circumstances after 12 years of such possession (unregistered land) or 10 years (registered land) the occupier may gain title to the land.
Adverse rights	Sometimes used to refer to the rights which someone other than the owner may have over land.
Agreement for sale	Another name for the contract setting the agreed terms of a sale.
Alienation clause	Provision in a lease which restricts the tenant's rights to assign or sub-let.
Apportionment	The process of adjusting the purchase price of land to take account of outgoings that affect it. In leasehold property, rent and service charges are normally paid in advance, so on completion of the sale the buyer will have to pay to the seller an extra sum equivalent to the payments in advance made by the seller.
Appurtenant	A right benefiting a piece of land (eg, an easement) can be said to be 'appurtenant' to that land.
Arbitration clause	A clause in an agreement (eg, a lease) requiring disputes to be referred to a third party for resolution in accordance with the Arbitration Acts.
Arm's length	A transaction between parties who are not associated in any way.
Assign	To transfer a right in property over to another. Usually used to signify the transfer of a lease.
Assignee	The person who receives the property being assigned.
Assignment	The document by which property is assigned — usually used in relation to the transfer of leases.
Assignor	The person who transfers the property.
Attestation clause	The part of a document containing the signatures of the parties.

Bailiff	An officer of the court charged with serving documents and enforcing judgments.
Banker's draft	A cheque drawn by a bank (rather than by a private individual) usually on its own head office. It is generally accepted as the equivalent of cash, although it needs to be paid in through the bank's 'clearing system' in the same way as any other cheque.
Beneficial owner	The person who is entitled to enjoy the benefit of property (as opposed to a trustee who owns land for the benefit of someone else).
Benefit (of a covenant)	The right to enforce compliance with it.
Body of deed	The operative part of a deed — as opposed to the recitals.
Boiler plate clause	Standard provision included in a legal document.
Break clause	Clause in a lease which allows one party to terminate the lease before its normal expiry date.
Bridleway	A path or road over which the public have the right to pass on foot or with horses and bicycles, but not with vehicles.
Building lease	Long lease under which the tenant is obliged to carry out some building work on the demised property.
Building regulation approval or consent	Confirmation that the plans for proposed building work show that it will comply with the Building Regulations. All building work has to comply with prescribed standards and the local authority is charged with ensuring compliance (although the NHBC will normally undertake such responsibility in relation to a new house to be covered by its structural insurance).
Burden (of a covenant)	The obligation to comply with it.
Call option	An agreement under which a party can, within a defined period, 'call' on (or compel) the other to sell their property.
Caution	Under LRA 1925 a method of protecting a third-party right in registered land. This could be entered on the register without the consent of the proprietor. Cautions can no longer be used under LRA 2002, but existing registrations remain effective.
Caveat emptor	Let the buyer beware — emphasising that it is the buyer's responsibility to discover problems with the property, not the seller's to disclose them.
Cesser	The premature ending of a right.
Charge	An interest in land securing the payment of a debt; a mortgage.
Chattels	Items of property other than land, eg, furniture. They will be excluded from the sale of land — unless there are specific provisions in the contract to the contrary.
Chief rent	Used in certain parts of the country to describe a rentcharge.

Clear lease	A lease under which the landlord is under no liability to pay for insurance and repairs, ie, the rental income is 'clear' of these obligations.
Comfort letter	A letter under which an assurance is given that the sender will behave in a particular way, eg, that the sender will provide funds for a particular purpose.
Common land	Land over which the inhabitants of a locality can exercise rights, eg, grazing.
Common parts	The parts of a development used in common by all the occupiers, eg, the hallways and stairs in a block of flats or the car park in a business park.
Concurrent lease	A lease granted to run at the same time as an existing lease. The tenant under the concurrent lease will then become the landlord of the tenant under that existing lease. Sometimes used in flat management schemes.
Conservation area	An area of special architectural or historic interest so designated by the local authority in order to preserve or enhance its character or appearance. Special planning rules will apply restricting development in the area.
Conveyance	The document used to transfer ownership to another. Usually used in unregistered land.
Corporeal hereditament	Physical property, eg, land, buildings, as opposed to incorporeal hereditaments such as easements.
Counterpart lease	A lease is normally drawn up in two identical copies: the lease signed by the landlord and the counterpart signed by the tenant. Each party then keeps the part signed by the other.
Covenant	An obligation entered into by a landowner. In certain circumstances this can be binding on subsequent owners of the land.
Covenantee	The person to whom the promise is made, ie, taking the benefit of the covenant.
Covenantor	The person making the promise, ie, bearing the burden of the covenant.
Curtilage	Old fashioned term used to refer to the land occupied along with a property, eg, the garden of a house.
Dedication	Giving rights over land for public use, eg, the dedication of land for use as a highway.
Deed	A document executed in accordance with various formal requirements. It must be signed and witnessed and then delivered.
Defective title insurance	Insurance taken out to protect a buyer and/or lender against the consequences of a specified defect in title up to the financial limit specified in the policy.
Delivery	One of the formal requirements for a deed. A deed will be delivered when the signatory intends it to be binding on them. This is usually on payment by a buyer of the purchase price.

Demise	A lease; the grant of a lease. Sometimes used to indicate the property granted by a lease.
Devise	A gift of property by a will.
Disbursements	Payments made by a solicitor on behalf of the client, eg, search fees.
Dominant tenement	The piece of land which benefits from an easement.
Due diligence	The proper steps to be taken by a professional in connection with a particular transaction to ensure that it is lawful.
Easement	A right over one piece of land for the benefit of another, eg, a right of way.
Enfranchisement	In leases, the process of tenants acquiring the freehold in their land.
Engrossment	The final version of a document which will be signed by the parties. Traditionally prepared on better quality paper than mere 'drafts' of the document.
Epitome of title	A chronological list of the documents which prove title to unregistered land. It will usually be accompanied by photocopies of the documents.
Escrow	A deed which has been signed but only delivered conditionally. It will not become operative until the condition (eg, the payment of money) is fulfilled.
Estate rentcharge	A rentcharge imposed on freehold land to ensure the running of the burden of postitive covenants.
Execution	Signing and delivering a deed to make it legally effective.
Fair wear and tear	Damage caused by the ordinary operation of natural causes. Sometimes in a lease a repairing obligation does not include damage caused in this way.
Fine	A non-returnable lump sum payable by a tenant to a landlord on the grant of a lease in addition to rent. A premium.
Fixtures	Items fixed to land which become part of it and will pass to a buyer on a sale unless specifically excluded by the terms of the contract.
Flying freehold	A part of a freehold property which lies over land belonging to someone else.
Forfeiture	A landlord's right to terminate a lease prematurely due to the tenant's breach of their obligations.
Good leasehold title	One of the classes of title conferred by Land Registry. It guarantees the ownership of the lease but not that the landlord had the right to grant that lease.
Ground rent	The rent payable to a landlord, particularly in relation to leasehold houses and flats where the tenant will have paid a premium on the grant of the lease to cover the cost of the house and will effectively just be renting the 'ground' on which the building stands.

Guarantee	Promise given by a guarantor
Guarantor	Person who promises to perform an obligation if there is default by the person who has taken on the obligation, eg, the tenant under a lease.
Habendum	The part of a deed which describes the property being transferred.
Head-lease	A lease granted directly by the freeholder. Used where the tenant under that lease has then granted a sub-lease of all or part of that property.
Heads of terms	The fundamental terms of an agreement which will then form the basis of the formal contract between the parties when it is drawn up by the lawyers.
Hereditament	Real property; land.
HMRC	His Majesty's Revenue and Customs. The government department responsible for the administration and collection of taxes such as Value Added Tax and Stamp Duty Land Tax, roles formerly undertaken by the Inland Revenue and HM Customs and Excise.
Holding	The area of land demised to a tenant.
Holding over	The act of a tenant remaining in possession of the land at the end of a lease.
Improvements	Changes to property which increase its value.
Incorporeal hereditament	An intangible right over land, eg, an easement.
Incumbrance	An adverse right affecting a property, eg, a mortgage or a covenant.
Indemnity	An agreement to reimburse or compensate someone in relation to some possible future liability.
Indemnity covenant	A promise to indemnify someone against a possible future loss or expense. Often included in a transfer to protect a seller against a possible breach of obligation by the buyer for which the seller could be liable.
Indenture	A deed made between two parties. Historically, each party was given their own copy both of which had been written on. The same document was then cut into two using a wavy line.
Inhibition	Under LRA 1925 a method of protecting third-party rights over the land. Any disposition was prevented in the circumstances prescribed, eg, on bankruptcy.
Joint and several	An obligation entered into by two or more persons under which they are 'severally' or individually liable (eg, for the full amount of a debt) as well as jointly liable with the others.
Laches	Delay in enforcing a right.
Lady Day	25 March. The feast of the Annunciation of the Virgin Mary. One of the usual quarter days.

Landlord	The grantor of a lease.
Lease	Used interchangeably to mean a leasehold interest in land and also the document creating that interest.
Lessee	Tenant under a lease.
Lessor	Landlord under a lease.
Lien	The right to hold onto another's property as security for a debt.
Managing agent	Someone appointed to oversee the day-to-day maintenance of a property, eg, a block of flats or a shopping centre.
Mesne	Intermediate.
Mesne profits	Compensation due to a landowner for the unlawful occupation of their land, eg, by a tenant who holds over without the landlord's consent.
Messuage	Old fashioned term for a dwelling house.
Michaelmas	29 September. The feast of St Michael. One of the usual quarter days.
Midsummer Day	24 June. The feast of St John the Baptist. One of the usual quarter days.
Minor interest	Under LRA 1925, an interest which had to be protected by an entry on the register in order to bind a purchaser.
Office copies	The name formerly used for official copies — but still often used in practice.
Official copies	Copies of the register entries relating to a title.
Party wall (or fence)	A wall (or fence) owned jointly by adjoining landowners over which both have rights and responsibilities as to maintenance.
Peppercorn rent	A nominal rent.
Perpetuity	Forever.
Planning permission	Permission required from the local authority to develop land.
Possessory title	One of the classes of title the Land Registry may grant. Often granted when the owner claims to have lost the title deeds, or to have acquired ownership by adverse possession.
Pre-emption	A right of first refusal.
Premium	A non-returnable lump sum payable by a tenant on the grant of a lease in addition to rent.
Prescription	The acquisition of legal easements by long user — often 20 years user as of right will suffice.
Public bridleway	A path or road over which the public have the right to pass on foot or with horses and bicycles, but not with vehicles.

Public footpath	A path over which the public have rights to pass on foot only.
Public highway	A road over which the public have rights to pass on foot and with vehicles.
Put option	A contract under which a party has the right, but not the obligation, to sell their land to another.
Quarter days	25 March; 24 June; 29 September; 25 December. The days on which (traditionally) rent was payable. Still much used in commercial leases as rent payment days.
Rack rent	Open market rental.
Reddendum	The part of a lease which specifies the rent payable.
Rentcharge	A sum of money payable by the owner of freehold land.
Reversion	The interest which the lessor retains after the grant of a lease, ie, the right to repossession when the lease terminates — if the lease was granted by the owner of the freehold the grantor then has a freehold reversion.
Riparian rights	The rights of a landowner over a non-tidal river adjoining their land, eg, rights to fish.
Sale and leaseback	An arrangement in which a landowner sells the freehold and then takes back a lease of the property from the new freeholder. Often used to free up capital tied up in freehold land.
Seisin	Old-fashioned term denoting the possession of freehold land.
Service charge	Payment made by an owner of property towards the landlord's costs of the upkeep of the 'common parts', eg, the repair and maintenance of a block of flats or shopping centre.
Side letter	A letter accompanying a legal document, eg, a contract, explaining or clarifying the intentions of the parties.
Stamp Duty Land Tax	Tax payable to the Government (inter alia) on the purchase of property or the grant of a lease. Known as stamp duty until 1 December 2003.
Sub-lease	A lease granted by a person who is a tenant. Must be of a shorter duration than the head-lease.
Sub-lessor and sub-lessee	The parties to a sub-lease.
Surety	Person who promises to perform an obligation if there is default by the person who has taken on the obligation; a guarantor.
Surrender	The premature termination of a lease by agreement between landlord and tenant.
Tenancy	Often used instead of lease for short term, eg, 10 years, 21 years or periodic tenancies.

Tenant	The person to whom a lease is granted.
Tenant's fixtures	Chattels fixed to leasehold property by a tenant which, although strictly fixtures, can be lawfully removed by the tenant.
Term	The duration of the lease.
Term of years	A leasehold interest in land (an archaic alternative to lease).
Title	The ownership of a piece of property. Often also used to signify the documents used to prove ownership.
Transfer	The document used to pass the ownership of land to another. Usually used in relation to registered land.
Travelling draft	The draft of a document that 'travels' between the parties and on which the various amendments required are made. Will nowadays often be sent electronically.
Tree preservation order	An order made by the local planning authority preventing the felling or lopping of trees without permission from the local authority.
Trigger notice	A notice required to initiate some procedure — usually used in relation to a notice required to initiate a rent review under a lease.
Turnover lease	A lease (eg, of retail premises) where the rent is fixed as a percentage of the annual turnover.
User	The use to which a property can be lawfully put.
Usual quarter days	25 March; 24 June; 29 September; 25 December. Days on which rent was traditionally payable. Still frequently used in commercial leases as rent payment days.
Vacant possession	Having no tenant or other person in occupation.
Waiver	The abandonment of a right, eg, of the right to forfeit a lease.
Warranty	A promise as to the truth of a statement.
Yield up	To give up possession at the end of a lease.

Table of Abbreviations

AGA	authorised guarantee agreement
ATED	annual tax on enveloped dwellings
CGT	capital gains tax
CHAPS	Clearing House Automated Payment System
CIL	Community Infrastructure Levy
CLLS Protocol	City of London Law Society Land Law Committee Protocol for Discharging Mortgages of Commercial Property
CMA	Competition and Markets Authority
CPSE	Commercial Property Standard Enquiries
CRA 2015	Consumer Rights Act 2015
CRAR	Commercial rent arrears recovery
EPA 1990	Environmental Protection Act 1990
EPC	Energy Performance Certificate
ERRA 2013	Enterprise and Regulatory Reform Act 2013
F&C	Fittings and Contents Form (TA10)
FCA	Financial Conduct Authority
GPDO	Town and Country Planning (General Permitted Development) Order 1995
HMRC	His Majesty's Revenue & Customs
LCA 1972	Land Charges Act 1972
LDF	Local Development Framework
LPA	local planning authority
LPA 1925	Law of Property Act 1925
LP(R)A 1938	Leasehold Property (Repairs) Act 1938
LRA 1925	Land Registration Act 1925
LRA 2002	Land Registration Act 2002
LTCA 1995	Landlord and Tenant (Covenants) Act 1995
MEES	Minimum energy efficiency standard
MHCLG	Ministry of Housing, Communities and Local Government
NHBC	National House Building Council
NLIS	National Land Information Service
NPPF	National Planning Policy Framework
NPV	Net Present Value
OMRV	open market rental valuation
PD	Particulars Delivered
PIF	Property Information Form (TA06)
PR	privately rented
PRA	Prudential Regulation Authority
SC	Standard Conditions
SCPC	Standard Commercial Property Conditions
SDLT	stamp duty land tax
SRA	Solicitors Regulation Authority
TCEA 2007	Tribunals, Courts and Enforcement Act 2007
TCPA 1990	Town and Country Planning Act 1990
TID	Title Information Document
UCO	Town and Country Planning (Use Classes) Order 1987
VAT	value added tax
VATA 1994	Value Added Tax Act 1994

PART I

ESSENTIAL BACKGROUND

CHAPTER 1

Introduction to Property Law and Practice

LEARNING OUTCOMES

After reading this chapter you will be able to:

- identify the two land systems in existence in England and Wales and how they differ
- explain the current status of e-conveyancing

1.1 WHAT IS 'PROPERTY LAW AND PRACTICE'?

Property Law and Practice is the law and practice involved in the transfer and creation of interests in land, an area of practice that has historically been gathered together under the umbrella term 'conveyancing'. For many, conveyancing means the process of buying and selling a home, allegedly one of the most stressful times in a person's life. It is the conveyancer, or property lawyer, who must manage this process and endeavour to make it as efficient and painless as possible.

Residential conveyancing is, however, only one aspect of a typical property lawyer's work. The property lawyer will often be much more involved in conducting commercial transactions. These will range from acting on the sale or purchase of a small corner shop, to the multi-million sale or purchase of a large office development or shopping centre. Property lawyers will also be involved in the sale and purchase of land that is going to be the site of some major new development such as a housing estate, or a commercial or industrial site. Most commercial or industrial developments will not be occupied by their owners; instead, they will be leased out to business as shops, offices or factories. The grant and approval of commercial leases and the management of the on-going relationship between a landlord and a tenant also fall within the ambit of a typical property lawyer's work.

There are many reasons why property practice, and the procedures associated with it, have developed in the way they have. Two are worth mentioning at the outset. First, land is a comparatively complex form of property, and it can be subject to or have the benefit of many different kinds of rights and restrictions. Identifying what these are (and ensuring that any problems associated with them are dealt with) forms an important part of the property lawyer's day-to-day job. The stages that make up a typical property transaction have, in part, evolved to facilitate this. Secondly, the sums of money involved in buying a property are often considerable. Managing the financial aspects of a transaction therefore also forms an important part of the property lawyer's work. In the residential context, in particular, this is likely to involve acting for the lender as well as the borrower, ensuring the lender is willing to release the funds it has agreed to advance, but also ensuring that lender's security is properly protected in the form of a mortgage. Again, these demands have helped shape the form that a typical property transaction takes.

1.2 APPROACH TAKEN BY THIS BOOK

This book is intended as an introductory work for those who have little or no experience of conveyancing in a practical context. It is set out in a chronological sequence, taking the reader through the steps in a simple transaction from beginning to end in the order in which they would occur in practice. In order to set this in context, **Chapter 2** gives an overview of a typical transaction.

Most land is owned freehold, and the major part of this book concentrates on the procedures relating to freehold tenure. In many respects, the procedure adopted in a leasehold transaction is identical to that used in freehold conveyancing. Where leasehold procedure differs from that for freeholds, this is considered in **Part VII** of this book. An introduction to the drafting and approving of commercial leases and the security of tenure given to business tenants is also included.

The procedures used in residential and commercial conveyancing are broadly similar to one another. Commercial transactions may involve more money than residential ones, but the objective of both types of transactions remains the same, namely, the safe, speedy and efficient transfer of ownership from seller to buyer. If the solicitor does not achieve this, whether in the domestic or the commercial sphere, they will not have done their job properly and risk being sued for negligence. Where the steps to be taken in a commercial transaction differ from those in a residential transaction, this is indicated at the appropriate stage of the proceedings.

In order to assist the reader, this book has eight appendices which contain materials supplementing the main text. This includes **Appendices 2** and **3**, which contain copies of the two main forms of standard contractual provisions used by property practitioners. The Standard Conditions of Sale (which will be referred to in the format 'SC 1.1.1' etc in this book) are the form most commonly used in residential transactions. The Standard Commercial Property Conditions (which will be referred to in the format 'SCPC 2.2.2') are based on the Standard Conditions of Sale but have been tailored to deal with the specific demands of commercial transactions.

1.3 THE RELATIONSHIP OF CONVEYANCING AND LAND LAW

Property law and practice is about buying and selling interests in land, and so a decent understanding of underlying principles of land law is inevitably required. In order to assist, **Chapters 3** and **4** contain an overview of the main issues.

It should be understood, however, that the property practitioner encounters land law in a practical context, and so uses land law as a tool in order to address the client's needs rather than as a thing in itself. By way of example, a buyer will not be interested in the technical requirements that must be met in order for a right of way to qualify as a legal easement. Instead, they will want to know whether the property has the rights of way it needs and is not subject to any that will diminish its value. The task of the property lawyer is to address both the practical and the technical aspects of this.

1.4 REGISTERED AND UNREGISTERED LAND

Strictly, it is the *title* to the land rather than the land itself that a seller sells to a buyer in a conveyancing transaction. It is important, therefore, to remember that there are two systems in existence in England and Wales by which title to land is proved. These are the registered and unregistered systems. The main difference between the two lies in the way in which the seller proves their ownership of the property to an intending buyer. Although the basic format of a property transaction is the same irrespective of whether title is registered or unregistered, some of the detailed steps differ as a result, and these will be considered where they occur as appropriate throughout this book.

However, given the fundamental importance of this distinction, the difference between the two systems will now be briefly explained.

1.4.1 The unregistered system

Under the unregistered system, a seller proves their title by establishing that they have been in undisturbed possession of the land for a long time. Possession, and thus ownership, is proved by the seller producing the deeds by which title has changed hands (historically called 'conveyances') and other documents dealing with the ownership of the land during that time. Collectively these are known as the 'title deeds'. The seller is required to show the buyer title deeds that demonstrate the seller's undisputed ownership of the land from the present day to a point in time at least 15 years before.

There is logic in this method, as if the seller can prove that they have been in undisturbed possession for this length of time and has the title deeds, it is fair to assume that they are the owner. If anyone else had rights in relation to the land, the logical assumption is that they would not have let the seller remain on the land for so long without claiming possession. However, the process of producing and then checking all the documents needed to establish this chain of ownership is cumbersome, time-consuming and expensive, and must be repeated each time the land is sold. The system is also not without its flaws, since a competent forger would have little difficulty in producing an authentic and convincing set of fake documents. Further, deeds and documents can always get lost.

1.4.2 The registered system

In order to simplify and speed up conveyancing, and to lessen the opportunities for fraud, the registered system of conveyancing was introduced.

The idea of the registered system is that the Government maintains a register of title to land, land transfers take place by notifying the registry of the change of ownership, and the details recorded at the registry are amended accordingly. This is a concept similar to the DVLA, which keeps a central record of motor vehicles and which must be notified on the change of ownership of a vehicle.

The register for each title shows the extent of the land concerned by reference to a plan based on the Ordnance Survey map. The register sets out the benefits enjoyed by the land (eg, the benefit of a right of way over neighbouring land) and also contains details of the burdens attached to it (eg, restrictive covenants which have to be observed by the owner).

When an intending buyer wants to check the title which they are buying, a quick search of the register at Land Registry will confirm the information needed.

Placing all the land in England and Wales on the register is a time-consuming process, but it will lead to the gradual elimination of the unregistered system.

1.4.3 The systems exist in parallel

The registered system now dominates conveyancing, but there are still large pockets of land, some in rural areas, others owned by large trusts, which continue to be unregistered.

The progress of the registered system was achieved by gradually making designated areas of the country 'compulsory' areas, so that within these areas, when land was sold, it was obligatory to register it and, afterwards, to carry out all further dealings with the land using only the registered system. By this approach, much land was entered on the register, but it was only in 1990 that the last compulsory registration order was made, so that it became compulsory to register land on any freehold sale throughout England and Wales. It was only from 1 April 1998 that changes of ownership following death and gifts of land became compulsorily registrable.

Although all areas of the country are now 'compulsory' as far as registration is concerned, broadly, registration occurs only when there is a triggering event (see **4.3.2.1**). Thus, although the amount of land governed by the unregistered system is getting gradually smaller, some land will remain unregistered for the foreseeable future. For this reason, property lawyers need to know and to understand the mechanics of both systems. A brief explanation of the operation of each system is set out in **Chapter 4**.

1.5 E-CONVEYANCING

For several years, from the turn of the new millennium, Land Registry has been working towards a system that would allow the whole conveyancing process to be effected electronically, by the use of documents drafted and signed electronically. The thinking is that this will streamline and speed up the process. The Land Registration (Amendment) Rules 2018 (SI 2018/70), which came into force on 6 April 2018, allow for registrable dispositions of registered land to be carried out using electronic documents with electronic signatures. However, this is only available when the Chief Land Registrar is satisfied that adequate arrangements are in place and publishes a notice to this effect. At the time of writing, no such notice has been published by the Chief Land Registrar.

Nonetheless, certain e-services are already provided by Land Registry through two online channels, the portal and Business Gateway. These services are only available to customers who have signed up to them and include:

(a) *Information Services*. Customers can request information from Land Registry online. So they can lodge searches of the index map with supporting plans, official searches of whole or part and conduct land charges and bankruptcy searches in the Land Charges Department.

(b) *Network Services*. Certain applications to change the register can be lodged online. For example, customers can change proprietors' names due to marriage and remove the name of a deceased joint proprietor from the register. A standard form electronic charge (which has been executed electronically by the borrower), known as e-CSF, can also be registered electronically. (See <http://www.landregistry.gov.uk/professional/business-e-services/network-services>.)

(c) *Lender Services*. Mortgage lenders can discharge their mortgages over the Internet, using the e-DS1 system (see **30.7.1.10**).

(d) *Digital Registration Service*. This service allows customers to electronically submit substantive applications based on scanned images of the original paper registration documents and any supporting evidence. The service calculates the fee automatically and provides prompts to upload relevant documents. It can be used to update registered titles (amongst other things) but cannot yet be used for first registration applications.

(e) *Digital Mortgage Service*. This is available to a restricted number of users where there will be no simultaneous change of registered proprietor (eg a re-mortgage). A digital mortgage is a mortgage deed that has been created, signed and dated electronically, without the need for a witness as the identity of the signatory has been identified in advance.

Despite these steps towards an online e-conveyancing system, the process is still predominantly paper based, although further developments in the future are anticipated.

1.6 PRACTITIONER TEXTS

As indicated, this book offers a comprehensive but broad overview of property law and practice. Readers will find it useful to refer to more detailed texts on specific topics, and at the end of most chapters, relevant sources have been identified for this purpose. However, the following is some guidance on texts that are of general use.

1.6.1 General textbooks

F Silverman, *The Law Society's Conveyancing Handbook* (published annually). This contains The Law Society's recommended methods of practice.

The loose-leaf work, *Emmet & Farrand on Title* (Sweet & Maxwell) is a recognised authority on many aspects of conveyancing law, especially those relating to legal title. *Ruoff and Roper: Registered Conveyancing* (Sweet & Maxwell), another loose-leaf service, is perhaps the major work on registered land. *Woodfall on Landlord and Tenant* (Sweet & Maxwell) is a valuable resource on matters relating to leasehold land.

For a fuller explanation of the land law principles on which conveyancing is based, reference should be made to a standard land law textbook such as *Megarry & Wade: The Law of Real Property* (10th edn, 2024).

1.6.2 Precedents

Many precedent books (which are used to assist in drafting documents that may be required in a transaction) also exist. The well-known examples are: *The Encyclopedia of Forms and Precedents*, vols 35–38 (Butterworths), which carries a comprehensive range of model documents and clauses designed to fit most situations; and TM Aldridge, *Practical Conveyancing Precedents* (Sweet & Maxwell), which contains a selection of precedents drafted in simple, modern language.

1.6.3 The Internet

The Land Registry website (www.landreg.gov.uk) is valuable resource containing practice and other guides as well as many of the forms that are used when dealing with registered titles.

In addition, government departments with responsibility for matters which impact on property are a useful source of information, in particular the Ministry of Housing, Communities and Local Government, whose website at <www.gov.uk> contains much concerning town and country planning and related matters.

SUMMARY

- There are two land systems in existence in England and Wales – unregistered and registered.
- The registered system dominates the conveyancing process, but large pockets of land remain unregistered.
- Certain dealings with registered land may be dealt with electronically. The intention of Land Registry is that, in the future, the whole conveyancing transaction will be undertaken electronically. However, plans to implement an electronic form of transfer have recently been put on indefinite hold, due to concerns over the risk of fraud.

CHAPTER 2

OUTLINE OF A SIMPLE TRANSACTION

LEARNING OUTCOMES

After reading this chapter you will be able to:

- outline the steps in a simple conveyancing transaction
- explain the implications of linked transactions
- explain the purpose of the Law Society Conveyancing Protocol.

2.1 HOW A CONVEYANCING TRANSACTION WORKS

A typical conveyancing transaction divides into three stages:

(a) the pre-contract stage;

(b) the post-contract (or pre-completion) stage; and

(c) the post-completion stage.

In terms of time, the pre-contract stage is the longest, and much of the legal work involved in the transaction is done at this time. Assuming that matters proceed smoothly, the pre-contract stage of a residential transaction may take four to six weeks from the date when instructions are first received. The post-contract stage may then be much shorter, often no longer than two weeks, and the post-completion stage represents the 'tidying up loose ends' process after the buyer has bought the property. It is unrealistic in most circumstances to expect the transaction to be accomplished in less than about six to eight weeks from start to finish, and sometimes, due to delays caused by parties over whom the solicitor has no control (eg, delays by a local authority in returning a search application, or delays by a lender in processing a buyer's mortgage application), the transaction may take much longer than either the solicitor or the client feels is reasonable.

In commercial transactions, different considerations apply, and a much shorter timescale has often to be achieved in order to meet the needs of the clients. However, the procedure to be followed is basically the same.

This chapter contains a brief overview of the form a typical transaction takes to give context for the remainder of the book. A flowchart showing the steps is to be found at the end of the chapter.

2.2 OUTLINE OF A SIMPLE TRANSACTION

2.2.1 Marketing the property

The transaction will begin with the seller putting the property on the market in the hope of finding a buyer. The seller will usually engage an estate agent to assist in this process. Before marketing can start, the seller (or the estate agent) will need to have commissioned (but not necessarily received) an Energy Performance Certificate (EPC). Detail on the timing and function of this document is considered in **Chapter 8**. Estate agents are required to provide 'material information' on all residential property listings, defined in detail in s 230(2) of the Digital Markets, Competition and Consumers Act 2024 for conduct taking place on or after 6 April 2025, and in the Consumer Protection from Unfair Trading Regulations 2008 for conduct taking place before this date, as 'information which the average consumer needs, according to the context, to take an informed transactional decision'. Guidance is contained in 'Material Information in Property Listings (Sales)', available at <www.national trading standards.uk>, and includes the price, Council Tax, tenure, physical characteristics of the property, utilities and restrictions and rights.

Once a buyer is found and a price agreed, the conveyancing process can then begin. It should be understood that, at this stage, the parties have not entered into any legally-binding relationships with each other, and either of them can walk away from the transaction at any point until exchange of contracts. The steps that make up the remainder of a conveyancing transaction are the steps that are needed ensure that this happens in a smooth and safe manner, so that the property is validly transferred from the seller to the buyer. These steps will now be considered in turn.

2.2.2 Taking instructions

From 6 December 2018, all firms regulated by the SRA have to comply with the SRA's Transparency Rules 2018, which require them to publish price and service information for certain areas of law on their website, or on request if the firm does not have a website. One of the areas to which this applies is residential conveyancing, specifically freehold or leasehold residential sales or purchases, mortgages and remortgages. The information to be provided includes the total cost of the service (or the average cost or range of costs), the basis for the charges, including any hourly rates or fixed fees, a description of, and the cost of, any likely disbursements (or the average cost or range of costs) and whether any fees or disbursements attract VAT. This is so that individual and business consumers have the information they need to make an informed choice of legal services provider.

Once the solicitor is retained by the client, instructions must be taken. Those instructions should normally be confirmed to the client in writing, together with written information relating to the costs which the client will have to pay for the work to be done by the solicitor. At this stage it will also be necessary to obtain documentary proof of the client's identity – whether buyer or seller – in order to comply with anti-money laundering regulations. Following this, the seller's and buyer's solicitors must attend to different aspects of the transaction.

2.2.3 The pre-contract stage

Having taken instructions, the seller's solicitor must prepare the pre-contract package for the buyer. This comprises:

(a) the draft contract, showing what land the seller is selling and on what terms they are prepared to sell it;

(b) evidence of the seller's legal title to the property, to prove that they own and are entitled to sell the land; and

(c) sometimes, the results of pre-contract searches which the seller has made and other information about the property.

The package may also include such items as copy local authority planning permissions, which the buyer's solicitor will want to see to make sure that the property which the client is buying was permitted to be built on the site.

When the buyer's solicitor receives the pre-contract package from the seller's solicitor, they will check all the documents supplied very carefully to ensure that the terms of the contract accord with their instructions and do not reveal any problems which might make the property an unsuitable purchase for their client. Although the seller has a limited duty to disclose defects in their legal title (but not physical defects), the *caveat emptor* principle ('let the buyer beware') applies to conveyancing, so that it is the buyer's responsibility to find out all the information which they need to know about the property before committing to the purchase.

2.2.3.1 Title

The pre-contract package will include documents showing proof of the seller's ownership of the land. The buyer's solicitor must check these documents carefully to ensure that the seller is entitled to sell what they are purporting to sell. Any queries arising out of the title documents are raised with the seller's solicitor by means of 'requisitions'. These are questions or 'requests' addressed to the seller, requiring them to resolve any apparent problems with the seller's ownership, or 'title' as it is usually referred to. The contract normally contains a clause excluding the buyer from questioning the seller's title once contracts for the sale and purchase have been entered into. In such a case it is essential, therefore, for any problems with title to be raised and resolved prior to a binding contract being entered into. If the buyer's solicitor discovers problems with the seller's title at this stage, the buyer can withdraw from the transaction without penalty since no formal contract yet exists between the parties.

2.2.3.2 Searches

It is the application of the *caveat emptor* principle which makes pre-contract searches necessary. These searches, many of them made with public bodies such as the local authority or Land Registry, will reveal a large amount of information about the property, all of which will help the buyer to make up their mind whether or not to proceed with the purchase. In some cases, the seller's solicitor will submit the search applications and pass their results to the buyer's solicitor with the pre-contract package. If this has happened, the buyer's solicitor still needs to check that the correct searches have been made and that their results are satisfactory. In most cases, the buyer's solicitor will make the search applications themselves. In this situation the search applications need to be sent to the relevant authorities as soon as firm instructions to proceed have been obtained, otherwise the time taken to receive search replies may cause a delay in the transaction. The National Land Information Service (NLIS) provides an Internet-based 'one-stop shop', enabling information kept by a variety of public and other bodies to be accessed more efficiently and speedily than by requesting the information separately from each individual body.

2.2.3.3 The buyer's finances

The buyer's solicitor must check that their client is able, in financial terms, to proceed with the transaction. Unless the client has sufficient available cash to purchase the property, they must have received a satisfactory offer of finance and have available sufficient money overall to afford the transaction, including associated costs such as stamp duty land tax. The client must also be able to fund the deposit which traditionally is payable on entering into a contract to buy land. Traditionally, this was 10% of the purchase price and a sum that lenders would expect the buyer to provide separately to the amount advanced under the mortgage. Although banks will offer mortgages at higher loan to value ratios, since the 'credit crunch' they are moving back to offering their most attractive deals only to those borrowers who can provide a decent deposit. It should be noted that in commercial transactions, sometimes no deposit at all will be paid.

2.2.3.4 The draft contract

When the buyer's solicitor is satisfied with their search results, with the proof of the seller's ownership (title) and with the terms of the draft contract (they may have negotiated some amendments to the contract with the seller's solicitor), they will be ready to return the draft contract to the seller's solicitor, telling them that the buyer has approved the terms and is now ready to enter the contract. The contract is then prepared for the clients' signatures. Two copies of the contract, incorporating any agreed amendments, are printed off; the seller signs one, the buyer the other. The contract comes into existence by 'exchange of contracts' (ie, the buyer receives the copy signed by the seller and the seller the copy signed by the buyer). However, prior to physical exchange, which is effected through the post, it is usual for the parties to agree over the telephone that the contract should come into existence at the moment of the telephone call. This is often referred to as 'telephonic exchange'.

2.2.4 Exchange of contracts

The exchange of contracts marks the stage in the transaction at which a binding contract comes into existence. Until exchange, no contract exists between buyer and seller, and either is free to change their mind about the transaction and withdraw from it. It is this aspect of conveyancing procedure that is most frequently criticised; remember, in a residential transaction, there could well be six weeks or more between a solicitor being instructed and contracts being exchanged, and if either party withdraws at the last minute before exchange, this can cause great inconvenience to the other party. Once exchange has taken place, a binding contract exists and usually neither party can withdraw without incurring liability for breach of contract. On exchange, the buyer will normally pay a deposit. This was customarily 10% of the purchase price and will be held by the seller's solicitor until completion. The money serves as a 'statement of intent' by the buyer that they are serious about the transaction and intend to fulfil their contractual obligations. If the buyer fails to complete, the seller can usually forfeit the deposit and retain the money.

2.2.5 Post-contract stage

Since most of the important stages of the transaction have now been accomplished, the pre-completion, or post-contract, stage of the transaction should be less onerous for both sides. Although it is often necessary for the buyer to insure the property on exchange, the first step is normally for the buyer to 'raise requisitions' with the seller. Historically, the purpose of requisitions was to clarify any queries which had arisen out of the seller's proof of ownership of the property, but in modern conveyancing, where proof of title is invariably a pre-contract issue, requisitions are more likely to be directed at the resolution of procedural queries relating to the mechanics of completion itself. For example, the buyer needs to know precisely how much money is required from them to complete the transaction, where completion is to take place and who holds the keys to the property. These queries are usually raised on a standard form which is sent to the seller's solicitor for their replies.

2.2.5.1 The draft transfer deed

At the same time as sending the requisitions, the buyer's solicitor sends the draft transfer deed to the seller's solicitor, for their approval. In registered land, this will take the form of a transfer, as prescribed by the Land Registration Rules. In unregistered land, it may take the form of a traditional conveyance, although usually a form of Land Registry transfer is used.

Although it was the seller's solicitor's duty to prepare the contract, customarily it was the buyer's solicitor who prepared the transfer deed itself. However, it is increasingly common for the contract to provide that the seller will draft the transfer. This will then be provided to the buyer at the same time as the draft contract. This can help to prevent delays between exchange and completion. The contract states what the parties have agreed to do; the transfer deed carries it out. In other words, the transfer deed activates the terms of the contract and brings them alive; this deed must therefore be drafted to reflect the terms of the contract (no new terms can be introduced at this stage) and the seller's solicitor will check the draft deed to ensure that the buyer's solicitor has done the job properly (if the buyer's solicitor has prepared it). The seller's solicitor's approval of the draft transfer deed is normally notified to the buyer's solicitor at the stage when the seller's solicitor replies to the buyer's solicitor's requisitions. The transfer deed can then be 'engrossed', ie a copy is prepared containing any agreed amendments; this is the copy which will be signed by the parties.

The seller must always sign the transfer deed, otherwise the legal estate in the land will not pass. Usually the buyer also signs, but there are circumstances in which it is not necessary for them to do so.

2.2.5.2 The buyer's lender

At the same time as the transfer deed is being prepared, it is also necessary for some work to be done on behalf of the buyer's lender. At the time when a mortgage offer was made to the buyer, the lender would have instructed solicitors to act for it in connection with the loan. The lender needs to be certain that the property which it is accepting as security for the loan has a good title (ie, it needs to carry out the same investigations as were carried out on behalf of the buyer in this respect) and various documents need to be drawn up to put the mortgage into effect.

2.2.5.3 Acting for the buyer and the lender

Frequently, in a residential transaction, the solicitor who is acting for the buyer will also be instructed to act for the buyer's lender. Acting for more than one party in a transaction is restricted by para 6.2 of the SRA Codes of Conduct, but acting for buyer and lender in a residential transaction is usually permitted; see **Chapter 5**. The solicitor who is acting for the buyer's lender must:

(a) draw up the mortgage deed for signature by the borrower (buyer);
(b) certify to the lender that the legal title to the property is in order (a report on title); and
(c) obtain a clear bankruptcy search against the borrower, since the lender will be reluctant to lend money to a person who is the subject of bankruptcy proceedings.

The buyer's solicitor must also ensure that they are put in funds to complete the transaction. The seller's solicitor will have informed them of the exact amount of money needed to complete the transaction, either in answer to the buyer's requisitions or on a separate document called a 'completion statement'. In residential transactions, the amount needed to complete is often simply the balance of the purchase price, taking into account the deposit which was paid on exchange. In other cases, other sums may be due, for example payment for stock-in-trade in the case of the purchase of a business. The buyer's solicitor will notify their client of the amount due to complete the transaction by sending them a statement of account. The client will also be sent (where appropriate) a copy of the completion statement and, in residential cases, the solicitor's bill showing the fees and disbursements payable in respect of the transaction.

Commonly in house purchases, a large part of the purchase price will be provided by way of loan from the lender and/or by the proceeds of sale of the buyer's present property. This fact will be shown on the statement of account, so that the amount which the client has to find from their own funds is comparatively small.

The money which the client has to pay the solicitor to make up the balance due on completion must be paid to the solicitor in sufficient time before completion to allow that money to be cleared (ie, the normal banking process of clearing a cheque) before the solicitor uses that money to complete the transaction. The mortgage loan from the lender must similarly be obtained, so that at the time when the money is required to be sent to the seller's solicitor, all the necessary funds are cleared and are in the buyer's solicitor's client account. Usually, however, the mortgage advance will not be paid by cheque but will be transmitted directly to the solicitor's bank account.

2.2.5.4 Preparation for completion

A few days before completion the buyer's solicitor makes their pre-completion searches to ensure that no last-minute problems have occurred with the title to the property.

At the same time as the buyer's solicitor is preparing for completion, the seller's solicitor is also taking steps to ensure that completion will proceed smoothly and without delay.

2.2.5.5 Discharge of seller's mortgage

Very often the seller will have a mortgage on the property which they will have agreed contractually with the buyer to remove on completion. The seller's solicitor must now confirm with the seller's lender the exact amount of money which is required to discharge the seller's mortgage (usually referred to as the 'redemption figure'), and generally make sure that they have in their possession all the documents required to complete the transaction. This may involve the preparation of a form of discharge of the seller's mortgage if (as is usual) the seller's solicitor is also acting for the seller's lender in connection with the discharge.

2.2.5.6 Final checks

Both parties' solicitors check through their respective files and make a 'checklist' of what is to happen at completion. This is to ensure that nothing has been overlooked: no two transactions are identical, and even the most straightforward of residential transactions can throw up unforeseen last-minute complications. An appointment can then be made for completion actually to take place.

2.2.6 Completion

Traditionally, completion took place by the buyer's solicitor attending personally at the seller's solicitor's offices to hand over the money in return for the deeds, but personal attendance at completion is an expensive and time-consuming operation, especially in the context of residential transactions. It is more common today for the parties to agree to complete 'through the post'. In effect, a postal completion means that the seller's solicitor is temporarily appointed to be the agent for the buyer's solicitor, and while acting as such must carry out all the steps which the buyer's solicitor instructs them to do (ie, all the things which the buyer's solicitor would be doing if they were physically present at completion).

The method by which completion is to be effected will have been agreed by the respective solicitors at the 'requisitions' stage of the transaction. If a postal completion is to take place, the time at which completion is due will have been agreed in the course of a telephone conversation between the parties' solicitors, and the buyer's solicitor will have given the seller's solicitor precise instructions as to what is required to be done. This is in accordance with the guidelines for postal completions issued by The Law Society (the 'Code for Completion by Post') (see **Appendix 5**).

On the morning of completion day, the first priority is to transmit to the seller's solicitor the money which is required to complete the transaction. Without tangible evidence that the buyer has paid, the seller will not complete. With a postal completion, the money is usually sent to the seller's solicitor's bank account by an electronic transmission of funds from the buyer's solicitor's bank account to the seller's solicitor's account. No physical transfer of the money takes place: the buyer's solicitor's account is debited with the requisite sum, a corresponding credit being entered in the seller's solicitor's account. This is still sometimes referred to by the old term 'telegraphic transfer' or 'TT'.

When the seller's solicitor's bank receives the funds from the buyer's solicitor's bank, the bank should notify the seller's solicitor that the funds have arrived, so that the seller's solicitor can proceed with completion itself. In practice, this is little more than a formality. The deeds may have to be checked on behalf of the buyer's solicitor, the transfer deed dated, the estate agent informed that completion has taken place (so that the agent can release the keys of the property to the new owner), and the deeds themselves sent by first-class post to the buyer's solicitor. The seller's solicitor will then telephone the buyer's solicitor to inform them of the safe arrival of the money and that completion has taken place in accordance with their instructions.

The clients themselves do not attend completion but should be informed by telephone immediately after completion that it has taken place: the sellers are told that they are now in funds with the proceeds of sale; the buyers are told that they now own, and can take possession of, their new property.

2.2.7 Post-completion

2.2.7.1 The seller's solicitor

The seller's solicitor now has some loose ends to tie up. First they must send to the seller's lender the amount required to pay off the seller's mortgage, obtain a receipt for that money and send the receipt to the buyer's solicitor, who will need this receipt to prove to Land Registry that the mortgage has been discharged. They must also account to their client for the proceeds of sale and, if not already done, prepare and submit their bill of costs. The proceeds of sale should be dealt with on the day of completion, or as soon as is possible. A solicitor who delays in returning money to a client may have to pay interest on that sum to the client under the SRA Accounts Rules 2019. The seller's solicitor can close their file when they have dealt with these matters.

2.2.7.2 The buyer's solicitor

The buyer's solicitor must deal with the payment of stamp duty land tax (SDLT). More detail about rates of tax and the method of payment is to be found in **Chapters 6** and **31**. Where SDLT is payable, it must usually be paid within 14 days of completion; failure to pay within this time attracts fines and penalties. Particulars of the transaction (ie, who has sold what to whom and at what price) must be delivered to HMRC after completion in the form of a land transaction return. A certificate is then issued by HMRC as proof that these requirements have been complied with. Without this certificate it is not possible to register the transaction at Land Registry. Without registration the buyer will not acquire legal ownership to the property.

After these formalities have been completed, the buyer's solicitor must apply to Land Registry for their client's title to be registered. Land Registry will provide the buyer with a Title Information Document (TID) which contains a copy of the register showing the buyer as the new registered proprietor as confirmation of ownership. When they have checked that the details contained in the TID are correct, the buyer's solicitor should forward the TID, together with any other relevant documents, to the lender or, if the property is not subject to a loan, to the buyer, for safe-keeping. However, due to increasing costs of storage, most mortgage lenders do not wish to receive any documents relating to the mortgaged property and the solicitor must either pass them to the client or store them themselves. After they have received an acknowledgement from the lender or buyer and all other outstanding matters have been satisfactorily dealt with, the buyer's solicitor may send their file for storage.

2.3 LINKED TRANSACTIONS

In many residential transactions, the client will be selling one house and buying another. The intention is to move from one to the other on the same day, using the money obtained from the sale transaction towards payment of the purchase price of the house they are buying. In such a case, the sale and purchase transactions are inextricably linked: the client cannot afford to buy the new house unless they can also sell the old one; neither does the client want to sell the existing house unless they can buy a new one in which to live, since a sale without a related purchase would leave the client homeless. This is sometimes described as the 'no home/two homes' syndrome; neither situation is desirable from the client's point of view. The solicitor's objective is to ensure that at any one time the client owns only one house and that at no time is the client without a home. The sale and purchase transactions must therefore be synchronised, and failure to achieve synchronisation where the client has instructed it will prima facie be negligence on the part of the solicitor. It follows that, where the solicitor is acting in linked transactions, they will at the same time be carrying out the steps described above relating to both the seller's and the buyer's solicitor, one set of procedures being relevant to the sale transaction, the other to the simultaneous purchase.

2.4 THE CONVEYANCING QUALITY SCHEME AND THE LAW SOCIETY CONVEYANCING PROTOCOL

In 1990, The Law Society issued the first edition of the National Protocol for residential conveyancing. The Protocol was designed to standardise the conveyancing process, using uniform documentation under the brand logo 'TransAction'. A new version, entitled 'The Law Society Conveyancing Protocol', was issued in 2011 and updated in 2019. All firms that undertake residential conveyancing and want to be members of The Law Society's TransAction – Conveyancing Quality Scheme (CQS) are required to sign up to comply with the Protocol, a Client Service Charter, and mandatory training and enforcement procedures. Membership of CQS is essential for any firm wanting to be on the panels of solicitors approved by the residential mortgage lenders to act for lenders where the buyer is taking out a residential mortgage. The procedures laid down by the Protocol are intended to regulate the relationship between the seller's and buyer's solicitors, and do not affect dealings with third parties such as estate agents or lenders. Broadly speaking, the requirements of the Protocol reflect what is already standard practice within the profession and no special procedures are involved. For the sake of brevity, in the residential context, reference will be made to the parties following the Protocol as, even if the parties have not formally chosen to adopt its use, they may well use the TransAction forms in any event.

The text of the Protocol is set out for reference in **Appendix 1** and provides a further useful checklist of the procedural stages in a simple transaction.

GENERAL FREEHOLD CONVEYANCING

OUTLINE OF A SIMPLE CONVEYANCING TRANSACTION

<table>
<tr><th>SELLER</th><th>BUYER</th></tr>
<tr><td>TAKE INSTRUCTIONS</td><td>TAKE INSTRUCTIONS</td></tr>
<tr><td>PREPARE PRE-CONTRACT PACKAGE</td><td></td></tr>
<tr><td></td><td>PRE-CONTRACT SEARCHES AND ENQUIRIES</td></tr>
<tr><td></td><td>INVESTIGATE TITLE</td></tr>
<tr><td></td><td>APPROVE DRAFT CONTRACT</td></tr>
<tr><td colspan="2">EXCHANGE CONTRACTS</td></tr>
<tr><td></td><td>PREPARE TRANSFER DEED</td></tr>
<tr><td>APPROVE TRANSFER DEED</td><td></td></tr>
<tr><td></td><td>PRE-COMPLETION SEARCHES</td></tr>
<tr><td>PREPARE FOR COMPLETION</td><td>PREPARE FOR COMPLETION</td></tr>
<tr><td colspan="2">COMPLETION</td></tr>
<tr><td>POST-COMPLETION MATTERS</td><td>POST-COMPLETION MATTERS</td></tr>
</table>

The chart above shows the responsibilities of the parties' solicitors at each stage of the transaction and serves as a reminder of the various procedures which are involved and the stages in the transaction at which they take place.

SUMMARY

- A typical conveyancing transaction is broken down into three stages – pre-contract, post-contract/pre-completion and post-completion.
- Each stage consists of several key steps that the solicitors acting for the seller, buyer and lender conduct.
- In residential transactions the solicitor will often need to synchronise a sale and purchase so that one transaction does not take place without the other.
- The Law Society Conveyancing Protocol standardises the residential conveyancing procedure for those firms that adopt it.

CHAPTER 3

UNDERLYING LAND LAW PRINCIPLES – RIGHTS AND INTERESTS

LEARNING OUTCOMES

After reading this chapter you will be able to:

- identify the legal estates, legal interests and equitable interests that affect land
- explain the legal formalities necessary for property contracts and the transfer or creation of legal estates
- identify what third-party interests would bind on the purchase of a property
- describe the two forms of co-ownership and their implications for a property transaction.

3.1 INTRODUCTION

Conveyancing is concerned with the buying and selling of interests in land. As such, it is necessary to have an understanding of the underlying principles relating to land law in England and Wales in order to be able to conduct a transaction successfully. The following two chapters therefore contain an overview of the main principles. They do not pretend to be a comprehensive guide to land law, for which the reader is referred to one of the standard texts on the subject.

Chapter 3 introduces the main types of interest that are likely to be encountered in a conveyancing transaction. **Chapter 4** will explain the ways in which title is shown and how the main types of interest identified in **Chapter 3** are protected. These chapters attempt to put the basic principles of land law into the context in which you will come across them in a conveyancing transaction, and the reader may find it helpful to refer to them when reading later chapters as a reminder of particular land law topics as they arise. **Chapters 3** and **4** concentrate primarily on the principles relating to freeholds; a more detailed analysis of the underlying law relating to leasehold interests is to be found in **Chapter 34**.

3.2 LEGAL ESTATES, LEGAL INTERESTS AND EQUITABLE INTERESTS

3.2.1 Legal estates

Since 1925 there can be only two legal estates, namely an estate in fee simple absolute in possession (the freehold estate) and a term of years absolute (the leasehold estate).

3.2.2 Legal interests

The most important legal interests which can subsist today are:

(a) an easement for an interest equivalent to a fee simple absolute in possession or term of years absolute; and
(b) a charge by way of legal mortgage.

3.2.3 Equitable interests

Virtually all other estates, interests and charges in or over land other than those mentioned above will take effect as equitable interests (Law of Property Act (LPA) 1925, s 1).

3.3 FORMALITIES

3.3.1 Contracts for the sale of land

A contract for the sale or creation of an interest in land must comply with the Law of Property (Miscellaneous Provisions) Act 1989, s 2. This requires all contracts for the sale or other disposition of land (or an interest in land) to be made in writing and signed by the parties. The writing must incorporate all the terms which have been expressly agreed by the parties, and the document must then be signed by or on behalf of all the parties.

Where contracts are to be exchanged, each part of the contract must contain all the agreed terms and be signed by the appropriate party; it is not necessary for both parties to sign both parts of the contract. It is possible for the signed document to refer to another document which itself contains some or all of the agreed terms. If the document does not contain all the agreed terms, an order for rectification may be sought. The statutory requirements are normally satisfied by the preparation by the seller's solicitor of a formal contract, which is usually produced in two identical parts based on standard conditions of sale amended to fit the particular circumstances of the transaction.

There are limited exceptions where the requirement for a written contract does not apply. These include contracts to grant a lease for a term not exceeding three years taking effect in possession at the best rent without a fine (ie a capital payment) and contracts made at a public auction (where the contract is made on the fall of the hammer).

Options, equitable mortgages and side letters (variations of contract) issued in connection with sale of land transactions do need to satisfy the requirements of s 2 of the 1989 Act. Failure to satisfy the requirements of s 2 results in there being no contract at all between the parties. The court has no equitable jurisdiction to allow the enforcement of a contract which does not comply with s 2.

3.3.2 Deeds

As a general rule, a deed is required to convey or create a legal estate or interest. An important exception is in the case of the grant a lease for a term not exceeding three years taking effect in possession at the best rent available without a fine. Such a lease requires no formalities and can even be created orally. However, any subsequent assignment of it can only be effected by deed.

If the requirements of a deed are not satisfied, the transaction may still operate in equity if the conditions in the Law of Property (Miscellaneous Provisions) Act 1989, s 2 are satisfied. The example of the creation of an equitable easement in such circumstances is considered at **3.5.1.1**.

The requirements for execution as a deed are considered at **16.10**.

3.4 PROTECTING THIRD-PARTY INTERESTS

When acquiring a property, a key question to consider is whether any interests affecting that property belonging to a third party will continue to bind the new owner following acquisition. The way in which such interests are protected depends upon whether the title to the land is registered or unregistered and is considered in more detail in **Chapter 4**. In summary, in registered land, interests need be protected by entry on the register in order to bind, unless they fall within a list of interests which are said to be 'overriding' which will bind even if no entry appears in respect of them. In unregistered land, most legal interests bind automatically. Other interests will either be covered by the Land Charges Act 1972 (LCA 1972), or be binding where a buyer has notice of them. For those interests covered by the LCA 1972, registration at the Central Land Charges Registry will be necessary if they are to bind (see **4.2.2**).

3.5 EASEMENTS

An easement confers the right to one landowner to use the land of another in some way, or to prevent it being used in a certain way. Examples are a right of way (the right to cross the land of another) and a right of light (the right to have light pass into a defined aperture from over the land of another without that light being blocked). There are certain conditions which must be satisfied before an easement can exist:

(a) there must be a dominant and a servient piece of land (ie a piece of land that has the benefit of the easement and piece of land that has the burden);

(b) the right must benefit the dominant land;

(c) the dominant and servient pieces of land must not be both owned and occupied by the same person; and

(d) the right must be capable of being granted by deed and therefore must usually be:

   (i) within the general nature of rights capable of being easements, and

   (ii) sufficiently definite.

3.5.1 Creation of easements

There are three main ways in which easements may be created.

3.5.1.1 Express grant or reservation

Easements are most frequently created expressly, usually where an owner of land sells part of the property. Consideration of the creation of easements will therefore concentrate on this method. If an individual owns a piece of land fronting a road, and decides to sell part of the rear to someone, they might need to *grant* the buyer a right of way in favour of the land sold to get to the road. Equally, if the individual decides to keep the rear portion and sell the front, they might need to *reserve* a right of way in favour of the land retained.

In order to take effect as a legal easement, the right has to be created by deed and granted for a period that is equivalent to an estate in fee simple in possession or a term of years absolute. Where the land has an unregistered title, a legal easement is automatically binding and needs no further protection. Where the land has a registered title, a legal easement should be registered on the charges register of the servient tenement. Where both the servient and dominant titles are registered, a legal easement (except those already in existence on 13 October 2003) should be registered against both titles.

Express equitable easements can arise in two main ways. First, where the easement is granted for a period that is not equivalent to a fee simple or term of years. Secondly, where the formalities for a deed have not been satisfied, but the easement is created for value and satisfies the formalities for a contract for an interest in land (see **3.3.1**). Where the land has a registered title, the equitable easement should be registered on the charges register of the servient tenement. If the land is unregistered, the easement will bind only if a purchaser has notice.

3.5.1.2 Implied grant or reservation

Implied easements can be created only on a sale of part. In certain circumstances legal easements may be impliedly *granted* to the buyer of the part sold or *reserved* in favour of the land retained even though the parties have failed to provide for their express creation. The detail is considered in the context of sales of part (see **41.3**), but for the moment, it must be understood that the rules leading to the implied grant of easements are more extensive and more generously interpreted than those leading to implied reservation. It is standard practice to exclude the operation of these rules (in respect of implied grant in particular) and instead have express provisions. This will lead to greater certainty generally, and also means that the parties can address important issues such as, for example, who is to be responsible for maintenance in the case of rights of way.

Where the land has an unregistered title, a legal easement created by implied grant or reservation is automatically binding and needs no registration. Where the land has a registered title, provided certain conditions are satisfied, such easements will take effect as overriding interests.

3.5.1.3 Prescription

A legal easement may be presumed to have been granted if the claimant can show long and continuous user as of right. A claim may be made under common law rules, but more usually it is made under the Prescription Act 1832 where the period of uninterrupted user must be at least 20 years. Where the land has an unregistered title, a legal easement created by prescription is automatically binding and needs no registration. Where the land has a registered title, provided certain conditions are satisfied, such easements will take effect as overriding interests.

3.5.2 Extinguishment of easements

Easements may be extinguished in three ways:

(a) Unity of ownership of the dominant and servient tenements. If this happens the easement will not automatically revive if the tenements are subsequently split up again.

(b) Express release by deed by the dominant owner.

(c) Implied release, ie, where the circumstances imply that the dominant owner has abandoned the easement, eg, non-user for more than 20 years.

3.5.3 Easements and public rights of way

A public right of way, often encountered in conveyancing, is not an easement but a right exercisable by anyone, by virtue of the general law, to cross another's land. The surface of the land over which a public right of way exists is known as a highway.

A public right of way can be created at common law by dedication by the owner to the public, either expressly or by implication, and by the public accepting that dedication as a highway. It can also be created by statute, for example under the Highways Act 1980.

Whether or not such a highway is maintainable at the public expense is a separate matter.

3.5.4 Easements and conveyancing

Easements have a dual importance in a conveyancing transaction. First, a buyer needs to ensure that the land being purchased has the benefit of all the easements over adjoining land that are needed for the full enjoyment of the land being acquired. So, for example, if the only access to the land is over land belonging to another, a buyer should ensure that right of way over that land exists. Secondly, a buyer is concerned to see what easements affect the land being bought. So, if land is being bought for development purposes, the existence of rights of way, or drainage or other easements over it, could cause problems to that development, and thus need discovering at an early stage.

3.6 COVENANTS

3.6.1 Covenants affecting freehold land

A covenant is simply a promise made in a deed, and land may be subject to covenants which affect its use in some way. Such covenants are usually first imposed on a sale of part, where the parties need to enter covenants to govern the use of what will in effect become two new parcels of land following the completion of that transaction.

Consideration is given below to enforcement of freehold covenants. The position in respect of covenants in leases is considered in **Chapter 34**.

3.6.2 Types of covenant

Covenants imposed on land may be positive or restrictive/negative. Positive covenants are characterised by requiring active steps to secure compliance, whilst restrictive covenants limit the use of the land in some way and do not require positive acts to secure compliance. The test is the substance of the covenant, not its wording. Thus a covenant 'to leave the land uncovered by buildings' is restrictive even though it is worded in a positive form: it means 'not to build'. Equally, a covenant 'not to allow land to fall into disrepair' is positive as, even though expressed in the negative, it in effect means 'to keep in repair'. This distinction is of particular importance when considering the enforcement of freehold covenants.

3.6.3 Enforcement of covenants

As a matter of contract, the original parties to a covenant will have the benefit and burden of it and so the person to whom the covenant was given (who has the benefit of it) may sue the person by whom it was given (who has the burden of it) in the event of breach. However, a feature of land is that it does not remain with one owner forever and will pass to successive individuals over time. In order to understand what happens where this has occurred, it is sensible to take the burden and benefit of covenants separately.

3.6.3.1 Burden

The burden of a positive covenant cannot run with the land to which it is attached and so will not be enforceable directly against a successor in title. Under the rule in *Tulk v Moxhay* (1848) 2 Ph 774, however, the burden of a restrictive covenant can run with the land in equity if:

(a) it touches and concerns the burdened land;

(b) it was entered into for the benefit of the benefited land and is capable of benefiting that land;

(c) the original parties intended that the burden of the covenant should run with the burdened land and not be a purely personal matter between them; and

(d) all successors in title to the land burdened buy with 'notice' of the covenant.

The first three requirements are normally clear from the wording of the covenant. A well-drafted covenant will always say that the burden is intended to affect the land (and each and every part of it) and to run with it so as to bind successors in title (LPA 1925, s 79 implies this anyway). As regards notice, this depends on whether the land is registered or unregistered, and is considered in more detail in **Chapter 4**.

3.6.3.2 Benefit

The benefit of both positive and restrictive covenants can run with the retained land at common law and in equity. In practice, however, since the *burden* of a positive covenant cannot run with the land, the issue of running of benefit is generally of more concern with restrictive covenants.

Well-drafted covenants will always state that the benefit of the covenant is given for each and every part of the benefited land, and is intended to run with it to benefit successors in title of that land (that it is 'annexed' to it). Annexation is anyway implied by LPA 1925, s 78.

3.6.4 Indirect enforcement of covenants

The burden of a positive covenant does not run with land and the burden of a negative covenant runs only if certain conditions are met, and this may not always be the case (especially in respect of the notice requirement). There are, however, a number of ways in which the burden of both positive and negative covenants can be made indirectly enforceable in any event.

3.6.4.1 Indemnity covenants

Unless otherwise provided, the person who originally gives a covenant remains liable in contract for breach of that covenant forever, even after they have parted with the burdened land. This means that they could be sued for a breach committed by a successor in title. As a result of this, when they dispose of the property, they should obtain a covenant from the new owner indemnifying against any breach. This means that if the covenant is breached by the new owner and the original covenantor is sued, they can then in turn sue the new owner under the indemnity. Thus, even if the new owner cannot be sued directly by the person who has the benefit (because the covenant is, say, positive in nature), the threat of being made to pay up under the indemnity will have the indirect effect of getting them to comply.

A consequence of the new owner indemnifying the original covenantor is that the new owner in effect also becomes liable for breaches of covenant whenever they occur. On disposing of the property, the new owner should therefore obtain an indemnity from their successor in turn, and so on. What develops is a chain of indemnity covenants, with each successive owner indemnifying their predecessor. In practice, the procedure is extremely cumbersome, and the longer the chain the greater the risk that a former land owner cannot be traced or did not give an indemnity covenant.

It is possible to avoid the need for a chain of indemnity covenants by limiting liability under the original covenants to the period of ownership only. This approach to drafting is not, however, that common, as it may not be acceptable to the original covenantee, especially in respect of positive covenants.

3.6.4.2 Who claims the benefit must submit to the burden

Although the burden of a positive covenant cannot run with the land, there is a common law rule that a person who claims the benefit of a deed must also submit to any associated burdens contained in it (*Halsall v Brizell* [1957] Ch 169). In that case an easement of way over the roads on a housing estate had been granted to house owners, coupled with a positive obligation to contribute to maintenance of the roads. It was held that a subsequent purchaser of one of the houses who wished to use the roads must submit to the burden of the positive obligation in respect of maintenance. In order for this principle to work, the burden assumed must be linked to the benefit enjoyed, eg a payment related to services that the payer actually uses (see *Thamesmead v Allotey* [1998] 3 EGLR 97).

3.6.4.3 Deed of covenant protected by a restriction

This is the most commonly used way of making the burden of positive covenants run on land that is registered or subject to compulsory first registration. As well as entering into the original covenant, the original covenantor (owner of the burdened land) also covenants that they will not dispose of their land without procuring from the buyer a deed of covenant in favour of the covenantee (the owner of the benefitted land and their successors) in the same terms as the original covenant. To secure that obligation, the covenantor registers a restriction on the burdened land. The restriction states that no disposition of the land in the title should be registered without a certificate signed by a conveyancer confirming that the requirement to provide a deed of covenant has been met. When the time comes to sell, the original covenantor obtains the deed of covenant from the buyer (who has been alerted to the need for the deed by the presence of the restriction on the title). The original covenantor also ensures that the transfer to the buyer contains a covenant from the buyer that they will not dispose of the burdened land until they have procured an equivalent deed of covenant from their buyer. This procedure is followed every time the property changes hands, so that the covenantee has a directly enforceable covenant from each successive owner of the burdened land.

Other ways of securing the performance of positive covenants include reserving a rentcharge annexed to a right of entry and reserving a freehold right of re-entry (similar to a right of forfeiture under a lease). These methods are less commonly used and are beyond the scope of this book. It is also possible for one owner to offer the other owner a long lease rather than a transfer of the freehold title as the burden of positive covenants does run with leasehold land.

3.6.5 Covenants in the context of a conveyancing transaction

As with easements, covenants have a double impact on a transaction. First, a buyer will be concerned about the terms of the covenants burdening the land, as these may conflict with their plans or may mean that they are buying the property subject to an existing breach. Secondly, a buyer will be concerned to ensure that the property has the benefit of covenants as appropriate, for example in respect of maintenance of any shared driveways.

3.7 TRUSTS OF LAND

Where land is subject to a trust, in all but a small number of cases it will be held under what is known as a 'trust of land'. This is defined as 'any trust of property which consists of or includes land'. This includes express, implied, resulting and constructive trusts, trusts for sale, and bare trusts. Trusts of land are governed by the Trusts of Land and Appointment of Trustees Act 1996. Such trusts can be created expressly or will arise under statute, for example where land is held by co-owners or where land passes to personal representatives on the death of the owner.

Under a trust of land the legal estate is vested in the trustees, and there can be no more than four such trustees. Trustees have all the powers of an absolute owner, but restrictions may be imposed on such powers by requiring that consent be obtained, for example from a beneficiary, before a power is exercised. On the death of a trustee, the legal estate automatically vests in the surviving trustee(s) without the need for any document.

In order to buy a property which is subject to a trust of land free of that trust, the mechanism of overreaching should be employed. This is achieved by paying the purchase money to all the trustees, being at least two in number, or to a trust corporation. In such cases, the trust affecting the property is detached from it and transfers to the proceeds of sale. As such, the trust is overreached.

A small number of trusts (called 'strict settlements') are still governed by the Settled Land Act 1925 rather than being treated as trusts of land. Since 1 January 1997, no new strict settlements can be created and are not considered in detail here. Instead, a standard text should be consulted for further information.

3.8 CO-OWNERSHIP

Co-ownership arises whenever two or more people have simultaneous concurrent interests in land. The most common example is two people buying a house together. Whenever co-ownership occurs, a trust of land arises, with the legal estate being held by those to whom it is conveyed as trustees for themselves beneficially. The legal interest can only be held under a joint tenancy. As far as the beneficial interest is concerned, it may be held either under a joint tenancy or under a tenancy in common.

A conveyance or transfer deed to co-owners should state how the beneficial interest is to be held, and this is conclusive as to the position at the date of transfer. If it does not so state, it will be held as joint tenants unless either words of severance have been used in the transfer deed or an equitable presumption of a tenancy in common arises. 'Words of severance' would include phrases such as 'in equal shares', 'equally', 'half and half' and will usually create a tenancy in common.

An equitable presumption of a tenancy in common may arise where property is purchased as a partnership asset, or where the purchasers make unequal contributions towards the purchase price. The law in this area is complex, particularly where a family home is involved (see, for example, *Jones v Kernott* [2011] UKSC 53). A specialist land law text should be consulted for further detail.

3.8.1 Joint tenancy

Joint tenants are all equally entitled to the whole property and do not have individual shares. If the property is sold, they are entitled to share the sale proceeds equally. Thus three joint tenants would receive a third each.

A crucial characteristic of a joint tenancy is the 'right of survivorship'; in other words, when a joint tenant dies, their interest automatically accrues to the remaining joint tenants. Thus if three individuals buy a property as joint tenants, on the death of the first of them, the deceased person's share will pass to the survivors who will then continue to hold the property as joint tenants. On the death of the second of them, the survivor becomes the absolute owner of the property, as both the legal and equitable interest will have become vested in them alone by operation of the same rule.

3.8.2 Tenancy in common

Where the equitable interest is held as tenants in common the right of survivorship does not apply and, on the death of one of the co-owners, the equitable interest passes under the will or intestacy of the deceased co-owner. Further, tenants in common may hold equal or unequal shares in equity.

A tenancy in common in equity is suitable where the co-owners wish to control the devolution of the equitable interest either in a private or commercial context. Private individuals may decide to hold as tenants in common, but it is also particularly appropriate for partners in a business who would not normally wish their share in the partnership to accrue to their surviving partners automatically. Thus if two individuals are business partners, holding as tenants in common, on the death of one of them, the beneficial share of the deceased will pass under their will or intestacy. The legal estate (held under a joint tenancy) will vest exclusively in the surviving business partner (because of the rule of survivorship), who will hold it on trust for themselves and the estate of the deceased partner. As such, the trust of land continues and a second trustee must be appointed on sale to ensure that the trust is successfully overreached (see **3.7**).

In order to avoid subsequent disputes and litigation, it is essential that the shares of each tenant in common are expressly agreed and recorded in a deed of trust (or certified copy transfer) which is signed by the co-owners and kept in safe custody. This statement or declaration as to the division of the beneficial interest can be altered only by mutual consent of the parties.

3.8.3 Land Registry practice

Where the co-owners have indicated on the transfer that they will be holding the property as tenants in common, Land Registry will place the following restriction on the proprietorship register of the title:

> No disposition by a sole proprietor of the registered estate (except a trust corporation) under which capital money arises is to be registered unless authorised by an order of the court.

This serves as a warning to any third party dealing with the proprietors that a trust of land is in existence, and that any disposition of the legal estate must be effected by a minimum of two trustees. Although this restriction indicates that a tenancy in common exists, it does not state the proportions in which the co-owners have divided the equitable interest between them. The division of the equitable interest is not a matter with which Land Registry is concerned; it is a private matter between the co-owners. No such restriction appears on the proprietorship register if the co-owners have indicated that they wish to hold the beneficial interest as joint tenants.

3.8.4 Severance of a joint tenancy

It is possible to 'sever' a joint tenancy of the equitable interest (though not of the legal estate). Severance turns the joint tenancy into a tenancy in common in equity. It can be achieved in a variety of ways, including by written notice by one joint tenant to the other. Severance must take place whilst the parties are alive: it cannot be done by will. Bankruptcy of any joint tenant also automatically severs their beneficial interest.

3.8.5 Sale by a sole surviving co-owner

Where land has been owned by co-owners and all but one have died, a buyer purchasing from the survivor will be concerned to check that the survivor has power to dispose of the land alone, or whether it will be necessary appoint a second trustee in order to overreach the trust.

3.8.5.1 Tenants in common

In the case of tenants in common, the position is simple: a second trustee will need to be appointed. The second trustee can be appointed at any time before completion of the transaction and does not have to be appointed before the contract for sale is made. If the second trustee is appointed before the contract, they should be made a party to the contract and their name should appear as one of the sellers. This is because the second trustee now holds the legal estate as trustee and must act jointly with the other trustee. The second trustee could be any third party (eg the seller's solicitor) and does not have to be the beneficiary who has inherited the equitable interest. The buyer should also obtain a copy of the death certificate of the deceased tenant in common.

3.8.5.2 Joint tenants

On the face of it, the position in respect of joint tenants is even simpler, in that the sole survivor of joint tenants becomes the absolute owner and so has the power to sell alone without any further requirement. However, a beneficial joint tenancy can always be severed (converting the joint tenancy into a tenancy in common), and a buyer needs to take steps to ensure that when they buy a property from a sole surviving joint tenant, they are safe in assuming that this is the case.

In registered land, the buyer is entitled to rely on the register of title. If there is no restriction on the register, the buyer may assume that the co-owners were joint tenants and will take a good title from the survivor. Even if there has been a severance, if it has not been recorded by the lodging of a restriction, the buyer will generally take free of any beneficial interests that remain (but see **4.3.7.2**). The buyer should obtain a copy of the death certificate of the deceased joint tenant.

In unregistered land, protection is provided by the Law of Property (Joint Tenants) Act 1964. If certain conditions are satisfied (see **16.4.2**), a buyer is entitled to assume that the survivor is solely and beneficially entitled and so buy from the survivor alone. The buyer should obtain a copy of the death certificate of the deceased joint tenant. If the conditions explained at **16.4.2** are not satisfied, the buyer cannot rely on the Act and should require the seller to appoint a second trustee to overreach the equitable interests. Note that the Act does not apply to registered land.

3.8.6 Legal title held by one individual on behalf of themselves and others

So far, consideration has been given to the situation where the co-owners acquire the legal and equitable interest together. A related, and not uncommon, situation is for just one individual to own the legal estate, but to hold it on trust for themselves and one or more others. If the beneficiary is in occupation of the property, their equitable interest will be binding on a buyer of registered land as an overriding interest under Sch 3 to the LRA 2002. In unregistered land, if the beneficiary is in occupation, their interest is likely to be binding under the doctrine of notice. From a buyer's perspective, therefore, the status of any occupier should be checked carefully. If necessary, a second trustee should be appointed to ensure that any trust is overreached, and the occupier should agree in writing to leave the property on completion.

3.8.7 'Home rights' for 'non-owning' spouses or civil partners

The Family Law Act (FLA) 1996 applies where one spouse or civil partner owns legal title to the matrimonial home and the other does not, either having no proprietary interest or having only a beneficial one. There is the risk that the legal owner could seek to exclude their partner from the property – or even seek to sell it – relying on their sole legal ownership to do so. The FLA 1996 gives statutory rights of occupation (called 'home rights') to the non-owning spouse or civil partner. If the spouse or civil partner is in occupation of the matrimonial home, they have a right not to be excluded from it without a court order, and if the spouse or civil partner is not in occupation, they have a right to enter into occupation with a court order (s 30(2)).

It is important to note that these rights apply only to married couples or civil partners, not to cohabitees. The overreaching of any trust must also be considered as a separate matter, if applicable.

Home rights bind a purchaser for value only if they are registered. They can be registered at any time before the owner completes the sale of the home. In the case of registered land, they should be entered as a notice on the charges register of the owner's title. Home rights cannot be overriding interests. In the case of unregistered land, home rights should be registered as a Class F Land Charge in the Central Land Charges Registry against the name of the legal owner.

Family Law Act rights cannot be overreached by appointment of a second trustee. They must be waived (or removed, if already registered) by the non-owning spouse or civil partner.

Even if such rights are not presently protected by registration, the spouse or civil partner may still effect a registration at any time until actual completion of the sale of the home. It will be a condition of the contract that any such registration is removed before completion (FLA 1996, Sch 4, para 4). Negotiations must be entered into with the spouse's or civil partner's solicitors for the removal of the charge, and a satisfactory solution obtained before exchange of contracts.

It is unsafe to assume that the spouse or civil partner will not exercise the right to register a charge under the FLA 1996 prior to completion, and instructions should be obtained directly from the spouse or civil partner (through a separate solicitor if there is any possibility of conflict of interests) to confirm their agreement to the proposed sale. A formal release of rights and agreement not to enforce any such rights against the seller should be prepared for signature by the non-owning spouse or civil partner before exchange.

A registration under the FLA 1996 can be removed on production of one of the following:

(a) an application made by the person with the benefit of the rights;

(b) a decree absolute of dissolution of the marriage or civil partnership;

(c) a court order for removal of the charge;

(d) the death certificate of the spouse or civil partner.

3.9 MORTGAGES

A mortgage is a transaction where the borrower ('mortgagor') borrows money from the lender ('mortgagee') and transfers to the lender, as security for the loan, a legal or equitable interest in land. It is possible to create more than one mortgage over the same property, and as a general rule, earlier mortgages will have priority over later ones.

To be legal a mortgage must be created by deed. If the mortgaged land is registered, the mortgage must be registered as a registered charge in the charges register of the borrower's title. The lender does not obtain a legal interest until this is done. In the case of unregistered land, a first legal mortgage of a freehold will trigger first registration of the title to the land. The mortgage will appear as a registered charge on the charges register of the title. Second and subsequent legal mortgages of unregistered land (called 'puisne' mortgages) will not trigger first registration.

3.9.1 The power of sale

3.9.1.1 General

The lender under a legal mortgage has a number of remedies available in the event of default by the borrower (including simply suing for the debt) but the power of sale is one of the most important. The power of sale *arises* 'when the legal date for redemption is past' (ie when the loan is repayable). Most mortgages contain a condition providing that the power of sale will arise as soon as the mortgage is created. Under s 103 of the LPA 1925 the power of sale does not, however, become *exercisable* (ie cannot be used by the lender), until:

(a) the borrower has defaulted in a repayment of capital for three months;

(b) a repayment of any interest due is two months or more in arrear; or

(c) the borrower has broken some provision in the mortgage.

This section can be changed by agreement to the contrary, and most mortgages say that the power shall be exercisable as from the creation of the mortgage.

Note that a purchaser from a lender exercising a power of sale will take a good title if the power of sale has *arisen*. They do not have to check whether it has become exercisable, and still takes the legal estate if in fact it has not. (The lender will, however, be liable to the borrower for wrongful exercise of the power.)

3.9.1.2 Effect of exercise of power of sale

Sale by a lender under the power of sale vests the borrower's legal title in the buyer, subject to incumbrances in existence prior to the mortgage but free from those subsequent to the mortgage. So, if a lender exercises the power of sale in respect of a property that has a prior legal easement but is subject to a later, second mortgage, the buyer will take subject to the legal easement but free from the first and second mortgages. The lender exercising the power of sale will use the purchase price to pay off the expenses of sale and its own mortgage, and then hand the entire balance to the second lender which is next in priority. The borrower will receive any balance left after that mortgages have been paid off. If there is not enough money to go round, any disappointed lender will sue the borrower for debt.

The lender who is selling cannot defeat a prior mortgage. However, its statutory power of sale entitles it to promise to sell free of this prior mortgage. To fulfil the promise, the selling lender will have to redeem (ie, pay off) the prior lender from the proceeds of sale before paying off its own mortgage and handing on any balance.

If the borrower is in occupation of the mortgaged property, the selling lender will first have to obtain a possession order from the court so that the sale can be made with vacant possession.

3.9.2 Mortgages in the residential context

3.9.2.1 Suspension of possession

The Administration of Justice Acts 1970 and 1973 apply where the mortgage is of a dwelling house and the lender is bringing a claim for possession. If the court is satisfied that the borrower is likely to be able, within a reasonable period, to pay sums due under the mortgage, or to put right a breach of any other obligation in the mortgage, it can adjourn the proceedings or suspend the effect of an order for possession for a period the court thinks to be reasonable.

If the mortgage is an instalment mortgage with a provision that, if any instalment is unpaid, the entire principal becomes instantly due, the borrower has only to satisfy the court that they can pay off the outstanding instalments within a reasonable time, not the entire capital.

3.9.2.2 The borrower's spouse, civil partner or cohabitee

If husband and wife, civil partners or cohabitees co-own the legal estate, both will have executed the mortgage and both are likely to be evicted if the mortgage payments are not made (subject to obtaining relief under the Administration of Justice Acts).

If only one party owns the legal estate, a lender lending to a spouse, civil partner or cohabitee on the security of a home will still be concerned about any rights the other spouse, civil partner or cohabitee might have. There are two main reasons for this. The first is that the lender might find itself bound by an equitable interest belonging to the other spouse, civil partner or cohabitee. If the lender is so bound, it might mean that it cannot get an order for possession against that individual, because if that individual is a beneficiary of a trust of land, the court may not order possession if the beneficiary has a right to occupy the trust land (see Trusts of Land and Appointment of Trustees Act 1996, s 12). Further, even if the lender is able to get vacant possession, it will have to share the proceeds of sale with the spouse, civil partner or cohabitee. Secondly, a spouse or civil partner (but not a 'mere' cohabitee) who does not co-own the legal estate will have 'home rights' under the FLA 1996, s 30 (see **3.8.7**) whether or not they co-own in equity.

3.9.2.3 Undue influence

One important additional factor is that of undue influence. The rules governing undue influence provide protection to spouses, civil partners and other cohabitees, and are of particular concern to lenders as, if undue influence can be shown to have occurred, a party may be able to claim that they are not bound by the mortgage (and therefore can have it set aside) if they executed the mortgage only under the pressure of that undue influence.

This is perhaps best illustrated by example. Suppose that a husband and wife live together in the family home. The husband wishes to raise money to meet his business debts. The bank from which he proposes to borrow insists that any loan be secured by a mortgage of the house. His wife thinks this is imprudent and is reluctant to sign the mortgage documents. He puts pressure on her to do this and she finally agrees. They both therefore sign mortgage documents in favour of the bank. The bank could be at risk in these circumstances unless it took reasonable steps to try to ensure that the wife understood the nature and effect of the transaction, and that her consent to it was an informed consent.

The leading case on this area is *Royal Bank of Scotland v Etridge (No 2)* [2001] 4 All ER 449. The procedures to be followed to avoid the risk are considered at **5.5**.

The principles apply in all cases where there is an emotional relationship between the cohabitees. It covers not only relationships such as marriage or civil partnerships, but others, such between child and parent, if the co-owner 'reposes trust and confidence' in the borrower. The principle can apply not only where the co-owner is asked to execute the mortgage because they are a co-owner of the legal estate, but also where they are asked to execute a mortgage or to sign any form of waiver because it is thought that they might have an equitable interest in the property.

3.9.3 Leases of mortgaged property

Where mortgaged property is subject to a lease and the lender seeks to exercise a power of sale, the tenant will need to know whether their lease is binding on the lender. If it is not, the lender can sell free of it and the tenant will have to vacate the property. If the lease was granted prior to the creation of the mortgage, whether the lender can sell free depends on whether the lender was bound by the lease under basic land law principles which will be considered in **Chapter 4**.

If the lease was granted after the mortgage, the matter is governed by s 99 of the LPA 1925 which gives a borrower who is in possession of the mortgaged property a power to grant leases that will bind the lender, provided the leases meet certain criteria. This power is unpopular with lenders and can be, and almost invariably is, removed by a provision in the mortgage deed, or made subject to the lender's prior consent. If the lease is granted without the consent of the lender, the lender who wishes to sell can obtain a court order for possession against the tenant. The tenant will have no rights against the lender and will have to leave.

3.10 ADVERSE POSSESSION

The principle of adverse possession (sometimes, erroneously, referred to as 'squatters' rights') is based on the concept of the limitation of actions, in other words, that where a cause of action arises, litigation must be begun within a certain time and, if not, the claimant loses the right to sue. Applying this to trespass to land, in simple terms, if an owner fails to sue within the relevant limitation period, the trespasser cannot be sued and in effect obtains title by default. Historically, subject to certain limited differences, the principle of adverse possession applied in broadly similar ways to registered and unregistered titles. The LRA 2002 introduced major changes in the case of registered land, and so the position as regards registered and unregistered land needs to be considered separately.

In either case, the trespasser will need to provide evidence to support their case, such as statutory declarations demonstrating the length and nature of their possession of the land in question.

3.10.1 Unregistered land

In the case of the law of trespass, the limitation period is 12 years (Limitation Act 1980, s 15). In order to obtain title by adverse possession, the trespasser needs to show that they had actual possession of the land coupled with an intention to so possess the land for that period: they must combine dealing with the land in question 'as an occupying owner might have been expected to deal with it' and demonstrate 'the intention ... to exclude the world at large including the owner with the paper title ... so far as is reasonably practicable and so far as the processes of the law will allow' (*Powell v McFarlane* (1970) 38 P & CR 452). The possession of successive trespassers can be accumulated.

The effect of establishing adverse possession for the 12-year period is to defeat the title of the true owner. The trespasser in effect becomes the new owner of the land, but will take subject to any existing third-party rights, such as an easement. In certain circumstances (such as where the true owner is under a disability), the 12-year period can be extended. Further, it is possible for time to stop running, such as, for example, if the true owner begins proceedings against the trespasser, or if the trespasser acknowledges the title of the true owner to the property (Limitation Act 1980, ss 29–30).

3.10.2 Registered land

The concept of adverse possession did not fit well with the principle that the register should set out the precise details of ownership of land, and so the LRA 2002 introduced major changes in respect of registered land. Although the meaning of adverse possession has not changed (in other words, the trespasser must show the requisite amount of actual possession coupled with the necessary intention), the 12-year period has been disapplied in respect of registered land.

Instead, a squatter in adverse possession for 10 years can apply to be registered as proprietor of the land. Notice of the application will be given to the registered proprietor and certain others (eg, the proprietor of any registered charge). Any such person so notified has the right to give notice of objection to the Registrar within a specified time limit. If such notice is given then the squatter will not be registered unless one of the following conditions is met.

(a) it would be unconscionable because of an equity by estoppel for the registered proprietor to dispossess the applicant and the circumstances are such that the applicant ought to be registered; or

(b) the applicant is for some other reason entitled to be registered as proprietor; or

(c) the land in question is adjacent to land belonging to the applicant and the exact boundary has not been determined under Land Registry rules. Also, for at least the last 10 years of the adverse possession prior to the application, the applicant (or any predecessor in title) reasonably believed that the land belonged to them and the estate in the land in question was registered more than 12 months prior to the date of the application.

Where the squatter is not entitled to be registered under these provisions, the registered proprietor then has two years to obtain possession as against the squatter. If the registered proprietor does not do so, and the squatter remains in possession for the further two years, the squatter can once again apply for registration as proprietor. The squatter will then be registered as proprietor.

There are transitional provisions (set out in Sch 12 to the LRA 2002) which preserve the position of a squatter who had been in adverse possession for the requisite period (say 12 years) as at 13 October 2003. Such a person will still be entitled to apply to be registered under the old rules.

3.11 FURTHER READING

Megarry and Wade: The Law of Real Property (10th edn, 2024).

SUMMARY

- There are two legal estates in land – freehold and leasehold.
- A contract for the sale of land must comply with the formalities set out in s 2 of the Law of Property (Miscellaneous Provisions) Act 1989.
- A deed is needed to create or transfer most legal estates or interests in land.
- A buyer of registered land will take subject to interests that are protected by an entry on the register and interests that override.
- A buyer of unregistered land will take subject to:
  - certain legal interests (regardless of notice); and
  - interests properly registered under the LCA 1972; and
  - non-registrable equitable interests of which they have notice.

CHAPTER 4

Underlying Land Law Principles – Registered and Unregistered Land

LEARNING OUTCOMES

After reading this chapter you will be able to:

- explain how the main types of land estate and interest are protected in the unregistered and registered systems
- identify which estates and interests may be registered voluntarily at Land Registry and which require registration
- list the classes of title that may be given to registered land and identify when each is appropriate
- describe the sections of a registered title.

4.1 INTRODUCTION

The two ways in which ownership of title is proved in England and Wales were briefly introduced in **Chapter 1**. In essence, in the case of unregistered land, title is shown by title deeds proving the history of the ownership of the land and identifying any rights that benefit or burden that land. Unregistered title has largely been replaced by a system of land registration, in which ownership and any rights that benefit and burden the land are recorded on a government register, the Land Registry. When a title is registered, a record of the fact is recorded against a geographical map, called the Index Map.

Chapter 3 contained an outline of the main types of estates and interests that can exist in respect of land in England and Wales. **Chapter 4** will address how these are dealt with in both the unregistered and unregistered systems, and the important question of the circumstances in which such estates and interests will bind third parties, such as a buyer of land in a conveyancing transaction. As registered land is by far the more commonly encountered of the two systems, most consideration will be given to this system, including explaining the format of the register and what events will trigger the conversion of an unregistered title into a registered one.

4.2 UNREGISTERED LAND

4.2.1 Legal estates and interests

Subject to one exception (see **4.2.2.1**), legal estates and interests automatically bind the land. Any individual who buys unregistered land, or receives it by way of gift, will therefore take subject to such an estate or interest. In this way, if an owner sells the freehold of some land which is, for example, subject to a legal easement, the buyer will take subject to that easement.

4.2.2 Other interests

As regards all other interests, protection fundamentally depends upon whether an individual had notice of the interest. Interests are divided into two types for this purpose.

4.2.2.1 Interests governed by the LCA 1972

If an interest is governed by the LCA 1972, notice is achieved by registration of that interest at the Central Land Charges Department. If the third party has registered their right, it will be binding on all persons, registration being deemed to be actual notice. If it is registrable but has not been registered then the precise effect of failure to register will depend on the nature of the right, but in broad terms failure to register will render the right void as against a buyer. The fact that the buyer may actually know of the third-party right is irrelevant.

The following are the main classes of land charge encountered in practice:

Class C(i)	A puisne mortgage (ie, a legal mortgage not protected by the lender's possession of the title deeds).
Class C(iv)	An estate contract (ie, a contract to create or convey a legal estate, eg a contract to sell land or grant a lease).
Class D(ii)	A restrictive covenant entered into on or after 1 January 1926.
Class F	A spouse's or civil partner's right of occupation of the matrimonial home under the FLA 1996.

It should be noted that a recipient of property by way of gift will not take free of such interests as they become void for non-registration only against buyers. Once defeated by a buyer, however, any subsequent donee will also take free.

4.2.2.2 Interests not governed by the LCA 1972

All other interests, such as a beneficial interest under a trust of land or pre-1926 restrictive covenants, will bind a buyer unless the buyer falls within the definition of being a bona fide purchaser for value of the legal estate without notice. Notice here includes not only actual notice (ie, what the buyer actually knew), but also imputed notice (ie, within the actual or constructive knowledge of their solicitor) and constructive notice (ie, of matters a person would have discovered had they made the enquiries they ought reasonably to have made).

As with interests governed by the LCA 1972, it is important to note that a recipient of property by way of gift will not take free of such interests as they become void for lack of notice only against a buyer. Again, however, once defeated by a buyer, any subsequent donee will also take free.

It should be noted that a beneficial interest under a trust (but not other equitable interests such as an equitable easement) can be overreached (see **3.7**). In such a case it will not be binding on a buyer, even if they have notice of it.

4.3 REGISTERED LAND

4.3.1 What title may be registered

The register is a register of the 'title' (or ownership) of various rights over the land. The following may be registered:

(a) the freehold (ie, the fee simple absolute in possession);
(b) a lease that has more than seven years unexpired;
(c) leases of any length where the right to possession is discontinuous (eg, a time share);
(d) leases of any length granted to take effect in possession more than three months after the date of grant;
(e) a rentcharge that is either perpetual or for a term of which more than seven years are unexpired;
(f) a *profit à prendre* in gross (eg, a fishing right) that is either perpetual or for a term of which more than seven years are unexpired;
(g) a franchise (eg, a right to hold a market) that is either perpetual or for a term of which more than seven years are unexpired.

It should be noted that it is the title to each of these rights that is registrable. So there will be a separate entry on the register for each of these rights, even though they relate to the same piece of land; there will not be one entry which deals with the ownership of all the rights affecting a given piece of land.

4.3.2 First registration

4.3.2.1 Events triggering first registration

The owners of the above interests in unregistered land can voluntarily apply for registration at any time, but due to the slow take-up of voluntary registration, a system of compulsory registration was introduced many years ago. Today, the requirement to 'convert' land from the unregistered to the registered system occurs when a 'trigger' event happens in relation to unregistered land.

The most frequently encountered trigger events are as follows:

(a) a transfer of an unregistered freehold estate in land, including those:
   (i) for valuable or other consideration,
   (ii) by way of gift,
   (iii) in pursuance of an order of any court,
   (iv) by means of an assent,
   (v) by a deed appointing a new trustee;
(b) a transfer of an unregistered leasehold estate in land with more than seven years to run at the time of the transfer;
(c) a grant of a new leasehold estate in land:
   (i) for a term of more than seven years, or
   (ii) for a term of any length to take effect in possession after a period of three months from the date of the grant;
(d) a first legal mortgage of an unregistered freehold or leasehold. In the case of leasehold, this applies if, at the time of the mortgage, the lease has more than seven years unexpired.

Where the trigger event involves the creation, transfer or mortgage of a lease, it is only the leasehold estate that is subject to compulsory first registration.

Once the title has been registered, any subsequent dispositions must themselves be registered in order to be legally effective.

4.3.2.2 Conveyancing implications

If the title is not registered within two months of any of the above events, the disposition will become void as regards the legal estate. It is, however, possible to apply to the Registrar for an extension of this period.

Although the requirements for compulsory registration have applied on a sale of the freehold to the whole of England and Wales since 1 December 1990, different areas of the country became subject to compulsion at different times prior to this over a period of more than 100 years. Similarly, it is only since 1 April 1998 that registration has become compulsory after a gift, the grant of a first legal mortgage or an assent, and only since 13 October 2003 that leases with more than seven years unexpired have become registrable. Prior to this, only leases for more than 21 years were capable of registration. It has only been compulsory to register following the appointment of a trustee by deed since 6 April 2009.

When buying unregistered land, it is therefore always necessary to check whether the title should already have been registered, which should include checking the date when the area in which the property is situated became subject to compulsory registration. If it is discovered that the land should have been registered after some earlier disposition but has not been, the seller must be required to register the title before the transaction. It is not satisfactory to purchase the unregistered title from the seller and then for the buyer to apply for first registration, because the buyer has no guarantee that the unregistered title being offered to them by the seller will be accepted for registration by Land Registry. The buyer's lender will also insist that the defect in the seller's title is corrected before completion of the buyer's purchase.

4.3.3 Title Information Documents and land and charge certificates

Once land is registered, title to that land depends on what is entered on the register at Land Registry; thereafter the State guarantees the title. Proof of ownership no longer depends on the deeds to the land.

Prior to 13 October 2003, a copy of the entries on the register was issued to the registered proprietor in the form of a land certificate. If there was a mortgage over the land, a charge certificate in similar form, but having the original mortgage deed attached, was issued instead to the lender, the land certificate being retained in the Registry. Land and charge certificates were abolished as from 13 October 2003 and existing certificates are no longer required on a subsequent registration. Land Registry now issues a Title Information Document (TID) to a registered proprietor, which contains a copy of the entries on the register. It is not admissible as evidence of ownership, though, and does not need to be produced on a subsequent disposition of the land.

It is the register itself which is the proof of ownership, and official copies can be obtained which are admissible as proof of ownership.

4.3.4 Devolution of registered land

Once an estate in land becomes registered, all devolutions from that title must also follow the registered system. A separate title number identifies each estate in registered land, so that each separate estate in one physical parcel of land will have its own distinctive title number. The title number of an estate in registered land is its sole distinguishing feature and must be referred to in any dealing with that estate. An entry is made on the Index Map to record the fact that the title is registered.

If, for example, a landowner registered the freehold estate in a parcel of land, a registered title would be created, identifying the physical area of land which belonged to them. The title would also identify the estate as freehold and give them a title number by which to identify the land. If that landowner then grants a 999-year lease of the whole of the land to a tenant, the tenant under that lease has a registrable interest in the land and, on registration of the lease, a second and separate registered title would be created, again showing the physical extent of the land (in this example this will be identical to that shown on the freehold title), stating that the interest held is leasehold, giving brief details of the lease itself, and giving the tenant an identifying title number which is different from that used by the freehold estate.

On registration of the lease, the freehold title will be cross-referenced to show the existence of the lease. Similarly, the leasehold title will contain a reference to the freehold title. This cross-referencing system ensures that the tenant of a registered lease is able to trace their landlord should the need to do so arise, and that, because the existence of the lease is noted on the freehold title, a buyer of the freehold cannot buy in ignorance of the existence of the lease.

If the lease had a been a lease of part, a similar process would have taken place, only the physical extent referred to in the title to the lease and cross-referenced on the freehold title would have reflected the actual extent let.

4.3.5 Classes of title

Once land is entered on the register, the State guarantees the title and compensation is payable in certain circumstances if a defect is found in a registered title. Four classes of title are available (reflecting the quality of the unregistered title provided on first registration) and, when an application is made for first registration, the Registrar will decide which class of title should be allocated to the interest which is being registered. The class of title which has been given to the interest is shown on the proprietorship register of the title (see **4.3.6**).

The four different classes of title are considered below.

4.3.5.1 Absolute title

The vast majority of registered titles are classed as 'absolute', which in effect means the title is as near perfect as it can be (see further below). This class of title can be given to either a freehold or a leasehold interest in the land.

The proprietor of an interest which is registered with an absolute title has vested in them the legal estate, together with all appurtenant rights, and subject only to:

(a) entries on the register;

(b) unregistered interests within Schs 1 or 3 to the LRA 2002 (see **4.3.7.2**);

(c) where the proprietor is a trustee, minor interests (third-party rights) of which they have notice, for example the interests of the beneficiaries under the trust; and

(d) where the land is leasehold, the express and implied covenants and obligations under the lease.

On an application for first registration, the Registrar has a discretion under s 9(3) of the LRA 2002 to overlook minor defects in the title and to grant an absolute title, so curing the defect.

It must not be assumed that just because a piece of land is registered with absolute title this means that the title to the land is perfect. The State guarantee takes effect subject to entries on the register (eg covenants and easements) which might make the land totally unsuitable for a client's needs. Further, Land Registry often makes 'non-guaranteed' entries on an absolute title, ie entries that do not carry the State guarantee. So the register might state that a particular deed 'is expressed' to have some effect. This means that Land Registry does not guarantee that it does have that effect.

4.3.5.2 Possessory title

Registration with a possessory title has the same effect as registration with absolute title, except that the proprietor is also subject to all adverse interests existing at the date of first registration. Possessory title will be granted where the applicant is in possession of the land

and, for example, they have lost the title deeds or claim title through adverse possession under the Limitation Act 1980. Although initially only a possessory title will be granted in these circumstances, it may be possible to upgrade the title to absolute after a period of time. Possessory titles are encountered quite frequently in practice, although statistically they represent less than 1% of all registered titles. This class of title can be given to either a freehold or a leasehold interest in the land.

4.3.5.3 Qualified title

A qualified title, which in practice is very rare, is granted where the title submitted for registration shows a specific identified defect which the Registrar deems to be of such a nature that they cannot use their discretion to overlook the defect and grant an absolute title. The registration has the same effect as registration with an absolute title, except that the State's guarantee of the title does not apply to the specified defect. Such a title might be awarded where, for example, the title submitted for first registration showed that a transaction within the title had been carried out in breach of trust. In this situation, the proprietor would take their interest in the land subject to the interests (if any) of the beneficiaries under the trust. This class of title can be given either to a freehold or to a leasehold interest in the land.

4.3.5.4 Good leasehold title

As its name suggests, a good leasehold title applies only to leasehold estates. This class of title will be awarded where the Registrar is satisfied that the title to the leasehold interest is sound but, having no access to the title to the superior reversionary interest, they are not prepared to guarantee the lease against defects in the freehold title, or to guarantee that the freeholder had the right to grant the lease. Such a title will therefore be given only where the title to the freehold reversion is unregistered, or where the freehold is registered with less than an absolute title and where the applicant for registration of the leasehold interest does not submit evidence of title to the freehold reversion when making their application. A good leasehold title is regarded by lenders as being unsatisfactory, and for this reason is sometimes difficult to sell or mortgage.

4.3.5.5 Upgrading title

The Registrar may upgrade a title on their own initiative, or the proprietor may apply for upgrading as follows:

(a) A possessory title may be upgraded to an absolute title (or, in the case of leasehold land, to a good leasehold title) if either the Registrar is satisfied as to the title, or the land has been registered with possessory title for at least 12 years and the Registrar is satisfied that the proprietor is in possession.

(b) A qualified title may be upgraded to absolute (or, in the case of leasehold land, to a good leasehold title) if the Registrar is satisfied as to the title.

(c) A good leasehold title may be converted to an absolute title if the Registrar is satisfied as to reversionary freehold title and any intermediate leasehold title. This could occur after the registration of the reversion or of a superior lease.

4.3.6 The form of the register

The register kept at Land Registry shows the true state of the title. Land Registry Offices now have computerised records and the official copy issued is a computer-generated printout of the register entries. An example showing typical register entries is to be found at the end of this chapter.

The register is divided into three sections:

(a) the property register;

(b) the proprietorship register; and

(c) the charges register.

Each title has a title plan, based on the Ordnance Survey, showing the physical extent of the property. As appropriate – if, for example, there are rights such as easements affecting the land – the routes of these may be shown and will be cross-referenced to the entries on the register.

Each of the three sections of the register will now be considered in turn.

4.3.6.1 The property register

The property register describes the estate in land which is registered (ie, freehold or leasehold), identifies the property by a short verbal description (eg, its postal address) and shows the physical area of the land which is the subject of the registration, usually by reference to the title plan. The property register will also give details of any rights which benefit the land (eg, the right to use a pathway over adjacent land). It may also contain reference to easements to which the property is subject. In appropriate cases, the register will contain cross-references to superior and inferior titles (eg, to the freehold reversion in the case of a head lease and to any sub-leases granted out of the head lease).

Although the right does exist for a land owner to have their boundaries determined by Land Registry, this right is rarely used and the boundaries shown on the plan supplied by the Registry will give only a general indication of the position of the boundaries. Extraneous evidence (eg, from pre-registration deeds) may be required to prove the exact position of boundaries. This is a reason to retain pre-registration deeds, in case of a dispute relating to boundaries at a later date.

Where the land is leasehold, brief details of the lease under which the land is held will be given on the property register.

4.3.6.2 The proprietorship register

The proprietorship register states the class of the title which is registered. Although the vast majority of titles are absolute, this part of the register must be checked carefully to ensure that a registration with a title other than absolute is not inadvertently overlooked. This part of the register will also give the name(s) and address(es) of the registered proprietor(s). The address entered on the register is the address which the Registrar will use if for any reason they need to contact the land owner about the land. It is therefore important that this address is kept up-to-date. It is possible for a proprietor to have up to three addresses for service noted on the register, one of which can be an e-mail address.

If there are any restrictions on the proprietors' powers to deal with the land, for example if they hold as trustees for another person, a note of the restriction will be entered on this part of the register. It should be noted that the register only details the ownership of the legal estate in the land and beneficial interests under trusts are kept off the register. The register may therefore reveal the existence of a trust through the presence of a restriction, but will never reveal the details of it, such as who the beneficiaries are or their respective interests in the trust.

Any personal covenants given by the current registered proprietors can also be noted on the proprietorship register. The most common situation where this occurs is when the current registered proprietors have entered into an indemnity covenant with the previous owner. The function of indemnity covenants was considered at **3.6.4.1** and they are of importance in securing the indirect enforcement of positive covenants in particular. Indemnity covenants are commonly noted on the proprietorship register of the title, although there is no obligation on Land Registry to do so.

In the case of proprietors registered on or after 1 April 2000, the register will also normally include details of the price paid for the property by those proprietors.

4.3.6.3 The charges register

The charges register contains details of charges or incumbrances which currently affect the title. Here will be found a note of the burden of easements and covenants which bind the land, often with a reference to a schedule attached to the register. The schedule will contain extracts of the documents which imposed the easements or covenants, with a verbatim copy of the wording of the incumbrance. Only covenants which endure through a change of ownership of the land are noted on the charges register. Covenants which are purely personal in nature, such as an indemnity covenant, are commonly noted on the proprietorship register (see **4.3.6.2**).

Positive covenants (eg to repair a fence) are often seen in the charges register, particularly if they are mixed up with negative covenants. However, the fact that a positive covenant is on the register does not make it binding; under normal land law rules, the burden of a positive covenant cannot run with the land even if it is on the register (see **3.6**).

Details of mortgages of the land are also found on the charges register. Two entries are recorded for each mortgage, the first stating the fact that the mortgage exists and the date on which it was created, the second showing the name and address of the proprietor of the charge, ie lender.

4.3.7 Third-party rights in registered land

Third-party rights in registered land fall into one of the following three categories:

(a) registered charges;

(b) unregistered interests which override the disposition; and

(c) interests which must be protected by an entry on the register.

4.3.7.1 Registered charges

The most usual way of protecting a mortgage of registered land is by substantive registration of the charge, which will be noted in the charges register of the mortgaged land. The priority of mortgages in registered land is governed by the date of registration of the charges. The LRA 2002 has changed the rules with regard to the tacking of further advances, but this is beyond the scope of this book.

Other methods of creating a mortgage of registered land do exist, but they are rare in practice and beyond the scope of this book.

4.3.7.2 Unregistered interests which override a registered disposition

The Land Registration Act 1925 (LRA 1925) set out various rights which would be binding on the proprietor of registered land, even though they did not appear on the register and irrespective of whether they had notice of them. These were known as 'overriding interests', and although the LRA 2002 strictly no longer uses this terminology, it is still used in practice.

The LRA 2002 introduced important changes to the treatment of overriding interests, the first being is that a distinction is now made between those unregistered interests which will override a first registration and those which will override a disposition of land already registered. These are now considered in turn.

Unregistered interests which will override a first registration

These are set out in Sch 1 to the LRA 2002 and are designed to reflect the fact that whether a first registered proprietor is bound by an interest depends upon the rules relating to the purchase of unregistered land, and that first registration should reflect that existing position.

There are 15 such interests, the most common being:

(a) leases for seven years or less;

(b) an interest belonging to a person in actual occupation;
(c) a legal easement or profit; and
(d) a local land charge (see **17.5**).

Unregistered interests which will override a registered disposition

These are set out in Sch 3 to the LRA 2002 and have been rationalised from the list of overriding interests contained in LRA 1925, the second major change introduced by the LRA 2002 in respect of overriding interests.

There are 15 such interests, the most common being:

(a) legal leases for terms for seven years or less;
(b) an interest belonging to a person in actual occupation;
(c) certain legal easements and profits; and
(d) local land charges (see **17.5**).

The second and third of these will now be considered in more detail, given their importance and comparative complexity.

An interest belonging to a person in actual occupation

It is this head that produced the most case law under the old system laid down by the LRA 1925, and this case law will still be relevant to the provisions under the LRA 2002, despite the changes made. As from 13 October 2003, the rights of a person in actual occupation will override a disposition *except* for:

(a) an interest under a Settled Land Act settlement;
(b) an interest of a person of whom enquiry was made before the disposition and who failed to disclose the right when they could reasonably be expected to do so;
(c) an interest of a person whose occupation would not have been obvious on a reasonably careful inspection of the land at the time of the disposition and of which the person to whom the disposition was made did not have actual knowledge at the time of the disposition; and
(d) a lease granted to take effect in possession more than three months after the date of the grant and which had not taken effect in possession at the time of the disposition.

It is important to understand that it is not the fact of occupation that creates an overriding interest. Mere occupation by itself is of no effect. Rather, what is required is for an individual to have a proprietary right (ie one recognised under normal land law principles) over a property. If that individual couples the interest with actual occupation of the property, it is the proprietary interest that will become overriding.

A common example of when this might occur is where property is held subject to a trust, for example if a spouse, civil partner or other cohabitee holds the legal title as registered proprietor in trust for themselves and their partner. The interest of the partner should have been protected by entry of a restriction, but if not, the partner's interest is protected as an overriding interest if the partner is in occupation. Equally, the interest of a beneficiary of a deceased tenant in common's estate could be similarly protected even though no restriction had been entered on the register to reflect the existence of that tenancy in common.

Three final points should be noted about interests that are protected in this way. First, protecting a proprietary interest by virtue of occupation is a fall-back position and the interest should ideally be protected by substantive registration. Secondly, an overriding interest which arises under a trust of land can always be overreached on a disposition by all the trustees being at least two in number: see *City of London Building Society v Flegg* [1988] AC 54. Thirdly, rights under FLA 1996 (see **3.8.7**) cannot override.

Easements and profits

Under the LRA 1925, all legal easements (and some equitable easements) were capable of being overriding interests. Under the LRA 2002, an easement that is expressly granted or reserved on or after 13 October 2003 can never be overriding. Neither can equitable easements. Other legal easements and profits (ie, those created impliedly or by long user under the Prescription Act 1832) will be overriding *except* for an easement or profit which, at the time of the disposition:

(a) was not within the actual knowledge of the person to whom the disposition was made; and

(b) would not have been obvious on a reasonably careful inspection of the land; *unless*

(c) it had been exercised within the 12 months ending with the day of the disposition.

However, there are again transitional provisions. Any easement or profit that was an overriding interest immediately prior to 13 October 2003 will retain that status.

Ensuring that unregistered interests are registered

Although these interests that override a first registration or a registered disposition form a major flaw in the concept that the register itself should be conclusive as to ownership, this should prove to be less so over a period of time. The Land Registration Rules 2003 (SI 2003/1417) contain provisions requiring an applicant for registration (whether on a first registration or a disposition) to provide details to the Registry of any interests that would override the disposition so that they can then be entered on the register. They will then cease to override, although they will be binding by virtue of their registration.

4.3.7.3 Interests which must be protected by an entry on the register

All interests affecting a registered estate (except registered charges and overriding interests) have to be protected by some entry on the register in order to bind a successor. Under the LRA 1925, these were referred to as 'minor interests', but the LRA 2002 no longer uses that term. The easiest way to recognise which interests need protecting by an entry on the register is by a process of elimination. Is the interest a registered charge? If not, does it fall within the list of overriding interests which will bind even though no entry appears on the register in respect of it? If not, it should be protected by an entry on the register.

The LRA 1925 set out four methods of protecting 'minor interests' by entries on the register. These were notices, cautions, restrictions and inhibitions. Under the LRA 2002, cautions and inhibitions are abolished for the future (although existing registrations will remain and so will be encountered in practice). Notices (which have now been split into two types) are now the appropriate method of protection for interests intended to be binding on future proprietors of the land. Restrictions operate to prevent a disposition being registered without conformity with the conditions laid down in the restriction.

Cautions

Under the LRA 1925, a notice could be entered only with the consent of the registered proprietor. Where the entry of a notice was not possible (eg, where the proprietor did not consent to the application – perhaps because they disputed the claim) a caution could be used. This, however, provided only temporary protection for the owner of the interest claimed. On an application to register a subsequent disposition, the claimant would be given a limited period of time to establish their rights. Also, at any time the proprietor could require the Registrar to 'warn off' the caution. The claimant would be warned that unless they could justify their claim to an interest, the caution would be removed from the register. If they could justify the claim, the interest would receive permanent protection (eg, by the entry of a notice).

Cautions appeared on the proprietorship register. Although no new cautions can be entered on or after 13 October 2003, existing ones will remain until 'warned off' and so will still be encountered in practice.

Inhibitions

Inhibitions were used under the LRA 1925 to prevent dispositions being made in certain defined circumstances. So, an inhibition would be used when a court injunction had been obtained to freeze the disposition of land, or on the insolvency of the proprietor to prevent any disposition which might be in breach of the insolvency laws. Although no new inhibitions can be registered on and from 13 October 2003, existing registrations will remain.

Notices

Notices have always been the usual method of protecting third-party rights and appear on the charges register. So easements, restrictive covenants and estate contracts will be protected in this way. Under the LRA 1925, most interests could be protected only by notice and could be registered only with the consent of the registered proprietor, hence the need for cautions.

As from 13 October 2003, there are two types of notice: agreed and unilateral. Agreed notices will usually still need the consent of the registered proprietor. As before, a spouse's or civil partner's home rights under the FLA 1996 can still be entered as an agreed notice without the proprietor's consent.

Unilateral notices are registrable on and from 13 October 2003 and replace cautions. Unlike cautions, however, they appear in the charges register. As the name suggests, unilateral notices can be entered on the register without the consent of the proprietor. When this happens, however, Land Registry notifies the registered proprietor. A procedure similar to the 'warning off' procedure for pre-LRA 2002 cautions exists, but the terminology actually used in Land Registry Practice Guide 19 is the 'cancellation' of the notice. The registered proprietor, or their solicitor, applies to Land Registry for cancellation of the notice. Land Registry will then notify the beneficiary (the person who entered the unilateral notice) on the register that an application for cancellation has been made, and the beneficiary then has 15 business days to respond and attempt to prove the validity of the interest claimed. It is then a matter for Land Registry to establish whether the unilateral notice protects a valid interest. If a valid interest is indeed established, Land Registry would confirm this but the detail of the entry itself would not change (unless the beneficiary applied for more specific details to be set out). If not (or if the beneficiary does not respond during the 15 business day period) the unilateral notice is 'cancelled'. Where the beneficiary asks for the unilateral notice to be withdrawn, the notice is, to use Land Registry's terminology, 'removed'.

The court also has an inherent jurisdiction to determine a claim to cancel a unilateral notice (*Nugent v Nugent* [2013] EWHC 4095 (Ch)). A party to a dispute may prefer to go to court rather than use Land Registry procedures under the Land Registration Act 2002 as it may be quicker.

Restriction on the proprietorship register

Where the registered proprietor's powers of disposition are restricted in some way, this will be signified by the entry of a restriction in the proprietorship register. The restriction must be complied with, otherwise any disposition will not be registered. Typically, such an entry is made where co-owners hold as beneficial tenants in common, where the land is held on trust or strict settlement, or where the proprietor is a limited company or a charity subject to restrictions on its powers of disposition. Where tenants in common are registered as proprietors the following restriction will be entered:

> No disposition by a sole proprietor of the registered estate (except a trust corporation) under which capital money arises is to be registered unless authorised by an order of the court.

Under the LRA 2002, restrictions will be used in circumstances where inhibitions were used under the LRA 1925 (eg, on insolvency).

4.3.8 Caution against first registration

A caution against first registration should not be confused with the caution which was used under the LRA 1925 to protect third-party rights and which has been abolished as from 13 October 2003 (see **4.3.7.3**). A caution against first registration can be lodged by a person who has an interest in land which is currently unregistered. The caution warns any person who attempts to deal with the land that another person purports to have an interest in that land. When a dealing with the affected land is lodged at Land Registry, the cautioner is 'warned off' and given a limited period of time in which to establish their rights over the land, failing which the dealing will proceed and the cautioner will lose their interest. A person must not lodge a caution without reasonable cause and if they do so, they may be liable for damages to a person adversely affected.

The LRA 2002 limits the use of cautions against first registration as from 13 October 2003. They cannot be used if the applicant is the owner of the freehold or a lease for more than seven years in the land over which the right is being registered. Prior to this limitation, a caution might be used, for example, by a landowner where the precise boundaries of the land are uncertain. Registration of a caution against first registration would ensure that the landowner was notified of any purported dealing with the land and would be given an opportunity to defend their rights if a neighbour deliberately or inadvertently attempted to register the land as their own. Whilst cautions registered to protect this type of interest prior to 13 October 2003 continue to be effective, they cannot be used on or after this date in relation to such interests. Instead, an application for first registration should be made to resolve the problem. However, a caution against first registration can still be used to protect someone who has the benefit of an easement or profit and wants to ensure that it will be noted against the servient land if that is registered.

4.3.9 Mistakes on the register

Where there is a mistake on the register, it may be possible to seek rectification of the register. Compensation (indemnity) is payable where an error in the register is not rectified, where the register is rectified but loss is still suffered, where loss is suffered as a result of rectification or for any other error in the registration system, such as an error in the result of an official search. The conditions for claiming rectification and/or indemnity are stringent and are beyond the scope of this book.

4.4 OVERSEAS ENTITIES

An overseas entity is defined in s 2 of the Economic Crime (Transparency and Enforcement) Act 2022 as a legal entity that is governed by the law of a country or territory outside the United Kingdom. An overseas entity which already owns registered property in the UK (since 1 January 1999), or wishes to acquire such property, is required to register with Companies House and identify its beneficial owners. The information about the beneficial owners is registered on the Register of Overseas Entities and the overseas entity is issued with an overseas entity ID number. Overseas entities (unless exempt under regulations made under s 34(6) of the Act) are prohibited from becoming a registered proprietor of a freehold estate in land or a leasehold estate in land for a term of more than seven years at HM Land Registry without an overseas entity ID number.

If an overseas entity is registered as the proprietor of a freehold estate or a leasehold estate in land for a term of more than seven years, HM Land Registry must enter a restriction in the register which prohibits certain dispositions by the overseas entity unless it is a registered overseas entity or an exempt overseas entity at the time of the disposition. These dispositions include a transfer of a registered estate and the grant of a lease for more than seven years from the date of grant out of a registered estate (in each case by or to an overseas entity) and the grant of a charge over a registered estate by an overseas entity. Appendix 3 of HM Land Registry Practice Guide 78 (overseas entities) gives examples of such dispositions and guidance as to the evidence required for applications.

4.5 FURTHER READING

RB Roper et al, *Ruoff and Roper: Registered Conveyancing* (looseleaf)

C Harpum and J Bignell, *Registered Land: Law and Practice under the Land Registration Act 2002* (2024).

4.6 EXAMPLE OF A REGISTERED TITLE

Official copy of register of title

Title number LM 12037 Edition date 01.05.2009

- This official copy shows the entries subsisting on the register on 5 September 2025 at 10.55.59.
- This date must be quoted as the "search from date" in any official search application based on this copy.
- The date at the beginning of an entry is the date on which the entry was made in the register.
- Issued on 5 September 2025.
- Under s.67 of the Land Registration Act 2002 this copy is admissible in evidence to the same extent as the original.
- For information about the register of title see Land Registry website www.landregistry.gov.uk or Land Registry Public Guide 1- A guide to the information we keep and how you can obtain it.
- This title is dealt with by Land Registry Hull Office

A: Property Register

This register describes the land and estate comprised in the title.

COUNTY	DISTRICT
CORNSHIRE	MARADON

1. (19 February 1960) The freehold land shown and edged with red on the plan of the above title filed at the Registry and being 47, Queens' Road, Loamster, Maradon, Cornshire CS1 5TY

B: Proprietorship Register

This register specifies the class of title and identifies the owner. It contains any entries that affect the right of disposal.

Title Absolute

1. (1 May 2009) Proprietor (s): ROGER EVANS of 47, Queens' Road, Loamster, Maradon, Cornshire CS1 5TY
2. (1 May 2009) The price stated to have been paid on 15 April 2009 was £275,000.
3. (1 May 2009) The transfer to the proprietor contains a covenant to observe and perform the covenants referred to in the Charges Register and of indemnity in respect thereof.

C: Charges Register

This register contains any charges and other matters that affect the land.

1. (19 February 1960) A Conveyance of the land in this title dated 9 August 1952 made between (1) Sir James Fawcett (Vendor) and (2) Harold Hawtree (Purchaser) contains the following covenants:

   "The Purchaser with the intent and so as to bind the property hereby conveyed and to benefit and protect the retained land of the Vendor lying to the south of the land hereby conveyed hereby covenants with the Vendor that he and their successors in title will at all times observe and perform the stipulations and conditions set out in the schedule hereto."

   THE SCHEDULE ABOVE REFERRED TO

   "Not to build or allow to be built on the property any building without the written consent of the Vendor or their successors in title."

2. (1 May 2009) REGISTERED CHARGE dated 19 April 2009 to secure the moneys including the further advances therein mentioned.

3. (1 May 2009) Proprietor(s): HUMBERSHIRE AND COUNTIES BANK PLC of County House, Westford, Humbershire HS11 8YU.

END OF REGISTER

Note: *A date at the beginning of an entry is the date on which the entry was made in the Register.*

Land Registry Cymraeg			TITLE NUMBER **LM 12037**	
ORDNANCE SURVEY PLAN REFERENCE	COUNTY CORNSHIRE	SHEET	NATIONAL GRID TH 100	SECTION D
Scale: 1/1250			© Crown copyright 2008	

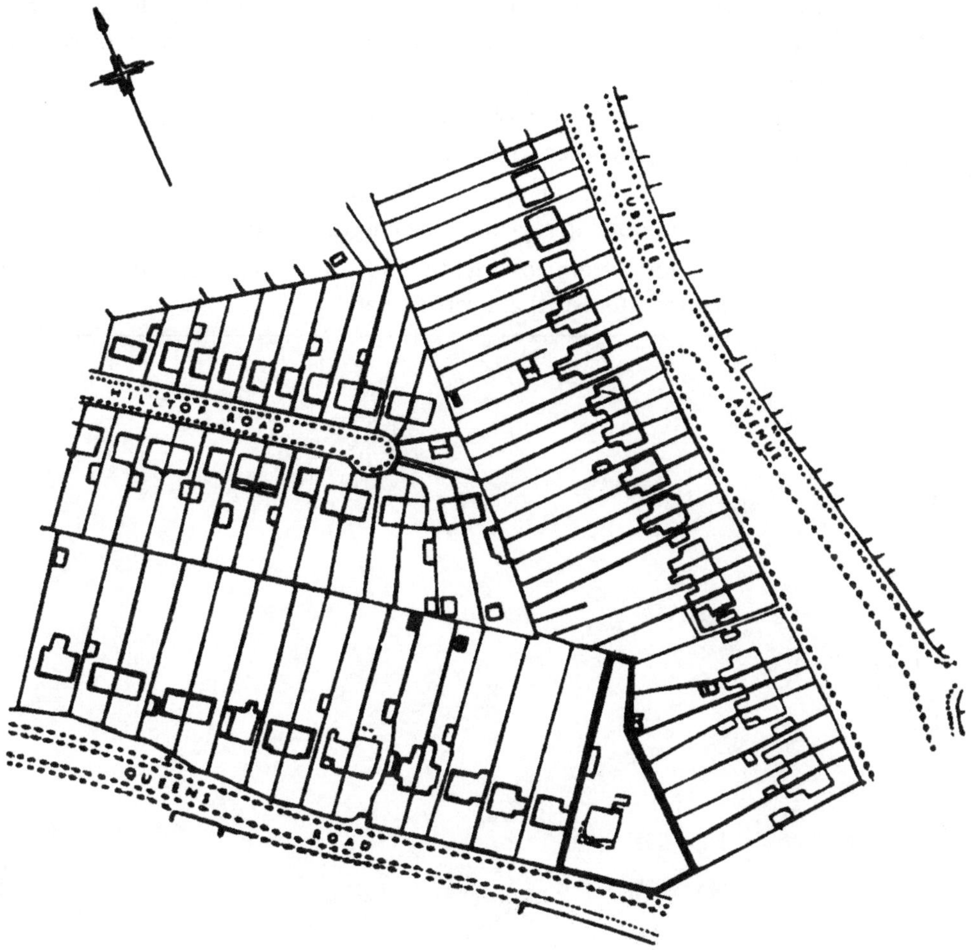

This official copy issued on 5th September 2025 shows the state of this title plan on 5th September 2025 at 10:55.59.

Admissible in evidence to the same extent as the original (s67 Land Registration Act 2002)

This title plan shows the general position, not the exact line, of the boundaries. It may be subject to distortions in scale.

Measurements scaled from this plan may not catch measurements between the same points on the ground. See Land Registry Public Guide 7 – Title Plans

This title is dealt with by Land Registry Hull Office

SUMMARY

- Certain registration requirements exist in both the registered and unregistered systems.
- In the unregistered system, interests governed by the LCA 1972 must be registered at the Central Land Charges Department if they are to be binding.
- Certain dealings with land will trigger a compulsory requirement for registration at Land Registry. These include any transfer or first legal mortgage of the land and the grant of a lease for more than seven years. Failure to register within two months renders the disposition void.
- Upon registration at Land Registry, an estate will be awarded one of four classes of title – absolute, qualified, possessory or good leasehold.
- The register maintained by Land Registry is divided into three parts – property register, proprietorship register and charges register.
- In the registered system, in order to bind, interests must appear on the register of title unless they are interests that override.

CHAPTER 5

Conduct Issues Relevant to Conveyancing

LEARNING OUTCOMES

After reading this chapter you will be able to:

- advise on how the Codes of Conduct deal with acting for different parties in a property transaction
- advise (in accordance with the Codes of Conduct) on various ethical issues that may affect a property lawyer
- explain the requirements of the Money Laundering, Terrorist Financing and Transfer of Funds (Information on the Payer) Regulations 2017
- explain the implications of acting for a client involved in mortgage fraud.

5.1 INTRODUCTION

This chapter contains a summary of the conduct issues which are most likely to be encountered during the course of a conveyancing transaction. Those matters which are exclusive to conveyancing are dealt with in detail. Other more general principles are mentioned in outline only, and further detail of these can be found in the companion textbook ***Legal Foundations***.

Solicitors are regulated by the Solicitors Regulation Authority (SRA), which publishes Codes of Conduct that must be complied with. A solicitor's conduct is governed by the Code of Conduct for Solicitors, and a firm's conduct is governed by the Code of Conduct for Firms (the 'SRA Codes'). Both SRA Codes are contained in the SRA Standards and Regulations published by the SRA. A failure to comply with the rules contained in the SRA Codes may lead to the SRA taking regulatory action against the solicitor who is acting, the firm itself as an entity, or its managers or compliance officers.

The SRA has issued guidance to assist in the practical application of SRA Codes. This can be accessed on the SRA website.

5.2 ACTING FOR SELLER AND BUYER

Occasionally, the parties to a conveyancing transaction ask if one solicitor or one firm of solicitors can act for both parties. The parties may feel that the deal has been done at the outset when the terms of the sale and purchase are recorded by the selling agent, and that thereafter they can avoid duplication of time and expense if one solicitor or one firm does the work of both the buyer's and seller's solicitors. Sometimes, both seller and buyer have been clients of the same firm and neither wants to instruct a new firm.

Paragraph 6.2 of the SRA Codes supports Principle 7 and lays down a basic rule that, subject to certain exceptions discussed below, a solicitor or firm cannot act if the solicitor or firm has a conflict of interest or a significant risk of such a conflict. According to the SRA Glossary, a conflict of interest is 'a situation where your separate duties to act in the best interests of two or more clients conflict'. So a conflict of interest may exist right from the start, or may arise during the transaction, for example where the parties start off with an agreed deal but something comes to light as a result of the searches and enquiries which causes the buyer to want to reduce the purchase price or insert conditionality clauses into the contract.

The decision as to whether acting for buyer and seller does or is likely to involve a conflict of interest rests with the solicitor and the firm. Whilst the SRA Codes do not prohibit acting for both buyer and seller, it is worth noting that guidance issued by the SRA in relation to the SRA Codes states that one client selling or leasing an asset to another client is an example of a circumstance that can give rise to a conflict of interest or a significant risk of one. The guidance goes on to say that 'you should not normally act for two or more clients in these scenarios'. Law Society guidance issued on 18 June 2020 states that 'there is a high risk of a conflict of interest if you act for both a buyer and a seller'. Factors to take into account when determining whether a conflict of interest exists, or is likely to arise, include:

(a) the complexity of the matter and length of the conveyancing chain involved. The more complex the transaction, the greater the risk of a conflict of interest;

(b) the likelihood of negotiations having to take place. In higher value or complex transactions, there is a greater likelihood of substantial contract negotiations, increasing the risk of a conflict;

(c) the bargaining power of the parties and any particular vulnerability of either party. Where there is unequal bargaining power, it makes it more difficult to act in the best interests of both clients.

Examples where a solicitor or firm would have a conflict of interest if acting for both buyer and seller include:

(a) where a buyer should be advised to renegotiate the purchase price following an adverse survey or search result; such advice would clearly be to the detriment of the seller and so the duty to act in both their interests would conflict;

(b) where a term in the contract would be advisable to protect the interests of one party but detrimental to the other (for example, a term requiring the seller to bear the risk of any VAT liability in the event of the VAT status of the transaction changing between exchange and completion). Neither the firm nor solicitor can act in the best interests of both clients in this situation: if you advise the buyer to insert the term, you are not acting in the best interests of the seller; if you stay silent, you may not be acting in the best interests of the buyer.

If there is a conflict, or a significant risk of one, the solicitor or firm can only act for both parties if one of the two exceptions contained in para 6.2 applies. Under para 6.2(a), a solicitor can act for more than one party even if there is a conflict where the clients have a 'substantially common interest' in relation to a matter or a particular aspect of it and the conditions set out in para 6.2(i)–(iii) are satisfied (see **5.4**). According to the SRA Glossary, a 'substantially common interest' is a situation where there is a clear common purpose between the clients and a strong consensus on how it is to be achieved. Law Society guidance issued in June 2020 states that this exception 'does not apply to a property purchase. Although both clients have a common interest in completing the sale, they also have different interests, since one is buying and one is selling.'

The other exception to the general prohibition in para 6.2 is contained in para 6.2(b) and applies when the clients are competing for the same objective. This cannot apply to a seller and buyer in a conveyancing transaction as they are not competing for the same asset and therefore do not satisfy the definition of 'competing for the same objective'.

So a solicitor or firm may only act for both parties in a conveyancing transaction in the rare instances where they are satisfied that there is no existing conflict of interest and no significant risk of a conflict arising in future, or there is a conflict of interest but the parties share a substantially common interest. This will be difficult to establish where the land or interest in land is being transferred for value. It might be possible to act, for example, where the land is being gifted, or transferred between related parties, ie in the context of private individuals, where the parties are related by blood, adoption, marriage, civil partnership or living together; and in the commercial context, where the parties are associated companies (one is a holding company and the other is its subsidiary, or both are subsidiaries of the same holding company). However, if a conflict arises during a transaction or they cease to share a substantially common interest, the solicitor or firm would have to stop acting for at least one of the clients and could only continue acting for the other if the duty of confidentiality to the former client is not at risk. The client (or clients) for whom the solicitor or firm could no longer act would have to incur the disruption and additional expense involved in instructing a new solicitor or firm in the middle of a transaction. Many solicitors and firms therefore take the view that it is best never to act for both buyer and seller in a property transaction, even where this could be justified under the SRA Codes.

If, however, a decision is made at the outset of the transaction that there is no conflict of interest under para 6.2, then it is advisable (although not required by the SRA Codes) to:

(a) inform the clients in writing of the risks (in terms of costs and inconvenience) should a conflict arise and the firm have to cease acting;
(b) obtain the client's consent to the firm acting;
(c) record the factors considered in reaching a decision to act;
(d) ensure that each is party is represented by a different fee earner within the firm.

If a decision is made to act under the 'substantially common interest' exception then the conditions in para 6.2(i)–(iii) *must* be complied with. These require:

(i) the parties to have given 'informed consent' (in writing or evidenced in writing) to the solicitor or firm acting for both of them, meaning that the parties must appreciate the issues and risks of the solicitor or firm acting for both of them;
(ii) the firm (where appropriate) to put in place effective safeguards to protect the parties' confidential information; and
(iii) the solicitor to be satisfied that it is reasonable to act for both parties, meaning that the solicitor should consider if one client will be prejudiced (for example due to vulnerability or unequal bargaining power) if not separately represented.

5.3 ACTING FOR JOINT BUYERS

It is usually acceptable to act for joint buyers, provided that no conflict of interest exists or is likely to arise. It may be necessary to advise residential buyers separately about their rights in the property, particularly where the prospective joint buyers are not married to each other nor in a civil partnership (see **Chapter 10**).

5.4 ACTING FOR BORROWER AND LENDER

As soon as the buyer's solicitor receives instructions to act for the lender, they are effectively acting for both parties in one transaction (ie, for both lender and borrower). They have two clients and owe a duty to both (see *Mortgage Express v Bowerman & Partners (A Firm)* [1996] 2 All ER 836). Acting for borrower and lender is possible unless, under para 6.2 of the SRA Codes, the solicitor or firm has a conflict of interest or a significant risk of a conflict (see **5.2**).

Examples of a conflict of interest when acting for both a buyer and a lender may include where:

(a) the terms of the mortgage offer are unfair to the borrower (eg, an extortionate rate of interest is being charged);

(b) instructions reveal that the buyer would be in breach of one of the terms of the offer (eg, by allowing tenants into possession of the property);

(c) the buyer is unable to comply with the lender's terms (eg, to provide the balance of the purchase price from their own funds);

(d) the mortgage documentation requires negotiation between the parties.

Examples (a)–(c) would preclude the firm or solicitor from acting for both borrower and lender or continuing to act (if instructions had initially been accepted from both). However, example (d) requires further analysis to identify when such negotiation is likely to take place. In residential transactions, the borrower will often be borrowing from a high street bank or building society where the mortgage is offered on standard terms and conditions, ie the material terms of the mortgage documentation are not negotiated between the lender's and borrower's solicitors, and a prescribed (and even pre-printed) form of mortgage deed is used. It is arguable that where the mortgage is on 'standard terms', there is either no conflict of interest or, if there is, there is a 'substantially common interest' under para 6.2 in that both the borrower and the lender want a good and marketable title to the property to be acquired. Indeed, Law Society guidance issued in June 2020 indicates that it may be acceptable to act for both borrower and lender where the mortgage is on standard terms, a significant part of the lender's activities consists of lending, the mortgaged property is the borrower's private residence and the certificate of title required by the lender is in the form approved by the Law Society and UK Finance.

The Law Society guidance states that the risk of conflict is high 'if the mortgage is not a standard mortgage ... of property to be used as the borrower's private residence'. This suggests that the Law Society is of the view that acting for borrower and lender on a commercial transaction presents a high risk of conflict. Indeed, in practice, the borrower and lender in commercial transactions are often separately represented from the outset because the mortgage documents (which would typically include a facility letter/agreement as well as a charging document) are likely to be the subject of significant negotiation between the solicitors for the two parties, so will not be on 'standard terms'. Even where standard mortgage documents are used, many lenders prefer to instruct their own solicitor (often from a panel of preferred law firms). Sometimes, the lender may ask the borrower's solicitor to act for both the lender and the borrower on the title investigation and searches and enquiries but instruct its own solicitors to negotiate the loan documentation. However, if the mortgage is a standard mortgage, or the mortgage is between related parties, it may be possible for a firm or solicitor to decide that there is no conflict of interest existing or likely to arise, or that a substantially common interest can be demonstrated. This conclusion would enable the firm or solicitor to act for both lender and borrower, but is unlikely to happen routinely given the Law Society guidance and lenders' preference for separate representation.

In either residential or commercial cases, if a firm or solicitor is acting for a borrower and a lender and a conflict of interest occurs during the transaction (or the parties cease to have a substantially common interest), the firm or solicitor cannot continue to act for both parties, and may continue to act for one of them only if the duty of confidentiality to the other can be fulfilled.

If a solicitor is aware that their buyer client is attempting to perpetrate a mortgage fraud, they must stop acting for that client immediately and their duty of confidentiality to the buyer client is discharged (see **5.12**).

5.5 ACTING FOR JOINT BORROWERS – UNDUE INFLUENCE

Provided no conflict of interest exists or is likely to exist, there is no rule of law or conduct which prevents the same solicitor acting for joint borrowers. However, problems can arise in the common situation where, for example, a husband needs to borrow money for the purpose of his business and the bank requires security, but the only asset is the matrimonial home which is in the joint names of the husband and his wife. If the wife agrees to a mortgage over the house for the benefit of her husband's business but the husband defaults, the bank may well seek to enforce its security to the wife's detriment. In such circumstances, the wife may seek to have the mortgage set aside on the basis of undue influence.

The House of Lords, in the case of *Royal Bank of Scotland v Etridge (No 2) and Other Appeals; Barclays Bank plc v Coleman; Bank of Scotland v Bennett; Kenyon-Brown v Desmond Banks & Co (A Firm)* [2001] 4 All ER 449, laid down detailed guidance for solicitors acting in such a situation.

The burden of proof that a landowner entered into a charge because of undue influence rests on the landowner. Where there is a special relationship (parent and child; solicitor and client; but not husband and wife), there is a rebuttable presumption that there has been undue influence. In the case of husband and wife, there is no such presumption. However, where a wife proposes to charge the matrimonial home as a security for a bank loan to her husband, or to a company through which he operates his business, a lender is put on enquiry because, prima facie, such transaction is not to the wife's advantage.

Where the lender is put on such enquiry, it need do no more than take reasonable steps to satisfy itself that the practical implications of the proposed transaction have been brought home to the wife in a 'meaningful way', so that she enters into the transaction with her eyes open so far as its basic elements are concerned. Normally, it will be reasonable for the lender to rely on confirmation from a solicitor acting for the wife that they have advised her appropriately. In ordinary cases, any deficiencies in the advice given by the solicitor are matters between the wife and her solicitor. The lender is entitled to proceed on the basis that the solicitor advising the wife has done so properly.

In light of the above, the solicitor should:

(a) explain to the wife the purpose for which they (the solicitor) have become involved;
(b) explain that, if it becomes necessary, the lender will rely on the solicitor's involvement to counter any suggestion that the wife has been unduly influenced or has not fully understood the nature of the transaction; and
(c) obtain confirmation from the wife that she wishes the solicitor to act for her in the transaction, and to advise her on the legal and practical implications of the transaction.

The nature and extent of the advice given will depend on the facts of the case, but should include an explanation of the nature of the documents and the practical consequences to the wife of her signing them, and a warning as to the seriousness of the risks involved. It must be clearly explained to the wife that she has a choice as to whether or not to go ahead with the transaction, emphasis being placed on the fact that the choice is hers and hers alone.

The solicitor must check if the wife wishes to proceed. She should be asked whether she wants the solicitor to write to the lender confirming that matters have been explained to her.

The solicitor must not write to the lender confirming these matters unless they have express instructions from the wife to do so. The solicitor should ensure that all the relevant documents have been received from the lender, and should refuse to make the confirmation to the lender until they have been received. The lender should supply the following financial information:

(a) the purpose for which the facility is being made available;
(b) the current amount of the husband's indebtedness;
(c) the amount of the current overdraft facility;
(d) the amount and terms of the new facility; and
(e) a copy of any written application made by the husband for the facility.

The lender cannot release this information without the consent of the husband; and if the consent is not forthcoming, the transaction cannot proceed.

The solicitor's discussion with the wife should take place at a face-to-face meeting in the absence of the husband, and the advice should be given in non-technical language. It is not for the solicitor to veto the transaction, but if the solicitor thinks that the transaction is not in the wife's best interests, they should give reasoned advice to that effect. Ultimately, the decision is one for the wife. If she wishes to enter into a financially unwise transaction, that is a matter for her. However, the *Etridge* guidelines on what advice should be given and how it should be given must be followed, even where a wife insists on a very short meeting and appears determined to proceed regardless of the solicitor's advice (*Padden v Bevan Ashford Solicitors* [2011] EWCA Civ 1616). If it is 'glaringly obvious' that the wife is being 'grievously wronged', the solicitor should decline to act.

The House of Lords also considered the issue of whether the wife (or other guarantor) should be advised by a different solicitor to the one acting for her husband (or other principle borrower). However, it decided that the cost disadvantages outweighed the benefits. Therefore, if a solicitor or firm is satisfied that it can act under the SRA Codes, there is no rule of law preventing one solicitor acting for both the husband and wife. To act for both, a firm or solicitor would need to be satisfied it could comply with para 6.2 of the SRA Codes (see **5.2**).

Note that although the *Etridge* case involved husband and wife, the same principles will apply to civil partners or cohabitees. The same principles will also apply to any situation where property is being charged in return for a loan that is not being made to the property owners. So if parents mortgage property to secure a loan made to a child, the same guidelines should be followed.

5.6 CONFIDENTIALITY

Paragraph 6.3 of the SRA Codes states that a solicitor must keep the affairs of clients confidential unless disclosure is required or permitted by law, or the client consents. Disclosure may be permitted, or even required, by law where there is a potential commission of a crime by a client, such as money laundering. Where the client consents to the disclosure of confidential information, the SRA guidance states that the consent must be clear, so that the client knows to whom their information should be made available, when and for what purpose.

See **5.12** for where problems arise when the solicitor has been acting for borrower and lender and has information that the lender would consider relevant to granting the loan, but the borrower does not want the solicitor to tell the lender.

5.7 CONTRACT RACES

A contract race occurs when a seller enters into the conveyancing process with two or more prospective buyers at the same time. The buyers are competing with each other, and the winner of the race is the buyer who is ready to exchange contracts first. The 2011 SRA Code required the solicitor to inform all buyers immediately of the seller's intention to deal with more than one buyer. Whilst there is no such explicit requirement in the 2019 SRA Codes, the solicitor and firm are required to comply with para 1.2 and must not abuse their position by taking unfair advantage of clients or others. Under para 1.4, the solicitor and firm must not mislead others, either by their own acts or omissions or allowing or being complicit in the acts or omissions of the seller. The Law Society practice note on Conflict of interests advises that it would be sensible to continue the practice of informing all buyers immediately of the seller's intention to deal with more than one buyer, provided that the seller consents to the disclosure.

Where a solicitor is acting for the seller, they must explain to their client that they are required to comply with paras 1.2 and 1.4. Since buyers are often wary of entering into contract races because of the wasted time and expense incurred by the losers, the seller should also be warned of the danger of losing all the prospective buyers if a race is commenced. If the seller wants to proceed with the contract race, having obtained their client's authority, the seller's solicitor should disclose the seller's decision to conduct a contract race direct to the solicitor acting for each prospective buyer, or, where no solicitor is acting, to the prospective buyer(s) in person. It is advisable to make clear to each of them the precise terms of the race, ie what has to be done by a buyer in order to secure the property. Commonly, the terms of the race are that the first buyer who presents a signed contract and deposit cheque at the seller's solicitor's office will secure the property. If the seller refuses to allow the solicitor to notify all the prospective buyers of the contract race, the solicitor cannot disclose the contract race to the prospective buyers as they have a duty of confidentiality to their client under para 6.3. Instead, if they consider that paras 1.2 or 1.4 would be breached by the non-disclosure, they must decline to act to avoid breaching Principle 2 (acting with integrity).

A solicitor must not accept instructions to act for both seller and any of the buyers in a contract race as there will be a clear conflict of interest and para 6.2 (see **5.2** above) will apply. There will also be a clear conflict of interest if the solicitor acts for more than one prospective buyer in a contract race. However, in certain circumstances, it may be possible to act under the exception in para 6.2(b), as the clients have a conflict of interest but are competing for the same objective, particularly where the clients are sophisticated users of legal services and effective safeguards, such as information barriers, can be put in place, as this will make it more likely that the conditions in para 6.2(i)–(iii) have been complied with. In considering whether it is reasonable to act for both buyers, the Law Society practice note on Conflict of interests identifies inequality of bargaining position, client vulnerability and whether one client has more to lose than the other as relevant factors.

5.8 WITHDRAWAL OF PAPERS

Where, having supplied a prospective buyer with a draft contract, the seller later receives a further offer for the property which they would prefer to accept, the seller may withdraw their acceptance of the first offer and the draft papers from the first prospective buyer before accepting the second prospective buyer's offer and submitting draft papers to them. In this situation, only one buyer is in possession of a draft contract at any one time, and thus a contract race does not exist.

5.9 UNDERTAKINGS

An undertaking is a statement, made by a solicitor or their firm, that the solicitor or the firm will do something or cause something to be done, or refrain from doing something, given to someone who reasonably places reliance on it. It can be given orally or in writing and need not include the words 'undertake' or 'undertaking'. A solicitor is not obliged to give or accept undertakings. However, there will be many situations in conveyancing practice where a solicitor will be asked to give an undertaking on their client's behalf. For example, an undertaking may be required to enable the buyer client to obtain a bridging loan for the deposit. Similarly, an undertaking may be required from the seller's solicitor that they will discharge their client's mortgage over the property (see **26.2**). In both cases, The Law Society has agreed standard wording for undertakings. Even where an undertaking is presented to the solicitor in the 'standard' form (or in a familiar and frequently used form of wording), the entire wording should be read carefully in the light of the particular transaction to ensure that it is appropriate for those circumstances. If the wording is not wholly appropriate to the circumstances in hand, it should be amended.

All the general rules on undertakings apply equally in the context of conveyancing. An undertaking must be performed within the agreed timescale or, in the absence of an agreed timescale, within a 'reasonable amount of time' (see para 1.3 of the SRA Codes).

Failure to honour an undertaking constitutes professional misconduct. Because of the personal liability which attaches to undertakings, it is important that both the giver and recipient of the promise understand precisely what the terms of the promise are. It is recommended that oral undertakings be confirmed or recorded in writing so there can be no doubt as to the content. Once an undertaking is given and the recipient has relied upon it, it can be withdrawn only by agreement.

Particular care should be taken when accepting an undertaking given by an incorporated law firm, ie an LLP or a limited company. Following the decision of the Supreme Court in *Harcus Sinclair v Your Lawyers* [2021] UKSC 32, it is clear that, unlike an undertaking given by an individual solicitor or a traditional partnership, an undertaking given by an incorporated law firm is not capable of being enforced under the court's supervisory jurisdiction over solicitors as officers of the court. Whilst a personal undertaken given by a solicitor working within an LLP or limited company would be enforceable against that solicitor personally, the Law Society has advised solicitors working for incorporated firms against giving personal undertakings (due to the risks involved for the individual solicitor). An incorporated law firm regulated by the SRA that breaches an undertaking would still be subject to the SRA's disciplinary powers, and some commentators believe that the prospect of disciplinary action will mean the risk of an undertaking being breached is low. However, the SRA is not able to order the performance of an undertaking given by an incorporated law firm, nor can it award compensation for the breach of an undertaking given by an incorporated law firm. Any solicitor receiving an undertaking from an LLP or limited company should be aware of its limitations and clients should be advised accordingly. The Law Society has advised that thought should be given as to whether an undertaking from an incorporated law firm should be supported by consideration (in order that it be enforceable as a contract) or be created by deed (so that it can be enforced through the courts without the need for consideration). Solicitors should check their firm's policy on accepting undertakings from an incorporated law firm in light of this case.

5.10 DEALING WITH NON-SOLICITORS

Where the other party to the transaction is not represented by a solicitor, precautions may have to be taken to ensure that the transaction proceeds smoothly and that the interests of the solicitor's client are properly protected.

5.10.1 Licensed conveyancers and legal executives

Licensed conveyancers and legal executives are bound by the rules of their own regulatory bodies, which are similar to those that apply to solicitors. However, licensed conveyancers and legal executives are not officers of the court and therefore their personal undertakings are not enforceable through the courts as they are for solicitors. Instead, a complaint relating to a breached undertaking would have to made to the appropriate regulatory bodies. See **5.9** for a discussion on the issues of accepting undertakings that are not enforceable through the courts.

5.10.2 Dealing with unqualified persons

The Legal Services Act 2007 makes it an offence to carry on reserved legal activities through an unqualified person, including preparing a contract, transfer or charge for the purposes of the Land Registration Act 2002. At the start of a transaction which apparently involves an unqualified person, the solicitor should write to the unqualified person asking for satisfactory evidence that no offence will be committed. The solicitor's client should also be informed of the situation.

Undertakings should not be accepted from unqualified persons because there is no method of enforcing them. Therefore, where a seller who is represented by an unqualified person has a mortgage to be discharged at completion, the buyer's solicitor must require the seller to produce a signed Form DS1 (or receipted mortgage) at completion and must not accept an undertaking for its discharge.

5.10.3 Acting for the lender

A solicitor acting for a lender where the borrower is represented by an unqualified person is under no obligation to undertake work which the buyer's solicitor would normally carry out (eg, drafting the transfer) and should not give the unqualified person additional assistance. However, in such a situation, the solicitor must bear in mind that the interests of their lender client in obtaining a good title to the property are paramount. The advance should be sent to a solicitor, licensed conveyancer or person properly authorised to receive the money by the borrower. Similar principles apply on redemption of a mortgage.

5.10.4 The buyer or seller is not represented at all

The solicitor is under a duty in conduct to act in the best interests of their client (Principle 7), but also to act with integrity (Principle 5) and not to take unfair advantage of third parties (para 1.2 of the SRA Codes). Where two or more Principles come into conflict, the Introduction to the SRA Codes states that those which safeguard the wider public interest take precedence over an individual client's interest. For example, when an unrepresented opponent provides badly-drawn documentation, the solicitor should suggest that the opponent obtains legal advice; but if they do not do so, the solicitor should strike a balance between doing the best for the client and not taking unfair advantage of the opponent's lack of legal knowledge and drafting skills. However, in maintaining that balance, great care must be taken not to create a contractual relationship with the unrepresented opponent (thereby putting the solicitor in breach of para 6.2 of the SRA Codes), or to become involved in possible breaches of the Legal Services Act 2007.

Where a transaction is over £5,000 in value and one of the parties is unrepresented, Land Registry requires a solicitor making certain applications (including applications to register a transfer or discharge a mortgage) to provide certified details and evidence of the unrepresented party's identity. These requirements are part of the wider initiative to combat money laundering and mortgage fraud (see **5.11** and **5.12**). Further details of the requirements may be found in Land Registry Practice Guide 67.

5.11 MONEY LAUNDERING

Broadly speaking, money laundering is the conversion, concealment or disguise of the proceeds of crime, so as to make it appear that they come from a legitimate source. Conveyancers need to be aware of the possibility of clients using their services in order to launder money, which may expose the solicitors themselves to criminal offences. Conveyancers are at particular risk, since money passes through the client account on a regular basis and property investment is a common way of investing laundered funds. Warning signs of money laundering include:

- a client making a payment using large sums of cash;
- sudden or unexplained changes in ownership of the property;
- a third party providing the finance for the purchase but the property being registered in someone else's name;

- cash changing hands directly between clients;
- an unusual sale price;
- a client paying a deposit but then withdrawing from a transaction without good reason and requiring their deposit to be repaid to them.

Assisting a money launderer or failing to report a client where there is a suspicion of money laundering could render the solicitor liable to prosecution under the Proceeds of Crime Act 2002.

In addition to offences under the Proceeds of Crime Act 2002, practitioners must also be aware of their obligations under the Money Laundering, Terrorist Financing and Transfer of Funds (Information on the Payer) Regulations 2017 (SI 2017/692) ('the Regulations'). Those caught by the Regulations include legal professionals participating in real property transactions, and failure to comply with the Regulations is a criminal offence. Obligations imposed on firms by the Regulations include the following:

- To assess the risk of money laundering and terrorist financing to which the business is subject (reg 18) and thereafter maintain written policies, controls and procedures to manage the identified risks (reg 21).
- To appoint a 'nominated officer' to receive reports from within the firm concerning any instances of suspected money laundering and to liaise, if necessary, with the National Crime Agency (reg 21(3)). In addition, a firm must appoint a senior manager to be responsible for compliance with the Regulations (reg 21(a)).
- To obtain, at the beginning of the business relationship or transaction, verification of the identity of each of the firm's clients (referred to as 'customer due diligence' in the Regulations). This can be done by either 'simplified', 'standard' or 'enhanced' due diligence, according to the type of client involved and the risk of money laundering. Standard due diligence will apply to most clients and obliges the solicitor to verify identity using documents or information from a reliable source, independent of the person whose identity is being verified (reg 28). Where the client is a company, trust or partnership, the firm will have to take steps to verify the identity of the beneficial owner or owners of the client.

The Legal Sector Affinity Group, the anti-money laundering supervisors for the legal sector, issues guidance on anti-money laundering for the legal profession. A court is required to consider this guidance in assessing whether a solicitor committed an offence or took all reasonable steps and exercised all due diligence to avoid committing an offence. The guidance covers warning signs, beneficial ownership information and terrorist property offences (among other things) and is published by the Solicitors Regulation Authority.

Further detail on both the Regulations and offences under the Proceeds of Crime Act 2002 is contained in ***Legal Foundations***.

5.12 MORTGAGE FRAUD

Mortgage fraud occurs where individuals defraud a lender through the mortgage process. A mortgage fraud may be committed in many ways: perhaps the borrower overstates their income in order to obtain a higher mortgage, or a husband forges his wife's signature, or the price shown in the transfer is not the price actually paid by the buyer. Some frauds are carried out on a large scale and involve the use of, for example, nominee buyers or multiple properties.

A solicitor must uphold the rule of law (Principle 1) and act with integrity (Principle 5). Continuing to act for a client when doing so would involve the solicitor in a breach of the law or a breach of the SRA Codes may result in the solicitor being disciplined by the SRA, a criminal prosecution for having aided and abetted a fraud, and/or a civil claim for negligence brought by the lender. Moreover, under the Proceeds of Crime Act 2002, a solicitor risks committing a money laundering offence (see **5.11**) if they enter into an arrangement with respect to or transfers the value of a mortgage obtained through fraud.

The Law Society has published a Mortgage Fraud Practice Note (available at <www. lawsociety. org.uk>) to help conveyancers spot the warning signs of mortgage fraud and protect their firms against it. The Practice Note also contains guidance on a solicitor's obligations under the 2019 SRA Codes. In summary, the guidance indicates that a solicitor will have a conflict of interest if they have information about the transaction that the lender would consider relevant to granting the loan but the borrower does not want them to disclose it to the lender. There is an obligation to disclose all relevant information to the lender client, but the solicitor also has a duty of confidentiality to the borrower client. Accordingly, the solicitor must seek consent from the borrower to disclose the information to the lender, but if that consent is not given the solicitor must refuse to continue to act for the borrower and the lender.

The duty of confidentiality to the borrower is discharged only where the solicitor is satisfied of a strong prima facie case that the borrower is using them to further a fraud or other criminal purpose. The Law Society suggests that this test may be satisfied if a client makes a deliberate misrepresentation on their mortgage application. If this is the case, the information may be passed to the lender. In addition, the solicitor must consider whether a disclosure should be made to the National Crime Agency, as fraudulently obtained mortgage funds, if received into the client's or solicitor's bank account, constitute money laundering and give rise to offences under the Proceeds of Crime Act 2002 (see **5.11**). If the duty of confidentiality is not released, the solicitor should return the mortgage documents to the lender, stating only that they are ceasing to act due to professional reasons. In practice, this may result in the lender withdrawing its mortgage offer.

The Law Society issued an additional Practice Note, entitled Property and Registration Fraud, in October 2010. The SRA has also issued warning cards on fraudulent financial arrangements, money laundering and property fraud. This is a very difficult area and further advice may be obtained from the SRA's Professional Ethics Helpline.

5.13 PROPERTY AND TITLE FRAUD

The Law Society and the Land Registry have jointly published an advice note on property and title fraud. The advice note contains examples of title fraud encountered in practice, such as impersonating registered proprietors, creating false conveyancing firms and submitting forged documents. The advice note also contains case studies on suspicious client behaviours, recommendations to mitigate the risk of property fraud and details of professional bodies so that the identity of the conveyancer acting for the other party can be verified.

Buyers' solicitors should be aware of the Court of Appeal decision in *P&P Property Ltd v Owen White & Catlin LLP and Another; Dreamvar (UK) Ltd v Mishcon De Reya and Another* [2018] EWCA Civ 1082. Both cases were heard together as they contained similar facts. In both cases, a fraudulent seller had purported to sell a high value London property to an innocent buyer. In fact the fraudsters did not own the properties, but this was not discovered until after the purchase monies had been handed over. The Court of Appeal held that, although there was no negligence on the part of the buyers' solicitors, they were liable for the losses suffered by their buyer clients. This was on the basis that the buyers' solicitors had received the money from their clients on trust to use for a genuine completion. As there had, in fact, not been a genuine completion, the buyers' solicitors were in breach of trust. This was despite the fact that, in the *Mishcon De Reya* case, the seller's solicitor had not carried out adequate identity checks on its own client. The Court held that the seller's solicitor was not liable in tort to the buyer or its solicitor, as it had no general duty of care to them. However, the buyer's solicitor could claim a contribution from the seller's solicitor towards the buyer's losses, as the previous edition of the Law Society's Code for Completion by Post (see **30.8.1**), which the parties had adopted, required the seller's solicitor to use the purchase money for a genuine completion.

These cases are alarming for buyers' solicitors, as the losses stem from the actions of a party who is not their client and whose identify and status they are not in a position to easily check. The Law Society has considered the implications of the case and published a new edition of its Code for Completion by Post. The Code expressly provides that the seller's solicitor holds the purchase moneys on trust for the buyer and is under a fiduciary duty not to deal with that money other than in accordance with the terms of the Code. The seller's solicitor also undertakes that they have authority from the true owner of the property to receive the money and that the person named as the owner in the contract is entitled to transfer the property to the buyer. The Law Society has also suggested that buyers' solicitors consider asking sellers' solicitors questions, for example, about whether they have carried out their anti-money laundering investigations. It is advised that additional questions of sellers' solicitors should also be raised by buyers' solicitors where there are indicators of potential fraud of the type highlighted in the HM Land Registry/Law Society joint note on property and title fraud.

5.14 DATA PROTECTION

The General Data Protection Regulation (EU) 2016/679 (GPDR) and the Data Protection Act 2018 (DPA 2018), which came into force on 25 May 2018, require those who are 'controllers' or 'processors' of personal information to handle it in particular ways, and they impose penalties on processors who are in breach of their duties. The precise details of the duties and penalties are beyond the scope of this book, but, broadly, personal information is defined in the GDPR as 'any information relating to an identified or identifiable natural person', controlling means determining the purpose and manner in which personal data is processed, and processing includes collecting, recording organising, storing and disclosing such information, whether by automated or manual methods. A data processor must comply with all six principles set out in the GDPR (eg personal data must be accurate and, where necessary, kept up to date), and a data controller is responsible for, and must be able to demonstrate compliance with, these principles. A data controller can only process data on one or more of the six legal grounds in the GDPR or a public interest ground set out in the DPA 1998. A data processor may have to obtain express consent from a person about whom data is collected and stored ('a data subject'), and the data subject will have rights over their data, including the right to see the data by making a subject access request and to have the data erased in certain circumstances.

There are some property transactions which are likely to involve personal data. For example, where a property is being sold subject to leases, the personal details of tenants may have to be retained in case of claims and also passed on to the new landlord for management purposes. Where the rent payable under a lease is determined by reference to the tenant's turnover, the tenant may be disclosing personal information relating to employees and customer relationships. Personal data may also be disclosed when a tenant applies to the landlord for licence to assign or underlet, or where a guarantor is asked for references and financial information. Property lawyers will therefore need to consider whether they are a controller or a processor, the legal basis for processing personal data and whether they have policies and procedures in place to ensure compliance with the relevant GDPR duties.

SUMMARY

- A solicitor cannot act for more than one party in a property transaction if there is a conflict of interest or a significant risk of a conflict of interest.
- Acting for a buyer and seller in the same transaction carries a high risk of conflict of interest and should not occur routinely.
- It will often be possible to act for both buyer and lender in a residential transaction if the mortgage is on standard terms.
- In commercial transactions, the lender will usually be represented separately. It may be possible for a solicitor to act for both if the mortgage is on standard terms.

- A solicitor should follow the guidelines laid down in *Royal Bank of Scotland v Etridge (No 2) and other Appeals* [2001] 4 All ER 449 if acting for joint borrowers.
- A solicitor must, in most circumstances, keep the affairs of their client confidential.
- A solicitor dealing with more than one buyer in a 'contract race' must comply with paras 1.2 and 1.4 of the SRA Codes.
- Undertakings are frequently given in property transactions, but a failure to comply with an undertaking constitutes professional misconduct.
- The Legal Services Act 2007 makes it an offence for an unqualified person to prepare a property contract, transfer or charge.
- The Money Laundering, Terrorist Financing and Transfer of Funds (Information on the Payer) Regulations 2017 impose customer due diligence requirements on property lawyers.
- A solicitor must be able to spot the warning signs of money laundering, mortgage fraud, property fraud and title fraud, and should read the Law Society's guidance on these subjects.

CHAPTER 6

PROPERTY TAXATION

LEARNING OUTCOMES

After reading this chapter you will be able to explain the implications for property transactions of:

- capital gains tax
- value added tax
- stamp duty land tax
- annual tax on enveloped dwellings.

6.1 CAPITAL GAINS TAX

6.1.1 Basic principles

A liability to capital gains tax (CGT) may arise on the disposal of an interest in land by an individual. A seller's solicitor should be aware of the possibility of CGT being chargeable and advise their client accordingly. Equally, a solicitor acting for a buyer should advise their client of the potential for liability on any future disposal where appropriate. With effect from April 2015, owners of residential property who are not resident in the UK will also be liable to pay CGT on gains made after April 2015, in the same way as UK residents. Set out below is a brief explanation of the basic principles relating to CGT, followed by a more detailed consideration of the principal private residence relief, which is of particular importance in the context of residential conveyancing.

Capital gains tax is charged on gains made on 'chargeable assets' within the meaning of Taxation of Chargeable Gains Act 1992. This includes freehold and leasehold property, and the interests of co-owners in the case of jointly-owned property. Some transactions that are incidental to the sale of land also give rise to a charge to CGT, for example where a separate payment is made for the release or modification of an easement or covenant. Gifts also fall within the meaning of 'disposal' for the purpose of CGT.

The gain is calculated by deducting the purchase price of the property (or its base value in 1982 if purchased earlier than this) from its current sale price. Certain forms of expenditure incurred in acquiring or improving the property can also be deducted in appropriate cases. The gain is chargeable at a rate set by the Government after allowing for the individual's annual exemption. For a more detailed analysis of CGT generally, including reliefs that may be available in certain situations, see ***Legal Foundations***.

Companies can also be liable under corporation tax for gains realised by them on the basis of similar principles.

6.1.2 Private residence relief

Gains made on the disposal by sale or by gift of an individual's dwelling house used as their only or main residence (including grounds of up to 0.5 hectares) are exempt from CGT (Taxation of Chargeable Gains Act 1992, s 222).

6.1.2.1 Qualifying conditions

To qualify for the relief, the seller must have occupied the dwelling house as their only or main residence throughout their period of ownership. If an individual has more than one residence, it is a question of fact which one constitutes their only or main residence. However, the taxpayer can determine the question by making an election within two years of acquiring a second property, backdated for up to two years.

6.1.2.2 Absences

Under s 223 of the Taxation of Chargeable Gains Act 1992, certain periods of absence are disregarded when calculating the amount of relief:

(a) the last 18 months of ownership (in order to facilitate the purchase of another property);

(b) the first 12 months of ownership due to the owner undertaking repairs or redecoration;

(c) any period(s) not exceeding three years in total throughout the period of ownership. Absence within this exception may be for any reason (eg, an extended holiday) and can be made up of several separate periods of absence, provided that the total under this exception does not exceed three years;

(d) any period(s) during which the owner was working outside the UK. This exception applies to employees only, not to self-employed persons;

(e) any period(s) during which the owner was prevented from living in their dwelling house because they were employed elsewhere. This exception would apply, for example, to a school caretaker who was required to live in accommodation provided by the school, or an employee taking a job in another part of the country.

If the taxpayer is absent for longer periods, the proportion of the gain attributable to periods in excess of those mentioned in cases (c) to (e) above loses the benefit of the relief, and so becomes chargeable. Thus, if an individual made a gain of £120,000 on a property owned for 12 years out of which they spent four years travelling, three of the four years' absence fall within case (c). The gain attributable to one year out of the 12 years' ownership will be chargeable ($\frac{1}{12}$ × £120,000 = £10,000).

6.1.2.3 Letting the property

To the extent that the property is let during the period of ownership, it ceases to be the individual's only or main residence (unless such absence can be disregarded under **6.1.2.2**). The proportion of the gain attributable to the period of letting will be chargeable, but only to the extent (if any) to which it exceeds the lesser of £40,000 and the part of the gain that is not a chargeable gain.

Thus, in the example considered in **6.1.2.2** above, if the individual had let their house during their absence, the £10,000 gain would be exempt as it is under £40,000 (and £40,000 is less than the £110,000 non-chargeable gain attributable to their occupation). On the other hand, if the gain attributable to the period of letting had been £50,000 and the non-chargeable gain still £110,000, then £10,000 (ie, the excess of £50,000 over £40,000) would be chargeable.

6.1.2.4 Houses with large grounds

Where a dwelling house has grounds of more than 0.5 hectares, the excess is on the face of it taxable, but HMRC has discretion to allow land in excess of 0.5 hectares to be included within the private residence relief if the extra land can be shown to be necessary for the reasonable enjoyment of the house.

6.1.2.5 Sale of land alone

The sale of land alone, where the ownership of the house is retained, may enjoy the benefit of the relief so long as the area of the grounds does not exceed 0.5 hectares. If the house is sold and land retained, a subsequent sale of the land will usually attract CGT.

6.1.2.6 Part business user

Where part of a principal private dwelling house is used exclusively for business purposes (eg, a doctor who has a consulting room in their home), a proportion of the relief may be lost, relative to the area of the 'business premises' in relation to the total area of the dwelling house. If a 'duality of user' can be shown, the full relief may be available. Thus, a person who works from home, but who does not have a separate room for their business from which the other members of the family are excluded, may still take full advantage of the principal private residence relief.

6.1.2.7 Married couples and civil partnerships

Only one relief is available to couples who are married or in civil partnerships. Where such couples own more than one house, they must choose which property is to take the benefit of the relief. However, an election is not irrevocable and can thus be changed (eg, if one property is increasing in value more than the other).

6.1.2.8 Trustees

The private residence relief is available where the disposal is made by trustees, provided that the person in occupation of the property was a person who was entitled to be in occupation under the terms of the settlement (eg, a tenant for life) (Taxation of Chargeable Gains Act 1992, s 225). By virtue of s 12 of the Trusts of Land and Appointment of Trustees Act 1996, a beneficiary under a trust of land now has a statutory right to occupy the trust property.

6.1.2.9 Tenants in common

Tenants in common may be liable for CGT on their respective shares in the equitable interest in the property.

6.1.2.10 Four key questions

When taking instructions from an individual in relation to the sale of a dwelling house, the answers to the following four questions will indicate whether there is likely to be a CGT liability on the property. If the answers to the questions set out below match the suggested answers, there is unlikely to be a CGT liability on the transaction. If any of the client's answers differ from those suggested, further enquiries should be raised.

	Question	**Answer**
1.	Did you move into the house immediately after you bought it?	Yes
2.	Have you lived anywhere else since moving into this house?	No
3.	Does the garden extend to more than 0.5 hectares?	No
4.	Do you (or your spouse) own another house?	No

6.1.3 Buy-to-let properties

An individual who disposes of a dwelling house as part of a property-letting business will be subject to CGT. The gain is calculated by deducting the purchase price (including legal costs, SDLT and the cost of any capital improvements) from the sale price (less legal costs and estate agent's commission). Private residence relief will not be available because the dwelling house was acquired for the purpose of realising a gain from its disposal.

6.2 VALUE ADDED TAX

6.2.1 Introduction

A property lawyer will frequently have to consider the impact of value added tax (VAT) on the transaction. Value added tax is chargeable in respect of a supply of goods or services made in the course of a business. Supplies can be exempt, zero-rated or standard-rated depending upon the circumstances. Standard-rated supplies are subject to VAT at the current standard rate; zero-rated supplies are taxable, but, as the name suggests, are subject to VAT at 0%. Exempt supplies are not subject to tax.

The current standard rate of VAT is 20%.

Value added tax paid by a business on supplies made to it ('input tax') can be recovered from HMRC, provided that it was incurred in making taxable (ie, standard-rated or zero-rated, but not exempt) supplies. The VAT charged by a business on supplies it makes ('output tax') has to be accounted for to HMRC. In practice, the input tax incurred in making those supplies is deducted from the output tax and only the balance is paid over to HMRC. Deducting the input tax is colloquially referred to as 'recovering the VAT'.

Value added tax affects property transactions as follows:

(a) Residential properties:
  (i) sale of a green field site: exempt, but subject to option to tax (see **6.2.2**);
  (ii) construction and civil engineering works: zero-rated;
  (iii) legal and other professional services: standard-rated; and
  (iv) sale or lease of a new house: zero-rated.

(b) Commercial properties:
  (i) sale of a green field site: exempt, but subject to option to tax (see **6.2.2**);
  (ii) construction and civil engineering services: standard-rated;
  (iii) legal and other professional fees: standard-rated;
  (iv) sale of a new freehold building: standard-rated;
  (v) sale of an old freehold building: exempt, but subject to option to tax (see **6.2.2**); and
  (vi) grant or assignment of a lease; exempt, but subject to option to tax (see **6.2.2**).

6.2.2 The option to tax

When an exempt supply is made, any input tax incurred in connection with that supply cannot be recovered from HMRC. The purpose of the option to tax is to enable an individual to convert an exempt supply into a taxable one, enabling them to recover any input tax incurred. Thus, a developer who has incurred VAT on constructing or refurbishing a property may opt to charge VAT on its disposal so that the VAT incurred getting it ready for sale can be recovered. The details of how to effect this option (sometimes confusingly referred to as an 'election to waive exemption') are outside the scope of this chapter. However, notification of the option to HMRC is necessary for it to be effective.

6.2.3 VAT and residential property

In the case of residential property, the impact of VAT is relatively uncomplicated. The sale or lease of a new house by the person constructing it is zero-rated. The subsequent sale of a dwelling (either freehold or leasehold) by a private individual will not be made in the course of a business. The sale of a buy-to-let property is an exempt supply. So in none of these cases will the seller be charging the buyer VAT in addition to the purchase price.

In the case of residential development, the purchase of land by a developer will be an exempt supply, unless the seller has opted to charge tax (see **6.2.2**). The construction work will be zero-rated and so no input tax will be incurred on this, but input tax will be paid on the professional fees. The sale of the houses will be zero-rated and, as this is a taxable supply (albeit at 0%), the developer will be able to recover the input tax incurred from HMRC.

6.2.4 VAT and commercial property

The VAT implications here are much more extensive.

The sale of a 'new' freehold commercial building is standard-rated, which will enable a developer to recover the potentially significant amounts of input tax incurred in developing the site. For these purposes, a 'new' building is one completed within the three years prior to the sale. The input tax incurred may well be substantial as the construction and other works will be standard-rated. Further, although the purchase of land in the first place will prima facie have been an exempt supply, the seller to the developer might have opted to charge tax.

The freehold sale of a commercial property which is more than three years old and the grant of a lease of commercial property (whatever the age of the building) are exempt, but subject to the option to tax. The only point in the seller/landlord opting to tax is to enable them to recover any input tax incurred. If none has been incurred, they are unlikely to so opt because this will make the property unattractive to VAT-sensitive buyers/tenants (see **6.2.5**). However, VAT may have been incurred in carrying out repair and refurbishment works on the building, and as this cannot be recovered on making an exempt supply, the seller/landlord can opt to tax and recover their input tax by setting it off against the output tax being charged to the buyer/tenant.

Where the property is a 'new' freehold or 'old' property where the option to tax has been exercised (so that the standard rate would normally apply), if the property is let and the buyer intends to continue the letting business, it may be possible to treat the sale of the property as a transfer of a business as a going concern (TOGC). If the transaction is a TOGC, no VAT will be chargeable on the transaction. The seller and buyer must both be VAT registered, and the buyer must opt to tax the property and notify HMRC prior to the tax point for the transaction. The detailed provisions concerning TOGCs are outside the scope of this book.

6.2.5 VAT-sensitive buyers/tenants

Potential buyers and tenants who make mainly standard-rated or zero-rated supplies in the course of their businesses (eg, retail foodstores or solicitors) will not be adversely affected by a charge to VAT on the purchase price or rent, since they will be able to recover the VAT. They will do this either by offsetting the input tax against their output tax (in the case of those making standard-rated supplies) or by reclaiming it from HMRC (in the case of those making zero-rated supplies). However, for those businesses that make only exempt supplies (eg, banks, building societies, insurance companies), any VAT they pay on the purchase price or the rent will be irrecoverable. Such businesses may, for example, be reluctant to purchase 'new' freehold properties or take a lease of a property where the landlord has opted to tax. Alternatively, they may seek to pay a reduced price or rent to compensate for the irrecoverable VAT.

6.2.6 Conveyancing points

If VAT is chargeable in a property transaction, it is necessary to ensure that the documentation deals with it adequately. Under general principles, a price is deemed to be inclusive of VAT unless the contrary is stated. The terms of the contract between the parties have to be considered.

6.2.6.1 Sale of new commercial freehold

The sale of a new freehold commercial building is standard-rated. The seller will need to ensure that the contract allows them to charge VAT in addition to the agreed purchase price. The contract for sale is likely to incorporate one of the two standard sets of conditions (see **Chapter 18**). Where the Standard Conditions (SCs) are used, SC 1.4.1 states that the price is inclusive of VAT, and so a special condition will have to be incorporated to allow the seller to charge VAT in addition to the agreed purchase price. Where the Standard Commercial Property Conditions (SCPCs) are used, SCPC 2 provides that VAT at the standard rate will be payable by the buyer. Under the SCPCs, the seller will therefore be able to require the buyer to pay VAT in addition to the purchase price, without the need for a special condition. The buyer's solicitor should make the client aware of the obligation to pay the VAT in addition to the purchase price at the earliest opportunity, as the extra amount payable may affect the buyer's financial arrangements.

6.2.6.2 Sale of old commercial freehold

On the sale of an *old* commercial building, whether VAT is payable on the purchase price depends on whether the seller has opted to tax prior to completion (see **6.2.2**). If the seller has opted to tax and the SCs are used, SC 1.4.1 states that the price is inclusive of VAT, so a special condition will have to be incorporated to allow the seller to charge VAT. Where the SCPCs are used, as discussed, SCPC 2 provides that VAT at the standard rate will be payable by the buyer. As a result, if the SCPCs are used and the seller opts to tax prior to completion, the buyer is required to pay VAT in addition to the purchase price.

In consequence, the buyer should be warned of the danger of the seller opting to tax prior to completion in respect of an old commercial building. The danger also exists in respect of any other exempt supply of land (eg the sale of a greenfield site). If the buyer does not want to pay VAT and is using a contract incorporating the SCPCs, then the buyer's solicitor should seek to negotiate a provision in the contract to ensure VAT is not payable by the buyer. The buyer's solicitor should consider the following:

(a) Incorporating condition A1 in Part 2 of the SCPCs. Condition A1 provides that the sale does not constitute a supply for VAT purposes and that the seller will not opt to tax. As a result, if condition A1 is incorporated into the contract, the buyer cannot be required to pay any VAT, subject to one exception. The exception is provided for in A1.3 in Part 2. This provides that if there is a change in the law between exchange and completion that makes the sale of the property a VATable supply, the buyer will have to pay VAT. So, if the Government were to pass legislation after the buyer had exchanged contracts to make the sale of an old commercial freehold a standard-rated supply for VAT purposes, the buyer would then have to pay VAT.

(b) Incorporating a special condition that disapplies SCPC 2 and provides that the purchase price is inclusive of any VAT. This will mean that should VAT become payable on the sale for any reason (eg a change in the law or an option by the seller to tax), the buyer will not have to pay it. This will, however, have consequences for the seller (see **6.2.6.4**). As a result, the seller's solicitor may resist such a provision.

If the buyer's solicitor is unable to negotiate an appropriate contractual provision to protect the buyer from liability for VAT, the buyer should again be advised to make their financial arrangements on the assumption that VAT will be payable in addition to the agreed price.

6.2.6.3 Landlord and tenant

The grant of a commercial lease, whether of a new or old building, is an exempt supply, subject to the option to tax. If the option is made after the grant of the lease, s 89 of the VATA 1994 allows the rent to be increased by the amount of VAT, unless there is a clause in the lease making the rent inclusive of VAT. If an election is made before the grant of a lease, s 89 will not apply, and so the landlord will be able to add VAT to the rent only if there is a provision in the lease permitting this. From the landlord's point of view, therefore, there ought to be such a provision in every lease.

6.2.6.4 What if the seller/landlord cannot add on VAT?

If the option to tax is made, or a standard-rated supply is made and the seller/landlord is unable to charge VAT in addition to the agreed price, the seller is still liable to account for VAT to HMRC out of the agreed price. So, for example (on the basis of the current 20% rate), a price of £750,000 is agreed for a sale of land. If the seller can add VAT, the buyer will hand over £900,000, £750,000 of which will be kept by the seller, the other £150,000 being handed over to HMRC. If the seller is unable to add on the VAT, the buyer need only pay £750,000 on completion. The seller will then have to account for the VAT element of the £750,000 received. As the £750,000 amounts to 120% of the purchase price, the seller will have to account for £125,000 to HMRC: ($\frac{750,000}{120} \times 20$). As a result, the seller will keep only £625,000.

6.3 STAMP DUTY LAND TAX

6.3.1 Introduction

Stamp duty land tax (SDLT), which replaced stamp duty as from 1 December 2003, is charged on property transactions, freehold and leasehold, residential and commercial. However, it is charged at different rates depending on the type of property and the value of the transaction. Stamp duty land tax is payable to HMRC within 14 days of completion (see **31.7** for the method of payment). Non-payment or evasion of SDLT gives rise to fines and penalties, for which the client and their solicitor may face prosecution.

In Wales, with effect from April 2018, SDLT has been replaced with Land Transaction Tax (LTT). LTT is beyond the scope of this book but details can be found at www.gov.wales.

6.3.2 Rates of SDLT

6.3.2.1 Residential freehold property

Since 4 December 2014, SDLT on residential property transactions has been charged using a separate rate of tax on each portion of the purchase price. For those who are not first-time buyers, the rates and bands from 1 April 2025 are as follows (although see **6.3.2.3** for 'special rates' that apply to certain transactions and **6.3.2.4** for exemptions and reliefs (including those that apply to first-time buyers)):

Part of consideration	Rate
So much as does not exceed £125,000	0%
So much as exceeds £125,000 but does not exceed £250,000	2%
So much as exceeds £250,000 but does not exceed £925,000	5%
So much as exceeds £925,000 but does not exceed £1,500,000	10%
The remainder	12%

For example, a second-time buyer who pays £275,000 for their home will pay SDLT of £3,750 (0% on the first £125,000, 2% on the next £125,000 and 5% on the remaining £25,000). The position is different for first-time buyers (see **6.3.2.4**).

6.3.2.2 Non-residential or mixed use freehold property

Since March 2016, SDLT on non-residential and mixed use properties has (like residential properties) been charged using a separate rate of tax on each portion of the purchase price.

The rates and bands are as follows:

Part of consideration	Rate
So much as does not exceed £150,000	0%
So much as exceeds £150,000 but does not exceed £250,000	2%
So much as exceeds £250,000	5%

For example, a buyer of freehold commercial property for £275,000 will pay SDLT of £3,250 (0% on the first £150,000, 2% on the next £100,000 and 5% on the final £25,000). If VAT is charged, SDLT is payable on the VAT-inclusive sum.

6.3.2.3 Special rates

There are different SDLT rules and rate calculations for certain types of transaction (see <www.gov.uk> for full details). These include:

(a) purchases by corporate bodies: a SDLT rate of 17% applies to residential purchases of over £500,000 by certain corporate bodies and 'non-natural persons';

(b) purchases of six or more residential properties in one transaction: such purchases will be subject to the rates for non-residential property (see **6.3.2.2**);

(c) shared ownership properties;

(d) multiple purchases or transfers between the same buyer and seller (linked transactions). The buyer pays SDLT on the total of value of all linked transactions;

(e) purchases of 'additional' residential properties: since 1 April 2016, an extra surcharge on top of the normal SDLT rates has been payable by any buyer whose purchase results in them owning more than one residential property and on acquisitions of dwellings by companies. From 1 April 2025 the surcharge will be 5%. A buyer can claim a refund of this additional SDLT charge if the second property is intended as a replacement for their main residence and the main residence is sold within 36 months of the purchase of the second property. There are also certain purchases that are not subject to the higher rates (see **6.3.2.4**).

6.3.2.4 Exemptions and reliefs

Certain transactions may be entitled to relief from SDLT, although a land transaction return will still need to be filed in order to claim the relief (see **31.7**). Those purchasing their first home for £500,000 or less can claim relief so that they do not pay any SDLT up to £300,000 and pay 5% on the portion from £300,001 to £500,000. Other examples where reliefs are available include transfers between group companies and purchases by charities.

Certain transactions are exempt from the obligation to apply SDLT and submit a land transaction return altogether. These include where property is left in a will or is transferred following divorce or dissolution of a civil partnership.

In addition, certain purchases of 'additional' residential property do not attract the higher rates of SDLT referred to at **6.3.2.3(e)**. These include purchases for less than £40,000 and purchases of purpose-built student accommodation or mobile homes.

Full details on reliefs and exemptions and the conditions applicable to them can be found by visiting <www.gov.uk>.

It should be noted that whilst the above exemptions and reliefs can legitimately reduce a buyer's SDLT liability, the SRA has issued a Warning Notice to solicitors about advising clients to participate in artificial tax arrangements designed to avoid SDLT. The SRA warns that professionals who facilitate a tax avoidance scheme that HMRC later defeats may face a new penalty that HMRC intends to bring into force.

6.3.3 Apportionment of SDLT for chattels

Stamp duty land tax is payable only on the consideration for the land, not on that separately attributed to chattels. If the sale includes chattels, it is sometimes possible to reduce the liability to tax by apportioning some of the price to the chattels included in the sale, for example carpets and curtains. The amount apportioned to the chattels must, of course, be a fair reflection of their value, otherwise both solicitor and client could be liable to criminal sanctions.

Guidance issued by HMRC states that 'the valuation of any chattels should represent the open market value (including depreciation) at the ... date of the transaction ... bearing in mind the age, quality and condition of each item. Where an item is regarded as a chattel, HMRC would generally expect the open market value for some of these items to be substantially lower than their acquisition cost.'

6.3.4 Leasehold property and SDLT

For SDLT on the grant of a lease, see **35.11.2.1**. For SDLT on the assignment of a lease, see **36.10.1**.

6.4 ANNUAL TAX ON ENVELOPED DWELLINGS

The annual tax on enveloped dwellings (ATED) is chargeable on companies, collective investment vehicles and partnerships with company members who own UK residential property valued at over a certain threshold level. The threshold for returns from 1 April 2016 is £500,000. The property is said to be 'enveloped' because the ownership sits within a corporate 'wrapper' or 'envelope' (rather than with an individual). The amount of ATED is worked out using a banding system based on the value of the property. Its primary purpose is to discourage the use of corporate wrapper schemes as a method of avoiding SDLT. There are a number of reliefs from ATED designed to exempt properties held in corporate wrappers for genuine business reasons, such as property development, heritage, charity or farming purposes.

6.5 RESIDENTIAL PROPERTY DEVELOPER TAX

Part 2 of the Finance Act 2022 introduces a new tax – the Residential Property Developer Tax (RPDT). RPDT applies from 1 April 2022 for a period of 10 years and is intended to partially fund the removal of unsafe cladding from high rise blocks of flats.

RPDT only applies to companies and groups of companies who are involved in residential property development (although non-profit housing companies are excluded). RPDT is only payable on profits that exceed the RPDT annual allowance (currently £25 million) and so will only apply to larger developers.

If payable, RPDT is paid at the rate of 4% of the developer's taxable profits above the annual allowance (although there are certain reliefs available). It applies to profits from development activities on residential land, where those activities are carried out by companies with an interest in the land. These concepts are defined further in the Finance Act 2022 (see ss 35–37). An RPDT developer must include its residential property development profits or losses in its corporation tax return.

6.6 COUNCIL TAX AND BUSINESS RATES

Owners of residential properties will have to pay Council Tax to their local council. The amount of tax depends on what band the property falls into (the banding being based upon the property's value). The property's banding will normally be revealed by the agent's particulars and the pre-contract enquiries raised with the seller. Buyers of residential properties should be aware that councils have the power (from April 2025) to charge owners of second homes (not used as a sole or main residence) 100% extra council tax under the Levelling Up and Regeneration Act 2023.

Owners of commercial properties will have to pay business rates to their local council instead of Council Tax. Business rates are based on the property's 'rateable value' which is an estimate by the Valuation Office Agency of how much it would cost to rent the property for a year. A buyer of a commercial property should check the amount of business rates payable for the property prior to committing to purchase it.

SUMMARY

- A liability to CGT may arise on the disposal of an interest in land.
- Gains made on the disposal of a principal private dwelling house are exempt from CGT.
- The sale of a residential property by a private individual will not give rise to VAT.
- The sale of a residential property by a developer will be zero rated for VAT purposes and so no VAT will be paid by the buyer.
- The sale of a new commercial building is standard rated for VAT purposes.
- The sale of an old commercial building is exempt, but subject to the option to tax.
- If VAT is (or could become) chargeable on a property transaction, the contract must contain provisions to deal with it.
- Stamp duty land tax is charged on freehold and leasehold property transactions at different rates depending on the type of property, the purchase price and (in the case of leasehold property) rent.

CHAPTER 7

Town and Country Planning, Building Regulations and Related Matters

LEARNING OUTCOMES

After reading this chapter you will be able to:

- identify when planning permission and building regulation approval are required
- explain the implications of failure to obtain planning permission or building regulation approval
- advise on a solicitor's responsibilities for planning and related matters in a property transaction
- explain the implications of buying contaminated land.

7.1 TOWN AND COUNTRY PLANNING

7.1.1 Outline of the planning system

The planning system exists to ensure that development of land is carried out in a planned and appropriate fashion. Responsibility for town and country planning vests in the local planning authority (LPA), usually the district, unitary or London borough council for that area. The LPA is responsible, amongst other things, for the grant or refusal of planning permission and taking enforcement action in respect of breaches of planning control.

In carrying out many of these functions, the LPA will be guided by a variety of central and local government policies. This will include the 'development plan' for the area. The development plan incorporates what is known as the Local Development Framework (LDF) for an area. The LDF is a collection of planning documents outlining how an LPA will manage development and land use in its area. The development plan will also include any 'saved policies' from the old-style local plans that pre-dated LDFs.

In addition to the development plan, the central government department responsible for planning control, the Ministry of Housing, Communities and Local Government (MHCLG), also publishes important policy guidance to which the LPA will need to have regard. In the past, that guidance took the form of numerous circulars, guidance notes and policy statements, but from 27 March 2012 most of the guidance has been consolidated into one document, the National Planning Policy Framework (NPPF). The NPPF sets out the Government's economic, social and environmental planning policies for England (excluding only policies for traveller sites, nationally significant infrastructure projects and national waste).

Central to the NPPF is the presumption of sustainable development, which Resolution 42/187 of the United Nations General Assembly (cited in the NPPF) defines as meeting the needs of the present without compromising the ability of future generations to meet their own needs. The planning system has three overarching objectives – economic, social and environmental – which are interdependent and are to be pursued in mutually supportive ways. The NPPF sets out a number of specific planning policies, including delivering a sufficient supply of homes, ensuring the vitality of town centres, building a strong, competitive economy, promoting sustainable transport, protecting green belt land, meeting the challenge of climate change, flooding and coastal change and conserving and enhancing the natural and historic environments. The presumption of sustainable development must be taken into account in the preparation of development plans and the determination of planning applications. Development proposals that accord with the relevant development plan should be approved without delay, and where the development plan is absent, silent or contains out-of-date policies, planning permission should be granted unless the adverse impacts of so doing would significantly outweigh the benefits, or specific policies in the NPPF indicate that development should be restricted.

Note that since devolution, the Welsh Assembly has had responsibility for the overall planning framework in Wales. Differences will therefore arise when dealing with properties in Wales. A Welsh planning toolkit can be found at <uk.practicallaw.thomsonreuters.com>.

7.1.2 Legislation

The principal legislation is the Town and Country Planning Act 1990 (TCPA 1990) supplemented by numerous statutory instruments. This chapter draws attention to the principles of planning law only in so far as they affect the normal conveyancing transaction and is not a comprehensive guide to the topic.

7.1.3 Relevance of planning to the transaction

Planning law affects whether a building can be built, altered or extended, and also specifies the particular use to which a property can be put. It is therefore important for a buyer to be satisfied that the building which they are buying has permission to be on the site where it has been built, and also that it is being used for its authorised purpose. Heavy fines can be imposed for breach of planning control and, since planning matters (both permission granted and breaches committed) usually run with the land, action for any breach which is outstanding at completion could be brought against the buyer after completion, even though the breach was committed by a predecessor in title.

In addition, it may be the case that the buyer intends to carry out works to, or change the use of, the property after purchase. Such activity may require planning permission and the buyer's solicitor needs to advise their client on this before exchange of contracts. If planning permission is indeed needed, consideration needs to be given either to ensuring that planning permission is obtained before exchange or to making the contract conditional upon obtaining that permission.

7.1.4 When is planning permission needed?

7.1.4.1 Planning permission required for the carrying out of 'development'

At the heart of the planning system is the idea that planning permission is needed in respect of any activity which constitutes 'development'. This term is defined in s 55 of the TCPA 1990 as the carrying out of either the following:

(a) *The carrying out of building, engineering, mining or other operations in, on, over or under land.* This can include the erection of new buildings and alteration to existing buildings; and/or

(b) *The making of any material change in the use of any buildings or other land.*

Note that provided any one of these elements is present, the possibility of the need for planning permission must be considered. It is possible for there to be building works but not a change of use and, equally, for there to be a change of use without building work: in either case, the proposals may amount to development and so require planning permission. As regards change of use, only a *material* change in use requires permission. 'Material' is not defined and is a question of fact and degree in each particular case.

7.1.4.2 Matters which do not constitute 'development'

Certain matters which would otherwise fall within the definition of development (and so require planning permission) are specifically excluded from that definition by the TCPA 1990 and statutory instruments made under it. The most commonly encountered exceptions are as follows:

(a) Works for the maintenance, improvement or other alteration of a building which affect only the interior or do not materially affect the external appearance of a building.

(b) The use of buildings or land within the curtilage of a dwelling house for any purpose incidental to the use of the dwelling house (eg, using an existing garage as a playroom). The 'curtilage' of a dwelling house is the land immediately surrounding the house and, except where the grounds are extensive, will normally encompass the whole of the garden area.

(c) Change of use within the same use class as specified by the Town and Country Planning (Use Classes) Order 1987 (SI 1987/764) (UCO). The UCO contains lists of uses grouped together into use classes denoted by a letter of the alphabet and, in most cases, a number (thus, B2 and B8 are each separate use classes whereas E(a) and E(b) are in the same class E). A change of use from one use within a class to another within the same class will not require planning permission. The use classes have been amended on a number of occasions, but have recently undergone major changes in England as a result of significant amendments to the UCO which took effect on 1 September 2020. The main use classes in England from 1 September 2020 are set out in the table below:

B2 General industrial	Use for industrial process other than one falling within class E(g)
B8 Storage or distribution	This class includes open air storage.
Class C1: hotels	Use as a hotel or boarding or guest house where no significant element of care is provided.
Class C3: dwelling houses	Use as a dwelling house whether or not as a sole or main residence by: (a) a single person or by people to be regarded as forming a single household; or (b) not more than six residents living together as a single household, whether or not care is provided, other than a use falling within Class C4.

Class C4: houses in multiple occupation	Use of a dwellinghouse by not more than six residents as a 'house in multiple occupation' (known as an 'HMO').
Class E: commercial, business and service	
E(a)	Display or retail sale of goods, other than hot food
E(b)	Sale of food and drink for consumption (mostly) on the premises
E(c)	Provision of:
	(i) financial services, **(ii)** professional services (other than health or medical services), or **(iii)** other appropriate services in a commercial, business or service locality.
E(d)	Indoor sport, recreation or fitness (not involving motorised vehicles or firearms or use as a swimming pool or skating rink)
E(e)	Provision of medical or health services (except the use of premises attached to the residence of the consultant or practitioner)
E(f)	Creche, day nursery or day centre (not including a residential use)
E(g)	Uses which can be carried out in a residential area without detriment to its amenity:
E(g)(i)	Offices to carry out any operational or administrative functions,
E(g)(ii)	Research and development of products or processes
E(g)(iii)	Industrial processes
Class F: local community and learning	
F1 Learning and non-residential institutions	Use (not including residential use) defined in 7 parts:
F1(a)	Provision of education
F1(b)	Display of works of art (otherwise than for sale or hire)
F1(c)	Museums
F1(d)	Public libraries or public reading rooms
F1(e)	Public halls or exhibition halls
F1(f)	Public worship or religious instruction (or in connection with such use)
F1(g)	Law courts
F2 Local community	Use as defined in 4 parts:
F2(a)	Shops (mostly) selling essential goods, including food, where the shop's premises do not exceed 280 square metres and there is no other such facility within 1000 metres

F2(b)	Halls or meeting places for the principal use of the local community
F2(c)	Areas or places for outdoor sport or recreation (not involving motorised vehicles or firearms)
F2(d)	Indoor or outdoor swimming pools or skating rinks

As an example, a change of use from a bookshop (E(a)) to a café (E(b)) would not require planning permission as they are both within class E.

Where the UCO is being relied upon, the following points should be taken into account before any advice can be considered to be complete:

(i) Whilst changing uses *within* a use class does not amount to development, a change of use *between* use classes is likely to amount to a material change of use and so will require planning permission.

(ii) The TCPA 1990 expressly provides that changing a single dwelling house into two or more dwelling houses constitutes a material change of use and so is within the definition of development. It will thus require planning permission.

(iii) Some uses (sometimes referred to as 'sui generis' uses) are expressly excluded from any category in the UCO. These are uses which could potentially have particular adverse effects on their locality, such as use as a petrol station, night club, scrapyard, hot food takeaway or casino. Changes to and from a sui generis use will always require planning permission (although see **7.1.4.3** for the possibility that changes from a sui generis use will be granted automatically without the need for a planning application and an express planning permission).

7.1.4.3 Matters which do not require express planning permission

The Town and Country Planning (General Permitted Development) Order 2015 (SI 2015/596) (GPDO) (which applies to England) and the Town and Country Planning (General Permitted Development) Order 1995 (SI 1995/418) (which applies to Wales) automatically grant planning permission to development which falls within their scope without the need for an express planning application. This does not mean that planning permission is not needed, merely that there is no need to make an express application for it to the LPA. In England, the GPDO contains a list of over 40 different categories of development for which planning permission is granted in this way. The categories most commonly encountered in a typical conveyancing transaction are as follows:

(a) *Development within the curtilage of a dwelling house* This permits a variety of forms of development, including the erection of extensions and porches to the dwelling house itself and the laying down of a hard surface such as a car port.

(b) *Minor operations* This permits a variety of minor operations including the erection of fences and gates and the painting of the exterior of a building.

(c) *Changes of use* The GPDO permits certain changes of use that constitute development and would otherwise require an express application for planning permission. The changes permitted have expanded considerably over the years and an up-to-date version of the GPDO must always be consulted when advising on this area, particularly as there are exclusions and conditions applicable to some of the categories.

Some (but not all) of the permanent changes of use permitted in England by the GPDO are shown in the table below:

From	**To**
B2 (general industrial)	**B8** (storage and distribution) up to 500m^2

C1 (hotels)	**State-funded school (F1a)**, subject to meeting all limitations and conditions, including Prior Approval. It may also change back to its previous use.
C2 (residential institutions) / **C2A** (secure residential institutions)	**State-funded school (F1a)**, subject to meeting all limitations and conditions, including Prior Approval. It may also change back to its previous use.
C3 (dwellinghouses)	**C4** (small houses in multiple occupation)
C4 (small houses in multiple occupation)	**C3** (dwellinghouses)
E (commercial, business and service)	**C3** subject to meeting all limitations and conditions, including Prior Approval **State-funded school (F1a)**, subject to meeting all limitations and conditions, including Prior Approval. It may also change back to its previous use. A **mixed use** comprising any of a **betting office**, a **pay day loan shop**, **E**; and up to two flats (**C3**) may also be permitted subject to meeting all limitations and conditions, including Prior Approval. It may also change back to its previous non-residential use.*
Agricultural buildings (Sui generis)	**C3** up to 5 separate dwellings, subject to meeting all limitations and conditions, including Prior Approval A **flexible use** within one of **B8**, **C1**, **E** up to $500m^2$, subject to meeting all limitations and conditions, including Prior Approval **State-funded school (F1a)** up to $500m^2$, subject to meeting all limitations and conditions, including Prior Approval
Amusement arcades/ centres (Sui generis)	**C3** up to $150m^2$, subject to meeting all limitations and conditions, including Prior Approval
Betting offices (Sui generis)	**C3** up to $150m^2$, subject to meeting all limitations and conditions, including Prior Approval, including Prior Approval (includes those already in mixed use with C3) **E** (commercial, business and service) A **mixed use** comprising any of a **betting office**, a **pay day loan shop**, **E**; and up to two flats (**C3**) may also be permitted subject to meeting all limitations and conditions, including Prior Approval. It may also change back to its previous non-residential use.*

Casinos (Sui generis)	**C3** up to $150m^2$, subject to meeting all limitations and conditions, including Prior Approval **E** (commercial, business and service)
Hot food takeaways (Sui generis)	**C3** up to $150m^2$, subject to meeting all limitations and conditions, including Prior Approval **E** (commercial, business and service)
Launderettes (Sui generis)	**C3** up to $150m^2$, subject to meeting all limitations and conditions, including Prior Approval (includes those already in mixed use with C3)
Pay day loan shops (Sui generis)	**C3** up to $150m^2$, subject to meeting all limitations and conditions, including Prior Approval (includes those already in mixed use with C3) **E** (commercial, business and service) A **mixed use** comprising any of a **betting office**, a **pay day loan shop**, **E**; and up to two flats (**C3**) may also be permitted subject to meeting all limitations and conditions, including Prior Approval. It may also change back to its previous non-residential use.*
Public house, wine bar, or drinking establishment / Drinking establishment with expanded food provision (Sui generis)	A **Public house, wine bar, or drinking establishment** may change in use to or from a **Drinking establishment with expanded food provision**.

* Where the original use is a class E use, the change of use permitted under the GPDO is limited to a mixed use comprising of any class E use with up to two flats. The GPDO does not allow a change from a class E use to a betting shop or pay day loan shop simply by incorporating up to two flats.

(d) *The extension or alteration of an office building, shop, financial or professional services establishment, industrial unit or warehouse* Such works are subject to restrictions (see (a)(ii) and (a)(iii) below).

Where the GPDO is being relied upon, the following points should be considered before any advice can be considered to be complete:

(a) Each category of development permitted by the GPDO has conditions attached to it within the GPDO itself (the GPDO sets out what development is permitted and then the conditions). These conditions must be strictly observed, and if they cannot be complied with, express permission for the development is needed. For example, volume and height restrictions apply to any extension to a building permitted under category (a) or (d) above. Some changes of use are subject to 'Prior Approval'. This will require that an application is made to allow the local authority to assess the impact of the permitted development on, for example, flood and contamination risk, transport and highways. It is important that an up-to-date version of the GPDO is consulted before any advice is given to a client on this area.

(b) The rights contained within the GPDO do not apply to all properties and each of the rights may be excluded or varied in certain cases. So, for example, some rights will not apply to properties in conservation areas or areas of outstanding natural beauty. Again, an up to date copy of the GPDO must be consulted prior to advising.

(c) The LPA has power to restrict the GPDO in whole or in part in relation to its area. This is done by the LPA passing an order under art 4 of the GPDO known as an 'Article 4 Direction'. The existence of any such Direction can be discovered by making a local search (see **Chapter 17**).

Local planning authorities also have the power to issue 'local development orders'. These operate like permitted development under the GPDO, and may be site-specific or cover the whole or part of an LPA's area. There are limitations on the types of development that may be permitted under local development orders, and the LPA must also consult with interested bodies (such as English Nature and the Mayor of London in the case of a London Borough) as appropriate before the order can be confirmed.

In England, the Localism Act 2011 has also introduced a power for the LPA to make 'neighbourhood development orders' (orders that grant planning permission in a particular neighbourhood for the development specified in that order) and 'community right to build orders' (a type of neighbourhood development order which gives a community organisation a right to carry out a particular development in its local area without the need for planning permission). The Town and Country Planning (Permission in Principle) Order 2017 (SI 2017/402) (which applies to England but not Wales) allows a local planning authority to grant permission in principle to a site by entering the site on its brownfield land register. Such an entry triggers a grant of permission in principle for that land (see **7.1.5.2**).

7.1.4.4 Demolition

The position in respect of demolition works needs further consideration. Powers exist for the Secretary of State to make directions excluding the demolition of certain types of building from the definition of 'development'. The Town and Country Planning (Demolition – Description of Buildings) Direction 2014 (which applies to England but not Wales) excludes the *total* demolition of the following from the definition of 'development':

(a) any building of less than 50 cubic metres volume;

(b) any means of enclosure (such as a gate, fence or wall), except if it is in a conservation area.

Whilst the total demolition of other types of building or structure does require planning permission, in most cases this will be granted automatically (although subject to conditions) under the GPDO. The following should, however, be noted:

(a) Demolition of certain buildings that are unlisted but in a conservation area will require express planning permission (see **7.2**).

(b) Demolition likely to have a significant effect on the environment will require express planning permission (see *R (Save Britain's Heritage) v Secretary of State for Communities and Local Government* [2011] EWCA Civ 334).

(c) Demolition of a listed building does not require express planning permission but will require listed building consent (see **7.2**).

(d) *Partial* demolition of a building constitutes a building operation and is generally considered, therefore, to require express planning permission.

7.1.5 Obtaining planning permission

7.1.5.1 General

If an express application for planning permission is required, this should be made to the relevant LPA on a form supplied by that authority. A fee is payable, which is calculated using regulations made under the TCPA 1990. It is not necessary for the applicant to be the owner of the freehold of the land over which permission is sought but, if the applicant is not the landowner, they are required to notify the owner of the application. Regulations made under the TCPA 1990 also impose requirements relating to the content of the application (eg most applications will need to have a 'design and access statement') and also to consultation and publicity (such as the posting of notices on the site in question).

7.1.5.2 The type of planning application

Application for outline planning permission

Applications for outline planning permission seek to establish whether the scale and nature of a proposed development would be acceptable to the local planning authority, before a fully detailed proposal is put forward. Outline planning permission can be obtained for the erection of a building but cannot be granted for an application where the only development is a material change of use.

This type of planning application allows fewer details about the proposal to be submitted. Once outline permission has been granted, the applicant will need to ask for approval of the details before work can start. These details will be the subject of a 'reserved matters' application at a later stage.

An outline permission allows the applicant to know if its proposal is acceptable before incurring the costs involved in submitting the full drawings and specifications required for full planning permission.

Application for full planning permission

An application for full planning permission will deal with all aspects of a given development proposal and involve the submission of full plans and specifications to the local authority. However, whilst initially more costly than outline permission, once obtained, development can proceed without the need for a further reserved matters application to the local planning authority.

Application for permission in principle

The permission in principle consent route is an alternative way of obtaining planning permission for small scale 'housing-led' development (ie development for housing purposes or mixed development where housing occupies the majority of the floor space of the overall scheme). This route has two stages: the first stage (or permission in principle stage) establishes whether a site is suitable in principle; and the second stage ('technical details consent') is when the detailed development proposals are assessed. The granting of technical details consent has the effect of granting planning permission for the development. Certain types of development are excluded from a grant of permission in principle, including householder development, 'major' development and development where an environmental impact assessment is required.

7.1.5.3 The LPA's decision

The LPA may refuse the application or grant planning permission which will usually be subject to detailed conditions. In making this decision (including considering what conditions to impose), the LPA must have regard to the development plan. It must also have regard to other material considerations such as the NPPF and other planning-related factors specific to the proposal (such as the impact of the proposal on the amenity of the neighbourhood and any planning obligation – see **7.1.5.5** below). Although the LPA can restrict a permission to a named individual, or limit it in time, most planning permissions are not so limited and can therefore be sold with the land.

The LPA must make its decision within certain time limits (depending on the nature of the development), and failure to do so gives the applicant the right to appeal.

7.1.5.4 Duration of planning permission

Once planning permission has been granted, development must be started within a certain time limit. This is usually dealt with expressly in the permission and differs according to the type of permission. An ordinary (ie, full) permission is now normally subject to a condition that development must be started within three years (and if the permission is silent on a time limit, this period will be implied by the TCPA 1990).

An outline permission is usually subject to conditions that an application for approval of reserved matters must be made within three years and that development must be begun within two years of the approval of the reserved matters.

An express permission in principle consent is usually subject to a condition that technical details consent must be obtained within three years. A full planning permission is achieved by the grant of the technical details consent, meaning a development must then be commenced within three years of the technical details consent.

Note that different time limits may apply to permissions granted before 24 August 2005 and care should be taken to check the time limits for such permissions.

Although there is a time limit within which the development must be *commenced*, there is no time limit within which it must be *completed*. However, if the development has not been completed within a reasonable time, the LPA has the power to issue a 'completion notice' specifying a time limit within which this must be done. If it is not, the planning consent is treated as being withdrawn.

7.1.5.5 Planning obligations

Case law and government policy limit what matters the LPA can deal with by a condition attached to planning permission. In particular, a developer cannot be required to make a payment in return for the grant of planning permission. There will be situations, however, where a development proposal could place demands on local infrastructure that would legitimately require just such a contribution from a developer (eg, a housing development that creates a need for additional school classrooms). In such cases, matters can be dealt with by a planning obligation under s 106 of the TCPA 1990. This is a separate agreement entered into between the developer and the LPA, and will be a material consideration when deciding whether the planning permission should be granted.

In order to prevent abuse, reg 122 of the Community Infrastructure Levy Regulations 2010 (SI 2010/948) provides that a planning obligation may constitute a reason for granting planning permission only if the obligation is:

(a) necessary to make the development acceptable in planning terms;
(b) directly related to the development; and
(c) fairly and reasonably related in scale and kind to the development.

The Planning Act 2008 introduced the Community Infrastructure Levy (CIL), a form of discretionary tax that an LPA may choose to charge on developments which impact on local infrastructure. The CIL is based on a formula that reflects the size and type of development, and is set out in a charging schedule published by the LPA. The aim is for it to fund the infrastructure requirements previously dealt with by planning obligations, but in a more open and accountable way. Where the CIL is in use, planning obligations continue to have a part to play in dealing with site-specific matters, but their role and use will be significantly reduced.

7.1.6 Enforcement

7.1.6.1 Time limits

If there is a breach of planning control, the LPA must take enforcement action within 10 years of the alleged breach. However, for breaches involving operational development (such as building works) or changing the use of a building to use as a single dwelling house that took place before 25 April 2024, the time limit is the one that applied before this date, which is within four years of the alleged breach. An LPA can apply to a magistrates' court for a planning enforcement order to enable enforcement action to be taken when the statutory time limits have expired and the breach of planning control has been concealed.

7.1.6.2 The LPA's enforcement powers

The LPA has a wide variety of enforcement powers available to it, including:

(a) *Enforcement notice* The notice must state the matters alleged to constitute the breach, the steps required to remedy the breach and the time within which these must be taken. These might be, for example, the removal of buildings or the cessation of any activity on the property. A recipient can appeal against the service of an enforcement notice which is then suspended pending the outcome of the appeal. From 25 April 2024, LPAs in England have the power to issue enforcement warning notices when it appears that there has been a breach of planning control. The enforcement warning notice is an invitation to the recipient to regularise the breach by applying for a retrospective planning permission.

(b) *Stop notice* This can be only be served in conjunction with an enforcement notice and will stop the activity stated in it pending the outcome of any appeal against the enforcement notice by the recipient.

(c) *Temporary stop notice* This allows the LPA to prevent activity stated in the notice for 56 days (in England) or 28 days (in Wales) whilst it considers whether further, more permanent action should be taken.

(d) *Breach of condition notice* This may be served in respect of a breach of a condition attached to a consent. Unlike an enforcement notice, the recipient cannot appeal against its service and the defences available are limited.

(e) *Injunction.*

Non-compliance with an operative enforcement or other notice is a criminal offence which may carry heavy penalties.

Note: stop notices and temporary stop notices cannot be used to stop use as a dwelling house.

7.2 LISTED BUILDINGS AND CONSERVATION AREAS

Additional controls exist in respect of listed buildings and conservation areas.

Where it is considered that a building is of outstanding historic or architectural interest, it may be 'listed'. Responsibility for this rests (in England) with the Department for Digital, Culture, Media and Sport, and (in Wales) the Welsh Parliament and Cadw. The effect of the listing depends on which grade of listing is given. Part only of a building may be subject to listing. The consequences of listing are, principally, that tighter controls are exercised over development than is the case with an unlisted building and that, in general, the exceptions from development (examples of which are considered at **7.1.4.2**) do not apply. Consequently, listed building consent is required for the total demolition of a listed building and alterations or extensions that affect the building's character as a building of special interest.

However, with the aim of reducing the number of listed building consent applications, the Enterprise and Regulatory Reform Act 2013 ('ERRA 2013') introduced the ability for the Secretary of State to make a consent order allowing alterations or extensions to listed buildings nationally ('Listed Building Consent Order') or to certain types of listed building or listed buildings in a specific area ('Local Listed Building Consent Order'). Neither type of consent order will permit demolition of a listed building, and they are intended to permit works that are not considered to affect the building's special architectural interest. Under the ERRA 2013 a listed building owner may also enter into a 'heritage partnership agreement' with a local authority by which it can agree (amongst other things) the types of works that would, or would not, affect a building's special character. Finally, the ERRA 2013 introduced the ability for a person unsure as to whether works require listed building consent to apply to the local authority for a determination of the issue. If the works in question do not require such consent, the local authority must issue a certificate to that effect ('Certificate of Lawfulness of Proposed Works').

There are criminal sanctions for non-compliance and no time limits for bringing enforcement proceedings. Details of listed buildings in England may be found on the online database, The National Heritage List for England (www.historicengland.org.uk).

In addition to the above, the LPA may designate as a conservation area any part of its area which is of special architectural or historic interest, the character or appearance of which it is desirable to preserve or enhance. As a general rule, any non-listed building in a conservation area cannot be demolished without planning permission. There may also be other restrictions on development.

7.3 BUILDING REGULATION CONTROL

7.3.1 General

As a separate issue from the need to obtain planning permission, the need to obtain building regulation consent from the building control authority must be considered whenever building works are to be undertaken. Introduced for building works from February 1966, building regulation control is concerned with the health and safety aspects of the building to be erected or altered, and regulates the types of materials and construction methods used in carrying out the work. Building regulation consent may be required irrespective of whether the works constitute development for the purposes of planning control. Many 'home improvement' schemes, for example, will require consent, such as installing replacement windows, or installing a central heating system, certain new electrical installations, certain drainage and plumbing alterations.

7.3.2 Compliance

A person intending to carry out building or home improvement works that require building regulation consent will make the application in one of two ways: a 'full plans' application requires the submission of detailed plans and full details of the construction; while a 'building notice' application requires only the submission of a simple form describing the proposed works. In both cases, a building control officer will carry out inspections of the work. Once the final inspection has taken place, the building control authority will issue a certificate of compliance. This should be kept safe along with other documents relating to the property, as evidence of compliance with building regulation control.

Several 'self-certification' schemes have been established to enable competent contractors to self-certify their own work, eg the FENSA (Fenestration Self Assessment) scheme in relation to replacement windows/double glazing and the like. These schemes are regulated by the trade's own governing body, which sets and tests the competency of installers and their understanding of the building regulations specific to their trade or profession. A self-certification certificate is issued by the contractor at the completion of the work, and the relevant governing body then sends a notification of the works to the local authority.

7.3.3 Non-compliance

Care must be taken by the buyer whenever the seller is unable to produce proof of compliance with building regulations. This is for two main reasons:

(a) *Building control authorities' enforcement powers.* A building control authority can bring a prosecution for breach of building regulation control. There is now no time limit for bringing a prosecution: prior to 1 October 2023 the prosecution had to be brought within six months of the breach being discovered and within two years of completion of the building work. A building control authority can also serve an enforcement notice requiring the alteration or removal of work carried out in breach of building regulations control. Such a notice must be served within 10 years of completion of the building work alleged to be in breach, but other enforcement options, including injunctions, can be still be used after this date (see *Cottingham v Attey Bower* [2000] Lloyd's Rep PN 591).

(b) *Structural concerns.* Building works carried out without complying with building regulation control will raise questions concerning the future suitability and safety of the structure of the building, which could require expensive repairs or remedial work, or impact on the future marketability of the property. A solicitor acting for a buyer should strongly advise their client to consider obtaining a full structural survey to assess the potential cost.

The buyer should consider asking the seller to obtain a regularisation certificate from the local authority which will list the work required to bring the building up to the correct standard. Insurance can be obtained in cases where proof of building regulation consent is not forthcoming, but this will usually cover only the cost of compliance with the regulations should the local authority bring enforcement proceedings. It will not cover personal injuries or loss of trade caused by the defective buildings.

The buyer's lender must also be informed of any breach, and may be reluctant to lend on a property where such a breach exists, or may impose conditions on the terms of the loan (such as an retention of some of the mortgage advance against the cost of remedial works) to ensure that the building work is brought up to standard. A lender may insist on a full survey being done.

7.4 RESTRICTIVE COVENANTS AND PLANNING AND BUILDING REGULATIONS CONTROL

Just as the planning and building regulations regimes are separate and independent of each other (and so it is important to check that both have been complied with), it is important to remember that any private controls on the land, such as restrictive covenants, must also be considered, as these too are a separate issue. An important consequence flows from this, which is that it is perfectly possible, for example, for planning permission to be granted for a given proposal (or for it not to amount to 'development' in the first place), but for that proposal to contravene a valid restrictive covenant over the land. The contravention of the covenant will need to be dealt with as a separate issue, even though the planning issues have been resolved.

7.5 TRANSACTIONAL MATTERS

7.5.1 Acting for the seller

Although planning and related matters do not necessarily fall within the seller's duty of disclosure, the buyer's solicitor will be reluctant to proceed with the transaction unless they are satisfied that the buildings and use of the property comply with current planning and other regulations. It is therefore sensible for the seller's solicitor to satisfy themselves as to these matters at an early stage so as to be able to anticipate any problems which might otherwise arise. Accordingly, the seller's solicitor should check the following and consider the implications for the transaction:

(a) The date when the property was first built and the use to which it has been put since then.

(b) Whether any additions, alterations or extensions have been made to the property or within its grounds since it was first built and, if so, the date of each addition, etc.

(c) If any activity has been carried out that could potentially have required planning permission, that either planning consent was obtained (either expressly or by virtue of the GPDO) or that such consent was not required. Any conditions attached to the planning consent (or GPDO) should be checked to ensure that they have been complied with.

(d) Whether any alterations, changes of use etc, have taken place in breach of any covenants which affect the title. If the property is leasehold, this will involve consideration not only of the covenants that bind the freehold, but also consideration of any covenants controlling development contained in the lease.

(e) Whether the property is a listed building or in a conservation area.

(f) Where alterations or additions to the property have been made, whether building regulation control has been complied with (and if appropriate, that any necessary certificates of compliance or self-certification certificates have been obtained).

7.5.2 Acting for the buyer

The buyer's solicitor needs to ensure that there are no problems with any planning or related matters, and should address the issues identified in **7.5.1**, this time on the buyer client's behalf. Enquiries of the seller and local authority will provide valuable information in this respect (see **Chapter 17** for more details). Any irregularity revealed by the answers either should be corrected at the seller's expense or, depending on the nature of the breach, an indemnity should be taken from the seller in the contract.

The above will identify any problems arising out of the seller's use of the property. In addition, instructions should be obtained from the buyer in respect of their plans for the property following acquisition. If the buyer proposes to carry out works to the property or change the use, it will be necessary to consider if planning permission will be needed. Consideration should be given to obtaining this before exchange of contracts or making the contract conditional upon it being obtained. In addition, issues relating to restrictive covenants and building regulations should be considered.

A planning case study is included at 7.7 below.

7.6 ENVIRONMENTAL ISSUES

7.6.1 General

The presence of contaminants in land may have very serious consequences. First, use of the property may be impossible without extensive clean-up works being undertaken. Secondly, a property may become 'blighted', making it difficult to sell or mortgage. If the land is to be developed, the LPA might impose onerous conditions concerning the removal or control of any contaminants. Lastly, the presence of contaminants could lead to liability under the Environmental Protection Act 1990 (EPA 1990) (or other environmental control legislation) or at common law (see *Scott-Whitehead v National Coal Board* (1987) 53 P & CR 263; cf *Cambridge Water Co v Eastern Counties Leather plc* [1994] 1 All ER 53).

Remediation can be very expensive, depending upon the nature and extent of the contamination. It might consist of excavating and then safely disposing of the contaminated soil, or encapsulating it so that the contaminants cannot escape.

In all conveyancing transactions (whether a purchase, a mortgage or a lease, and whether the property involved is residential or commercial), the solicitor should consider whether contamination is an issue and, in all purchases, leases or mortgages (unless instructed otherwise), undertake a CON29 search to ascertain whether the land has been designated as contaminated land by the local authority. If it appears that contamination is an issue and the solicitor is acting for a buyer, tenant or lender, the solicitor should advise the client of the potential liabilities associated with it and the further steps that can be taken to assess the risks (see the Law Society's practice note, 'Contaminated land').

In the case of new houses, the cover given by the NHBC includes the cost of cleaning up contamination of the site should this be subsequently discovered (see **42.2.3.1**), but it must be remembered that the cover provided lasts only 10 years.

7.6.2 The Contaminated Land Regime under the EPA 1990

In terms of statutory controls, the main source of liability arises in the context of the 'contaminated land' regime which was introduced by the EPA 1990 as amended.

Each local authority (or the Environment Agency in the case of certain large-scale sites) is under a duty to inspect its area for contaminated sites. Once a site has been identified as contaminated, the local authority must then serve a remediation notice specifying the steps necessary to clean up the site so that it is suitable for its intended use. This is served on the person or persons who caused or knowingly permitted all or some of the contaminating materials to be present in, on or under the land. This might be the original polluter (but might also potentially catch a buyer once it has bought the property). If such a person cannot be identified after reasonable inspection, liability falls on the current owner or occupier. Either way, a buyer could be faced with liability under the regime.

7.6.3 Planning and the environment

If land is to be developed, it is likely that planning permission will be required. If there are environmental issues concerning the site, the LPA is likely to impose conditions which require the site to be cleaned up before development can take place, or which require investigations to be made to ascertain the full extent of any potential contamination. In fact, this is the way which much contamination is dealt with.

Part 6 of the Environment Act 2021 sets out a new general condition to all planning permissions in England (with some exemptions), which requires that a biodiversity gain plan must be submitted and approved before development can commence. The biodiversity gain plan should contain an assessment of the value of natural habitats before and after development and ensure that at least a 10% net gain is achieved.

7.6.4 Searches and enquiries and other investigations

It is important to be able to spot when a property might give rise to concerns in respect of contamination and then obtain further information so that full advice can be given to the client. This will come from conducting appropriate searches and enquiries, the detail of which is set out in **Chapter 17**.

7.7 A PLANNING CASE STUDY

Roger Evans owns 47, Queens' Road, Loamster, Maradon, Cornshire CS1 5TY. Title to the property is registered and the Official Copy is reproduced at **4.5**. Mr Evans has agreed to sell the property on the terms set out in the Attendance Note at **8.7**. The solicitor for the prospective buyers is trying to establish the planning status of the property. This can be done by using the checklist set out in **7.5.1**.

(a) *The date when the property was first built and the use to which it has been put since then.*

A plaque on the front of the property suggests that it was constructed in 1897. This means that there will not be a planning permission for its original construction as the requirement for a planning permission was not introduced until after 1947. The seller has lived in the property since 2009 and has confirmed that the property has only been used for residential purposes all the time he has lived there. Even if there has been a change of use in breach of planning control before that time, the LPA would now be outside the period of four years for taking enforcement action for change of use to a single dwelling house that applied before 25 April 2024.

(b) *Whether any additions, alterations or extensions have been made to the property or within its grounds since it was first built and, if so, the date of each addition, etc.*

Mr Evans' solicitors have confirmed, on their client's behalf, that the property was significantly extended in 2018. The volume and height of the extension was such that it was not possible to take advantage of the GPDO, so planning permission was obtained.

This planning permission is reproduced on the following pages, together with the Building Regulation Final Certificate for the extension works. The seller has confirmed that there have been no other additions, alterations or extensions in the seller's period of ownership, so even if there had been building works which required planning permission before 2009, the LPA would now be outside the period of four years for taking enforcement action that applied to building works that took place before 25 April 2024.

(c) *If any activity has been carried out that could potentially have required planning permission, that either planning consent was obtained (either expressly or by virtue of the GPDO) or that such consent was not required. Any conditions attached to the planning consent (or GPDO) should be checked to ensure that they have been complied with.*

The planning permission for the 2018 extension is reproduced on the following pages. It grants full planning permission for a single rear extension to the property, subject to three conditions:

1. The roof area shall be used for maintenance access only and not for sitting out space.
2. The development shall be begun not later than three years from the date of the permission.
3. The development shall be carried out in accordance with the approved plans.

Presumably the second condition has been fulfilled, as the Building Regulation Final Certificate is dated 4 March 2019 and states that the works have been completed. If the first and third conditions have been breached then the LPA is well within the period of 10 years for taking enforcement action. If the LPA has already taken enforcement action, this will be revealed in the reply to Enquiry 3.9 of the CON29 Enquiries of the Local Authority (see **17.6**), so this must be checked particularly carefully. The seller should also be asked in the pre-contract enquiries of the seller (see **17.7**) to confirm that he is not aware and has not received any notice of breach of any of these conditions. If the buyers are still concerned about the third condition then a surveyor could be asked to inspect to see whether the extension on the ground matches that shown on the approved plans.

Irrespective of whether there has been a breach of the first planning condition, the buyers' attention should be drawn to it as the restriction on use will continue into the future.

(d) *Whether any alterations, changes of use etc, have taken place in breach of any covenants which affect the title. If the property is leasehold, this will involve consideration not only of the covenants that bind the freehold, but also of any covenants controlling development contained in the lease.*

This is a matter of concern, as the official copy in **4.5** contains, in the charges register, a restrictive covenant not to build any building on the property without the written consent of Sir James Fawcett or his successors in title to unknown land lying to the south of the property. The building of the extension could be a breach of this restrictive covenant and this must be raised with the seller's solicitor immediately. It is possible that the seller obtained the necessary consent or took out restrictive covenant indemnity insurance against its enforcement (see **16.9**).

(e) *Whether the property is a listed building or in a conservation area.*

A building of this age is unlikely to be listed but may be in a conservation area. This may be checked by contacting the LPA. A conservation area designation may also be revealed in the local land charges search (see **17.5**). If the building is listed or in a conservation area, this must be raised with the seller, as additional consents would have been needed for the 2018 extension.

(f) *Where alterations or additions to the property have been made, whether building regulation control has been complied with (and if appropriate, that any necessary certificates of compliance or self-certification certificates have been obtained).*

A Building Regulation Final Certificate dated 4 March 2019 has been produced by the seller and is reproduced on the following pages.

SUMMARY

- Planning permission is needed for any activity that constitutes 'development'. Building, engineering, mining or other operations ('BEMO') constitutes 'development', as does a material change of use.
- The GPDO automatically grants planning permission for certain types of 'development'.
- An express application may be made either for full or for outline planning permission.
- A failure to obtain necessary planning permission may result in enforcement action by the LPA.
- Enforcement action must be taken within 10 years for a breach of planning control occurring on or after 25 April 2024. If the breach relates to building works substantially completed before 25 April 2024 or change of use to a single dwelling occurring prior to 25 April 2024, the enforcement action must be taken within four years of the breach.
- Additional controls exist in respect of listed buildings and those in conservation areas.
- Building regulation consent is needed for building works.
- A failure to obtain building regulation approval casts doubt on the safety of the building works and may result in enforcement action by the local authority.
- A buyer's solicitor should ensure that a property has all necessary planning permissions and building regulation approvals.
- There are significant liabilities associated with ownership and occupation of contaminated land, and appropriate due diligence must be done on purchase to ascertain the risk of contamination.

Cornshire

Environment and Regeneration

Planning Decision Notice

Jane Roberts S&R Architects 56 High Quarters Loamster Maradon Cornshire CS3 9DN	Planning Service PO Box 3389 222 Upper Street Maradon Cornshire CS1 6RT Case officer: Roy Grey Issue date: 22 May 2018

Dear Sir/Madam

TOWN AND COUNTRY PLANNING ACTS
PERMISSION FOR DEVELOPMENT (CONDITIONAL)

Notice is hereby given that the Maradon Borough Council, the Local Planning Authority, in pursuance of its powers under the above mentioned Acts and Rules, Orders and Regulations made thereunder, resolved to GRANT planning permission to the development described in the undermentioned schedule subject to the conditions set out therein and in accordance with the plans submitted, save insofar as may be otherwise required by the said conditions.

Your attention is drawn to the enclosed statement of Applicants Rights and General Information (Endorsed on Part II of this notice under form Ref: TP6A/9A)

SCHEDULE:	Type of Application:	Full Planning Application
	Date of Application:	06-Sep-2017

LOCATION: 47, Queen's Road, Loamster, Maradon, Cornshire CS1 5TY

DEVELOPMENT:

Single storey extension with removal of some existing external walls and windows, creation of new party walls to side of extension, new beam and block floor and new flat roof with single ply membrane

PLAN NOS:

113A_200, 113_201, 113A_202, 113A_203, 113_204, 113A_205 and 113A_206

REASON TO GRANT:

This application has been approved under delegated authority as the development replaces an existing structure and has resulted in minimal additional loss of neighbouring amenity. Furthermore it has a design which is in keeping with the host building and surrounding area.

This development has been approved following consideration of all the relevant policies in the Development Plan 2002 and other material considerations; the proposal is generally considered to comply with the UDP, and in particular policies D1 (Overall Design) and D11 (Alterations and Extensions). Other policies may have been considered but in this instance are not considered to have such weight as to justify a refusal of permission.

SUBJECT TO THE FOLLOWING CONDITIONS:

1. **CONDITION:** the roof area of the extension shall be used as a means of access for maintenance only, and shall not be used as an amenity or sitting out space of any kind whatsoever.

   REASON: To avoid overlooking of the neighbouring properties and to comply with the requirements of policy D3 (Site Planning).

2. **CONDITION:** The development hereby permitted shall be begun not later than the expiration of three years from the date of this permission.

REASON: To comply with the provisions of section 91(1)(a) of the Town and Country Planning Act 1990 as amended by the Planning and Compulsory Purchase Act 2004 (chapter 5).

3. **CONDITION:** The development hereby approved shall be carried out in accordance with the following approved plans:

 113A_200, 113_201, 113A_202, 113A_203, 113_204, 113A_205 and 113A_206

 REASON: To comply with section 70(1)(a) of the Town and Country Planning Act 1990 as amended and the Reason for Grant and also for the avoidance of doubt and in the interests of proper planning.

Your attention is drawn to any informatives that may be listed below: [Not reproduced]

Yours faithfully

Laurie S Taylor

Laurie Taylor

Head of Service – Development Manager and Proper Officer

Cornshire Building Control Ltd

International House, 1–8 Ludgate Place, Maradon, Cornshire CS1 6GH

Approved by the Construction Industry Council in accordance with section 49(1) of the Building Act 1984 and the Building (Approved Inspectors etc) Regulations, Serial Number 128

FINAL CERTIFICATE

Section 51 of the Building Act 1984 and the Building (Approved Inspectors etc) Regulations

Project Ref: 12/7218/JCA

This certificate relates to the following work:

Initial Notice Dated: 22/05/2018

Description: Single storey extension with removal of some existing external walls and windows, creation of new party walls to side of extension, new beam and block floor and new flat roof with single ply membrane

Location: 47, Queen's Road, Loamster, Maradon, Cornshire CS1 5TY

1. We are an Approved Inspector and the work described above was the whole of the work described in an initial notice given to us and dated as above.
2. The work described above has been completed and we have performed the functions assigned to us by regulation 11 of the 2010 Regulations.
3. Final certificates have now been issued in respect of all the work described in the initial notice referred to in paragraph 2 above.
4. With this certificate is the declaration, signed by the insurer, that the named scheme of insurance approved by the secretary of state applies in relation to the work to which the certificate relates [not reproduced].
5. The work is minor work ('Minor Works' has the meaning given in regulation 10(1) of the 2010 Regulations).
6. We have had no financial or professional interest in the work described above since giving the initial notice described above.

Signed **TOBAN**

Date 04-March-2019

For and on behalf of:
Cornshire Building Control Ltd
Corporate Approved Inspectors

PART II

THE CONVEYANCING TRANSACTION: INITIAL STAGES

CHAPTER 8

MARKETING THE PROPERTY AND TAKING INSTRUCTIONS

LEARNING OUTCOMES

After reading this chapter you will be able to:

- explain when and why Energy Performance Certificates are required
- explain the purpose and methods of taking instructions
- identify the matters on which instructions should be taken.

8.1 MARKETING THE PROPERTY, ENERGY PERFORMANCE CERTIFICATES AND THE MINIMUM ENERGY EFFICIENCY STANDARD

The conveyancing process begins when an individual decides to put their property on the market. This might be a private individual selling their current home, or a large developer selling a newly-built office to an institutional investor such as a pension company. The seller will usually employ an estate agent to advertise the property, and once a buyer is found the conveyancing process proper can begin.

8.1.1 Energy Performance Certificates

At this stage, it is worth considering Energy Performance Certificates (EPCs), which the seller will need to have in hand at an early stage. EPCs should be obtained from an accredited energy assessor, who will carry out the assessment and produce the EPC. Most estate agents will be able to assist a seller in contacting an appropriate assessor.

EPCs were introduced to comply with the European Energy Performance of Buildings Directive (Directive 2002/91), which has now been revoked and replaced by the Energy Performance of Buildings Directive 2010 (EPB Directive 2010/31/EU). Nearly 40% of the UK's energy consumption arises from the way in which our 25 million buildings are lit, heated and used. Even comparatively minor changes in the energy performance of each building, and the way in which we use it, will have a significant effect in reducing energy consumption and therefore carbon emissions.

The requirements for EPCs are contained in the Energy Performance of Buildings (England and Wales) Regulations 2012 (SI 2012/3118). These require, where a building is to be sold or rented out, that the seller or landlord must make an EPC available free of charge at the earliest opportunity. The EPC must have been commissioned (even though not received) before the property can be marketed and there is an obligation to use all reasonable efforts to ensure that it is received within seven days of marketing. If it is not received within the seven days, there is a further 21 days in which to obtain it. Once an EPC has been received, the estate agent must provide a copy of the EPC (the first page only for residential properties) with the sale particulars and ensure the energy performance rating of the property is contained within any advertising. It remains the responsibility of the seller or landlord to ensure that a valid EPC has been given, free of charge, to the person who ultimately becomes the buyer or tenant. There are financial penalties (enforceable by Trading Standards Officers) for failing to comply with the Regulations.

Nearly all buildings in the UK that are constructed, sold or rented out will have to have an EPC. This applies to both commercial and residential property. There are exceptions, amongst others, for buildings about to be demolished. The Regulations also impose obligations for air-conditioning systems exceeding stated power outputs to be subject to an energy assessment every five years, and for the inspection reports to be lodged with the central EPC register.

EPCs are issued by specially qualified inspectors. The EPC contains an indicator of the amount of energy estimated to be needed for the standard use of the building. This 'asset rating' is expressed as a number and on a graph with coloured bands labelled A to G (A being the most energy efficient). The EPC also contains certain recommendations for improving the energy performance of the building, together with the potential ratings which might be achieved for the building if all the recommendations were implemented.

From April 2018 it has been unlawful to grant or renew tenancies of buildings that do not have at least a rating of E (see **8.1.3**).

8.1.2 Green Deal

The EPC will also disclose to the buyer the existence of a Green Deal plan. The Green Deal was launched in January 2013 and is a government initiative that enables property owners and tenants to carry out a range of energy efficiency measures with no upfront cost. The finance is provided by Green Deal providers (private companies, charities and local authorities) and the repayments are spread over a period of up to 25 years through a separate charge added to the property owner's electricity bill. The charge (which should not be more than the estimated energy bill savings) is payable by the occupier from time to time, so on a sale and purchase it will transfer to the buyer. The seller is therefore obliged to provide prospective buyers with an EPC containing the required Green Deal plan information and ensure that the contract for sale includes an acknowledgement by the buyer that the bill payer at the property is obliged to make payments under the Green Deal plan (see Energy Act 2011, ss 12 and 14).

If the seller fails to disclose the existence of a Green Deal plan or obtain the necessary acknowledgment from the buyer, the Secretary of State may (but is not obliged to) cancel the liability of the buyer to make payments under the Green Deal plan and may require the seller to pay compensation (which in most cases would equate to the amount outstanding on the Green Deal plan less a discount for early settlement). The seller's solicitor should therefore ensure that they inspect the EPC before drafting the contract, so that any required acknowledgment can be inserted into the contract for sale. It would be prudent for the buyer's solicitor to do the same, as when deciding whether to cancel liability the Secretary of State will consider what knowledge of the Green Deal the buyer had. If the information is contained on a disclosed EPC (even if it has not been acknowledged by the buyer in the contract), there is a risk that the Secretary of State may decline to cancel the obligation to pay the charge. It should be noted that the duty of disclosure and acknowledgement also applies to a landlord on the letting of a property, if the occupier is to pay the energy bills.

Take-up for the Green Deal has been small, largely because of doubts about how mortgage lenders and prospective buyers will react to the prospect of the increased energy bills. In July 2015, the Government stopped funding the Green Deal Finance Company, set up to lend money to Green Deal providers, although new applicants may still be able to get Green Deal funding from providers financing the scheme themselves.

8.1.3 Minimum energy efficiency standard

Since April 2018, landlords of certain domestic or non-domestic buildings cannot lawfully grant new tenancies or renew existing tenancies if the building does not meet the minimum energy efficiency standard (MEES), which is EPC rating E. MEES was introduced by the Energy Efficiency (Private Rented Property) (England and Wales) Regulations 2015 (SI 2015/962) (the MEES Regulations), which also provide that a landlord cannot continue to let a domestic privately rented (PR) property on or after 1 April 2020, or a non-domestic PR property on or after 1 April 2023, unless the property complies with MEES. A domestic PR property is, in general terms, a property let under an assured, regulated or agricultural tenancy, but certain tenancies are excluded, such as those not required to have an EPC. A non-domestic PR property is a building which is not a dwelling and is let under a tenancy in England and Wales, although certain properties are excluded, such as those not required to have an EPC and those let on tenancies of less than six months or over 99 years.

A landlord who wishes to let a 'sub-standard' property (ie a domestic PR property or a non-domestic PR property where the valid EPC is F or G rated) will have to undertake 'relevant energy efficiency improvements' that improve efficiency in the use of energy in the property and which are listed in the Schedule to the Green Deal (Qualifying Energy Improvements) Order 2012 (SI 2012/2105), unless the landlord has obtained an opinion that the improvement will have a negative impact on the fabric or structure of the property. There are also exemptions from the relevant part of the MEES Regulations (Part 3) for a landlord who has tried to increase the EPC to band E but failed because the tenant's consent has not been forthcoming, or who has obtained a report from a surveyor stating that making the relevant energy efficiency improvement would result in a reduction of more than 5% in the market value of the property. Landlords will also be able to obtain a temporary exemption for six months in certain circumstances.

A breach of the MEES Regulations is not a criminal offence. If a landlord lets out a building which does not meet MEES, it may be subject to a fine and/or adverse publicity (by entry of details of the breach on a publicly accessible register). The validity of the lease granted in breach of the MEES Regulations is not affected. Enforcement of the MEES Regulations will be carried out by Trading Standards and it remains to be seen how proactively breaches are pursued.

8.2 PURPOSE OF TAKING INSTRUCTIONS

The purpose of taking instructions is for the solicitor to obtain from their client sufficient information to enable them to carry out the whole of the client's transaction, not just to enable them to take the first or next step in that transaction. This does not mean that the client is contacted only once during the course of the whole conveyancing transaction; the client must be regularly informed as to the progress of the transaction. From time to time, further instructions will be needed. However, obtaining as much information as possible in one interview at the commencement of the transaction will save time (both the client's time and that of the solicitor) and will enable the solicitor to obtain a full picture of the transaction and thus to advise the client fully and correctly about their proposals.

Unless full instructions are taken, the solicitor is in danger of overlooking matters which are relevant to the transaction but which the client had not thought to mention specifically to them (eg, a liability to pay CGT on the proceeds of sale).

8.2.1 Personal interview

Wherever possible, instructions should be taken from the client in person. The personal interview gives the client the opportunity to ask questions of the solicitor, and the solicitor the benefit of being able to explain matters to the client in an informal and friendly manner. The Law Society's Practice Notes on Anti-Money Laundering and on Mortgage Fraud both advise of the need for taking special care in cases where the solicitor never meets the client.

8.2.2 Indirect instructions

Indirect instructions, for example where an estate agent sends the solicitor instructions to act on behalf of one of the estate agent's clients, must be confirmed directly with the client, preferably by personal interview, to ensure that there is no misunderstanding about the instructions and that they comply in all respects with the SRA Codes. This principle applies equally to the situation where instructions are taken from one only of two or more co-sellers or co-buyers (see *Penn v Bristol and West Building Society and Others* [1995] 2 FLR 938). Direct confirmation of instructions must be obtained from all persons who are to be clients of the solicitor.

A solicitor who acts for a client without authority may be liable to anyone who suffers loss as a result of this under the principle of breach of warranty of authority. Under the law of agency, an agent (ie the solicitor) is deemed to warrant that they have the authority to act on behalf of their principal (ie the client) and is liable for any loss suffered by someone who relies on this. So, in the *Penn* case (above), a solicitor who had no instructions to act for one co-owner was liable to the buyer's lender who advanced money to fund a purchase in which that co-owner's signature on the transfer had been forged by the other co-owner. The forgery rendered the transfer (and thus the mortgage) void.

8.2.3 Preparing for the interview

The methods of preparation for the interview and interviewing techniques are dealt with in ***Skills for Lawyers*** and are not discussed further in this book, except for the comments which appear below which are particularly relevant to conveyancing.

Before the interview, the solicitor should find out whether the firm has acted for this client previously in property matters. If it is found that the firm acted on the client's purchase of the property which they are now proposing to sell, the old purchase file should be retrieved from storage and its contents examined before interviewing the client for the purpose of taking instructions on the sale. Much of the information required on the sale transaction may already be contained in the purchase file (eg, who owns the boundaries of the property), and it will save time at the interview if this information can be confirmed with the client (to ensure that it has not changed) rather than fresh and full instructions being taken on every point.

8.2.4 Acting for both parties

Paragraph 6.2 of the SRA Codes prevents a solicitor from acting for both seller and buyer in the same conveyancing transaction, except in limited circumstances (see **Chapter 5**). Before interviewing the client, the solicitor should check that the firm has not already accepted instructions to act for the other party in the same transaction or that, if it has, acting for this client complies with the general principles relating to conflict of interests and does not infringe any other practice rule or principle of professional conduct.

8.2.5 Using checklists

Although checklists cannot be expected to cover every eventuality in every transaction, they are useful in standard transactions to ensure that all necessary information is acquired during the course of the interview. Checklists focus the interviewer's mind on the relevant information, reducing preparation time and, ultimately, saving time in the interview itself, but they do need to be used sympathetically so that the client does not feel they are being processed in an impersonal way. Where checklists are used, it is helpful to have them printed on a distinct colour of paper so that they are easily located in the file, either by the solicitor themselves or by another member of their staff who has to work on the file.

An example of an attendance note made using such a checklist appears at **8.7**.

8.2.6 Evidence of identity

Money laundering and fraud of all types is on the increase. Since 1 March 2004, solicitors have been required to play their part in combating such criminal activity by obtaining documentary proof of the identity of clients involved in property transactions, whether as a seller or a buyer. This should be obtained as soon as possible after first contact with the client is made. See **5.11** for details of the requirements of the Money Laundering Regulations.

8.3 MATTERS ON WHICH INSTRUCTIONS MUST BE OBTAINED

A reminder of the matters which will be discussed at a first interview with a client is set out in **8.4** and **8.5**. Although much of the information needed when acting for a seller is the mirror image of, or identical to, the information needed when acting for a buyer, some issues are exclusive to each side of the transaction. For that reason, separate checklists for seller and for buyer are given.

8.4 ACTING FOR THE SELLER

8.4.1 Full names and addresses of seller(s) and buyer(s), and home and business telephone numbers of seller(s)

The full names and addresses (including post codes) of all parties involved in the transaction are needed because they have to be inserted in both the contract and transfer deed. 'Full names' includes all middle names (ie, names exactly as they appear on the client's birth certificate or passport). The client's home and business telephone numbers are needed in order to be able to contact them during the course of the transaction. If a limited company is involved, details of the company's registered office and its registered number should also be obtained. The company's constitution should also be checked to ensure that it does not have any restrictions on its power to buy, sell or mortgage land, as the case might be.

8.4.2 Name, address and person to contact at estate agents

Where an estate agent is involved in the sale, the name, address and telephone number of the person at the agents who is dealing with the sale is needed for contact purposes and in case any queries need to be resolved with the agents.

8.4.3 Name and address of other party's solicitors

The name, address and telephone number of the person dealing with the matter as solicitor or representative of the other party to the transaction must be obtained for contact purposes.

8.4.4 Full address of the property to be sold

The full address (including post code) and description of the property to be sold is required for insertion in the draft contract and, later, in the transfer deed.

8.4.5 Tenure

Whether the property is freehold or leasehold will need to be stated in the contract. Where the property is held on a lease, the terms of the lease must also be set out in the contract. The client may well not know this information. In any event, it should always be checked with the title documents, when they have been obtained.

8.4.6 Price

The price at which the property is agreed to be sold must be stated in the contract and the transfer deed.

8.4.7 Has any preliminary deposit been paid?

There is no requirement for the buyer to pay any money to the seller before the contract is entered into. However, sometimes a small sum of money (a preliminary deposit) is paid by the buyer to the seller's estate agent pending negotiations for the sale. This sum should be noted on the seller's solicitor's file, with a copy of the receipt for its payment, and taken into account when calculating the deposit needed later in the transaction (see **Chapter 21**). The commonest situation in which a preliminary deposit is payable is when the seller is a builder or developer selling a new house (see **Chapter 42**).

8.4.8 Fixtures and fittings

It is essential to obtain clear instructions relating to which fixtures and fittings are to remain at the property after completion of the sale, and which are to be removed by the seller (see **Chapter 11**).

Consideration should be given to whether any fittings (eg, carpets and curtains) which are included in the sale are included in the purchase price or are to be paid for separately by the buyer (see **6.3.3**).

8.4.9 Enquiries of the seller

The seller will be expected to provide answers to enquiries raised by the buyer in respect of various matters regarding the property, such as whether there have been any boundary disputes or whether any alterations have been made to the property (see **17.7**).

Where the buyer is a 'consumer' (an individual acting for purposes that are wholly or mainly outside that individual's business) and the seller is a 'trader' (anyone acting for purposes relating to that person's business), the Digital Markets, Competition and Consumers Act 2024 will apply to the transaction for conduct taking place on or after 6 April 2025 (the Consumer Protection from Unfair Trading Regulations 2008 will apply for conduct that took place before that date). Although this has not yet been tested by the courts, these provisions may also apply to the seller's solicitor in a sale or letting of property to a person for personal use or private investment even when the seller is not a trader. There are criminal penalties for those that engage in unfair commercial practices in dealings with consumers. The Law Society has published a practice note entitled 'Consumer Protection Regulations in conveyancing', which identifies the concern for residential conveyancing practitioners and sets out guidance on good practice in relation to the 2008 Regulations. The guidance states that the solicitor should make the seller client aware at the outset of the transaction that neither the seller nor the solicitor must mislead the buyer by providing incorrect or ambiguous information, or by omitting to provide material information. The seller should also be advised that certain information will be revealed through searches and enquiries and that the buyer will have rights of redress against the seller, including the right to unwind the sale and damages. The guidance also states that the seller's solicitor may wish to encourage the seller to make all known disclosures as early in the transaction as possible to prevent delays.

In commercial transactions, the seller will also be required to reply to enquiries raised by the buyer; a different standard form, the Commercial Property Standard Enquiries, is in use in this case (see **17.7**).

8.4.10 Anticipated completion date

The client should be asked when they anticipate completion taking place. A 'normal' residential transaction takes on average 8–10 weeks from start to finish, although in certain circumstances a shorter time-span can be achieved. Sometimes a longer period of time may be desired by the client owing to particular circumstances (eg, where the client finds a buyer for the property in September, but does not want to move until the children have completed the full academic year at their school the following July).

8.4.11 The present use of the property

Information relating to the present use of the property should be checked against its authorised use for planning purposes (see **Chapter 7**) and any restrictive covenants affecting the use of the property, to ensure in both cases that no breaches have been committed.

8.4.12 Does the transaction attract VAT?

Most residential property transactions are not within the scope of the charge to VAT; VAT is, however, an important consideration in a commercial sale. In the case of a 'new' commercial property, it is mandatory for VAT to be charged on the sale; in the case of other commercial properties, the seller may elect to charge VAT. The seller will need to so elect if they wish to reclaim any input tax incurred in connection with the property. If VAT is chargeable on the sale, the seller's solicitor should ensure that the terms of the contract with the buyer enable VAT to be added on to the agreed price (see **6.2.6.1**).

8.4.13 Who is in occupation of the property?

If someone other than the seller(s) is in occupation of the property, it will be necessary to ensure that they will vacate on or before completion. Details of any tenancies to which the property is subject must also be obtained, as these will have to be disclosed to the buyer.

8.4.14 Synchronisation

Whether the transaction is dependent on the purchase or sale of another property is one of the most important questions to be raised at the first interview. In residential transactions, the client will often wish to sell their existing house and to use the proceeds of sale to purchase another house in which they will then live. The purchase of the new house cannot be undertaken without the proceeds of sale of the old house. Similarly, if the old house is not sold, the client has no use for the new house – they do not want or need two houses. Where the sale and purchase transactions are interdependent, the solicitor must ensure synchronisation of the two transactions, ie no sale without purchase and vice versa. Failure to do this constitutes professional negligence.

8.4.15 Whether any terms have been agreed between the parties

It is usually a good idea to ask whether the parties have agreed any other terms between them, ie terms which have not come to light in the interview so far. These terms may have been agreed informally by conversation between the parties, or may be recorded in correspondence between them. The solicitor should be aware of all the terms which have been agreed so that they can be incorporated into the contract which is drawn up between the parties.

8.4.16 Money

The client must be advised as to the costs of the transaction, and a financial calculation should be made to ensure that the sale will yield sufficient funds to carry out the client's proposals (eg, to pay off the existing mortgage and to purchase a new house).

8.4.17 Whereabouts of title deeds and documents

The seller's solicitor will need to obtain the title deeds to the property to check that the seller does own and can sell the property, and to enable the contract to be drafted. The whereabouts of the deeds should, therefore, be ascertained from the seller. Often they will be in the possession of an existing lender. Under the LRA 1925, a land certificate was issued to the registered proprietor, and this was needed before any subsequent registration could be made.

However, under the LRA 2002, land certificates are no longer issued and any existing certificate is no longer required on a disposition.

8.4.18 Outstanding mortgages

Where the client has an outstanding mortgage on the property, the solicitor will need to contact the lender to obtain the title deeds. The client should be asked to supply their mortgage roll number or account number so that the solicitor can obtain the information and documents which they need from the client's lender. Under the LRA 1925, a charge certificate was issued to each mortgage lender, and this was needed before any subsequent registration could be made. The LRA 2002 has now abolished them, and any existing certificates are no longer required on a disposition. However, the mortgage lender may have other documents in its possession (eg, planning permissions) that will be required on the sale. Increasingly, however, mortgage lenders are unwilling to store any documentation, and it may well be that the client or the client's previous solicitors will have custody of this documentation. Most clients will have a mortgage over their property; some have more than one. All outstanding mortgages will normally need to be discharged before completion of the sale, and therefore the solicitor needs to enquire of the client:

(a) whether there are any further charges over the property;
(b) if so, how many;
(c) who the lender is in each case; and
(d) in each case, how much money (approximately) is outstanding on the loan. The information yielded by this question affects the financial calculation.

8.4.19 Amount of deposit

It is customary for a deposit equivalent to 10% of the purchase price to be paid by the buyer to the seller when a contract is entered into. If it is contemplated that a lower deposit will be paid in this case, the seller should be fully advised of the consequences of this step (see **Chapter 21**).

8.4.20 Proceeds of sale

In many residential cases, the question of what is to happen to the proceeds of sale of the property will be self-evident – the proceeds are to be used towards the purchase of another property. If the answer to this question is not clear from the information already supplied by the client, the solicitor must find out what the client's wishes are. The proceeds of sale must be dealt with as quickly as possible after completion takes place, otherwise the client may be entitled to interest on their money from the solicitor. If the proceeds are to be sent to the client's bank account, the solicitor needs to know the name and address of the relevant bank and the client's account number.

8.4.21 Capital gains tax

In certain cases, the sale of the property will be a disposal for CGT purposes (see **Chapter 6**).

If CGT is payable, this should be pointed out to the client at the earliest possible opportunity. The fact that tax is chargeable on the disposition may affect the financial viability of the sale and the seller's decision to sell.

8.5 ACTING FOR THE BUYER

Most of the information required when acting for a buyer client is either the same as, or the mirror image of, that required when acting for the seller, with the following modifications.

8.5.1 Use of the property

In addition to knowing what the present use of the property is, the buyer's solicitor will need to know what the buyer intends to use the property for after completion. In many cases, the answer to this question will be apparent from the circumstances of the transaction (eg, the client wants to buy a house to live in it). The buyer's solicitor will need to consider whether any additional steps are required as a result of the proposed use. For example, any change of use of the property or alteration to its physical structure may require planning permission (see **Chapter** 7), which must be addressed before the client is committed to buy the property. If the client is intending to let out the property following purchase, the implications of the MEES Regulations should be considered and any works required by these Regulations costed (see **8.1.3**).

8.5.2 Money

A financial calculation must be undertaken to ensure that the client potentially has sufficient money to purchase the property and pay the related costs of purchase including, in appropriate cases, Land Registry fees and SDLT. Land Registry fees are payable for registering the land or registering a dealing at Land Registry after completion; fees are payable on a scale published by Land Registry, and the client can therefore be told the exact amount of this cost. The rates of SDLT and the possibility of apportioning part of the purchase price to chattels to save on SDLT are discussed in **6.3**.

The source of the funds should also be considered. Where a residential property is being purchased with the aid of a mortgage, the *Lenders' Handbook* (see **Appendix** 7) requires the solicitor to ascertain the source of the remainder of the purchase price and advise the lender if it is not being provided from the buyer's own funds. Very often family members will provide part of the purchase price, and this must then be reported to the lender with the client's authority. If authority is not forthcoming then the solicitor must cease to act, as a conflict will have arisen.

The Law Society's Anti-Money Laundering Practice Note also reminds solicitors of the need to exercise caution in this area (see **5.12**). If, for example, a client states that £100,000 of the purchase price is to be provided from savings, this will be a factor to take into account in deciding whether the transaction should be referred to the firm's Nominated Officer. The key factor in money laundering issues is Customer Due Diligence. Is it reasonable to expect that this client has £100,000 in savings, or could the money be the proceeds of crime?

Particular care should be taken if the buyer advises that part of the purchase price has been/is to be paid directly to the seller. Again, according to the *Lenders' Handbook*, this should be reported to the lender, and again may give rise to money laundering issues.

8.5.3 Deposit

The buyer will usually be required to pay a deposit of 10% of the purchase price on exchange of contracts, although often the seller can be persuaded to accept a lower figure. The client may not have ready access to cash to be used for the deposit and the solicitor will have to discuss with their client how the deposit is to be funded. Often it will be possible to use the deposit paid to the client on the sale of their existing property to fund the deposit required on their purchase. Otherwise a bridging loan may be necessary (see **21.4.2**).

8.5.4 Mortgage

Most clients will require some type of mortgage funding to assist with the purchase of the property. Some clients will already have arranged finance before going to see the solicitor; residential clients may require assistance with the sources and types of finance available (see **Chapter 9**).

8.5.5 Survey

The maxim *caveat emptor* applies (with limited exceptions) to conveyancing: it is for the buyer to make sure of their bargain. It is sensible for the buyer to commission an independent survey of the property to ensure that the property does not have more problems associated with it than the client had bargained for. The solicitor should therefore discuss with their buyer client the need for a survey in appropriate cases (see **Chapter 12**). The need for an environmental survey should also be discussed (see **7.6**).

8.5.6 Situation of the property

Enquiries should be made as to the situation of the property, for example its proximity to canals, rivers, etc, which may indicate the need for special searches to be undertaken (see **Chapter 17**).

8.5.7 Insurance

The risk in the property for insurance purposes will often pass to the buyer when a contract is entered into. The client should be warned of this and that the solicitor will arrange such insurance on their behalf at the client's expense. Additionally, there may be a need to discuss with the client arrangements for life assurance (it may be a term of the client's mortgage offer that they take out a life policy) and buildings contents insurance.

8.5.8 Who is buying the property?

Where the prospective buyer is married or is intending to live in the property with a cohabitee or friend, the lender who is providing the mortgage finance for the property will insist that the legal title to the property is held in joint names, or that the cohabitee or friend sign a waiver of any rights they may have in favour of the lender. Where the purchase is to be in more than one person's name, the clients must be advised in relation to co-ownership (see **Chapter 10**). The problems of conflict of interests must be borne in mind when dealing with this issue.

8.5.9 Custody of deeds

Where there is to be a mortgage of the property, the client's lender would normally in the past have taken custody of the charge certificate and other documents after completion. The LRA 2002 abolished charge certificates and many mortgagees are no longer prepared to store documents because of the costs involved. In all cases, therefore, the client's instructions in relation to custody of the deeds should be obtained. The client may, for example, wish to have the deeds sent to their home or to their bank, or for the solicitor to store them.

8.5.10 The client's present property

In a residential transaction, it must be ascertained where the client is presently living, and whether it is necessary to sell the client's present house before buying the new one (see **8.4.14**). If the client is presently living in rented accommodation, they may need to be advised about giving notice to the landlord to terminate that tenancy.

8.6 INSTRUCTIONS IN SPECIAL CASES

Information additional to that outlined above will be required where the transaction concerns a newly-constructed property (see **Chapter 42**), a leasehold (see **Chapters 35** and **36**), or a dealing with part only of the seller's property (see **Chapter 41**).

8.7 SPECIMEN INSTRUCTIONS

Set out on the following page is an example of an attendance note recording instructions from a client which would have been obtained using the sort of checklist referred to in **8.2.6**. Many firms have their own checklists and this is merely one suggested format. The client, Roger Evans, is the current owner of 47, Queens' Road, Loamster, the title to which has already been seen at **4.5**.

Bucks & Co Solicitors
Attendance Note

Client:	Roger Evans
Matter:	Sale of 47, Queens' Road, Loamster. Purchase of 10, Bladen Road, Overton.
In attendance:	A Solicitor Roger Evans
Date:	1 September 2025

Money laundering identity check Passport seen and copy on file.[1]

Sale

Property and tenure:	47, Queens' Road, Loamster, Maradon, Cornshire, CS1 5TY. Freehold
Seller:	Roger Evans (tel mob 08885 456988).
Buyer:	Catherine and Joanne Reade, 24 Leeming Road, Bridgeton, Cornshire, CS3 4DD.
Buyer's solicitors:	SLT Solicitors (contact details to be confirmed).
Estate Agents:	Mercury Estate Agents (Anne Norwood – mob 08888 324536).
Price (including fixtures and fittings):	£350,000. Various items of garden furniture and washer drier and fridge freezer being sold for an additional £500.
Deposit:	No preliminary deposit paid. £20,000 deposit agreed.
Completion date:	As soon as possible, but ideally before the end of October as this fits in with buyer's plans.
PIF and F&C:	Handed client PIF and F&C and explained purpose. Client to complete and return next week.
Mortgage:	Mortgage with Humberside and Counties Bank, £50,000 outstanding. Title documents at the Loamster Branch.
Miscellaneous:	
• Current use • Any works carried out to property • Occupiers • CGT/VAT	The property is the client's home and was extended in 2018. Otherwise, apart from minor decoration, the client has not carried out works to the property. There are no other occupiers.

Purchase	
Property and tenure:	10, Bladen Road, Overton, Cornshire, CS1 6AU. Freehold.
Seller:	Neil Stuart. Address as above.
Seller's solicitors:	Fining and Co, Overton Office. Jayne Peters (01366 695444)
Estate Agents:	Cranswick Properties. Overton Office.
Price (including fixtures and fittings):	£252,000 including £2,000 for chattels (antique dining furniture).
Deposit:	No preliminary deposit paid. 5% deposit agreed. Explained that the deposit received on sale of 47, Queens' Road might be used to fund this.[2] Client would prefer this but has savings to fund if necessary.
Completion date:	As with sale. Seller is moving abroad but has no deadline.
Survey:	Client has already commissioned a survey.
Mortgage:	None. Purchase to be funded from equity released on sale of current property.
Miscellaneous:	Roger Evans is retiring and buying 10, Bladen Road as his retirement home. The seller, Neil Stuart, is recently widowed and is moving overseas. NS is keen to complete as soon as possible, but has no specific deadline for doing so. Explained to client that apportioning the £2,000 specifically to fixtures and fittings will save a small amount of SDLT. Client confirmed that £2,000 represents proper market value for the items in question. 10, Bladen Road has recently been extended (client thinks two years ago) with a conservatory to the rear overlooking the nearby river. This was one of the selling points to the client as there is also access to the river for the purposes of fishing.
Financial	Reviewed estimate of figures with client and will confirm in writing:[3]

Sale		**Purchase**	
Sale price	350,000	Purchase price	250,000
		Furniture	2,000
Less:			
Mortgage	50,000	Plus:	
Our fees (incl VAT)	[ ]	Our fees (incl VAT)	[ ]
Estate agents fees (incl VAT)	[ ]	Disbursements	[ ]
		Survey	[ ]
		SDLT	2,500
		Land Registry electronic fee	150

Balance of proceeds of sale to be sent to client on completion. Recommended Private Client department for advice on financial and estate planning.

Notes

1. For more detail on this issue, see **8.2.7**.
2. For more information on funding the deposit, see **Chapter 21**.
3. This specimen attendance note identifies the major financial elements of a typical residential transaction. Clients may be unaware of some of the costs involved (particularly significant sums such as SDLT) and so must be made aware of them when taking instructions. Disbursements would include searches and enquiries, for which see **Chapter 17**. Note that potential clients will often shop round before choosing a solicitor and so care needs to be taken in explaining the basis of, level of, and reasons behind the fees charged.

SUMMARY

- An EPC is required for most buildings sold or rented out in the UK, and should be obtained by the seller as soon as marketing begins.
- Once a sale is agreed, full instructions on the transaction should be taken at an early stage and documentary evidence of client identity obtained by the solicitor.
- Personal details of the client (and other relevant parties) should be confirmed by the solicitor, together with details of the property and terms agreed for the sale (including the amount of any deposit).
- The solicitor should advise of the costs of the transaction and carry out a financial calculation to check that sufficient funds exist to pay off outstanding mortgages (in the case of the seller) or to complete the purchase (in the case of the buyer).
- The solicitor should advise of any CGT and VAT implications of the transaction.
- In the case of a sale, the need for a mortgage, survey and insurance should be discussed by the solicitor, together with the proposed use of the property.
- In residential transactions, instructions must be taken as to whether the client needs to synchronise a sale and purchase.
- The solicitor should identify whether the client requires any particular completion date.

CHAPTER 9

FINANCE FOR THE BUYER

LEARNING OUTCOMES

After reading this chapter you will be able to:

- identify the sources of debt finance available to a buyer
- explain the types of mortgage available
- advise on the factors affecting the amount of loan available
- appreciate the impact of the Financial Services and Markets Act 2000 when acting for a client in connection with a mortgage.

9.1 INTRODUCTION

The buyer's solicitor should check that the client has sufficient funds available to meet the cost of the purchase and related expenses. This matter should be raised with the client when taking instructions, and a further check should be made just before exchange of contracts to ensure that any factors which have altered since instructions were first obtained have been taken into account in calculating the client's financial situation. The client should be advised against entering into a binding contract for purchase unless the financial arrangements are settled and adequate to meet the commitments involved.

This chapter is concerned with debt finance, where the lender lends money in return for interest. There are other ways of obtaining finance for property purchase and development (including sale and leaseback and equity funding) but these are beyond the scope of this book.

This chapter is also restricted to secured lending, where the borrower grants the lender a legal mortgage over the property and, where appropriate, additional security such as a fixed charge over fixtures, plant and machinery, an assignment of the rental income and, if the borrower is a company, a floating charge over all the assets not covered by the other security. It is possible to obtain unsecured loans for property transactions, but the loan amount will be smaller and the interest rate higher than for secured loans to reflect the fact that if the borrower becomes insolvent, the lender will be an unsecured creditor and will rank below all secured creditors in any distribution of the borrower's assets and may, therefore, lose some or all of its money.

9.1.1 The client has already arranged a mortgage

Many clients will have already considered the financial implications of the transaction before instructing the solicitor to act, in which case all that the solicitor needs to do is to check through the figures with the client to ensure that all necessary items of expenditure have been taken into account. In this situation, the client is likely to have submitted a mortgage application to a lender already, and will not require advice on the sources and types of finance available for the purchase of property. The solicitor should not interfere with arrangements which the client has made, but if it appears that the mortgage arrangements are patently unsatisfactory (eg, an exorbitant interest rate is to be charged on the loan), there may be a duty on the solicitor to suggest that the client reconsiders their choice of finance on the basis that more advantageous terms could be obtained from another source.

9.1.2 Financial Services and Markets Act 2000

If you are carrying out a 'specified activity' in relation to a regulated mortgage contract, you must be authorised under the Financial Services and Markets Act 2000 (FSMA 2000). 'Specified activities' will include arranging or advising on a regulated mortgage contract, unless you are arranging the execution of a mortgage chosen independently by the client or on the advice of an authorised person. General advice as to what type of loan to take out will not require authorisation as it will not amount to a 'specified activity'.

A regulated mortgage contract is a contract which meets the following conditions at the time it is entered into:

(a) the borrower is an individual or a trustee;

(b) the lender takes a first legal charge over property in the UK; and

(c) at least 40% of the property is occupied by the borrower or a member of their immediate family, or is intended for their occupation.

If a specified activity is involved and you are not authorised by the Financial Conduct Authority (FCA) or the Prudential Regulation Authority (PRA) to carry out regulated activities (which most firms will not be), you will need to rely on the so-called 'professional firms exemption'. This exemption will allow firms operating under it to arrange or advise on a regulated mortgage contract, subject to certain conditions, even though they are not authorised by the regulators. It should be noted that the ability to 'advise' under the professional firms exemption does not include recommending a client to enter into a regulated mortgage contract, except where that advice consists of an endorsement of a recommendation given to the client by an authorised person. For further detail on this complex area, see ***Legal Foundations***.

9.2 SOURCES OF FINANCE

Where the client has not made any financial arrangements prior to instructing the solicitor, they may require advice on the sources of mortgage finance and types of loan available. In some cases, the client may require assistance with making the mortgage application. The solicitor may have an arrangement with a lender for the introduction of clients; any such arrangement must comply with the SRA Codes.

9.2.1 Sources of mortgage finance

The main sources of mortgage finance available for the purchase of land in England and Wales are:

(a) banks;

(b) building societies;

(c) the client's employer;

(d) a private mortgage (eg, a loan from a relative or from a trust fund); and

(e) finance houses.

9.2.2 Building societies and banks

Loans from building societies and banks represent the largest slice of the mortgage market. There is little to distinguish between the terms offered by these two types of institutions: both will offer long-term loans at commercially competitive interest rates.

Banks have the reputation of being slightly more flexible in the application of their lending criteria and of being more willing to consider unusual property (eg, a derelict barn which is to be converted) and higher-value loans. Loans for commercial property and business expansion are also more likely to be funded by banks.

9.2.3 The client's employer

Some large company employers (eg, banks) offer mortgages at concessionary rates to their employees. The terms of these loans may enable an employee to borrow a substantially higher sum at a lower rate of interest than could be obtained on the open market.

Where the rate of interest payable on such a loan is less than the commercial rate being charged by other lenders, the employee may be deemed by HMRC to be in receipt of a benefit in kind which is taxable in the hands of a higher-paid employee. Even with this tax burden, the loan from the employer still usually represents good value for money. The main drawback to such an arrangement is that the employee with this type of loan will find it more difficult to change their job, since ending their employment will result in the withdrawal of the concessionary rates and a consequent increase in mortgage repayments.

9.2.4 Private mortgage

A client may sometimes be able to arrange mortgage finance through a loan from a relative or from a private trust fund. The terms of such a loan are a matter for agreement between the parties involved, which must always be separately advised. Even where the loan is between related parties, a potential conflict of interests between lender and borrower will preclude the same solicitor from acting for both parties.

9.2.5 Finance houses

Mortgage funding is available from finance houses, but they are not generally considered to be a primary source of finance for a client who is seeking a loan for the purchase of property, particularly a residential client. The terms offered by a finance house may be less generous than those offered by the banks and building societies (ie, a shorter period of loan and higher rate of interest).

However, a client might approach a finance house for a second loan (eg, for improvements to the property). Second mortgages from finance houses may be affected by the notice provisions contained in s 58 of the Consumer Credit Act 1974.

9.2.6 Government schemes

The Government has introduced various schemes to attempt to alleviate the difficulties buyers have experienced in funding house purchases due to tight lending criteria and rises in property prices not matched by salary rises. The availability and criteria for the schemes change from time to time and the latest information can be found at <www.gov.uk/affordable-home-ownership-schemes>.

9.3 AMOUNT OF THE LOAN

All lenders have slightly different criteria or status qualifications for granting a loan. In broad terms, the maximum sum that a borrower can hope to obtain on mortgage is linked to the borrower's income, taking into account any other debts and financial commitments. A residential borrower will typically be asked to provide evidence of salary and details of the number of dependants, debts and household outgoings. A commercial borrower will be asked to provide financial projections, business plans and audited accounts. In both cases, lenders will look more favourably on borrowers with a positive credit rating and a stable financial position, and will charge a higher rate of interest to borrowers who are unable to demonstrate this or, in current market conditions, refuse to lend to them at all. For example, self-certification mortgages, designed for borrowers whose income is difficult to assess using the standard methods adopted by most mortgage lenders, are now available only in very limited circumstances for the self-employed, and require the borrower to contribute a deposit of 25% or more.

This maximum sum is usually subject to the further qualification that the amount of the loan does not exceed a fixed percentage of the lender's valuation of the property (not the purchase price). The fixed percentage (sometimes known as the 'loan-to-value ratio') will vary depending on the lender and the type of property involved. In current market conditions, it is difficult for a residential client to obtain a loan of more than 90% of the valuation, although the Government's 'NewBuy and 'Help to Buy' schemes may assist residential buyers (see **9.2.6**). In the commercial market, lenders are unlikely to lend more than 70–80% of the value of the property, although higher amounts may be available if the borrower can provide additional personal guarantees.

It must also be remembered that the lender's valuation of the property is frequently less than the asking price for the property. Where the lender agrees to lend a sum in excess of the normal percentage of the valuation, it may be a term of the loan that the borrower pays for a single premium insurance policy ('a mortgage guarantee policy' or 'MIG') which is taken out by the lender. If the lender has to exercise its power of sale, it is insured against any loss it may incur due to having lent more than the normal percentage of the value. These mortgage guarantee policies have been much criticised since, although they are paid for by the borrower, they protect only the lender. The borrower has no rights under them on a sale at a loss. Indeed, the insurer often has a right of subrogation to reclaim any loss it has had to meet from the borrower. Many lenders now no longer require such policies, or will meet the cost themselves.

Where the property is let, the lender will also apply the interest rate cover ratio. The lender wants to ensure that the borrower has enough money coming in to make the interest payments throughout the term of the loan; with a let property, this money will come from the rent that the tenants are paying. Typically, a lender will insist that the expected rental income must exceed the mortgage repayments by a certain percentage, which in the case of residential 'buy-to-let' mortgages may be as high as 130%.

9.4 TYPES OF MORTGAGE

Each lender will apply a different name to the various loan packages which it advertises. The first decision for the borrower is whether to take out a repayment mortgage or an interest-only mortgage.

9.4.1 Repayment mortgage

A repayment mortgage is the most straightforward type of loan available. In return for the loan, the borrower grants a mortgage of the property to the lender. Throughout the term of the loan the borrower will make monthly repayments to the lender, part of which represents a repayment of the capital sum borrowed. The balance is interest on the loan. At the end of the mortgage term, the loan has been completely repaid and the mortgage is discharged. If the borrower wants to sell the property before the end of the mortgage term, they will pay off the mortgage out of the proceeds of sale of the property, and any sum over and above this amount will belong to them.

9.4.2 Interest-only mortgage

With an interest-only mortgage, the borrower pays off only the interest on the loan, so that the whole of the capital remains outstanding at the end of the loan term. The borrower will usually enter into a separate investment plan, such as an endowment policy, an ISA or a pension plan, to enable them to pay off the outstanding capital. The advantage is that interest-only mortgages usually have lower monthly repayments than repayment mortgages, but they are more risky in that there is no guarantee that the investment plan will generate sufficient funds to pay off the outstanding capital.

Another option is a combined mortgage, where a proportion of the loan is interest only and a proportion is repayment, particularly for those borrowers who already have an investment plan in place prior to taking out the new mortgage.

9.4.3 The interest rate (residential mortgages)

Whether the mortgage is interest-only or repayment, the borrower will have to choose the method by which the interest on the loan is set. The simplest option is the standard variable rate mortgage based on the lender's basic mortgage rate (its 'Standard Variable Mortgage Rate'), which rises and falls in response to changes in the UK base rate set by the Bank of England. For borrowers who want greater certainty, particularly in the initial period of the loan, a fixed rate mortgage may be preferable. The interest rate will be set for a specified period, resulting in a guaranteed monthly payment. Alternatively, a capped rate mortgage puts a maximum limit on the interest rate; a discount rate mortgage offers a percentage discount from the lender's Standard Variable Mortgage Rate; while a tracker mortgage will have a rate of interest set as a percentage above the UK base rate set by the Bank of England. In each case, the mortgage will usually revert to the lender's Standard Variable Mortgage Rate once the fixed, capped, discount or tracker period ends. It should also be noted that in most cases, the lender will charge a fee (a 'redemption penalty') if the borrower repays the loan during the special rate period.

9.4.4 The interest rate (commercial mortgages)

Commercial mortgages are offered on a repayment or an interest-only basis, and the interest rates may be fixed or variable. However, commercial mortgages are considered to be a higher risk than residential ones, so interest rates tend to be higher and loan terms shorter (eg, 15 years instead of 25).

9.4.5 Payment protection (residential mortgages)

Problems will arise if the borrower or one of the co-borrowers dies, suffers a critical illness or becomes unemployed during the term of the mortgage. This is particularly the case with a repayment mortgage: if the borrower dies before the mortgage is paid off, the whole of the outstanding balance of the loan becomes immediately repayable from the deceased's estate. This may cause problems if the deceased borrower was the main salary earner for a family, leaving a non-earning spouse and children to cope with the repayment of the mortgage. Lenders will sometimes require the borrower to take out a 'mortgage protection policy', which guarantees to repay the balance outstanding on the mortgage in the event of the borrower's death. Some policies will also cover permanent disability through accident or illness which prevents the borrower from earning their living. These policies are readily available and, in the case of co-owners, are taken out over joint lives, so that even if one co-owner is not contributing financially to the mortgage, the repayment of the loan is guaranteed in the event of the death of either of them. Insurance cover for critical illness and income protection can also be obtained separately.

Solicitors should be aware that such policies will be regulated by the FSMA 2000 (see **22.6**). For further detail on this complex area, see ***Legal Foundations*** and the SRA Financial Services (Scope) Rules 2019.

9.4.6 Islamic mortgages

Most loans require the payment (and receipt) of interest. There are, however, various finance schemes that are Sharia compliant and avoid the payment of interest.

The Murabaha involves a bank buying the property and then reselling it to the actual buyer at a higher price. This price is then paid to the bank by instalments over a period of years.

Alternatively, the Ijara and Diminishing Musharaka schemes allow the bank to purchase the property and then lease it to the buyer in return for rent. At the end of the lease, the bank agrees to transfer the property to the buyer.

SUMMARY

- A buyer may get finance for their purchase from a bank, building society, employer, relative or finance house.
- Commercial lenders will have lending criteria that must be met in order to obtain finance. They often have a maximum loan to value ratio and will usually carry out their own valuation of the property.
- A buyer will usually choose from a repayment mortgage or an interest only mortgage. The interest rate on the loan may be fixed, variable or capped, or track the base rate set by the Bank of England.
- Residential mortgages are specified investments for the purposes of the FSMA 2000, and so advising on or arranging such a mortgage is a regulated activity.

CHAPTER 10

ADVISING JOINT BUYERS

LEARNING OUTCOMES

After reading this chapter you will be able to:

- explain when sole ownership and co-ownership are appropriate
- advise on the distinction between a joint tenancy and a tenancy in common
- explain when joint tenancies and tenancies in common are appropriate
- record the method of co-ownership at the time of purchase.

10.1 ADVISING THE CLIENT

Where it is apparent from instructions that the property is to be occupied and/or financed by two or more adults, the solicitor should discuss with their client(s) the advantages and disadvantages of co-ownership and the various methods by which the client's wishes can be carried out. A note of the client's instructions should be made on the file to ensure that they are implemented at the appropriate stage of the transaction (ie, in the transfer deed).

There are three possible options which need to be discussed with the clients:

(a) sole ownership by one of the clients; or

(b) ownership by all as joint tenants; or

(c) ownership by all as tenants in common.

The following points should be borne in mind.

(a) Instructions should be obtained directly from all proposed co-owners. It is not sufficient to accept the word of one co-owner that their co-buyer agrees to the proposals.

(b) Advising more than one party in the same transaction (ie, the two or more co-buyers) may give rise to a conflict of interests between them, for example where the beneficial interest in the property is to be held in unequal shares. The solicitor must ensure that the co-buyers receive separate independent advice in any situation where a conflict arises or is likely to arise (see **Chapter 5**).

10.2 SUITABILITY OF EACH METHOD

When advising clients in this area, regard should be had to the underlying principles relating to trusts and co-ownership (see **Chapters 3** and **4**), and these should be borne in mind in the context of the following paragraphs.

10.2.1 Sole ownership

This is generally suitable only where the other occupier is not contributing to the purchase price in any way. This is because the non-owning occupier will legally have no say in any future disposition of the property. However, a spouse or civil partner will have rights of occupation under the Family Law Act 1996 and may prevent a sale by registering those rights.

If the occupier is making a financial contribution, it may well be preferable to consider one of the forms of co-ownership. Whatever type of co-ownership is chosen, all co-owners have to join in (and thus agree to) any disposition. However, if there is to be a mortgage on the property, all co-owners will be required to join in this and thus make themselves personally liable to repay the loan. This may well not be what the parties intend.

If an occupier making a contribution were not to become a legal co-owner, it may well still not be possible for a sale or other disposition to be made without their consent. The occupier may have a beneficial interest because of the contribution, which could be an overriding interest under Sch 3 to the LRA 2002 and, as such, will be required to release those rights on a disposition; otherwise they will be binding on a purchaser irrespective of notice. In theory, the sole owner of the legal estate can appoint another trustee and thus overreach the overriding interest of the occupier (see *City of London Building Society v Flegg* [1988] AC 54). However, in practice, if a sale is contemplated and the occupier is refusing to leave, it may well still be necessary to obtain a court order to evict the occupier and thus give a buyer vacant possession.

The possibility of a conflict of interest arising should very carefully be borne in mind in advising in this area.

10.2.2 Joint tenancy

All cases of co-ownership give rise to a trust of land (see **3.8**). The legal estate will be held under a joint tenancy and the maximum number of legal owners is four. As with any form of co-ownership, all of the legal co-owners must join in any future disposition of the property. In case of a dispute, an application may be made to the court under s 14 of the Trusts of Land and Appointment of Trustees Act 1996. The court may make whatever order it thinks fit, but will particularly take into account the purpose for which the land was bought.

In equity, there is a choice between holding as joint tenants or as tenants in common. On the death of a joint tenant the right of survivorship will apply, and this will make a joint tenancy particularly suitable for married couples, civil partners and others in a permanent relationship who want their interest in the house to go to the other party on their death. If the parties wish to be able to leave their respective shares by will, eg where they have children from a previous relationship, then a tenancy in common will be necessary.

A joint tenancy can subsequently be 'severed', ie converted into a tenancy in common. This will then destroy the right of survivorship and allow an owner's share to be left by will to whomsoever the owner pleases.

However, joint tenants always have equal rights in the property, irrespective of their contributions to the purchase price. Thus, if A and B buy as joint tenants, A having contributed 90% of the price and B only 10%, on a subsequent severance B will acquire a half share in the land. If the parties want recognition to be given to their respective contributions then a tenancy in common will be required from the outset.

10.2.3 Tenancy in common

This would be usual in the case of business partners and other circumstances where the parties do not wish the right of survivorship to apply, for example where the parties are not married or in a civil partnership, are not cohabiting or not in a long-term relationship, or want to be able to make provision for others out of their interest on death, or want the amount of their contribution to the purchase price to be recognised in the size of their share in the land. It is essential in a tenancy in common for the respective shares of the co-owners to be expressly recorded (see **10.3**).

As with a joint tenancy, all of the co-owners of the legal estate must join in a disposition. Disputes may again be resolved by the court under s 14 of the Trusts of Land and Appointment of Trustees Act 1996.

10.3 RECORDING THE METHOD OF CO-OWNERSHIP

The cases of *Stack v Dowden* [2007] 2 AC 432 and *Jones v Kernott* [2010] 3 WLR 2401 have highlighted the problems that can occur when joint owners of a property fail to declare how they hold their beneficial interests at the outset. Land Registry and the Law Society have issued a Practice Note entitled 'Joint ownership', advising solicitors that they should make their clients aware of the potential consequences of not making a declaration of trust at the time of the purchase, ie that a dispute might arise, necessitating expensive litigation, with the court eventually dividing the property in a way that is different to what the parties intended.

Once the clients have been advised and made their decision on how they want to hold their beneficial interests, that decision can be recorded in:

(a) the Land Registry transfer form (see panel 10 of Form TR1 at **27.9**);
(b) Land Registry Form JO (see below);
(c) a separate declaration of trust.

A separate declaration of trust is usually more detailed than the trust declaration panels on the Land Registry forms and may include information on how much each party contributed to the purchase price, the share of the beneficial interest that each party intends to hold, how the proceeds of sale are to be divided if the parties separate and who is going to pay the mortgage and other outgoings.

A separate declaration of trust is particularly suitable if the clients want the details of their interests in the property to be private. Also, in the case of business partners, it is preferable for the exact shares of the partners not to be recorded in the Land Registry forms. This is because those shares might change due to a reorganisation of the partnership, for example on the admission of a new partner. It is preferable for the shares of the co-owners to be dealt with exclusively by the partnership agreement and for the Land Registry forms to make it clear that they hold as tenants in common in the shares as set out in the partnership agreement.

In the domestic context, the parties may wish to use a pre-nuptial, post-nuptial or separation agreement to declare their interests. Form JO and all the Land Registry's transfer, assent and prescribed clauses leases have declaration of trust panels which allow for details of a separate declaration of trust to be given.

Land Registry will automatically enter a Form A restriction in the register whenever two or more people apply to be registered as joint proprietors of an estate in land, unless it is clear that they will be holding the property for themselves alone as joint tenants (see **3.8.3**).

Land Registry
Trust Information

JO

This form may accompany an application in Form AP1, FR1 or ADV1 where:

- panel 9 of Form FR1 or ADV1 has not been completed and the applicant is more than one person, or
- the Form AP1 relates to a transfer (in Form AS1, AS3, TP1, TP2, TR1, TR2 or TR5) or a prescribed clauses lease (within rule 58A of the Land Registration Rules 2003) of a registered estate to more than one person (the Joint Owners), and
  - the declaration of trust panel in the transfer or lease has not been completed and/or the transfer has not been executed by the Joint Owners, andthe estate transferred or leased is not a rentcharge, franchise, profit or manor.

Guidance	Panel
Enter the same information as either in the transfer or lease to the Joint Owners or in panel 6 of Form ADV1. Leave blank if this form accompanies a Form FR1.	1 Title number(s) of the property:
Insert address including postcode (if any) or other description of the property as it appears either in the transfer or lease to the Joint Owners, in panel 3 of Form ADV1 or in panel 2 of Form FR1.	2 Property:
	3 Date:
Give full name(s) and address(es), as in either the transfer or lease to the Joint Owners, panels 6 and 7 of Forms ADV1 or panels 6 and 8 of Form FR1.	4 Joint Owners:
Complete either this or panel 6. Place an 'X' in the appropriate box. If completing the fourth box, insert details either of the trust or of the trust instrument under which the Joint Owners hold the property. The registrar will enter a Form A restriction in the register if an 'X' is placed: – in the second or third box, or – in the fourth box, unless it is clear that the Joint Owners hold on trust for themselves alone as joint tenants. If this panel is completed, each Joint Owner must sign. Please refer to Land Registry's *Public Guide 18 – Joint property ownership* and *Practice Guide 24 – Private trusts of land* for further guidance. These guides are available on the website www.landregistry.gov.uk	5 ☐ The Joint Owners declare that they are to hold the property on trust for themselves alone as joint tenants ☐ The Joint Owners declare that they are to hold the property on trust for themselves alone as tenants in common in equal shares ☐ The Joint Owners declare that they hold the property on trust for themselves alone as tenants in common in the following unequal shares: *(complete)* ☐ The Joint Owners are to hold the property (*complete*): Signature of each of the Joint Owners ____________________ ____________________ Date:

	6 Under the term of a written declaration of trust dated (*complete*) the Joint Owners ☐ hold the property on trust as joint tenants for themselves alone ☐ do not hold the property on trust as joint tenants for themselves alone
If this panel is completed, a conveyancer must sign.	Signature of conveyancer ________________ Date:

WARNING
If you dishonestly enter information or make a statement that you know is, or might be, untrue or misleading, and intend by doing so to make a gain for yourself or another person, or to cause loss or the risk of loss to another person, you may commit the offence of fraud under section 1 of the Fraud Act 2006, the maximum penalty for which is 10 years' imprisonment or an unlimited fine, or both.

Failure to complete this form with proper care may result in a loss of protection under the Land Registration Act 2002 if, as a result, a mistake is made in the register.

Under section 66 of the Land Registration Act 2002 most documents (including this form) kept by the registrar relating to an application to the registrar or referred to in the register are open to public inspection and copying. If you believe a document contains prejudicial information, you may apply for that part of the document to be made exempt using Form EX1, under rule 136 of the Land Registration Rules 2003.

SUMMARY

- There are three possible forms of ownership: sole ownership, co-ownership as tenants in common, co-ownership as joint tenants.
- In most case where two or more persons contribute to the purchase price, co-ownership will be most suitable.
- If the co-owners hold as joint tenants, they will have equal rights in the property and, on the death of one co-owner, the deceased's share will pass to the survivor.
- This makes a joint tenancy particularly suitable for those in a permanent relationship.
- If the co-owners hold as tenants in common, the shares of the co-owners should be recorded expressly.
- On the death of a tenant in common, their share in the property will pass according to their will or the intestacy rules.
- This makes a tenancy in common particularly suitable for business partners or anyone wishing to bequeath their interest in the property on death.
- Once co-owners have been advised and have decided how they are to hold the beneficial interest in the property, that decision should be recorded.

CHAPTER 11

FIXTURES AND FITTINGS

LEARNING OUTCOMES

After reading this chapter you will be able to:

- recognise the difficulties in distinguishing between fixtures and fittings
- explain how to deal contractually with fixtures and fittings.

11.1 FIXTURES AND FITTINGS – INTRODUCTION

The distinction between fixtures and fittings is an important one. Fixtures are treated as forming part of the land, and so (except where the seller has reserved the right to remove specific items) the buyer can expect to take over the ownership of fixtures on completion. They are part of the property which they have purchased and their value is included in the purchase price. Generally some degree of attachment to the land is required in order for an item to be a fixture. By contrast, fittings (or chattels) do not form part of the land, and so are not included as part of the property on sale of the land unless the seller expressly agrees to leave them behind. Fittings may or may not be included in the sale price for the property (although there may be tax advantages to having a separate price for fittings – see **11.4**). Often the issue is dealt with estate agent's particulars of sale; but if not, parties will need to reach agreement over what fittings are to be left following sale and whether an additional price is to be paid for them.

11.2 DIFFICULTY OF DISTINGUISHING BETWEEN FIXTURES AND FITTINGS

In order to distinguish between fixtures and fittings, a two-stage test has evolved which looks at the degree to which an object is attached to the land and the purpose for which it is so attached. Although the test is, on the face of it, comparatively straightforward, its practical application is at the mercy of the complexity of human living arrangements. There have been reported cases where items such as greenhouses and garden ornaments have been held to be fixtures, and other cases where similar types of items have been held to be fittings (see, eg, *TSB Bank plc v Botham* (1997) 73 P & CR D1).

11.3 NEED FOR CERTAINTY IN CONTRACT

The problems considered above can be avoided by the parties dealing with the issue as part of the conveyancing process. When acting for a seller, it will be necessary to ascertain from the client which items are to be removed, which items they expect to remain at the property and whether any price in addition to the price of the land is required for the fittings. The buyer's solicitor should make similar enquiries of their client in terms of what items the buyer thinks are (and are not) to be included in the sale, and at what cost. The position should be communicated between the parties so that any discrepancies may be sorted out.

In appropriate circumstances the contract can then be used to resolve any uncertainty by being made expressly to deal with:

(a) fixtures which the seller intends to remove on or before completion;

(b) fittings which are to remain at the property;

(c) any additional price which the buyer is to pay for the fittings;

(d) postponement of passing of title to fittings until completion; in the absence of such a condition, s 18 of the Sale of Goods Act 1979 will provide that title to the fittings passes to the buyer on exchange (this provision is contained in SC 9.4 (SCPC 12.4));

(e) a warranty that fittings are free of incumbrances (eg, subsisting hire-purchase agreements). In the absence of an express special condition dealing with this matter, SC 9.2 and SCPC 12.2, by making the contract one for the sale of goods, implicitly import s 12 of the Sale of Goods Act 1979 which contains such a warranty.

11.4 APPORTIONMENT OF PURCHASE PRICE

The sale of chattels does not attract SDLT. The value of chattels which have been included in the purchase price of the land can therefore be deducted from the total purchase price, producing a reduction in the value of the land and a possible consequent reduction in the amount of tax payable by the buyer (see **6.3.3** for more details).

11.5 FITTINGS AND CONTENTS FORM

The Protocol (see **2.4** and **Appendix 1**) requires the seller's solicitor to obtain information relating to fixtures and fittings from the seller, using the Fittings and Contents Form (F&C), so that the completed form can be sent to the buyer's solicitors with the draft contract. Special Condition 3 on the reverse of the Standard Conditions of Sale form makes reference to a list of contents and, in appropriate cases, requires it to be annexed to and form part of the contract. The F&C may be used for this purpose. This arrangement should address the issues raised in **11.2** and **11.3** in the case of residential transactions.

SUMMARY

- Ownership of fixtures (but not fittings) will pass with the sale of the land to which they are attached.
- Whilst fixtures will generally have some degree of attachment to the land, it is hard to categorise all fixtures and fittings with certainty.
- The sale contract should specify any fittings that are to remain post completion and any price agreed for them.
- If the seller wishes to retain any items that might be categorised as fixtures, the right to remove them should be provided for in the contract.
- Stamp duty land tax is not payable on chattels and therefore an appropriate apportionment of the purchase price to chattels may be made to reduce the client's overall SDLT bill.

CHAPTER 12

SURVEYS

LEARNING OUTCOMES

After reading this chapter you will be able to:

- explain why a survey should be carried out
- list and explain the main types of survey available
- advise as to when a full survey is desirable
- identify the circumstances in which a specialist survey is appropriate.

12.1 WHEN SHOULD A SURVEY BE COMMISSIONED?

In an ideal world, the client should always have a survey carried out before exchange of contracts, but many buyers of residential property, particularly first-time buyers for whom the expense of a survey is a major consideration, do not commission an independent survey, preferring to rely instead on the valuation undertaken by their lender.

A valuation will be undertaken by the buyer's lender in order to establish whether the property being purchased will be adequate security for the amount of the loan. The buyer pays the cost of this valuation and is usually permitted to see the valuer's report, but the report will not necessarily reveal sufficient information about the state of the property to allow the buyer to make a reasoned judgement as to whether or not to proceed with the purchase. As its name suggests, it just assesses the value of the property; it will not contain a detailed commentary on the state of the structure of the property. If the lender has concerns about the condition of the property, it may insist on a full survey as a condition of the mortgage offer.

12.2 REASONS FOR A SURVEY

The *caveat emptor* rule places on the buyer the onus of discovering any physical faults in the property agreed to be sold. For this reason alone, a survey is always advisable in order to discover physical defects which are not readily apparent on inspection of the property by the lay client.

12.3 TYPES OF BUILDING SURVEY

From June 2020, surveyors undertaking residential surveys should be offering standardised forms of survey at three differing levels of detail (and therefore cost). Survey level 1 will be the cheapest option, and will involve a visual inspection that is less extensive than for the other levels. The most comprehensive report will be the level 3 survey (which is essentially a full structural survey) consisting of a detailed visual inspection of the building, its services and grounds.

Surveys of commercial properties are not standardised in the same way as residential surveys and the extent of the survey will depend on the scope of the instructions. However, a buyer of commercial property should be encouraged to consider a comprehensive survey, given the principle of *caveat emptor* (see **12.2**).

In both residential and commercial transactions, whilst the potential expense of a full survey deters many clients, the client might be reminded that incurring the cost of a survey is preferable to discovering that many thousands of pounds need to be spent on carrying out structural repairs to the property they have just purchased without the benefit of a survey. A full structural survey will provide a detailed commentary on the condition of the structure of the building and is particularly important if:.

(a) the property is of a high value;
(b) the amount of the buyer's intended mortgage represents a low proportion of the purchase price;
(c) the property is more than 100 years old;
(d) the buyer intends to alter or extend the property after completion;
(e) the property is not of conventional brick and mortar construction;
(f) the property is close to features that may cause subsidence or other structural problems (eg, mines, rivers, clay sub-soils); and
(g) the property is not detached.

12.4 ADDITIONAL TYPES OF SURVEYS

12.4.1 Drainage survey

A surveyor, even when instructed to carry out a full structural survey, will not normally investigate drainage or electrical systems. A property which does not have the benefit of mains drainage will require a separate drainage survey from an expert in that field, since the cost of repair or replacement of a private drainage system can be prohibitive. Liability for escaping effluent can also involve civil and criminal penalties.

12.4.2 Environmental survey

For properties at high risk of contamination, an environmental survey undertaken by a specialist environmental consultant should be considered (see **17.9**).

12.4.3 Asbestos survey

The Control of Asbestos Regulations 2012 (SI 2012/632) impose a duty to identify and manage asbestos in non-domestic buildings. A buyer of commercial property should therefore be advised to undertake an asbestos survey and request copies of any existing asbestos management plan from the seller.

12.5 FLATS AND OTHER ATTACHED PROPERTIES

Where the property to be purchased is a flat or is a property which is structurally attached to neighbouring property, a full survey is desirable. The structural soundness of the property being bought is, in these circumstances, dependent on the soundness of the neighbouring property too, and the surveyor must therefore be instructed to inspect the main structure of the building and the adjoining property (if possible) as well as the property actually being purchased.

If buying a flat in (or the freehold of) a high rise residential building, the solicitor should consider the application of the Building Safety Act 2022 (see **38.4.1**). The surveyor should be asked to consider the fire safety aspects of the building and, in particular, the potential presence of combustible cladding as there are considerable cost implications for removing such cladding and uncertainty as to who will bear those costs. The Law Society has issued a guidance note entitled 'The Building Safety Act 2022: a guide for conveyancers'. This should be reviewed by any conveyancer acting in a transaction involving a high rise residential building.

12.6 SURVEYOR'S LIABILITY

The surveyor owes a duty of care to their client to carry out their survey with reasonable skill and care. This common law duty is reinforced by statutory provisions which imply into a contract for services a term that the work will be carried out with reasonable skill and care (see the Supply of Goods and Services Act 1982, s 13 and the Consumer Rights Act 2015, s 49(1)). Where a client suffers loss as a result of a negligent survey, a claim may lie against the surveyor, subject to the validity of any exemption clause which may have formed part of the surveyor's terms of work. The normal rules relating to remoteness of damage apply, thus the client will not sustain a successful claim unless the area of the client's complaint lies within the scope of what the surveyor was instructed to do, hence the importance of giving full and explicit instructions when the survey is commissioned.

Where the client suffers loss after having relied on a lender's valuer's report, a claim in tort may lie against the surveyor. No claim in contract can be sustained because the survey was commissioned by the lender, and so there is no contractual relationship between the buyer and the surveyor. The success of such a claim may again depend on the validity of any exclusion clause contained in the valuation. However, it was held by the House of Lords in *Smith v Eric S Bush (a Firm)* [1990] 1 AC 831 that a valuer instructed by a lender to carry out a mortgage valuation of a modest house, in the knowledge that the buyer would rely on the valuation without obtaining an independent survey, owed a duty of care to the buyer to exercise reasonable care and skill in carrying out the valuation.

SUMMARY

- The onus is on the buyer to discover physical defects in the property they are buying, and they should therefore consider a survey.
- There are different types of report available, ranging from a basic valuation of the property to a full structural survey.
- Particular consideration should be given to a full structural survey where the property:
  - is of high value; or
  - presents a greater risk of physical problems than usual; or
  - is to be altered after purchase.
- In certain circumstances additional environmental, asbestos or drainage surveys may also be appropriate.

CHAPTER 13

Action Following Instructions

LEARNING OUTCOMES

After reading this chapter you will be able to explain the steps required to be taken by both parties' solicitors following initial instructions.

13.1 AFTER THE INTERVIEW: BOTH PARTIES

13.1.1 Attendance note

An attendance note (see **8.7**) should be made as soon as possible after the interview, recording exactly what took place at the interview, the instructions received and the advice given. The time spent in the interview should be noted on the attendance note for time-recording purposes.

It is important that a detailed written record of the interview exists on the solicitor's file. The written record provides a reminder to the solicitor of what needs to be done, and evidence of what took place between solicitor and client in case of a later dispute between them.

13.1.2 Confirming instructions to the client

In order to ensure that no misunderstanding exists between solicitor and client, instructions should always be confirmed to the client in writing as soon as possible after the interview has taken place. The letter should contain a full record of what happened at the interview, including a repetition of the instructions given by the client and the advice given by the solicitor. The letter should also deal with information as to costs, confirm any action agreed to be taken by the solicitor, and remind the client of anything which they promised to do (eg, obtain their building society account number). To comply with the SRA Codes of Conduct, the letter must also give details of how complaints about the solicitor's services and/or charges can be made and of the client's right to complain to the Legal Ombudsman (together with details of how to contact the Ombudsman and the timeframe for doing so).

13.1.3 Letters to other parties

If not already done, contact should be established with the representatives of the other parties involved in the transaction, such as the other party's solicitor, the estate agent, and the client's lender. Any such letter is likely to be merely introductory, saying that the solicitor has been instructed to act in the transaction, on what terms the client has agreed to proceed, and that the solicitor will contact the third party further in due course.

13.1.3.1 'Subject to contract'

For historical reasons, it used to be customary for all correspondence preceding the contract, including this type of introductory letter, to be headed 'Subject to contract'. The purpose of the inclusion of this phrase was to ensure that no contract was inadvertently entered into between the seller and buyer before they fully intended to do so. In view of the provisions of the Law of Property (Miscellaneous Provisions) Act 1989 (see **3.3**), it is extremely unlikely that a client could inadvertently form a contract by letter, so the inclusion of the 'Subject to contract' phrase is unnecessary on pre-contract correspondence, but it is still encountered in practice.

13.1.3.2 Telephone call

A telephone call to the third party (provided it is recorded by means of an attendance note on the file) would suffice in place of a letter in these circumstances. The object of the exercise is to establish contact between all the parties who are involved in the transaction, and any method of doing this quickly is therefore acceptable. Sending correspondence by fax is also routinely used to speed up transactions; more and more solicitors also use e-mail as a method of communication.

13.1.3.3 The estate agent

Apart from confirming to the estate agent that the solicitor is instructed, it is always useful to have a copy of the estate agent's particulars of sale on file. These particulars can provide useful information relating to the area in which the property is sited, which may indicate to the solicitor that particular searches and enquiries may be required. They will also contain details of the fixtures and fittings at the property, and whether or not these are to be included in the sale (see **Chapter 11**).

13.2 FOR THE SELLER

13.2.1 Obtain title deeds and documents

The seller's solicitor needs to have access to the title documents in order to check that the seller owns and is entitled to sell what they have instructed the solicitor to sell, and to draft the contract of sale.

If the seller does not have a subsisting mortgage on the property, they may have the title documents in their possession, or they might be kept, for example, in the solicitor's strongroom or in a bank safe deposit box. The whereabouts of the documents will have been ascertained from the seller in the initial interview.

Although land and charge certificates have been abolished by the LRA 2002, they will be already in existence for all titles registered prior to 13 October 2003. Although they are not required in order for a disposition to be registered, it will still be necessary to ask the client for the title documents. There may be other documents accompanying the land or charge certificate which will be required for the sale (eg, planning consents or guarantees for any building work carried out).

Where there was a subsisting mortgage over the property, it used to be the case that the deeds (charge certificate in registered land) and other documents would be kept by the mortgage lender. However, in recent years, mortgage lenders concerned about the cost of storage of such documents have increasingly taken advantage of s 63 of the LRA 1925, under which a lender can request the Registry to retain the charge certificate in the Registry. Where this has happened, an entry to that effect will be found in the charges register. In such a case, it will still be necessary to obtain any other documents held by the lender, as explained above. However, some lenders are reluctant to retain any documents after completion of the mortgage, and in such a case it will be necessary to ascertain their whereabouts from the client.

Where the lender is holding documents, it will be reluctant to hand them over without a guarantee that the loan will be repaid. The lender will thus require an undertaking from the solicitor with regard to repayment.

When writing to the lender to ask for the title deeds, it is customary to pre-empt the lender's request about the repayment of the loan, and to include in the letter an undertaking that the solicitor will either repay the loan to the lender (thus ending the mortgage and entitling the seller to the return of their deeds) or, at the lender's request, return the deeds to the lender. This type of undertaking is normally acceptable to the lender, who will then release the deeds to the solicitor on the terms of the undertaking. The undertaking is a solicitor's undertaking, subject to the usual rules as to enforceability, and care must therefore be taken in wording it to ensure that what it promises to do is within the solicitor's control to perform (see ***Legal Foundations***).

13.2.2 Amount outstanding on mortgage

When writing to the lender, it may also be prudent to ascertain the approximate amount outstanding on the seller's mortgage (a redemption figure) to ensure that there will be sufficient funds from the sale to pay off (redeem) the mortgage and the costs associated with the sale, and that the surplus (if any) is sufficient for the seller's requirements (eg, to put towards the purchase of another property). At this stage, an approximate redemption figure only need be obtained (eg, to the nearest £500); nearer completion an exact figure can be confirmed with the lender. Where the seller has several mortgages on the same property, redemption figures should be obtained from each lender.

13.2.3 Official copies of the register

When the land being sold is an interest in registered land, the seller's solicitor should make an application to the Land Registry for official copies of the register entries. This application is usually done electronically using the Land Registry Portal. Where additional documents are known to be filed at Land Registry (eg, a copy of a conveyance imposing restrictive covenants), it may be necessary to apply for copies of these documents too. Whilst these additional documents can be applied for via the Land Registry Portal, some may be delivered electronically and some delivered by post. A fee is payable for obtaining official copies, but this can be paid by credit account.

13.2.4 Investigation of title

The purposes of obtaining official copies are:

(a) To check that the information supplied by the seller in relation to their title, and that contained in the land or charge certificate or TID, is supported by the information contained in the official copies. The official copies are an official and up-to-date copy of the actual register entries, which therefore represent the true state of the title at the date of their issue. The land or charge certificate or TID in the solicitor's possession may not have been updated by Land Registry for several years (eg, since the seller bought the land) and it is important for the seller's solicitor to know precisely what entries are now present on the register so that they can take account of these in drafting the contract of sale.

(b) During the course of the transaction, the seller will need to prove their ownership of the property to the buyer. In registered land this is done by supplying the buyer with (inter alia) official copies of the register entries.

When the official copies are received from Land Registry, they should be examined to ensure that they do not contain anything of which the solicitor was previously unaware (if they do, instructions must be obtained immediately), and a photocopy should be taken. The seller's solicitor will need to keep a copy of the register entries in their own file to refer to during the transaction, and they must supply the buyer with the original of the official copies.

This procedure is known as 'investigating title' and has to be carried out by the seller's solicitor before the contract can be drafted. The precise procedure to be followed in investigating title to both registered and unregistered titles is set out in **Chapters 15** and **16.**

In all cases where the seller is a company, a company search should be commissioned to ascertain that the company:

(a) exists (it could have been struck off the register for failure to file annual returns);
(b) has powers to buy and sell land (although these are normally implied);
(c) has no undisclosed fixed or floating charges which affect the land being sold; and
(d) is not in administration, receivership or liquidation.

A solicitor acting for a company which has been struck off or lacks legal capacity may be personally liable to a buyer or a lender who suffers loss as a result of this under the principle of breach of warranty of authority (see **8.2.2**).

In the case of unregistered land, the deeds should be studied (see **15.4** as to the procedure to be followed) to ensure that the seller does have the power to sell the property and to ascertain what third party rights affect it. Also, the date at which the area became subject to compulsory registration should also be ascertained from Land Registry Practice Guide 51, to ensure that there have been no dealings since that date that would have induced compulsory registration. In all cases an Index Map search should also be commissioned from Land Registry using Form SIM to ensure that the land has not already been registered and that no caution against first registration affects the land.

13.2.5 Preparation of the pre-contract package

The seller's solicitor should then start preparing the pre-contract package which will have to be sent to the buyer. This will contain, as a minimum, two copies of the draft contract (see **Chapter 18**) and details of the seller's title to the property (see **Chapter 14**), but if the Protocol is being adopted it will also need to contain the following:

(a) the PIF;
(b) the F&C;
(c) in unregistered land, an Index Map search at Land Registry. This is to ensure that the land is indeed unregistered and that there are no interests registered at Land Registry adverse to the seller's title; and
(d) in unregistered land, a land charges search against the seller and all other previous estate owners revealed by the title deeds against whom there is not already a search with the deeds upon which it is safe to rely (see **Chapter 17**). This will reveal incumbrances affecting the property and whether any insolvency proceedings have been commenced against the seller.

It is also good practice to include: copies of planning permissions and building regulation consents relating to the property; and copies of any other certificates, consents, etc, relating to the property (eg, a guarantee in relation to the insertion of a new damp proof course).

The object of this package is to supply the buyer with all the information needed to decide whether or not to proceed with the transaction. If the buyer is supplied with a complete package of information at the start of the transaction, it is likely to run more smoothly and speedily, as time will not be wasted in the buyer having to make repeated requests for information and documents from the seller.

13.3 FOR THE BUYER

13.3.1 Search applications

The buyer's solicitor should, as soon as is practicable, put in hand such pre-contract searches as are appropriate to the property in question (see **Chapter 17**).

13.3.2 Mortgage and survey arrangements

The buyer's solicitor should deal with their client's mortgage and survey arrangements if required to do so. In many cases, the client will already have approached a lender and submitted a mortgage application form before seeing the solicitor, and this step will therefore be unnecessary (see **Chapter 9**). Surveys are dealt with in **Chapter 12**.

13.3.3 The pre-contract package

When the pre-contract package is received from the seller's solicitor, its contents must be studied carefully to ensure that what is being offered for sale by the seller matches the instructions given by, and expectations of, the buyer.

SUMMARY

- An attendance note should be made of the initial interview and the instructions confirmed in writing.
- Introductory letters should be sent to the other side, the acting agents and any lender.
- The seller's solicitor should obtain the title deeds and documents for the property, and should investigate title to it before preparing the pre-contract package for the buyer.
- The seller's solicitor should check the amount of any outstanding mortgage to ensure that the sale proceeds will be sufficient to redeem it.
- The buyer's solicitor should put in hand pre-contract searches and ensure the buyer's mortgage and surveys are in hand (if required).
- Once received, the buyer's solicitor will need to consider the pre-contract package carefully.

PART III

THE CONVEYANCING TRANSACTION: PROCEDURE LEADING TO EXCHANGE

CHAPTER 14

Deduction of Title

LEARNING OUTCOMES

After reading this chapter you will be able to:

- explain what is meant by deduction of title
- explain how and when title is deduced
- advise on what constitutes a 'good root' of title and the dangers of accepting a 'short root'.

14.1 DEDUCTION OF TITLE

'Deduction of title' is the expression used to signify the seller's obligation to prove to the buyer their ownership of the interest which they are purporting to sell. Ownership is proved to the buyer by producing documentary evidence of title. The method of doing this varies according to whether the land in question is registered or unregistered.

14.2 TIME FOR DEDUCTION

Historically, deduction of title took place only after contracts had been exchanged, so that the buyer had to take the seller's title on trust up until that time and to rely on their right to rescind the contract if the title later turned out not to reflect what the seller had contracted to sell.

Modern practice (reflected in the Protocol) is for title to be deduced before exchange. As the buyer will therefore have entered into the contract with full knowledge of the title, their right to raise questions about the title after exchange should be limited. This is reflected in both the Standard Conditions of Sale and Standard Commercial Property Conditions (SC 4.2.1 and SCPC 7.2.1).

14.3 SELLER'S OBLIGATIONS

The seller's obligation in relation to the deduction of the title is to supply sufficient documentary evidence to the buyer to prove that they have the right to sell the land.

14.4 METHOD OF DEDUCTION FOR REGISTERED LAND – OFFICIAL COPIES

Both the Protocol and SC 4.1.2 (SCPC 7.1.2) require the seller to supply official copies of their title to the buyer. Official copies are copies prepared directly from the register and should always be supplied since they show the up-to-date position of the register. The seller should pay for the official copies. Under the Protocol, the official copies should be less than six months old.

14.5 METHOD OF DEDUCTION FOR UNREGISTERED LAND – EPITOMES AND ABSTRACTS

14.5.1 Format

Title to unregistered land is proved by the title deeds which, obviously, the seller will not be prepared to release to the buyer until completion. Instead, the seller will prove their ownership of the title by supplying the buyer with an abstract or epitome of the documents comprised in it. In some cases the evidence supplied will be made up of a combination of these two styles of presentation. An example of an epitome appears in **Chapter 16**.

An abstract of title is in essence a précis of all the documents comprised in the title. Abstracts of title have largely been superseded by epitomes, but are still sometimes encountered in the case of older titles.

An epitome of title is a schedule of the documents comprising the title accompanied by photocopies of the documents themselves. On the epitome, the documents should be numbered and listed in chronological order. Each document should be identified as to its date, type (eg, conveyance, assent, etc), the parties to it, whether a copy of the document is supplied with the epitome and whether the original of the document will be handed to the buyer on completion. Photocopies of the documents which accompany the epitome must be of good quality and marked to show the document's corresponding number on the list shown by the epitome. Any plans included in the documents must be coloured or marked so that they are identical to the original document from which the copy was made.

14.5.2 The root of title

Whatever format is chosen, title in unregistered land begins with what is known as the root of title. At common law the epitome must commence with a good root of title at least 15 years old (LPA 1925, s 44 as amended). A good root of title is a document which:

(a) is at least 15 years old;
(b) deals with or shows the ownership of the whole legal and equitable interest contracted to be sold;
(c) contains a recognisable description of the property; and
(d) contains nothing to cast any doubt on the title.

However, s 44 of the LPA 1925 only applies if the contract does not provide otherwise, and a typical contract will specify the root of title and go on to state that title has been deduced prior to exchange and that the buyer accepts the title as deduced and is precluded from raising any objection or requisition on it (see SC 4.2.1 and SCPC 7.2.1). The document specified in such a contract as the root of title could in theory be of any age, but a buyer should not generally accept a root that does not comply with the common law position (ie, is not a 'good' root). The reason for this is explained in **14.5.2.2**. If a shorter root is accepted by the buyer in the contract, this will override the seller's common law obligation to provide a root at least 15 years old.

14.5.2.1 Documents capable of being good roots of title

A conveyance on sale or legal mortgage which satisfies the above requirements is generally acknowledged to be the most acceptable root of title, because it effectively offers a double guarantee. The buyer in the present transaction will be investigating the seller's title back for a minimum period of 15 years, and the buyer under the root conveyance would similarly have investigated title over a period of at least 15 years prior to when they bought the property. Thus the present buyer is provided with the certainty of the soundness of the title over a minimum period of at least 30 years.

In the absence of both a conveyance on sale and legal mortgage, title may be commenced with either a voluntary conveyance or an assent dated after 1925. Since voluntary conveyances and assents both effect gifts of the land, no investigation of prior title may have taken place at the time when they were executed, and therefore they do not provide the double check which is given by the conveyance on sale or legal mortgage. For this reason they are less satisfactory to a buyer when offered as roots of title.

14.5.2.2 The dangers of accepting a 'short root'

A good root of title (ie, one that satisfies s 44 of the LPA 1925) effectively acts as a longstop in the buyer's investigation of title. Under s 44, a buyer is bound by matters that would be revealed by a title that begins with a good root, but does not have notice of any additional matters that would have been revealed by a title that began with an earlier root. The danger for a buyer who accepts a title that begins with a document that does not satisfy s 44 – such as one that is less than 15 years old – is that the buyer will therefore be bound by matters that would have been revealed had the title begun with a good root, but they will be unaware of what those matters are. In addition, the title is unlikely to be registered with absolute title at Land Registry.

In fact, it is only in rare cases that the seller will be unable to provide the buyer with a good root of title. However, a buyer who is offered a short title should not accept the situation until they have received a satisfactory explanation from the seller of the reasons for the short root. It will also be necessary to get the agreement of the lender before accepting such a root of title. The possibility of obtaining defective title insurance should also be considered.

14.5.2.3 Documents and events to be included in the abstract or epitome

All documents and events affecting the ownership of the land from the root to the present day must be included. There should be an unbroken chain of ownership from the root to the present seller. This includes the following:

(a) conveyances on sale and by gift;
(b) deaths;
(c) grants of representation to deceased owners' estates;
(d) changes of name of estate owners (eg, on marriage, or by deed poll or statutory declaration);
(e) leases;
(f) mortgages;
(g) discharge of legal mortgages;
(h) documents prior to the root which contain details of restrictive covenants which affect the property;
(i) memoranda endorsed on documents of title (eg, recording a sale of part, assent to a beneficiary, or severance of a beneficial joint tenancy);
(j) powers of attorney under which a document within the title has been executed;
(k) documents of record (eg, death and marriage certificates).

14.5.2.4 Documents which need not be included in the abstract or epitome

Certain documents need not be included in the abstract or epitome, although in some cases their inclusion will be helpful to the buyer. These include:

(a) land charges department search certificates. It is, however, good practice to include search certificates so that the buyer can see which searches have been correctly made in the past, in which case the buyer need not repeat the search during their own investigation of the title;
(b) leases which have expired by effluxion of time;

(c) documents which pre-date the root of title, except where a document within the title refers to the earlier document (LPA 1925, s 45). Where a document within the title has been executed under a power of attorney, the power must be abstracted whatever its date.

14.5.3 Production of original documents

Standard Condition 4.1.3 (SCPC 7.1.3) requires the seller to produce to the buyer (at the seller's expense) the original of every relevant document, or an abstract, epitome or copy with an original marking by a solicitor of examination, either against the original or against an examined abstract or against an examined copy. 'Marking' is a certification by a solicitor that the copy has been examined against, and is a true copy of, the original.

14.5.4 Documents which will not be handed over on completion

The epitome must specify which documents will be handed to the buyer on completion and which will be retained by the seller. On completion the buyer is entitled to take the originals of all the documents within the title, except those which relate to an interest in the land which is retained by the seller. For example, on a sale of part, the seller will retain the title deeds in order to be able to prove their ownership of the land retained. Similarly, a general power of attorney may be retained by the seller, because the donee of the power needs to keep the original document in order to deal with other property owned by the donor. Personal representatives will retain their original grant in order to administer the remainder of the deceased's estate.

14.6 LEASEHOLDS

Deduction of title to leaseholds is discussed in **Chapters 35** and **36**.

SUMMARY

- Deduction of title is the process by which the seller shows evidence of their right to sell a property.
- Typically title is deduced before the contract for sale is exchanged.
- Where registered land is being sold, the seller will supply official copies of the register.
- Where unregistered land is being sold, the seller will supply an abstract or epitome of title.
- An abstract or epitome should begin with a good root of title satisfying s 44 of the LPA 1925 and contain all documents affecting ownership from the date of the root till the present day.
- A buyer who accepts a 'short root' may be bound by matters of which they are unaware and should consider defective title insurance.
- The seller should hand over the original title documents (or certified copies) on completion.

CHAPTER 15

INVESTIGATION OF TITLE – HOW TO INVESTIGATE TITLE

LEARNING OUTCOMES

After reading this chapter you will be able to:

- explain who investigates title and why
- explain how to investigate both registered and unregistered title.

15.1 INTRODUCTION

Investigation of title is one of the most important (and intellectually rewarding) elements of a conveyancing transaction; it is, after all, the *title* to the land that a seller is actually selling in the transaction. As such it is important to grasp the fundamental technical issues and techniques involved in carrying out this process. The topic is therefore considered over the next two chapters.

Chapter 15 begins by considering the reasons why the various parties to a transaction need to carry out investigation of title in the first place, before moving on to examine how investigation of title is, from a practical point of view, carried out. The form in which title will be deduced depends upon whether the title is registered or unregistered, and so each will be looked at in turn.

Having established how to investigate title, **Chapter 16** will move on to consider three further issues. First, there are certain situations which may throw up particular challenges to a conveyancer: what these issues are and how they can be resolved is dealt with in **16.1**. Next, issues relating to verifying title and raising queries on issues raised during the investigation of title are considered. **Chapter 16** ends with a worked example of an investigation of, first, a registered and then an unregistered title.

The key to successful investigation of title is the keeping of systematic and thorough notes of issues raised by that investigation and the steps taken to resolve those issues. The precise format of this may vary from individual to individual (and the worked examples at the end of **Chapter 16** reflect merely one approach). The fact that the format may vary should not detract from the need to keep a thorough and systematic record.

15.2 REASONS FOR INVESTIGATING TITLE

15.2.1 Seller's investigation of title

There are two main purposes behind the seller's solicitor's investigation of title. First, it is the seller's solicitor's responsibility to draft the contract for the sale of the property. This will contain the terms of the agreement between the parties, including what it is that the seller is actually selling to the buyer, ie the title to the property (see **Chapter 18**). The seller's solicitor will therefore need to carry out a thorough investigation of title in order to be able to embody the detail of this accurately in the contract. Secondly, investigation of title will enable the seller's solicitor, at an early stage, to anticipate and, if possible, deal with any problems that might be revealed by the title, and this can help smooth the passage of the transaction as a whole.

Although the seller's reasons for investigating title are different from those of the buyer, the method that they will use to do so will be identical to that undertaken by a buyer's solicitor.

15.2.2 Buyer's investigation of title

When the seller has supplied the buyer with evidence of the title, the buyer's task is twofold: first, to ensure that the seller is able to transfer what they have contracted to sell; secondly, to identify whether there are any defects in, or problems raised by, the title which could adversely affect the interests of the buyer. Any matters which are unclear or unsatisfactory on the face of the documentary evidence supplied by the seller may be raised as queries (requisitions) with the seller.

Modern practice is for title to be deduced and investigated before exchange of contracts, and for any issues that arise from this process to be resolved before that point. If this is the case, as the buyer will already have had the opportunity to raise any queries and will have entered into the contract with full knowledge of what the title contains, it is usual to find that the contract will contain a provision preventing the buyer raising requisitions on some or all aspects of the title once exchange has taken place (see SC 4.2.1 and SCPC 7.2.1). If, exceptionally, title is deduced after exchange, the contract will usually contain a timetable for the raising of, and responding to, requisitions (see SC 4.3 and SCPC 7.3).

15.2.3 Lender's investigation of title

If a lender is lending money in the form of a mortgage to help finance the acquisition of a property, it will be concerned to ensure that the property is worth the money that has been advanced. If the borrower defaults on the mortgage, the lender may ultimately need to exercise its power to sell the property to recover the loan, but this power will be of limited value if defects or problems on the title reduce the market value of the property so that the lender is unable to recover the money owed to it. Any lender will therefore want to ensure that the title is investigated to protect its position.

Where the same solicitor is acting for both the buyer and their lender in a transaction, investigation is carried out only once, but will be done on behalf of both the borrower and lender client, taking into account the particular interests of each. Where the lender is separately represented, the solicitor acting for the lender may undertake their own investigation of title. However, in commercial property transactions, the borrower's solicitor may be required instead to provide the lender with a 'Certificate of Title'. This is a certificate signed by the borrower's solicitors certifying that the borrower has a 'good and marketable' title to the property. This certificate will be relied on by the lender in lieu of its own investigation of title. Special care should be taken in giving such certificates, as the lender will be able to sue the borrower's solicitors should there in fact be any problem with the title. The City of London Law Society has produced a standard form of certificate which is in widespread use.

15.3 INVESTIGATING TITLE IN REGISTERED LAND

The buyer's investigation of title will involve two main elements. Title will be deduced by the seller in the form of official copies of the entries on the register and the title plan, and so, first, a thorough examination of these must be undertaken. Secondly, the buyer needs to carry out investigations to discover if there are any overriding interests affecting the property, as such interests will bind the buyer even though the register contains no mention of them. Information in this respect will come from a variety of sources, the detail of which is considered at **15.3.4**.

Having made their investigation of title, the buyer will need to carry out certain checks before completion to update the information revealed and to ensure that no changes have taken place since the investigation of title was carried out. These checks are considered in **Chapter 28**. Part of this process involves carrying out a search at Land Registry to confirm that no new entries have been added to the register since the official copies were issued. Land Registry will not perform this search on official copies that are more than 12 months old and so, when title is deduced, a buyer should not accept official copies that are outside, or close to, this time limit.

15.3.1 Points to look out for on the official copies and title plan

The following are the particular issues that the solicitor should look out for when examining the official copies and title plan.

15.3.1.1 The property register

(a) Does the description of the land agree with the contract description?
(b) Does the title number match the one given in the contract?
(c) Is the estate freehold or leasehold? Does this accord with expectations from the contract?
(d) Which easements are enjoyed by the property? Do these match the needs of the client?

15.3.1.2 The proprietorship register

(a) Is the class of title correct?
(b) Is the seller the registered proprietor? If not, who has the ability to transfer the land?
(c) Are there any other entries? What is their effect?

15.3.1.3 The charges register

(a) Are there any incumbrances?
(b) How do these affect the buyer?
(c) Which of them will be removed or discharged on completion?
(d) Have you agreed in the contract to buy subject to the incumbrances which remain?

15.3.1.4 The title plan

(a) Is the land being bought included within the title?
(b) Are there any colourings/hatchings which may indicate rights of way, the extent of covenants or land which has been removed from the title?

15.3.2 Adverse entries

Any adverse entries revealed by a reading of the official copies will need to be considered carefully and a full report made to the buyer and lender clients. Any problems that are identified should be resolved before exchange of contracts. It should be remembered that rights can be protected in a variety of ways in registered land, depending on the nature of the interest involved. The practitioner should be familiar with, and be able to anticipate and deal with, issues arising from all of these different methods. For more detail on how third-party interests can be protected on the register, see **Chapter 4**.

15.3.3 Documents referred to on the register

Sometimes, documents or plans are filed with the title at Land Registry and will be referred to as such in the official copies. Where this is the case, a copy of any such items should be obtained and examined in the same way as the official copies themselves.

15.3.4 Overriding interests

The existence of most overriding interests can be discovered through:

(a) disclosure by the seller in the contract;
(b) pre-contract enquiries of the seller, under which the seller will normally be asked to reveal details of adverse interests and occupiers' rights;
(c) a local land charges search (local land charges are overriding interests);
(d) inspection of the property before exchange, which may reveal evidence of such matters as non-owning occupiers, easements and adverse possession.

15.4 UNREGISTERED LAND

Investigation of title to unregistered land comprises:

(a) An Index Map search at Land Registry, which should be made in all cases when dealing with interest in unregistered land. Application is made to the Land Registry Office for the area in which the land is situated on Form SIM, accompanied by a large-scale plan of the property and the fee. The search result will reveal whether the land is already registered, or is subject to a pending application or caution against first registration.
(b) An examination of the documents supplied in the abstract or epitome to check that:
    (i) the root document is as provided for by the contract – if the wrong document has been supplied, the buyer is entitled to insist on the correct document being supplied in its place;
    (ii) there is an unbroken chain of ownership beginning with the seller in the root document and ending with the present seller, ie the documents show the progression of the title from A to B, from B to C, from C to D and so on, with no apparent breaks in the chain; and
    (iii) there are no defects in the title which will adversely affect the buyer's title or the interests of their lender.
(c) Verification, ie inspection of the original deeds (in practice this is frequently postponed until completion and not carried out at this stage of the transaction).
(d) Checking for evidence of occupiers (this is normally done by inspection of the property).
(e) Pre-completion searches. These are carried out for similar reasons to pre-completion searches in registered land. The detail is set out in **Chapter 28**.

15.4.1 Events triggering first registration

One crucial question that should be borne in mind throughout an investigation of unregistered title is whether any transaction in the title's history should have triggered first registration. The detail of the events that trigger first registration and the conveyancing consequences of not doing so are dealt with in **Chapter 4**. When looking at each document in the title in turn, it is sensible to begin consideration of it by dealing with this question.

15.4.2 Method of investigation of an unregistered title

In unregistered land, title will be deduced in the form of an abstract or epitome of title. Whilst a systematic approach and the taking of notes are needed in any investigation of title, both are particularly important when investigating a title that is unregistered. Unlike registered land (where the title is in the format of user-friendly official copies), an unregistered title can be made up of many documents, presenting the person investigating it with a significant challenge in terms of document management. The following is suggested as an approach that has proven to work well and is followed in the worked example that appears at the end of **Chapter 16**. It is based around a mnemonic: RLSDIES (Robert Louis Stevenson DIES).

Begin by reading over the title to get a broad overview of the history of the property and what has happened to it over the years. Having done that, identify the document that is to form the root of title for this property. This forms the foundation for the title, and the investigation should proceed from the date of the root to the present day. Having identified the root, it is then necessary to work through each document in turn, starting with the root itself. The key is to be systematic and to subject each document to the same standard scrutiny. It is with this that the mnemonic above is designed to assist.

The abbreviation RLSDIES stands for:

(a) root of title;
(b) links in the chain;
(c) stamp duties;
(d) description;
(e) incumbrances;
(f) execution; and
(g) searches.

Each element will now be considered in turn.

15.4.2.1 Root of title

Check that the epitome begins with the root of title specified in the contract. Ideally this should be a 'good' root of title for the purposes of s 44 of the LPA 1925 (see **14.5.2**) for the reasons explained at **14.5.2.2**.

The contract should specify what document is to form the root of title, and generally it is not possible (or necessary) to require evidence of title prior to the root (LPA 1925, s 45). It is possible, however, in the following circumstances:

(a) when an abstracted document is executed by an attorney, the buyer is always entitled to a certified copy of the power, whenever that might be dated;
(b) when the property is described by reference to a plan in a pre-root document, the buyer is entitled to see that plan; and
(c) when the property is sold subject to or together with matters contained in a pre-root document (eg, the land is sold subject to pre-root covenants), the buyer is entitled to a copy of those matters.

15.4.2.2 Links in the chain

There should be an unbroken chain of ownership from the root of title up to the present seller. Legal estates can be transferred only by means of some form of document (usually a deed), so there should be documentary evidence of every change of ownership. There should be a chain of ownership which shows the transfer from A to B and then from B to C and so on, up to the present seller.

Any changes in the names of owners should also be evidenced, for example a marriage certificate if a name was changed on marriage.

15.4.2.3 Stamp duties

For documents dated prior to 1 December 2003, it is necessary to ensure that the requirements for the payment of stamp duty were complied with. (Stamp duty was replaced with respect to most documents as from 1 December 2003 by SDLT, to which different considerations apply.) Unstamped or incorrectly stamped documents are neither good roots of title nor good links in the chain. They cannot be produced in evidence in civil proceedings, neither will they be accepted by Land Registry on an application to register the title. The buyer must therefore check that all the title deeds have been correctly stamped. The payment of duty is evidenced by an embossed stamp (or stamps) placed on the deed, usually in the top margin. If stamping defects are discovered, the buyer is entitled to insist that the seller remedies the deficiency at their own expense. Interest and a penalty are usually charged if stamp duty is not paid at the correct time. Any contractual provision requiring the buyer to meet the cost of putting the defect right will be void (Stamp Act 1891, s 117).

The following points should be considered:

(a) Ad valorem duty. A conveyance on sale is liable to an ad valorem duty, ie a duty varying according to the amount of the consideration. Rates of duty have changed over the years and in practice a table of stamp duties should be used to check the applicable rates for a particular document. For some lower-value properties a reduced rate or total exemption from duty was possible if the consideration was below a certain threshold; again, this has changed over the course of time. However, the reduced rates could be claimed only if a certificate of value was included in the conveyance. The wording of the certificate is:

> It is hereby certified that the transaction hereby effected does not form part of a larger transaction or of a series of transactions in respect of which the amount or value or the aggregate amount or value of the consideration exceeds .... pounds.

Therefore, a conveyance on sale which does not have a certificate of value in it and does not bear an ad valorem stamp has not been correctly stamped.

(b) Stamp duty does not have to be paid on mortgages executed after 1971.

(c) A conveyance or transfer by way of gift, and an assent by which property is being passed by personal representatives to a beneficiary under a will, in each case executed after 30 April 1987, are exempt from stamp duty, provided they contain a certificate that they are instruments within one of the categories of exempt documents under the Stamp Duty (Exempt Instruments) Regulations 1987 (SI 1987/516). This is an example of such a certificate:

> The Donor certifies that this deed falls within category B in the Schedule to the Stamp Duty (Exempt Instruments) Regulations 1987.

The category differs according to the circumstances of the transaction, which should be checked with the Regulations. Category B shown in the example relates to transfers to a beneficiary under a will.

(d) A power of attorney is not liable for stamp duty (Finance Act 1985, s 85).

(e) Particulars delivered stamp. The Finance Act 1931 provided that certain documents must be produced to the Inland Revenue (now HMRC), together with a form giving particulars of the documents and any consideration received. The form was kept by the Inland Revenue (it provided useful information for the assessment of the value of the land) and the document was stamped with a stamp (generally called the 'PD stamp') as proof of its production. Without the PD stamp the document was not properly stamped and the person who failed in their responsibility to produce it (ie the original buyer) could be fined. The document had to be produced, irrespective of whether any ad valorem duty was payable. The documents that needed a PD stamp were:

(i) a conveyance on sale of the freehold;

(ii) a grant of a lease for seven years or more; and

(iii) the transfer on sale of a lease of seven years or more.

15.4.2.4 Description

The buyer should check that the description of the property corresponds with the contract and is consistent throughout the epitome, ie that the ownership of the land presently being sold is included in the deeds. Particular care should be taken where the deeds show that part of the land included in the root document has been sold off separately. Copies of any plans referred to should be obtained, even if they are pre-root.

15.4.2.5 Incumbrances

Particular care should be taken with incumbrances. The solicitor should check to ensure that there are none disclosed by the deeds other than those disclosed in the contract. Copies of all covenants, easements and other burdens affecting the land should be supplied, even if they are pre-root. Burdens should be checked to ensure that have not been breached and that they will not impede the client's proposed use for the property. If they appear to do so, the solicitor should consider whether they will in fact bind the client if they buy the land, applying normal land law principles. So, for example, in the case of a restrictive covenant, the solicitor should check if it has been registered as a Class D(ii) land charge; it will not be binding on a purchaser otherwise.

The steps to take in the case of 'problem' covenants are considered in more detail at **16.9**.

15.4.2.6 Execution

The solicitor should check that all deeds and documents in the title have been properly executed. In particular, in order to transfer the legal estate, the requirements for execution as a deed must be satisfied. The detailed law on the execution of deeds can be found at **16.10**.

15.4.2.7 Searches

Although not essential, a seller should supply copies of all previous land charges and company searches made against the previous owners of the land with the epitome. These would have been made prior to previous dispositions of the land. If the Protocol is being used, a search against the seller should also be produced. Before they can safely buy the land, a buyer needs clear, correctly made searches against the names of all the estate owners revealed by the epitome. However, the buyer need not repeat searches that have been made previously (with the exception of the seller, who must be searched against again), if they have been made correctly. The following matters should, therefore, be checked carefully:

(a) Was the search made against the correct name of the person as set out in the deeds? The full name must be searched against and the spelling must be correct.

(b) Was the search made for the full period of the person's ownership? The years of ownership searched against are set out on the search result, and whether it is the correct period can be checked from the epitome.

(c) Was the transaction which followed the search completed within the priority period of the search? The priority period is set out on the result of the search and this should be compared with the date on the appropriate deed.

(d) In the case of changes of name (eg, on marriage), is there a search against both old and new versions of the name?

If the above checks reveal any problems, for example a transaction not completed within the priority period, there is a danger that other entries could have been on the register which would not have been revealed by the search but which would be binding on a buyer. It will therefore be necessary to repeat any such searches to ensure that there are no problems.

The approach to note taking adopted in the worked example at the end of **Chapter 16** is designed to assist in the task of checking central land charge searches for suitability, by closely following the format of the search result for that particular system.

SUMMARY

- The seller's solicitor should investigate title to anticipate problems that may arise, and obtain the necessary information to draft the contract for sale.
- The buyer's solicitor should investigate title to check that the seller is able to sell what they contract to sell, and to discover any defects or problematic incumbrances.

- The lender's solicitor should investigate title to ensure the property is worth the money lent to the borrower.
- In registered land the solicitor will review the official copies and title plan, and carry out due diligence to discover any interests that override and are not recorded on the registers of title.
- In unregistered land the solicitor will review the documents in the abstract or epitome. They will also carry out an Index Map search and central land charges searches, and review the results. Due diligence to discover undocumented third-party interests will also be necessary.
- When reviewing the abstract or epitome the solicitor should check for a good root, unbroken chain of ownership, correct stamp duties and proper execution. The description of the property should be consistent throughout the abstract or epitome and should match the contract.
- In both unregistered and registered land, any third-party interests revealed by investigation of title must be considered carefully. If they affect the property or client adversely, they must be discussed with the client and any available solutions considered.

CHAPTER 16

INVESTIGATION OF TITLE – PARTICULAR PROBLEMS AND WORKED EXAMPLES

LEARNING OUTCOMES

After reading this chapter you will be able to:

- identify those areas that present particular difficulty when investigating title
- explain why those areas are problematic
- advise on what steps may be taken to overcome such problems.

16.1 PARTICULAR PROBLEM AREAS

Whilst studying the official copies (in registered land) or the abstract or epitome (in unregistered land), the transaction with the seller and any past transactions revealed should be considered to see if they raise any issues or situations which can cause particular difficulties. It is these problem areas that are considered in this chapter. The points raised apply to both registered and unregistered land, unless otherwise stated. At the end of the chapter are worked examples of an investigation of title in both registered and unregistered land, which can be used either by way of example or as practice.

16.2 TRUSTEES OF LAND

16.2.1 Registered land

In registered land, a restriction may be entered on the proprietorship register which will indicate to the buyer what must be done to overreach the beneficiaries' interests. Provided the terms of the restriction are complied with, the buyer will get good title. In all cases, the disposition must be made by all the trustees, being at least two in number, or a trust corporation.

16.2.2 Unregistered land

Since 1 January 1997, trustees of land (including trustees for sale) have the same powers of disposition as a sole beneficial owner, unless the trust deed varies these or imposes a requirement for consents to be obtained. If the trust deed indicates that consents are required to a sale, a buyer is not concerned to see that the consents of more than two persons are obtained and is never concerned with the consent of a person under mental incapacity. Where the person whose consent is required is not of full age, the consent of the minor's parent or guardian must be obtained. A buyer must pay their money to all the trustees, being at least two individuals or a trust corporation, to take the land free from the equitable interests of the beneficiaries (see LPA 1925, ss 2 and 27). A sale by trustees for sale prior to 1 January 1997 will be subject to similar rules, but the provisions of the LPA 1925, ss 26–28 should be checked in transactions other than a sale, or where consents are required.

16.2.3 Appointing a further trustee

If there is only one trustee then the buyer must insist that a second trustee is appointed in order to overreach the interests of the beneficiaries. The appointment will usually be made by the surviving trustee (although the trust deed can confer the power of appointment on someone else). The appointment can be made prior to the contract for sale being entered into. In this case, the new trustee will thus be a party to the contract and bound by its terms. This is particularly useful where the new trustee is also in occupation of the property (see **18.8.4**). Alternatively, the sole trustee can enter into the contract on their own and then appoint a further trustee prior to completion in order to receive the purchase price and thus ensure overreaching takes place. A special condition can be included in the contract requiring the seller to appoint the further trustee, although the seller would be under an obligation to do so anyway in order to comply with the duty to make good title.

16.2.4 Conveyance by trustees to themselves

In the case of a disposal by trustees or personal representatives to one of themselves, enquiry must be made into the circumstances of the transaction because, on the face of it, such a disposal is in breach of trust and is voidable by the beneficiaries. Such a transaction can be justified if one of the following situations exists:

(a) there is proof of a pre-existing contract in favour of the trustee or personal representative;

(b) the personal representative was a beneficiary under the will or intestacy of the deceased;

(c) the consent of all the legally competent (ie adult and sane) beneficiaries was obtained to the transaction;

(d) the conveyance was made under an order of the court;

(e) the transaction was sanctioned by the trust instrument.

16.3 PERSONAL REPRESENTATIVES

16.3.1 General

Personal representatives enjoy the same wide powers as trustees of land. If there is only one proving personal representative, they have all the powers of two or more personal representatives, and consequently (unlike a sole individual trustee) can convey the land on their own and give a valid receipt for the proceeds of sale. If, however, the grant of probate is made to two or more personal representatives, they must all join in the assent or conveyance. A buyer must therefore call for the grant to see who has or have been appointed as personal representative(s), and must insist that all the personal representatives named in the grant join in the assent or conveyance, or call for evidence of the death of any personal representative who will not be a party to it.

16.3.2 Registered land

On production of the grant of probate, personal representatives may become registered as proprietors of the land, in which case, provided the buyer deals with the registered proprietors and complies with any restriction on the register, the buyer will get good title. However, personal representatives would not normally register themselves as proprietors unless they intended to hold on to the land without disposing of it for some period of time, for example during the minority of a beneficiary. In other cases, the personal representatives will produce their grant of probate to the buyer as proof of their authority to deal with the land. Provided the buyer takes a transfer from all the proving personal representatives and submits an office copy or certified copy of the grant with the application for registration, the buyer will obtain a good title. An assent made by personal representatives to a beneficiary must be in the form prescribed under the Land Registration Rules 2003 (SI 2003/1417). Unlike unregistered land (see **16.3.3** below), there is no danger of the same piece of property being mistakenly disposed of twice.

16.3.3 Unregistered land

16.3.3.1 Assents

An assent made by personal representatives must be in writing in order to pass the legal estate in the land to the beneficiary. The beneficiary who is to take the land must be named in the document, which must be signed by the personal representatives. If the document contains covenants given by the beneficiary (eg indemnity in respect of existing restrictive covenants), it must be by deed. Even where the beneficiary is also the sole personal representative (eg where a widow is her deceased husband's sole personal representative and sole beneficiary), a written assent is required (*In re King's Will Trusts; Assheton v Boyne* [1964] Ch 542). A buyer from an assentee (or a subsequent buyer where there is an assent revealed in the title, must check that a memorandum (written record) of that assent was endorsed (written or typed) onto the grant of representation. Otherwise there is a danger that a later sale by the personal representatives to a buyer (who has given value) will deprive the assentee (who has not given value) of the legal ownership (see **16.3.3.2** below).

16.3.3.2 Section 36 statement

The purpose of s 36 of the Administration of Estates Act 1925 is to provide protection for a buyer who purchases from personal representatives. It is based on the premise that personal representatives, not dealing with their own property, and perhaps dealing with a large, complicated estate, may be more likely than other owners of land to attempt (mistakenly) to dispose of the same property twice. A buyer will take good title from personal representatives, even if there has been a prior disposition by them, provided that:

(a) the conveyance to the buyer contains a statement given by the personal representatives that they have not made any previous assent or conveyance of the same land; and
(b) no memorandum of a previous conveyance or assent of the land is endorsed on the grant; and
(c) any prior disposition is not for valuable consideration.

The effect of this provision is that an assentee (who will not have provided valuable consideration) is at risk of losing title to a later buyer from the personal representatives who relies on s 36 and ensures that the three criteria set out above are met. To prevent this happening, the assentee should have insisted that a memorandum of the assent was endorsed on the grant of probate.

Where, as it almost always will, the transaction induces first registration, an endorsement on the grant of probate is not required. The need for registration of any disposition will prevent any land being disposed of twice.

16.3.3.3 Acknowledgement for grant

A disposition by personal representatives should contain an acknowledgement of the right to production of their grant of probate, because this is a document of title the inspection of which may be required by subsequent buyers of the land. The grant should be inspected to check for endorsements which have been made on it.

16.3.3.4 Naming the beneficiary

An assent or conveyance by personal representatives of a legal estate is sufficient evidence in favour of a buyer that the person in whose favour it is made is the person entitled to have the legal estate conveyed to them, unless there is a memorandum of a previous assent or conveyance on the grant. In effect, this means that a buyer from an assentee of land, having checked the grant and found no adverse endorsements, does not have to look at the deceased's will to check that the assentee was entitled to the land, but this provision will not protect the buyer if it is apparent from some other source (eg, the assent itself) that it was made in favour of the wrong person (see the Administration of Estates Act 1925, s 36).

16.3.3.5 Investigation of title points

The result of all the above is that, when investigating an unregistered title, the following points should be checked:

(a) On a sale by personal representatives:
   (i) inspect grant of probate to check authority of personal representatives;
   (ii) ensure all proving personal representatives are joined in conveyance;
   (iii) check grant of probate contains no memorandum of a prior disposition of the land;
   (iv) check conveyance contains a s 36 statement;
   (v) check conveyance contains an acknowledgement for production of the grant.

(b) On an assent by personal representatives:
   (i) inspect grant of probate to check authority of personal representatives;
   (ii) ensure all proving personal representatives are joined in assent;
   (iii) check grant of probate contains no memorandum of a prior disposition of the land;
   (iv) check grant of probate does contain a memorandum of the assent;
   (v) check assent contains an acknowledgement for production of the grant.

16.4 CO-OWNERS

Co-owners hold land on a trust of land, and the remarks relating to trustees in **16.2** apply.

16.4.1 Registered land

16.4.1.1 Tenants in common

If the co-owners are tenants in common in equity, a restriction will be entered on the proprietorship register. In the event of death of one or more of the co-owners, so that at the time of sale there is only one surviving trustee, the restriction ensures that a second trustee is appointed to join with the survivor in the transfer. This is the preferred and safest method of dealing with this situation. Alternatively, the buyer can deal with the survivor alone, provided that the restriction is removed from the register because the seller has been able to prove that they have become solely and beneficially entitled to the whole legal and equitable interest in the land as explained at **16.4.2.1**. Proof of death of the deceased must also be provided.

The wording of the restriction in use as from 13 October 2003 is:

> No disposition by a sole proprietor of the registered estate (except a trust corporation) under which capital money arises is to be registered unless authorised by an order of the court.

Note, however, that the previous version of this restriction may well still be encountered with regard to registrations made prior to 13 October 2003:

> No disposition by a sole proprietor of the land (not being a trust corporation) under which capital money arises is to be registered except under an order of the registrar or the court.

16.4.1.2 Joint tenants

If the co-owners are joint tenants in equity, no restriction is placed on the register and a buyer may generally deal safely with the survivor alone on proof of the death of the deceased co-owner. It is possible that the equitable joint tenancy could have been severed, but in the absence of a restriction, only if the beneficiary of the deceased has an overriding interest under the LRA 2002 by virtue of being in occupation of the property will a problem arise. Pre-contract searches and enquiries will reveal information about any occupiers and so the matter should come to the buyer's solicitor's notice in order that it can be dealt with in the ordinary course of the transacion.

16.4.2 Unregistered land

The conveyance under which the co-owners bought the land should be inspected to see whether they held as joint tenants or tenants in common in equity.

16.4.2.1 Tenants in common

Although the whole of the legal estate passes automatically by survivorship to the survivor of two co-owners of the legal estate, the whole of the equitable interest held as tenants in common does not pass automatically to the survivor because a tenancy in common is capable of passing by will or on intestacy, so the trust still subsists. A buyer from the survivor should therefore insist on taking a conveyance from two trustees in order to overreach any beneficial interests which may subsist under the trust. This is the safest and preferred method when dealing with the survivor of tenants in common. Alternatively, if the survivor has become solely and beneficially entitled to the whole legal and equitable interest in the land, they may convey alone as sole owner on proof to the buyer of this fact. Such proof would consist of a certified copy or office copy of the grant of probate and an assent made in favour of the survivor. A copy of the deceased's death certificate could also be produced, but the grant strictly makes this unnecessary.

16.4.2.2 Joint tenants

The survivor of beneficial joint tenants becomes entitled to the whole legal and equitable interest in the land, but a buyer from the survivor will accept a conveyance from the survivor alone only if they can be satisfied that they will benefit from the protection of the Law of Property (Joint Tenants) Act 1964. The problem is that the joint tenancy could have been severed, turning it into a tenancy in common.

This Act (which is retrospectively effective to 1925) allows the buyer to assume that no severance of the joint tenancy had occurred before the death of the deceased joint tenant if the transfer by the surviving joint tenant to the buyer contains a statement that the surviving joint tenant is solely and beneficially entitled to the land and neither of the following has occurred before the date of the transfer:

(1) A memorandum (written record) of severance endorsed on the conveyance of the property to the joint tenants.

(2) Bankruptcy proceedings registered against either of the joint tenants at the Land Charges Registry.

Otherwise, the surviving joint tenant must be treated as a surviving tenant in common and the procedure (at **16.4.2.1**) relating to tenants in common must be followed.

Should it be necessary to appoint a further trustee, the procedure outlined in **16.2.3** should be followed.

16.5 DISPOSING LENDERS

16.5.1 Existence of the power of sale

Section 101 of the LPA 1925 gives a power to sell the legal estate vested in the borrower, subject to prior incumbrances but discharged from subsequent ones, to every lender whose mortgage is made by deed. Thus, unless expressly excluded, the power is available to a lender under a legal mortgage. In relation to registered land, only the proprietor of a registered charge has a power of sale. Where a lender sells in exercise of its power of sale, the mortgage deed will not bear a receipt, but the buyer nevertheless will take free from it and any subsequent mortgages over which the lender exercising the power of sale has priority.

16.5.2 Power of sale arises

The power of sale arises when the mortgage money becomes due under the mortgage, ie on the legal date for redemption, which is usually set at an early date in the mortgage term. The power becomes exercisable by the lender only as provided for in the mortgage deed, or when one of the events specified in s 103 of the LPA 1925 has occurred. These events are:

(a) a demand has been made for the principal sum outstanding on the mortgage and this demand is unpaid for three months; or

(b) any interest due under the mortgage is in arrears for two months; or

(c) there is breach of any other covenant in the mortgage.

A buyer from the lender must check (by looking at the mortgage deed) that the power of sale has arisen, but need not enquire whether the power has become exercisable.

16.6 DISCHARGED MORTGAGES

16.6.1 Registered land

A mortgage over registered land which has been discharged will be deleted from the charges register of the title and is thus of no further concern to the buyer. As far as the seller's existing mortgage is concerned, the buyer should raise a requisition requiring this to be removed on or before completion. Discharge of a mortgage of registered land is effected by filing a completed Form DS1 at Land Registry or by use of the ED or e-DS1 system (see **31.3.5**).

16.6.2 Unregistered land

Discharged legal mortgages should be provided by the seller and checked by the buyer's solicitor to ensure that the discharge was validly effected.

Where a lender has sold the property in exercise of its power of sale, the mortgage deed will not bear a receipt.

16.6.2.1 Building society mortgages

Provided that the receipt (usually endorsed on the mortgage deed) is in the form of wording prescribed by the Building Societies Act 1986 and is signed by a person authorised by the particular society, the receipt may be treated as a proper discharge of the mortgage without further enquiry being made.

16.6.2.2 Other mortgages

By s 115 of the LPA 1925, a receipt endorsed on the mortgage deed operates to discharge the mortgage, provided it is signed by the lender and names the person making repayment. However, where the money appears to have been paid by a person not entitled to the immediate equity of redemption, the receipt will usually operate as a transfer of the mortgage. Thus, if the person making repayment is not the borrower named in the mortgage, or a personal representative or trustee acting on their behalf, the receipt should make it expressly clear that the receipt is to operate as such and is not intended to be a transfer of the mortgage to the person making payment.

16.7 ATTORNEYS

16.7.1 Powers of attorney

A power of attorney is a deed under which the donor appoints someone (the attorney or donee) to carry out certain actions on their behalf. In the context of conveyancing, it might be necessary for a seller to give someone a power of attorney to execute documents on the seller's behalf because the seller was going abroad and would not be available when the documents needed to be signed.

16.7.2 Types of power

There are five types of power of attorney:

(a) a general power, under s 10 of the Powers of Attorney Act 1971, entitles the attorney to deal with all of the donor's assets;

(b) a special power, which permits the attorney to deal only with certain specified assets or categories of assets;

(c) a trustee power, which is used where property is held on trust;

(d) an enduring power, which is made under the Enduring Powers of Attorney Act 1985. This type of power endures through the donor's mental incapacity (subject to registration of the power);

(e) a lasting power, which has replaced the enduring power as from 1 October 2007.

These powers are examined in more detail below.

16.7.3 Revocation

Subject as below, a power of attorney may be revoked expressly by the donor, or will be revoked automatically on the donor's death, mental incapacity or bankruptcy. Once registered, enduring powers are irrevocable except by order of the court.

A person who buys from an attorney (and subsequent buyers) will get good title if the power:

(a) authorises the transaction which is to take place between the attorney and the buyer; and

(b) is valid and subsisting at the date of completion of the transaction.

The buyer is therefore concerned to ensure that the power had not been revoked at the date of completion of their purchase from the attorney. A summary of the protection given to the buyer by the Powers of Attorney Act 1971 is set out below.

16.7.4 Copy of power

The buyer is entitled to a certified copy of any power of attorney which affects the title (even if the transaction involves land which is unregistered and the power is dated earlier than the root of title). If the land is registered or registrable, Land Registry will require the original or a certified copy of the power on registration of a disposition made in exercise of the power.

16.7.5 Terms of the power

By checking the terms of the power itself, the buyer should ensure that the transaction was authorised by the power. A general power of attorney under s 10 of the Powers of Attorney Act 1971 entitles the attorney to take any action the donor could have taken with regard to any of the donor's property. Other types of power should be checked carefully to ensure that they authorise the particular transaction in relation to the particular property concerned.

16.7.6 General, special and trustee powers

A person who deals with an attorney holding these types of powers of attorney will take good title under s 5(2) of the Powers of Attorney Act 1971, provided they acquire in good faith without knowledge of the revocation of the power. Death revokes such a power, thus the buyer cannot take good title if they are aware of the death of the donor. A subsequent buyer (including but not limited to a person who buys from the person who dealt with the attorney), in this paragraph referred to as 'C', obtains the protection of s 5(4) of the Powers of Attorney Act 1971 if either:

(a) the dealing between the attorney and the person who dealt with them (P) took place within 12 months of the grant of the power; or

(b) the person (P) who dealt directly with the attorney made a statutory declaration before or within three months of completion of a purchase by C to the effect that they (P) had no knowledge of the revocation of the power.

If either (a) or (b) applies, it will be presumed in favour of the buyer that the person who dealt with the attorney did not know of any revocation of the power. As a result, the buyer will obtain good title, even if in fact the power had been revoked.

16.7.7 Enduring and lasting powers

An enduring power of attorney is one made under the Enduring Powers of Attorney Act 1985. This Act has been repealed and enduring powers are now governed by provisions contained in Sch 4 to the Mental Capacity Act 2005. Until the incapacity of the donor, the power takes effect as an ordinary power and the Mental Capacity Act contains provisions to protect buyers which are similar to those outlined above. On the incapacity of the donor, the attorney's authority to act becomes limited to such acts as are necessary for the protection of the donor and their estate until such time as the power is registered with the Office of the Public Guardian. The Public Guardian is a Government-appointed individual responsible for dealing with various matters in respect of persons who lack mental capacity. Once registered, the power is incapable of revocation and the attorney's full authority to act is restored.

Where a person is buying from an attorney who holds an enduring power, they should make a search at the Office of the Public Guardian to ensure that no application for registration of the power is pending. If an application is pending, this would suggest mental incapacity on the part of the donor. In these circumstances, the buyer should wait until the registration has been completed and the attorney's authority to act is restored. If the power has already been registered, the attorney should produce the registration certificate to the buyer. An office copy of the power can be produced as evidence both of the contents of the power and of its registration.

The Mental Capacity Act 2005 (in force 1 October 2007) replaced enduring powers with a new form of power called a lasting power. Existing enduring powers (whether registered or not) continue to be valid and operate as above. Lasting powers give an attorney power to deal with the donor's personal welfare and/or their property and affairs, including authority to deal with such matters when the donor no longer has capacity. As with enduring powers, the lasting power is required to be in a prescribed form but, unlike enduring powers, comes into effect only when registered with the Office of the Public Guardian. Where the buyer is buying from an attorney who holds a lasting power, they should obtain an office copy of the power from the Office of the Public Guardian as evidence that the lasting power is registered with the Office of the Public Guardian and to check that the attorney is acting within the scope of their authority. The buyer from the attorney will be protected unless they knew the power was invalid (by s 14(3) of the Mental Capacity Act 2005) or were aware of circumstances which would have terminated the attorney's authority to act (by s 5(2) of the Powers of Attorney Act

1971). A subsequent buyer will be protected under either s 14(3) of the Mental Capacity Act 2005 or s 5(4) of the Powers of Attorney Act 1971 if the sale by the attorney to the first buyer was completed within 12 months of the date on which the power was registered, or the first buyer makes a statutory declaration within three months of completion of the subsequent purchase, that they had no reason to doubt that the attorney had authority to sell them the property at the time of the purchase.

16.7.8 Trustees and powers of attorney

The law regarding the use of powers of attorney by trustees was changed, non-retrospectively, as from 1 March 2000 by the Trustee Delegation Act 1999.

In the case of powers of attorney created prior to that date (even if exercised after it), trustees could not use a general power. They had to use a trustee power under s 25 of the Trustee Act 1925. However, this permitted delegation for a maximum of 12 months only and could not be used to delegate in favour of a sole human co-trustee. This had profound implications in relation to co-owners, who hold the land under an implied trust. Take the case of a husband and wife who were co-owners. They could not use a general power; and if using a trustee power, they could not appoint the other as attorney – a stranger would have to be appointed. However, due to the wording of s 3 of the Enduring Powers of Attorney Act 1985, one co-owner could validly appoint the other as attorney if an enduring power was used.

16.7.8.1 Powers created prior to 1 March 2000

The rules set out above continue to apply. However, any enduring powers created prior to 1 March 2000 in favour of a sole human co-trustee cease to be effective in relation to the trust property on registration of the power with the Office of the Public Guardian or on 28 February 2001, whichever is the earlier, unless the donor has a beneficial interest in the land. In such a case, the power will continue to be effective in relation to the trust property. Thus an enduring power made by one co-owner in favour of the other in (say) 1999 can still be used today, as the donor has a beneficial interest under the implied trust under which the co-owners hold the land.

16.7.8.2 Powers created on or after 1 March 2000

Trustees can now use a general power, provided the donor of the power has a beneficial interest in the land. In favour of a buyer, this is to be taken conclusively if the donee of the power, ie the attorney, makes a statement to that effect either at the time of the disposition by them, or within three months afterwards.

Section 25 of the Trustee Act 1925 has been rewritten to provide for a new general trustee power of attorney. This still allows delegation only for a maximum period of 12 months. Such a power can be an enduring power.

Co-owners may thus use either an ordinary general power or a general trustee power, and can in both cases validly appoint a sole co-owner as attorney. The 1999 Act makes it clear, however, that a person acting both as trustee and as attorney for the other trustee, cannot give a valid receipt for capital money; remember that the receipt of two trustees is required to overreach the beneficial interests under a trust.

So, the end result of these complicated provisions is that if one of two co-owners wishes to appoint an attorney to execute a deed selling the land, the co-trustee cannot be appointed, as such co-trustee will not be able to give a valid receipt. In such a case, a stranger will need to be appointed, and this rule cannot be evaded by using an enduring power.

16.8 TRANSACTIONS AT AN UNDERVALUE

Where in the chain of title there is a transaction for no consideration or at an undervalue, care needs to be exercised, since the transaction could be set aside under the Insolvency Act 1986 (as amended by the Insolvency (No 2) Act 1994).

The rules could apply to pure gifts, inter-spouse transfers on marriage breakdown (including those made by court order) and any inter vivos transaction where the consideration received by the seller is significantly less than was paid on the original purchase. Note that an assent is also a transaction for no consideration, but although there is a theoretical risk that it could be set aside, the steps outlined below are not in this case usually followed in practice because it is assumed that the personal representatives will have made extensive enquiries about debts and creditors before assenting any part of the estate to the beneficiary.

16.8.1 Transactions by an individual

A transaction at an undervalue by an individual within the five years immediately preceding the current transaction may be set aside by the trustee in bankruptcy if the donor is made bankrupt under s 339 of the Insolvency Act 1986.

16.8.2 Transactions by a company

If a transaction at an undervalue was made by a company within the two years preceding the date of the current transaction, it may be set aside by the liquidator on the company's subsequent insolvency under s 238 of the Insolvency Act 1986.

16.8.3 Defences available to a subsequent buyer

The basic principle is that a subsequent buyer is protected, provided that they have acquired in good faith and for value from a person other than the insolvent company or bankrupt individual (Insolvency Act 1986, s 241(2)(a) and s 342(2)(a)).

The buyer is presumed not to be in good faith in either of the following cases:

(a) when the buyer acquired the property, they had notice of the insolvency or bankruptcy proceedings and that the disposition by the insolvent company or bankrupt individual was at an undervalue; or

(b) the buyer was connected with or an associate of the company or individual who made the original transaction at an undervalue. A 'connected' person includes directors, shadow directors and associates. 'Associate' is widely defined to include a person's spouse or ex-spouse, members of their family and their spouse's family, their partner and their partner's family, and their employees.

Registration of bankruptcy proceedings will amount to notice, so a buyer will need to make a bankruptcy search against the individual making the transaction at an undervalue not for the period of that person's ownership, but for a period of five years from the date of the transaction at an undervalue. This is to ensure that the buyer is not presumed to be lacking in good faith under (a) above. If the search reveals bankruptcy entries against the individual making the transaction at an undervalue within five years of that transaction, the purchase cannot proceed. Similarly, if the buyer is an associate of either the individual making the transaction at an undervalue or the person who bought the property from them, the sale likewise cannot proceed if the onset of bankruptcy took place within five years of the transaction at an undervalue.

The above applies to dispositions made by companies, but in that case the relevant time period is two years.

16.8.4 Registered land

In the case of dispositions registered on or after 1 April 2000, the register includes details of the price paid by the proprietor. If this appears to be nil or something of low monetary value, the provisions of the Insolvency Act 1986 should be borne in mind. Where first registration is based on a transaction at an undervalue, a note will be added in the proprietorship register to the effect that the title is subject to the provisions of the Insolvency Act 1986. Where such a note appears, a buyer from that proprietor will need to consider the effect of the Insolvency Act 1986 as outlined above.

16.8.5 Summary

A buyer who buys for value and in good faith will generally now be protected under the Insolvency Act 1986 (as amended by the Insolvency (No 2) Act 1994). However, some lenders are reluctant to lend on property where there has been a transaction at an undervalue within the past two years (companies) or five years (individuals), unless an insurance policy is obtained covering the possibility of the donor's insolvency within these periods.

16.9 RESTRICTIVE COVENANTS

Many properties are subject to restrictive covenants imposed on a previous sale of the land. In most cases, the nature of the covenants is consistent with the type of property being sold. It is common, for example, to find covenants imposed on residential property which restrict the use of the property to a private dwelling house in the occupation of a single family, which prevent alterations from being made to the property without the consent of a named third party, and which prohibit the keeping of animals other than ordinary domestic pets. In such cases, provided that they will not seriously impede the buyer's intended use of the property, no further action need be taken other than informing the buyer of the extent of the covenants and telling them that they have a liability for breach of the covenants.

16.9.1 Problematical covenants

Instructions may reveal that the buyer's intended use of the property after completion will cause a breach of existing covenants. For example, if there is a restrictive covenant which prevents use of the property except as a single private dwelling house and the client wants to convert the property into flats, a breach of covenant will occur.

The first step to be taken in such cases is to check to see whether the covenants are registered. Post-1925 covenants which are not registered either on the charges register of a registered title or as Class D(ii) entries in unregistered land are unenforceable. Usually the covenants are registered. Next, look at the wording of the covenants to see whether they have been annexed effectively to the land and are prima facie binding. Unless it is very clear on the face of the covenants that they are invalid, it is safest to assume that they are enforceable and to consider whether it is possible to obtain an insurance policy which will cover liability for the future breach of covenant. An insurance company will usually need the following information or documents when considering whether or not to issue a policy:

(a) A copy of the document imposing the covenant or, if this is not available, a copy of the exact wording of the covenant.

(b) The exact nature of the breach which has occurred, or details of the action which is contemplated which will cause the breach.

(c) The date when the covenant was imposed.

(d) Whether or not the covenant is registered.

(e) The nature of other properties in the immediate neighbourhood. This is to enable the insurance company to assess the risk of enforcement of the covenant. Taking the example given above of a potential breach being caused by a conversion of a dwelling into flats, if many of the neighbouring properties have already been converted into flats, the likelihood of this particular covenant being enforced if breached is more remote than if the surrounding properties remain in single ownership. A plan which shows the property in the context of the surrounding locality is often useful.

(f) A copy of any planning permission which permits the development to be undertaken by the client.

(g) What steps have been taken (if any) to trace the person(s) with the benefit of the covenant and the results of those enquiries.

If a policy is issued, it is normally a single premium policy (a single sum is paid on the issue of the policy). The benefit of the policy may be passed on to successors in title. The buyer's lender should be consulted about the proposed breach of covenant and their approval obtained to the terms of the insurance policy. In arranging or advising on such a policy, the solicitor is carrying out a 'regulated activity' for the purposes of the FSMA 2000. For most solicitors, this will mean that they must ensure that they fall within the professional firms exemption to avoid committing a criminal offence (see **22.2.2**).

16.9.2 Other methods of dealing with covenants

If no policy can be obtained (the risk of enforcement might cause the insurance company to charge a prohibitive premium), consideration might be given to one of the solutions suggested below. If, however, it appears that valid and enforceable covenants will impede the client's proposed use of the land and that no viable solution to this problem can be achieved, the client should be advised not to proceed with the proposed purchase.

16.9.3 Approaching the person with the benefit of the covenant

Approaching the person with the benefit of the covenant is occasionally a viable option. This person will be the present owner of the land for the benefit of which the covenant was taken. Such a person may be prepared to modify the problematic covenant, or even release the buyer from the covenant entirely. Alternatively they may be prepared to consent to a particular activity. Often they will require payment in exchange for a modification, release or consent.

There are also other potential difficulties. The person with the benefit of the covenant may be hard to trace or unwilling to agree to the buyer's proposals. If the land benefitting from the covenant has been divided up between several owners, the consent of all the owners of that land will be needed. Further, if you have unsuccessfully approached the person with the benefit of the covenant, you are very unlikely subsequently to obtain restrictive covenant indemnity insurance. This is because you have put the person with the benefit on notice of a possible breach, thereby increasing the risk of action to enforce the covenant.

16.9.4 Application to the Upper Tribunal (Lands Chamber)

The Upper Tribunal (Lands Chamber) (formerly Lands Tribunal) has power in certain circumstances under the LPA 1925, s 84 to grant a modification or discharge of a restrictive covenant, but this solution may not be quick or cheap to pursue. The county court enjoys a similar, but more limited, jurisdiction.

16.9.5 Competition legislation and restrictive covenants

16.9.5.1 Application to land agreements

Anyone drafting or considering a restrictive covenant in connection with either freehold or leasehold land should be aware of the Competition Act 1998. This prohibits any agreement which may affect trade within the UK and which prevents, restricts or distorts competition within the UK. Since April 2011 this prohibition has applied to land agreements, which include transfers of freehold and leasehold interests together with leases themselves. It only applies to agreements between businesses and not to individuals (unless they are acting as a business), so most residential transactions will be unaffected. It is retrospective, thus the date of the covenant is irrelevant. It is not possible to exclude the Act.

16.9.5.2 What type of restrictions may be prohibited?

In 2011, the Office of Fair Trading (OFT) issued guidance on the application of the Competition Act to land agreements. This guidance as now been adopted by the OFT's successor body, the Competition and Markets Authority (CMA). The guidance gives the following examples of restrictions that may be anti-competitive:

(a) a restriction preventing a high street retail unit from being used for the sale of the same products that are being sold in the premises adjacent to it;

(b) a restrictive covenant on the sale of land not to sell it to a competitor of the seller;

(c) a covenant by a landlord not to permit another business of the same type as the tenant to open in its shopping centre.

However, unless the covenant has an 'appreciable effect' on the market affected by the agreement, it will not fall within the competition legislation. Whether such provisions have an appreciable effect depends on a number of factors, including the scope of the relevant market and the degree of market power of the parties.

It is worth noting that the guidance suggests that only a minority of restrictions in land agreements will be anti-competitive.

16.9.5.3 The consequences of being anti-competitive

The CMA can impose fines of up to 10% of a firm's worldwide turnover if it discovers a prohibited restriction. An agreement that contains a prohibited restriction is also void and unenforceable, although the CMA takes the view that a court may consider it possible to sever the prohibited restriction and let other terms of the agreement remain valid.

Further guidance on the application of the Competition Act to land agreements may be found on the gov.uk website.

16.9.6 Restrictive covenants and the groceries market

Certain land agreements in connection with grocery retailing activities are subject to additional control under the Groceries Market Investigation (Controlled Land) Order 2010 (the 'Controlled Land Order'). This is an attempt to address the adverse effects on competition resulting from the control of land by large grocery retailers. It requires large grocery retailers to release certain specified restrictive covenants and prohibits them from entering into new covenants that may restrict grocery retailing. A further specialist text should be consulted for more information.

16.10 EXECUTION OF DEEDS

A solicitor should check that all deeds and documents in the title have been properly executed. In order to transfer a legal estate in land, it is usually necessary to do so by deed, and this part of the chapter considers the requirements necessary to ensure that a deed has been properly executed as such.

16.10.1 Registered land

In the case of registered land, title is updated by Land Registry whenever there is a dealing in respect of that title. As part of this process, Land Registry will scrutinise the execution of the document giving effect to that dealing before recording its effect on the register. Accordingly, it should not be necessary for a solicitor to scrutinise the execution of historic documents in respect of registered land.

16.10.2 Unregistered land

In the case of unregistered land, title is proven by title deeds, and each document needs to be scrutinised in turn to ensure that it satisfies the relevant formalities for its valid execution.

16.10.3 Execution of deeds by an individual

The formalities for execution of a deed changed on 31 July 1990. For deeds executed on or after 31 July 1990, the following rules apply. When made by an individual, a document will be a deed only if:

(a) it is signed by its maker;
(b) that signature is witnessed and attested. This means that the signing of the deed by a party must be witnessed by another person, who then also signs the deed to signify that they were present when the deed was so signed. There is no need for the same person to witness all of the signatures;
(c) it is clear that the document is intended to be a deed. That intention can be made clear either by describing the document as a deed (eg, 'This Deed of Conveyance is made 1 September 1993 ...'), or because the document is expressed to be executed as a deed (eg, the attestation clause might say 'executed by the seller as a deed in the presence of ...'); and
(d) the document is delivered as a deed. A deed is delivered by a seller when it is signed by them with the intention that they will be bound by it. In the case of a transaction involving the disposition or creation of an interest in land, where a solicitor, notary public or licensed conveyancer purports to deliver a document on behalf of a party to the document, a purchaser is conclusively entitled to presume that the solicitor, etc has authority to deliver that document.

It is possible for an individual to direct another person to sign a deed on their behalf, provided that the signature is made in their presence and there are two attesting witnesses.

As regards deeds executed before 31 July 1990, the rule was that the document had to be signed and sealed by its maker, and delivered as their deed. The seal was usually only a red, self-adhesive circular piece of paper. However, it was still essential that a seal was placed on the conveyance before the maker signed. If a document purporting to be a deed does not bear a seal, evidence is needed that a seal (or something representing a seal, such as a printed circle) was in position at the time of execution. If a seal was never there then the document is not a deed, and could not have conveyed a legal estate.

The delivery of the deed was a matter of intention. A deed was delivered when it was signed by the maker with the intention that they were to be bound by it. If a person signed and sealed a deed, it was inferred from this that the deed was also delivered, so no evidence that a deed was delivered should be required.

16.10.4 Execution by a company

As with individuals, the rules relating to the execution of deeds by a company underwent significant change on 31 July 1990. Other changes were introduced for documents executed on or after 15 September 2005 (as indicated). Further changes were introduced by s 44 of the Companies Act 2006 as from 6 April 2008.

In the case of deeds executed by a company on or after 31 July 1990, the following rules apply. A document can be executed in one of three ways:

(a) *By the affixing of the company seal.* It must be clear on the face of the document that is intended to be a deed. If this method of execution is used, the document is deemed, in favour of a purchaser, to have been duly executed, provided that the seal purports to have been affixed in the presence of and attested by two members of the board of directors or a director and the secretary. For deeds executed prior to 15 September 2005, this protection only applied where the seal was affixed and attested in front of a director and secretary.

The following is an example of an attestation clause that would comply with the above conditions and would be accepted by Land Registry:

Executed as a deed by affixing the common seal of *(insert name of company)* in the presence of:	*Common seal of company*

____

Signature of director

____

Signature of [director][secretary]

(b) *By being signed by a director and the secretary, or by two directors of the company, provided that the document is expressed to be executed by the company.* In other words, it must be clear that the signatures amount to execution by the company, rather than execution by the directors personally. If this method of execution is used, the document is deemed, in favour of a purchaser, to have been duly executed, provided that it purports to be signed by a director and the secretary or by two directors.

The following is an example of an attestation clause that would comply with the above conditions and would be accepted by Land Registry:

Executed as a deed by *(name of company)* acting by [a director and its secretary] [two directors}	*Signature* director *Signature* [secretary] [director]

(c) For documents executed on or after 6 April 2008 only, a third method is available. *A deed can be executed by being signed by a single director in the presence of a witness who then attests that signature.*

The following is an example of an attestation clause that would comply with these conditions and would be acceptable to Land Registry:

Executed as a deed by *(name of company)* acting by a director In the presence of Signature of witness	*Signature* director

Name (in BLOCK CAPITALS)

Address

[Note that from September 2019, the words 'signed as a deed' is not an acceptable form of execution in prescribed form deeds executed by companies so far as the Land Registry is concerned.]

In addition to being *executed* as a deed, the document must also be *delivered* as such. A document which makes it clear on its face that it is intended to be a deed is presumed to have been delivered on execution: this presumption can be rebutted by a contrary intention. Note that for deeds executed prior to 15 September 2005, in favour of a purchaser, if the deed was executed by being signed by a director and secretary (or two directors), it would seem that this presumption of delivery is irrebuttable.

As regards deeds executed by a limited company before 31 July 1990, the execution was valid if the conveyance was executed in accordance with the company's articles of association. By s 74 of the LPA 1925, if the company seal had been affixed in the presence of the secretary and director, the deed was deemed to have been duly executed, even if in fact the articles demanded different formalities. Further, a buyer could assume that the deed had been executed so as to satisfy s 74 if there was on the deed a seal that purported to be the company seal, and signatures that purported to be those of secretary and director.

16.10.5 Land Registry Practice Guide

Land Registry publishes a number of forms of advice, and Land Registry Practice Guide 8, which can be accessed from Land Registry website <www.landregistry.gov.uk>, contains detailed information on Land Registry's current requirements.

16.11 VERIFICATION OF TITLE

Verification of title consists of checking the evidence of title supplied by the seller against the original deeds. In registered land, the true state of the register can be confirmed by the buyer when making a pre-completion search at Land Registry.

In unregistered land, the abstract or epitome should be checked against the seller's original deeds. In most cases the buyer's solicitor will postpone their verification until completion. If they then find an error on the title which had not previously been disclosed by the seller, although SC 4.3.1 (SCPC 7.3.1) allows a further period of six working days to raise further requisitions, there will inevitably be a delay in completion. In reality, where photocopies of the original deeds have been supplied with the epitome, verification will normally be a formality.

Standard Condition 4.1.3 (SCPC 7.1.3) requires the seller, at their own expense, to produce to the buyer the original of every document within the title or, if the original is not available, an abstract, epitome or copy with an original marking by a solicitor of examination either against the original, or against an examined abstract or against an examined copy.

16.12 RAISING REQUISITIONS

If the buyer's solicitor's investigation of title reveals any problem then the buyer should raise a 'requisition on title' of the seller's solicitor. A requisition is a question asked about the problem which requires a remedy from the seller.

If the seller ultimately cannot show good title then the buyer may consider whether defective title indemnity insurance is available (perhaps at the seller's cost) in order to protect them should they decide to proceed and accept the defect. If such insurance is unavailable, or the defect is such that it may affect the buyer's enjoyment of the property, the buyer is unlikely to proceed.

The buyer (and the buyer's lender) should be advised of any defects in title as soon as they become apparent.

Traditionally, title was deduced by the seller only following exchange. In such a situation, the seller's inability to make good title would have constituted a breach of contract entitling the buyer to withdraw from the contract and/or claim damages. Where requisitions are raised prior to exchange, a buyer will have no remedy should they choose to withdraw because of defects in title as there is no contract between the parties. Equally, of course, the seller would have no remedy if the buyer chose to withdraw for no good reason.

Standard Condition 4.3.1 (SCPC 7.3.1) requires the buyer to raise requisitions within six working days of the later of exchange or the delivery of the epitome. It is usual in modern practice for the title to be deduced prior to exchange (see **14.2**) and in such cases both sets of conditions of sale (SC 4.2.1 and SCPC 7.2.1) prohibit the raising of requisitions after exchange. However, these prohibitions only apply to matters disclosed by the seller prior to exchange. So if the buyer discovers a title problem after exchange which had not been previously disclosed, they can still raise requisitions in the usual way. They must do so within six working days of the particular matter coming to their attention (see SC 4.2.2 and SCPC 7.2.2).

16.13 WORKED EXAMPLE OF INVESTIGATION OF A REGISTERED TITLE – 10, BLADEN ROAD, OVERTON, CORNSHIRE

The chapter ends with two worked examples of how to investigate title which offer a suggestion as to how the task may be approached. The first is in respect of a registered title and the second in respect of an unregistered title. As investigation of title is a skill, you may find it useful to attempt the investigations yourself before looking at the worked examples to see how many issues you were able to identify.

The first worked example picks up on the case study introduced at **8.7**. You act for Roger Evans who is selling his current property, 47, Queens' Road, Loamster and buying a new home, 10, Bladen Road, Overton. Official copies for 47, Queens' Road are shown at **4.5**. This is the property being sold by Roger Evans and so, as the solicitor acting on the sale of this property, it will be necessary for you to investigate this title for the reasons set out in **15.2.1**. In fact, the title to 47, Queens' Road does not reveal any particular problems, and so the major reason for carrying out the investigation will be in order to draft the contract for sale. A worked example of this contract will be considered in **Chapter 18**. The worked example that follows assumes that the official copies for 10, Bladen Road (the property Roger Evans is buying) have now been received and need to be investigated from a buyer's perspective (see **15.2.2**). The title to this property may prove more problematic. If you wish to use this title to practice investigation of title in registered land, you will find that it is important to re-read the instructions taken at the end of **Chapter 8** before you do so.

The second worked example involves the investigation of an unregistered title and is a free-standing exercise. In unregistered land, title could be deduced in the form of an abstract or an epitome. In the example, the epitome format has been used, as this is the format that is most commonly met in practice.

In both cases, the worked examples merely suggest one way of approaching the task – other, equally valid approaches exist. Whichever, is taken, however, it should be in writing and equally systematic.

16.13.1 The official copies

Official copy of register of title

Title number LM 6042 Edition date 30.04.2023

- This official copy shows the entries subsisting on the register on 14 September 2025 at 10:55:50
- This date must be quoted as the 'search from date' in any official search application based on this copy.
- The date at the beginning of an entry is the date on which the entry was made in the register.
- Issued on 14 September 2025.
- Under s.67 of the Land Registration Act 2002 this copy is admissible in evidence to the same extent as the original.
- For information about the register of title see Land Registry website www.landregistry.gov.uk or Land Registry Public Guide 1 – A guide to the information we keep and how you can obtain it.
- This title is dealt with by Land Registry Hull Office

A: Property Register

This register describes the land and estate comprised in the title.

COUNTY	DISTRICT
CORNSHIRE	OVERTON

1. (18 December 2000) The freehold land shown edged with red on the plan of the above title filed at the Registry and being 10, Bladen Road, Overton, Cornshire, CS1 6AU.
2. (18 December 2000) The property has the benefit of a right of way granted by deed of grant dated 19 April 1969 and made between (1) Ivan Walton and (2) Jonathan Hartley.
   NOTE: Copy filed

B: Proprietorship Register

This register specifies the class of title and identifies the owner. It contains any entries that affect the right of disposal.

Title absolute

1. (18 December 2000) PROPRIETOR(S): NEIL STUART AND ANITA STUART of 10, Bladen Road, Overton, Cornshire, CS1 6AU.
2. (18 December 2000) The price stated to have been paid on 3 December 2000 was £180,000.
3. (18 December 2000) RESTRICTION: No disposition by a sole proprietor of the registered estate (except a trust corporation) under which capital money arises is to be registered unless authorised by an order of the court.
4. (18 December 2000) The transfer to the proprietor contains a covenant to observe and perform the covenants referred to in the Charges Register and of indemnity in respect thereof.

C: Charges Register

This register contains any charges and other matters that affect the land.

1. (18 December 2000) A conveyance of the land in this title dated 1 April 1968 and made between (1) Ivan Walton and (2) Jonathan Hartley contains the following covenants:
   "The Purchaser with the intent and so as to bind (as far as practicable) the property hereby conveyed and to benefit and protect the retained land of the Vendor lying to the west of the land hereby conveyed hereby covenants with the Vendor that he and his successors in title will at all times observe and perform the stipulations and conditions set out in the schedule hereto."

THE SCHEDULE ABOVE REFERRED TO

"1. Not to use the property other than as a single private dwelling house; and

2. Not to build or allow to be built any new building on the property nor alter or allow to be altered any building currently erected on the property without the written consent of the Vendor or his successors in title; and

3. To keep the wall on the northern boundary of the property in good repair and condition."

2. (18 December 2010) CHARGE dated 3 December 2010 to secure the monies including the further advances therein mentioned.

3. (18 December 2010) PROPRIETOR – NORTHERN WEST BUILDING SOCIETY of 54 Maine Road, Manchester, M2 3ER.

4. (30 April 2023) CHARGE dated 14 April 2023 to secure the monies including the further advances therein mentioned.

5. (30 April 2023) PROPRIETOR – HOME IMPROVEMENT LOANS LIMITED, 12 Hanging Lane, Liverpool Street, London, EC1 2MM.

END OF REGISTER

Note: A date at the beginning of an entry is the date on which the entry was made in the Register

Authors' note: These official copies should be accompanied by an official copy of the title plan. This has not been reproduced for the purposes of this worked example.

16.13.1.1 Worked example of investigation of title as revealed by official copies

	NOTES
Date of Official Copies	*14 September 2025*(1)
Title Number	LM6042(2)
Property Register	
Address:	*10, Bladen Road, Overton, Cornshire, CS1 6AU.*(2)
Entries:	**Note:** *Entry 2: Benefit of right of way. Copy filed – request from seller.*(3)
Proprietorship Register:	
Class of Title:	*Absolute* (4)
Registered Proprietor(s):	*Neil Stuart and Anita Stuart*(5)
Entries:	**Note:** *Entry 3. NS and AS held property as tenants in common. AS is deceased. Request death certificate. Will need to appoint second trustee to overreach. Ensure this is done before exchange or insert special condition requiring appointment before completion.*(6) **Note:** *Entry 4. Indemnity covenant.*(7)
Charges Register: Entries:	**Note:** *Entry 1. Property subject to covenants. Residential user only. No building or alterations without consent. Instructions indicate extension built two years ago. Request evidence of consent. Will need to check planning and building regulations. Positive covenant to maintain boundary wall.*(8) **Note:** *Entries 2–5. Two registered charges.*(9)

16.13.1.2 Commentary

The notes are laid out in a structured format which follows the layout of the official copies themselves: the right-hand column has space for the solicitor acting for Roger Evans to make notes on the title. These notes will enable the solicitor to consider (and, if necessary, amend) the contract for the sale of 10, Bladen Road, and also to identify any problems with the title that need following up.

The following footnotes expand upon the comments made in the worked example:

(1) This is relevant as Land Registry will not permit a pre-completion search to be made for a period exceeding 12 months (see **28.5.1**).

(2) This information is necessary for checking the contract when received from the seller.

(3) The property benefits from a right of way, details of which are contained in a copy of the deed of grant that has been filed with the title. It will be necessary to obtain a copy in order to find out the exact route of this easement. It may well be the path down to the river referred to in Roger Evans's instructions.

(4) This information is necessary for checking the contract. Title is absolute, which is the best class obtainable, but if the title were registered with a lesser class, this would need to be investigated and the buyer client advised accordingly (see **4.3.5**).

(5) & (6) Anita Stuart has recently died, as indicated in Roger Evans's instructions. The restriction indicates that Anita and Neil Stuart were tenants in common, and so her share will pass to her estate. It will be necessary to appoint a second trustee in order to overreach the trust of land. A note has been made of the necessary steps here.

(7) Neil and Anita Stuart entered into an indemnity covenant with their sellers when they purchased the property. This means that Neil Stuart will remain liable for the covenants that affect the property even after he has sold to Roger Evans (see **3.6.4.1**). As a result Neil Stuart should obtain an indemnity covenant from Roger Evans on the sale of the property.

(8) Roger Evans's instructions indicate that the property has recently been extended and the covenants referred to in Entry 1 on the Charges Register indicate that consent for this should have been obtained. Steps will need to be taken to resolve this (see **16.9** for more detail). In addition, consideration needs to be given to the need for planning permission and building regulations consent (see **Chapter 7**). There is also a positive covenant to maintain a boundary wall. The burden of positive covenants does not run with the land. However, as Roger Evans will be expected to enter into an indemnity covenant, he will be indirectly liable for performing the positive covenant. The state of the wall should therefore be checked by a surveyor and enquiries raised with Neil Stuart about previous repairs.

(9) The final four entries in the Charges Register indicate that there are two mortgages on the property (the second may well have been taken out to finance the extension mentioned above). These will need to be discharged, and the solicitor acting for Roger Evans will need to ensure that the contract sells 10, Bladen Road free from both of them.

16.14 WORKED EXAMPLE OF INVESTIGATION OF AN UNREGISTERED TITLE – 15, MILL STREET, TORRIDGE, HUNTSHIRE

In this worked example, the title concerns 15, Mill Street, Torridge, Huntshire. The property is being bought by first-time buyers, David Ecclestone and Nadia Sutcliffe, as their home, from Jennifer Dawes. Jennifer has lived in the property since 1996 when she was given the property by her step-parents.

16.14.1 The epitome of title

EPITOME OF TITLE

of freehold premises known as

15, Mill Street, Torridge, Huntshire

No. of Doc.	Date	Description of document including parties or event	Evidence now supplied	Whether original will be handed over on completion
1	21.8.1960	Conveyance by David Henderson to Bryan Tyndal	Photocopy	Yes
2	8.12.1987	Central Land Charges Search	Photocopy	Yes
3	10.12.1987	Conveyance by Danielle Popham to Bernard Holmes and Catherine Eden	Photocopy	Yes
4	10.12.1987	Mortgage by Bernard Holmes and Catherine Eden to Huntshire Building Society	Photocopy	Yes
5	16.12.1996	Deed of Gift by Bernard Holmes and Catherine Eden to Jennifer Dawes	Photocopy	Yes

Document 1

INLAND REVENUE PRODUCED	£50

THIS CONVEYANCE is made the 21st August 1960 BETWEEN DAVID HENDERSON of 15, Mill Street, Torridge in the county of Huntshire (hereafter referred to as "the Vendor") of the one part and BRYAN TYNDAL of 17 Roland Street, Redenhill in the County of Cornshire (hereafter referred to as "the Purchaser") of the other part

WHEREAS the Vendor is seised of the property hereby assured for an estate in fee simple in possession subject as hereinafter mentioned but otherwise free from incumbrances

AND WHEREAS the Vendor has agreed to sell the said property to the Purchaser for the sum of Five thousand pounds

NOW THIS DEED WITNESSETH as follows:

1. In consideration of the sum of Five thousand pounds (£5,000) paid by the Purchaser to the Vendor (the receipt of which the Vendor hereby acknowledges) the Vendor as BENEFICIAL OWNER HEREBY CONVEYS unto the Purchaser ALL THAT piece or parcel of land with the dwelling house erected thereon known as 15 Mill Street, Torridge in the County of Huntshire TO HOLD unto the Purchaser in fee simple SUBJECT to the restrictive covenants referred to in a conveyance dated 25th February 1955 and made between Thomas Terry of the one part and the Vendor of the other part.
2. THE PURCHASER (with the object of affording to the Vendor a full indemnity in respect of any breach of the said restrictive covenants but not further or otherwise) HEREBY COVENANTS with the Vendor that the Purchaser and the persons deriving title under him will at all times hereafter perform and observe such restrictive covenants and keep the Vendor and his estate and effects indemnified against all actions claims demands and liabilities in respect thereof so far as the same affect the property hereby conveyed and are still subsisting and capable of being enforced

IN WITNESS whereof the parties hereto have set their respective hands and seals the day and year first before written

SIGNED SEALED and DELIVERED
by the said DAVID HENDERSON
in the presence of: } *David Henderson* ○

Hilary Miller
Torridge
Secretary

SIGNED SEALED and DELIVERED
by the said BRYAN TYNDAL
in the presence of: } *Bryan Tyndal* ○

Damian Noble
Torridge
Builder

Document 2

FORM K18

CERTIFICATE OF THE RESULT OF SEARCH

CERTIFICATE NO.	CERTIFICATE DATE	PROTECTION ENDS ON
2220398	8th December 1987	31st December 1987

It is hereby certified that an official search in respect of the undermentioned particulars has been made in the index to the registers which are kept pursuant to the Land Charges Act 1972. The results of the search is shown below.

PARTICULARS SEARCHED					
COUNTY OR COUNTIES: HUNTSHIRE					
NAME(S): Particulars of Charge				**PERIOD**	**FEES £**
THOMAS TERRY* No subsisting entry				1926–1955	.50p
DAVID HENDERSON* (1) D(ii) No. 0198 Dated 3/3/1955 (2) 15, Mill Street (3) Torridge (4) Huntshire				1955–1960	.50p
BRIAN TYNDAL* No subsisting entry				1960–1987	.50p
DANIELLE POPHAM No subsisting entry				1960–1987	.50p
APPLICANT'S REFERENCE: JP	Ternant & Co	APPLICANT'S KEY NUMBER	56456	AMOUNT DEBITED	£2.00
Ternant and Co 8 London Road Torridge Hunts HT1 6DR				Any enquiries concerning this certificate to be addressed to: The Superintendent Land Charges Department Burrington Way Plymouth PL5 3LP IMPORTANT: PLEASE READ THE NOTES OVERLEAF	

Document 3

INLAND REVENUE PRODUCED	**£550**

THIS CONVEYANCE is made the 10th day of December 1987 BETWEEN DANIELLE POPHAM of 15, Mill Street, Torridge in the county of Huntshire (hereinafter called "the Vendor") of the one part and BERNARD HOLMES AND CATHERINE EDEN of 45, Mayer Crescent, Godhall in the County of Huntshire (hereinafter called "the Purchasers") of the second part

WHEREAS the Vendor is seised of the property hereinafter described for an estate in fee simple in possession and has agreed to sell the same to the Purchasers for the sum of Fifty-five thousand pounds AND WHEREAS the Vendor is solely and beneficially entitled to the said property

NOW THIS DEED WITNESSETH as follows:

1 IN consideration of the sum of Fifty-five thousand pounds (£55,000) paid by the Purchasers to the Vendor (the receipt whereof the Vendor hereby acknowledges) the Vendor as BENEFICIAL OWNER HEREBY CONVEYS unto the Purchasers ALL THAT piece or parcel of land with the dwelling house erected thereon known as 15, Mill Street, Torridge in the county of Huntshire TO HOLD the same unto the Purchasers in fee simple as beneficial joint tenants SUBJECT TO the covenants referred to in a conveyance of the property herein conveyed dated the 21st day of August 1960 and made between David Henderson and Bryan Tyndal.

2 THE PURCHASERS (with the object of affording to the Vendor a full indemnity in respect of any breach of the said restrictive covenants but not further or otherwise) HEREBY JOINTLY AND SEVERALLY COVENANT with the Vendor that the Purchasers and any person deriving title under them will at all times hereafter perform and observe such restrictive covenants and keep the Vendor and her estate and effects indemnified against all actions claims demands and liabilities in respect thereof so far as the same affect the property hereby conveyed and are still subsisting and capable of being enforced.

IN WITNESS whereof the parties hereto have set their respective hands and seals the day and year first before written

SIGNED SEALED and DELIVERED on behalf of the above named DANIELLE POPHAM by her attorney Albert Pardew in the presence of: } *Albert Pardew* ○

Colin Scales
Fernhill
Clerk

SIGNED SEALED and DELIVERED by the said BERNARD HOLMES and CATHERINE EDEN in the presence of: } *Bernard Holmes* *Catherine Eden* ○

Stephan McGuiness
Teacher

Document 4

Huntshire Building Society

MORTGAGE DEED

Account Number:	**Hol/EDE.1576**	Date: **10 December 1987**
Society:	**HUNTSHIRE BUILDING SOCIETY**	
Mortgage Conditions:	Huntshire Building Society Mortgage Conditions 1987	
Borrower:	**BERNARD HOLMES AND CATHERINE EDEN** 15, Mill Street, Torridge, Huntshire	
Property:	15, Mill Street, Torridge, Huntshire	
Title No:	**N/A**	

1. This Mortgage Deed incorporates the Mortgage Conditions a copy of which has been received by the Borrowers.
2. The Borrowers as beneficial owners charge the Property by way of legal mortgage with payment of all moneys payable by the Borrowers to the Society under the Mortgage Conditions.
3. This Mortgage Deed is made for securing further advances.

Signed sealed and delivered by the Borrowers in the presence of the Witness.

Borrowers:	Witness (signature, name and address)
Bernard Holmes	**Kevin Knowles, Fernhill, Musician**
Catherine Eden	**Kevin Knowles, Fernhill, Musician**

RECEIPT

The Huntshire Building Society hereby acknowledges receipt of the loan secured by this mortgage.

IN WITNESS whereof the Common Seal of the Society has been affixed this 20th day of June 1990 in the presence of:

John Crouch

DIRECTOR

Lee Bell

SECRETARY

Huntshire B.S.

Document 5

THIS DEED OF GIFT is made the 16th December 1996 between (1) BERNARD HOLMES and CATHERINE EDEN both of 14, Steed Mews, Cleveland Street, London W9 1HB ('the Donors') and (2) JENNIFER DAWES of Carshalton Mansions, Hawarden Street, London, W9 1NL ('the Donee')

WHEREAS the Donors are seised of the property hereinafter described for an estate in fee simple in possession and out of natural love and affection have decided to convey the same to the Donee.

NOW THIS DEED WITNESSETH as follows:

1 IN consideration of natural love and affection, the Vendors as TRUSTEES HEREBY CONVEY unto the Donee ALL THAT piece or parcel of land together with the dwelling house erected thereon known as 15, Mill Street, Torridge in the county of Huntshire TO HOLD the same unto the Donee in fee simple SUBJECT TO the covenants referred to in a conveyance dated the 21st August 1960 and made between David Henderson and Bryan Tyndal.

2. THE DONEE (with the object of affording to the Donors a full indemnity in respect of any breach of the said restrictive covenants but not further or otherwise) HEREBY COVENANTS with the Donors that the Donee and any person deriving title under her will at all times hereafter perform and observe such covenants and keep the Donors and their estates and effects indemnified against all actions claims demands and liabilities in respect thereof so far as the same affect the property hereby conveyed and are still subsisting and capable of being enforced.

3. The Donor certifies that this deed falls within category L in the Schedule to the Stamp Duty (Exempt Instruments) Regulations 1987.

Signed as a deed and delivered by BERNARD HOLMES and CATHERINE EDEN in the presence of: }	*Bernard Holmes* *Catherine Eden*

Matthew Pleasance
Trainee Solicitor
London

Signed as a deed and delivered by JENNIFER DAWES in the presence of: }	*Jennifer Dawes*

Petra McNulty,
Managing Director
Torridge

16.14.2 Worked example of investigation of title as revealed by epitome of title

Dates	Parties	Notes
	Compulsory registration: December 1990[(1)]	
1960–1987	Danielle Popham	Refers to covenants in 1960 conveyance. Obtain copy of conveyance.[(2)] Seller executes by attorney. Need to see power of attorney.[(3)] BH and CE buy as joint tenants.[(4)] BH and CE give indemnity covenant.[(5)]
1987–1995	Bernard Holmes and Catherine Eden	1987. BH and CE buy with aid of mortgage. Receipted 1990 and so discharged.[(6)]
1995–date	Jennifer Dawes	Deed of gift. Do search against BH and CE to ensure no bankruptcy.[(7)] JD gives indemnity covenant.[(8)]
	Pre-root	
1926–1955	Thomas Terry	
1955–1960	David Henderson	1960 conveyance refers to plan and covenants in 1955 conveyance. Obtain copy.[(9)] Buyer gives indemnity covenant.[(10)] CLCR Search reveals D(ii) against David Henderson (see below).[(11)]
1960–1987	Bryan Tyndal	
	Central Land Charges Searches[(12)]	
~~1926–1955~~	~~Thomas Terry~~	
~~1955–1960~~	~~David Henderson~~	D(ii) registered. 1955 covenants?
1960–1987	Bryan Tyndal	Name misspelt in 1987 search. Re-do search.
1960–1987	~~Danielle Popham~~	
1987–2001	Bernard Holmes and Catherine Eden	Check to 2001 for insolvency due to gift in 1995.
1996–date	Jennifer Dawes	

16.14.3 Commentary on investigation of title

The history of 15, Mill Street is broadly as follows. In 1955, Thomas Terry sold the property to David Henderson and imposed new covenants on the buyer in that conveyance (it is possible that this was a sale of part of a bigger plot of land at this stage). In order to ensure that the negative covenants bound successive owners of 15, Mill Street, Thomas Terry registered them as D(ii) land charges against the buyer's name. David Henderson then owned the property for about five years before selling it in 1960 to Bryan Tyndal. It is not entirely clear who owned the property between 1960 and 1987, but what we do know is that sometime between 1960 and 1987 Bryan Tyndal sold the property and Danielle Popham bought it. We do not know who owned it in the meantime, but that does not matter: this took place pre-root and there is no need to trace an unbroken chain of ownership pre-root.

In 1987, in what should form the good root of title, Danielle Popham sold the property to Bernard Holmes and Catherine Eden. Danielle, Bernard and Catherine form the first links in the chain that needs to be built up from the owners in the good root of title to the seller. Bernard and Catherine bought with the aid of a mortgage to Huntshire Building Society, but this was paid off in 1990 as evidenced by the receipt to be found attached to the mortgage itself.

In 1995, Bernard and Catherine gave 15, Mill Street to Jennifer Dawes, completing the chain of ownership from the seller in the root of title, Danielle Popham, down to present day. The fact that the property was given to Danielle raises issues relating to setting aside gifts in the event of bankruptcy, and it will be necessary to check that neither Bernard nor Catherine became insolvent in the five years following the gift.

16.14.4 Specific points on the worked example

(1) It is necessary to check when registration became compulsory for the area in which the property is situated in case any of the dispositions revealed by the epitome mean that title should have already been registered (see **4.3**). The area became subject to compulsory registration in 1990.

(2)–(5) The 1987 conveyance from Danielle Popham forms the root of title and, subject to what follows, should satisfy the definition of a good root (see **14.5.2**). It is from the seller in this document that an unbroken chain of ownership needs to be traced.

- (2) The 1987 conveyance refers to covenants in a 1960 conveyance, which in turn refers to covenants in a 1955 conveyance, and so this pre-root document needs to be requested (see **15.4.2.1**).
- (3) As revealed by the attestation clause, the 1987 conveyance was executed by the seller under a power of attorney. A copy of this will need to be obtained and checked for the issues raised in **16.7**. If this is unavailable or the execution of the 1987 conveyance is called into question, the conveyance will not be a good root and, further, represents a serious flaw in the title.
- (4) Bernard Holmes and Catherine Eden buy as joint tenants: should one of them die, this is important information affecting how the title would then devolve.
- (5) As buyers, Bernard and Catherine gave an indemnity covenant. This indicates the presence of a chain of indemnities which means the current buyers, David Ecclestone and Nadia Sutcliffe, will be expected to give such a covenant themselves.

(6) Bernard Holmes and Catherine Eden bought with the aid of a mortgage. This was paid off in 1990 and so is not an issue; but any mortgage on the title should be checked to ensure that a receipt is indeed present.

(7) In 1995, Bernard and Catherine give the property to Jennifer Dawes. An unbroken chain from the seller in the good root to the current owner is made out, but care must be taken because of the fact this was a gift. In the event of insolvency within five years of the gift, it can be set aside (see **16.8**). A Central Land Charges Search will need to be done to cover this period (ie, up to 2001) to check that Bernard and Catherine did not become insolvent.

(8) Jennifer gave an indemnity covenant, continuing the chain down to the present day. See item (5) above for the consequences to the current buyers.

Having investigated title from the good root to the present day, it is now necessary to consider the pre-root documents. Although, generally, a buyer is not entitled to see pre-root documents, in certain circumstances this is not the case (see **15.4.2.1**).

(9) The 1960 conveyance (in which David Henderson sells to Bryan Tyndal) has been provided as the good root of title states that there are covenants referred to in it. Unfortunately, these covenants are not actually contained in the 1960 conveyance, merely referred to (as is a plan of 15, Mill Street). So, in turn, the 1955 conveyance (between a Thomas Terry and David Henderson, the seller in 1960), containing both the covenants and the plan, should be obtained.

(10) An indemnity covenant is given. See item (5) above for the consequences of this.

(11) The Central Land Charges search reveals that a D(ii) land charge has been registered against David Henderson. This will almost certainly relate to the covenants that he gave when he bought the property in 1955. Official copies of the entries should be obtained. The consequence is that such covenants will bind the land and, so, if David Ecclestone and Nadia Sutcliffe acquire 15, Mill Street, they will take subject to them.

(12) Central Land Charges searches will need to be done against the names of all owners revealed by the title for the period during which they owned the property. This will include the names of individuals revealed in pre-root documents.

Where it is unclear when an individual acquired or disposed of the property, the dates should deal with this uncertainty by covering all possibilities. Thus, although we know Bryan Tyndal bought the property in 1960, we do not know when he sold it, but it must have been sometime in or before 1987 at the latest as Danielle Popham owned it by then. Hence a search will need to be done against Bryan Tyndal's name from 1960 to 1987. Where the solicitor has had to approximate periods of ownership in this way, he has done so by indicating this in italics.

If a Central Land Charges search has been provided as part of the epitome, this may mean that certain searches do not need to be repeated. As such, the names of Thomas Terry, David Henderson and Danielle Popham have been crossed through as satisfactory searches have been provided in respect of their names. The search against Bryan Tyndal is not acceptable, as the search was done against an incorrect spelling of his name. As you will see, the layout of the solicitor's notes into 'date' and 'parties' columns, replicates the format of the Central Land Charges search to facilitate the process of checking old searches.

The search against Bernard and Catherine will need to be carried out not merely for the periods during which they owned the property, but for a further five years after that, due to the insolvency issues surrounding the gift to Jennifer, and so the search against their names will need to be from 1987 to 2001.

SUMMARY

- A buyer from trustees must pay the purchase price to all the trustees, being at least two in number, or a trust corporation.
- A buyer from personal representatives must check the grant of representation and buy from all proving personal representatives. If title is unregistered, the buyer must ensure that the requirements of s 36 of the Administration of Estates Act 1925 are met.
- A buyer of unregistered land purchasing from assentees must check that a memorandum of the assent has been endorsed on the grant of probate and that there is no memorandum of a prior disposition.
- A buyer from co-owners must pay the purchase monies to all living co-owners.
- On the death of a co-owner, the buyer must see evidence of the death; if the co-owners held as tenants in common, a second trustee must be appointed to sell.

- In unregistered land, a buyer from a sole surviving joint tenant must ensure that the conditions of the Law of Property (Joint Tenants) Act 1964 are satisfied.
- A buyer from a lender must check that the lender's power of sale has arisen.
- A buyer should ensure that all subsisting mortgages are validly discharged.
- A buyer from an attorney must be satisfied that the power of attorney authorises the attorney to sell the property, and that the power is valid and subsisting at the time of the sale.
- A buyer of property previously sold at an undervalue should carry out bankruptcy searches against the individual or company who sold at an undervalue for the period of five years (if an individual) or two years (if a company) from the date of the undervalue transaction.
- A buyer must be advised of restrictive covenants affecting the property, particularly if they are being breached by the current owners or likely to be breached by the buyer.
- It may be possible to insure against losses arising from the successful enforcement of a restrictive covenant. Such insurance is called restrictive covenant indemnity insurance, and its availability will depend upon the risk posed by the covenant in question.
- Alternatively, a problematic restrictive covenant could be dealt with by obtaining the consent of (or seeking a release from) the person with the benefit of the covenant. An application to the Upper Tribunal is a further option.
- Anti-competitive restrictive covenants between businesses are prohibited under the Competition Act 1998.
- A buyer of unregistered land must ensure that all documents within the title have been executed validly. Different formalities for execution exist before and after 31 July 1990. An additional method of execution for companies came into existence on 6 April 2008.
- If investigation of title reveals a problem, the buyer's solicitor should raise a requisition with the seller's solicitor. If the problem cannot be resolved, it may be possible to obtain insurance against the risks associated with the defect. This is called defective title indemnity insurance.

CHAPTER 17

Searches and Enquiries Before Contract

LEARNING OUTCOMES

After reading this chapter you will be able to:

- explain who should make searches and enquiries before contract, and why they are made
- identify what searches and enquiries should be made in a particular transaction
- advise on what matters may be revealed by the search and enquiry results.

17.1 REASONS FOR MAKING SEARCHES

It is the responsibility of the buyer's solicitor to find out as much as possible about the property before allowing their client to enter into a binding contract to buy. At this stage the buyer can freely withdraw from the transaction if they discover something about the property they do not like; if something was discovered after exchange which might lead the buyer to wish to withdraw, they may well not be able to do so without incurring liability for breach of contract. As we shall see (at **18.8.1**), when drafting the contract the seller has only a very limited duty to disclose certain matters affecting the title to the property. The seller does not have to disclose physical defects, hence the need for a structural survey (see **Chapter 12**), or matters such as the authorised use of the property for planning purposes, or whether a new motorway is to be built just over the back hedge. The buyer's solicitor must, therefore, as far as possible, take steps to ensure that the property is suitable for the buyer's purpose.

Failure by the buyer's solicitor to make these searches may give rise to liability in negligence to the buyer client if, as a result, the buyer suffers loss (see *Cooper v Stephenson* (1852) 21 LJQB 292).

It is, of course, not sufficient just to make the searches; the buyer's solicitor must ensure that the buyer is fully advised of the information discovered and its implications for the proposed purchase. Then the buyer will be able to make an informed decision about whether or not to proceed with the purchase, or whether the terms of the draft contract need to be amended in some way.

17.2 WHO SHOULD MAKE THE SEARCHES AND ENQUIRIES?

Since the risk of buying the property subject to undiscovered defects rests with the buyer, it is for the buyer to ensure that all necessary pre-contract searches have been made and that the results are satisfactory.

The *Lenders' Handbook* requires, when acting for a mortgage lender, that all searches be no more than six months old at the date of completion (*Lenders' Handbook*, para 5.4.3), but many conveyancers would regard any search more than three months old as being too out-of-date to be acceptable to a buyer.

17.3 HOW ARE THE SEARCHES MADE?

How the search is made will vary from search to search and from law firm to law firm. However, many searches can now be undertaken electronically, and law firms often subscribe to property data hubs that allow different searches to be undertaken via a single portal (such as the National Land Information Service (NLIS)). The results, regardless of how the search is made, may not be instantaneous and, in the case of searches made with local authorities, can take several weeks.

There is a large amount of free information available online which can provide useful background information on a property. However, it is often only official searches for which a fee is paid that will provide the buyer with an adequate remedy in the event of an error in the result.

17.4 WHICH SEARCHES SHOULD BE MADE?

17.4.1 Recommended on every transaction

The following searches are regarded as 'usual' in every transaction:

(a) search of the local land charges register;
(b) enquiries of the local authority and, if appropriate, additional enquiries;
(c) pre-contract enquiries of the seller;
(d) water and drainage enquiries;
(e) environmental search;
(f) personal inspection.

These searches should be made whether the property being purchased is residential or commercial.

17.4.2 Additional searches

Depending on the circumstances of the transaction, the following search results and reports may need to be obtained:

(a) chancel repair search;
(b) Index Map search;

(c) in unregistered land, a Land Charges Department search against the seller's name (for insolvency) and against other previous owners of the land (to discover incumbrances);

(d) company search;

(e) flood search;

(f) any of the location specific searches which may be applicable in the circumstances (see **17.16**);

(g) survey reports (see **Chapter 12**).

This chapter summarises only the main searches which are relevant to a normal conveyancing transaction. For a detailed explanation of the contents of the various search forms and of the less usual searches, reference should be made to a specialist work such as Silverman and Hewitson, *Conveyancing Searches and Enquiries*, 5th edn.

17.5 LOCAL LAND CHARGES SEARCH

Local land charges are financial charges or restrictions on land that have been imposed by public authorities under statute. Examples of these are shown at **17.5.3**. They will bind a buyer of the land, even though they are unlikely to be apparent from an inspection of the land or from investigation of title. Local authorities are bound by statute to hold a register of local land charges in their area, although this duty is gradually being passed in phases (beginning summer 2018) to Land Registry (see **17.5.5**).

It is essential that a search of the register of local land charges is made in every transaction.

17.5.1 Making the search

How and where to make the search depends on whether the register for the relevant area is maintained by the local authority or Land Registry. This can be checked at https://search-local-land-charges.service.gov.uk and the relevant search made electronically via this link if the local land charges register for the relevant area is held by Land Registry.

Where the local authority still has responsibility for holding the local land charges register, the local land charges search is made by submitting form LLC1 to the relevant local authority for the area in which the property is situated.

A fee is payable for an official search made in either way.

17.5.2 The search result

The search result is given by way of certificate, digitally signed by an officer of the council or Land Registry, which shows whether any, and if so how many, entries are revealed by the search. This certificate is accompanied by a schedule which contains a summary of the relevant entries and, if the search is at Land Registry, a link to source information about the charge. If further detail of the entries is required, it can be obtained either by attending at the council offices to inspect documents, or by obtaining office copies of documents from the council. A fee is payable for copies of documents.

17.5.3 What the search reveals

The local land charges search result will reveal any entries kept under the statutory obligations mentioned above. Some of this information (for example, Article 4 directions) might also be revealed by the local authority when enquiries are raised with it on Form CON29 (see **17.6**). However, even though there is some overlap, both searches should be undertaken to ensure due diligence is complete. Matters revealed by the local land charges result may include the following:

(a) financial charges (eg, for adoption of estate roads; see **42.2.4**);

(b) tree preservation orders (which prevent the protected tree(s) being felled without permission);

(c) smoke control orders (which restrict the use of non-smokeless fuels in domestic fireplaces);
(d) some compulsory purchase orders (which make it lawful for an acquiring authority to take steps to acquire the land without the owner's consent);
(e) planning permissions granted;
(f) any restrictions on permitted development (eg, 'Article 4 Direction': see **7.1.4.3**);
(g) orders revoking or modifying planning permissions;
(h) conservation area designation orders made since 31 August 1974. Orders made prior to that date will be revealed by the replies to the enquiries of the local authority (CON29, Enquiry 3.11; see **17.6**);
(i) listed building status (this can also be checked with English Heritage, particularly if the property may have been recently listed, as the local authority may not yet have made an entry on the local land charges register).

The buyer should be advised of the entries affecting the property and their significance – for example, in the case of a tree preservation order, that the tree in question cannot be felled or lopped without permission. Consideration should also be given as to how the entries will affect the buyer's proposed use for the property. Where a planning permission has been revealed, the seller should be required to produce copies (failing which, the buyer's solicitor can obtain copies from the local authority at extra cost) so that the buyer's solicitor can check that the client's proposed use is the authorised use for planning purposes and that there are no conditions in the planning permission which might interfere with that use (see **Chapter** 7). If financial charges are revealed, the seller should be requested to discharge these prior to completion, or to reduce the purchase price accordingly.

17.5.4 Liability

Where a person suffers as a result of an error in an official certificate of search, compensation may be payable under s 10 of the Local Land Charges Act 1975.

17.5.5 Land Registry to take over the register of local land charges

At the moment, each of the 348 local authorities keeps the local land charges register for its area. The method of data collection, the format and cost of the search and the turnaround time vary from authority to authority. The Infrastructure Act 2015 (ss 34, 35 and Sch 5) provides that Land Registry will take over responsibility as the sole registering authority for local land charges in England and Wales. Land Registry will become the statutory owner of a single digitised local land charges register, to which the local authorities will provide updated entries. Although the relevant sections of the Infrastructure Act 2015 came into force in April 2015, the Act does, however, contain certain transitional provisions enabling Land Registry to take over responsibility for local land charges in stages. Land Registry will publish a notice once it has taken over the local land charges data from a relevant local authority.

17.6 ENQUIRIES OF LOCAL AUTHORITY

17.6.1 Making the search

Enquiries of the local authority should be made in every transaction by submitting Form CON29 to the appropriate unitary, district or London borough council in which the property is situated. The fee for this search varies from authority to authority.

The CON29 enquiries are relevant to every transaction and are covered by the authority's quoted fee. The CON29O enquiries are more specialised in nature, and not all the questions will be relevant in every transaction. It should always be considered which, if any, of the CON29O enquiries should be raised in each transaction, and those enquiries which are raised should then be indicated by placing a tick in the box against the relevant question number at the foot of the front page of the search form. A separate fee is chargeable for each CON29O enquiry raised.

If it is necessary to raise additional enquiries covering matters which are not dealt with by the printed questions, such additional questions should be typed on a separate sheet of paper and submitted in duplicate with the search application. An extra fee is chargeable for each additional question raised. Some local authorities refuse to answer questions other than those on the printed form.

17.6.2 What the searches reveal

A local authority keeps records of a great quantity of information relating to a large number of different matters, extending beyond the limited confines of the local land charges register. It is this enormous quantity of non-statutory information which the search application is designed to reveal. The information revealed by this search will assist the buyer to build up a complete picture of the property they are proposing to buy, and is essential to the decision as to whether or not to proceed with the purchase. Examples of the type of information which might be revealed in the replies to the CON29 enquiries are as follows:

(a) *Enquiry 1* – whether any planning consents or building regulations approvals have been granted, or are pending, or have been refused (in which case, in relation to planning consents, the seller should be required to produce copies (or copies should be purchased from the local authority) so that the buyer' solicitor can check that the client's proposed use is the authorised use for planning purposes and that there are no conditions in the planning permission which might interfere with that use (see **Chapter** 7));

(b) *Enquiry 2.1* – whether the roads serving the property are maintained at the public expense (if not, the buyer will be liable for the costs of maintenance and may be charged for the cost of bringing them up to standard if the local authority decides to adopt them (see **42.2.4**);

(c) *Enquiry 2.2* – whether the property is crossed by a public path or bridleway (in which case the public cannot be denied access across the property and the owner will not be able to build over the path or bridleway unless they can have it diverted using lengthy statutory procedures);

(d) *Enquiries 3.4 and 3.5* – whether there are any new roads and railways proposed within 200 metres of the property, or if there are any proposals for a railway, tramway, light railway or monorail within the local authority boundary (in which case there might be disturbance to the buyer's use and enjoyment of the property). This latter enquiry should assist a buyer in identifying if a property may be affected by proposed schemes such as High Speed Rail and whether additional enquiries should therefore be made (see **17.17.4**);

(e) *Enquiry 3.6* – whether there are any proposals for permanently stopping up roads or footpaths, or putting any other traffic schemes into operation, for example one-way streets, parking restrictions, etc;

(f) *Enquiries 3.8 and 3.9* – whether any proceedings for breach of building regulations have been authorised or whether planning enforcement and stop notices have been served in respect of a breach of planning control and, if so, whether they have been complied with (see **7.1.6**); whether the property is affected by any Article 4 direction restricting permitted development or by a tree preservation order (TPO) (Article 4 directions and TPOs will also be revealed by LLC1 (see **17.5.3**));

(g) *Enquiry 3.12* – whether there are any proposed compulsory purchase orders;

(h) *Enquiry 3.13* – whether any notices have been served in relation to remediation of contaminated land (in which case the buyer may incur liability for clean-up if they proceed with the purchase, see **7.6** and **17.9**);

(i) *Enquiry 3.14* – whether the property is in an area affected by radon gas; and

(j) *Enquiry 3.15* – whether the property is an asset of community value (for example a pub or village shop), meaning that if it is to be sold, community groups must be given a fair chance to prepare a bid to purchase it.

The CON29O enquiries include the following:

(a) *Enquiries 11 to 14* – whether the property is within an area afforded a special designation (eg as an enterprise zone); such areas benefit from government policies (such as tax breaks) to stimulate economic growth;

(b) *Enquiry 18* – whether any environmental and pollution notices have been served (see **17.9**); and

(c) *Enquiry 22* – whether the property, or land abutting it, is registered as common land or village green under the Commons Registration Act 1965 (see **17.17.2**).

Further information on the CON29O enquires can be found in the Practical Law Practice Note, 'Searches: enquiries of the Local Authority'.

As with the LLC1 (see **17.5**), the replies should be considered carefully and the client advised accordingly. The buyer's solicitor must also think about what has not been revealed that they would have expected to see. For example, if no planning permission is revealed, how is the use of the property authorised (see **7.1.4**)? If the property has recently had work done on it, why has no building regulation consent been revealed (see **7.3**)?

The client should also be advised that, generally, both the LLC1 and the CON29 enquiries merely reveal matters directly affecting the land being bought; they will not reveal matters relating to adjoining land which may indirectly affect the property. So if a new supermarket is planned for the field at the rear of the house, this will not be revealed. The main exceptions to this are new roads and railways. Those planned within 200 metres of the property will be revealed. However, a new motorway 300 metres away would not be revealed and might still cause disturbance to the occupiers of the property.

17.6.3 Liability

Subject to the validity of the exclusion clause printed on the front sheet of the search application form, a local authority could be sued in negligence for an erroneous reply to the printed enquiries.

17.6.4 Differences between Forms LLC1 and CON29/O

In practice, the three search applications are often submitted simultaneously to the same authority, with one fee covering all three searches (although this will change as Land Registry gradually assumes responsibility for local land charges searches). It is unusual to do an LLC1 search without CON29/O searches, and for that reason, the three searches are often treated as being indistinguishable and are together referred to as 'the local search'. In fact they are three totally separate and distinct searches having different functions. Their differences are summarised below:

(a) Form LLC1 will only reveal matters which fall within the statutory definition of a local land charge (eg, planning permissions granted); Forms CON29/O cover a wider range of subject matter and are not restricted to land charges (eg, planning applications made, including refusals).

(b) The liability of the issuing authority for errors is different (see **17.5.4** and **17.6.3**). For the CON29/O enquiries, negligence has to be established; this is not necessary for the LLC1 search.

(c) Form LLC1 is restricted to information which is on the register at the moment the search is made; Forms CON29/O may reveal information which has affected the property in the past (eg, history of planning applications made on the property) or will do so in the future (eg, a compulsory purchase order which is pending but which has not yet been registered as a local land charge).

17.6.5 Personal searches

It can take several weeks for local authorities to provide results to the LLC1 and CON29 searches even where the search is submitted electronically. Where speed is essential, it is possible to undertake a personal search using an agent who will (for a fee) attend personally at the offices of the appropriate local authority and make the search personally.

A slightly different approach is taken by organisations such as OneSearch Direct. This particular organisation maintains its own database of the information that would be revealed by a local search, and offers a speedy service at a set fee.

In any case where an official search is not made, it will be necessary to ensure that the personal search is acceptable to any mortgage lender which is advancing money on security of the property. Some mortgage lenders will not accept personal searches, or state that they will do so only at the solicitor's own risk. Where a personal search is to be used, the solicitor must ensure that it has been made by a properly trained person and that the results are backed by adequate insurance. A Search Code has been sponsored by the Council of Property Search Organisations (COPSO) to ensure adequate consumer protection. The Search Code will be monitored and enforced by the independent Property Codes Compliance Board.

17.7 PRE-CONTRACT ENQUIRIES OF THE SELLER

17.7.1 Purpose of the search

Pre-contract enquiries of the seller are the third of the 'usual' searches and are made in every transaction. The purpose of this search is to elicit from the seller information, mainly relating to the physical aspects of the property, which they are not bound by law to disclose (see **18.8.1.4**).

Since the object of the exercise is to obtain information which the seller is not by law bound to disclose, it follows that the seller could refuse to answer the buyer's enquiries altogether. Such a refusal would, however, be unusual and would serve no useful purpose, since it would make the buyer suspicious and would, at best, hinder the speedy progress of the transaction or, at worst, cause the buyer to abort the purchase. The seller, and their solicitor, should also consider whether the Digital Markets, Competition and Consumers Act 2024 applies (see **8.4.9**).

17.7.2 Residential property

In cases where the Protocol is used, the seller's solicitor should ask their client to complete a Property Information Form (TA06) or the Leasehold Information Form (TA07) for leasehold properties. The Law Society also publishes a Leasehold Property Enquiries Form (LPE1), a Leasehold Consumer Summary Form (LPE2) summarising the key financial obligations, and a Freehold Management Enquiries Form (FME1) for freehold properties that have services in common with other properties. These forms contain various questions about the property, phrased in layman's language so that the average client should be able to complete these forms with minimal help from their solicitor. The TA7 and LPE1 forms may provide information about the height of the building and whether the building is a 'relevant building' for the purposes of the Building Safety Act 2022 (see **17.18.5**).

Whilst the forms are designed to be completed with minimal input from a solicitor, The Law Society does recommend that the seller's solicitor should go through the answers with the client to ensure that the questions have been answered correctly.

An erroneous or misleading reply to these questions could give rise to liability in misrepresentation. So, for example, in *Doe v Skegg* [2006] PLSCS 213, a seller who incorrectly answered the question regarding disputes was held liable for fraudulent misrepresentation when sued by the buyer for damages of £150,000. See also **17.7.6**.

The form is then submitted to the buyer's solicitor as part of the pre-contract package.

17.7.3 Commercial property

Law stationers produce a standard form of pre-contract enquiries and many solicitors have their own version. In order to try to bring some uniformity to preliminary enquiries, the Commercial Property Standard Enquiries (CPSE) have been drafted for use in commercial transactions. The CPSE have been endorsed by the British Property Federation. Supplementary enquiries are available for use where the property is tenanted or is leasehold.

The CPSE Form 1, which should be used in every transaction, includes questions on the following areas:

(a) boundaries;
(b) adverse rights;
(c) access to the property;
(d) fire safety;
(e) compliance with planning and building regulations;
(f) the VAT status of the transaction.

Other CPSE forms are available for use in addition to CPSE 1:

(a) CPSE 2 for use on the sale of property subject to tenancies;
(b) CPSE 3 for use on the grant of a new lease;
(c) CPSE 4 for use on the assignment of a lease.

These forms are updated regularly. The latest versions (together with guidance notes) may be obtained at <http://property.practicallaw.com>.

CPSE 7 is a shorter alternative to CPSE 1 and may be preferred to CPSE 1 in the following situations:

(a) on the grant or assignment of a commercial property lease with vacant possession;
(b) on a refinancing, where full replies to CPSE 1 were recently given to the buyer or borrower;
(c) on a straightforward share purchase where, in addition to replies to enquiries, the buyer is also relying on warranties;
(d) on auction sales.

17.7.4 Additional enquiries

Where there are areas of enquiry which are not covered by the questions on the standard forms, but which are relevant to the buyer's situation, these should be raised as separate additional enquiries. Additional enquiries may extend to queries arising out of the provisions of the draft contract, from due diligence or from replies given to the standard form enquiries.

They may also arise from matters revealed by the survey (eg a survey that revealed combustible cladding would necessitate further enquiries about the removal of such cladding, costs involved and liability for such costs).

17.7.5 Liability

An incorrect reply to pre-contract enquiries may lead to liability in misrepresentation. Any exclusion clause purporting to avoid or minimise liability for misrepresentation will be subject to the reasonableness test in s 11 of the Unfair Contract Terms Act 1977, and cannot therefore be guaranteed to afford protection to the seller (see SC 7.1.1(b) (SCPC 10.1) and *Walker v Boyle* [1982] 1 All ER 634). Some forms of pre-contract enquiries also contain an exclusion clause.

Where the erroneous reply stems from the seller's solicitor's negligence, they will be liable to their own client (*CEMP Properties (UK) Ltd v Dentsply Research and Development Corporation (No 1)* (1989) 2 EGLR 192), but in this respect they do not owe a duty directly to the buyer (see *Gran Gelato v Richcliffe (Group)* [1992] 1 All ER 865).

It is common for the seller's solicitor to answer enquiries as vaguely as possible with the intent of avoiding any possible liability for misrepresentation. So answers such as 'Not so far as we are aware' or 'Not so far as the seller is aware' are common. However, it should be noted that the effect of *William Sindall plc v Cambridgeshire CC* [1994] 1 WLR 1016 is that such a reply indicates not only that the seller has no actual knowledge of a matter, but also that they have undertaken all reasonable enquiries that a prudent conveyancer should have made.

Some conveyancers try to avoid the need to make such enquiries by inserting a condition in the contract to the effect that such replies are not to be taken to mean that extra enquiries have been made. The effectiveness of such a condition is unclear.

17.8 WATER AND DRAINAGE ENQUIRIES

Information about water and sewerage matters should be made using the application form published by the water service company serving the property. These enquiries should be made in every transaction. The enquiry will reveal (amongst other things) the following:

(a) whether the property has foul water drainage to the public sewer;

(b) whether the property has surface water drainage to the public sewer;

(c) whether there is a water main, public sewer, disposal main or lateral drain within the boundaries of the property; and

(d) whether the property is connected to the public water supply.

If the property does not drain into a public sewer, the buyer will be liable for the costs of maintaining the drains and sewers, and may be liable for the costs of bringing them up to adoption standard if the water authority decides to adopt them (see **42.2.5**).

If there is a public sewer on the property, the water company's consent will be needed to any development over or within the vicinity of the sewer. In October 2011 the water companies took over ownership of and responsibility for existing private sewers serving two or more properties and all new sewers being built in England and Wales. The transfer means that a higher proportion of developments will require water company consent. Newly-adopted public sewers will be added to the water companies' records as the companies become aware of them, but these records are likely to be incomplete for some time.

Buyers should be made aware that water companies have statutory rights of access to properties on which they hold assets.

17.9 ENVIRONMENTAL SEARCHES AND SURVEYS

People have become much more aware of environmental issues in recent years, and these are matters which ought to be considered on a purchase of land. One obvious problem is the possibility of the land being contaminated – see **7.6**. Apart from the potential expense of clean-up liabilities, the dangers posed by the contamination to the owners and occupiers must also be taken into account. The advice to be given to clients is discussed at **7.6**.

Other environmental matters might also affect the potential buyer's decision whether or not to proceed. Is the property near a landfill site, or are there factories in the area discharging hazardous substances? Because of issues such as these, it is now regarded as best practice to obtain an environmental report in all property transactions.

Until recently, it was not thought necessary to make enquiries with regard to potential contamination when buying residential property. However, after several cases where land on which new houses had been built was found to be contaminated, the need to make enquiries about environmental matters should be considered in every case, especially, say, where the property is on former (or near current) industrial land.

In commercial transactions, and particularly when contemplating the purchase of a previously undeveloped ('green field') or recycled ('brown field') site for development, it will always be necessary to undertake certain checks and enquiries to ensure that the land which is being acquired is clean or, if not, that the steps needed to clean up the land are clearly understood by the client.

17.9.1 Environmental searches

The first step is to assess risk. There are a number of professional search providers which offer packaged environmental reports, collating information from a variety of sources, priced on a tariff relating to the value and nature of the property. A specialist environmental consultant can be employed to prepare a more tailored and detailed report. As such reports (whether packaged or more tailored) draw on documentary evidence, they are often referred to as being 'desk-top' environmental searches.

17.9.2 Environmental surveys

If an environmental search report reveals that the property is at risk of contamination, the client will need to decide whether they wish to instruct environmental consultants to undertake an environmental survey of the land. If an environmental survey is undertaken, samples of the soil will be taken on a systematic basis using established techniques, and will then be tested in order to discover the extent and nature of the contamination. An environmental survey should establish if the site is contaminated and, if so, to what extent.

17.10 CHANCEL REPAIR SEARCHES

For historical reasons, certain properties in certain parishes could be under an obligation to pay the cost of repairing the chancel of the parish church. The costs associated with a chancel repair liability can be considerable (£186,000 in the case of *Aston Cantlow and Wilmcote with Billesley Parochial Church Council v Wallbank* [2003] UKHL 37) and the liability may not be apparent from the title deeds or known to the seller. Parishes where such liability might occur are those with a medieval church with a vicar, although a property may be liable even if some distance from the church. The obligation used to override both first registration and registered dispositions, but this overriding status ended on 13 October 2013. The consequences of this are as follows:

17.10.1 Registered land

Chancel repair liabilities can still be protected by notice in the registers of title of the burdened property at any time until a transfer for value occurs on or after 13 October 2013. Once a transfer for value of the burdened property occurs on or after 13 October 2013, the liability will not bind any subsequent buyer unless already protected by notice.

If no such transfer has occurred, then it would be advisable for the buyer's solicitor to carry out a screening search to ascertain whether the property is within a liable parish. This is because there is a risk of being bound by a chancel repair liability protected by a notice entered after the buyer has completed their title investigation but prior to registration of the transfer. If the screening search result shows that the property is within a liable parish, insurance can be obtained against the potential liability. It is possible to make a personal search at the National Archives in Kew to ascertain whether a particular property is in fact liable for chancel repairs, but insurance will normally be the cheaper and quicker option. In addition, if a personal search did find that a property had such a liability, it would not then be possible to obtain insurance against the liability and the property would be very difficult to sell.

If a transfer for value of the property on or after 13 October 2013 has occurred, the buyer should not be bound by a chancel repair liability unless a notice has already been entered on the registers of title. It might be logical to conclude, therefore, that no screening search is necessary in such circumstances. Practitioners should be aware, however, that Land Registry will continue to register Unilateral Notices to protect chancel repair liabilities, regardless of whether a transfer for value after 13 October 2013 has been made. This is because Land Registry does not assess the legitimacy of the Unilateral Notice application; it is for the registered proprietor to challenge the Unilateral Notice if it considers it does not protect a valid interest. There will inevitably be legal costs involved in challenging the Unilateral Notice, although if the challenge is successful, it may be possible to recover these from the party who lodged the Unilateral Notice. Nonetheless, some commentators have suggested that insurance against the costs associated with chancel repair liability may assist in meeting these costs and this may be a reason to continue with the screening test (and if appropriate its associated insurance). Of course, this is also a new and untested area of law and, for this reason also, some practitioners may wish to continue with a screening search for the foreseeable future.

17.10.2 Unregistered land

A buyer (for value) will only be bound if the chancel repair liability is referred to in the title deeds or protected by a caution against first registration lodged prior to first registration. If a caution against first registration is lodged and the chancel repair liability proved to the satisfaction of Land Registry, a notice of the liability will be entered on the registers of title on first registration. A buyer can, of course, undertake an Index Map Search prior to completion to check for cautions against first registration (see **17.3.1**). However, there is a theoretical risk that a caution could be lodged after completion but prior to first registration (in the so-called 'registration gap'). The only way to protect against such a risk would be to continue with the screening search when purchasing unregistered land.

17.10.3 Transfers without consideration made on or after 13 October 2013

Those acquiring property without giving consideration (for example by way of a gift) will retain any chancel repair liability. Such liability will remain until a sale (for value) to a third party occurs on or after 13 October 2013. This is so even if the obligation has not been protected as detailed at **17.10.1** and **17.10.2**.

17.10.4 Summary – when should a screening search be carried out?

Unregistered land	Registered land
Do screening search	If the previous transfer for value occurred on or after 13 October 2013 – no screening search may be necessary (but check your firm's policy on this issue) If the previous transfer for value occurred prior to 13 October 2013 – do screening search

17.11 CENTRAL LAND CHARGES DEPARTMENT SEARCH – UNREGISTERED LAND

A Land Charges Department search should be made in all cases when dealing with unregistered land. Although this search is sometimes undertaken at a later stage of the transaction, it is sensible to make the search prior to exchange to obtain an early warning of potential problems (eg the seller's bankruptcy, Family Law Act 1996 rights, estate contracts). The search is made by submitting Form K15 to the Land Charges Department at Plymouth, or it can be made electronically via Land Registry's business portal. Fees can be paid by credit account, provided the applicant's solicitor's key number is stated on the application form.

17.11.1 Form of the register

The register comprises a list of the names of estate owners of land, with details of charges registered against those names. The search is therefore made not against the land itself but against the names of the estate owners. A fee is payable for each name searched. The search must be made against the names of all the estate owners whose names appear on the abstract or epitome of title supplied by the seller, including those who are merely referred to in the bodies of deeds (as opposed to being parties to the deeds themselves) or in schedules attached to deeds which form part of the title. There is no need to repeat searches where a proper search certificate made against previous estate owners has been supplied with the abstract of title.

The register is maintained on a computer which will search only against the exact version of the name as shown on the application form. It is therefore important to check that the name inserted on the application form is identical to that shown on the title deeds and that, if any variations of that name appear in the deeds, for example if Samuel Smith is variously referred to as 'Sam Smith', 'Samuel James Smith' and 'Samuel Smyth', all the given variations of the name are separately entered on the search form and a separate fee paid in respect of each. Guidance on filling in the application form, together with a list of accepted abbreviations and variations which the computer will search against, is given in Land Registry Practice Guide 63.

17.11.2 Period to be searched against

It is generally only possible for an effective entry to be made against a name in relation to that person's (or company's) period of estate ownership of the land in question. It is therefore usually only necessary to search against a name for the period during which the estate owner owned the land and for the period between the death and the date of the appointment of personal representatives. For the purposes of the search form, periods of ownership must be stated in whole years and can be ascertained by looking at the abstract or epitome of title supplied by the seller.

If the estate owner's period of ownership is not known, as will be the case when searching against the name of the person who was the seller in the document forming the root of title, the search is, in practice, made from 1926 (the year when the register was opened). Where there is a voluntary disposition in the title which is, at the date of the contract, less than five years old, it is necessary to search against the donor's name for a period up to and including the current year to ensure that no bankruptcy of the donor occurred during this period. The bankruptcy of the donor during this period could lead to the disposition being set aside by the trustee in bankruptcy (see **16.8**).

17.11.3 Description of the land

Unless a description of the land is inserted on the search application form, the computer will produce entries relating to every person of the given name in the whole of the county or counties specified. In order to avoid having to read through and then reject multiple search entries revealed by the certificate of search, a brief description of the land, sufficient to identify it clearly, should be included on the application form. Although the intention of describing the land is to curtail the number of irrelevant entries produced by the computer, care should be taken in supplying the description, because an inaccurate description of the land may result in a relevant entry not being revealed by the search.

Particular care is needed when the abstract shows that the land formerly was part of a larger piece of land (eg, when buying one plot on a building estate where the estate is being built on land which was previously part of a farm), because the land may previously have been known by a description other than its current postal address. If the search is limited to the present postal address, entries registered against its former description will not be revealed by the search. In such a case, both the present address and former description of the land should be entered on the search application form.

There is a possibility that because of local government reorganisation the land was formerly situated in a different administrative county from that in which it is now. For the reasons given above, both the present and former county must be included in the description of the land given on the search application form. Where the postal address of the property differs from its actual address (eg, the village of Rogate is in the administrative county of West Sussex, but its postal address is Hampshire), the search must be made against the actual address of the property, not its postal address.

17.11.4 Pre-root estate owners

The buyer does not need to search against estate owners who held the land prior to the date of the root of title supplied to them, except in so far as the names of such persons have been revealed to them in documents supplied by the seller.

17.11.5 Official certificate of search

An official certificate of search is conclusive in favour of the searcher, provided that the search has been correctly made, ie it extends over the whole period of the title supplied by the seller and has been made:

(a) against the correct names of the estate owners for this period;
(b) against the correct county or former county; and
(c) for the correct periods of ownership of each estate owner.

In order to ensure that the buyer gains the protection afforded by the search and the accompanying priority period, it is vital to check that the search application form is accurately completed.

17.11.6 Search certificates supplied by the seller

Where the seller provides previous search certificates as part of the evidence of title, it is not necessary to repeat a search against a former estate owner provided that the search certificate supplied by the seller reveals no adverse entries and:

(a) was made against the correct name of the estate owner as shown in the deeds;
(b) was made for the correct period of ownership as shown in the title deeds;
(c) was made against the correct county or former county of the property as shown in the deeds; and
(d) the next disposition in the chain of title took place within the priority period afforded by the search certificate.

If any of the conditions outlined above is not met, a further search against the previous estate owner must be made.

17.12 BANKRUPTCY SEARCH

If the buyer's solicitor is also acting for the lender, it will be necessary at some time, whether the land is registered or unregistered, to make a bankruptcy search against the buyer/borrower to ensure that there are no bankruptcy orders or proceedings affecting them. If the result of the search reveals an entry against the name of the borrower, the lender will not advance the money unless the solicitor is prepared to certify that the entries do not relate to the actual borrower but to someone else with the same name.

The search is made by submitting either Form K15 (as part of a full search for unregistered land – see **17.11.1**) or Form K16 (bankruptcy only search for registered land) to the Land Charges Department at Plymouth, or it can be made electronically via Land Registry's business portal. It is usual to make this search immediately before completion (see **28.7**); however, if any entries are revealed, completion will inevitably be delayed due to the time necessary to resolve the matter. Some conveyancers therefore recommend making this search prior to exchange, when there is more time to resolve any problems. If it were to be made at this stage, however, it would still be necessary to repeat the search prior to completion to guard against any last-minute entries.

17.13 COMPANY SEARCH

17.13.1 Who should be searched against?

17.13.1.1 Unregistered land

Company searches should be carried out against any companies revealed as estate owners within the epitome of title.

17.13.1.2 Registered land

A company search should be carried out against a corporate seller.

17.13.1.3 If acting for the lender

If acting for a lender where the borrower is a company, a company search will be needed against the borrower.

17.13.2 When should the search be undertaken?

There is no priority period offered by a company search. It is a snapshot of the company at the point at which the search is undertaken. For this reason, it will be prudent to undertake the search both before exchange (to identify any issues before the buyer is contractually bound) and again before completion (to ensure the results are as up to date as possible).

17.13.3 What is revealed by the search?

There is no standard company search and so the solicitor must decide which documents lodged at Companies House should be inspected. The solicitor can obtain copies of these documents directly from Companies House or instruct a specialist firm to obtain these and produce a company search report for the solicitor. In either case there will be a fee payable. The following matters should be checked:

17.13.3.1 Solvency

The solicitor should check that the company exists and is not in administration, receivership or liquidation and has not been wound up. If a selling company is subject to insolvency proceedings then the buyer should deal with the administrator, receiver or liquidator and not the seller.

17.13.3.2 Undisclosed charges

The solicitor should check the register of charges for the selling company maintained at Companies House. This will contain details of all charges created by the company and will allow the buyer's solicitor to check whether a corporate seller has created any fixed or floating charges over the property that it has failed to disclose when deducing title.

A floating charge is a charge that companies (as opposed to human individuals) can create and is analogous to a mortgage. The charge 'floats' over all the assets of the company. The company is free to deal with its assets without the lender's consent, so it can sell some (free of the charge) to a third party and buy others (which become subject to the charge as soon as they are acquired by the company). The charge ceases to float and instead fixes and attaches to particular assets of the company (which then cannot be dealt with without the lender's consent) only when it crystallises. Crystallisation occurs when a specified event happens which makes the sum due under the mortgage payable (eg, default in payment of an instalment).

In registered land, neither fixed nor floating charges will bind the buyer unless protected by registration in the charges register of the property at Land Registry. No action is therefore needed in relation to charges registered at Companies House, but not protected by registration at Land Registry. These will not bind the buyer. The only exception to this is where the transaction involves the sale of chattels. If there are chattels included in the sale, and any charge purports to attach to those chattels, it will need to be dealt with. A fixed charge affecting chattels would need to be discharged on or before completion (see **30.7.1.10**). As a floating charge will not attach to chattels unless it crystallises, a certificate of non-crystallisation (given in a letter signed by the lender) should be obtained where a floating charge is revealed.

In unregistered land, any fixed charge affecting the property being sold should be discharged on or before completion. Likewise, if a floating charge is revealed, a certificate of non-crystallisation should be obtained.

17.14 FLOOD SEARCH

The Environment Agency estimates that one in six homes in England (approximately 5.2 million properties) are at risk from flooding. Flooding does not just occur in properties that are near to rivers or coasts. The Environment Agency estimates that 2.8 million homes are at risk of surface water flooding, which arises where heavy rainfall overwhelms the drainage capacity in an area. Flooding can also occur when sewers become blocked ('sewer flooding') or when underground water levels rise above surface level ('groundwater flooding').

In recent years, the number of flooding incidents in the UK has risen. Given the potential impact on property values and saleability, on 23 May 2013 The Law Society issued a practice note on flood risk. The advice given includes the following:

(a) In all conveyancing transactions, the solicitor should mention the issue of flood risk to their client and, if appropriate, make further investigations.
(b) A solicitor should consider advising a buyer to do the following before exchange of contracts:
    (i) Establish whether insurance for flood risk is available and, if so, on what terms and at what cost. A Government-backed scheme known as 'Flood Re' ensures that flood cover is provided for most residential properties. Flood Re provides flood insurance for homes over a 25-year period from April 2016, but premiums will be adjusted as time passes, so that by the end of the 25-year period, the premium will actually reflect the flood risk of a property. Certain property (such as commercial property, buy to let properties, residential property built since 1 January 2009 and blocks of flats) is not covered by the scheme and, where such excluded property is at risk of flooding, insurers may charge high premiums or excesses, or decline insurance entirely.
    (ii) Discuss the level of flood risk with the building surveyor or, if necessary, a flood risk consultant.

If, after discussion with the client, further investigations are deemed appropriate (or if they are required by a lender), the following sources of information can be considered:

17.14.1 Environment Agency and Land Registry

A free screening search for river, coastal, surface water and reservoir flooding can be made using the property's postcode on the flood maps on the Agency's website at <www.environment-agency.gov.uk>. This will show the extent of possible flooding and give a flood risk assessment for the area. Land Registry also provides a 'Flood Risk Indicator Online', which may be found in the 'Find-a-Property' section of the Land Registry website. This is a search available to private individuals to enable them to assess the risk to registered titles arising from coastal and river flooding.

It should be noted that The Law Society's practice note states that neither the Environment Agency flood maps nor the Flood Risk Indicator should be used as the sole means of assessing flood risk: neither is property-specific and neither shows groundwater flooding.

17.14.2 Commercial search providers

Given the damage caused by flooding, the possibility of a commercial flood search should be discussed with the client on every transaction, but specific instructions should be obtained before undertaking it due to the cost.

Such searches vary in terms of their cost and the range of information provided. It is possible, however, to carry out commercial searches that will provide surface water and groundwater flooding information. The Law Society advises that the solicitor should consider the terms and conditions on which the search or report is given, including any limits on the liability of the provider. When reporting on the results of any flood search, the solicitor should make it clear that they are not qualified to advise on technical matters regarding the search results. Any such question should be raised with the client's surveyor or the consultant who produced the report.

17.14.3 Enquiries of the seller

Both the PIF (see **17.7.2**) and the CPSE (see **17.7.3**) ask for details of flooding that has affected the property. The Law Society states that the reply to these enquires should not be the only source of information relied upon in relation to flooding risk.

17.14.4 Specialist surveys

Depending on the risk identified from other sources, a client may consider commissioning a specialist flood risk survey. This can provide information on steps to mitigate flood damage, as well as advice on flood risk. It may be that any costs associated with such steps can be deducted from the purchase price, but this is clearly a matter for negotiation between buyer and seller. As with commercial search results, any questions from the buyer as to technical matters should be addressed to the surveyor producing the report.

17.15 INDEX MAP SEARCH

17.15.1 What is an Index Map Search?

Land Registry keeps a computerised map based on the Ordnance Survey map. This computerised map provides an index of the land in every registered title and pending application for first registration.

An official search of the index map, using form SIM, will show whether or not the property is registered, subject to a pending first registration application or subject to a caution against first registration (see **4.3.8**). If the land is registered, it will reveal all relevant title numbers.

17.15.2 When should it be done?

This search should always be done if the land being sold appears to be unregistered.

In theory there is no need to carry out a SIM where the land is registered, since it will simply confirm what you already know. However, it is considered good practice to do one in the following circumstances:

(a) If purchasing a site comprising more than one registered title. This is to ensure that no part of the site falls under a title number not deduced to you.

(b) If mines and minerals are excluded from the registration of the title. A SIM will reveal if those mines and minerals are registered under a separate title, enabling identification of the owner of those mines and minerals and any associated rights.

17.16 INSPECTION OF THE PROPERTY

Inspection of the property should be undertaken by the client in all cases. There is no obligation on the solicitor, either in law or conduct, to carry out an inspection in every transaction, but they should do so if their client so requests, or if matters reported by the client's inspection give rise to suspicion on the part of the buyer's solicitor. The client should be advised to look for (and to report their existence to their solicitor) any of the following matters:

(a) a discrepancy or uncertainty over the identity of or boundaries to the property;
(b) evidence of easements which adversely affect the property (eg, evidence suggesting that a right of way over the property exists);
(c) the existence and status of non-owning occupiers;
(d) a discrepancy between the fixtures and fittings which the client understood to belong to the property and those actually existing.

17.17 LOCATION SPECIFIC SEARCHES

The buyer's solicitor should be aware of any features of the property or its location which indicate that one of the less usual searches may be appropriate to the situation. The buyer will usually be bound by any incumbrances which exist over the property, whether or not a search was made. A solicitor who fails to carry out a relevant search in circumstances where they should have done so may be liable in negligence to their client (see *G & K Ladenbau (UK) Ltd v Crawley and De Reya* [1978] 1 All ER 682).

Examples of some of the location specific searches appear below.

17.17.1 Mining searches

A coal mining search should be carried out if the property is located in a coal mining claim area. Information as to whether the property is situated in an area where a coal mining search is recommended is available on the Mining Remediation Authority's website at <www.groundstability.com>.

An application for a search should be made on Form CON29M (2018), accompanied by the fee and a large-scale plan of the property, to the Mining Remediation Authority. The result of the search will reveal whether the property is in an area where mining has taken place in the past or is likely to take place in the future, the existence of underground workings which may cause problems with subsidence, and whether compensation for subsidence damage has been paid in the past or any claim is pending. Although this search covers only coal mining activities, similar search schemes are available in areas potentially affected by other types of mining. These include:

(a) tin in Cornwall, Devon and Somerset;
(b) clay in Cornwall, Devon and Dorset;
(c) limestone in Dudley, Sandwell, Telford, Walsall and Wolverhampton;
(d) brine and salt in Cheshire.

17.17.2 Common land; town and village greens

Councils in England and Wales are required to maintain a register of common land and a register of town and village greens (TVGs) under the Commons Registration Act 2006. Land so registered may not be developed and may be be subject to third party rights (such as rights of grazing or rights to use the land for recreational purposes). In recent years a number of applications have been made to register land as a TVG (including applications relating to a beach and a skate park), in order to prevent development of them. Although restrictions on applying for TVG status have been introduced by the Growth and Infrastructure Act 2013 to limit such applications, it is clearly important to be aware if the property to be purchased is on the registers.

A search can be made of the registers of common land and TVGs by ticking the box for Enquiry 22 in the Enquiries of the Local Authority Form CON29O (see **17.6**).

This enquiry should be made in any case where the property to be purchased abuts a village green or common land, or where a verge strip, not owned by the property, separates the property from the public highway. It should also be made where the land being purchased is undeveloped or newly developed or where access to the land is across undeveloped land.

It should be noted some land does not appear on the registers maintained by councils, even though it is widely recognised as common land today. Exempted areas include the New Forest and Epping Forest as well as a number of urban recreational commons.

17.17.3 Land adjoining rivers, streams or canals

If the property is next to a river or canal, a search can be made with the Canal & River Trust to check on, for example, responsibility for maintenance of the waterway, its banks and (in the case of canals) associated towpath. The search will also reveal if any contribution to flood defence structures is required and any relevant proposals relating to the waterway or non-statutory rights benefiting the waterway.

17.17.4 Railways

It should be obvious from a personal inspection of the property whether it adjoins an existing railway. Replies to CON29 enquiries (see **17.6.1**) should confirm whether the property might be affected by a proposed rail scheme. In either case, additional enquiries should be made.

In the case of properties adjoining a railway line, it used to be possible in the days of (nationalised) British Rail to make enquiries as to whether there were any obligations on the property owner to maintain the boundary walls and fences separating the land from the railway. However, nowadays Network Rail will no longer answer such enquiries. It is therefore necessary to raise such issues with the seller as additional pre-contract enquiries. The buyer should also be advised that Network Rail has a statutory right of access onto the adjoining land in order to undertake repairs to railway property. Network Rail should be contacted before carrying out any building work next to the railway line, as there may be restrictions on this. Searches are available in relation to other existing and proposed railway undertakings, eg Docklands Light Railway, London Underground, Crossrail and the Newcastle Metro. Crossrail and HS2 (high speed rail) searches can also be made through NLIS (see **17.3**).

17.17.5 Highways search

The replies to Enquiries 2, 3.4 and 3.6 of Form CON29 (see **17.6.2**) will provide certain information about whether the roads adjoining the property are publicly adopted or subject to any road or traffic schemes. However, the information provided may not be very detailed (particularly as to pavements and verges), so it may be necessary to make specific enquiries of the relevant highway authority to confirm the exact boundaries of the publicly maintainable highways abutting or crossing the property. This will be particularly relevant where the property is to be redeveloped in a different configuration, or where there appears to be land, such as a grass verge, between the title boundary of the property and the public road. Such land may be in third party ownership, and if it is not publicly adopted, it may become a 'ransom strip' if access over it is needed for the use of the property.

There is no set form for this search; specific enquires are usually made by letter, enclosing a detailed plan of the property with a request for the highways authority to mark onto it the boundaries of the publicly maintainable highways (including verges) in and about the property.

17.18 RESULTS OF SEARCHES

On receiving the results of searches, the buyer's solicitor must check the answers given to ensure that the information supplied complies with their client's instructions. Any reply which is unclear must be pursued with the appropriate authority (or seller in the case of pre-contract enquiries) until a satisfactory explanation is received. Failure to pursue an unsatisfactory reply which results in loss being suffered by the client, may result in the buyer's solicitor being liable to their own client in negligence (*Computastaff Ltd v Ingledew Brown Bennison & Garrett* (1983) 7 ILR 156).

Any reply which is not satisfactory must be referred to the client for further instructions. The contract should not be finally approved by the buyer's solicitor or exchanged until satisfactory results of all searches have been received. A summary of the information received from the searches should be communicated to the buyer by their solicitor. The individual searches should not be looked at in isolation; rather, the information from each should be correlated and considered in the light of the title investigation, the draft contract and any particular circumstances of the case. The following scenarios are commonly encountered and need special care.

17.18.1 Property built within last 10 years

(a) For residential properties, check that you have copies of NHBC documentation. This provides insurance cover against many structural defects (see **42.2.3**). Revealed by pre-contract enquiries of the seller.

(b) Check that there is planning permission and you have copies (see **7.1.6** for enforcement if planning controls are breached). Revealed by pre-contract enquiries of the seller, LLC1 and CON29.

(c) Check that any conditions attached to the planning permission have been complied with. Enforcement revealed by CON29 (see **7.1.6**).

(d) Check that building regulation consent was obtained and a copy provided (see **42.2.2**). Revealed by pre-contract enquiries of the seller; proceedings for breach revealed by CON29.

(e) Check that the roads and drains are adopted, or that agreements and bonds exist (see **17.6.2**). Copies should be provided. Revealed by CON29DW.

(f) If the roads, etc are not adopted, check that adequate easements exist for access. Check title documents.

If no agreements and bonds exist, consider whether a retention should be made from the purchase price until the roads and services are adopted.

17.18.2 Access to property or services to property across neighbouring land

(a) Revealed by pre-contract enquiries of the seller. Check title to ensure that there are easements for access, etc. If no express easements exist, will they be implied or presumed by long user? Can seller get a deed of grant now from neighbouring owners?

(b) What are the arrangements for maintenance and repair? Are there express arrangements in title documents, or are there any informal arrangements?

Unless the property has been built recently, adoption by the local authority will be unlikely.

17.18.3 Occupiers

(a) Revealed by pre-contract enquiries of the seller.

(b) Do the occupiers claim an equitable interest or a tenancy?

(c) If so, ensure that they will sign agreement to give up rights/surrender the tenancy and leave on completion (see **18.8.4**).

(d) In the case of a non-owning spouse, have rights of occupation under the Family Law Act 1996 been registered? Whether or not such rights have already been registered, the spouse should be required to agree to leave and remove any registration prior to completion (see **18.8.4**).

17.18.4 Building works or change of use carried out by previous owner

(a) Are there any guarantees for building works? (See pre-contract enquiries of the seller.)

(b) Was planning permission required/obtained? (See **7.1**.)

(c) Have copies of any required planning permission been obtained?

(d) Have any conditions attached to planning permission been complied with?

(e) Have any covenants on the title been complied with, for example consents for work or change of use?

(f) If consent was required but not obtained, can it be obtained now, or insurance cover obtained?

(g) Was building regulation consent obtained for building works? (See **7.3**.)

(h) Did the survey cover any building works to check that they were carried out to a proper standard?

17.18.5 High rise residential buildings

The Building Safety Act 2022 (BSA 2022) (see **38.4.1**) was enacted following the 2017 Grenfell Tower fire, where faulty external cladding contributed to a catastrophic fire resulting in many fatalities. The BSA 2022 is a very complex piece of legislation, intended to improve the safety of high rise residential buildings. Unfortunately, however, there is uncertainty about its application and the implications for owners of flats within high rise developments. As a result, some solicitors have been reluctant to act on the purchase of properties that may be affected by the BSA 2022, due to concern over their liability and whether their professional indemnity insurance will cover them in relation to such transactions. The Law Society has issued a guidance note entitled 'The Building Safety Act 2022: a guide for conveyancers'. This should be reviewed by any conveyancer acting in a transaction involving a high rise residential building.

17.19 IMPUTED KNOWLEDGE

Knowledge acquired by the solicitor while acting on their client's behalf is imputed to the client (regardless of whether the client had actual knowledge of the matter in question). Thus, a seller may be liable in misrepresentation to the buyer for a statement made by their solicitor without their knowledge. In such a case, indemnity against the seller's liability could be sought from the seller's solicitors (see *Strover v Harrington* [1988] Ch 390).

17.20 RELYING ON SEARCHES MADE BY A THIRD PARTY

The results of searches are not personal to the searcher, thus their benefit may be transferred to a third party. Where the seller makes pre-contract searches and passes their results to the buyer, the buyer and their lender may take the benefit of the results. The buyer must check that the seller has undertaken all the searches and enquiries which the buyer deems necessary for the transaction in hand, and if not, they must carry out the additional searches themselves. If the buyer is not satisfied with the results of the searches made by the seller because, for example, they consider that insufficient questions have been raised, they should repeat the searches. Similarly, a lender may rely on searches made by a buyer's solicitor.

17.21 CONCLUSION

The results of these searches and enquiries provide valuable information about the property being bought, and thus about the viability of the transaction and the buyer's proposals for it. The search results should be studied carefully, and the buyer kept fully informed about them and their implications. The buyer's solicitor should not finally approve the contract and the buyer should not be allowed to exchange contracts until all outstanding queries have been resolved. The solicitor should also remember that if they are acting for the buyer's lender as well as the buyer, they should keep the lender client informed about any matters affecting the value or saleability of the property, or which otherwise might affect the lender's decision to lend on the security of the property.

SUMMARY

- The buyer's solicitor must carry out appropriate searches and enquiries to find out as much as possible about the property before the client contracts to buy it.
- On every transaction the buyer's solicitor should carry out the following searches and enquiries before exchange of contracts:
  - a search of the local land charges register (LLC1). This reveals information the local authority is bound by statute to keep (eg tree preservation orders and compulsory purchase orders);
  - enquiries of the local authority (CON29). This will reveal non-statutory information on the property held by the local authority, including information on planning permissions granted and the adoption of roads. Optional enquiries may also be raised (CON29O), although these may not be relevant to every transaction;
  - pre-contract enquiries of the seller. These will contain various questions about the property, usually on a standard form.
  - water and drainage enquiries. These will reveal, amongst other things, whether the property is connected to the public sewer and public water supply;
  - environmental searches. There are a number of professional search providers providing 'desk-top' environmental reports assessing the risk of contamination. Depending on the level of risk revealed, the buyer may consider a physical environmental survey;
  - a personal inspection of the property by the client.
- Depending on the circumstances of the transaction, the following searches may need to be made before exchange of contracts:
  - a mining search, if the property is within an area where there has been, or currently is, mining activity. The results should allow the buyer's solicitor to advise whether there is an additional risk of subsidence;
  - an Index Map search. This is to check that no one has registered (or is trying to register) any part of the land at Land Registry and that there are no cautions against first registration. This is always done if the land is unregistered, but in certain circumstances is also undertaken if the land is registered;
  - a chancel repairs search. Certain properties may have an obligation to contribute to the costs of repairing the chancel of the parish church. A chancel repairs screening search will identify whether the property is within a liable parish. If it is, insurance is normally taken out;
  - a central land charges search. If the land is unregistered, a full central land charges search on Form K15 should be made against all estate owners of the property. This will reveal any third-party interests protected as land charges (eg restrictive covenants). If acting for a lender in a registered land transaction then a bankruptcy only search on Form K16 may be made against a borrower to check their solvency;

- a company search. This is to check solvency, charges against the property and the company's power to deal with the property;
- a flood search, to see if the property is susceptible to coastal, river or surface water flooding;
- additional searches or enquiries arising from the location of the property (eg commons registration, river, canal, railway, highways).

- The buyer's solicitor should also discuss obtaining appropriate survey reports with their client (see **Chapter 12**).
- The solicitor must consider the results of all searches, enquiries and surveys, and report appropriately to their client on them.

CHAPTER 18

THE DRAFT CONTRACT

LEARNING OUTCOMES

After reading this chapter you will be able to:

- identify the elements of a contract for the sale of land
- explain the purpose of standard and special conditions of sale
- advise on the matters commonly covered by special conditions
- understand what to look for when considering a draft contract and how to amend it.

18.1 INTRODUCTION AND CONTEXT

As explained in **Chapter 2**, in a traditional conveyancing transaction, prior to the actual transfer of title to a property (which occurs on what is known as 'completion'), the parties first enter into a binding contract to do so. This contract defines the extent of the land to be sold and sets out the terms on which the seller is prepared to sell, including specifying when the day of completion is to be. Although title is actually transferred in the transfer deed on completion, it is important to understand that the terms of the transfer deed are fixed by the terms of the contract.

It is the seller who drafts the contract, since only they will know precisely what they are prepared to sell and on what terms. Although it is the seller's prerogative to dictate the terms on which they are prepared to sell, this does not necessarily mean that the seller can draft a contract which is entirely in their own favour. The contract terms are open to negotiation with the buyer, and unless the bargaining strength of the seller is very strong, the seller must be prepared to concede points in the buyer's favour. For example, if the survey reveals problems with the physical structure of the property, the price may have to be renegotiated to reflect this. Ultimately, contract drafting is an exercise in the art of compromise. The seller's solicitor must ensure that the terms of the contract adequately protect their own client's interests, but at the same time provide a sufficiently attractive package to persuade the buyer to proceed with the purchase.

This chapter outlines the legal formalities and contents of a contract for the sale of land, but it does not discuss drafting techniques. These are considered in ***Skills for Lawyers***.

18.2 PREPARING TO DRAFT THE CONTRACT

The seller's solicitor will have taken instructions and will seek to embody in the contract the agreement that has been reached by the parties. This will involve dealing with any aspects particular to the transaction, but will always involve investigating title, for the reasons set out in the following paragraphs and in **15.2**.

18.3 SELLER'S CAPACITY

While investigating the seller's title, it is necessary to check that the seller is entitled to sell the whole of the estate in the land which they intend to sell. A sole owner, who owns the whole of the legal and equitable interest for their own benefit (a 'beneficial owner'), will normally have unlimited powers of disposal. However, the following circumstances require further consideration.

18.3.1 Trustees (including co-owners)

The issues surrounding a sale by trustees are covered in detail in **16.2** and **16.4**. If a second trustee is necessary to overreach any beneficial entitlement, this must be dealt with in the contract. Either the second trustee must be a party to the contract, or a special condition may be included in the contract requiring the seller to appoint a second trustee to be a party to the transfer. See **16.2.3** for further explanation.

18.3.2 Personal representatives

The issues surrounding a sale by personal representatives are covered in detail in **16.3**. If there is only one proving personal representative, they can contract on their own to sell the land. However, if the grant of representation is made to two or more personal representatives, they should all be a party to the contract as seller.

18.3.3 Mortgage lenders

The issues surrounding a sale by a mortgagee are covered in detail in **16.5**. In order to sell the property, the lender must have an express or implied power of sale, and that power must have arisen and become exercisable. The seller's solicitor will normally draft recitals for the contract that recite the details of the mortgage document, the fact the mortgagee is now in possession of the property and that the mortgagee is selling under its power of sale.

18.3.4 Companies

A company which was incorporated under the Companies Act 1985 may deal with land, provided the transaction is within the scope of the objects clause of its memorandum of association (one of its constitutional documents). A company incorporated under the Companies Act 2006 will not have an objects clause, but it may deal with land unless its power to do so is restricted by its articles of association.

It would be unusual for a normal trading company to lack the power to hold or dispose of an estate in land, although restrictions on granting mortgages may be encountered. In the case of registered land, if the company's powers are limited, an appropriate restriction will be entered on the proprietorship register. The buyer's solicitor should carry out a company search, if the contract names a company as seller (see **17.12**).

18.3.5 Persons suffering from mental disability

A contract for the sale or purchase of land entered into by a person who is suffering from mental incapacity sufficient to deprive them of understanding of the nature of the transaction is voidable at the option of the incapacitated party, provided they can prove that, at the time of the transaction, the other contracting party was aware of the disability (*Broughton v Snook* [1938] Ch 505).

A person who lacks capacity may have a finance deputy appointed by the Court of Protection under the Mental Capacity Act 2005 to deal with their property, subject to the court's approval. If the deputy is the registered proprietor or has requested that a restriction be entered on the title, no disposition of the land will be registered unless made pursuant to an order of the court.

18.4 ELEMENTS OF A CONTRACT

The contract will state that the seller agrees to sell the property and the buyer to buy it, and it will set out the terms of the sale. By virtue of s 2 of the Law of Property (Miscellaneous Provisions) Act 1989, any contract for an interest in land must be in writing, signed by all the parties and contain all its terms, either expressly or by being incorporated by reference in the contract.

A contract for the sale of land usually comprises three distinct elements:

(a) the particulars of sale;
(b) the standard conditions of sale; and
(c) the special conditions.

Each of these elements is dealt with in detail in the following paragraphs.

18.5 THE PARTICULARS OF SALE

The particulars of sale describe the estate in land which is being sold, ie whether it is freehold or leasehold, and the physical extent of that land. They may also contain a reference to easements and covenants which benefit the land (eg, the benefit of a right of way). The aim of the particulars is to give a clear and concise description of the property. Where the land being sold can be identified by a regular postal address and has clearly marked boundaries, describing it by reference to its postal address and, in the case of registered land, its title number will suffice. In other cases, a fuller description and a plan may be needed.

18.5.1 Plans

A plan must be used on a sale of part of land and may be desirable in other cases, for example where the boundaries of the property are not self-evident. A plan is generally not necessary for the sale of the whole of a freehold registered title. Whatever type of plan is used, it must be of sufficient size and scale to enable the boundaries and other features of the property to be identified readily. Land Registry has numerous and detailed requirements for plans submitted to it, and these may be found in Land Registry Practice Guide 40. Where the value or complexity of the transaction justifies the expense, an architect or a surveyor may be instructed to prepare a plan. If there is any doubt as to the size or extent of the property, an inspection should be carried out and measurements taken. The seller usually bears the cost of the preparation of the plan.

18.5.1.1 Showing features on the plan

If a plan is used, the contract and the transfer will need to make reference to it and its various features. Markings on the plan should therefore be clear and precise.

The land to be sold is usually outlined or coloured in red. Land retained by the seller should be outlined or coloured in a different colour: practitioners often use blue. Other land referred to (for example a driveway over which the buyer is to have a right of way) should be coloured or hatched in other distinct colours. Any agreed ownership of boundaries should be indicated by 'T' marks. The stem of the 'T' should rest on the relevant boundary, the 'T' being on the side of the boundary which is responsible for the maintenance. Routes of services that are referred to in the contract should be marked with broken or dotted lines of a distinct colour, with each end of the route being identified with separate upper-case (capital) letters. A key should be included to explain the meaning of the various colours and lines used on the plan.

18.5.1.2 Referring to the contract plan

If a plan is used, there should be no discrepancy between the verbal description of the property and the plan. If there is, it will be a question of construction as to whether the verbal description or the plan will prevail. The contract (and subsequent transfer) may refer to the plan as being 'for identification purposes only', or may describe the land as being 'more particularly delineated on the plan'. These two phrases are mutually exclusive and a combination of the two serves no useful purpose (*Neilson v Poole* (1969) 20 P & CR 909).

'Identification purposes only'

Where there is a discrepancy between the land shown on the plan and the contract description, and the plan has been described as being for identification purposes only, the verbal description of the land will normally prevail over the plan. This type of plan is unacceptable for use in connection with registered land and will be returned by Land Registry.

'More particularly delineated'

In the event of a discrepancy between the verbal description of the land and the plan, the plan will prevail over the words where the phrase 'more particularly delineated' has been used. This phrase should not be used unless the plan is to scale.

Note, however, that in many cases there will be no verbal description as such. So, for example, the land being sold may be described as 'All that land edged in red on the plan ... and forming part of property known as ...'. Here the only means of identifying the property is the plan itself, and so there can be no question of a discrepancy between the verbal description and the plan.

18.5.2 Easements and rights benefiting the property

The seller's investigation of title will have revealed whether or not the property has the benefit of easements or other rights. These may be included in the particulars of sale, although this is not essential as the benefit of them will pass to the buyer in any event under s 62 of the LPA 1925. On a sale of part of land, new rights (eg, a right to lay a new water pipe) may be granted to the buyer, and these must be provided for in the contract (see **Chapter 41**).

18.5.3 Errors in the particulars

A mistake in the particulars of sale, for example describing a freehold property as leasehold, or describing the extent of the land as 5 hectares when in fact it is only 3 hectares, may give the buyer a remedy in misdescription or misrepresentation. These remedies are both explained in **Chapter 33.**

18.6 THE STANDARD CONDITIONS

Whilst the particulars describe the land being sold, the conditions will set out the terms of the sale. As many of the conditions of sale which are needed in a contract are common to all transactions, standard sets of these conditions, which have been drafted by experts and will be familiar to the buyer's solicitor, will usually be incorporated into the contract. There are two such sets of standard conditions widely used in practice: the Standard Conditions of Sale, Fifth Edition–2018 Revision ('SCs') and the Standard Commercial Property Conditions, Third Edition–2018 Revision ('SCPCs'). These may be found in **Appendix 2** and **Appendix 3.** Whilst a practitioner will see many different versions of a property contract, almost invariably a contract for the sale of land will incorporate one of these sets of conditions. The SCPCs are designed for use in more complex or high value commercial property transactions and are divided into two parts: 'Part 1 conditions' and 'Part 2 conditions'. Part 1 conditions are of general application and will apply in their entirety to any contract incorporating the SCPCs unless varied by special condition. Part 2 conditions contain provisions on VAT, capital allowances and reversionary interests in flats that will only be relevant to certain transactions.

As a result, these Part 2 conditions will only apply if specifically incorporated by special condition. The SCs are a less extensive set of conditions and are designed for use in residential or lower value, straightforward commercial property transactions. However, it is up to the solicitors advising the parties to decide which of the sets of conditions (if any) to incorporate into the sale and purchase contract.

Whichever set of standard conditions is incorporated, the contract will also usually fall into one of the following categories.

18.6.1 The printed form of contract purchased from stationers

It is possible to purchase in hard-copy or electronic form, a pre-printed form of contract, containing gaps into which the seller's solicitor inserts the relevant details of the transaction. Two versions of such contracts are widely used in practice. The first incorporates the SCs and is intended for use in residential transactions. Some solicitors also use it for low value, straightforward commercial property work. The second incorporates Part 1 of the SCPCs, which is more suitable for use in commercial transactions, particularly where the property is of high value or subject to occupational leases. Examples of the front and back pages of these two versions may be found at **18.11.1** to **18.11.4** below. The centre pages of these documents will be the SCs or SCPCs (as appropriate).

18.6.2 The firm's precedent contract

Many solicitors will not use a printed form of contract purchased from a law stationers but will produce their own word-processed version, incorporating by reference one or other set of standard conditions. This is particularly the case with commercial property, where the terms of the transaction may be complex. The word-processed version will normally include numerous variations and additions to the standard conditions. Although such a contract may look very different in terms of its structure, it will deal with the same content, and the draftsman must make the same decisions about what particulars and special conditions to put in it. A worked example of a word-processed contract incorporating the SCPCs is set out at **18.11.6**.

18.7 THE SPECIAL CONDITIONS

18.7.1 The purpose of special conditions

Special conditions are those drafted by a solicitor for one of two reasons. First, a special condition may be necessary to deal with the particular circumstances of the transaction. For example, if the seller had agreed to provide the buyer with defective title insurance to cover a defect in the property's title, this would need to be dealt with by way of special condition. The purchase price for the property and details of any contents being sold will be dealt with by special condition. Such matters are peculiar to the transaction and cannot be dealt with by generic standard conditions. Secondly, a special condition may be needed to vary the standard condition position. This may be because the particular transaction requires such a departure. For example, if the parties have agreed that the deposit monies will be held by the seller's solicitor as agent for the seller (see **21.6.3**), this will usually require a special condition. The reason for this is that SC 2.2.6 and SCPC 3.2.2 generally provide for the seller's solicitor to hold the deposit as a stakeholder (see **21.6.4**). However, more often than not, if a solicitors' firm is using its own precedent contract, the precedent will contain variations to the standard conditions the firm considers favour its seller clients and which apply regardless of the specifics of the transaction.

18.7.2 Conflict with the standard conditions

What happens if a contract incorporates one of the sets of standard conditions but then a special condition is added which contradicts the standard condition position? Which should prevail? Standard Condition 1.1.4 and SCPC 1.1.4(a) deal specifically with this issue by providing that the special condition will prevail in such a scenario. However, in practice, the standard condition in question will often be expressly stated to be excluded in the interests of certainty. Where a printed-form contract purchased from law stationers is being used (see **18.6.1**), an amendment to the standard conditions must be made by special condition on the reverse of the contract form. It is not sufficient merely to strike out or alter the offending condition in the centre pages of the contract form. An example is shown at special condition 5 of the worked example set out at **18.11.5**.

18.8 MATTERS TO BE COVERED BY SPECIAL CONDITION

The seller's solicitor will have to decide what special conditions need drafting for the contract. The following areas should be considered.

18.8.1 The seller's duty to disclose incumbrances

Standard Condition 3.1.1 and SCPC 4.1.1 state that the seller will sell the property free from incumbrances other than those listed in SC 3.1.2 and SCPC 4.1.2. In other words, unless the contract varies the SC or SCPC position, the only incumbrances the buyer agrees to take subject to are those set out in SC 3.1.2 and SCPC 4.1.2. In consequence, the seller's solicitor must list in a special condition all incumbrances not covered by SC 3.1.2 or SCPC 4.1.2.

Some practitioners take the view that it is better to list all incumbrances revealed by the seller's solicitor's investigation of title in a special condition, regardless of whether they are already covered by SC 3.1.2 or SCPC 4.1.2. This is because the two sets of conditions are very different in the way they deal with incumbrances registered at Land Registry, Land Charges Registry and Companies House (see SC 3.1.2(e) and SCPC 4.1.2(d) referred to at **18.8.1.1** and **18.8.12**). As a result of these differences, practitioners switching between the SCs and the SCPCs in different transactions risk failing to disclose an incumbrance covered by the SCPCs but not covered by the SCs. Listing all incumbrances in a special condition avoids the risk of non-disclosure. In order to list the incumbrances, the seller's solicitor will need to investigate their client's title to the property thoroughly. Provided the incumbrances are listed in a special condition, the buyer will take subject to them due to SC 3.1.2(a) and SCPC 4.1.2(a), which make the sale subject to incumbrances 'specified in the contract'.

What happens, then, if the seller's solicitor fails to expressly disclose an incumbrance that the property is burdened by? The answer depends on whether the incumbrance is covered by the remaining paragraphs of SC 3.1.2 and SCPC 4.1.2. If the incumbrance is covered by one of those paragraphs then the seller will be deemed to have disclosed it and the buyer will be without remedy. If it is not so covered then the buyer might have the right to rescind the contract and/or claim damages (see **Chapter 33**).

18.8.1.1 Incumbrances under the SCs

The matters covered by SC 3.1.2(b) to (f) (and therefore deemed to be disclosed if the SCs are used) are as follows:

Matters discoverable by an inspection of the property before the contract (SC 3.1.2(b))

This means that an obvious incumbrance (eg a clearly used right of way) need not be disclosed expressly. However, to avoid any dispute as to whether a matter is or is not discoverable by an inspection, it is usual to disclose all such incumbrances in the contract, whether or not they could be discovered by an inspection.

Matters the seller does not and could not reasonably know about (SC 3.1.2(c))

This is necessary to counteract the strictness of the rule that the property is being sold free from all incumbrances. Note that for a matter to come within this provision, it is not enough that the seller did not know about the incumbrance; they must also show that they could not reasonably have known of it. In reality, it is most unlikely that there would be any incumbrances which the seller both did not know about and could not have known about had the seller's solicitor investigated title properly.

Matters, other than mortgages, which the buyer knows about (SC 3.1.2(d))

This means that the property is being sold subject to any incumbrance the buyer knows about, regardless of whether the information has come from the seller, conveyancing searches and enquiries, inspection, survey or third parties such as neighbours or estate agents. Mortgages are excluded as these are usually paid off immediately after completion, and it is not usually the intention that the buyer will take the property subject to them.

Entries made before the date of the contract in any public register except those maintained by Land Registry or Land Charges Registry or by Companies House (SC 3.1.2(e))

This means that any incumbrances registered at Companies House, or entered on the register in registered land or registered as land charges in unregistered land, are not deemed to be disclosed and should be expressly mentioned in the contract. Even if they are discoverable by an inspection (and so deemed disclosed under SC 3.1.2(b)) or already known to the buyer (and so deemed disclosed by SC 3.1.2(d)), it is good practice to expressly disclose them as incumbrances in the contract so as to avoid later argument about what the buyer actually did know or should have known. On the other hand, matters entered in other public registers, eg the Local Land Charges Register (see **Chapter 17**), need not be expressly disclosed in the contract.

Public requirements (SC 3.1.2(f))

Public requirements are defined in SC 1.1.1(j) as being any notice, order or proposal given or made (whether before or after the date of the contract) by a body acting on statutory authority. This would therefore include matters likely to be revealed by the Enquiries of the Local Authority, for example a public right of way affecting the land (see **Chapter 17**). Therefore, these need not be expressly disclosed to the buyer in the contract.

18.8.1.2 Incumbrances under the SCPCs

The matters covered by SCPC 4.1.2(b) to (e) (and therefore deemed to be disclosed if the SCPCs are used) are as follows:

Matters discoverable by an inspection of the property before the contract (SCPC 4.1.2(b))

As with the SCs, this means that an obvious incumbrance (eg a clearly used right of way) need not be disclosed expressly. However, to avoid any dispute as to whether a matter is or is not discoverable by an inspection, it is usual to disclose all such incumbrances in the contract, whether or not they could be discovered by an inspection.

Matters the seller does not and could not reasonably know about (SCPC 4.1.2(c))

As with the SCs, this is necessary to counteract the strictness of the rule that the property is being sold free from all incumbrances. Note that for a matter to come within this provision, it is not enough that the seller did not know about the incumbrance; they must also show that they could not reasonably have known of it. In reality, it is most unlikely that there would be any incumbrances which the seller both did not know about and could not have known about had the seller's solicitor investigated title properly.

Matters, other than mortgages, disclosed or which would have been disclosed by the searches and enquiries which a prudent buyer would have made before entering into the contract (SCPC 4.1.2(d))

This paragraph is included in the SCPCs only and is much wider than the equivalent SC 3.1.2(e) (above). It means that the sale is subject to all entries on the title at Land Registry even if not specifically mentioned in the contract. The only exceptions to this are mortgages. In consequence, where the SCPCs form the basis of the contract, there is strictly no need for the seller's solicitor to insert a special condition listing the incumbrances revealed in the registers of title. However, in practice, as previously discussed above, many sellers' solicitors simply list in a special condition all incumbrances revealed by their investigation of title, regardless of whether their contract incorporates the SCs or SCPCs.

Public requirements (SCPC 4.1.2(e))

Public requirements are defined in SCPC 1.1.1(l) as being any notice, order or proposal given or made (whether before or after the date of the contract) by a body acting on statutory authority. This would therefore include matters likely to be revealed by the Enquiries of the Local Authority, for example a public right of way affecting the land (see **Chapter 17**). Therefore, these need not be expressly disclosed to the buyer in the contract.

18.8.1.3 Defects in title

Standard Condition 3 and SCPC 4 provide that the seller is selling free from incumbrances other than those mentioned in SC 3.1.2 and SCPC 4.1.2. This implies that there are no other flaws or defects in the title. Accordingly, if there are any such defects, they should be specifically disclosed in the contract by a special condition. Failure to do so may give the buyer remedies for non-disclosure (see **Chapter 33**). It is also standard practice when specifically disclosing a defect to state that the buyer will not be entitled to raise any objection to the defect. This will prevent any suggestion by the buyer, after exchange, that the seller should (if it is possible) remedy the defect. By way of example, if the defect in question is an incorrectly executed conveyance, the following special condition might be inserted into the contract:

> The Buyer will assume that the conveyance dated ... and made between ... and ... is correctly executed and will raise no requisition or objection in respect of it.

It must of course be remembered that a defect in title (such as missing details of covenants) might be revealed on the registers of title. If the SCPCs were used and the defect was apparent from the registers of title, it would not technically need to be disclosed by special condition (see SCPC 4.1.2(d)). Neither would there need to be a special condition prohibiting the raising of requisitions on the defect as, providing the title has been deduced before exchange, SCPC 7.2.1 precludes any such requisitions. Nonetheless, some practitioners prefer to expressly disclose any such defect and bar out requisitions or objections relating to it. Whilst not legally required where the SCPCs are used, this ensures that the issue is brought to the buyer's attention and dealt with prior to exchange.

18.8.1.4 Green Deal

If a Green Deal plan exists (see **8.1**), the seller's solicitor must ensure that the contract includes an acknowledgment by the buyer that the bill payer at the property is liable to make payments under the Green Deal plan and that certain terms of that plan are binding on the bill payer (see Energy Act 2011, s 14 and **8.1**).

18.8.1.5 Matters that do not require disclosure

Matters that will not bind the buyer do not require disclosure. They would include, for example, the interests of the beneficiaries under a trust of land which will be overreached on a sale by two trustees. Physical defects need not be disclosed (see SC 3.2.1 and SCPC 4.2.1), hence the need for the buyer to commission a survey. However, if the seller deliberately conceals a physical defect (eg, 'papering over the cracks'), this may give rise to a claim in the tort of deceit.

18.8.1.6 Insurance for breach of a restrictive covenant or other defect in title

If investigation of the title reveals a breach of a restrictive covenant or other defect in title (eg a missing title deed), consideration should be given to seeking insurance. Restrictive covenant indemnity insurance and defective title insurance are available in the insurance market, subject to the insurer finding the level of risk acceptable.

Who obtains and pays for such insurance is a matter for negotiation between buyer and seller. If it is the buyer's intended use of the property that will lead to a breach of covenant, it will often be the buyer who will arrange and pay for the insurance, in which case there is usually no need for it to be dealt with in the contract. However, if the title being offered for sale is defective in some way, or the seller is using the property in breach of covenant, it would be usual for the seller to assume this responsibility.

If insurance is available and the parties agree that the seller will arrange and pay for such insurance, a special condition to this effect should be inserted in the contract. This should detail the sum insured (usually the market value of the property) and, from the buyer's perspective, allow them to approve the terms of the policy. The seller should be obliged to hand over the original policy documentation on completion. Restrictive covenant indemnity insurance is considered in more detail at **16.9.1**.

18.8.2 Deduction of title

Standard Condition 4.1 (SCPC 7.1) sets out what documentary evidence of title the seller is to provide. However, as title is invariably deduced prior to exchange of contracts, these provisions will rarely be relied upon and will usually have been complied with by the time of exchange (see **14.2**). If, exceptionally, the seller has been unable to comply with the requirements set out in SC 4.1 (SCPC 7.1), they should include a special condition to stipulate how title will be proved. For example, if the seller has acquired title by adverse possession, their title will normally be evidenced by a statutory declaration.

The buyer's solicitor should be aware that if title has been deduced before exchange, no requisitions can be raised on that title (SC 4.2.1 and SCPC 7.2.1). See **26.1** for further discussion of this.

18.8.3 Title guarantee

By including 'key words' in the transfer, it is possible to give the buyer the benefit of certain implied covenants under the Law of Property (Miscellaneous Provisions) Act 1994. It is usual to specify in the contract which (if any) of the implied covenants the seller is prepared to give. The inclusion of the statement 'the seller sells with full title guarantee' (or its Welsh equivalent) will give the buyer the benefit of the full range of covenants implied by the 1994 Act (see **18.8.3.1**). A more limited set of covenants is implied if the seller uses the expression 'the seller sells with limited title guarantee' (or the equivalent Welsh expression) (see **18.8.3.2**). It is possible for the seller to state that they are giving no title guarantee (see **18.8.3.4**).

Where the contract is silent and makes no reference to title guarantee, both sets of standard conditions provide that the seller will sell with full title guarantee (SC 4.6.2 and SCPC 7.6.2). So, if the seller does not wish to sell with full title guarantee, their solicitor will need to include a special condition in the contract amending SC 4.6.2 or SCPC 7.6.2 (as appropriate). Note that the implied covenants for title are implied into the transfer and not the contract. The sole purpose of putting the provision into the contract is to tell the buyer what covenants will be included in the transfer when that is executed.

18.8.3.1 Covenants implied in full title guarantee

With full title guarantee, the covenants implied into the transfer can be summarised as follows:

(a) A covenant that the seller has the right to dispose of the land.

(b) A covenant that the seller will do all they reasonably can to transfer the title.

(c) If the land disposed of is leasehold land, a covenant that the lease is subsisting at the time it is disposed of, and that there is no breach of covenant making the lease liable to forfeiture.

(d) A covenant that the land is disposed of free from incumbrances, other than those the seller does not know about and could not reasonably know about. Whilst this implied covenant can seem rather wide, s 6 of the 1994 Act does limit its effect (see **18.8.3.3**).

18.8.3.2 Covenants implied in limited title guarantee

With limited title guarantee, the implied covenants set out at (a) to (c) in **18.8.3.1** above are also given. However, the freedom from incumbrances covenant referred to at (d) in **18.8.3.1** is more limited. With limited title guarantee the seller is promising that they have not incumbered the land, and that they are not aware that anyone else has done so since the last disposition for value. So, for example, a seller who purchased the land for value will only be covenanting that incumbrances have not been created since they acquired the property.

18.8.3.3 Matters that will not breach the implied covenants.

Section 6 of the 1994 Act states that the seller is not in breach of the implied covenants in respect of any of the following:

(a) *Matters to which the disposition is expressly made subject.* It will have been seen from **18.8.1** that under the SCPC and the SC, the sale will be expressly subject to various incumbrances set out in the contract. To ensure these are covered by s 6 and that no breach of the implied covenants arises, some commentators recommend the seller should require the transfer deed to contain a provision that the transfer is subject to all the matters to which the contract is made subject. Other commentators consider that listing an incumbrance in the contract is sufficient to ensure it is a matter 'to which the disposition is expressly made subject' in accordance with s 6(1) of the 1994 Act. Standard Commercial Property Condition 7.6.3 attempts to deal with the issue by providing that the transfer is to have effect as if it were expressly made subject to all the matters covered by SCPC 4.1.2. However, not all commentators agree that SCPC 7.6.3 is sufficient and some still recommend that matters the sale is made subject to are repeated in the transfer deed. If the seller's solicitor does require such matters to be repeated in the transfer deed, the contract should contain a special condition to this effect.

(b) *Matters about which the buyer knows at the time of the disposition* (s 6 of the 1994 Act). This means that a buyer of registered title could not sue the seller for a breach of the implied covenants in respect of an overriding interest, if the buyer knew at the time of the transfer that the overriding interest existed.

(c) *Matters which at the time of the disposal were entered on the registers of title (in relation to registered land).* If the seller's solicitor still has concerns about the extent of the implied covenants, the seller can modify their effect in the transfer deed, provided such modification has been provided for in the contract (s 8 of the 1994 Act) (see **18.8.3.5**).

18.8.3.4 Deciding upon the title guarantee

When drafting the contract on behalf of the seller, the seller's solicitor must decide whether the seller will promise to dispose of the land with 'full title guarantee' or with 'limited title guarantee', or refuse to give any title guarantee at all.

If the seller promises, for example, a 'full title guarantee', that phrase will appear in the subsequent transfer, ie 'the Seller transfers to the Buyer with full title guarantee ...'. The inclusion of the phrase in the transfer will imply the covenants for title into the transfer. Which kind of title guarantee is chosen will depend upon the circumstances of the seller and the state of their title to the land.

The seller's solicitor will investigate their client's title before the contract is drafted. If the client has a good title and knowledge of the incumbrances that affect the property, the seller has no reason to refuse to promise a full guarantee, as the covenants implied into the transfer by the 1994 Act will be no wider than the promises about title the seller gives in the agreement.

On the other hand, if the seller has very little knowledge of the property, it may be appropriate for them to give only a limited title guarantee. This might apply to trustees holding on trust for people other than themselves, and to personal representatives selling a property to a third party or assenting a property to the beneficiary.

Where the seller has no title to the land, or a questionable title (eg, title might be based on adverse possession under the Limitation Acts), a special condition will be inserted in the agreement to negate the implied promise that the seller has a good title. Equally, the seller will not want to give any title guarantee in the transfer. So, the contract should make it clear on the front page, or by special condition, that no title guarantee is to be given. Other sellers who commonly refuse to give any title guarantee include a donor making a deed of gift of a property, or a receiver/administrator selling the assets of a bankrupt or insolvent seller.

When a lender sells under its power of sale, there seems no reason why limited guarantee cannot be given to the buyer; however, in practice, it is common for no title guarantee to be given.

If a landlord grants a lease with full or limited title guarantee, the same covenants for title given by the seller to the buyer on a sale will be impliedly given by the landlord to the tenant in the lease. A tenant who is taking a long-term lease and paying a substantial premium is likely to ask for full guarantee to be given. Title guarantee is less common in a short-term lease.

When acting for the lender on a mortgage, the lender's instructions must be checked to see if the lender requires the borrower to give a full title guarantee in the mortgage, or is willing to accept a limited title guarantee. Usually, full title guarantee is required.

18.8.3.5 Modifying the implied covenants

If the seller wishes to modify any of the covenants implied by either full or limited title guarantee, those modifications should be agreed in the contract (although they will need to appear in transfer deed). For example, it is usual on the sale of a lease to modify the implied covenants (see **36.7.1**). Standard Condition 4.6.3 and SCPC 7.6.4 provide for the transfer deed to contain an appropriate modification to the implied covenants on the sale of a lease. However, a special condition in the contract should agree the exact wording of the modification that will appear in the transfer.

18.8.3.6 Grant of a lease

If a landlord grants a lease with full or limited title guarantee, the covenants for title will be implied into the lease. A tenant who is taking a long-term residential lease and paying a substantial premium is likely to ask for a guarantee to be given. Title guarantee is not usual in a short-term lease.

18.8.4 Vacant possession

The seller's solicitor will need to specify by special condition whether the property is being sold with vacant possession or subject to occupational leases. On the back pages of the standard form contracts purchased from law stationers there are two pre-printed options dealing with the alternatives. These conditions may be seen at **18.11.2** and **18.11.4**. The condition that does not apply should be struck out, as in the worked example at **18.11.5**. If the property is sold subject to leases or tenancies, copies should be supplied to the buyer with the draft contract so that they can see the terms of those agreements.

If vacant possession is intended, but someone apart from the seller is in occupation of the property (eg a non-owning spouse), it will be necessary to ensure that that person will vacate the property on completion. Clearly the buyer would need to be satisfied that the occupier had no legal interest in the property and that any equitable interest of the occupier was overreached. Even if the buyer is so satisfied, it is good practice to get the occupier to confirm that they will vacate in the contract for sale. The buyer does not wish to arrive at the property on the completion date to find the occupier still in possession. Although an occupier with no binding rights will have no defence to a possession claim, the buyer will much prefer to avoid court action. By asking the occupier to confirm in writing that they will leave, this should ensure that any potential problems will be revealed at an early stage of the transaction should the occupier refuse to sign such an agreement. Some pre-printed forms of contract incorporating the SCs contain appropriate wording for this. In other cases, a suggested form of wording is as follows:

> In consideration of the Buyer entering into this Agreement, I .... [name of occupier] ...... agree:
>
> (1) to the sale of the Property on the terms of this Agreement; and
>
> (2) not to register any rights I may have in relation to the Property (whether under the Family Law Act 1996 or otherwise); and
>
> (3) to remove any registrations made by me in relation to these rights before completion; and
>
> (4) to give vacant possession of the Property on completion.

This form of wording is appropriate for inclusion in the contract; alternatively, it could be amended slightly and set out as a separate document. If the occupier is not the seller's spouse or civil partner, the reference to the Family Law Act 1996 should be deleted.

An alternative solution, if the occupier is claiming an equitable interest in the property, is to appoint the occupier as a second trustee of the property (see **18.3.1**).

18.8.5 Date and time for completion

Instructions will have been obtained from the client as to their desired date for completion, but it is not usually possible at this stage of the transaction to insert a definite date for completion in the contract. The actual date for completion agreed between the parties will be inserted in the relevant place in the contract on exchange. Until that time, this space is left blank. Many factors, including the progress of any related purchase transaction, affect the timing of completion, and at the stage when the contract is drafted it is too early to make a positive decision on the actual date for completion.

If no completion date is inserted in the contract on exchange, SC 6.1.1 (SCPC 9.1.1) sets completion at 20 working days after the date of the contract.

Standard Condition 6.1.1 (SCPC 9.1.1) also provides that time is not to be of the essence as regards the completion date, except where a notice to complete has been served. Where time is not of the essence, a delay in completion beyond the contractual date will not automatically allow the party not in default to repudiate the contract. Although time can be made of the essence by varying this standard condition by special condition, this is not usually desirable and the condition is usually left unamended. Problems relating to time being of the essence and to notices to complete are discussed in **Chapter 32**.

Neither set of standard conditions deals with the precise time on the day of completion by which the transfer must be completed. Standard Condition 6.1.2 (SCPC 9.1.2), which refers to the time of completion, relates only to the payment of compensation for late completion (see **18.8.6**) and does not impose a time limit on completion itself.

It may be desirable in chain transactions for this matter to be dealt with by express special condition in the contract, for example 'completion shall take place by 2 pm'. This is to ensure that there is sufficient time on the day of completion for the seller to use the funds to complete the dependent purchase. The buyer, of course, must be satisfied that it can comply with such a condition before accepting it. Delays in the banking system for transferring funds electronically can mean that it takes several hours for funds transmitted electronically to reach their intended recipient.

18.8.6 Compensation for delayed completion

The contract normally provides for compensation to be paid by one party to the other in the event of completion being delayed beyond the contractual date. Standard Condition 6.1.2 (SCPC 9.1.2) states that if the completion monies are received after 2.00 pm then, for the purposes of calculating compensation, completion is deemed to have occurred on the next working day. The 2.00 pm cut off can be changed by special condition if the parties agree.

In the case of the SC, either the buyer or the seller may pay compensation, depending on who is most at fault (see **32.4**). Under the SCPC, the buyer will pay compensation to the seller if the buyer has defaulted in some way and completion is delayed, but the buyer has no contractual right to compensation if the seller defaults (see **32.6**).

Standard Condition 7.2 (SCPC 10.3) contains provisions for the payment of compensation for late completion, and states that the amount of such payment shall be assessed at the 'contract rate' as defined. According to SC 1.1.1(e) (SCPC 1.1.1(e)), the contract rate, unless altered by special condition, is 'The Law Society's interest rate from time to time in force'. The Law Society's interest rate is published weekly in the *Law Society's Gazette* and is set at 4% above the base lending rate of Barclays Bank plc.

The object of inserting an interest rate is both to provide an incentive to complete on the due date and to provide monetary compensation to the innocent party for any financial losses caused by the delay in completion. In practice, an interest rate of 4% above the base lending rate of a major bank is accepted as being normal. If, therefore, the draft contract provides for a higher interest rate, this should be resisted by the buyer. The forms of contract purchased from law stationers for both sets of standard conditions contain a space on the front page in which the contract rate may be inserted. If it is wished to rely on Condition 1.1.1(e), this may be left blank. However, it is often used to state expressly that The Law Society's interest rate is to be used. Alternatively, many solicitors will substitute a rate of their own choosing, usually linked to the base rate of their own bankers. Providing for a fixed interest rate (eg, 'the contract rate shall be 10% pa') is not normally considered to be desirable in case rates of interest change radically between the time when the contract is drafted and the time when the interest becomes payable. If that were to occur and the rate were fixed, it might no longer reflect a reasonable rate of interest from either the seller's or the buyer's perspective.

18.8.7 Deposit

Although not required by law, it is customary for the buyer to pay a deposit of 10% of the purchase price on exchange of contracts. This acts both as part-payment of the price and as a guarantee of performance by the buyer, since the buyer cannot usually afford to lose this amount of money. If the buyer subsequently defaulted on the contract, the seller would have the right to forfeit that deposit. Standard Condition 2.2 (SCPC 3.2) provides for payment of a 10% deposit to be held by the seller's solicitor in the capacity of stakeholder. A special condition relating to the deposit is needed only if it is desired to vary the capacity in which the deposit is to be held. The buyer should consider a change from stakeholder to agent for the seller very carefully (see **21.6**). In the forms of contract purchased from law stationers for both sets of standard conditions, the amount of the deposit is inserted in the space provided for this towards the bottom of the front page of the contract form. If the amount inserted is less (or more) than 10% of the purchase price, this will override SC 2.2 (SCPC 3.2).

If a lower deposit is accepted by the seller, it may be agreed that it is held as agent for the seller rather than as stakeholder. Certain large corporations may not be required to pay a deposit at all. Special conditions in the contract varying the amount of the deposit and/or the capacity in which it is held will be required. These are discussed fully in **Chapter 21**.

18.8.8 Indemnity covenants

If the seller entered into a covenant when they purchased the property, whether positive or restrictive, they will remain liable on that covenant even after they have disposed of the property, unless the wording of the covenant makes it clear that they are not to be bound after they have sold. Where the seller remains bound, it means that if the buyer breaks the covenant, there is a risk of the seller being sued in respect of that breach. To protect themselves, therefore, the seller needs to take an indemnity covenant from the buyer in the transfer. In their turn, a buyer who has entered into an indemnity covenant at the time of purchase will need to take an indemnity from their buyer when they come to sell the property. However, like other matters, the indemnity may be included in the transfer only if this is provided for in the contract. Standard Condition 4.6.4 (SCPC 7.6.5) makes provision for such an indemnity. Even so, some practitioners prefer to provide expressly for an indemnity covenant by special condition in the contract. An example of this may be found in clause 8.3 of the worked contract example at **18.11.6**. By providing expressly for the indemnity covenant, its exact wording can be agreed and the matter is drawn specifically to the attention of the buyer.

18.8.9 Fixtures and fittings

Fixtures (items which are attached to the land, eg the central heating system) automatically pass with the land unless a special condition is included giving the seller the right to remove them. Fittings or chattels (eg carpets and curtains) which are to be included in the sale must be specifically identified in the contract, either by special condition or by making use of a printed special condition, which refers to the chattels as 'contents' which are itemised on a list attached to the contract. In residential cases, an F&C may be used for this purpose (see **11.5**). Any separate consideration for the contents should be expressly stated, as SDLT is not payable on consideration payable for contents (see **6.3.3** and **11.4**). Fixtures and fittings are dealt with in detail in **Chapter 11**.

18.8.10 Value added tax

Both party's solicitors will need to consider whether the sale of the property will attract VAT (see **6.2.3** and **6.2.4**). If it might, consideration needs to be given as to how the contract deals with the issue. A failure to deal with this issue adequately can have serious repercussions for either party. From the seller's perspective, if the sale constitutes a taxable supply but the contract does not allow VAT to be added onto the purchase price, the seller will have to deduct the VAT from the purchase monies received and hand it over to HMRC. If the contract does allow VAT to be added to the purchase price and the buyer is not alert to the issue, the buyer might end up handing over considerably more money on completion than anticipated. The position under both sets of standard conditions is dealt with in detail at **6.2.6**.

18.9 UNFAIR CONTRACT TERMS

The solicitor drafting the contract will need to be aware of the possible application of Part 2 of the Consumer Rights Act 2015 (CRA 2015). This Act regulates contracts made between a 'consumer' and a 'trader'.

'Consumer' means an individual acting for purposes that are wholly or mainly outside that individual's trade, business, craft or profession (CRA 2015, s 2(1)). 'Trader' means a person acting for purposes relating to that person's trade, business, craft or profession, whether acting personally or through another person acting in the trader's name or on the trader's behalf (CRA 2015, s 2(2)).

It is envisaged that the following contracts for the sale of land would be caught by the Act:

(a) a contract for the sale of a house or flat by a builder/developer to a private buyer;

(b) a contract for the sale of a repossessed house or flat by a lender to a private individual.

Any contract caught by the CRA 2105 must be 'transparent' (ie, legible and expressed in plain and intelligible language) and 'fair'. A term is unfair (and therefore not binding on the 'consumer') if, contrary to the requirement of good faith, it causes a significant imbalance in the parties' rights and obligations under the contract to the detriment of the consumer. The requirement for the contract to be 'fair' does not apply to the price specified in the contract, provided that the price is 'transparent' and prominent. Part 1 of Sch 2 to the CRA 2015 contains examples of terms that may be regarded as unfair.

18.10 BUYER'S CONSIDERATION OF THE CONTRACT

Except where the buyer is purchasing a plot on a building estate (a new house in the course of construction), the terms of the contract will usually be open to negotiation between the parties, and the buyer's solicitor should therefore consider the terms of the draft contract in the light of their instructions and of the information revealed by the other documents in the pre-contract package.

Style of drafting is to an extent a matter of individual taste, and the buyer's solicitor should not seek to amend the contract simply because it is drafted in a style which they do not like. Amendments should be made only where they are both necessary and relevant to the transaction. The primary questions in looking at the contract from the buyer's point of view are as follows:

(a) Does the clause accord with the client's instructions?

(b) Does the clause do what it is intended to do?

(c) Does the clause represent a fair balance between the respective parties' interests?

If the answers to these questions are 'yes', leave the wording alone. If not, alter the clause until it does meet the above criteria.

18.10.1 How to amend the contract

Traditionally, the buyer's solicitor would insert amendments to one copy of the draft contract in manuscript, usually in red. They would retain a coloured copy of the amended version and return the original, with their marked-up amendments, to the seller's solicitor for consideration. On the front of the amended document they would write 'amended in (red) on (date)'. Further amendments (by either party) followed the same procedure and were made in distinctive colours not previously used, so that it was possible to identify each layer of changes. More commonly now, where significant amendments to a draft contract may be anticipated, the solicitors send each other electronic copies of the draft. Most word-processing packages (eg, Microsoft Word) have a 'tracking' facility, enabling amendments and additions to be made and then clearly shown when the other party reviews the document. This, together with the use of e-mail, will speed up the process of agreeing the final version of the document. A document which passes back and forth between the parties in this way is often referred to as a 'travelling draft'.

Sometimes only minor amendments are needed, and this process may be shortened by agreeing the necessary amendments over the phone.

When final agreement is reached over the contents of the contract, a 'clean' or 'fair copy' should be produced by the seller's solicitor incorporating all the agreed amendments. This too should be sent to the buyer's solicitor to approve. Assuming it accurately reflects their final agreement, the buyer's solicitor can return the fair copy 'approved as drawn' (ie without further amendment). Copies for signature by the parties (referred to as 'engrossments') can then be produced by the seller's solicitor.

18.10.2 What to look for when considering the draft contract

The following are matters which the buyer's solicitor should bear in mind when considering the draft contract:

(a) Are the full names and addresses of the parties correctly included?

(b) Is every person who needs to be a party to the contract included as seller? (See **18.3**.)

(c) Does the description of the property tie in with that on the register or in the deeds, and is any plan used acceptable? (See **18.5.1**.)

(d) Does the property have the benefit of all the easements necessary for the use to which the buyer intends to put the property or any other reasonable use? (See **18.5.2**.)

(e) Is the estate being sold (freehold or leasehold) stated correctly?

(f) Is the class of title stated (registered land)?

(g) Is the root of title a 'good root' (unregistered land)? (See **15.4.2.1**.)

(h) Is the title number stated correctly (registered land)?

(i) What incumbrances is the property sold subject to, and will they restrict the buyer's proposed use of the property in any way? (See **18.8.1**.)

(j) Is full title guarantee being offered? If not, why not? (See **18.8.3**.)

(k) Is the contract rate more than The Law Society's rate (ie, more than 4% above base rate)? (See **18.8.6**.)

(l) Is the purchase price as agreed?

(m) Is the amount of the deposit as agreed?

(n) How is the deposit to be held? If as agent for the seller, does the buyer appreciate the risks of this? (See **18.8.7**.)

(o) How is VAT dealt with, and is this acceptable to the buyer? (See **18.8.10**.)

(p) Is the amount payable for fittings/contents and the identity of the contents as agreed? (See **18.8.9**.)

(q) Is any balance stated correct?

(r) Is vacant possession to be given on completion? If not, was this agreed? (See **18.8.4**.)

(s) Has title been investigated, and have all enquiries and requisitions been satisfactorily dealt with prior to exchange? (See **18.8.2**.)

(t) Have any of the standard conditions been amended/made inapplicable by a special condition? If so, will this adversely affect the buyer?

(u) Will the buyer need to insure on exchange? (See **Chapter 22**.)

(v) Have the parties agreed any matters that require a special condition (eg is the seller to procure restrictive covenant indemnity insurance)?

18.11 CONTRACT DRAFTING: WORKED EXAMPLES

Drafting any document is a skill that develops and improves over time. It is a good idea to build up a 'precedent bank' made up of documents commonly encountered in practice, with guidance on how they should be completed. To assist you in developing this skill you will find the following:

(a) At **18.11.1** and **18.11.2** are the front and rear pages of a pre-printed form of contract purchased from law stationers incorporating the SCs. At **18.11.3** and **18.11.4** are the front and rear pages of a pre-printed form of contract incorporating the SCPCs. The middle section of each contract would simply include the relevant set of standard conditions. Guidance on how to complete each section of the front and rear pages has been provided.

(b) At **18.11.5** is a worked example of the SC form purchased from a law stationers. This has been completed for the sale of 47 Queens' Road using the attendance note at **8.7** and the official copies at **4.5**. A commentary on the worked example follows on from it.

(c) At **18.11.6** you will find a word-processed contract incorporating the SCPCs for the same transaction. This is the kind of contract you are likely to find in a law firm's precedent bank. Such documents vary from firm to firm. Whilst they will all usually cover the same substantive areas, each will do so in a slightly different way. It will be the buyer's solicitor's job to ensure that the contract is satisfactory from their client's point of view. Footnotes are included as an aid to drafting and reviewing such a document.

18.11.1 Standard Conditions of Sale: front page

For conveyancer's use only
Buyer's conveyancer: ....
Seller's conveyancer: ....
Law Society Formula: [A / B / C / Personal exchange]

CONTRACT

Incorporating the Standard Conditions of Sale (Fifth Edition–2018 Revision)

Date	:
Seller	: Insert full name and address of (each) seller(s)
Buyer	: Insert full name and address of (each) buyer(s)
Property (freehold/leasehold)	: 1. Delete leasehold or freehold on left as appropriate 2. Insert existing description of property taken from official copies (reg land) or title deeds (unreg land) (if boundary unclear or sale of part refer to plan which should then be affixed to the contract)
Title number/root of title	: 1. Delete title number/root of title on left as appropriate 2. (Reg land) Insert title number and class of title; or 3. (Unreg'd) Insert root by document, date & parties eg "The Conveyance dated [ ] made between (1) [Seller] & (2) [Buyer]"
Specified incumbrances	: (1) List all incumbrances that will bind the buyer (exclude mortgages to be redeemed on sale) (2) (Reg land) Identify by incumbrance + register + entry eg "The [easements] referred to in entry number [4] of the [Charges] Register" (3) (Unreg) Identify by incumbrance and document eg "The [covenants] referred to in a conveyance dated [ ] between [ ] & [ ]"
Title guarantee (full/limited)	: Full or limited
Completion date	:
Contract rate	: Insert specific contract rate or leave blank and rely on SC 1.1.1(e)
Purchase price	: Insert purchase price <u>for property only</u>
Deposit	: 10% of <u>purchase price of property</u> or as agreed (if different)
Contents price (if separate)	: Insert agreed price for contents
Balance	: Purchase price + contents price – deposit = balance

The seller will sell and the buyer will buy the property for the purchase price.

WARNING	Signed
This is a formal document, designed to create legal rights and legal obligations. Take advice before using it.	Seller/Buyer

18.11.2 Standard Conditions of Sale: rear page

SPECIAL CONDITIONS

---

1. (a) This contract incorporates the Standard Conditions of Sale (Fifth Edition–2018 Revision).

   (b) The terms used in this contract have the same meaning when used in the Conditions.

2. Subject to the terms of this contract and to the Standard Conditions of Sale, the seller is to transfer the property with either full title guarantee or limited title guarantee, as specified on the front page.

3. (a) The sale includes those contents which are indicated on the attached list as included in the sale and the buyer is to pay the contents price for them.

   (b) The sale excludes those fixtures which are at the property and are included on the attached list as excluded from the sale.

   Spec Cond 3 – Add list if chattels to be sold.

4. The property is sold with vacant possession.

(or) 4. The property is sold subject to the following leases or tenancies.

   Spec Cond 4 – Delete second alternative where selling with vacant possession. If selling subject to leases, delete first alternative and list leases here.

5. Conditions 6.1.2 and 6.1.3 shall take effect as if the time specified in them were [ ] rather than 2.00 p.m.

   Spec Cond 5 – Insert time after which compensation will become payable if 2.00 pm unsatisfactory.

6. **Representations**

   Neither party can rely on any representation made by the other, unless made in writing by the other or his conveyancer, but this does not exclude liability for fraud or recklessness.

7. **Occupier's consent**

   Each occupier identified below agrees with the seller and the buyer, in consideration of their entering into this contract, that the occupier concurs in the sale of the property on the terms of this contract, undertakes to vacate the property on or before the completion date and releases the property and any included fixtures and contents from any right or interest that the occupier may have.

   Note: this condition does not apply to occupiers under leases or tenancies subject to which the property is sold

Name(s) and signature(s) of the occupier(s) (if any):

Name ....

Signature ....

Notices may be sent to:

Seller's conveyancer's name:

E-mail address:*

Buyer's conveyancer's name:

E-mail address:*

* Adding an e-mail address authorises service by e-mail: see condition 1.3.3(b)

18.11.3 Standard Commercial Property Conditions: front page

CONTRACT

Incorporating the Standard Commercial Property Conditions (Third Edition–2018 Revision)

Date	:	
Seller	:	Insert full name and address of (each) seller(s)
Buyer	:	Insert full name and address of (each) buyer(s)
Property (freehold/leasehold)	:	1. Delete leasehold or freehold on left as appropriate 2. Insert existing description of property taken from official copies (reg land) or title deeds (unreg land) (if boundary unclear or sale of part refer to plan which should then be affixed to the contract)
Title number/root of title	:	1. Delete title number/root of title on left as appropriate 2. (Reg land) Insert title number and class of title; or 3. (Unreg'd) Insert root by document, date & parties eg "The Conveyance dated [ ] made between (1) [Seller] & (2) [Buyer]"
Specified incumbrances	:	(1) List all incumbrances that will bind the buyer (exclude mortgages to be redeemed on sale) (2) (Reg land) Identify by incumbrance + register + entry eg "The [easements] referred to in entry [4] of the [Charges] Register" (3) (Unreg) Identify by incumbrance and document eg "The [covenants] referred to in a conveyance dated [ ] between (1) [ ] & (2) [ ]"
Completion date	:	To be inserted on exchange of contracts
Contract rate	:	Insert specific contract rate or leave blank and rely on SCPC 1.1.1(e) (see **18.8.6**)
Purchase price	:	[ ] exclusive of any VAT Insert purchase price for land and chattels
Deposit	:	10% of purchase price or as agreed (see **18.8.7**)
Balance	:	Insert balance due by deducting amount of deposit from purchase price

The seller will sell and the buyer will buy the property for the purchase price.

WARNING	Signed
This is a formal document, designed to create legal rights and legal obligations. Take advice before using it.	Authorised to sign on behalf of Seller/Buyer

18.11.4 Standard Commercial Property Conditions: rear page

SPECIAL CONDITIONS

---

1 (a) This contract incorporates the Standard Commercial Property Conditions (Third Edition – 2018 Revision).

(b) The terms used in this contract have the same meaning when used in the Standard Commercial Property Conditions.

2 Neither party can rely on any representation made by the other, unless made in writing by the other or its conveyancer, but this does not exclude liability for fraud or recklessness.

If the box next to any of Special Conditions 3 to 8 is checked, that Special Condition applies, provided that (in the case of Special Conditions 6 and 7 and the second alternative for 8) the gaps in the printed text have been filled in.

3 ☐ The property is sold with limited title guarantee, which replaces the reference to full title guarantee in condition 7.6.2.

Special Condition 3. Tick box if seller is not prepared to transfer with full title guarantee (see **18.8.3**).

4 ☐ The property is sold with vacant possession on completion.

[or]

4 ☐ The property is sold subject to the leases or tenancies set out on the attached list but otherwise with vacant possession on completion.

Special Condition 4. Tick second alternative if selling subject to leases and attach list of those leases. Otherwise tick the first alternative.

5 ☐ (a) The sale includes those contents which are indicated on the attached list as included in the sale

☐ (b) The sale excludes those fixtures which are at the property and are indicated on the attached list as excluded from the sale.

Special Condition 5. Tick (a) if chattels to be sold and attach list of chattels. Tick (b) if seller intends to remove fixtures from property and attach list of those fixtures. If the parties wish to apportion an amount of the purchase price to the chattels, an additional special condition will be needed (see **18.8.9**).

6 ☐ In conditions 3.2.2 and 9.7, as an alternative to payment from a conveyancer's account, the payment may be made from an account held by [ ] at [ ]

If payment of monies due under the contract is to be accepted from an account other than a conveyancer's account, tick this box and insert details of the account holder and where the account is held. Anti-money laundering checks will be required if this box is ticked.

7 ☐ Conditions 9.1.2 and 9.1.3 are to have effect as if the time specified in them were [ ] am/pm rather than 2:00pm.

If seller requires purchase monies prior to 2:00pm, tick this box and insert earlier time (see **18.8.6**).

8 ☐ Where after the transfer the seller will be retaining land near the property, the transfer is to be in the form of the attached draft transfer.

If the sale is of part of the seller's property and the parties have agreed the form of the transfer deed, tick this box and attach the agreed form of transfer.

[or]

8 ☐ Where after the transfer the seller will be retaining land near the property, the transfer is to contain the additional express terms:

(a)

(b)

If the sale if of part of the seller's property and the transfer deed will contain new covenants, easements or other provisions, tick this box and set out the agreed terms.

9 The conditions in Part 2 shown against the boxes ticked below are included in the contract:

☐ Condition A1 (VAT: not a taxable supply)

[or]

☐ Condition A2 (VAT: transfer of a going concern)

☐ Condition B (capital allowances). The amount of the purchase price apportioned to plant and machinery that are fixtures for the purposes of the Capital Allowances Act 2001 is £

☐ Condition C1 (flats: no tenants' rights of first refusal)

[or]

☐ Condition C2 (flats: with tenants' rights of first refusal in auction sales)

Special Condition 9

Box 1 – Leave blank if a VATable transaction. Tick if not VATable (see **18.8.10**).

[Boxes 2–5 are additional boxes dealing with other matters relating to transfers of going concerns, capital allowances and tenants' rights of first refusal under the Landlord and Tenant Act 1987. These are specialist issues and are outside the scope of this example.]

Notices may be sent to:

Seller's conveyancer's name:

Fax number:*

E-mail address:*

Buyer's conveyancer's name:

Fax number:*

E-mail address:*

*Adding a fax number authorises service by fax and an e-mail address authorises service by e-mail: see condition 1.3.3

18.11.5 Worked example of the contract

For conveyancer's use only

Buyer's conveyancer: ....
Seller's conveyancer: ....
Law Society Formula: [A / B / C / Personal exchange]

CONTRACT
Incorporating the Standard Conditions of Sale (Fifth Edition–2018 Revision)

Date	
Seller	: ROGER EVANS of 47, Queens' Road, Loamster, Maradon, Cornshire, CS1 5TY
Buyer	: CATHERINE READE and JOANNE READE both of 24, Leeming Road, Bridgeton, Cornshire, CS3 4DD
Property (freehold/~~leasehold~~)	: 47, Queens' Road, Loamster, Maradon, Cornshire CS1 5TY
Title number/~~root of title~~	: LM 12037 (Absolute Title)
Specified incumbrances	: The covenants referred to in entry No. 1 of the Charges Register
Title guarantee (full/limited)	: Full
Completion date	:
Contract rate	: The Law Society's interest rate from time to time
Purchase price	: £350,000
Deposit	: £20,000
Contents price (if separate)	: £500
Balance	: £330,500

The seller will sell and the buyer will buy the property for the purchase price.

WARNING	Signed
This is a formal document, designed to create legal rights and legal obligations. Take advice before using it.	Seller/Buyer

SPECIAL CONDITIONS

1. (a) This contract incorporates the Standard Conditions of Sale (Fifth Edition–2018 Revision).

   (b) The terms used in this contract have the same meaning when used in the Conditions.

2. Subject to the terms of this contract and to the Standard Conditions of Sale, the seller is to transfer the property with either full title guarantee or limited title guarantee, as specified on the front page.

3. (a) The sale includes those contents which are indicated on the attached list as included in the sale and the buyer is to pay the contents price for them.[1]

   ~~(b) The Sale excludes those fixtures which are at the property and are indicated on the attached list as excluded from the sale.~~

4. The property is sold with vacant possession.

(or) ~~4. The property is sold subject to the following leases or tenancies.~~

5. Conditions 6.1.2 and 6.1.3 shall take effect as if the time specified in them were 12 noon rather than 2.00 p.m.

6. **Representations**

   Neither party can rely on any representation made by the other, unless made in writing by the other or his conveyancer, but this does not exclude liability for fraud or recklessness.

~~7.~~ **Occupier's consent**

~~Each occupier identified below agress with the seller and the buyer, in consideration of their entering into this contract, that the occupier concurs in the sale of the property on the terms of this contract, undertakes to vacate the property on or before the completion date and releases the property and any included fixtures and contents from any right or interest that the occupier may have.~~

~~Note: this condition does not apply to occupiers under leases or tenancies subject to which the property is sold~~

Name(s) and signature(s) of the occupier(s) (if any):

~~Name~~ ....

~~Signature~~ ....

~~Notices may be sent to:~~

Seller's conveyancer's name: Buck & Co

E-mail address:*

Buyer's conveyancer's name: SLT Solicitors

E-mail address:*

* Adding an e-mail address authorises service by e-mail: see condition 1.3.3(b)

[1] *Author's note*: Not attached for the purposes of this example.

The following comments may be made on the worked example of the contract.

Date

The contract is left undated at the draft stage. The date is inserted on actual exchange of contracts.

Parties

The full names and addresses of the parties, as they will later appear on the transfer, should be inserted. The seller's solicitor may not at this stage know the full names of the buyer, and if necessary this information can be supplied later by the buyer's solicitor. Note the inclusion of postcodes in the parties' addresses.

Property

The property is freehold, so the word 'leasehold' can be deleted. Since the property is registered with an absolute title and is a suburban property with well-defined boundaries, it will suffice to describe it merely by its postal address. This constitutes the 'particulars' of the contract. No plan is needed in this case. Note the inclusion of the postcode in the description of the property; it is Land Registry practice to include this on the register.

Title

The property is registered, therefore the reference to 'root of title' is irrelevant and can be deleted. The title number and confirmation that the class of title is absolute should be inserted here.

Incumbrances

As the mortgage is to be discharged on completion, this need not be mentioned. The restrictive covenants must be stated to comply with SC 3. There is no need, however, to set out the covenants verbatim as long as a copy is provided; in this case as it is registered land, official copies will be supplied in any event.

Title guarantee

The seller is a sole owner and will give full title guarantee. It is customary to insert this on the front page of the contract form, even though in this case the words inserted repeat SC 4.6.2.

Completion date

The completion date is left blank at this stage and inserted on actual exchange.

Contract rate

Even though it is not intended to vary SC 1.1.1(e), confirmation of that fact is included on the front page of the contract form. Unless there are special circumstances, the solicitor would normally decide on the rate of interest to be included in the contract and this is not a matter on which the client's instructions are sought.

Price

The price, amount of deposit, amount (if any) payable for contents and balance due on completion are inserted in the appropriate space towards the bottom of the front page of the contract form. Note that the deposit is normally calculated as being 10% of the price for the property. This is to comply with SC 2.2.1. However, here the instructions at **8.6** indicate that a deposit of £20,000 has been agreed.

Agreement for sale

The words 'The seller will sell and the buyer will buy the property for the purchase price' above the two boxes at the bottom of the front page of the contract form constitute the agreement for sale. A box is provided for the seller/buyer to sign. This is left blank at this stage and will be signed by the client close to exchange.

Printed Special Condition 1

Printed Special Condition 1 incorporates the text of the Standard Conditions of Sale (Fifth Edition–2018 Revision) from the centre pages of the contract form. These pages are not reproduced in this example. This Condition should not be deleted, since to remove it is to remove the effect of the Standard Conditions.

Printed Special Condition 2

This Condition refers to the implied covenants which are given to the buyer under the Law of Property (Miscellaneous Provisions) Act 1994. In this case, the seller is selling with full title guarantee, and this fact is included on the front page of the contract form.

Printed Special Condition 3

This is necessary to ensure the contents are included in the sale. A list of the relevant items needs to be attached.

Printed Special Condition 4

This Condition provides two options, depending whether the property is to be sold with vacant possession (as here) or is subject to tenancies. In the latter case the details of the tenancies would be given in the condition.

Printed Special Condition 5

The completion time has been brought forward by two hours as this is a chain transaction and the additional time will assist all the sellers and buyers in the chain to complete on a single day.

Printed Special Condition 7

This has been deleted as there are no occupiers other than the seller in this property.

Conveyancers

The names (and if desired the addresses and references) of the parties' conveyancers are inserted at the foot of the back page of the contract form.

18.11.6 Worked example of a word-processed contract

THIS AGREEMENT is made the ...... day of ....

BETWEEN:

ROGER EVANS of 47 Queens' Road, Loamster, Maradon, Cornshire ('the Seller')[1] and CATHERINE READE and JOANNE READE both of 24 Leeming Road, Bridgeton, Cornshire[2] ('the Buyer')

1 **Definitions and interpretation**

In this Agreement:

1.1 'this Agreement' means this document as varied by any subsequent documentation;

1.2 'the Buyer's Solicitors' means SLT Solicitors[3];

1.3 'the Chattels' means the items listed in the Second Schedule;

1.4 'the Completion Date' means [ ];[4]

1.5 'the Completion Money' means the Purchase Price (or any outstanding balance of it) as adjusted by all sums due between the parties at Completion;

1.6 'the Contract Rate' means the Law Society's Interest rate from time to time;[5]

1.7 'the Deposit' means £20,000;[6]

1.8 'the Property' means the freehold property described in the First Schedule;

1.9 'the Purchase Price' means £350,500;[7]

1.10 the Seller's Solicitors' means Buck & Co;[8]

1.11 'the Standard Conditions' means the Standard Commercial Property Conditions (3rd Edition–2018 Revision);

1.12 'the Transfer' means the transfer of the Property;

1.13 'VAT' means an amount equal to the value added tax as charged in accordance with the VATA or any equivalent or substituted tax;

1.14 'VATA' means the Value Added Tax Act 1994 or any equivalent tax Act; and

1.15 'VAT invoice' means an invoice complying with the provisions of regulations 13 and 19 of the VAT Regulations 1995.

2 **Agreement for sale**

2.1 The Seller shall sell and the Buyer shall buy the Property and the Chattels for the Purchase Price.

2.2 The Purchase Price of £350,500 shall be apportioned as follows:

2.2.1 to the Property: £350,000;

2.2.2 to the Chattels: £500.[9]

3 **Deposit**

3.1 The Deposit shall be paid to the Seller's Solicitors to hold as stakeholders.[10]

3.2 The Law of Property Act 1925 Section 49(2) shall not have effect.

---

1. Insert details from the official copies.
2. Insert details from instructions.
3. Insert details from instructions.
4. Insert agreed date on exchange of contracts.
5. See **18.8.6**. No definition of this is needed as it is defined by SCPC 1.1.1 (e). However, it is not uncommon to find it specified in the special conditions.
6. See **18.8.7**. The SCPC position has been changed and a deposit of less than 10% provided for.
7. Insert details from instructions.
8. Insert details from instructions.
9. Insert as per instructions. The consideration for chattels will not attract stamp duty land tax. See **18.8.9**.
10. See **18.8.7**.

4 Completion

4.1 Completion of the sale and purchase and payment of the Completion Money shall take place on the Completion Date on or before 1.00 pm at the offices of the Seller's Solicitors or where they may reasonably direct.[11]

4.2 If the Completion Money is received after 1.00 pm on the Completion Date or on a day which is not a working day Completion shall be deemed for the purposes of the Standard Conditions to have taken place on the next working day after receipt.[12]

4.3 The Seller is not obliged to complete the sale of the Property unless it has also received the price for the Chattels.

5 Title guarantee

The Seller sells the Property with full title guarantee.[13]

6 Vacant possession

The Property is sold with vacant possession subject to the presence of any third party chattels.

7 Title

7.1 The title to the Property is registered at Land Registry and in relation to such title the Seller shall provide to the Buyer official copies of the items referred to in rules 134(1)(a) and (b) and 135(1)(a) of the Land Registration Rules 2003 as amended except charges or incumbrances registered or protected on the register which are to be discharged or overridden at or before completion.[14]

7.2 Title having been deduced prior to the date of this Agreement the Buyer accepts the Seller's title to the Property and shall be deemed to purchase with full knowledge of the title in all respects and shall not raise any requisitions or make any objection in relation to the title but the Buyer may raise requisitions arising out of:

7.2.1 events occurring after the date of this Agreement,

7.2.2 matters revealed by pre-completion searches which are not registered at the date of this Agreement,

7.2.3 matters which a prudent buyer could not be aware of at the date of this Agreement.[15]

8 Incumbrances

8.1 The Property is sold subject to and (where appropriate) with the benefit of the matters contained or referred to in the property proprietorship and charges registers of the title to the Property except any subsisting financial charges,

8.2 The Buyer or the Buyer's Solicitors having been supplied with copies of the documents referred to in clause 8.1 above the Buyer shall be deemed to purchase with full notice and knowledge of the same and shall not raise any requisition or make any objection in relation to them.[16]

8.3 The Transfer shall contain a covenant by the Buyer that the Buyer will (by way of indemnity only) observe and perform the covenants conditions and other matters contained or referred to in the documents referred to in clause 8.1 above and will indemnify and keep the Seller and its estate indemnified against all actions, proceedings, damages, costs, claims and expenses which may be suffered or incurred by the Seller or its estate in respect of future breach or non-observance or non-performance of those covenants and conditions and obligations.[17]

---

11. This amends the position under the SCPC which do not contain a time for completion. The buyer should consider its ability to comply with such a time limit (see **18.8.5**).
12. This amends the position under SCPC 9.1.2 by reducing the time the buyer has to transmit funds (see **18.8.6**).
13. This mirrors SCPC 7.6.2. The buyer should be wary of accepting anything less than full title guarantee (see **18.8.3**).
14. This mirrors SCPC 7.1.2. See **18.8.2**.
15. This provision presupposes title will have been deduced prior to exchange and therefore bars out requisitions on it. This mirrors SCPC 7.2.1 (see **18.8.2**).
16. As in n 2 above.
17. SCPC 7.6.5 does provide for an indemnity covenant to be given but practitioners often prefer to expressly agree the wording of the indemnity in the contract (see **18.8.8**).

9 Matters affecting the Property

The Property is sold subject to the following matters:

9.1 all local land charges whether registered or not before the date of this Agreement and all matters capable of registration as local land charges whether or not actually so registered;

9.2 all notices served and orders, demands, proposals or requirements made by any local public or other competent authority whether before or after the date of this Agreement;

9.3 all actual or proposed charges, notices, orders, restrictions, agreements, conditions, contraventions or other matters arising under any statute;

9.4 all easements, quasi-easements, rights, exceptions or other similar matters including rights of way, drainage, water, watercourses, light, rights of adjoining owners affecting the Property and liability to repair or covenants to repair roads, pavements, paths, ways, passages, sewers, drains, gutters, fences and other like matters whether or not apparent on inspection or disclosed in any of the documents referred to in this Agreement and without any obligation on the Seller to provide evidence of the creation of or to define or apportion any such liability;

9.5 matters referred to in Standard Condition 4.1.2;

9.6 matters relating to the Property about which the Seller does not know;

9.7 matters disclosed or which would be disclosed by any searches or as a result of enquiries (formal or informal and made in person in writing or orally) made by or for the Buyer or which a prudent buyer ought to make; and

9.8 unregistered interests which override first registration or registered dispositions listed in the Land Registration Act 2002 Schedules 1 and 3 as amended as appropriate.[18]

10 Disclaimer

10.1 The Buyer admits that:

10.1.1 it has inspected the Property and purchases it with full knowledge of its actual state and condition and shall take the Property as it stands;

10.1.2 it enters into this Agreement solely as a result of its own inspection and on the basis of the terms of this Agreement and not in reliance upon any advertisement statement representation or warranty either written or oral or implied made by or on behalf of the Seller except as stated in clause 10.2 below;

10.1.3 no warranty statement or representation has been made or given to the Buyer that the Property can be used or developed in any particular way or for any particular purpose and the Seller shall not be liable to the Buyer if the Property cannot for any reason whatsoever be so used or developed.

10.2 This Agreement contains the entire agreement between the parties and incorporates all the terms agreed between them for the purposes of the Law of Property (Miscellaneous Provisions) Act 1989 Section 2 and there are no other terms or provisions agreed prior to the date of this Agreement which have not been incorporated into this Agreement.

11 Incorporation of conditions of sale and documents

11.1 The Standard Conditions shall apply to this Agreement and are incorporated in it in so far as they are applicable to a sale by private treaty and are not varied by or inconsistent with the terms of this Agreement.

11.2 If there is any conflict between the Standard Conditions and the terms of this Agreement the terms of this Agreement prevail.[19]

---

18. This clause 9 and clause 8.1 qualify SCPC 4.1.1 and 4.1.2 (see **18.8.1**). The buyer would need to consider whether they were happy to purchase subject to each of the incumbrances specified in this clause.
19. This contract incorporates the SCPC but does depart from them in places. A buyer would need to consider with care the acceptability of any departure from the SCPC.

12 Merger on completion

The provisions of this Agreement shall not merge on completion of the Transfer so far as they remain to be performed.

13 Chattels

13.1 The Purchase Price includes payment for the items specified in the Second Schedule.

13.2 The Seller warrants that it is entitled to sell the Chattels free from any charge, lien, burden or adverse claim.

14 VAT provisions

14.1 Standard Condition Part 2, condition A1 (VAT exempt supply) is included in this Agreement.[20]

14.2 Any VAT payable by the Buyer shall be paid at the same time as the payment on which it is chargeable.

14.3 The Seller shall provide the Buyer with a receipted VAT invoice for any VAT paid by the Buyer under this Agreement.

15 Jurisdiction and governing law

This Agreement shall be governed by and construed in accordance with English law and the parties submit to the jurisdiction of the English courts.

AS WITNESS this Agreement has been signed by the parties (or their duly authorised representatives) on the date stated at the beginning of this Agreement:

SIGNED by the Seller **SIGNED** by the Buyer

FIRST SCHEDULE

The Property

Description of the Property

All that freehold property situate at and known as 47 *Queens' Road, Loamster, Maradon, Cornshire* CS1 5TY registered with title absolute at Land Registry under title number LM 12037.

SECOND SCHEDULE

The Chattels

The following fittings belonging to the Seller in the Property:

[Insert details of any chattels as appropriate]

20. The effect of incorporating condition A1 in Part 2 of the SCPCs is that the seller warrants the sale of the property is not a taxable supply for VAT purposes. Therefore, no VAT will be payable unless the taxable status of the property changes as a result of a change in the law between exchange and completion (see **18.8.10**).

SUMMARY

- The seller's solicitor will draft the contract, which will then need to be reviewed by and agreed with the buyer's solicitor.
- The seller's solicitor will need to investigate their client's title prior to drafting the contract.
- The seller's capacity to sell the land will need to be checked. Special care must be taken if the sellers are trustees, personal representatives, mortgagees or companies.
- A contract for sale must be in writing, contain all agreed terms and be signed by all parties. It will normally comprise the particulars of sale, the standard conditions of sale and the special conditions of sale.
- The particulars should give a clear and concise description of the property and confirm whether it is leasehold or freehold. If the sale is of part, or the boundaries are unclear, a plan should be used.
- Most contracts will incorporate either the Standard Conditions of Sale (Fifth Edition–2018 Revision) or the Standard Commercial Property Conditions (Third Edition–2018 Revision). These have been produced by experts to deal with issues common to most property transactions.
- Special conditions will be needed to vary or supplement the position under the standard conditions, or to deal with matters specific to the transaction.
- Most contracts will contain special conditions dealing with the following:
  - the incumbrances subject to which the property is sold;
  - whether the property is sold with vacant possession or subject to tenancies;
  - the date for completion of the sale;
  - the rate of interest to be paid if completion is delayed ('the contract rate').
- The contract may (if relevant and required) contain special conditions:
  - providing for a deposit of less than 10%;
  - providing for the deposit to be held as agent, rather than as stakeholder;
  - disclosing a defect in title;
  - dealing with any agreed restrictive covenant indemnity insurance policy;
  - stating the seller is selling with limited title guarantee;
  - providing for an indemnity covenant to be given in the transfer deed;
  - detailing the fittings to be sold to the buyer and their price;
  - specifying any fixtures the seller is to remove and retain;
  - dealing with the payment of VAT.
- The buyer's solicitor will need to review the contract and make any amendments to it they consider appropriate. These amendments will then need to be agreed or negotiated with the seller's solicitor until an agreed form of contract exists.

CHAPTER 19

Conditional Contracts and Options

LEARNING OUTCOMES

After reading this chapter you will be able to:

- identify when a conditional contract may be appropriate
- advise as to the requirements for a valid conditional contract
- explain what an option is and when it might be used
- advise on how to create a valid option.

19.1 USE OF CONDITIONAL CONTRACTS

A conditional contract is one that requires satisfaction of a specified condition if the transaction is to complete. Conditional contracts are generally not desirable since they leave an element of doubt as to whether the transaction will proceed to completion. However, they are useful where the transaction cannot proceed without satisfaction of the condition but the parties do not wish to spend time and money satisfying the condition without a contract in place.

Most of the situations in which conditional contracts are used benefit the buyer more than the seller (eg, 'subject to planning permission'), and the seller should be aware of the risk of the condition not being satisfied and the transaction not completing.

Despite these risks and uncertainties, they may be considered for use in the following circumstances:

(a) where the buyer has not had the opportunity before exchange of contracts to make searches and enquiries, or to conduct a survey, or where their mortgage arrangements have not been finalised (such a condition is highly undesirable from the seller's perspective, as it is likely to give the buyer ample opportunity to withdraw);

(b) where the contract is dependent on planning permission being obtained for the property (contracts of this kind are common where the buyer is a developer);

(c) where the sale is dependent on permission being obtained from a third party (eg, landlord's consent) (this is usually the case where a commercial property lease is assigned).

19.1.1 Chain transactions

Conditional contracts should never be used where one or both of the parties has an unconditional sale or purchase contract which is dependent on the conditional contract. In this situation, if the conditional contract was rescinded for non-fulfilment of the condition, this would give rise to great difficulties in the fulfilment of the linked unconditional contract and could result in a breach of that contract.

19.1.2 Alternative solutions

Before agreeing to enter a conditional contract, the seller should consider whether there are any alternative solutions which could be used in preference to the conditional contract. For example, it may be preferable to delay exchange until the matter which was the subject of the condition has been resolved. An alternative solution may be to grant the buyer an option to purchase the property to be exercised within a stated period (see **19.4**).

19.2 REQUIREMENTS FOR A VALID CONDITIONAL CONTRACT

19.2.1 Certainty

In addition to the usual requirements for a land contract (see **18.4**), the terms of the condition must be clear and certain. In *Lee-Parker v Izzett (No 2)* [1972] 2 All ER 800, an agreement to sell a freehold house 'subject to the buyer obtaining a satisfactory mortgage' was held to be void because the word 'satisfactory' was too vague and there was, therefore, no certainty regarding the circumstances in which the buyer would validly be able to withdraw from the contract. Not all 'subject to mortgage' clauses will suffer the same fate. Provided that the condition is drafted to make it clear that 'satisfactory' mortgage offer means an offer satisfactory to the buyer acting as a reasonable person, the condition is likely to be valid. There is now an objective standard by which any mortgage offer received may be judged.

The need for certainty must also be borne in mind with regard to other common conditions. So, a contract subject to 'satisfactory searches' will again need a reasonableness provision inserting to prevent its being void. See **19.3.1** as to drafting contracts 'subject to planning permission.

If the condition is void for uncertainty then the whole contract between the parties will also fail.

19.2.2 Time for performance

It was held in *Aberfoyle Plantations Ltd v Cheng* [1960] AC 115, that the time for performance of the condition is of the essence and cannot be extended either by agreement between the parties or by the court. The same case also laid down the rules relating to the time for performance of the condition, which are summarised as follows:

(a) Where the contract contains a completion date, the condition must be fulfilled by that date, irrespective of whether time was of the essence of the contractual completion date.

(b) If a time is stated for the fulfilment of the condition, that time limit must be complied with or the contract will fail.

(c) If no time limit is specified the condition must be fulfilled within a reasonable time. This provision is clearly unsatisfactory since it leaves room for argument about what is a reasonable time, and so a time limit should always be stated.

19.3 DRAFTING

19.3.1 For all conditional contracts

The drafting of a condition requires extreme care to ensure that the requirements outlined in **19.2** have been satisfied. No such provision is included in either set of Standard Conditions, although a contract to assign a lease may be conditional on the landlord's consent being obtained under SC 8.3 (SCPC 11.3).

The following guidelines should be borne in mind:

(a) Consider the precise event(s) on which the contract is to be made conditional.
(b) By what time must the condition be fulfilled? (The specified time limit cannot be extended.)
(c) Consider the circumstances in which the contract may be rescinded.
(d) Make sure that there are no loopholes which would enable one party to escape from the contract other than for the non-fulfilment of the event(s) contemplated in (a) above.
(e) Use an established precedent, adapting it to fit the exact requirements of the client's circumstances.

19.3.2 For contracts 'subject to planning permission'

Where a contract is to be made 'subject to the buyer obtaining planning permission', the following matters should be dealt with in the drafting of the condition:

(a) the form of the planning application to be submitted and whether it is for detailed or outline consent;
(b) the obligations the buyer is under to submit and pursue the planning application;
(c) if conditions are attached to the consent, the type of conditions that would entitle the buyer to rescind;
(d) who should pay the fee for the application;
(e) whether the buyer can (or is obliged to) appeal if the local planning authority does not grant permission within a stated period or if the planning application initially is refused;
(f) the seller should agree not to oppose the buyer's application.

19.4 OPTIONS

19.4.1 What is an option?

An option is a right given to a prospective buyer which allows the buyer to insist on the seller selling the land to them if the buyer wishes to buy within a specified period. There is no obligation on the buyer to buy, but if they do choose to do so, the seller is obliged to sell. Options are common in commercial transactions, but less so in residential transactions.

19.4.2 Duration

The option agreement will state the time limit within which it must be exercised if the seller is to be obliged to sell. Since 6 April 2010 there has been no maximum permitted period (previously the maximum permitted period was 21 years under the Perpetuities and Accumulations Act 1964) but short periods (eg, 12 months) are common as the seller will not want to keep the property off the market for long.

19.4.3 Formalities

An option must comply with the normal requirements for a valid contract – offer, acceptance, consideration, etc. Although the consideration can be a nominal amount (and can be dispensed with altogether if the option is granted by deed), it is common to find that the seller will require a substantial amount to commit themselves in this way. The option will also have to provide how the actual sale price of the land is to be arrived at if the buyer exercises the option. If the option is exercisable only for a short period, a fixed price can be specified in the option. In an option exercisable over a period longer than (say) 12 months, the effects of inflation, etc, must be considered and a new price will have to be arrived at. In such a case, the requirements of certainty must be considered, so some formula will need laying down so that the price can be ascertained if the parties are unable to reach agreement. An appointment of a valuer whose decision is final is common. The buyer may wish the consideration for the option itself to be set off against the purchase price; this will need stating expressly.

In addition to the normal contractual rules, as this is a land contract, the provisions of s 2 of the Law of Property (Miscellaneous Provisions) Act 1989 will also need to be taken into account. This requires that the contract is in writing, must incorporate all the agreed terms and be signed by both parties. When the option is exercised, the contract to buy the land comes into existence at that moment. The exercise of the option does not need the signature of both parties.

As the contract for sale comes into existence on the exercise of the option, the terms of that sale contract need considering in the usual way and will need providing for in the option contract. Otherwise, an open contract will be created, which will be unsatisfactory for both buyer and seller. So the option agreement should state that the sale contract will be subject to (for example) the Standard Conditions of Sale, how title will be deduced, what incumbrances the land will be sold subject to, what special conditions will apply, etc, in the same way as if the seller were drafting an ordinary sale contract. The buyer will also need to consider these as they would any other contract.

19.5 PROTECTION OF CONDITIONAL CONTRACTS AND OPTIONS

In order to make the conditional contract or option binding on a subsequent buyer of the land, it should be protected by registration. This will be a Class C(iv) land charge in unregistered land and a notice in registered land.

SUMMARY

- A conditional contract is one dependent upon the satisfaction of a specified condition in order for the transaction to complete.
- As satisfaction of the condition cannot be guaranteed, a conditional contract carries with it certain risks for the parties.
- A conditional contract may be useful where, for example, the buyer requires planning permission or the consent of a third party is needed to the sale.
- The terms of the condition must be clear and certain or the contract will be void for uncertainty.
- An option may be an alternative to a conditional contract; it gives a prospective buyer a right to purchase the property within a specified window of time.
- An option agreement must satisfy all the usual requirements of a contract and, as a land contract, must also be in writing, contain all agreed terms and be signed by both parties.
- The parties will need to agree the time period within which the option must be exercised and a mechanism for determining the price to be paid when (and if) the option is exercised.
- The conditional contract or option should be protected either as a Class C(iv) land charge (unregistered land) or by a notice (registered land).

CHAPTER 20

THE MORTGAGE

LEARNING OUTCOMES

After reading this chapter you will be able to:

- identify the documentation that will be needed where the property is to be mortgaged
- explain what terms will be contained in a typical mortgage offer
- advise on the professional conduct issues that may arise when a mortgage is to be created
- identify the responsibilities of the solicitors for the lender and the borrower in connection with the mortgage.

20.1 THE MORTGAGE OFFER

When a lender is approached by a potential borrower seeking a loan to fund a property purchase, it first carries out checks on the financial position of the borrower (a process sometimes referred to as 'due diligence'). Once it is satisfied as to the borrower's credit-worthiness, the lender issues a document setting out the terms on which it is prepared to lend. In residential and simple commercial loans, this document is called a 'mortgage offer'. In complex commercial loans given by banks, the lender issues a 'commitment letter' with a 'term sheet' attached, followed by a 'facility agreement' setting out the detailed terms of the loan (see **20.7**). In whatever form it is produced, the solicitor for the borrower must ensure that the client has received and (where applicable) accepted a satisfactory mortgage offer before advising the client to exchange contracts.

If you are carrying out a 'specified activity' in relation to a regulated mortgage contract, you must be authorised under the FSMA 2000 (see **9.1.2**).

The types of mortgage available to the client are discussed in **Chapter 9**.

20.2 TERMS OF OFFER

A mortgage offer made by a lender in respect of a loan to be made for the purchase of property will normally deal with some or all of the matters listed below:

(a) a description of the property which is to be mortgaged, its purchase price and tenure (ie, freehold or leasehold);

(b) the amount of the advance (loan) and period of the mortgage (see **9.3**);

(c) whether the mortgage is to be repayment or interest-only (see **9.4**);

(d) the interest rate applicable to the loan (see **9.4**);

(e) the amount of the borrower's initial monthly repayments to the lender. This sum is subject to fluctuation if the interest rate charged under the mortgage is variable (see **9.4**);

(f) where the lender is to insure the property, the amount of cover and when that cover will start. The solicitor must ensure that the time when the lender's policy is to come into force coincides with the contractual provisions relating to insurance (see **Chapter 22**). The amount of cover taken out by the lender is usually index-linked and should cover the cost of rebuilding the property in the event of its total destruction. Where the property is not detached, it must also cover the cost of repairs to any adjoining or neighbouring property which is damaged by the incident;

(g) details of any repair works which the lender requires to be carried out to the property, including the time limit within which these works must be done. Where repairs are required, the lender may also decide to hold back a part of the loan until it is satisfied that the repairs have been completed. This 'retention' from the mortgage advance will cause a shortfall in the money available on completion, and a recalculation of the client's finances will be necessary to ensure that sufficient funds will be available both to complete the transaction and to carry out the necessary repairs;

(h) the amount of any 'guarantee premium' which is payable by the borrower. Where the lender is agreeing to lend a larger sum than it feels is advisable in the circumstances of the case, some lenders insist that an insurance policy is taken out to insure against the risk of the borrower defaulting on the mortgage and the lender not being able to recover the full amount owing on resale of the property. A single premium is payable for this insurance. The cost is usually borne by the borrower (see **9.3**).

It is usually a term of a mortgage offer for a mortgage over residential property that any existing mortgage which the client has (eg, over their present house) should be discharged on or before completion of the new loan. The buyer's solicitor must ensure that their client is aware of and can comply with this condition.

20.3 CONDITIONS ATTACHED TO OFFER

Before accepting the offer or committing their client to the purchase, the buyer's solicitor should ensure that their client understands the conditions and terms attached to the mortgage offer and will be able to comply with them. Conditions may be general (eg, a condition that the property must not be let to a tenant without the lender's consent) or special, having application to this offer only (eg, a condition that the buyer carries out certain repairs to the property).

The solicitor should check the offer to see whether or not the lender requires a formal acceptance of the offer. If a formal acceptance is required, the client must be advised to do this within the time limit stipulated by the lender. Failure to accept a formal offer (where required) will result in the mortgage funds not being available to complete the transaction.

Before advising the client to exchange contracts, the solicitor should also check to see whether the mortgage offer is expressed so as not to be legally binding on the lender, or is subject to a condition that allows the lender to withdraw even after formal acceptance and exchange of contracts by the borrower. For example, a commitment letter would usually contain a provision enabling the bank to withdraw the offer to lend if there is a material adverse change in the market or the borrower. The client should be advised if this is the case, as a client who has exchanged contracts will still be required to purchase the property, even if they are no longer able to obtain mortgage finance.

20.4 INSTRUCTIONS TO ACT

At the same time as a mortgage offer is sent to the client, the lender will instruct solicitors to act for it in connection with the grant of the new mortgage. These solicitors will receive a number of documents from the lender, including instructions to act (which contain similar information to the mortgage offer sent to the borrower), specimen mortgage deeds and any other documents relevant to the transaction. In commercial property cases the lender is likely to be separately represented, but in most residential cases the solicitor who is instructed to act for the lender will be the same solicitor who is acting for the borrower (see **5.4**). In the latter case, the objectives of the two clients coincide, in that both seek a property which is structurally sound and has a good, safe legal title; the risk of conflict of interests nevertheless exists (see **20.5**) and the solicitor must always bear in mind that they owe a duty to both clients (see *Mortgage Express v Bowerman & Partners (A Firm)* [1996] 2 All ER 836). Acting for both clients in this way has advantages in terms of time and costs, since the same solicitor can do the work required for both clients at the same time.

20.4.1 *The Lenders' Handbook* (residential property)

Most lenders who are active in the residential loan market have adopted the *Lenders' Handbook* promulgated by UK Finance. This is a set of standardised mortgage instructions, written in plain English. The instructions in the *Handbook* are in two parts. Part 1 applies to all lenders using the *Handbook*; Part 2 sets out the requirements of each individual lender in cases where they differ from Part 1. Part 1 of the *Lenders' Handbook* is set out in **Appendix** 7. It should be noted, however, that the *Handbook* is liable to change, and that a printed version should not be relied upon. An up-to-date version may be obtained from the UK Finance website at <www.cml.org.uk/lenders-handbook>, as can copies of Part 2 for any particular lender.

The solicitor must ensure that they carry out their lender client's instructions as set out in both parts of the *Lenders' Handbook*.

20.4.2 *The BSA Mortgage Instructions* (residential property)

The Building Societies Association (BSA) has developed a set of mortgage instructions for its members which has been available for use since January 2010. Use of these instructions is voluntary for BSA members, and BSA members who are members of UK Finance can continue to use the *Lenders' Handbook*. A solicitor acting for a building society using the *BSA Mortgage Instructions* must obtain a copy from the BSA website, <www.bsa.org.uk>, as the instructions are not available in printed format.

20.5 CONFLICT OF INTERESTS

Where the buyer's solicitor has also been instructed to act for the lender and, for example, some of the conditions attached to the mortgage offer are unacceptable or prejudicial to the buyer client, a conflict arises between the interests of the buyer client and those of the lender client. Unless the conflict can be resolved to the satisfaction of both clients, the solicitor cannot continue to act for both. For example, if it comes to the notice of the solicitor that the buyer client will be in breach of the terms of the mortgage offer, the solicitor's duty to their lender client is to inform the lender. However, where a conflict of interests exists between the buyer client and the lender client, the solicitor, acting in their capacity of adviser to the buyer, may disclose the nature of the conflict to the lender only with the consent of the buyer client (see *Halifax Mortgage Services v Stepsky* [1996] 1 FLR 620). Disclosure of information without the buyer client's consent will be a breach of the solicitor's duty of confidentiality to the buyer client. In such a case the *Lenders' Handbook* requires the solicitor to cease acting for the lender.

Note that the solicitor's duty of confidentiality to the buyer is discharged in a case of mortgage fraud (see **5.12**).

20.6 REPORTING TO THE LENDER

Whether the title investigation and analysis of the pre-contract search results is done by the solicitor acting for the borrower and the lender or by a separate lender's solicitor, the lender will want to know that the property is adequate security for the loan and has a 'good and marketable' title. In residential transactions the lender's solicitor will use the form of certificate approved by The Law Society and UK Finance. In commercial transactions, the lender's solicitor is likely to use the standard form certificate of title produced by the City of London Law Society.

20.7 THE MORTGAGE DOCUMENTATION

The number and nature of the documents used in a secured lending transaction depend on the amount of the loan, the number of properties to be mortgaged, the complexity of the loan arrangements and the type of lender. A mortgage of a residential property to be used as the borrower's home or a simple commercial property loan granted by an institutional lender (such as a high street bank or building society) is likely to involve a single mortgage deed in the lender's standard form. This deed is likely to incorporate by reference the lender's standard terms and conditions (a published booklet) and, in the case of a building society, the rules applying to members of the particular society. Both the standard terms and conditions and the rules are subject to change over the term of the loan. In this case, the lender will supply the printed mortgage form and the solicitor will merely fill in the blank spaces provided for the borrower's name and the property address. Alternatively, the lender may require the borrower to use Form CH1 produced by Land Registry for registered land, or a mortgage deed drafted by the firm of solicitors acting for the lender. Land Registry has begun testing an all-digital process to create, sign and register a mortgage deed, but this is still in the small pilot stage.

For a complex loan secured on commercial property, there may be a loan agreement (sometimes called a facility letter or credit agreement) and a separate charge by way of legal mortgage, or a debenture incorporating a charge by way of legal mortgage. Often the loan agreement is dealt with by the banking departments of the relevant firms, while the charging document is dealt with by the conveyancers.

Whatever form the documents take, the mortgage documentation is likely to have the following aspects in common:

(a) It will set out the commercial details of the particular transaction, such as the purpose of the loan, the date on which it is to be repaid, what interest will be paid in the meantime and whether, (and if so, on what terms) the borrower is allowed to redeem the mortgage early.

(b) As security for the loan, the property will be charged by way of legal mortgage. A legal mortgage creates an interest in favour of the lender equivalent to a 3,000-year lease (or for a leasehold property a term of one day less than the lease), and is considered better security than an equitable mortgage because the law relating to the remedies available to the lender on enforcement of an equitable mortgage is less settled.

(c) The document which charges the property will be a deed, so as to comply with the definition of a legal mortgage in s 87 of the LPA 1925.

(d) Depending on the type of property, the lender may be granted additional security, such as a fixed charge over any fixtures, plant and machinery not caught by the legal mortgage of the property, and an assignment of the rental income.

(e) If the borrower is a company, the lender may also take a floating charge over all the assets of the borrower not covered by the other security. A floating charge catches types of assets, such as stock-in-trade, goodwill and book debts, that it would be impossible or impractical to secure with a fixed charge (or of which the lender is unaware) and allows the borrower to deal with the assets in the ordinary course of business, including disposing of them, thus affording some flexibility to the borrower. Any assets acquired after the date on which the floating charge is created but which fall within an identified group of assets will be subject to the charge.

(f) It will state the liabilities owed by the borrower to the lender in respect of which the security is given. In many cases, the documents will create an 'all monies charge', which secures any sums owed by the borrower to the lender (perhaps under another loan, guarantee, credit card or overdraft on a current account), not just the loan made for the purchase of this particular property. So, in the event of the borrower's insolvency, the lender can use the proceeds of sale of the property to discharge any debts owed by the borrower to the lender.

(g) The borrower may be required to make representations and warranties about certain matters relating to their status (eg, that the borrower is solvent and, in the case of an organisation, has obtained all necessary internal consents and approvals to the taking out of the loan).

(h) The borrower will enter into covenants designed to ensure that they do not do things or omit to do things which would devalue the financial status of the borrower or the property (eg, a covenant to keep the property in good repair and not to invalidate the insurance, or not to grant a lease or licence without the consent of the lender).

(i) It will set out the events of default, the trigger events which will permit the lender to cancel the loan and demand immediate repayment (a procedure known as acceleration). The events of default will include failure to make the required payments of capital/interest, breach of a representation or warranty, breach of the financial or property covenants, and insolvency of the borrower.

(j) It will extend the statutory powers of sale, leasing, accepting surrenders given to mortgagees (see, eg, **3.9.1.1**) and exclude s 93 of the LPA 1925, thus allowing the lender to refuse to discharge the mortgage on the property until any loans secured on the borrower's other properties have also been repaid (a practice known as 'consolidation').

(k) It will prohibit the borrower from creating any other mortgages over the property, a clause that is often known as a 'negative pledge'. This gives the lender the power to refuse any request by the borrower to take out another loan secured on the property from a different lender, or to control the way in which it is done if it is minded to agree. The commercial purpose of the negative pledge clause is to prevent the borrower taking out a further loan which might make it more difficult for them to make the payments on the first loan. Also, at some point during the term of the loan, the first lender may want to make a 'further advance' to the borrower (lend them some additional money), and the first lender will want to be sure that this money is secured by its first legal mortgage, notwithstanding the creation of any subsequent mortgages (a process known as 'tacking'). Although tacking is possible, the rules are complicated and it is simpler to prohibit the creation of subsequent mortgages altogether. In addition, where the lender has also taken a floating charge, the negative pledge supports the floating charge and gives it effective priority. A properly registered first legal mortgage will automatically have priority over any legal mortgage created later in time. Any second mortgage that is granted in favour of a new lender will take priority over the floating charge unless the new lender has notice of the negative pledge at the time it takes the security. If it does have notice, priority is reversed and the new lender's security, although valid, will rank behind the floating charge. So, a negative pledge is an effective way to prevent the borrower creating a second mortgage which would take priority over the first lender's floating charge. Finally, if the borrower breaks the negative pledge, this will be an event of default and the lender will be entitled to demand immediate repayment of the loan.

The borrower's solicitor is under an obligation to explain the nature and effect of the mortgage documentation to the client in whatever level of detail is appropriate. A residential client may require more explanation as to the borrower's covenants, the events of default and the powers of the lender in the event of default. For example, almost all mortgage deeds will give the lender power, expressly or impliedly, to take possession of and/or sell the property in the event of default by the borrower (see **3.9**). Some residential borrowers are unaware of this fact, and the solicitor, without unnecessarily frightening the client, should point out to the client that these powers do exist and will be exercised by the lender if the need arises. It may therefore be sensible to check that the client is aware of their liability to make monthly repayments of the loan, and insurance premiums where appropriate, and that the amount of these monthly outgoings does not represent an unrealistically high proportion of the client's income.

20.8 PROTECTING THE SECURITY

The pre-completion searches that must be carried out specifically to protect the lender prior to the purchase of the property and the creation of the mortgage are discussed in **28.5**, **28.7** and **28.8**. After completion, the mortgage must be registered at Companies House and Land Registry; further details are given in **31.4.9** and **31.8** respectively.

SUMMARY

- In residential (or straightforward commercial) transactions, a lender will issue a 'mortgage offer' indicating the terms on which it is willing to lend. In more complex commercial transactions the offer will be in the form of a 'commitment letter', followed by a facility agreement containing the detailed terms of the lending arrangement.
- The solicitor should check the terms of the mortgage offer and advise the client:
  - if there is any 'retention' from the mortgage advance;
  - whether the buyer is obliged to pay a 'guarantee premium';
  - if the buyer is obliged to discharge an existing mortgage;
  - of any terms and conditions attached to the offer;
  - if a formal acceptance of the offer is required;
  - if the mortgage offer can be withdrawn by the lender.
- In residential transactions, the solicitor may be instructed to act for the buyer as well as the lender. In commercial transactions, buyer and lender are usually represented separately. A solicitor acting for both buyer and lender must consider the risk of a conflict of interest arising, and must be aware of their duty of confidentiality.
- If acting for a lender in a residential transaction, the solicitor will usually have to carry out standardised instructions as set out in the *Lender's Handbook* (see **Appendix 7**). The lender will require confirmation from the solicitor that the property has a good and marketable title.
- The lender's solicitor will need to put in place the mortgage documentation. In a straightforward residential or commercial transaction this will often simply require the completion of a mortgage deed in the lender's standard form, by which the property is charged to the lender. In more complex commercial transactions there may be a facility agreement, legal mortgage and floating charge. There may be further fixed charges over plant and machinery, and (if appropriate) an assignment of rental income.
- The borrower's solicitor must explain the nature and effect of the mortgage documentation to the borrower.
- The lender's solicitor must ensure that appropriate pre-completion searches are carried out and that the mortgage is registered at Land Registry and (if the borrower is a company) at Companies House.

CHAPTER 21

The Deposit

LEARNING OUTCOMES

After reading this chapter you will be able to:

- explain the purpose of a preliminary deposit and a deposit payable on exchange of contracts
- advise a seller client on the risks involved in accepting a deposit of less than 10% of the purchase price
- calculate the amount of the deposit correctly for the purposes of the contract
- understand the different ways in which a buyer client may fund the deposit
- explain the different capacities in which a deposit may be held, and advise on the associated risks for buyers and sellers
- pay the deposit to the seller's solicitor in the manner required by the contract
- understand how the Standard Conditions protect the seller against the possibility of the deposit cheque being dishonoured
- advise on whether the seller or the buyer will be credited with interest earned on the deposit between exchange and completion.

21.1 NEED FOR DEPOSIT

It is customary for a buyer, on exchange of contracts, to pay to the seller a deposit of 10% of the purchase price. Standard contractual conditions (such as SC 2.2 and SCPC 3.2) reflect this practice. In law, a deposit is unnecessary, and neither common law nor statute provides for any deposit to be payable.

21.1.1 Purpose of deposit

The payment of a deposit acts as part payment of the purchase price, demonstrates the buyer's good intentions of completing the contract and gives the seller leverage to ensure the fulfilment of the contract, since the seller is usually able to forfeit the deposit if the buyer defaults.

21.2 PRELIMINARY DEPOSITS

Neither party needs to pay a preliminary deposit since neither is committed to the sale and purchase until contracts have been exchanged. An estate agent will sometimes ask a prospective buyer to pay a preliminary deposit as an indication of the buyer's good intentions to proceed with negotiations. If a preliminary deposit is paid, the buyer should ensure that the agent has the seller's authority to receive the deposit. In the absence of the seller's authority, the buyer has no recourse against the seller if the agent misappropriates the money (see *Sorrell v Finch* [1977] AC 728). A preliminary deposit is normally fully refundable to the buyer if the transaction does not proceed.

21.2.1 Buying a newly-built house

A seller who is a builder or developer will invariably require a prospective buyer to pay a preliminary deposit. Since this type of preliminary deposit often buys an option to purchase a numbered plot at a stated price, it is not unusual to find that the deposit is not returnable to the buyer in any circumstances, although it will be credited as part of the purchase price if the matter proceeds.

21.3 AMOUNT OF DEPOSIT

No deposit at all is payable unless the contract expressly makes provision for one. A deposit of 10% of the purchase price has until recently been standard practice and is the figure provided for in both sets of Standard Conditions (SC 2.2 and SCPC 3.2) unless specifically amended. Deposits of less than 10% are not uncommon.

21.3.1 Reduced deposit

It is clearly to the seller's advantage to demand a 10% deposit. If, however, the seller is asked by the buyer to accept a reduced amount, the following matters should be considered by the seller's solicitor:

(a) The risk of the sale going off, with the consequent need to forfeit the deposit to compensate for loss.

(b) The amount of the buyer's mortgage offer. (It may be reasonable to accept a less than 10% deposit from a buyer who has a firm offer of advance for the whole of the balance of the purchase price, taking into account the amount of the reduced deposit.)

(c) The likely amount of loss which the seller would suffer if the buyer were to default (eg, the cost of bridging finance or interest needed to complete a related purchase, the length of time which will be taken to effect a resale and the costs of such a resale).

21.3.2 Seller's solicitor's duty

The seller's solicitor must explain the consequences of taking a reduced deposit to their client and obtain their client's express authority before agreeing to accept a reduced deposit. *Morris v Duke-Cohan & Co* (1975) 119 SJ 826 suggests that it may be professional negligence for a solicitor to accept a reduced deposit without the client's express authority.

21.3.3 No deposit payable

Only in exceptional circumstances should the transaction proceed without any deposit being taken. Examples might include family transactions, or sales to sitting tenants. However, in commercial transactions, some major institutions will refuse to pay a deposit on the basis that they are of such standing that there is no risk of loss to the seller.

21.3.4 Calculating the deposit

The amount of the deposit actually payable on exchange should take into account any preliminary deposit already paid. Under SC 2.2.1 it is calculated as 10% of the total of the purchase price and does not include the price payable for any contents included in the sale. Under SCPC 3.2.1 the deposit is 10% of the 'purchase price' and whether the 'purchase price' includes any chattels will depend upon the special conditions.

21.4 FUNDING THE DEPOSIT

Instructions should be obtained from the buyer client as to how they propose to fund the deposit. When initial instructions are taken from the client, it is best to assume that the seller will require payment of a full 10% deposit. If the buyer wishes to pay a reduced deposit, the matter will have to be raised during negotiations with the seller's solicitor.

21.4.1 From an investment account

Where the buyer intends to fund the deposit from money in an investment account held by them, the length of notice which the buyer needs to give to withdraw funds without losing a significant amount of interest should be borne in mind.

21.4.2 Bridging finance

Bridging finance from a bank or other lender may be needed in a situation where the purchase is dependent on a related sale. Bridging finance will be required in the situation where the buyer will have sufficient funds for all of the purchase price on completion (eg, because of a related sale), but does not have sufficient funds at exchange of contracts to fund the deposit. A loan will then be required to 'bridge the gap' between when the money is needed (exchange) and when it will be available (completion of the sale). It should be apparent at an early stage in the transaction that bridging finance will be required and arrangements should be made as soon as possible, so that the money is immediately available when required on exchange. An undertaking to repay the bridging loan out of the proceeds of sale of the client's existing property will often be required from the solicitor.

The client should be advised about the costs and risks of bridging finance, such as the high interest rate which will be payable over an uncertain period if the sale goes off, and the arrangement fees charged by the lender for negotiating the loan. If the client has a high cash flow passing through their current account, it may be more cost effective for them to take advantage of the lower interest rates payable on an overdraft on current account. It should be noted, however, that a secured bridging loan will be a regulated mortgage contract for the purposes of the FSMA 2000 (see **9.1.2**).

21.4.3 Deposit guarantees

A deposit guarantee, obtainable from some insurance companies, is an insurance policy which is bought by the buyer and tendered to the seller on exchange in place of payment of a money deposit. If the buyer wishes to fund the deposit in this way, the seller's consent must be obtained and the contract amended to provide for payment by way of the guarantee. The guarantee should be taken out in the sum required as deposit (ie, normally 10% of the purchase price). The seller will be able to enforce the guarantee against the insurance company, and so recover the deposit in cash in the event of the buyer defaulting on completion. Although guarantees which can be moved up through a chain of transactions can be obtained (ie, their benefit can be assigned), they are not popular with sellers and are not commonly used.

21.4.4 Use of deposit from related sale

If the buyer is also selling their existing house, they will be receiving a deposit on that sale. Can that money be used to fund (or partly fund) the deposit on the purchase? Standard Condition 2.2.5 permits this in certain circumstances (see **21.6.1**). If, as is likely, the deposit received on the sale is less than the deposit required on the purchase, the balance can be funded in one of the ways previously mentioned. Alternatively, it may be possible to persuade the seller to accept a reduced deposit, ie, to try to get the deposit reduced to the amount being received by the buyer on the sale of their present house.

Such a provision is obviously inapplicable in a commercial transaction and so the Standard Commercial Property Conditions do not include a similar provision.

21.5 CLEARING FUNDS

The buyer's solicitor must ensure that they receive the amount of the deposit from their own client in sufficient time to allow the client's cheque to be cleared through the solicitor's client account before drawing on it.

21.6 CAPACITY IN WHICH DEPOSIT IS HELD

The deposit can be held in one of the three capacities listed below:

(a) agent for the seller;

(b) agent for the buyer;

(c) stakeholder.

Most deposits are paid to the seller's solicitor in the capacity of stakeholder.

21.6.1 Which capacity applies?

Both sets of Standard Conditions provide for the deposit to be held by an auctioneer as agent (SC 2.3.6 and SCPC 3.3.6) but by a conveyancer as stakeholder (SC 2.2.6 and SCPC 3.2.2). However, SC 2.2.5 allows the seller to use the deposit as a deposit on a related purchase of a house for the seller's residence, provided that in such related purchase it will be held on the same terms as SC 2.2.5 and 2.2.6. This is a very important provision as it allows the seller to use the deposit to fund their own deposit on a related purchase without the need for the express permission of the buyer. It is widely taken advantage of in practice. Such a provision is inapplicable in a commercial transaction and so the SCPCs do not include a similar provision.

If the contract is silent on the issue, solicitors and estate agents hold in the capacity of agent for the seller, but an auctioneer holds as stakeholder (see *Edgell v Day* (1865) LR 1 CP 80; *Ryan v Pilkington* [1959] 1 All ER 689).

21.6.2 Agent for the buyer

The capacity of agent for the buyer is rarely used, since in most situations the seller will be reluctant to agree to the deposit being held in this way. It may, however, be necessary to use this capacity where the seller is represented by an unqualified person.

21.6.3 Agent for the seller

If the deposit is held as agent for the seller, the agent may hand the money over to the seller before completion. This capacity is advantageous to the seller who can, if they wish, use the money immediately for any purpose they wish. Where this occurs, although the buyer will have a lien over the property (see **21.10**), the buyer may have difficulty in recovering the money if the seller defaults on completion, because the money will have passed into the hands of a third party who may be unknown to the buyer and with whom the buyer has no contractual relationship.

If either set of the Standard Conditions is being used, a special condition will be required to state that this capacity is to apply if the deposit is to be held by the seller's solicitor. However, in the case of auction sales, SC 2.3.6 and SCPC 3.3.6 provide for the deposit to be held by the auctioneer as agent for the seller. It is also usual on the purchase of a new house from a builder to find that the deposit is to be held as agent. This is to allow the builder to use the money to fund the building work. The risk here is that the builder may become insolvent, but any loss in such a situation would be fully recoverable as long as the builder is selling the house with NHBC or similar insurance cover (see **42.2.3**).

21.6.4 Stakeholder

A stakeholder is a middleman standing between both parties, and where this capacity is used, the money cannot generally be handed to either party without the consent of the other. This capacity is disadvantageous to the seller (because they cannot use the money), but advantageous to the buyer who knows that the money is safe in the solicitor's bank account and will therefore be recoverable in the event of the sale going off due to the seller's default. However, SC 2.2.5 mitigates this disadvantage to the seller by allowing them to use the deposit on a related purchase of a house for their residence, provided that in such purchase the deposit will be held on the same terms as SC 2.2.5 and 2.2.6. So, even if the deposit is passed along a chain of related purchases, it will ultimately be held by a solicitor as stakeholder.

21.7 METHODS OF PAYMENT OF DEPOSIT

Standard Condition 2.2.4 and SCPC 3.2.2 require the deposit to be paid by electronic means from a solicitor's account with a clearing bank to the seller's solicitor's bank account. Under the SCs, it is also permissible to use a cheque drawn on a solicitor's or licensed conveyancer's client bank account. These provisions are designed to avoid problems with the payment of cheques drawn on the buyer's personal bank account which might be dishonoured when presented for payment. Both sets of Standard Conditions do allow payment by a personal cheque in the case of auction sales, but this is often varied by a special condition to provide for a more secure form of payment.

21.8 THE DEPOSIT CHEQUE BOUNCES

If a cheque taken in payment of the deposit bounces, this constitutes a fundamental breach of contract which gives the seller the option either of keeping the contract alive, or of treating the contract as discharged by the breach, and in either event of suing for damages (*Millichamp v Jones* [1983] 1 All ER 267). A separate cause of action arises out of the cheque itself. However, the option of treating the contract as discharged is of little consolation to a seller who, on the strength of their sale contract, has exchanged contracts for the purchase of another property. Provision should therefore be made in the contract to ensure that the deposit is payable by a method which will be honoured on presentation (see SC 2.2.4 and SCPC 3.2.2 referred to at **21.7**). The seller should insist on compliance with these conditions.

If the deposit cheque bounces, SC 2.2.2 allows the seller to give notice to the buyer that the contract has been discharged by the breach, provided that they do so within seven working days of being informed of the cheque being dishonoured. Standard Commercial Property Condition 3.3.7 contains similar provisions where a cheque is paid at auction.

21.9 INTEREST ON THE DEPOSIT

Where the deposit is held by a solicitor, irrespective of the capacity in which the money is held, interest may be payable under Rule 7.1 of the SRA Accounts Rules 2019. Standard Condition 2.2.6 (SCPC 3.2.2) provides that where the deposit, or part of it, is held in the capacity of stakeholder, interest on the deposit will be payable to the seller on completion. If the buyer negotiates an agreement that they are to be credited with interest on the deposit, a special condition must be inserted in the contract to that effect.

21.10 BUYER'S LIEN

From the moment when they pay the deposit to the seller in the capacity of agent (but not stakeholder), the buyer has a lien over the property for the amount of the deposit. The lien is enforceable only by a court order for sale of the property and may be protected as a notice (registered land) or Class C(iii) land charge (unregistered land). If the buyer is in occupation, their lien may be an overriding interest in registered land under the LRA 2002. It is not usual to register the lien unless problems arise in the transaction.

SUMMARY

- The purpose of a deposit is to demonstrate the buyer's commitment to the purchase.
- The deposit is usually 10% of the purchase price. There are risks to the seller in accepting a deposit of less than 10%, and the risks must be explained to a seller client.
- The 10% may be calculated on the purchase price of the property alone, or on the purchase price of the property and chattels included in the sale. This will depend on which form of contract is used.
- A buyer client may need to fund the deposit from an outside source between exchange and completion.
- A deposit is usually held by the seller's solicitor in the capacity of stakeholder. There are risks associated with the deposit being held in the capacity of agent, and these risks must be explained to a buyer client.
- The contract will usually require that the deposit is paid in a way that does not expose the seller to the risk of a bounced cheque.
- Interest earned on the deposit between exchange and completion is usually paid to the seller.

CHAPTER 22

INSURANCE

LEARNING OUTCOMES

After reading this chapter you will be able to:

- explain why it is important that the buyer insures the property from exchange of contracts
- ensure that the property is properly insured on the buyer's behalf immediately on exchange
- understand how both sets of Standard Conditions protect the buyer from problems arising when both the seller and the buyer are insuring the property between exchange and completion
- advise a buyer client on which other types of insurance might be useful after exchange of contracts.

22.1 RISK IN THE PROPERTY

At common law, and under both sets of Standard Conditions , the risk of accidental damage to the property passes to the buyer from the moment of exchange of contracts. The buyer bears the risk of loss or damage, except where it can be shown that the loss or damage is attributable to the seller's lack of proper care (*Clarke v Ramuz* [1891] 2 QB 456; *Phillips v Lamdin* [1949] 2 KB 33). The buyer should therefore normally insure the property from exchange of contracts onwards. A solicitor who fails to advise their client of the consequences of failure to insure, or who fails to carry out their client's instructions to insure the property, will be liable in negligence if the client suffers loss as a result of the lack of insurance.

22.2 INSURING THE PROPERTY

22.2.1 Arranging insurance

It is essential that the buyer's insurance arrangements have been made in advance of actual exchange so that the policy will be effective immediately upon exchange. Insurance is generally effected by one of the following methods:

(a) By noting the property on a block policy held by the buyer's solicitor which covers all properties currently being handled by the firm.

(b) Where the buyer is financing the purchase with the assistance of a mortgage, the lender will normally insure the property on being requested to do so by the buyer's solicitor. The lender's standing instructions to solicitors should be checked to ensure that:

(i) the amount of cover will be adequate both in terms of the value of the property and the type of risks covered;

(ii) the property will be put on cover from the time of exchange;

(iii) the lender's insurance requirements do not conflict with the terms of the contract or of any lease to which the property is subject.

(c) By the buyer taking out a policy which will cover the property from exchange.

22.2.2 The FSMA 2000 and insurance contracts

If you wish to advise on or arrange an insurance contract for your client and you are not authorised by the FCA to carry out that activity (which most firms will not be), you will need to rely on the so-called 'professional firms exemption'. This exemption will allow firms operating under it to arrange or advise on an insurance contract, subject to certain conditions, even though they are not authorised by the FCA. Any firm operating under the exemption in relation to insurance contracts must be registered in the FCA Register and must appoint a compliance officer. It should be noted that such firms are not 'authorised' by the FCA even though they are on the FCA Register, and they are therefore still operating under the professional firms exemption. For further detail on this complex area, see ***Legal Foundations***.

22.3 PROPERTY AT SELLER'S RISK

In some cases, and commonly with new property which is in the course of construction, the contract will provide that the property is to remain at the seller's risk until completion. (This was the case in the previous edition of the Standard Conditions (the Fourth Edition), where SC 5.1 provided for the seller to bear the risk in the property until completion, and permitted rescission if the property was substantially damaged between exchange and completion.) Where the risk in the property remains with the seller, the buyer need not take out their own policy until completion. It will also be necessary to exclude the LPA 1925, s 47, which would otherwise give the buyer the right, in certain circumstances, to claim off the seller's policy in the event of damage to the property.

22.4 PROPERTY AT BUYER'S RISK

The Fifth Edition of the Standard Conditions and SCPC 8 take a completely different approach. They do not change the common law position that the risk passes to the buyer on exchange. Both SC 5.1.2 and SCPC 8.2.4(a) provide that the seller is under no obligation to insure the property, except where required by the terms of any lease or the contract of sale. It is therefore essential for a buyer to take out their own policy of insurance as from exchange.

However, in practice, it is likely that the seller will keep up the policy until completion, and if the seller has a mortgage, they will be required to do so. Standard Condition 5.1.5 and SCPC 8.2.4(b) deal with such a case of dual insurance. Where there are two policies on the same property, there is a danger that, on a claim being made, an insurance company would reduce the amount it was prepared to pay out because of the existence of the other policy. Standard Condition 5.1.5 and SCPC 8.2.4(b) thus provide that where there is a reduction in any payment made to the buyer because of the existence of the seller's policy, the purchase price is to be reduced accordingly. The seller could then claim that reduction from their insurers.

Both sets of Standard Conditions also envisage the possibility of a condition being included in the sale contract requiring the seller to maintain their insurance until completion. If such a special condition is included, SC 5.1.3 and SCPC 8.2.2 require the seller (amongst other things) to maintain the policy until completion. If, before completion, the property suffers damage, the seller must pay to the buyer all policy monies received, or assign to the buyer all rights under the policy. Similar provisions apply if the seller is obliged to insure the property under the terms of a lease. This might be the case where the property being sold is leasehold, and the seller, as tenant is obliged to insure under the terms of the lease, or where freehold property is being sold subject to a lease and the seller, as landlord, is similarly obliged to insure.

22.5 MAINTENANCE OF SELLER'S POLICY

Except where the seller is required by a condition of the contract of sale or their mortgage or lease to maintain their policy, they could cancel the insurance policy on exchange of contracts, but in practice the seller would be unwise to do so (eg, in case the buyer failed to complete). The seller should also be advised not to cancel any contents or other policies until completion.

22.6 OTHER TYPES OF INSURANCE

In appropriate cases, the buyer should be advised to take out other insurances, such as contents insurance and life assurance. A contents policy should be taken out when the buyer moves their fittings into the property (ie, normally on completion day). If required, life assurance policies should be taken out immediately after exchange of contracts, so that their proceeds would be available to the buyer's personal representatives in the unlikely event of the buyer dying before completion takes place. If the buyer did die at this stage of the transaction the personal representatives could be forced to complete the sale, and without the proceeds of a life policy they would not have the funds to do so since the buyer's mortgage offer would have been revoked by the death. Advice given by the solicitor to their client about the terms of a life insurance policy will be subject to the provisions of the FSMA 2000. This means that, as with a buildings insurance policy, most firms wishing to arrange a life insurance policy will need to rely on the professional firms exemption (see **22.2.2**). It should be noted, however, that even exempt firms are prohibited from recommending that their clients buy certain types of life policy (see rule 5 of the SRA Financial Services (Scope) Rules 2019).

SUMMARY

- The contract will normally provide that the buyer must complete the purchase even if the property is damaged or destroyed between exchange and completion.
- Therefore the buyer's insurance must be in place, on appropriate terms, immediately on exchange.
- In some cases, it may be appropriate for the seller to continue insuring the property as well as, or instead of, the buyer.
- The contract will usually protect the buyer against the possibility of their insurer reducing the pay-out because the seller has also insured the property.
- It may be appropriate for you to advise the buyer to take out life insurance from exchange and contents insurance from completion.

CHAPTER 23

PREPARING TO EXCHANGE

LEARNING OUTCOMES

After reading this chapter you will be able to:

- understand the importance of resolving all outstanding queries and making sure appropriate financial arrangements are in place before exchange of contracts
- ensure that the contract is signed by your client in a legally-effective manner.

23.1 INTRODUCTION

A binding contract will come into existence on exchange of contracts, after which time neither party will normally be able to withdraw from, or change the terms of, the contract without incurring liability for breach. It is therefore essential to check that all outstanding queries have been dealt with and that all financial arrangements are in order before the client is advised to commit themselves to the contract.

23.2 MATTERS TO BE CHECKED

Consideration should be given to the following matters before exchange takes place. The matters marked with an asterisk in the lists concern both seller and buyer; the unmarked items are mainly of concern to a buyer client.

23.2.1 Searches

(a) Have all necessary searches and enquiries been made?

(b) Have all the replies to searches and enquiries been received?

(c) Have all search and enquiry replies been checked carefully to ensure that the replies to individual questions are satisfactory and accord with the client's instructions?

(d)* Have all outstanding queries been resolved?

(e) Has a survey of the property been undertaken and, if so, is the result satisfactory?

23.2.2 Financial arrangements

(a) Has a satisfactory mortgage offer been made and (where necessary) accepted by the client?

(b) Are arrangements in hand to comply with any conditions attached to the mortgage advance (eg, obtaining estimates for repairs to the property)?

(c) Taking into account the deposit, the mortgage advance (less any retention) and the costs of the transaction (including disbursements), is there sufficient money for the client to proceed with the purchase?

(d)* Have arrangements been made to discharge the seller's existing mortgage(s) or, on a sale of part, to release the part being sold from the mortgage?

23.2.3 Deposit

(a)* How much (if any) preliminary deposit has been paid?

(b)* How much money is needed to fund the deposit required on exchange?

(c) Has a suitable undertaking been given in relation to bridging finance?

(d)* To whom is the deposit to be paid?

(e) Have the deposit funds been obtained from the client and cleared through the firm's clients' account?

23.2.4 The contract

(a)* Have all outstanding queries been satisfactorily resolved?

(b)* Have all agreed amendments been incorporated clearly in both parts of the contract?

(c)* Has the approved draft been returned to the seller?

(d)* Is a clean copy of the contract available for signature by the client?

(e)* Have the terms of the contract been explained to the client?

(f)* Has the list of fixtures and fittings (if any) been agreed between the parties?

23.2.5 Insurance

(a) Have steps been taken to insure the property immediately on exchange?

(b) Have steps been taken to obtain any life policy required under the terms of the buyer's mortgage offer?

23.2.6 Completion date

* Has a completion date been agreed?

23.2.7 Method of exchange

(a)* Which method of exchange is most suitable to be used in this transaction?

(b)* Where the client requires a simultaneous exchange on both sale and purchase contracts, are both transactions and all related transactions in the chain also ready to proceed?

23.2.8 Signature of contract

* Has the client signed the contract?

23.2.9 Occupiers

* Has the consent of all non-owning occupiers been obtained?

23.3 REPORTING TO CLIENT

When the buyer's solicitor has completed their searches and enquiries, and the form of the draft contract has been agreed, they should report to their client in writing, explaining the results of their investigations and the terms of the contract and mortgage offer to the client. Some firms prepare a 'Buyer's Report' for this purpose.

23.4 SIGNATURE OF CONTRACT

Both parties must sign the contract (or each must sign one of two identical copies) in order to satisfy s 2 of the Law of Property (Miscellaneous Provisions) Act 1989. The signature need not be witnessed. Signature by a duly authorised agent is sufficient.

23.4.1 Signature by the client

Signature by the client in the presence of their solicitor, the solicitor first having ensured that the client understands and agrees with the terms of the contract, is desirable but is not always practicable. Where the contract is to be sent to the client for signature, the accompanying letter should clearly explain where and how the client is required to sign the document. If not already done, the letter should also explain the terms of the contract in language appropriate to the client's level of understanding, and request a cheque for the deposit, indicating by which date the solicitor needs to be in receipt of cleared funds.

23.4.2 Signature by solicitor on behalf of client

A solicitor needs their client's express authority to sign the contract on behalf of the client (*Suleman v Shahsavari* [1989] 2 All ER 460). Unless the solicitor holds a valid power of attorney, it is recommended that such authority should be obtained from the client in writing, after the client has been informed of the legal consequences of giving such authority (ie, signature implies authority to proceed to exchange, and exchange creates a binding contract). Failure to obtain authority may render the solicitor liable in damages for breach of warranty of authority (*Suleman v Shahsavari* (above)).

23.4.3 Companies

Provided that the transaction has been authorised by the company, an officer of the company (usually a director or the secretary) may be authorised to sign on behalf of the company.

23.4.4 Electronic signature

In most cases a client will sign the contract in wet ink. However, in some cases a client will want to sign using an electronic signature, perhaps by typing their name into the contract, using a stylus and touchscreen to write the name into the contract, electronically pasting an image of the signature into an electronic version of the contract or by accessing a contract through a web-based e-signature platform and clicking to insert the signature into the contract in a handwriting font.

In July 2016, The Law Society and The City of London Law Society published a practice note entitled *Note on the Execution of a Document using an Electronic Signature*. The practice note, which is limited to contracts entered into in a business context, considers the requirements for valid execution, and contains the opinion that a contract for the sale or other disposition of an interest in land in England and Wales which is executed using an electronic signature satisfies the statutory requirement to be in writing and signed (see **23.4**).

Parties negotiating by email should be aware of the dangers of email-generated electronic signatures or name and contact details. In *Neocleous v Rees* [2019] EWHC 2462 (Ch), the court found that an automatically generated email footer containing the name and contact details of the sender constituted a signature for the purposes of s 2(3) of the Law of Property (Miscellaneous Provisions) Act 1989. As a result, a series of emails between the parties' solicitors with a footer containing the defendant's solicitor's name and contact details amounted to an enforceable contract. Parties wishing to avoid such an outcome should ensure all correspondence (including email) is marked 'subject to contract'.

23.4.5 Client's authority

Before exchanging contracts, the solicitor should ensure that the client's authority to exchange has been obtained. Clients should be made aware of the consequences of exchange, ie, that they can no longer withdraw from the transaction. In order to emphasise the importance of exchange, some firms require instructions to exchange to be given in writing.

SUMMARY

- It is important to resolve all outstanding queries and make sure appropriate financial arrangements are in place before exchange of contracts, because it is not usually possible for either party to withdraw from, or change the terms of, the contract after exchange.
- This chapter has provided you with a list of the matters to be checked before exchange takes place.
- The contract may be signed by the client, or by the client's solicitor.
- You should explain the effect of exchange to the client and obtain their authority to exchange before doing so.

CHAPTER 24

EXCHANGE OF CONTRACTS

LEARNING OUTCOMES

After reading this chapter you will be able to:

- appreciate that an exchange of contracts may be carried out in person, by telephone or by post
- ensure that the client is aware of the effect of exchange and of the need to synchronise related sales and purchases
- understand the purpose of The Law Society's formulae for exchange
- choose the most appropriate formula for the circumstances of your transaction.

24.1 THE PRACTICE OF EXCHANGE

The physical exchange of contracts between the parties is not a legal requirement for a contract for the sale of land, but where a contract is drawn up by solicitors acting for the parties it is usual for the contract to be prepared in two identical parts, one being signed by the seller, the other by the buyer. When the two parts are physically exchanged, so that the buyer receives the part of the contract signed by the seller and vice versa, a binding contract comes into existence. The actual time when the contract comes into being depends on the method which has been used to effect the exchange.

Since exchange is not a legal necessity, it is possible for the contract to comprise a single document which is signed by both parties. In such a case, the contract becomes binding and enforceable as soon as the second signature has been put on the document (*Smith v Mansi* [1962] 3 All ER 857). This situation is uncommon because the same solicitor is usually unable to act for both parties under para 6.2 of the SRA Code of Conduct for Solicitors.

24.2 AUTHORITY TO EXCHANGE

A solicitor who exchanges contracts without their client's express or implied authority to do so will be liable to the client in negligence. In *Domb v Isoz* [1980] 1 All ER 942, it was held that once the solicitor has their client's authority to exchange they have the authority to effect the exchange by whichever method the solicitor thinks most appropriate to the situation. However, if Formula C is to be used, the client's express permission must be obtained (see **24.3.2.3**).

24.3 METHODS OF EXCHANGE

Contracts are usually exchanged in person or by telephone. Whichever method is chosen, the exchange is usually initiated by the buyer indicating to the seller that they are now ready to commit to a binding contract. Once contracts have been exchanged, neither party will be able to withdraw from the contract. It is therefore essential that the parties' solicitors have checked that all necessary arrangements are in order before proceeding to exchange. Also, in residential transactions, where the purchase of one property is dependent on the sale of another, the solicitor must ensure that the exchange of contracts and completion dates on both properties are synchronised to avoid leaving their client either owning two houses or being homeless. Failure to synchronise the exchange where the client has instructed that their sale and purchase transactions are interdependent constitutes professional negligence. The solicitor must ensure, therefore, that they either exchange on both the sale and the purchase or exchange on neither; they do not want to be in the position of exchanging on one transaction, only to find that the other party to the dependent transaction has decided to withdraw. Ideally, the exchange on the two transactions should take place simultaneously in order to avoid this danger, but this is not practical. The best that the solicitor can do is to ensure that there is as little time delay as is practically possible between exchanging on one transaction and on the other.

24.3.1 Telephone

Exchange by telephone is now the most common method of effecting an exchange of contracts. Legal recognition of the practice was given by the Court of Appeal in *Domb v Isoz* [1980] 1 All ER 942. With the exception of personal exchange, this method represents the quickest way of securing an exchange of contracts and is particularly useful in a chain of transactions.

The method is not free of risk. Where exchange is effected by telephone, the contract between the parties becomes effective as soon as the parties' solicitors agree in the course of a telephone conversation that exchange has taken place. The telephone conversation is followed by a physical exchange of documents through the post, but the existence of the contract is not dependent on this physical exchange, the contract already exists by virtue of the telephone conversation. If one party were subsequently to change their mind about the contract, it would be easy to dispute or deny the contents of the telephone conversation and thus the existence of the contract itself. The problems arising out of a telephonic exchange are as follows:

(a) neither party is able to check that the other's contract has been signed;
(b) neither party is able to check that the other's contract is in the agreed form and incorporates all agreed amendments.

If one part of the contract has not been signed, or if the two parts are not identical, then there can be no contract, even if the parties purport to exchange. The seller may also be exchanging without having received a deposit. This would be professional negligence on the part of their solicitors.

To avoid the uncertainties arising out of this method of exchange, the parties' solicitors must agree prior to exchange that the telephonic exchange will be governed by one of The Law Society's formulae which were drawn up by the Society in response to the decision in *Domb v Isoz* (above). An accurate attendance note recording the telephone conversation must also be made as soon as possible. The formulae rely on the use of solicitor's undertakings to overcome these problems.

24.3.2 Use of the formulae for exchange

There are three Law Society formulae:

(a) Formula A: this is used where one solicitor (usually the seller's solicitor) already holds both parts of the contract before the exchange is initiated;

(b) Formula B: this is used where at the time of the telephone exchange each party's solicitor is still in possession of their own client's signed contract;

(c) Formula C: this is designed to be used in chain transactions.

The wording of the formulae is set out in **Appendix 4**. Whichever formula is used, the client's express authority to exchange must be obtained before the procedure to exchange is commenced. If any variation to a formula is to be made, that variation must be expressly agreed and noted in writing by all the solicitors involved before exchange takes place. Subject to agreed variations, the conditions attached to the formula in use must be strictly adhered to.

24.3.2.1 Formula A

This is little used in practice. The buyer's solicitor will have sent their client's part of the contract, together with the deposit cheque, to the seller's solicitor, with an instruction to hold both of these to their order. When ready to exchange, the buyer's solicitor will telephone the seller's solicitor and a completion date will be agreed. The seller's solicitor will then confirm that they hold their client's part of the contract duly signed by the seller and that this is in the agreed form. It will then be agreed that exchange takes place as at that moment. The seller's solicitor then undertakes to send their client's part of the contract to the buyer's solicitor on the same day.

In practice, Formula A is the safest of the three formulae to use because, before actual exchange takes place, the seller's solicitor has the opportunity of seeing the buyer's signed part of the contract and can check that it is identical to their own client's part. They are also usually in possession of the buyer's deposit cheque, which will have been sent to them with the buyer's part of the contract. Although the seller cannot bank the cheque until exchange has taken place, they are secure in the knowledge that the deposit will be paid.

24.3.2.2 Formula B

This is the most commonly used of the formulae. Each solicitor still holds their own client's part of the contract. In the telephone conversation, both will confirm that their respective parts of the contract are signed and in the agreed form. After the exchange has taken place each undertakes to hold their signed part of the contract to the other's order. Then both parties undertake to send their respective parts of the contract to the other, the buyer also undertaking to send the deposit.

24.3.2.3 Formula C

This is specifically designed for use in chain transactions and will avoid any risk of a client exchanging on one transaction without also exchanging on the dependent transaction. It also makes provision for the seller using the buyer's deposit towards the deposit they will need to pay on their dependent purchase. It is, however, somewhat complex and thus little used in practice in many areas of the country. Formula C consists of two parts. Under Part I, the parties will initially agree that they each hold signed parts of the contract (as in Formula B). Exchange does not take place at that time, however, but each party undertakes that they will exchange, provided that the other party contacts them by a specified time later that day. This thus gives time for both buyer and seller to enter into any dependent contract, secure in the knowledge that this first transaction will become binding provided that contact is made by the specified time. Part II of Formula C is activated later when contact is made by the specified time. Under this there is the usual undertaking as to exchange taking place, but also provision for buyer and seller to make use of a deposit due under a dependent sale. So the undertaking is that the buyer will either send the deposit 'that day' or 'arrange' for it to be sent. So a buyer can arrange for the buyer on their own sale to send it. And it is to be sent either to the seller or to such other solicitor as the seller nominates, so allowing the seller to use that same money as deposit on their own related purchase. Note, however, that before using Formula C, the client's express permission to use that formula must have been obtained (see Note 8 to Formula C in **Appendix 4**).

24.3.3 Personal exchange

By this method, the solicitors for the parties meet, usually at the seller's solicitor's office, and the two contracts are physically exchanged. A contract exists from the moment of exchange. Although this type of exchange represents the safest and most instantaneous method of exchange, it is frequently not practical to use personal exchange because the physical distance between the offices of the respective solicitors makes it impractical to do so. Personal exchange is infrequently used in residential transactions, but is still used in high-value commercial contracts. This method has two benefits: it is instantaneous, thus leaving no uncertainty over the timing of the creation of the contract; and it enables both parties to see the other party's part of the contract before exchange actually takes place, so that both can check that the parts of the contract are identical in form and have been properly signed. The seller can also ensure that they are in receipt of the deposit before exchanging.

24.3.4 Postal exchange

Where exchange is to take place by post, the buyer's solicitor will send their client's signed contract and the deposit cheque to the seller's solicitor who, on receipt of these documents, will post their client's signed contract back to the buyer.

Generally, a contract does not come into being until the buyer has received the seller's contract. Exchange of contracts by post forms an exception to this rule and the contract is made when the seller posts their part of the contract to the buyer (*Adams v Lindsell* (1818) 1 B and Ald 6813). It follows from the above that a contract will be formed even if the seller's part of the contract is lost in the post and never received by the buyer.

Using the post as a method of exchange is reasonably satisfactory when dealing with a single sale or purchase which is not dependent on another related transaction, but even in this situation there will inevitably be a delay between the buyer sending their contract to the seller and the seller posting their part back, during which time the buyer is uncertain of whether they have secured the contract. There is also no guarantee that the seller will complete the exchange by posting their part of the contract back to the buyer. Until the seller actually does so, they are free to change their mind and withdraw from the transaction. Although these risks are small where a single sale or purchase is being undertaken, they assume a much greater significance where a chain of transactions is involved and the use of postal exchange is not advised in linked transactions.

24.3.5 Document exchange

A document exchange, or DX, is a private postal system not under the control of the Post Office. Most solicitors belong to a document exchange. A document exchange may be used to effect an exchange of contracts in a similar way to the normal postal service and is subject to the same risks. The court has approved the use of document exchanges for the service and delivery of documents in non-contentious matters in *John Wilmott Homes v Reed* (1986) 51 P & CR 90. The rules on postal acceptance do not apply to document exchanges and, unless the contract contains a contrary provision, the contract will come into existence when the seller's part of the contract is received by the buyer. Where the standard conditions are used, Condition 2 (SC) and Condition 3 (SCPC) provide that the contract is made when the last copy of the contract is deposited at the document exchange.

24.3.6 Fax

The main use of fax in the context of exchange of contracts is to transmit the messages which activate the Law Society formulae. Fax is merely a substitute for using the telephone. Condition 1.3.3 in both sets of standard conditions does not permit fax to be used as a valid method of service of a document where delivery of the original document is essential (as it is with the contract), thus effectively ruling out an exchange by faxing copies of the signed contract. Further, an exchange of faxes is not a valid exchange of contracts under s 2 of the Law of Property (Miscellaneous Provisions) Act 1989 (*Commissioner for the New Towns v Cooper (Great Britain) Ltd* [1995] Ch 259).

24.3.7 E-mail

At the moment, contracts for the sale of land must be in writing so cannot be entered into electronically via e-mail or the Internet. However, e-mail can be used to transmit the messages activating The Law Society formulae.

The Government's proposals for electronic conveyancing would allow contracts to be made electronically. There would then be only one copy of the contract which would be stored and 'signed' electronically. Thus there would no longer be exchange of contracts; instead the contract, once 'signed' by both parties, would come into existence at a time agreed between the parties. An electronic 'signature' will consist of the transmission of an encrypted message which is certified as coming only from the person transmitting it.

24.4 STANDARD CONDITIONS OF SALE

Standard Condition 2.1 and SCPC 3.1 govern the making of the contract and allow contracts to be exchanged by document exchange, post or by telephone using the Law Society formulae.

24.5 INSURANCE

If the buyer is to insure the property from exchange (see **Chapter 22**), the buyer's solicitor should immediately after exchange put in hand the previously decided arrangements. So, for example, if the buyer's lender is to effect the insurance, the lender should be telephoned immediately and informed that contracts have been exchanged and that the property should be placed on risk. Written or faxed confirmation of the telephone call should also be given.

SUMMARY

- Contracts may be exchanged in person, by telephone or by post (using the Post Office or DX service). The contract will come into being at different points in time, depending on the method used.
- Personal exchange is the safest method, postal exchange is the least safe method.
- Telephone exchange is the most common method, but there may be problems if neither party is able to see the contract signed by the other.
- The Law Society has devised three formulae, based on mutual undertakings, to reduce these risks.
- The choice of formula will depend on which parts of the contract each solicitor holds and whether there is a related sale or purchase.
- Any deviation from, or variation of, the chosen formula must be agreed between the solicitors for both parties and recorded in writing.
- Exchange by fax or e-mail is not possible at the moment.

PART IV

THE CONVEYANCING TRANSACTION: AFTER EXCHANGE

CHAPTER 25

THE CONSEQUENCES OF EXCHANGE

LEARNING OUTCOMES

After reading this chapter you will be able to:

- explain how ownership of the property is shared between the seller and the buyer in the period between exchange and completion
- inform the relevant parties that exchange has taken place, and deal with the contracts and the deposit in the correct manner
- consider whether registration of the contract is appropriate
- protect your seller client if it is agreed that the buyer may occupy the property before completion
- if the property is tenanted, consider whether your buyer client's interests are adequately protected by the contract or whether special conditions are required
- explain the contractual position if either the seller or the buyer dies after exchange but before completion
- decide whether any of the pre-completion steps need to be carried out before exchange of contracts rather than after it.

25.1 THE EFFECTS OF EXCHANGE

Following exchange, a binding contract exists from which normally neither party may withdraw without incurring liability for breach. At common law, the beneficial ownership in the property passes to the buyer, who becomes entitled to any increase in value of the property but also bears the risk of any loss or damage; hence the need to ensure that insurance of the property is effective from the moment of exchange.

The seller retains the legal title to the property until completion, but holds the beneficial interest on behalf of the buyer. During this period, the seller is entitled to remain in possession of the property and to any rental income (unless otherwise agreed). The seller must also pay the outgoings (eg, community charge or business rates) until completion. The seller owes a duty of care to the buyer and will be liable to the buyer in damages if loss is caused to the property through neglect or wanton destruction (*Clarke v Ramuz* [1891] 2 QB 456; *Phillips v Lamdin* [1949] 2 KB 33). This duty continues as long as the seller is entitled to possession of the property, and does not terminate if the seller vacates the property before completion.

25.2 IMMEDIATELY AFTER EXCHANGE

25.2.1 The seller

The seller's solicitor should inform the client and selling agent that exchange has taken place, and enter the completion date in their diary or file-prompt system. Where exchange has taken place by telephone, the copy of the contract signed by the seller should immediately be sent to the buyer's solicitor to fulfil any undertaking given in the course of an exchange by telephone, it having first been checked that the contract is dated and contains the agreed completion date. Any deposit received must immediately be paid into an interest-bearing clients' deposit account.

25.2.2 The buyer

The buyer's solicitor should inform the client and their lender that exchange has taken place, and enter the completion date in their diary or file-prompt system. Where exchange has taken place by telephone, the buyer's solicitor should immediately send to the seller's solicitor the signed contract and deposit cheque in accordance with the undertaking given, having first checked that the contract is dated and contains the agreed completion date. Where appropriate, the contract should be protected by registration. Where the buyer is to insure (see **Chapter 22**), the buyer's solicitor should immediately put in hand the insurance arrangements previously decided upon.

25.3 REGISTRATION OF THE CONTRACT

Since completion of most contracts occurs within a very short period following exchange, in practice registration of the contract is uncommon. However, the contract should always be registered if any of the circumstances listed below applies:

(a) there is to be a long interval (eg, more than two months) between contract and completion;

(b) there is reason to doubt the seller's good faith;

(c) a dispute arises between the seller and buyer;

(d) the seller delays completion beyond the contractual date.

With registered land the contract is protected by entry of a notice on the register of the title. However, a buyer who is in occupation of the property may have an overriding interest within the LRA 2002, in which case protection of the contract by registration is not necessary.

With unregistered land, the contract is an estate contract within the Class C(iv) category of land charge and will be void against a buyer of the legal estate for money or money's worth if not registered. Registration must be made against the name of the legal estate owner for the time being.

25.4 THE BUYER IN POSSESSION

25.4.1 Buyer's occupation of the property before completion

In many cases, the seller will be in physical occupation of the property until completion and the question of the buyer taking possession before completion does not arise. The seller is entitled to retain possession until completion, unless they agree to do otherwise. The buyer's request to enter and occupy the premises before completion should be regarded with caution by the seller, because once the buyer takes up occupation they may lose their incentive to complete on the contractual completion date; and if, ultimately, the buyer does not complete the transaction at all, it may be difficult for the seller to regain possession of the property.

Where the seller has a subsisting mortgage on the property, the lender's consent must be obtained before the buyer is allowed into occupation.

Where the seller is prepared to let the buyer into possession before completion, it is essential to ensure that the buyer's occupation is as licensee and not as tenant in order to avoid problems relating to security of tenure arising from the buyer's occupation. Standard Condition 5.2 expressly states that the buyer's occupation is to be construed as a licence, and this statement will probably be effective in most circumstances to prevent an inadvertent tenancy from arising. Even where a licence is granted, a court order will always be necessary to remove a residential occupier who does not voluntarily vacate the property (see the Protection from Eviction Act 1977, s 2) and may be necessary in non-residential cases where the tenant will not peaceably surrender their occupation.

25.4.2 Conditions of the buyer's occupation

Where the seller agrees to allow the buyer into possession, some restrictions or conditions should be attached to the buyer's occupancy.

25.4.2.1 Standard Conditions of Sale

Standard Condition 5.2.2 provides that the terms of the licence are that the buyer:

(a) cannot transfer it;
(b) may permit members of their household to occupy;
(c) is to pay for or indemnify the seller against all outgoings;
(d) is to pay the seller a fee calculated at the contract rate on the balance of the purchase price;
(e) is entitled to any rents from the property;
(f) is to keep the property in as good a state of repair as it was when they took possession and not to make any alterations;
(g) if the property is leasehold, is not to do anything which would put the seller in breach of the lease;
(h) is to quit the property when the licence ends.

Either party can terminate the licence on five working days' notice.

The buyer may wish to renegotiate some of these terms. They may wish, for example, to take possession for the purpose of carrying out building works for alterations, improvements, etc, which is not permitted under Standard Condition 5.2.2. In deciding whether to agree to possession for this purpose, the seller should bear in mind that if the contract fails for some reason, they may be left with a property severely damaged because of half-finished works of alteration or improvement. Standard Condition 5.2.3 provides that the buyer is not deemed to be in occupation for the purposes of this condition if they are merely allowed access to carry out work agreed by the seller. Accordingly, if the seller does allow the buyer access for such purposes, express provision will need to be made as to termination of the licence, making good any damage caused, etc.

As an alternative solution, the seller may consider granting the buyer a licence for access only (eg, to obtain estimates for alterations to be made to the property after completion).

25.4.2.2 Standard Commercial Property Conditions

These standard conditions contain no provisions allowing the buyer to take possession prior to completion, nor any provisions regulating such occupation. Such matters will thus need negotiating individually between the parties. Similar factors as those mentioned above would need to be considered.

25.5 TENANTED PROPERTY

The SCPCs contain extensive provisions dealing with tenanted property, both where the leasehold interest is being sold and where the freehold is being sold subject to tenancies. Thus SCPC 5.2 deals with general management issues, and SCPC 6 with rent reviews, which might arise between exchange and completion. These recognise that the buyer is concerned as to the outcome of such matters. So under SCPC 5.2.6, the seller is not to give or formally withhold any licence or approval under the lease without the buyer's consent. Similarly under SCPC 6.1.5, neither party is to agree a new rent figure unless the other agrees.

25.6 DEATH OF A CONTRACTING PARTY

The death of one of the contracting parties between contract and completion does not affect the validity of the contract; the benefit and burden of the contract pass to the deceased's personal representatives who are bound to complete.

If completion does not take place on the contractual completion date, a breach of contract will occur (irrespective of whether time was of the essence of the completion date) and remedies (eg, compensation, damages) will be available to the innocent party.

If time was not originally of the essence of the completion date, it may be made so by service of a notice to complete addressed to the deceased and the executor(s) named in the seller's will. A copy of this notice must be sent to the Public Trustee. If the deceased died intestate, notice may be served on the Public Trustee.

25.6.1 Death of one co-seller

Property owned by beneficial co-owners is held on a trust of land, and all the trustees must join in any conveyance of the legal estate. The death of one trustee between contract and completion does not, however, affect the validity of the contract. Where, following the death, there still remain at least two trustees of the legal estate, the transaction can proceed to completion without delay. In other cases, another trustee may have to be appointed so that the minimum number of two trustees is accomplished. This will depend upon whether the co-owners held the land as beneficial joint tenants or tenants in common (see **16.4**). It will be necessary to produce the death certificate of the deceased in order to provide the buyer with evidence of the death, and the transfer deed will need to be redrafted to reflect the change of parties to the transaction.

25.6.2 Death of the buyer

The personal representatives step into the shoes of the deceased and will be bound to complete the contract. Some delay in completion may occur because the transfer deed will have to be redrafted to reflect the change in parties and the personal representatives cannot complete until they obtain the grant of representation. Where the purchase was due to be financed by a mortgage, the death of the buyer will usually mean that the mortgage offer is revoked, and the personal representatives may find themselves with insufficient funds to complete unless an alternative source of finance can be found, eg the proceeds of a life policy.

The survivor of joint buyers remains bound by the contract and can be forced to complete. Finance may have to be rearranged and a new mortgage deed prepared. Some delay will be inevitable, and the seller will have a claim against the buyer for loss caused by the delay.

25.7 PRE-COMPLETION STEPS

Once contracts have been exchanged, most of the legal work in the conveyancing transaction has already been done by the parties' solicitors, and the interval between exchange and completion is used to tidy up outstanding matters and to prepare for completion itself. There are, however, four important matters which must be dealt with at this stage:

(a) preparation of the transfer deed (see **Chapter 27**);
(b) dealing with redemption of the seller's mortgage (see **Chapter 30**) and the creation of the buyer's mortgage;
(c) pre-completion searches made by the buyer (see **Chapter 28**); and
(d) ensuring that the financial aspects of the transaction are in order.

25.8 THE INTERVAL BETWEEN EXCHANGE AND COMPLETION

The interval between exchange and completion was conventionally a four-week period, giving ample time for the tasks listed in **25.7** to be undertaken. In many cases, however, the clients will want completion to follow more quickly after exchange; a completion date which is 14 days or less after exchange is common, and in some transactions exchange and completion will take place simultaneously. In such a case, the solicitors will need to plan their timetable of pre-completion steps carefully to ensure that all necessary matters can be accomplished within the available time. Alternatively, some of the pre-completion steps may be brought forward and dealt with at the pre-contract stage of the transaction. Pre-completion searches should be made as close to the date of actual completion as possible (see **Chapter 28**) because of the protection period given to the buyer with the result of an official search. There is no reason, however, why the preparation of the transfer deed should not be undertaken as soon as the contents of the contract have been agreed between the parties, and indeed the Protocol invites a seller's solicitor to consider whether a draft transfer should be included in the contract bundle at the pre-exchange stage.

SUMMARY

- In the period between exchange of contracts and completion, the buyer is the beneficial owner of the property and the seller is the legal owner.
- Immediately after exchange, you must inform the client and relevant third parties (such as the estate agent and the lender), and deal with the signed contracts and deposit as required by the contract and any undertakings given on exchange.
- If you act for the buyer, you should consider whether it is necessary to register the contract as a notice (registered land) or a Class C(iv) land charge (unregistered land).
- The buyer is not normally allowed to enter or occupy the property until after completion. If the seller agrees to this, it may be possible to use SC 5.2.2 to protect the seller's interests. If not, alternative contractual protection will have to be agreed.
- If one of the parties dies after exchange but before completion, the personal representatives of the deceased person are bound to complete. There is likely to be a delay. The other party may terminate the contract using the notice to complete procedure in the Standard Conditions, or may choose to wait, complete and claim against the other party for losses caused by the delay.
- There may not be enough time between exchange and completion to carry out the pre-completion tasks, in which case some or all of these tasks may have to be done before exchange.

CHAPTER 26

Request for Completion Information

LEARNING OUTCOMES

After reading this chapter you will be able to:

- understand the purpose of the buyer's Request for Completion Information
- issue a Request for Completion Information in an appropriate form.

26.1 INTRODUCTION

After exchange of contracts, the solicitors for the buyer and the seller need to agree the practical arrangements for completion. The buyer's solicitor initiates this process by requesting completion information from the seller's solicitor. You will often hear this request referred to as 'requisitions on title'. This is because, historically, title was deduced to the buyer after exchange and 'requisitions on title' were raised by the buyer's solicitor, requiring the seller's solicitor to clarify and, if necessary, rectify matters which the buyer's solicitor found unsatisfactory. Although the standard form contracts still contain a timetable for raising and replying to requisitions on title after exchange (see SC 4.3.1 and SCPC 7.3.1), in most cases now, the seller's evidence of title will have been supplied to the buyer before exchange of contracts, and the contract will contain a clause excluding the buyer's right to raise requisitions once contracts have been exchanged (see SC 4.2.1 and SCPC 7.2.1). Note, however, that if after exchange the buyer's solicitor discovers an undisclosed incumbrance or other defect, they will still be able to require it to be remedied or assert their remedies for non-disclosure (see **Chapter 33**). Standard Condition 4.2.2 (SCPC 7.2.2) requires the buyer to raise any further title requisitions within six working days of any matter coming to their attention, and Standard Condition 4.3.1 (SCPC 7.3.1) requires the seller's solicitor to reply to requisitions four working days after receiving them from the buyer's solicitor.

26.2 STANDARD FORM REQUESTS FOR COMPLETION INFORMATION

Most law stationers produce a standard form which includes many commonly asked questions (eg, confirmation that the seller's mortgage on the property will be discharged on or before completion). In addition, the printed questions frequently deal with the administrative arrangements for completion itself (eg, method of payment of money, the time and place for completion, whether completion can take place by post, etc). Where title has been investigated before exchange, the only question relating to title is to ask the seller to confirm that nothing has altered since the date of exchange. Queries which are specific to the property may either be added to the end of the standard form, or be typed on a separate sheet. The buyer's solicitor should send two copies of the form to the seller's solicitor, who will return one copy with their answers, keeping the other copy on their own file for reference.

One of the key areas covered by the request for completion information is the discharge of the seller's existing mortgage. In Protocol cases, use of the TA13 Completion Information and Undertakings is required. This form contains a request for confirmation that existing mortgages will be discharged on completion. The answer to this question takes effect as an undertaking to discharge the mortgages referred to and avoids the need for such an undertaking to be handed over on completion. Other versions, such as the Solicitors Completion Requirements (SCR) published by PLC Property Law, ask whether an undertaking will be given and, if so, for a draft to be provided for the buyer's solicitor to approve. The wording approved by the Law Society for such an undertaking can be found at **30.7.1.10**.

The buyer's solicitor should ensure that the replies given in response to their request for completion information are satisfactory. Any unsatisfactory replies should be taken up with the seller's solicitor and further written enquiries raised until the matter is resolved.

SUMMARY

- The buyer's solicitor issues a Request for Completion Information to the seller's solicitor to check that none of the information provided about the property before exchange has changed, and to confirm the practical arrangements for completion, such as how the seller's mortgage is going to be discharged.
- To do this, most solicitors use a standard form, to which they add any additional questions which are specific to the property and/or the transaction.

CHAPTER 27

The Transfer Deed

LEARNING OUTCOMES

After reading this chapter you will be able to:

- understand who prepares the transfer deed and what form it must take
- prepare a transfer in a form acceptable to Land Registry
- ensure that the transfer is executed and delivered in a legally-effective manner.

27.1 PREPARATION OF THE TRANSFER

It is normally the buyer's duty to prepare the transfer, but the seller may, by s 48(1) of the LPA 1925, reserve the right by contractual condition to prepare the transfer themselves. This right is usually used in sales of new houses, where the seller will supply an engrossment (top copy) of the transfer, a draft of which was attached to the contract.

If prepared by the buyer, the transfer is usually prepared shortly after exchange of contracts and sent to the seller for their approval with the buyer's Request for Completion Information. By SC 4.3.2 (SCPC 7.3.2), the buyer is required to submit the draft transfer to the seller at least 12 working days before contractual completion date. However, under the Protocol, the seller's solicitor may include a draft transfer with the contract bundle. If they do not, the buyer's solicitor is required to submit the draft transfer to the seller's solicitor when they approve the draft contract, which may be well before exchange of contracts.

27.2 FORM OF THE TRANSFER

The transfer must be a deed in order to transfer the legal estate in the land to the buyer (LPA 1925, s 52). The transfer puts into effect the terms of the contract and so must reflect its terms. The form of the transfer varies, depending on whether the land concerned is registered or unregistered, freehold or leasehold. This chapter concentrates on the form of the transfer in freehold transactions. Leaseholds are dealt with in **Chapters 36** and **37**.

27.2.1 Registered land

Where the property being transferred is registered land, the form of the transfer is prescribed by rules made under the LRA 2002 and, subject to permitted variations, the prescribed form of wording must be used. Many of the standard Land Registry forms (eg TR1, TP1) can be reproduced electronically, and in straightforward transactions these may be used as the basis of the transfer. In more complex cases it will be necessary to produce an individually drafted transfer, but in either case the form of wording prescribed by the rules should be followed as closely as circumstances permit. A traditional conveyance cannot be used to transfer registered land.

27.2.2 Unregistered land

No prescribed form of wording exists for a conveyance of unregistered land. The buyer is thus free to choose their own wording, subject to the seller's approval and provided that it accurately reflects the terms of the contract. However, as the transaction will lead to an application for first registration of title after completion, instead of using a traditional conveyance the buyer will usually prepare a Land Registry transfer.

27.3 AGREEING THE TRANSFER

When drafting the transfer the buyer's solicitor needs to have access to:

(a) the contract, because the transfer must reflect the terms of the contract;

(b) the official copy entries/unregistered title deeds, because the contract may refer to matters on the title which need to be repeated or reflected in the transfer; and

(c) except in straightforward cases, a precedent on which to base the transfer under preparation.

When the draft has been prepared, two copies should be sent to the seller's solicitor for their approval. On receipt of the draft, the seller's solicitor should check it carefully to ensure that the document accurately reflects the terms of the contract. Amendments should be restricted to those which are necessary for the fulfilment of the document's legal purpose, bearing in mind that the choice of style and wording is the buyer's prerogative. Under both sets of Standard Conditions, the seller's solicitor is to approve or return the revised draft document four working days after delivery of the draft transfer by the buyer's solicitor (SC 4.3.2 and SCPC 7.3.2).

When amendments (if any) to the draft transfer have been finalised, the buyer's solicitor should prepare an engrossment (clean copy) of the transfer. The engrossment must be checked carefully to ensure that all agreed amendments have been incorporated. The completed engrossment should then be sent to the seller's solicitor for execution (signature) by their client.

Where the buyer is also required to execute the transfer (see **27.4**), it is common practice for them to do so before it is sent to the seller for their signature. By SC 4.3.2 (SCPC 7.3.2), the buyer must deliver the engrossment of the transfer to the seller at least five working days before completion.

27.4 EXECUTION AND DELIVERY OF THE TRANSFER

To be valid in law a deed must:

(a) indicate clearly that it is a deed;

(b) be signed by the necessary parties in the presence of a witness; and

(c) be delivered (Law of Property (Miscellaneous Provisions) Act 1989, s 1). (See also Land Registration (Execution of Deeds) Rules 1990 (SI 1990/1010).)

Signature by the seller is always required in order to transfer the legal estate (LPA 1925, s 52). The buyer is required to execute the transfer if it contains:

(a) a covenant by the buyer (eg an indemnity covenant); or

(b) a declaration by the buyer (eg a declaration relating to the trusts on which co-owners hold the property); or

(c) an application (eg for a restriction to be entered on the proprietorship register).

Where other parties are joined in the transfer (eg, on a sale of part of a property subject to a mortgage, a lender will join in the transfer to release the part of the property being sold from the mortgage), they should also sign the document. The provisions relating to execution of deeds are explained in **16.10**.

The Land Registry's position on electronic signatures is set out in Practice guide 82. It contains complex requirements that are beyond the scope of this textbook.

In addition to being signed, a deed must be delivered, ie the parties must intend to be bound by it. A deed takes effect on its delivery. When the buyer delivers the engrossment transfer to the seller for execution, the buyer does not normally intend the transfer to become effective at that time. It is therefore common practice for the buyer to deliver the transfer to the seller 'in escrow', ie conditionally, so that the operation of the transfer is postponed until completion.

27.5 EXPLAINING THE TRANSFER TO THE CLIENT

A solicitor should always ensure, before submitting a document for signature, that the client understands the nature and contents of the document. The letter which accompanies the transfer should:

(a) explain the purpose and contents of the transfer;
(b) contain clear instructions relating to the execution of the transfer;
(c) tell the client when the signed transfer must be returned to the solicitor; and
(d) ask the client not to date the transfer (it is dated on actual completion).

27.6 PLANS

If the contract provides for the use of a plan, the transfer will also refer to the plan. In other cases, the buyer is not entitled to demand that a plan is used with the transfer unless the description of the property as afforded by the contract and title deeds is inadequate without one. If the buyer wishes to use a plan in circumstances where they are not entitled to demand one, they may do so with the seller's consent, but they will have to pay for its preparation.

Where the sale is of the whole of the seller's property, use of a plan is not normally considered necessary. On a sale of part (including flats and office suites) a plan is highly desirable; and where the land is registered or to be registered a plan must be used. The plan(s) to be used with the transfer should be checked for accuracy, including all necessary colourings and markings, and firmly bound into the engrossment of the deed, which should in its wording refer to the use of the plan(s). In registered land cases, all parties who execute the deed must also sign the plan as an acknowledgement of its inclusion as an integral part of the document. Signatures on a plan need not be witnessed. Where a company seals the transfer, it should also seal the plan.

The preparation and use of plans are discussed at **18.5.1**.

27.7 TRANSFER OF WHOLE

A transfer of the whole of a registered title will usually follow Land Registry Form TR1. A blank copy of this form is set out at the end of this chapter. It is divided into a number of panels and is designed so that it can be reproduced on a word processor. A worked example of the TR1 for 47, Queen's Road, Loamster follows the blank form and incorporates explanatory notes.

27.8 CONVEYANCE

As a conveyance of unregistered land will lead to first registration, it is possible to use the usual form of Land Registry transfer, ie Form TR1 (see below). This is very commonly used in practice. The only amendments required to the printed form will be the omission of the title number in box 1 – as the land is not registered there will not be one – and the need to include a fuller description of the property in box 2. This need contain only a reference to another document in the title which contains a full description. This might read, for example:

> 10, Coronation Street, Weatherfield, GM4 8YY, as is more particularly described in a conveyance dated 4 February 1962 and made between . . .

It will also be necessary to include reference (in panel 11) to the incumbrances subject to which the property has been sold.

Where a traditional conveyance is to be used, it will contain the same information as in Form TR1, but in a different format.

An example of a conveyance drafted in a modern style is given in **27.8.1** below:

27.8.1 Specimen modern form: conveyance

This Conveyance is made on

between FREDERICK ALBERT BROWN and CLAIRE BROWN both of Brookside, 73A Manor Grove Avenue, Newton, Blankshire ('the Sellers') and LEONARD ARTHUR JOHNSON and JENNIFER JOHNSON both of 28 Albert Road, Newton, Blankshire ('the Buyers').

1. In consideration of ninety-nine thousand eight hundred pounds (£99,800) paid by the Buyers to the Sellers (the receipt of which the Sellers acknowledge) the Sellers convey to the Buyers with full title guarantee the freehold property known as Brookside 73A Manor Grove Avenue, Newton, Blankshire described in a Conveyance dated 18th November 1970 and made between John Edward Smith and the Sellers ('the Property') subject to the matters in that Conveyance so far as they affect the Property and are still effective.
2. The Buyers hold the Property on trust for themselves as joint tenants.
3. The Buyers jointly and severally covenant with the Sellers to observe and perform the restrictions covenants and conditions contained in a conveyance dated 23rd April 1938 and made between Hedley Verity of the one part and Wilfred Rhodes of the other and to indemnify the Seller against any future breach or non-observance.

Signed as a deed and delivered by
Frederick Albert Brown
and Claire Brown
in the presence of: }

Signed as a deed and delivered by
Leonard Arthur Johnson
and Jennifer Johnson
in the presence of: }

HM Land Registry
Transfer of whole of registered title(s)

TR1

Any parts of the form that are not typed should be completed in black ink and in block capitals.

If you need more room than is provided for in a panel, and your software allows, you can expand any panel in the form. Alternatively use continuation sheet CS and attach it to this form.

For information on how HM Land Registry processes your personal information, see our Personal Information Charter.

Leave blank if not yet registered.	1	Title number(s) of the property:
Insert address including postcode (if any) or other description of the property, for example 'land adjoining 2 Acacia Avenue'.	2	Property:
Remember to date this deed with the day of completion, but not before it has been signed and witnessed.	3	Date:
Give full name(s) of **all** the persons transferring the property. Complete as appropriate where the transferor is a company.	4	Transferor: For UK incorporated companies/LLPs Registered number of company or limited liability partnership including any prefix: For overseas companies (a) Territory of incorporation: (b) Registered number in the United Kingdom including any prefix:
Give full name(s) of **all** the persons to be shown as registered proprietors. Complete as appropriate where the transferee is a company. Also, for an overseas company, unless an arrangement with HM Land Registry exists, lodge either a certificate in Form 7 in Schedule 3 to the Land Registration Rules 2003 or a certified copy of the constitution in English or Welsh, or other evidence permitted by rule 183 of the Land Registration Rules 2003.	5	Transferee for entry in the register: For UK incorporated companies/LLPs Registered number of company or limited liability partnership including any prefix: For overseas companies (a) Territory of incorporation: (b) Registered number in the United Kingdom including any prefix:
Each transferee may give up to three addresses for service, one of which must be a postal address whether or not in the UK (including the postcode, if any). The others can be any combination of a postal address, a UK DX box number or an electronic address.	6	Transferee's intended address(es) for service for entry in the register:
	7	The transferor transfers the property to the transferee

Place 'X' in the appropriate box. State the currency unit if other than sterling. If none of the boxes apply, insert an appropriate memorandum in panel 11.	8 Consideration ☐ The transferor has received from the transferee for the property the following sum (in words and figures): ☐ The transfer is not for money or anything that has a monetary value ☐ Insert other receipt as appropriate:
Place 'X' in any box that applies. Add any modifications.	9 The transferor transfers with ☐ full title guarantee ☐ limited title guarantee
Where the transferee is more than one person, place 'X' in the appropriate box. Complete as necessary. The registrar will enter a Form A restriction in the register *unless*: – an 'X' is placed: – in the first box, or – in the third box and the details of the trust or of the trust instrument show that the transferees are to hold the property on trust for themselves alone as joint tenants, *or* – it is clear from completion of a form JO lodged with this application that the transferees are to hold the property on trust for themselves alone as joint tenants. Please refer to *Joint property ownership* and practice guide 24: *private trusts of land* for further guidance. These are both available on the GOV.UK website.	10 Declaration of trust. The transferee is more than one person and ☐ they are to hold the property on trust for themselves as joint tenants ☐ they are to hold the property on trust for themselves as tenants in common in equal shares ☐ they are to hold the property on trust:
Insert here any required or permitted statement, certificate or application and any agreed covenants, declarations and so on.	11 Additional provisions

The transferor must execute this transfer as a deed using the space opposite. If there is more than one transferor, all must execute. Forms of execution are given in Schedule 9 to the Land Registration Rules 2003. If the transfer contains transferee's covenants or declarations or contains an application by the transferee (such as for a restriction), it must also be executed by the transferee. If there is more than one transferee and panel 10 has been completed, each transferee must also execute this transfer to comply with the requirements in section 53(1)(b) of the Law of Property Act 1925 relating to the declaration of a trust of land. Please refer to *Joint property ownership* and practice guide 24: *private trusts of land* for further guidance. Examples of the correct form of execution are set out in practice guide 8: execution of deeds. Execution as a deed usually means that a witness must also sign, and add their name and address. Remember to date this deed in panel 3.	12 Execution

WARNING
If you dishonestly enter information or make a statement that you know is, or might be, untrue or misleading, and intend by doing so to make a gain for yourself or another person, or to cause loss or the risk of loss to another person, you may commit the offence of fraud under section 1 of the Fraud Act 2006, the maximum penalty for which is 10 years' imprisonment or an unlimited fine, or both.

Failure to complete this form with proper care may result in a loss of protection under the Land Registration Act 2002 if, as a result, a mistake is made in the register.

Under section 66 of the Land Registration Act 2002 most documents (including this form) kept by the registrar relating to an application to the registrar or referred to in the register are open to public inspection and copying. If you believe a document contains prejudicial information, you may apply for that part of the document to be made exempt using Form EX1, under rule 136 of the Land Registration Rules 2003.

27.9 WORKED EXAMPLE OF TR1

HM Land Registry
Transfer of whole of registered title(s)

TR1

Any parts of the form that are not typed should be completed in black ink and in block capitals.

If you need more room than is provided for in a panel, and your software allows, you can expand any panel in the form. Alternatively use continuation sheet CS and attach it to this form.

For information on how HM Land Registry processes your personal information, see our Personal Information Charter.

Guidance	Panel
Leave blank if not yet registered.	1 Title number(s) of the property: LM12037 [Note: This information can be obtained from the official copy entries supplied by the seller, see **4.5**]
Insert address including postcode (if any) or other description of the property, for example 'land adjoining 2 Acacia Avenue'.	2 Property: 47, Queen's Road, Loamster, Maradon, Cornshire CS1 5TY [Note: This information can be obtained from the official copy entries supplied by the seller, see **4.5**. The description should include the postcode.]
Remember to date this deed with the day of completion, but not before it has been signed and witnessed.	3 Date: [blank]
Give full name(s) of **all** the persons transferring the property. Complete as appropriate where the transferor is a company.	4 Transferor: ROGER EVANS [Note: This information can be obtained from the official copy entries supplied by the seller, see **4.5**. If the transferor is a company, the registered number should be included. There is no need to include the transferor's address.] For UK incorporated companies/LLPs Registered number of company or limited liability partnership including any prefix: For overseas companies (a) Territory of incorporation: (b) Registered number in the United Kingdom including any prefix:
Give full name(s) of **all** the persons to be shown as registered proprietors. Complete as appropriate where the transferee is a company. Also, for an overseas company, unless an arrangement with HM Land Registry exists, lodge either a certificate in Form 7 in Schedule 3 to the Land Registration Rules 2003 or a certified copy of the constitution in English or Welsh, or other evidence permitted by rule 183 of the Land Registration Rules 2003.	5 Transferee for entry in the register: Catherine Reade and Joanne Reade [Note: This information has come from the Attendance Note at **8.7**.] For UK incorporated companies/LLPs Registered number of company or limited liability partnership including any prefix: For overseas companies (a) Territory of incorporation: (b) Registered number in the United Kingdom including any prefix:

Each transferee may give up to three addresses for service, one of which must be a postal address whether or not in the UK (including the postcode, if any). The others can be any combination of a postal address, a UK DX box number or an electronic address.

6 Transferee's intended address(es) for service for entry in the register:
47, Queen's Road, Loamster, Maradon, Cornshire CS1 5TY

[Note: The address will be the one which is entered on the register and is intended as an address at which any notices concerning the property can be served. It should, therefore, be the address which will be relevant after the purchase. In the case of a house purchase, it will normally be the address of the property being purchased, assuming that the buyers do intend to reside there. In the case of a commercial property, it will normally be the registered office of the buyer. Note that up to three addresses for service can be stated, including an e-mail address, to ensure that any notices from Land Registry do come to the proprietor's attention.]

7 The transferor transfers the property to the transferee

Place 'X' in the appropriate box. State the currency unit if other than sterling. If none of the boxes apply, insert an appropriate memorandum in panel 11.

8 Consideration

☒ The transferor has received from the transferee for the property the following sum (in words and figures):
three hundred and fifty thousand pounds £350,000.00

[Note: The amount stated should be the total amount payable for the property (ie, not just the balance due on completion) but should exclude any amount payable in respect of contents. If contents are being purchased for an additional sum, a separate receipt will need to be prepared for this amount. Where VAT is payable, the amount stated should include VAT, as this forms part of the consideration for the property.]

☐ The transfer is not for money or anything that has a monetary value

☐ Insert other receipt as appropriate:

Place 'X' in any box that applies.

Add any modifications.

9 The transferor transfers with

☒ full title guarantee

☐ limited title guarantee

[Note: This is space to include any modifications to the covenants which may have been agreed in the contract. See **18.8.3.5**.]

Where the transferee is more than one person, place 'X' in the appropriate box.

Complete as necessary.

The registrar will enter a Form A restriction in the register *unless*:
- an 'X' is placed:
  - in the first box, or
  - in the third box and the details of the trust or of the trust instrument show that the transferees are to hold the property on trust for themselves alone as joint tenants, *or*
- it is clear from completion of a form JO lodged with this application that the transferees are to hold the property on trust for themselves alone as joint tenants.

Please refer to *Joint property ownership* and practice guide *24: private trusts of land* for further guidance. These are both available on the GOV.UK website.

10 Declaration of trust. The transferee is more than one person and

☐ they are to hold the property on trust for themselves as joint tenants

☒ they are to hold the property on trust for themselves as tenants in common in equal shares

☐ they are to hold the property on trust:

[Note: This panel is only relevant where there is more than one transferee. It requires the buyers to declare whether they will hold the land as joint tenants or tenants in common. If they are to hold as tenants in common other than in equal shares, it is necessary for the precise shares to be set out. If the trusts are complicated, they should be continued onto the prescribed continuation sheet (form CS). Alternatively, Form JO or a separate deed of trust can be drafted. A separate deed may be preferable, as any document sent to Land Registry is open to public inspection, and it may well be that the buyer will not want details of the trust to be open to public view. If a separate deed is used, this need not be sent to Land Registry, the TR1 or Form JO simply declaring that the property is held on the trusts declared by that deed (see **10.3**).]

Insert here any required or permitted statement, certificate or application and any agreed covenants, declarations and so on.	11 Additional provisions The transferees jointly and severally covenant with the transferor to: 11.1 (by way of indemnity only) observe and perform the covenants referred to in Entry No 1 of the charges register of the title referred to above ('the Covenants') so far as they are subsisting and capable of taking effect; and 11.2 indemnify the transferor against any liability incurred for any breach or non-observance of the Covenants occurring after the date of this transfer. [Note: This is a box in which any other agreed clauses can be inserted. The most common will be an indemnity covenant as above. Remember that additional clauses can be included only if they were agreed in the contract, so the contract should be consulted when completing this panel. Where the sale is subject to any obligation on which the seller will remain liable after the sale, SC 4.6.4 and SCPC 7.6.5 will provide that the buyer should enter into an indemnity covenant.]
The transferor must execute this transfer as a deed using the space opposite. If there is more than one transferor, all must execute. Forms of execution are given in Schedule 9 to the Land Registration Rules 2003. If the transfer contains transferee's covenants or declarations or contains an application by the transferee (such as for a restriction), it must also be executed by the transferee. If there is more than one transferee and panel 10 has been completed, each transferee must also execute this transfer to comply with the requirements in section 53(1)(b) of the Law of Property Act 1925 relating to the declaration of a trust of land. Please refer to *Joint property ownership* and practice guide 24: *private trusts of land* for further guidance. Examples of the correct form of execution are set out in practice guide 8: execution of deeds. Execution as a deed usually means that a witness must also sign, and add their name and address. Remember to date this deed in panel 3.	12 Execution Signed as a deed by ROGER EVANS in the presence of .... Signature of witness .... Name (in BLOCK CAPITALS) .... Address .... Signed as a deed by Catherine Reade in the presence of .... Signature of witness .... Name (in BLOCK CAPITALS) .... Address .... Signed as a deed by Joanne Reade in the presence of .... Signature of witness .... Name (in BLOCK CAPITALS) .... Address .... [Note: The seller must always execute the transfer. The buyer must also execute if the transfer contains buyer's covenants (such as an indemnity covenant), declarations (such as a declaration of trust in panel 10) or an application (such as an application for a restriction to be entered on the registers of title). For appropriate methods of execution, see **16.10**.]

WARNING
If you dishonestly enter information or make a statement that you know is, or might be, untrue or misleading, and intend by doing so to make a gain for yourself or another person, or to cause loss or the risk of loss to another person, you may commit the offence of fraud under section 1 of the Fraud Act 2006, the maximum penalty for which is 10 years' imprisonment or an unlimited fine, or both.

Failure to complete this form with proper care may result in a loss of protection under the Land Registration Act 2002 if, as a result, a mistake is made in the register.

Under section 66 of the Land Registration Act 2002 most documents (including this form) kept by the registrar relating to an application to the registrar or referred to in the register are open to public inspection and copying. If you believe a document contains prejudicial information, you may apply for that part of the document to be made exempt using Form EX1, under rule 136 of the Land Registration Rules 2003.

SUMMARY

- The transfer is usually prepared by the buyer's solicitor.
- It must be a deed, and where the land is registered it must comply with Land Registry requirements.
- The worked example set out at **27.9** will help you to complete a Land Registry TR1 correctly.
- The transfer must always be signed by the seller, and must also be signed by the buyer where it contains a covenant or declaration on the buyer's behalf.

CHAPTER 28

Pre-completion Searches

LEARNING OUTCOMES

After reading this chapter you will be able to:

- understand why pre-completion searches are necessary
- know which pre-completion searches are appropriate for a particular property transaction
- protect a buyer client by making the relevant searches at the right time
- take appropriate action if a search reveals unexpected information.

28.1 WHO MAKES THE SEARCHES?

It is the buyer's solicitor's responsibility to ensure that such pre-completion searches as are relevant to the transaction are carried out, and that their results are satisfactory to their client. The buyer's lender also has an interest in the soundness of the title to the property and the solvency of the borrower, so searches will need making on the lender's behalf also.

28.2 REASON FOR MAKING SEARCHES

The main reason for making pre-completion searches is for the buyer's solicitor to confirm that information obtained about the property before exchange remains correct.

28.3 WHEN TO MAKE SEARCHES

The searches must be made in sufficient time to guarantee that the results are received by the buyer's solicitor in time for completion to take place on the contractual completion date. Pre-completion searches should generally be made about seven days before the contractual completion date, but may be left until closer to completion date if, for example, a telephone or electronic search is to be made.

28.4 WHICH SEARCHES TO MAKE

The following searches should be made:

(a) for registered land, search against title number at the Land Registry (see **28.5**);

(b) for unregistered land, including an unregistered reversion to a lease, search at the Land Charges Department against names of estate owners of the land (see **28.6**);

(c) if acting for a lender, a bankruptcy search against the name of an individual borrower (see **28.7**) or a company search against a company borrower (see **28.8**);

(d) such other of the searches listed in **28.8–28.11** as are relevant to the transaction.

28.5 TITLE SEARCHES: LAND REGISTRY SEARCH FOR REGISTERED LAND

For registered land, a pre-completion search should be made at Land Registry. The object of the search is to ascertain whether any further entries have been made on the register of title to the property since the date of the official copies supplied prior to exchange. A fee is payable and the search can be made electronically (via the Land Registry Portal) or by post.

The search application should be made on Form OS1 where the transaction concerns the whole of a registered title, and on Form OS2 where the transaction concerns part of a registered title. The application will give details of the title number of the property to be searched, a brief description of its situation, ie, postal address, county and district, and the names of the registered proprietors. The applicant's name must also be given, together with the reason for making the search, ie, they intend to purchase/lease/take a charge on the land. If Form OS2 is being used, a plan will need to be submitted showing the land being purchased, leased or mortgaged.

Where the property is being purchased with a mortgage, the search application should be completed in the name of the lender. If this is done, both the buyer and the lender will be protected by the search, and a separate search in the buyer's name is unnecessary. However, a search made on behalf of the buyer will not protect a lender.

The search result will reveal any fresh entries which have been made on the register since a stated date, which will usually be the date of the official copy entries given to the buyer and must be a date no earlier than 12 months before the date of the search application. In most cases there will be no new entries and, if this is the case and the form has been submitted electronically, the search result will be obtained immediately. The search result also confers on the searcher a priority period of 30 working days from the date of the certificate. This provides protection to the buyer (and lender, if the search was made on their behalf) against any subsequent entries which may be placed on the register after the date of the search but before the buyer is registered as proprietor. The buyer will take free from any such entries, provided that they submit the application for registration within the priority period.

28.6 TITLE SEARCHES: CENTRAL LAND CHARGES DEPARTMENT SEARCH FOR UNREGISTERED LAND

This search is only of relevance to unregistered land and will usually have been made before exchange (see **17.11**). However, it will need to be repeated against the current seller's name unless the transaction can be completed within the 15 working day priority period conferred by the pre-exchange search. This is to ensure that no further entries have been made against the seller's name since the date of the previous search. No further entries can validly be made against the names of previous estate owners once they have disposed of the land, so these need not be searched against again.

28.7 BANKRUPTCY SEARCH FOR INDIVIDUALS

28.7.1 Against the buyer/borrower

Irrespective of whether the transaction relates to registered or unregistered land, a lender will require a clear bankruptcy search against the name of the buyer/borrower before releasing the mortgage funds. Unless a full search of the register has been made on Form K15 (which includes a bankruptcy search) (see **28.6**), the lender's solicitor should send Form K16 to the Land Charges Department or submit it electronically via Land Registry's business portal, completed with the full and correct names of the borrower(s). A search certificate will be returned by the Land Charges Department or be available to view electronically if Land Registry's business portal has been used. In the unusual event of there being an adverse entry revealed by the search, the lender's instructions must be obtained immediately. Paragraph 5.16.2 of the *Lenders' Handbook* makes it clear that the lender will not proceed to advance the loan unless the solicitor certifies that the entry does not relate to the borrower, ie, that it relates to someone else with the same name. If a solicitor certifies a search entry as not relating to their client, this certification is construed as an undertaking. Obviously, a solicitor must take great care in giving such a certificate.

The Insolvency Service website <www.insolvencydirect.bis.gov.uk> provides an Individual Insolvency Register Search, a free instant online search of current bankruptcies, debt relief orders, IVAs and fast track voluntary arrangements. The search will reveal the date of birth of the person concerned. This can then be compared with the client's birth details on the document used to prove identity. In case of any doubt, the matter must be reported to the lender which will make its own enquiries. However, a delay in completion will be inevitable and the lender may decide not to proceed with the loan. It is for this reason that it is suggested that this search should be made prior to exchange (see **17.9**). It will need repeating prior to completion to cover the possibility that the borrower has become bankrupt since the date of the previous search (although the chances of this are very slight) and it will ensure that many potential problems can be resolved at a time where they will not cause a delay in completion.

28.7.2 Against the seller

In relation to a seller who is an individual, if the transaction relates to unregistered land, a Form K15 search against the seller as estate owner will reveal any entries relating to bankruptcy (see **28.6**). In the case of registered land, most conveyancing solicitors do not consider it necessary to do a bankruptcy check on an individual seller as s 86(5) of the Land Registration Act 2002 provides that where no notice or restriction relating to the bankruptcy appears on the registered title, a buyer for value acting in good faith without notice of the bankruptcy petition or adjudication will take good title from the bankrupt seller, even though legal title to the land has vested in the trustee in bankruptcy. However, the bankruptcy searches described at **28.7.1** can be done where the transaction is for a particularly high value or there is reason to be concerned about the solvency of the individual seller.

28.8 COMPANY SEARCH FOR CORPORATE ENTITIES

A company search against a corporate seller or borrower may be done as one of the pre-contract searches (see **17.12**). If so, it should be updated at this stage of the transaction to ensure that none of the information has changed. In addition, where the transaction is for a particularly high value, or there is reason to be concerned about the solvency of a corporate seller or borrower, it is possible to do a telephone search at the Registry of Winding Up Petitions at the Companies Court on the day of completion. This will reveal recent winding up and administration orders and applications and petitions for winding up/administration which may not yet be appearing on the Company Search. Alternatively, there are online commercial search providers who, for a fee, will carry out insolvency checks.

28.9 ENDURING AND LASTING POWERS OF ATTORNEY

Where the transfer deed is to be executed by a person who is acting under the authority of an enduring or lasting power of attorney, a search should be made with the Office of the Public Guardian to check whether or not registration of the power has been effected or is pending. In the case of enduring powers, unless a registration is pending (which would suggest the mental incapacity of the donor), the transaction may proceed to completion, provided the buyer has no actual knowledge of any circumstances that would revoke the power. If the power has been registered, the attorney may deal with the land and thus, provided the donor is still alive, completion may proceed, because the power is no longer capable of revocation without notification to the Public Guardian. An office copy of the power should be obtained from the Office of the Public Guardian. Lasting powers come into effect only when registered with the Office of the Public Guardian and, again, an office copy should be obtained. Powers of attorney are discussed in further detail at **16.7.7**.

28.10 LOCAL LAND CHARGES SEARCH AND ENQUIRIES

These searches are invariably made before exchange of contracts and are discussed in **Chapter 17**. Although the local land charges search shows only the state of the register at the time of issue of the search certificate, and neither search confers a priority period on the buyer, a repeat of these searches before completion is not normally considered to be necessary, provided that completion takes place within a short time after receipt of the search results. Delay in receipt of the replies to these searches sometimes makes it impracticable for them to be repeated at this stage of the transaction. These searches should nevertheless be repeated prior to completion if:

(a) there is to be a period of two months or more between exchange of contracts and completion, and the search has not been covered by insurance or replaced by insurance; or

(b) information received by the buyer's solicitor suggests a further search may be advisable in order to guard against a recently entered adverse entry on the register; or

(c) the contract was conditional on the satisfactory results of later searches.

The discovery of a late entry on such a search is not a matter of title and will not entitle the buyer either to raise requisitions about the entry, or to refuse to complete, unless the contract was made conditional on the satisfactory result of searches. It is still, however, best for the client to be advised of any further entries so that they understand the position they will be in once the purchase has been completed.

Although para 5.4.3 of the *Lenders' Handbook* requires that all searches should be not more than six months old at the date of completion, many conveyancers consider that repeating the searches after two months is preferable. Some lenders will, however, accept search insurance in such a situation which will provide insurance indemnity against late entries.

28.11 INSPECTION OF THE PROPERTY

Inspection or re-inspection of the property may be necessary just before completion. Such a step is advisable in the case of the purchase of a house which is in the course of construction (and may be done by the buyer's lender's surveyor in such cases), or where there has been a problem with non-owning occupiers. Inspection of the property is dealt with at **17.14**.

28.12 RESULTS OF SEARCHES

Completion cannot proceed until the search results have been received and are deemed to be satisfactory to the interests of the client. In the majority of cases, the results of searches will either show no subsisting entries or merely confirm information already known. In such circumstances, no further action on the search results is required from the buyer's solicitor. If an unexpected entry is revealed by the search result, the buyer's solicitor should:

(a) if the entry appears adversely to affect the property, contact the seller's solicitor as soon as possible to find out exactly what the entry relates to (if that is unclear from the search results) and seek their confirmation that the entry will be removed on or before completion (if that is possible);

(b) in the case of a Land Charges Department search, apply for an official copy of the entry using Form K19 (the official copy consists of a copy of the application form which was submitted when the charge was registered and will reveal the name and address of the person with the benefit of the charge who may have to be contacted to seek their consent to its removal);

(c) keep the client, their lender and, subject to the duty of confidentiality, other solicitors involved in the chain of transactions informed of the situation, since negotiations for the removal of the charge may cause a delay in completion. Any such delay will give rise to contractual remedies for breach of contract. Further, if the seller is unable or unwilling to remove an entry which the contract did not make the sale subject to, this will also be a breach of contract. For remedies for breach of contract, see **Chapter 33**.

28.12.1 Removing an entry from the register

An application form for the removal of an entry from the register in either registered or unregistered land will be accepted by the Chief Land Registrar only if it is signed by the person with the benefit of the charge or a person acting on their behalf. An application form signed by the seller's solicitors, or an undertaking given by them on completion to secure the removal of the charge may not, therefore, suffice, unless the seller is the person with the benefit of the charge (see *Holmes v Kennard (H) and Son (A Firm)* (1985) 49 P & CR 202). The court has a discretion to remove entries which are redundant but which cannot be removed from the register because the person with their benefit either will not consent to their removal or cannot be contacted. Entries protecting a spouse's rights under the Family Law Act 1996 can be removed on production of the death certificate of the spouse or a decree absolute of divorce. In the absence of these items, the charge can be removed only with the consent of the spouse who has the benefit of the charge.

28.12.2 Irrelevant land charges entries

Charges which are registered at the Land Charges Department can only validly be entered against the name of an estate owner in relation to the period during which they were the owner of the land in question. Thus, an entry which was made before or after this time cannot prejudice the buyer. The computerised system which is used to process these searches will sometimes throw up entries which are clearly irrelevant to the transaction in hand, particularly where the name searched against is a very common one such as John Jones. Having checked that the entry is irrelevant, it may either be disregarded or, at completion, the seller's solicitor may be asked to certify the entry as being inapplicable to the transaction. A solicitor's certificate is construed as an undertaking and should therefore only be given where the solicitor is sure that the entry is irrelevant. Particular care is needed in relation to bankruptcy entries.

28.12.3 Entries that cannot be removed

If the seller is unwilling or unable to remove an adverse entry revealed by a pre-completion search, the terms of the contract will need to be consulted to identify if the seller is in breach of contract. Remedies for breach of contract are discussed in **Chapter 33**.

28.12.4 Official certificates of search

28.12.4.1 Registered land

An official certificate of search issued by Land Registry is not conclusive in favour of the searcher, who will thus take their interest in the land subject to whatever entries are on the register, irrespective of whether or not they were revealed by the search certificate (see *Parkash v Irani Finance Ltd* [1970] Ch 101). However, where a person suffers loss as a result of an error in an official certificate of search, they may be able to claim compensation under the LRA 2002.

28.12.4.2 Unregistered land

An official certificate of search issued by the Land Charges Department is conclusive in favour of the searcher, who will thus take their interest in the land free of any entries which are on the register but which were not revealed by the search certificate. Where a person suffers loss as a result of an error in an official certificate of search, they may be able to claim compensation from the Chief Land Registrar, but there is no statutory right to compensation in these circumstances. No liability will attach to the solicitor who made the search, provided that a correctly submitted official search was made (Land Charges Act 1972, s 12).

28.13 PRIORITY PERIODS

28.13.1 Registered land

An official certificate of search issued by Land Registry following a search made on Form OS1 or OS2 gives a priority period to the searcher of 30 working days from the Certificate Date in the search. A buyer will also take advantage of this protection where a search was made on their behalf in the name of their lender. The searcher will take priority over any entry made during the priority period, provided that completion takes place and a correct application for registration of the transaction is received by the appropriate Land Registry Office by 12 noon on the day when the priority period given by the search expires.

28.13.2 Unregistered land

An official certificate of search issued by the Land Charges Department gives a priority period of 15 working days from the date of the certificate, during which time the searcher will take free of any entries made on the register between the date of the search and the date of completion, provided that completion takes place during the priority period given by the search.

28.13.3 Date of expiry of priority period

The date of expiry of the priority period is shown on the search certificate. It should be marked on the outside of the client's file and entered in the solicitor's diary or file-prompt system to ensure that it is not overlooked. The priority period given by these searches cannot be extended, so if completion is delayed and cannot take place within the priority period given by the search, a new search application will have to be made. The new search certificate will give another priority period, but does not extend the original priority period from the first search. This means that entries made in the intervening period may be binding.

28.14 COMPARISON OF LOCAL AND CENTRAL LAND CHARGES SEARCHES

	Local	*Central*
Form:	LLC1	K15
When to make:	in every transaction	unregistered land only
Time to make:	before exchange	part of investigation of title
Send to:	local authority/Land Registry	Plymouth
Search against:	description of land	owners' names
Information revealed:	mainly public incumbrances	mainly private incumbrances
Protection of search:	none	priority for 15 working days

28.15 COMPARISON OF LAND REGISTRY AND LAND CHARGES DEPARTMENT SEARCHES

	Land Registry	*Land Charges Department*
Form:	OS1 or OS2	K15
When to use:	registered land	unregistered land
Search against:	title number	owners' names
Protection given:	search not conclusive but compensation available	conclusive in favour of searcher
Fee:	standard fee for each search	fee for each name searched
Priority period:	30 working days	15 working days

SUMMARY

- The purpose of pre-completion searches is to check that nothing adverse to the buyer has happened to the property or the seller since exchange, and to protect the buyer against any adverse change.
- Information about the property's title is obtained by a Land Registry search for registered land and a central land charges search for unregistered land.
- Both types of search protect the buyer by providing a priority period during which no other entries may be registered.
- The priority periods are different, and in each case the purchase must be completed within the relevant priority period or the priority will be lost.
- Information about the solvency of the seller is obtained by a bankruptcy search for an individual and a company search for a corporate entity. These searches do not confer the protection of a priority period and so should be done as close as possible to the date of completion.
- If a search reveals unexpected information adverse to the buyer, it may be possible to agree a satisfactory solution with the seller. If not, refer to **Chapter 33**.

CHAPTER 29

Preparing for Completion

29.1 INTRODUCTION

Both parties need to carry out a number of preparatory steps to ensure that completion proceeds smoothly. Most of these steps have been explained in other chapters of this book. This chapter contains a summary of the matters to be dealt with at this stage of the transaction by way of checklists, with some additional commentary.

29.2 SELLER'S CHECKLIST

(1) Check that the transfer deed has been approved and replies given to the buyer's Request for Completion Information.

(2) Receive engrossed transfer deed from buyer. Has buyer executed the deed (where appropriate) and plan (if used)?

(3) Obtain seller's signature (and witness) to transfer deed in time for completion.

(4) Obtain redemption figure(s) for seller's mortgage(s).

(5) Obtain last receipts, etc (eg, rent receipts for leasehold property) where apportionments are to be made on completion (see **29.5**).

(6) Prepare completion statement (ie, statement of amount due on completion) and send two copies to buyer in good time before completion (see **29.6**).

(7) Remind client to organise final readings of meters at the property.

(8) Prepare forms for discharge of land charges where necessary (unregistered land).

(9) Prepare any undertaking which needs to be given on completion (eg, for discharge of seller's mortgage if also acting for the lender).

(10) Contact lender to confirm final arrangements for discharge of seller's mortgage, method of payment, etc.

(11) Check through file to ensure all outstanding queries have been dealt with.

(12) Prepare list of matters to be dealt with on actual completion.

(13) Locate deeds and documents which will need to be inspected or handed over on completion and prepare certified copies for the buyer of those documents which are not being handed to the buyer on completion.

(14) Prepare two copies of schedule of deeds to be handed to buyer on completion.

(15) Prepare inventory of and receipt for money payable for chattels.

(16) Check arrangements for vacant possession and handing over keys.
(17) Receive instructions from buyer's solicitor to act as their agent on completion and clarify instructions with them if necessary.
(18) Make final arrangements with buyer's solicitor for time and place of completion.
(19) Inform estate agents of completion arrangements.
(20) Prepare bill for submission to client.

29.3 BUYER'S CHECKLIST

(1) Ensure the transfer deed has been approved and your Request for Completion Information satisfactorily answered.
(2) Engross transfer and mortgage deeds.
(3) Get buyer to execute mortgage deed, transfer deed and plan (if necessary) and return it to solicitor.
(4) Send (executed) transfer deed to seller's solicitor for their client's execution in time for completion.
(5) Make pre-completion searches and ensure their results are satisfactory.
(6) Make report on title to lender in format specified by lender (eg CLLS Certificate of Title – see **29.4.2**) and request mortgage advance in time for completion.
(7) Receive completion statement (see **29.6**) and copies of last receipts in support of apportionments (see **29.5**) and check they are correct.
(8) Remind client of arrangements for completion.
(9) Prepare and agree the form of wording of any undertaking which needs to be given or received on completion (eg, in relation to the discharge of the seller's mortgage).
(10) Contact lender to confirm final arrangements for completion.
(11) Ensure that any life policy required by the lender has been obtained and check with client that any other insurances required for the property (eg, house contents insurance) have been taken out.
(12) Check through file to ensure all outstanding queries have been dealt with.
(13) Prepare statement of account and bill for client and submit, together with a copy of the completion statement, requesting balance due from client to be paid in sufficient time for the funds to be cleared before completion (see **29.8**).
(14) Receive mortgage advance from lender and balance of funds from buyer. Pay into client account and clear funds before completion.
(15) Arrange for final inspection of property by lender's valuer if necessary.
(16) Prepare list of matters to be dealt with on actual completion.
(17) Check arrangements for vacant possession and handing over keys.
(18) Instruct seller's solicitor to act as agent on completion if completion not to be by personal attendance.
(19) Make final arrangements with seller's solicitor for time and place of completion.
(20) Ensure estate agents are aware of completion arrangements.
(21) Make arrangements to send completion money to seller's solicitor (or as they have directed).
(22) Ensure relevant SDLT forms completed and signed (see **29.7**).

29.4 THE CLIENT'S MORTGAGE

29.4.1 The seller

The seller's solicitor must ensure that they have obtained from the seller's lender(s) a statement, known as 'a redemption statement', which shows the exact amount required to discharge the seller's mortgage(s), on the day of completion. The lender will usually also indicate the daily rate which applies to the seller's mortgage so that the redemption figure can be adjusted if completion takes place earlier or later than anticipated.

The form of discharge of the mortgage must be prepared for signature by the lender. Form DS1 can be used for this purpose when dealing with registered land. However, many lenders now make use of the electronic ED or e-DS1 systems. Where these are in use, Land Registry will accept an electronic message from the lender notifying the discharge of the loan in place of Form DS1.

In the case of unregistered land, discharge is shown by a receipt endorsed on the mortgage itself.

29.4.2 The buyer

Once they have completed their investigation of title and are satisfied as to it, the solicitor acting for the buyer's lender will report to the lender that the title to the property is safe, marketable and acceptable as security for the loan. In a residential transaction, the form of certificate of title approved by The Law Society and UK Finance will be used. In commercial transactions the City of London Law Society's form of certificate is often used. Any problems or queries relating to the title should have been clarified with the lender before this stage of the transaction is reached.

It will also be necessary for the solicitor acting for the buyer's lender to make a formal request for the advance money from the lender. Depending on the practice of the particular lender, this request may form part of the report on title form or may be made on a separate form.

The mortgage deed should be prepared for signature by the borrowers. Many lenders insist that the mortgage deed is executed by the borrowers in the presence of their solicitor.

29.5 APPORTIONMENTS

Where completion does not take place on a date when outgoings (eg, rent or water rates) on the property fall due, outgoings which attach to the land can be split between the parties on completion. The calculations of the apportioned sums are shown on the completion statement.

Council tax and water rates can be apportioned, but it is normally considered better practice to inform the relevant authority after completion of the change of ownership and request it to send apportioned accounts to seller and buyer.

Standard Condition 6.3 deals with apportionments and allows a provisional apportionment to be made where exact figures are not available at completion (eg, in respect of service charges). The seller must produce the last demands or receipts for all sums which are to be apportioned so that the calculations of the amounts due or to be allowed on completion may be made. Copies of these receipts should be sent to the buyer with the completion statement to allow them to check the accuracy of the calculation.

Standard Commercial Property Condition 9.3 is similar, but includes more comprehensive provisions dealing with apportionments when the property is being sold subject to a lease. Note also that under SC 6.3.3, the *seller* is deemed to own the property for the whole of the day of completion, whereas under SCPC 9.3.3 the *buyer* is deemed to own the property for the whole of that day.

29.6 COMPLETION STATEMENT

A completion statement is prepared by the seller's solicitor which shows the amount of money required to complete the transaction and how that figure is calculated. The statement will be requested by the buyer when they send the Request for Completion Information to the seller.

It is necessary to provide the buyer with a completion statement only where the sum due on completion includes apportionments or other sums in excess of the balance of the purchase price (*Carne v De Bono* [1988] 3 All ER 485). Two copies of the completion statement should be sent to the buyer, together with copies of any receipts or demands relating to apportionments so that the buyer's solicitor can check the accuracy of the calculations.

The statement should show clearly the total amount due on completion, and how that total sum is made up. Depending on the circumstances, it may be necessary to deal with some or all of the following items:

(a) the purchase price, giving credit for any deposit paid;
(b) apportionments of outgoings;
(c) money payable for chattels;
(d) compensation if completion is delayed;
(e) a licence fee if the buyer has been in occupation of the property.

Often in a residential transaction only the balance of the purchase price will be payable and a completion statement will not be required.

29.7 STAMP DUTY LAND TAX RETURNS

After completion it will be necessary to make a stamp duty land tax (SDLT) return to HMRC giving details about the transaction and the buyer (see **31.7**). This is normally the case whether or not any SDLT is payable. The SDLT return can be submitted online (provided the buyer is legally represented) or by post using Form SDLT1. If submitted by post, it will need signing by the client. Some transactions require additional forms (for example Form SDLT4 is required where the buyer is a company).

If the buyer's solicitor is also acting for a lender, it is essential that the SDLT return is completed by the solicitor and approved by the buyer before the loan is used to finance the purchase. The solicitor should also ensure it has adequate cleared funds from the client to cover the payment of the SDLT. If a paper return is being used, this should also be signed by the client prior to completion. If these steps are not taken, but the loan is used and the buyer subsequently refuses to co-operate in filing the return and paying the SDLT, it will not be possible for the transaction – including the mortgage – to be registered at Land Registry. The lender will thus have no security for its loan – and the solicitor could be held liable for any loss suffered. See *Lenders' Handbook*, at **Appendix 7**.

29.8 STATEMENT TO CLIENT

The buyer's solicitor should prepare and send to their client a financial statement which shows clearly the total sum due from them on completion and how that sum is calculated. In addition to the matters dealt with on the completion statement, the financial statement should also take account of such of the following matters as are relevant to the transaction:

(a) the mortgage advance and any costs and/or retentions made in respect of it;
(b) disbursements (eg, SDLT and Land Registry fees);
(c) the solicitor's costs.

The financial statement, together with a copy of the completion statement and the solicitor's properly drawn bill, should be sent to the client in sufficient time before completion to allow the client to forward the required balance of funds to the solicitor so that those funds can be cleared by completion.

29.9 MONEY

As soon as the buyer's solicitor is informed of the amount required to complete, they should check the figures for accuracy. Any discrepancies must be clarified with the seller's solicitor. If at this stage it appears that there is any shortfall in the buyer's funds, the client must immediately be informed and steps must be taken to remedy the shortfall. If bridging finance or a further loan are necessary in order to complete the transaction, arrangements to secure these funds must be made, otherwise a delay in completion may occur. The buyer's mortgage advance and balance of funds received from the client should be obtained in sufficient time to allow the funds to be cleared through client account before completion.

A solicitor may be guilty of a criminal offence if they assist someone who is known or suspected to be laundering money generated by serious crime. The solicitor must therefore exercise caution in circumstances where the buyer client settles a large property transaction in cash or where payment for the property is made through a third party who is unknown to the solicitor. Reference should be made to The Law Society's guidance on money laundering. See **5.12**.

On the day of completion, arrangements must be made to send the amount due to the seller's solicitor in accordance with their instructions.

29.10 COMPLETION CHECKLIST

When preparing for completion, the solicitor should make a checklist of the matters which need to be dealt with on actual completion to ensure that nothing is overlooked. Where the buyer instructs a person to act as their agent on completion, they should, when instructing the agent, send a copy of the checklist so that the agent is aware of the matters which need to be dealt with.

Some or all of the items in the following checklist will need to be attended to on actual completion.

The list should contain an itemised list of the documents which need to be inspected, marked, handed over or received at completion.

(1) Documents to be available at completion:
    (a) contract;
    (b) evidence of title;
    (c) copy transfer deed;
    (d) replies to Request for Completion Information;
    (e) completion statement.
(2) Documents to be inspected by buyer:
    (a) title deeds, where in unregistered land these are not to be handed over on completion (eg, on a sale of part);
    (b) power(s) of attorney;
    (c) grant of administration;
    (d) receipts/demands for apportionments if not previously supplied.
(3) Documents, etc, to be handed to buyer on completion:
    (a) where the property is unregistered land, title deeds and a schedule of deeds and a certified copy of any memorandum endorsed on retained deeds;
    (b) original lease (on purchase of a lease);
    (c) executed transfer deed;
    (d) Form DS1/discharged mortgage or undertaking in respect of discharge of mortgage(s);
    (e) receipt for money paid for chattels;
    (f) keys of the property (if these are not available the seller's solicitor should be asked to telephone the key holder to request the release of the keys).

(4) Documents, etc, to be handed to seller on completion:
   (a) executed duplicate transfer deed/counterpart lease (where appropriate);
   (b) receipted schedule of any deeds received from seller;
   (c) release of deposit if held by third party in capacity of stakeholder.

(5) Unregistered land only, endorsements on documents (if required by buyer):
   (a) endorsement of sale on most recently dated retained document of title (sale of part);
   (b) abstract or epitome to be marked up as compared with the original deeds (in respect of any document the original of which is not handed over on completion).

PART V

THE CONVEYANCING TRANSACTION: COMPLETION AND POST-COMPLETION

CHAPTER 30

COMPLETION

LEARNING OUTCOMES

After reading this chapter you will be able to:

- explain the legal effect of completion and the contractual significance of the completion date and completion time contained in the contract
- identify what the contract says about the date, time and place for completion
- make appropriate arrangements in advance for the transmission of the completion monies and the discharge of the seller's mortgage
- effect the completion of the sale and purchase of a property
- make appropriate arrangements for the discharge of the seller's mortgage on or immediately after completion.

30.1 INTRODUCTION

For the client, completion is the culmination and climax of the transaction. It is the day on which they move into the new home, or take possession of the new shop unit. It is also the day on which the balance of the purchase price has to be paid to the seller.

For the solicitor, completion is a paperwork transaction frequently conducted via e-mail, the telephone and postal service from the solicitor's own office. It represents the climax of the past few weeks' work, but not the end of the transaction, since several matters will still need to be attended to by the solicitor even after the client has physically moved into the property (see **Chapter 31**).

The drama and excitement attached by the client to their move is not always shared by the solicitor, for whom this client's completion is just one of many which will be carried out by the solicitor on every working day. The drama of completion affects the solicitor only when things go wrong, for example if the money is not received by the seller and they will not allow the buyer into possession, or if the seller's mother-in-law refuses to move out of the property and the buyer's removal van is standing outside the gate waiting to unload its contents. An understanding of what happens at completion and why it happens, and careful planning of what appears to be a mundane event (until it goes wrong), will avoid most of the foreseeable problems attached to completion.

30.1.1 Effect of completion

The effect of completion differs according to whether the land concerned is registered or unregistered. In unregistered land, legal title to the property passes to the buyer at completion. In registered land, title does not pass to the buyer until the buyer becomes registered at Land Registry as proprietor of the land.

On completion, the contract merges with the transfer deed in so far as the contract and transfer deed cover the same ground, so that after completion it is not generally possible to bring a claim which arises out of one of the terms of the contract, unless that provision has been expressly preserved by a term of the contract itself. For this reason the contract usually contains a non-merger clause (see SC 7.3 and SCPC 10.4), which will preserve the right to sue on the contract even though completion has taken place. Claims not based on the contract (eg, in tort or for misrepresentation) are not affected by this rule (see **Chapter 33**).

30.2 DATE OF COMPLETION

The date of completion will be agreed between the parties' solicitors (after discussion with their respective clients) shortly before exchange of contracts. Where the buyer's purchase is dependent on their sale of another property, the completion dates in both contracts must be synchronised. It follows that the completion dates in all transactions in a chain of transactions must also be synchronised if the chain is not to break. In residential transactions, a completion date 14 days or less from the date of exchange is common. Sufficient time must be allowed between exchange and completion for the pre-completion steps in the transaction to be carried out. If the parties want to complete very quickly after exchange, arrangements can usually be made for some of the pre-completion steps, such as preparation of the transfer deed, to be done before exchange.

30.2.1 The Standard Conditions

In the absence of express agreement, SC 6.1 (SCPC 9.1) provides that completion shall take place on the twentieth working day after exchange. Time is not 'of the essence' of the completion date. This means that the stipulation as to time merely has the status of a contractual warranty and not a condition, so that although a delay in completion beyond the date fixed in the contract would give the innocent party the right to bring a claim in damages and would activate the compensation provisions of SC 7.2 (SCPC 10.3) (see **Chapter 32**), the delay would not of itself entitle the innocent party to withdraw from the contract at that stage.

Since delay in completion can occur for reasons beyond the control of the contracting parties (eg, postal delays), it is not generally a good idea to make time of the essence of the completion date. If the parties do want to make time of the essence (this would be very unusual in a residential transaction), an express provision to this effect can be inserted in the contract (eg, by adding the words 'as to which time shall be of the essence' alongside the insertion of the contractual completion date in the contract).

30.3 TIME OF COMPLETION

Where a buyer's purchase is dependent on the receipt of money from a related sale transaction, the solicitor must ensure that arrangements for completion day are made so that the sale transaction will be completed before the purchase transaction (otherwise there will be insufficient funds available to complete the purchase), and with a sufficient interval between the two transactions (eg, a minimum of an hour) to allow the money received from the sale to be transferred to and used in the purchase transaction. These arrangements will be made when final completion arrangements are made shortly before the day fixed for completion. Where the transaction is part of a long chain, the arrangements may be complex since, inevitably, the transaction at the bottom of the chain (which will usually involve a buyer who is not selling in a related transaction) must complete first, the money then progressing upwards through the chain. Note that many banks will not accept instructions for same day transmission of funds later than 3 pm. Such a transaction will frequently have to be completed early in the morning of completion day to allow all the subsequent transactions to take place within the same working day. A completion time earlier than 10 am is often difficult to comply with unless the money is sent to the seller on the previous day, because of restrictions on banking hours.

Even where a seller has no related purchase, they should ensure that the completion time agreed allows sufficient time for the proceeds of sale to be banked on the day of completion. If the money is not banked or sent to the lender (to discharge the seller's existing mortgage) until the following working day, the seller will suffer loss of interest on their money. For these reasons, a completion time later than 2.30 pm is inadvisable.

30.3.1 The Standard Conditions

In the absence of contrary provision, SC 6.1.2 and SCPC 9.1.2 provide that if completion does not take place by 2 pm on the day of completion, interest for late completion becomes payable, ie, completion is 'deemed' to have taken place on the next working day. Non-compliance with this condition is a deemed late completion which invokes the compensation provisions of SC 7.2 (SCPC 10.3), requiring payment of compensation at the contractual interest rate for the delay. Standard Condition 6.1.2 (SCPC 9.1.2) does not apply where the sale is with vacant possession and the seller has not vacated the property by 2 pm on the date of actual completion. These Conditions affect only the payment of compensation for late completion. They do not make it a term of the contract that completion shall take place by a specified time. If it is desired to make it a term of the contract that completion takes place by a specified time on contractual completion day, a special condition to this effect must be added to the contract.

30.4 PLACE OF COMPLETION

By SC 6.2 (SCPC 9.2), completion is to take place in England and Wales, either at the seller's solicitor's office or at some other place which the seller reasonably specifies. If completion is not to take place at the seller's solicitor's office, they should give the buyer's solicitor sufficient notice of the chosen venue to allow the buyer's solicitor to make their arrangements for attendance at completion and/or transmission of funds. If possible, the buyer's solicitor should be informed of the venue for completion in the answers given to their Request for Completion Information.

Where the seller has an undischarged mortgage over the property and the seller's solicitor is not also acting for the lender, completion may have to take place at the offices of the seller's lender's solicitors.

30.4.1 Chain transactions

Where there is a long chain of transactions, it may sometimes be convenient for some or all of the solicitors for the parties involved in the chain to meet at a mutually convenient location in order to complete several of the transactions in the chain within a very short interval.

30.4.2 Completion by post

Although traditionally the buyer's solicitor attends the seller's solicitor's office in person to effect completion, it is common today (especially in residential transactions) for completion to be effected by using The Law Society's Code for Completion by Post. In such cases, the actual place of completion is of little significance to the transaction as long as both parties' solicitors are able to contact each other by telephone or e-mail to confirm the transmission and receipt of funds on the day of completion itself (see **30.8** for completion by post).

30.5 THE MONEY

30.5.1 Method of payment

Both sets of standard conditions provide for payment to be made only by a direct transfer of cleared funds and an unconditional release of a deposit held by a stakeholder. (See SC 6.7 and SCPC 9.7.) The funds must come from a solicitor's account held at a clearing bank.

The banks' computerised money transfer system allows funds to be transmitted electronically from one bank account to another on a same-day basis, even if with a different bank. This is frequently referred to in practice as a 'telegraphic transfer' (or 'TT'), reflecting methods of money transfer in the pre-computer age. The seller's solicitor should inform the buyer's solicitor of the amount needed to complete the transaction and of the details of the account to which the funds are to be sent. This information is normally given in answer to the buyer's Request for Completion Information and is a standard enquiry on the TA13 Completion Information and Undertakings Form used in Protocol transactions.

The buyer's solicitor will then instruct their bank to remit a specific sum from the buyer's solicitor's client account to the account nominated by the seller's solicitor. The bank will charge a fee for this service. Instructions to the bank must be given sufficiently early on the day of completion to ensure that the funds arrive at their destination before the time limit for receipt of funds, as specified in the contract, expires. Some delay in the transmission of funds may be experienced where the funds are to be transmitted from one bank to another as opposed to transfers between different branches of the same bank. The seller's bank should be asked to telephone the seller's solicitor to inform them of the receipt of the funds immediately they arrive. Completion can proceed as soon as the seller's solicitor is satisfied about the arrival of the funds in their client account. The transmission of funds can be facilitated by the solicitor having a direct computer link with their bank. This will enable them to effect the transmission of funds themselves, rather than having to rely on a telephone call or personal visit to the bank and then waiting for a clerk to effect the transfer.

30.5.2 Cleared funds

Payment of completion money should only be made from cleared funds in client account. A solicitor who draws on uncleared funds risks the possibility of the funds failing to clear, meaning that the solicitor will have used other clients' funds and will have to replace them with the firm's own money. So the buyer's solicitor should ensure that they are put in funds by their client in sufficient time for the money to clear through client account before it becomes necessary to draw against them.

30.5.3 Discharge of seller's mortgage

The seller's existing mortgage over the property being sold will often be discharged immediately after completion of the sale using part of the proceeds of sale to make payment to the lender. Where payment is to be made by electronic transfer and the lender is represented by a different solicitor from the solicitor acting for the seller, the seller's solicitor may request that a direct transfer is made to the lender's solicitor, and a second transfer for the balance of funds due is made to the seller's solicitor.

30.5.4 Release of deposit

A deposit which is held in the capacity of agent for the seller belongs to the seller and does not need to be released expressly to their use on completion. Where a deposit is held by some person in the capacity of stakeholder, the buyer's solicitor should, on completion, provide the seller's solicitor with a written release addressed to the stakeholder, authorising payment of the deposit to the seller or as the seller directs.

Where the deposit is being held by the seller's solicitor as stakeholder, a written release is often neither asked for nor provided, the release being given orally once completion has taken place. If the deposit is being held by a third party (eg, an estate agent in the capacity of stakeholder) a written release will be required. This can be done by letter addressed by the buyer's solicitor to the stakeholder, informing the stakeholder that completion has taken place and that the funds are now released to the seller's hands.

30.6 METHOD OF COMPLETION

Completion may take place by personal attendance (**30.7**) or through the post using The Law Society's Code for Completion by Post (**30.8**) or by telephone using the CLLS Protocol (**30.10**). The method of completion will usually have been agreed by the parties' solicitors at the Request for Completion Information stage of the transaction.

30.7 COMPLETION BY PERSONAL ATTENDANCE

Personal attendance by the buyer's solicitor on the seller's solicitor or seller's lender's solicitor is the traditional method by which completion takes place, but it is not commonly used in uncomplicated transactions where, particularly in residential conveyancing, it is now more common for completion to take place through the post.

30.7.1 What happens at completion

30.7.1.1 Appointment for completion

A few days before the date arranged for completion, the buyer's solicitor should telephone the seller's solicitor to arrange a mutually convenient appointment for completion.

30.7.1.2 Transfer of funds

The buyer's solicitor should arrange with the bank to transmit the balance of the purchase price to the bank account(s) nominated by the seller's solicitor. The amount required will have been notified to the buyer's solicitor in the replies to the Request for Completion Information.

30.7.1.3 Documents to be taken to completion

The representative from the buyer's solicitors who is to attend completion (often a trainee) should take with them to the seller's solicitor's office the following items:

(a) the contract (queries which arise at completion can sometimes be resolved by checking the terms of the contract);

(b) evidence of title (in order to verify the title);

(c) a copy of the approved draft transfer deed and of any other document which is to be executed by the seller and handed over on completion (in case there is any query over the engrossments);

(d) replies to the Request for Completion Information (so that queries which arise (eg, over who has the keys) can be checked);

(e) the completion checklist and completion statement (see **Chapter 29**);

(f) any documents which are required to be handed over to the seller's solicitor on completion (eg, release of deposit held by a stakeholder).

30.7.1.4 Unregistered land: verifying title

Verification is the process of comparing the original deeds with the abstract or epitome provided to ensure that the abstract is a true copy of the original. It is usually left until completion and, if photocopies of the original documents have been provided with the epitome, is very much a formality. If discrepancies are discovered, the buyer would not be precluded from objecting to these by the usual clause preventing the raising of requisitions as this prevents only requisitions on matters discoverable from the abstract as presented by the seller. There would inevitably be a delay in the transaction however. In the case of registered land, verification is unnecessary since the official copies supplied by the seller's solicitor (as updated by the buyer's Land Registry search) will show the true, up-to-date position of the register.

30.7.1.5 Title documents

When the buyer's solicitor is satisfied as to the title, they should ask the seller's solicitor to hand over the documents necessary to complete the transaction. These documents will include the title deeds (in unregistered land) and will have been agreed previously in a list drawn up between the parties and itemised on the completion checklist. Except where these documents have recently been checked by verification, the buyer's solicitor should check each document to ensure it is as they expect to find it, and tick each off on their list as they receive it. Although land and charge certificates are no longer issued after 13 October 2003, existing certificates may well be still handed over on completion – the seller will have no need for them. However, it is no longer necessary for these to be handed over and they will not be required when an application to register the transaction is made at Land Registry. Also to be handed over will be any other documents requested during the transaction that have not already been sent to the buyer. These may include planning consents, building regulation approvals and indemnity insurance policies in relation to title defects.

30.7.1.6 Transfer deed

The transfer deed will be among the documents to be received by the buyer's solicitor and should be dated at completion, after being checked by the buyer's solicitor to ensure that it has been validly executed and has not been altered since the buyer last saw the document.

30.7.1.7 Schedule of deeds and documents

The seller's solicitor will have prepared a schedule of deeds and documents in duplicate. One copy should be handed to the buyer's solicitor to keep; the other should be signed by the buyer's solicitor when they are satisfied that they have received all the deeds and documents listed on it, and be returned to the seller's solicitor as evidence for their file of the handover.

30.7.1.8 Inspection of receipts

It may be necessary for the buyer's solicitor to inspect receipts where, for example, the last payments of outgoings have been apportioned on the completion statement. Copies of these receipts should have been supplied to the buyer's solicitor with the completion statement in order to allow them to check the amount of the apportionments.

30.7.1.9 Chattels

Where the sale includes fittings or chattels, a separate receipt for the money paid for those items should be signed by the seller's solicitor and handed to the buyer's solicitor. A copy of the receipt should be retained by the seller's solicitor. The receipt clause on the transfer deed only operates as a receipt for the money paid for the land, therefore a separate receipt for the money paid for chattels is necessary.

30.7.1.10 Discharge of seller's mortgage

Arrangements for the discharge of the seller's mortgage(s) over the property will have been agreed between the parties at the Request for Completion Information stage of the transaction. Where the mortgage is a first mortgage of the property in favour of a building society lender, the parties will frequently have agreed to permit the seller to discharge their mortgage after actual completion by using part of the proceeds of sale to make payment to the lender. In such a case, it will often have been agreed that the seller's lender's solicitor should hand to the buyer's solicitor, on completion, an undertaking, in the form of wording recommended by The Law Society, to discharge the mortgage and to forward the receipted deed or Form DS1 to the buyer's solicitor as soon as this is received from the lender. An undertaking to discharge the seller's mortgage should be accepted only from a solicitor or licensed conveyancer because of the difficulties of enforcement of undertakings against unqualified persons. The undertaking should also be in the form of wording approved by The Law Society as follows:

> In consideration of you today completing the purchase of [insert description of property] we hereby undertake forthwith to pay over to [insert name of lender] the money required to discharge the mortgage/legal charge dated [insert date of charge] and to forward the receipted mortgage/Form DS1 to you as soon as it is received by us from [insert name of lender].

Where the ED or e-DS1 system is used, the form of undertaking given above will need to be modified. Reference to forwarding the receipted mortgage/Form DS1 will need to be deleted. Instead, the seller's solicitor must undertake to send confirmation that notice of release of discharge in electronic form has been given to HM Land Registry as soon as it is received.

Of course, acceptance of such an undertaking is not entirely risk-free, as the undertaking may not be honoured and either the mortgage not discharged (for example, because the sale proceeds are insufficient to discharge it or the solicitor misappropriates the funds) or evidence of the discharge not supplied by the lender. Nevertheless, the court in *Patel v Daybells* [2001] EWCA Civ 1229 held that it was not negligent to rely on such undertakings except in 'exceptional circumstances' (which were left undefined). Law Society guidance (see *Law Society Gazette* of 30 May 2002, 'Accepting undertakings on completion') suggests, amongst other precautions, that:

- an undertaking should only be accepted where the lender is a member of UK Finance (to minimise the risk of the DS1 not being supplied);
- the amount required to redeem the mortgage should not exceed the minimum level of solicitors' indemnity insurance (currently £3 million for alternative business structures and limited liability partnerships, and £2 million for traditional partnerships and sole traders) to ensure that the undertaking can be successfully enforced against the seller's solicitor; and
- there should be no 'exceptional circumstances' that make it inappropriate to accept the undertaking (such circumstances are not specified).

If the buyer's solicitor has any concerns in accepting an undertaking, these should be explained to the buyer and their lender and instructions sought. Some of the concerns could be addressed by adopting the Protocol for the Discharge of Commercial Property Mortgages introduced in 2014 by the City of London Law Society Land Law Committee ('the CLLS Protocol'). See **30.7.1.11** and **Appendix 8** for further details on this.

Assuming that an undertaking is to be relied on, in Protocol cases this undertaking is given on the TA13 Completion Information and Undertakings Form.

Increasingly, lenders are making use of the Electronic Discharge (ED) system as a means of discharging registered charges. This consists of the lender sending an electronic message to the Registry, which automatically removes the charge from the register. No paper application is required. The e-DS1 is an electronic discharge submitted by lenders through the Land Registry portal.

30.7.1.11 The CLLS Protocol

The CLLS Protocol (see **30.10** and **Appendix 8**) is intended for use in commercial property transactions and high value residential transactions where the seller's lender will be releasing the property from its charge and the buyer has a lender taking a first legal charge over the property. Its adoption may address some of the concerns about relying on the usual undertaking outlined in **30.7.1.10**. The CLLS Protocol requires a number of steps to be carried out *prior to* completion in relation to the seller's mortgage, including:

(a) DS1 executed by the outgoing lender to be obtained and held undated by either the seller's solicitors or the outgoing lender's solicitors.

(b) Undertaking to be given by the seller's solicitors to the seller's lender's solicitors to forward the funds needed to redeem the mortgage immediately after completion. The amount needed to redeem the mortgage will have been agreed with the seller's lender's solicitors.

At completion, the buyer's solicitors would release the completion monies to the seller, and the seller's solicitors (or seller's lender's solicitors) would release the DS1 to the buyer. The seller's solicitors can then redeem the seller's mortgage using the completion monies, and the buyer's solicitors (if in personal attendance) are immediately in receipt of the DS1.

30.7.1.12 Documents to be handed to seller's solicitor

When the buyer's solicitor is satisfied with the documents received from the seller's solicitor and those which they have inspected, they should hand to the seller's solicitor any documents which the seller's solicitor requires in accordance with the list agreed prior to completion (eg, release of deposit held by an estate agent).

30.7.1.13 Copy documents

In some cases the buyer will be entitled to have only copies of documents relating to the seller's title and not the originals. This will mainly happen on a sale of part of unregistered land where the seller is entitled to keep the title deeds which relate to the retained land. Other examples include purchases from personal representatives where they are entitled to retain the original grant, and purchases from attorneys who hold a general or enduring power. Where a power is a special power, relating only to the sale of this property, the buyer is entitled to the original power.

In any case where an original document relevant to the title is not being handed over, the buyer's solicitor should call for the original document and examine their copy against the original. The copy should then be marked to show that it has been examined against the original and is a true copy of the original document. On a sale of part of unregistered land, all the documents contained in the abstract or epitome of title will have to be so marked, and each examined document should bear the wording:

> examined against the original at the offices of [insert name of seller's solicitors or as appropriate] signed [by buyer's solicitor's representative either in their own name or in the name of the firm] and dated [insert date of examination].

Where a certified copy of a document will be required (eg, by Land Registry of a grant of representation), the certification should be carried out by a qualified solicitor by writing on the document clearly and in a conspicuous position the words:

> I certify this to be a true copy of the [insert type of document] dated [insert date of document being certified] signed [signature of solicitor] and dated [insert date of certification].

30.8 COMPLETION THROUGH THE POST

In many cases, particularly with simple residential transactions, the buyer's solicitor will not want to attend completion personally. In such a case, arrangements can be made with the seller's solicitor to complete the transaction through the post. These arrangements should be made, at the latest, at the Request for Completion Information stage of the transaction.

30.8.1 The Law Society's Code for Completion by Post

The Law Society's Code for Completion by Post should be used. The text of the code is set out in **Appendix 5**. The buyer's solicitor should agree any variations to the code in writing with the seller's solicitor well before completion is due to take place. The buyer's solicitor should also send written instructions to the seller's solicitor, specifying precisely what the buyer's solicitor requires the seller's solicitor to do on the buyer's solicitor's behalf at completion, and agreeing a time on the day of completion itself when completion will take place.

30.8.2 The money

The buyer's solicitor must remit the necessary funds by electronic transfer to the seller's solicitor's nominated bank account to arrive there in time for completion to take place at the agreed time.

30.8.3 The seller's solicitor's role

The seller's solicitor will act as the buyer's solicitor's agent for the purpose of carrying out the completion procedure. The instructions given by the buyer's solicitor should cover such of the matters detailed in **30.7** as the buyer's solicitor would have carried out had they attended personally at completion. On being satisfied as to the proper payment of the completion money, the seller's solicitor must carry out the buyer's instructions and effect completion on their behalf. They should then immediately telephone, e-mail or fax the buyer's solicitor to inform them that completion has taken place, and post to the buyer's solicitor, by first-class post or document exchange, the documents which the buyer is entitled to receive on completion. Where documents are required to be marked, certified or endorsed, the seller's solicitor will carry out these operations on behalf of the absent buyer's solicitor. Under the Code, the seller's solicitor is not entitled to make a charge to the buyer's solicitor for acting as their agent in carrying out completion.

30.9 USING AN AGENT

If the buyer's solicitor is unable to attend personally at completion and does not wish to complete through the post, they can appoint another solicitor to act as their agent. The agent will attend completion in person and will carry out the same procedures that the buyer's solicitor would have done had they been present. This is not common in residential transactions.

30.10 COMPLETION BY TELEPHONE CALL

The Law Society's Code for Completion by Post is intended for residential transactions. The CLLS Protocol (see **30.7.1.11** and **Appendix 8**) was introduced in 2014 to deal with the lack of a Law Society-approved protocol for completion of commercial property transactions. The CLLS Protocol envisages that completion will take place by telephone call (although the steps set out could also be adopted if completion is by personal attendance) and that all parties (including the seller's and buyer's lenders) will be represented by solicitors. It envisages that a paper DS1 will be provided and will not be appropriate (without adaptation) where the outgoing lender uses an electronic release system. It does not have to be adopted in its entirety and the parties can agree to adapt it to suit the specifics of their transaction. Under the CLLS Protocol, the executed DS1 will already be held by the seller's solicitors (or the solicitors of their lender) by the time of completion. The DS1 will be released to the buyer in return for release of the completion monies (which will have been sent in advance of completion to the seller's solicitor and held to the order of the buyer's solicitor). The parties will agree to date all relevant documentation during the telephone calls, and the seller's solicitors will undertake to send the TR1, title deeds and DS1 to the buyer's solicitors.

30.11 LENDER'S REQUIREMENTS

The buyer's solicitor will often also be acting for the buyer's lender. In such a case, the buyer's solicitor should check the lender's requirements for completion when they are preparing their own checklist and making arrangements for completion. In most cases the lender's requirements will be identical to the buyer's solicitor's own requirements, but a check on the lender's instructions should always be made to ensure that nothing is overlooked.

SUMMARY

- The parties will agree a completion date and time, and insert them into the contract before exchange; but if completion is delayed, the non-defaulting party will not normally be able to terminate the contract at that stage.
- Compensation is sometimes payable by the defaulting party if completion takes place after the completion time on the completion date specified in the contract.
- At completion, the transfer will be dated and the completion monies will be paid/released to the seller.
- Certain deeds and documents will be handed over to the other party; those that are being retained by one of the parties may need to be checked and certified by the solicitor for the other party. This chapter helps you to decide what needs to be done for your particular property transaction.
- Completion may take place by personal attendance, through the post using The Law Society's Code for Completing by Post, or by telephone using the CLLS Protocol.

CHAPTER 31

AFTER COMPLETION

LEARNING OUTCOMES

After reading this chapter you will be able to:

- take the appropriate post-completion steps on behalf of a seller client in order to close the file
- take the appropriate post-completion steps on behalf of a buyer client in order to complete the transfer the property to the client in a legally-effective manner.
- take the appropriate post-completion steps on behalf of a lender client so that its mortgage over the property is properly protected and enforceable.

31.1 INTRODUCTION

The solicitor's role in the transaction does not end when completion has taken place; a number of matters still need to be attended to by both parties, some of which have stringent time limits attached to them. The steps outlined below should therefore be taken as soon as possible after completion has occurred.

31.2 REPORTING TO THE CLIENT

Whichever party the solicitor is acting for, the client is entitled to be informed that completion of their sale or purchase has taken place. The solicitor should therefore contact their client as soon as possible after completion to inform them of the successful outcome of the transaction. Where the solicitor is also acting for the client's lender, the lender should be informed of completion.

31.3 ACTING FOR THE SELLER

Not all of the steps listed below will be relevant in every transaction. Those which are relevant to the circumstances of the case should be carried out promptly.

31.3.1 Contact the buyer's solicitor

Where completion has taken place by post, telephone the buyer's solicitor to inform them that completion has taken place.

31.3.2 Contact the estate agent

Telephone the estate agent to inform them of completion and to ask them to release the keys of the property to the buyer.

31.3.3 Send documents to buyer's solicitor

Where completion has taken place by post, send the transfer deed, any title deeds and other relevant documents to the buyer's solicitor by first-class post or document exchange.

31.3.4 Deal with the proceeds of sale

If part of the proceeds of sale is to be used towards the purchase of another property on the same day, arrangements should be made for the transmission of these funds in accordance with instructions received. Where the client is undertaking simultaneous sale and purchase transactions, the interval between the time of completion of the sale and the proposed time of completion of the purchase may be as short as an hour. The funds for the purchase must, therefore, be dealt with as a matter of urgency. If instructed to do so, pay the estate agent's commission and obtain a receipt for the payment. Account to the seller's bank for the proceeds of sale in accordance with any undertaking given to them. Account to the client for the balance (if any) of the proceeds of sale in accordance with their instructions.

31.3.5 Discharge the seller's mortgage(s)

Deal with the discharge of the seller's existing mortgage(s) by electronic transfer or sending a client account cheque for the amount required (as per redemption statement previously obtained) to the lender. If the CLLS Protocol has not been used (see **30.7.1.11**) then an engrossment of the Form DS1 requesting the lender to discharge the mortgage and return the receipted Form DS1 as quickly as possible will also need sending. If the mortgage is over unregistered land, the lender will complete the receipt clause on the reverse of the mortgage deed and forward the receipted deed to the seller's solicitor instead of using a Form DS1. Where necessary, the benefit of a life policy which was assigned to the lender as collateral security in an endowment mortgage should be reassigned to the seller. A lender who has insured the property will also need to be told to cancel the property insurance cover. On receipt of the completed Form DS1 or receipted mortgage from the lender, check it to ensure that it is correct, then send it to the buyer's solicitor and ask to be discharged from the undertaking given on completion.

If the ED or e-DS1 system is being used (see **30.7.1.10**), Form DS1 will not be used. Instead, there will be a saving of work and time in that the notification of the discharge will be sent directly by the lender to Land Registry, instead of the lender completing Form DS1 and sending it to the seller's solicitors, who have to check it and then send it to the buyer, who then has to send it to Land Registry.

31.3.6 Send bill to the client

If not already done, a bill of costs should be drafted and sent to the client. Money which is being held by the solicitor on account of costs may be transferred to office account, provided that the client has expressly or impliedly agreed to this being done.

31.3.7 Letter to client

The client should be reminded to notify the local authority and water undertaker of the change of ownership of the property, and to cancel insurance cover over the property and its contents. In appropriate cases, the client may also be reminded about their liability to CGT.

31.3.8 Custody of deeds

Deal with the custody of deeds in accordance with the client's instructions. Most, if not all, original deeds will have passed to the buyer's solicitor on actual completion, but the seller will have retained custody of the deeds on a sale of part, or may have such documents as an original grant of representation or power of attorney.

31.3.9 Check file for outstanding matters

Check through the file to ensure that all outstanding matters have been dealt with before sending the file for storage.

31.4 ACTING FOR THE BUYER

Where relevant to the transaction, the following steps should be taken by the buyer's solicitor as soon as possible after completion has taken place.

31.4.1 Complete mortgage deed

Complete the mortgage deed by insertion of the date and any other information which still has to be completed (eg, date when first repayment is due).

31.4.2 Complete file copies of documents

Complete file copies of the mortgage, transfer deed and other relevant documents. These are spare copies of the documents which will remain in the file for future reference or, in some cases, will be used as duplicate copies to send to Land Registry.

31.4.3 Pay SDLT

Submit the land transaction return and attend to payment of SDLT on the transfer deed and other appropriate documents (see **31.7**).

31.4.4 Account for bridging finance

Account to the buyer's bank for any bridging finance in accordance with any undertaking given to it, and ask to be released from that undertaking.

31.4.5 Send bill to client

If not already done, draft and send a bill of costs to the client. Where money is being held by the solicitor on account of costs, it can be transferred to office account, provided that the client has expressly or impliedly agreed to this being done.

31.4.6 Discharged mortgage

On receipt of the completed Form DS1 (if ED or e-DS1 is not being used) or receipted mortgage from the seller's lender's solicitor, check it to make sure it is correct, acknowledge its receipt and release the sender from the undertaking given on completion.

31.4.7 Make copies of documents

Make copies of all documents which are to be sent to Land Registry to ensure that file copies exist, in case requisitions are raised by the Registry or the documents are lost or damaged before registration is complete. Make copies of any documents of which Land Registry requires copies (eg, the buyer's mortgage, a transfer or conveyance of part which imposes new restrictive covenants). Certify copy documents which are to be sent to Land Registry. Certification is effected by writing or typing on the document (in the margin, or at the foot of the document):

> I/We certify this to be a true copy of the [type of document] dated [insert date] [signed XYZ and Co].

The certification, which can be signed in the name of an individual or of a firm, can be carried out only by a solicitor who holds a current practising certificate. Except in the case of powers of attorney, which need to be separately certified on each page, one certificate on the reverse of a document will cover the whole document.

31.4.8 Register the title

Make application for registration of title using Form AP1 within the relevant priority period (land already registered) or using Form FR1 within two months of completion (application for first registration) (see **31.8**).

31.4.9 Register company charges

Register any charge created by a company at Companies House within 21 days of its creation, in accordance with the Companies Acts requirements. A fee is payable and must accompany a certified copy of the mortgage deed and a 'section 859D statement of particulars' in the Companies House Form MR01. This time limit is absolute and cannot be extended without an order of the court. Registration of the charge at Companies House gives constructive notice of the charge to all those who could reasonably be expected to search the register. Failure to register within the time limit may prejudice the lender's security. It renders the charge void against the company's liquidator or administrator, and also against the company's other creditors. The requirement to register under the Companies Acts is separate and additional to the requirement to register the charge at Land Registry.

31.4.10 Diary entry for registration to be effected

Make a diary or file-prompt entry recording the approximate date when registration is expected to be effected (as notified by Land Registry), and send a reminder to the Registry if confirmation is not received by that time.

31.4.11 Discharge entries protecting the contract

Where an entry was lodged to protect the contract (notice or Class C(iv) land charge), an application should now be made for the discharge of that entry which, completion having taken place, is now redundant.

31.4.12 Check register entries

Once the transaction has been registered, Land Registry will send a copy of the register to the solicitor lodging the application. Most firms receive the completed land registration results electronically through their Land Registry portal account, although first registration results are sent through the post. The entries should be checked carefully, and if they do not appear to be accurate, the solicitor should advise the Registry and ask for errors to be corrected.

31.4.13 Custody of deeds

The question of the custody of the deeds and other title documents needs to be addressed. Once land has been registered, there are no title deeds as such; Land Registry no longer issues land or charge certificates and the register itself is proof of ownership, but there may well be various other documents that will need to be produced on a subsequent sale. So there may well be planning consents, building regulation approvals, defective title insurance polices, guarantees for building work, etc which will need safe keeping. Where there is a mortgage on the property, the lender is entitled to these and the lender's instructions must be complied with. However, in the case of residential property, most lenders no longer wish to take custody of these documents due to the administrative expenses of receiving, storing and producing them when they are required for a subsequent sale. In such a case, or where there is no mortgage, the buyer's instructions on these documents should be obtained. The buyer may wish to retain custody of them, or may wish them to be sent to their bank or kept by the solicitor. These last two options will generally result in a storage fee being payable by the client. However, if the buyer wishes to keep the documents themselves, it must be emphasised that these must be kept safely as they will be required on a subsequent sale.

31.4.14 Check file for outstanding matters

Check through the file to ensure that all outstanding matters have been dealt with before sending the file for storage.

31.5 THE LENDER'S SOLICITOR

Where a separate solicitor has been instructed to act for the buyer's lender, the lender's solicitor will normally have taken custody of the transfer deed and other title deeds on completion, and they will deal with the stamping and registration of the documents instead of the buyer's solicitor.

31.6 UNDERTAKINGS

Any undertaking given must be honoured and any obligations accepted must be fulfilled without delay. A solicitor who has performed their undertaking (eg, to discharge the seller's mortgage) should formally ask the recipient to release the giver from the undertaking, so that the giver has written evidence of the fulfilment of the undertaking. The recipient may either acknowledge the giver's release by letter, or return the original undertaking to the giver. In either case, the evidence of release is to be kept on the giver's file.

31.7 SDLT RETURNS

Certain transactions attract SDLT, currently payable to HMRC within 14 days of completion. The tax is payable on the value of land, but not on chattels. The SDLT rates for different types and values of property are set out in **6.3**. Non-payment or evasion of tax gives rise to fines and penalties, for which the client and their solicitor may face prosecution. An SDLT return must be submitted for each transaction, containing details of the transaction and the parties to it. The buyer is personally responsible for completing this tax return – just as they would be for an income tax return – but it is normally completed by the buyer's solicitor. It should be noted that the SDLT return must be completed for most transactions, regardless of whether SDLT is actually payable. The SDLT return can be submitted online or by post.

If the SDLT return is submitted by post, then Form SDLT 1, together with the payment of any tax, is submitted to HMRC's Rapid Data Capture Centre in Netherton, Liverpool. Form SDLT1 must be signed personally by the buyer(s); it cannot be signed by the solicitor, except under a power of attorney. The transfer deed itself should not be submitted. HMRC will issue Form SDLT 5 to prove that the return has been submitted and any tax necessary paid. Without Form SDLT 5 the transaction will not be accepted for registration by Land Registry.

Most SDLT returns will be submitted online. The online system also permits the solicitor immediately to print off Form SDLT 5. Where it is submitted online, the solicitor must certify that the SDLT return has been approved by the buyer before submission. Although this approval can be in any medium as far as HMRC is concerned, it will be sensible for the solicitor to obtain approval in writing. The actual payment of the SDLT due can also be made online, or a cheque may be sent through the post.

31.8 REGISTRATION OF TITLE

It is essential that the relevant time limits for submission of an application for registration of a client's title are complied with. The time limits, and the effect of non-compliance with them, differ according to whether it is a first registration of land previously unregistered or whether it is a registration of a dealing with land already registered. Failure to make an application for first registration within two months of completion results in the transfer of the legal estate becoming void. Failure to make an application for registration of a dealing within the priority period of 30 working days given by a pre-completion Land Registry search may have the consequence of the client's interest losing priority to another application.

31.8.1 Registration of dealings

Where registered land is transferred, an application for registration of the dealing must be made on the appropriate application form, accompanied by the correct documentation and fee, and must be received by Land Registry within the priority period of 30 working days given by the Land Registry search made before completion. The application must be received by Land Registry by 12 noon on the day on which protection under the applicant's search expires, in order to preserve the applicant's priority over the registration of other interests. The period of protection under the search cannot be extended (although a second search conferring a separate priority period can be made) and failure to lodge the client's application within the priority period may result in their interest ceding priority to another application.

Since 3 August 2009, Land Registry has been operating an early completion policy. This applies to all applications to discharge the whole of a registered charge where other applications are made (such as an application to register the transfer of the property to the buyer) but no evidence of satisfaction of the charge is supplied (perhaps because the lender has been slow in executing the DS1). Land Registry will reject the discharge application but complete the other applications. Accordingly, a buyer purchasing a property with a new mortgage will be registered as the proprietor, but the seller's mortgage will remain on the title until evidence of discharge is provided, and the buyer's mortgage will rank in priority behind the seller's mortgage on the register. Where there is a restriction on the register preventing a disposal or the registration of a new charge without the consent of the existing lender, proof of satisfaction of the charge or evidence of compliance with the restriction must be provided to Land Registry within 20 working days (which can be extended to 40 working days on application); if this is not done, Land Registry will cancel the buyer's applications for discharge, transfer and charge. Further details of the early completion policy are set out in LR Practice Bulletin 16 entitled 'Early Completion'.

Where there is likely to be a delay in providing evidence of satisfaction to Land Registry, the solicitors for each party should consult The Law Society's Practice Note entitled 'Land Registry early completion (9 July 2009)' for advice on how to proceed with completion in the light of the early completion policy. This contains advice to seller's solicitors and buyer's solicitors on additional undertakings and assurances relating to early completion.

31.8.2 Transfer of whole

The following points apply to any transfer of the whole of the seller's registered title, regardless of whether the interest transferred is freehold or leasehold. Application for registration of the dealing on Form AP1, accompanied by the relevant documents, should be lodged within 30 working days of the date of issue of the applicant's pre-completion official search certificate. Since 30 June 2014, it has not been necessary to send any original documents with this type of application, and certified copies should be sent instead. This is the case whether the application is sent through one of Land Registry's electronic channels or through the post. The relevant documents are as follows:

(a) a certified copy of the transfer;

(b) the appropriate fee unless to be paid by credit account.

In addition, such of the documents listed below as are appropriate to the circumstances of the transaction should be submitted with the application:

(c) certified copy grant of representation where the seller was the personal representative of the deceased proprietor;

(d) certified copy power of attorney if the transfer has been executed under a power of attorney;

(e) SDLT certificate;

(f) Form DI (see **31.8.5**);

(g) office copy of the appropriate death certificate if a registered proprietor has died and, if a tenancy in common existed, a certified copy of the Deed of Appointment of the second trustee.

31.8.3 Additional applications

Where there has been a transfer of the seller's registered title, there may be other associated applications to be made to Land Registry. These applications can be made on the same Form AP1 as the transfer. The following applications will often be relevant:

31.8.3.1 Application to discharge a mortgage

If the seller had a mortgage over the property, then this should have been discharged on completion. If the lender used the ED system (or other electronic means of discharge) (see **30.7.1.10**), there is no need for the buyer's solicitor to make an application to discharge the mortgage. Instead, Land Registry suggests that Form AP1 is endorsed with the words 'Charge discharged electronically'.

If a paper form of discharge has been used (such as Form DS1), then the buyer's solicitor will need to apply to Land Registry for the charge to be discharged and submit a certified copy of the paper form of discharge.

31.8.3.2 Application to register a new legal charge

If the buyer has created a new mortgage over the property, then the buyer's solicitor will need to apply to Land Registry for the new legal charge to be registered. The following documents will be needed in support of the application:

(i) a certified copy of the mortgage deed; and

(ii) if the borrower is a company, a certified copy of the certificate of registration issued by Companies House; and

(iii) if the borrower is a company, the conveyancer's/lender's written confirmation that the certified copy mortgage deed being lodged for registration at Land Registry is the same as that filed at Companies House and is the mortgage to which the certificate of registration (referred to at (ii) above) relates.

31.8.4 First registration of title

An application for first registration of title (freehold or leasehold) must be made within two months of completion of the transaction which induces the registration on Form FR1.

The application form and fee (unless being paid by credit account), accompanied by the documents listed at **31.8.4** below, should be sent to the relevant Land Registry Office (see **31.8.1**). Documents accompanying the application must be listed in duplicate on Form DL. One copy of this form will be returned to the applicant's solicitor in acknowledgement of receipt of the application. The acknowledgement copy will also give an estimate of the likely time which the Registry expects to take to deal with the application. This anticipated time should be noted in the solicitor's diary or file-prompt system, and a reminder should be sent to the Registry if the Title Information Document has not been received within that period.

31.8.5 Documents to be submitted on application for first registration of title

The Registrar needs to investigate title on an application for first registration in order to decide which class of title can be allocated to the title. They therefore need to have access to all the documents which formed the evidence of title supplied to the applicant by the seller's solicitor. Between 28 November 2016 and 1 October 2024, certified copies of the deeds and documents accompanying the application were acceptable, but Land Registry has now reverted to its previous practice of requiring the original deeds and documents.

The documents should be numbered in chronological sequence on form DL and should include such of the following documents as are relevant to the transaction:

(a) all the documents which formed the evidence of title supplied by the seller's solicitor;
(b) all the buyer's pre-contract searches and enquiries relating to the title with their replies (including any variations or further information contained in relevant correspondence);
(c) the contract;
(d) requisitions on title with their replies;
(e) all pre-completion search certificates;
(f) the transfer deed with a certified copy;
(g) the seller's mortgage, duly receipted;
(h) if there is a new mortgage:
    (i) the mortgage deed and a certified copy of the mortgage deed; and
    (ii) if the borrower is a company, a certified copy of the certificate of registration issued by Companies House; and
    (iii) if the borrower is a company, the conveyancer's/lender's written confirmation that the mortgage deed being lodged for registration at Land Registry is the original mortgage deed, a copy of which has been filed at Companies House, and is the mortgage to which the certificate of registration referred to at (ii) above relates;
(i) where the property is leasehold, the original lease and a certified copy;
(j) SDLT certificate;
(k) cheque for fee (unless paid by credit account);
(l) Form DI (see **31.8.5**).

With effect from 14 June 2021, most documents submitted with applications for first registration are scanned by the Land Registry to enable them to be processed electronically and the originals returned. Original documents unsuitable for scanning are retained and returned by post on completion of the registration.

31.8.6 Disclosing overriding interests

As part of the policy to reduce the number of overriding interests, an applicant for registration must complete Form DI setting out any overriding interests that burden the title. These will then be entered on the register and thus cease to be overriding.

31.8.7 Identity requirements

Land Registry Forms AP1, DS2 and FR1 require the applicant to give details of the conveyancer acting for each party and, unless a party is not represented and the value of the property is £6,000 or less, provide evidence of that party's identity. Further details are set out in Land Registry Practice Guide 67.

SUMMARY

- Acting for the seller, you must inform the client, the estate agent and any lender that completion has taken place. You must send the relevant documentation to the buyer's solicitor and ensure that the seller's mortgage is discharged. Then you can close the file.
- Acting for the buyer, you will have to ensure that any SDLT payable on the purchase is paid within 14 days of completion. You must also ensure that the transfer of the property to the client is registered at Land Registry within the relevant time period. For land that is already registered, this will be the priority period conferred by the Land Registry search carried out before completion, and for land that is subject to first registration this will be within two months of completion.
- Acting for the lender, you must ensure that the mortgage of the property to the lender is registered at Land Registry within the same time period. Where the borrower is a company, you must also register the charge over the property at Companies House within 21 days of its creation.
- Failure to carry out these steps within the required time periods will prejudice your client's interests and may result in your being held liable in negligence.

PART VI

DELAY AND REMEDIES

CHAPTER 32

LATE COMPLETION

LEARNING OUTCOMES

After reading this chapter you will be able to

- appreciate the contractual significance of a delay in completion beyond the completion time on the completion date specified in the contract
- identify and explain the provisions in the contract dealing with the payment of compensation for late completion
- identify and explain the provisions in the contract dealing with the termination of the contract by service of a notice to complete.

32.1 INTRODUCTION

There are many reasons why completion may be delayed and does not take place on the contractual date. Common examples of causes of delay in completion are the buyer not being in receipt of funds from their lender, or the seller's solicitor not managing to get the transfer deed signed by their client. Where the transaction forms part of a chain of transactions, all the transactions in the chain may be delayed if there is a problem with one of the links in the chain. In the majority of cases, the delay in completion is merely a temporary hitch in the transaction, causing practical difficulties both to the solicitor and, particularly, to their client, who may not be able to move on the date when they wished to do so and may now have to alter the removal arrangements. Where the delay is caused by, for example, the buyer not having received the mortgage advance from the lender, there is generally no doubt that completion will occur, even if it takes place a few days later than the anticipated date stipulated in the contract.

The two sets of Standard Conditions each contain provisions for payment of compensation for late completion designed to compensate the innocent party for the losses suffered as a result of minor delays in completion. There are, however, two important differences between the two sets of Standard Conditions and these are explained at **32.4** and **32.5.1**.

32.2 BREACH OF CONTRACT

Any delay in completion beyond the contractual completion date will be a breach of contract entitling the innocent party to damages for their loss, but will not entitle them immediately to terminate the contract unless time was of the essence of the completion date (*Raineri v Miles* [1981] AC 1050).

32.2.1 Time of the essence

In both sets of Standard Conditions, time is not of the essence of the contract unless a notice to complete has been served (SC 6.1 and SCPC 9.1.1). If time is to be of the essence from the outset, it can be made so by express contractual condition.

32.3 RELATED TRANSACTIONS

Delay in completing one transaction may affect the client's ability to complete a related sale or purchase. If, for example, completion of the client's sale is delayed, they will not have the money (from the proceeds of sale) with which to complete the synchronised purchase transaction, and failure to complete that purchase on the contractual date for completion will be a breach of contract.

Although the solicitor should try to ensure that no breach of contract occurs (eg, by arranging bridging finance in order to complete the purchase transaction on time), they are also under a duty to act in their own client's best interests, and in these circumstances completion of the purchase with the assistance of bridging finance may not necessarily be the best course of action for the client to take. For example, in the situation outlined above, where the client's sale transaction is delayed, if the client does go ahead with completion of the purchase, not only will they incur a heavy charge in interest on the bridging finance used to complete the purchase, but they will also be in the position of owning two properties until the sale is completed. If the sale transaction is not completed within a short space of time, this will represent an onerous commitment for the client. The reason for the delay on the sale transaction and its likely duration must be taken into account when advising the client whether to complete the purchase on time, or to delay completion of the purchase and commit a breach of that contract.

In the converse situation, where the sale can proceed but the purchase is delayed, completion of the sale transaction on the contract date will result in the client becoming homeless for a potentially indefinite length of time, with resultant problems relating to alternative accommodation for the period of the delay and storage of furniture.

32.4 COMPENSATION FOR DELAY

Damages are payable under normal contractual principles (see **33.2.6**) for delayed completion. In addition, at common law, there are rules dealing with the payment of interest as compensation for late completion. However, these are generally considered inadequate and are replaced in the Standard Conditions of Sale by SC 7.2 and in the Standard Commercial Property Conditions by SCPC 10.3. These require the payment of compensation for delayed completion irrespective of whether the relevant party has suffered any loss. Where loss has been suffered in excess of the amount payable under SC 7.2 or SCPC 10.3 (eg, the cost of alternative accommodation), this can still be recovered in a claim for breach of contract. However, any compensation paid under SC 7.2 or SCPC 10.3 must be taken into account in a claim for breach of contract.

32.4.1 Standard Condition 7.2

Standard Condition 7.2 provides for the payment of compensation at the 'contract rate', which is defined by SC 1.1.1(e) as being 'The Law Society's interest rate from time to time in force' (as published weekly in *The Law Society's Gazette*), although the parties may substitute a different rate by special condition if they wish. Interest is payable on the purchase price, or, where the buyer is the paying party, on the purchase price less the deposit paid. Under SC 7.2, compensation is assessed using the 'concept of relative fault', so that whoever is most at fault for the delay pays the compensation; it is not simply a matter of the party who delayed in actual completion being liable to pay compensation.

32.4.2 Calculating compensation under SC 7.2

To calculate the liability for compensation, it is necessary to refer back to the timetable of events contained in SC 4.3.1 and 4.3.2 in order to establish whether the delay in completion has been caused by a delay in carrying out a procedural step earlier in the transaction. Delay occurring before completion is assessed by reference to the definition of a 'working day' contained in SC 1.1.1(m), but this definition ceases to apply once the completion date has passed, after which every day's delay counts towards the liability for compensation. Having apportioned the delay between the parties, the party who is most at fault for the delay pays compensation to the other for the period by which their delay exceeds the delay of the other party, or for the actual period of delay in completion, if this is shorter. Compensation under this provision is neither additional to nor in substitution for common law damages, but merely on account.

EXAMPLE

The seller was three days late in delivering their evidence of title under SC 4.3.1; the buyer was then five days late in delivering their requisitions on title and a further four days late in delivering the draft transfer deed, but completion itself was delayed two days because of the seller's fault.

To assess who is liable for compensation, it is necessary to add up the total periods of default of each party. Here the seller's total default amounts to five days, but the buyer's to nine days. The buyer's default therefore exceeds that of the seller by four days, and in this example the buyer would be liable to pay up to four days' compensation to the seller for the delay, even though the delay in actual completion was not their fault; however, since the actual delay was only two days, their liability is limited to two days' compensation.

The calculation of the delay under SC 7.2 is thus rather complicated, but does have the merit of recognising that the delay might not be the fault of the party who is actually unable to complete on time. Their delay might be the knock-on effect of the other party's delay earlier in the transaction. The complications of SC 7.2 are further exacerbated by the fact that the timetable laid down in SC 4.3.1 is based on the traditional practice of title being deduced after exchange, which rarely happens now, and by the fact that the timetable is based on a minimum period of 15 working days (ie, three weeks) between exchange and completion. Where, as is usual, completion is to take place earlier than 15 working days after exchange, the time limits laid down have to be reduced accordingly.

32.4.3 Standard Commercial Property Condition 10.3

Standard Commercial Property Condition 10.3, which deals with compensation for delays in completion, is very different from SC 7.2. The concept of relative fault is not adopted. Instead, a contractual entitlement to compensation is given to the seller where the buyer has defaulted in some way and completion is delayed. If the seller defaults and completion is delayed, there is no contractual right to compensation given to the buyer, who would have to bring a claim for damages for breach of contract.

32.4.4 Deemed late completion

In both sets of Standard Conditions (SC 6.1.2/6.1.3 and SCPC 9.1.2/9.1.3), where the sale is with vacant possession and the money due on completion is not paid by 2 pm on the day of actual completion (or such other time as may have been agreed by the parties), for the purposes of the compensation provisions only, completion is deemed to have taken place on the next following working day, unless the seller had not vacated the property by 2 pm (or other agreed time). If this time limit is not complied with, the buyer may find themselves liable to pay compensation to the seller. If, for example, completion was due on a Friday, and the buyer's money did not arrive until 2.15 pm, the seller would be able to treat completion as not having taken place until the following Monday and, subject to the application of SC 7.2 or SCPC 10.3, recover compensation for the delay (irrespective of actual loss). Since the 'working day' definition contained in SC 1.1.1(m) and SCPC 1.1.1(p) ceases to apply once completion has taken place, the seller in this example would be able to charge interest for three days, ie, Saturday and Sunday are included in the calculation.

32.5 SERVICE OF A NOTICE TO COMPLETE

Where it appears that the delay in completion is not likely to be resolved quickly (or at all), consideration may be given to the service of a notice to complete, which will have the effect of making time of the essence of the contract so that, if completion does not take place on the new completion date specified in the notice, the aggrieved party may then terminate the contract immediately, forfeit or recover the deposit (as the case may be) with accrued interest and commence a claim for damages to recover their loss. This then gives the aggrieved party the certainty of knowing that on a stated date they can make a definite decision, either to look for a new property to purchase (if a buyer) or to resell the property elsewhere (as a seller).

Making time of the essence imposes a condition which binds both parties. If, therefore, unforeseen events occur between the date of service of the notice and the new date for completion as specified by the notice, which result in the previously aggrieved party being unable to complete on the new date, the previously defaulting party could turn round and terminate the contract, leaving the aggrieved party in breach of contract themselves. For this reason a notice to complete should never be served as an idle threat. The server must be sure that they will be able to comply with the new completion date themselves before serving the notice.

32.5.1 Standard Conditions on notices to complete

Although permitted at common law, the contract normally contains a provision relating to the service of a notice to complete. Standard Condition 6.8 and SCPC 9.8 provide that, on service of a notice to complete, completion must take place within 10 working days (exclusive of the date of service) and makes time of the essence of the contract.

Standard Condition 6.8.3 (SCPC 9.8.3) requires a buyer who has paid less than a 10% deposit to pay the balance of the full 10% immediately on receipt of a notice to complete.

The parties' rights and obligations where a valid notice has been served but not complied with are governed by SC 7.4 and 7.5 or SCPC 10.5 and 10.6. Once served, a notice to complete cannot be withdrawn.

32.5.2 Non-compliance with a notice to complete

Non-compliance with a notice to complete gives the aggrieved party the right to terminate the contract, but is not in itself an automatic termination of the contract.

32.5.2.1 Buyer's failure to comply with a notice to complete

Standard Condition 7.4 and SCPC 10.5 provide that, in addition to rescinding the contract, the seller may:

(a) forfeit and keep the deposit and any accrued interest;

(b) resell the property included in the contract; and

(c) claim damages.

The seller is expressly stated to retain their other rights and remedies and so would be able to issue a claim for specific performance should they so wish.

32.5.2.2 Seller's failure to comply with a notice to complete

Standard Condition 7.5 and SCPC 10.6 provide that, in addition to rescinding the contract, the buyer is entitled to the return of the deposit and accrued interest. The buyer also keeps their other rights and remedies, so they would be able to issue a claim for specific performance or damages if they wished.

SUMMARY

- Compensation may be payable under the contract by a defaulting party if there is a delay in completion beyond the completion time on the completion date specified in the contract.
- Under the Standard Conditions of Sale, either party may be liable to pay contractual compensation. Under the Standard Commercial Property Conditions, only the buyer is liable to pay contractual compensation.
- Under both sets of standard conditions, when completion is delayed, the party who is ready, willing and able to complete may serve a notice to complete on the defaulting party. This will make time of the essence, and if completion does not take place within 10 working days of the service of the notice, the aggrieved party may terminate the contract.
- If it is the buyer who has failed to comply with the notice to complete, they will forfeit their deposit.
- In addition to these procedures specified in the contract, the non-defaulting party retains their other rights and remedies in respect of a breach of contract.

CHAPTER 33

REMEDIES

LEARNING OUTCOMES

After reading this chapter you will be able to:

- understand the type of problems that may occur in a property transaction
- explain the remedies available to the innocent party under the general law
- identify and explain the provisions in the contract which confer remedies or restrict the remedies available.

33.1 INTRODUCTION

The vast majority of property transactions proceed to completion without serious problems. However, sometimes completion is delayed, and in a few cases one of the parties may not be able and/or willing to complete at all. Alternatively, the buyer may discover after exchange (or even after completion) that the property is subject to an incumbrance that has not been disclosed by the seller, or that the property has been misdescribed in the sales particulars or that a reply to the pre-contract enquiries given on behalf of the seller is not true. The contract is likely to incorporate one of the two sets of standard conditions, and these contain provisions for the payment of compensation for late completion and termination of the contract for failure to complete following service of a notice to complete (see **Chapter 32**). However, these provisions may not apply to the particular problem, or if they do, they may not adequately compensate the innocent party for their losses. This chapter summarises the remedies for breach of contract and the other remedies that might be available to the innocent party in a land transaction.

33.2 BREACH OF CONTRACT

Remedies for breach of contract depend on whether the breach is of a condition in the contract, entitling the aggrieved party to terminate the contract and/or claim damages, or of a warranty, entitling the aggrieved party to claim damages only.

33.2.1 Conditions and warranties

A term of the contract will be a 'condition' if it is a major or fundamental term. Minor terms are classified as 'warranties'.

In some cases, it is not possible to classify a term as specifically falling into one or other of these categories until the consequences of the breach can be seen. Where the consequences are serious or far-reaching, the unclassified term will be treated as a condition; otherwise, it will be treated as a warranty. In conveyancing contracts, all terms are usually called 'conditions', but in law some of those terms will only have the status of warranties. The classification attached to a term by the parties is not necessarily conclusive as to its status.

33.2.2 Limitation periods

A claim on a contract not made by deed has a limitation period under the Limitation Act 1980 of six years, running from the date of the breach. A limitation period of 12 years applies where the contract was made by deed.

33.2.3 Merger

On completion, the terms of the contract merge with the transfer deed in so far as the two documents cover the same ground, and a claim on the contract is no longer sustainable after completion except where it is based on a contract term which remains in existence despite completion taking place. For this reason, both sets of standard conditions contain a non-merger clause (SC 7.3 or SCPC 10.4) which expressly allows a particular clause or clauses to remain alive after completion.

33.2.4 Exclusion clauses

Standard Condition 7.1 and SCPC 10.1 restrict the remedies available for a breach of contract. The buyer is entitled to damages only if there is a material difference in the tenure or value of the property. In addition, the buyer is entitled to treat the contract as at an end only if the error or omission results from fraud or recklessness, or where they would otherwise be obliged to accept property differing substantially in quality, quantity or tenure from what they had been led to expect. Thus, in the case of an undisclosed incumbrance, the buyer would be entitled to damages only if this caused a material difference in the value of the land. Similarly, they would be able to treat the contract as at an end only if there was fraud or recklessness on the seller's part, or if the value of the property was substantially reduced because of the incumbrance. Obviously, a covenant preventing building on land otherwise suitable for development, would have a much greater effect on its value than a covenant restricting a dwelling house to use as a house. Note, however, that if there is fraud or recklessness on the seller's part, the buyer will always be entitled to rescind no matter what the effect on the value of the property.

Exclusion clauses contained in contracts for the sale of land (except those relating to the exclusion of liability for misrepresentation) are not subject to the reasonableness test in the Unfair Contract Terms Act 1977. However, exclusion clauses in contracts for the sale of land between 'traders' and 'consumers' will be affected by the requirement to be 'fair' and 'transparent' contained in the Consumer Rights Act 2015 (see **18.9**).

33.2.5 Delayed completion

Unless time was of the essence of the completion date, or had been made so by service of a notice to complete, a delay in completion will be a breach of warranty entitling the aggrieved party to recover damages for any loss suffered as a result of the delay (*Raineri v Miles* [1981] AC 1050). Credit must be given for any compensation payable for delayed completion under SC 7.2 (see **32.4**) or under SCPC 10.3 (see **32.6**).

33.2.6 Damages for breach of contract

Damages for breach of a contract for the sale of land are assessed under the normal contractual principles established in *Hadley v Baxendale* (1854) 9 Exch 341. Subject to establishing causation, damages for losses naturally flowing from the breach may be claimed, as may damages for consequential loss within the parties' reasonable contemplation.

33.2.6.1 Quantum

The quantum of damages under the consequential loss head is limited to loss which was within the contemplation of the parties in the light of the facts known at the date when the contract was made (not at the date of the breach of contract). The starting point for damages for breach of a contract for the sale of land is the difference between the contract price and the market price of the property at the date of the breach. To this may be added actual financial loss suffered as a result of the breach, such as wasted conveyancing costs, legal costs involved in the purchase of another property, interest payable on a mortgage or bridging loan, costs of removal or storage of furniture, and/or costs of alternative accommodation pending purchase of another property (see *Beard v Porter* [1948] 1 KB 321).

33.2.6.2 Loss of development profit

Loss of development profit, or loss of profit on a sub-sale, can be claimed only if the defendant was aware of the claimant's proposals for the property at the time the contract was made (see *Diamond v Campbell Jones* [1961] Ch 22; cf *Cottrill v Steyning and Littlehampton Building Society* [1966] 2 All ER 295).

33.2.6.3 Resale by seller

Where the buyer defaults and the seller makes a loss on the resale, that loss can be claimed as damages; but if the seller makes a profit on the resale they would have to give credit for the amount of the profit in the claim, because the seller is entitled only to recover their financial loss and is not entitled to benefit from the buyer's breach. The purpose of contractual damages is to place the parties in the position in which they would have been had the contract been duly performed, not to punish the guilty party.

33.2.6.4 Mental distress

As a general principle of contractual damages, it is possible to recover for financial loss only, and no claim can be made in respect of mental distress suffered as a result of the defendant's breach. The practice of awarding a nominal sum in respect of damages for mental distress established by *Jarvis v Swans Tours* [1973] 1 QB 233 seems to be confined to holiday contracts and contracts for leisure activities. (See also *Bliss v South East Thames Regional Health Authority* [1987] ICR 700.)

33.2.6.5 Pre-contract losses

Damages can normally be claimed only in respect of losses which have occurred since the contract was made, thus there is generally no possibility of recovering expenses incurred at the pre-contract stage of the transaction (eg, for a wasted survey); but, in *Lloyd v Stanbury* [1971] 1 WLR 535, pre-contract expenditure including money spent on repairs to the property was recovered.

33.2.6.6 Mitigation

The claimant must have attempted to mitigate their loss, for example by trying to purchase another similar property (as disappointed buyer) or by attempting to resell the property (as disappointed seller). If no attempt to mitigate is made, the award of damages may be reduced because of the failure to mitigate. If the claimant attempts to mitigate and, in so doing, increases their loss, the defendant will be liable for the increased loss.

33.2.6.7 Giving credit for money received

Credit must be given in the claim for damages for any compensation received under SC 7.2 or SCPC 10.3, or for any deposit forfeited by the buyer to the seller.

33.3 RESCISSION

In this chapter the word 'rescission' is used in the context of contracts which involve a vitiating element such as misrepresentation, fraud or mistake, and refers to the remedy which is available in those circumstances.

Rescission entails the restoration of the parties to their pre-contract position by 'undoing' the contract and balancing the position of the parties with the payment of compensation by one party to the other. Damages in the conventional sense of that word are not payable, because there will have been no breach of contract. Since rescission is an equitable remedy, its operation is subject to the general equitable bars (eg, lapse of time).

33.3.1 Contractual right to rescind

Under both sets of standard conditions, the right to rescind is available in the following situations:

(a) for misrepresentation (SC 7.1; SCPC 10.1);

(b) where a licence to assign is not forthcoming in leasehold transactions (SC 8.3; SCPC 11.3);

(c) where either the buyer or the seller has failed to comply with a notice to complete (SC 7.4 and 7.5; SCPC 10.5 and 10.6).

Where the right to rescind is exercised under one of the above conditions, the parties' rights on rescission are governed by SC 7.1.2 or SCPC 10.2, which provide for the repayment of the deposit to the buyer with accrued interest, the return of documents to the seller and the cancellation of any registration of the contract at the buyer's expense.

33.3.2 Limitation periods

Where the right to rescind arises out of a contractual provision, it must be exercised within the time limits given within the condition or, if no time is specified, within a reasonable time. A claim based on a contractual rescission clause is subject to the normal six-year limitation period under the Limitation Act 1980 (unless the contract was by deed, when a 12-year limitation period would be available).

33.4 MISREPRESENTATION

33.4.1 Definition

A misrepresentation is an untrue statement of fact made by one contracting party which is relied on by the aggrieved party, which induces them to enter the contract, and as a result of which they suffer loss. The statement must be of fact, not law (see *Solle v Butcher* [1950] 1 KB 671). A statement of opinion is not actionable unless it can be proved that the opinion was never genuinely held (*Edgington v Fitzmaurice* (1885) 29 Ch D 459). A misrepresentation may be fraudulent (ie, deliberately dishonest) within the definition of fraud laid down in *Derry v Peek* (1889) 14 App Cas 337, negligent (ie, made carelessly without having checked the facts, but not necessarily negligent within the tortious meaning of that word), or innocent (ie, a genuine and innocently made mistake).

33.4.2 Fraudulent misrepresentation

Where the misrepresentation has been made fraudulently, the aggrieved party may issue a claim in tort for deceit, which may result in rescission of the contract and damages. The party who alleges fraud must prove fraud. This places a very onerous burden of proof on the claimant and, except where there is clear evidence of fraud, it is more usual to treat the misrepresentation as having been made negligently and to pursue a remedy under the Misrepresentation Act 1967.

33.4.3 Claims under the Misrepresentation Act 1967

In relation to contracts between 'consumers' and 'traders' regulated by the Consumer Rights Act 2015 (see **18.9**), s 2 of the Misrepresentation Act 1967 does not apply to the extent that the consumer has a right to redress under Part 4A of the Consumer Protection from Unfair Trading Regulations 2008. These Regulations prohibit traders from engaging in unfair commercial practices when dealing with consumers (see **8.4.9**) and will be superseded for these purposes by the Digital Markets, Competition and Consumers Act 2024 at a date to be appointed.

In other cases (consumer-to-consumer and business-to-business contracts), the claimant must show that they have an actionable misrepresentation, after which the burden of proof shifts to the defendant who has to disprove negligence. A misrepresentation is negligent if the defendant cannot prove that they had reasonable grounds for believing and did believe the statement they made was true up to the time the contract was made. There is therefore a duty to correct a statement which, although being true at the time when it was made, subsequently becomes untrue.

The remedies for a negligent misrepresentation are rescission of the contract and damages. If the defendant successfully establishes the defence of grounds and belief, thus showing that the misrepresentation was truly innocent, rescission is available, but not damages.

33.4.4 Rescission

The award of rescission lies within the equitable jurisdiction of the court and is thus discretionary and subject to the equitable bars. If none of the equitable bars applies but, nevertheless, the court decides not to grant rescission, it may instead award damages in lieu of rescission to the claimant under s 2(2) of the Misrepresentation Act 1967. Rescission is likely to be awarded only where the result of the misrepresentation is substantially to deprive the claimant of their bargain (see *Gosling v Anderson* (1972) *The Times*, 6 February; cf *Museprime Properties Ltd v Adhill Properties Ltd* [1990] 36 EG 114). Rescission is available even after completion, although this is subject to the usual equitable rules and so may not be possible where a third party (eg, a lender) has acquired an interest in the land.

33.4.5 Damages

Damages under the Misrepresentation Act 1967 are awarded on a tortious basis (*Chesneau v Interhome Ltd* (1983) *The Times*, 9 June). An award of damages can be made both as an award in lieu of rescission and as an award to compensate the claimant for their loss, subject to the overriding principle that the claimant cannot recover more than their actual loss, thus the awards under s 2(1) and (2) of the Misrepresentation Act 1967 are not cumulative.

33.4.6 Limitation period

A claim in misrepresentation does not arise out of the contract or out of tort. There is some doubt as to whether the limitation periods prescribed by the Limitation Act 1980 apply in this situation, or whether the limitation period for a claim based on misrepresentation relies on the equitable doctrine of laches. However, in *Green v Eadie and others* [2011] EWHC B24 (Ch), the High Court held that a claim for damages under s 2(1) of the Misrepresentation Act 1967 should become statute barred six years (not 12 years) from when the cause of action accrued. A claim in negligent misrepresentation accrues when damage is first suffered, which in this case was the time that the claimant entered into the contract to buy the property.

33.4.7 Incorporation as a term of the contract

Where a misrepresentation has become incorporated as a term of the contract it is possible, by s 1 of the Misrepresentation Act 1967 to treat the statement as a representation and to pursue a remedy under the Misrepresentation Act 1967. This option gives the claimant the right to ask for rescission of the contract as well as damages. If the claim was confined to breach of a minor contractual term, the only available remedy would be damages.

33.4.8 Imputed knowledge

Knowledge gained by a solicitor in the course of a transaction is deemed to be known by the solicitor's client, whether or not this is in fact the case. Thus where a solicitor gives an incorrect reply to pre-contract enquiries, the solicitor's knowledge, and also their misstatement, is attributable to the client who will be liable to the buyer in misrepresentation (*CEMP Properties (UK) Ltd v Dentsply Research and Development Corporation (No 1)* (1989) 2 EGLR 192). In such a situation, the solicitor would be liable to their own client in negligence. Similarly, if the seller makes a misrepresentation to the buyer personally but the misrepresentation is later corrected in correspondence between the seller's solicitors and the buyer's solicitors, the buyer is deemed to know of the correction (even if not actually told by their solicitor) and would not in such circumstances be able to bring a claim for misrepresentation against the seller (*Strover v Harrington* [1988] Ch 390).

33.4.9 Exclusion clauses

For consumer-to-consumer and business-to-business contracts, s 3 of the Misrepresentation Act 1967 provides that any clause which purports to limit or exclude liability for misrepresentation is valid only in so far as it satisfies the reasonableness test laid down in s 11 of and Sch 2 to the Unfair Contract Terms Act 1977. For contracts between traders and consumers, the relevant test is the fairness test in s 62 of the Consumer Rights Act 2015. If a clause is unfair, it will not be binding on the consumer. There is a non-exhaustive list of terms that are presumed to be unfair in Sch 2 to the 2015 Act. It is not yet clear whether this will produce different results to the reasonableness test.

The reasonableness test is applied subjectively, in the light of the circumstances which were known to the parties at the time when the contract was made. It therefore depends on the circumstances of each particular case as to whether the exclusion clause is valid in that situation.

There is no guarantee that any given form of wording will satisfy the test. Standard Condition 7.1 and SCPC 10.1 purport to limit the seller's liability for (inter alia) misrepresentation. Under the condition, damages are payable for a misrepresentation only if there is a material difference between the property as represented and as it really is. Similarly, rescission is available only where there is fraud or recklessness, or where the innocent party would be obliged to accept something differing substantially (in quality, quantity or tenure) from what they had been led to expect. Special condition 2 in the SCPCs is intended to prevent reliance on any misprepresentation that is not in writing and made by the other party or their solicitor while preserving liability for fraud or recklessness. The validity of these clauses is subject to its satisfying the reasonableness test on the facts of each particular case.

Some standard forms of pre-contract enquiries (but not the PIF used in Protocol transactions) have an exclusion clause printed on them. This exclusion clause is also subject to the reasonableness test (see *Walker v Boyle* [1982] 1 All ER 634, where an exclusion clause contained in a then current edition of a standard form of pre-contract enquiries failed the test).

33.5 MISDESCRIPTION

Misdescription occurs when an error is made in the particulars of sale of the contract, for example, misdescribing the tenure of the property as freehold when it is in fact leasehold, or wrongly describing the physical extent of the land to be sold. Standard Condition 7.1 and SCPC 10.1 (see **33.4.9**) control the remedies available for misdescription as well as for misrepresentation.

33.6 NON-DISCLOSURE

Non-disclosure arises out of the seller's failure to comply with their duty of disclosure (see **18.8.1**). Where standard conditions are in use, the remedies for non-disclosure are again governed by SC 7.1 and SCPC 10.1.

33.7 SPECIFIC PERFORMANCE

Although specific performance is an equitable remedy which is granted at the discretion of the court, an order for specific performance is not uncommon in sale of land cases where, since no two pieces of land are identical, an award of damages would be inadequate compensation for the injured party's loss. The claim can be made either on its own, or in conjunction with a claim for damages or rescission, depending on the circumstances.

33.7.1 General bars to the award

The award of a decree of specific performance is subject to the usual principles of equity. It will not therefore be awarded where (inter alia):

(a) an award of damages would adequately compensate for the loss sustained by the breach;
(b) the contract contains a vitiating element such as mistake, fraud or illegality;
(c) a third party has acquired an interest for value in the property;
(d) the seller cannot make good title.

33.7.2 Delay

The doctrine of laches (lapse of time) applies to equitable remedies. The remedy may therefore be barred if the innocent party delays in seeking an award.

33.7.3 Damages in lieu

If, in a situation where specific performance would otherwise be available to the injured party, the court decides not to make such an order, it can award damages in lieu of specific performance under the Senior Courts Act 1981, s 50. These damages are assessed using normal contractual principles as outlined in **33.2**. Where an award of specific performance has been made but has not been complied with, the injured party may return to the court asking the court to withdraw the order and to substitute the decree of specific performance with an award of damages (*Johnson v Agnew* [1980] AC 367).

33.8 RETURN OF DEPOSIT

Where the buyer defaults on completion the seller will want to forfeit the deposit, but s 49(2) of the LPA 1925 gives the court an absolute discretion to order the return of the deposit to the buyer. Where the seller retains the deposit, this must be taken into account in any assessment of damages for breach of contract.

Where the seller defaults on completion, the buyer will have a right to the return of the deposit under SC 7.5 (SCPC 10.6).

33.9 RECTIFICATION

33.9.1 Rectification of the contract

Where the parties have reached agreement over a particular matter but that matter is either omitted from the written contract in error, or is wrongly recorded in the written agreement, an application for rectification of the contract to correct the error can be made. Under s 2(4) of the Law of Property (Miscellaneous Provisions) Act 1989, where rectification is ordered, the court has a discretion to determine the date on which the contract comes into operation.

33.9.2 Rectification of the transfer deed

Where a term of the contract is either omitted from or inaccurately represented in the transfer deed, an application for rectification of the deed may be made to the court.

33.10 COVENANTS FOR TITLE

Certain covenants for title will be implied into the transfer deed, the nature of those covenants depending on whether the seller has sold with full or limited title guarantee (or none at all) (see **18.8.3**). In the case of unregistered land, liability on the covenants is strict. The limitation period of 12 years runs from the date of completion in the case of the 'right to dispose of the property' covenant, and usually from the date of actual breach in other cases. The covenants for title have equal application to registered land (except that liability is not strict), but the State guarantee of a registered title means that, in practice, claims on the covenants are less likely to occur with the transfer of registered land.

SUMMARY

- Where there has been a delay in completion, damages for breach of contract may be available to the innocent party for losses suffered (in excess of the amount of any compensation paid under SC 7.2 or SCPC 10.3).
- Where one of the parties has failed to complete following service of a notice to complete, the innocent party will have a right to rescind the contract and claim damages for losses suffered. (Again, credit must be given for the amount of any compensation paid under SC 7.2 or SCPC 10.3.) An innocent party who wants to force the defaulting party to complete may be able to obtain an order for specific performance.
- Where the seller has failed to disclose an incumbrance over the property, damages for breach of contract may be available to buyer, but only where the incumbrance causes a material difference in the tenure or value of the property. The buyer may treat the contract at an end only if there has been fraud or recklessness by the seller, or if the buyer would otherwise be forced to accept a property differing substantially in quantity, quality or tenure from what they had been led to expect.
- Where there has been a misrepresentation by the seller or the seller's solicitor, the buyer may be able to rescind the contract and claim damages. However, the contract contains an exclusion clause stating that rescission will be available only if the misrepresentation is fraudulent or reckless, or if the buyer would be obliged to accept a property differing substantially in quantity, quality or tenure from what they had been led to expect. The exclusion clause also states that damages will be payable only if there is a material difference between the property as represented and as it really is. The validity of this exclusion clause will depend on whether it passes the reasonableness test in the Unfair Contract Terms Act 1977 in the particular circumstances of the transaction.
- After completion, it may be possible to bring a claim for breach of the implied covenants for title in the transfer deed, although this remedy is used very rarely.

PART VII

LEASEHOLDS

CHAPTER 34

Introduction to Leasehold Property

LEARNING OUTCOMES

After reading this chapter you will be able to:

- understand why a property may be let on a lease rather than sold freehold
- explain the difference between the grant of a lease, the assignment of a lease and a sub-letting
- understand the requirements for the creation of a legal lease
- explain whether the liability of the landlord and the tenant for performance of the covenants in a lease will continue after an assignment of that lease
- advise on how a lease may be terminated
- advise a landlord on the remedies available when a tenant is in breach of their covenants in the lease.

34.1 INTRODUCTION

So far, this book has concentrated on the law and practice involved in the outright sale and purchase of freehold land. This part of the book will move on to consider the law and practice relating to the grant and assignment of leases. This chapter will explore the reasons why parties grant or take leases in the first place, examine the leasehold property market and introduce the underlying legal concepts relating to leasehold land which are necessary to understand the conveyancing process as it applies to leases. The word 'tenancy' is often encountered in place of 'lease' in this area and is simply an alternative word for the same thing. For the sake of clarity, the word 'lease' rather than 'tenancy' is predominantly used in this book.

34.2 ADVANTAGES AND DISADVANTAGES OF LEASEHOLDS

Leasehold land is encountered for a number of reasons. First, there can be a ready market for leasehold property, such as that for the short-term letting of residential premises. Secondly, for reasons explained below, where a property forms part of a building rather than the whole, it is usual to find that each unit within the building will be held under a lease rather than being sold freehold. This can apply to both commercial property, such as an office suite, and residential property, such as a flat. Further, in some parts of England and Wales, for reasons which are largely historic in origin, it is not uncommon to find residential property being sold leasehold rather than freehold.

34.2.1 Advantages

There can be advantages to both parties in leasing property. First, although the term of a lease must be fixed once granted, the length of the actual term chosen can, theoretically, be of any duration. This gives parties flexibility to meet their mutual needs. The example of the short-term residential letting market has been mentioned in **34.2** above. Such lettings give tenants a place to live whilst, say, saving for a deposit to buy a home of their own, but also provide landlords with income from the rent paid by the tenants. Further, from a landlord's perspective, not only do they enjoy the benefit of a steady income from the property, they also retain an interest (ie, the freehold estate) which is a saleable capital asset in its own right, which can be disposed of separately from the leasehold interest.

Another advantage is that the parties are more easily able to enforce covenants than is the case with freehold land. In freehold land, positive covenants (eg, a covenant to repair) are not directly enforceable against future owners of the land. In the case of leasehold land, almost all covenants, both positive and negative, are enforceable against such successors in title. Where the enforcement of both positive as well as negative covenants is of particular importance in respect of a given property, it is therefore common to find that leases are used. Thus, where a property forms part of a larger building, it is usual to find that each unit within the building is let rather than being sold freehold. This meets the needs of the landlord, in that the landlord can enforce positive covenants such as repair on the tenants of each unit, but it also meets the needs of the tenants, as they can ensure that common parts retained by the landlord are also maintained as appropriate. As regards this latter point, in practice the way this is usually dealt with is that one individual (normally the landlord or a management company) will be responsible for the maintenance of the common parts but will recover the costs incurred by way of a 'service charge' levied on the tenants of the individual units within the building. This obligation to pay the service charge is itself a positive covenant, the enforcement of which could present problems in the case of freehold land.

34.2.2 Disadvantages

The disadvantages of leasehold property are mainly on the tenant's side. First, as a lease is granted for a fixed period of time, it will eventually expire. Should the tenant wish to remain in the property in this event, they will have to approach the landlord for a renewal, which the landlord may not be willing to give. Further, if the lease has a capital value, the lease is in effect a wasting asset in the tenant's hands. This difficulty is alleviated to a degree, as some tenants have statutory rights to renew or extend the term in certain circumstances. The most important examples of these rights in the commercial context are considered in **Chapter 40**. The fundamental problem remains, however, especially where such rights are not available.

An additional disadvantage for tenants relates to covenants. Leases often impose considerable burdens on tenants, including covenants relating to repair, obligations to contribute towards the cost of maintaining the building of which the property let forms part, and restrictions on the tenant's ability to assign or otherwise deal with the property. This is compounded by the remedies available to the landlord to ensure compliance with these obligations (see **34.8** for more details). Ultimately, the landlord can forfeit the lease, bringing it to an end. This remedy is dramatic, particularly if the lease has a capital value, as this capital value will be lost along with the lease itself.

From the landlord's point of view, the main disadvantage of granting a lease rather than selling the property outright is that, together with the rights which they retain in the property, they may also retain various obligations in relation to matters such as repairs and insurance.

The burden of these obligations must, however, be set against the benefit of the income received from the rent of the property and the covenants agreed to be performed by the tenant.

34.3 COMMON ILLUSTRATIONS OF LEASEHOLD PROPERTY

34.3.1 The residential market

34.3.1.1 Short-term residential lettings

The market for the short-term letting of residential property has already been mentioned. Such leases are usually granted for a period of, say, a year at the full open market rent (or 'rack rent') for the property. The lease will therefore have no capital value in the hands of the tenant. The procedure on the grant of a short-term lease is normally very informal. Such lettings are often handled by letting agents. It is likely that neither party will be legally represented and the tenant will make no searches or enquiries at all about the property. The landlord will be most concerned about the status of the tenant rather than legal matters (ie, whether the tenant will be a 'good' tenant or not; whether they will pay the rent regularly and not damage the property). Further, it is usual for the lease to provide that the lease cannot be assigned by the tenant and so the only 'dealing' with the lease is when it is originally granted.

Given the comparatively 'informal' nature of such transactions, the usual conveyancing procedures seen in this book do not, in effect, apply, and for the remainder of this part of the book this will be assumed to be the case. Such lettings may, however, give rise to certain statutory rights and protections in favour of tenants, but these are beyond the scope of this book.

34.3.1.2 The residential long lease

Long residential leases are routinely encountered where the units being disposed of form part of a larger building, such as units in a block of flats or maisonettes. Such units are disposed of using a leasehold arrangement due to the greater ability to enforce both positive and negative covenants discussed at **34.2.1** above. In either case, the lease will usually be granted for a lengthy term (say 125 years) in return for a lump sum payment (a 'premium') and a low 'ground rent' (often no more than £100 or so per annum). In recent years, there have been increasing numbers of houses also sold as leasehold, with the home-owners being required to pay a ground rent and sometimes a service charge to cover the maintenance of common parts. The residential long lease has received a lot of negative press in recent years, due in part to a recent trend for developers to include escalating ground rent provisions in their leases (see **37.3.9.1**) and problems with excessive service charges. The previous and current Governments have declared an intention to reform leasehold law to better protect residential leaseholders. The first piece of legislation to seek to do this is the Leasehold and Freehold Reform Act 2024. This contains provisions requiring houses to be sold only as freehold and provisions to strengthen long leaseholders' rights to purchase their freeholds and to manage the services provided to their homes. However, around 25–30 pieces of secondary legislation are required to bring most of its provisions into force and as a result, at the time of writing, none of the most significant changes brought about by the 2024 Act are in effect. Further, a group of freeholders have been given permission to seek judicial review of the 2024 Act (on the basis, in broad terms, that it affects the value of their freehold reversions and income streams). The judicial review hearing should be heard by July 2025.

Despite these issues and uncertainties, there are still many residential properties held on long leases and these will be frequently encountered in practice. Such leases have a capital value (although this can be detrimentally affected by onerous terms) and, unlike short-term residential lettings, there are usually few controls on the tenant's ability to dispose of the property by way of assignment (although there may be more controls on a tenant's freedom to assign part – as opposed to the whole – and to sub-let). Such leases can therefore be bought and sold like freehold land. Indeed, if it were not for the need to ensure the effective enforcement of positive and negative covenants, the leasehold route would probably not need to be used in such cases at all.

The conveyancing aspects of long residential leaseholds in many ways therefore mirror the procedure for the sale of a freehold. This is the case both on the grant of the original lease and in the event of the subsequent assignment of that lease. On grant, the developer will charge a purchase price, just as it would on the sale of a house, and when the buyer tenant in turn comes to sell, they too will sell the lease for a capital sum. As such, the original tenant (in the case of the grant of a lease) or a purchaser from the tenant (in the case of a subsequent assignment) will need to investigate title and carry out searches and enquiries in the usual way, and will need to consider how to fund the acquisition, often with the aid of a mortgage. In addition, the freehold model of exchanging contracts before subsequently completing is also usually followed.

Given the length of such leases and the historically low yield provided in the form of rent, ownership of the freehold in such circumstances is not viewed as a particularly attractive investment. This is compounded by the fact that tenants of such properties have various statutory rights to extend the terms of their leases, so landlords are unlikely to be able regain vacant possession of the land and re-let. In the light of this, the developer landlord will often dispose of the freehold of the common parts to a management company (owned through its shares by the tenants of the individual units) rather than retain any interest in the development following completion of it. Solicitors acting for buyers of long leaseholds should, however, look out for long leases containing ground rents that are more than a nominal amount. Where the ground rent provides an income stream for the developer landlord, the developer is more likely to retain the freehold reversion or sell it on to an investor. This leaves the occupying tenants with a landlord who collects the ground rent and service charge and enforces the covenants. The interests of the freeholder and occupying tenant are not usually aligned and this can lead to disputes between landlord and tenant. Ground rent and service charges can be particularly problematic areas (see **37.3.9** and **Chapter 38**).

34.3.2 The commercial property market

It is less usual for commercial occupiers to own the freehold to their premises, and instead most commercial property is occupied under leases. There are a number of reasons for this. First, businesses can be attracted by the flexibility a lease provides. To take an example of a new start-up business, this might prosper and so wish to move to larger premises. Alternatively, the business might not be such a success, and a move to smaller, cheaper premises might be desired. A short-term lease allows greater flexibility in this context. Secondly, the cost of buying a freehold will often be prohibitively expensive, and in any case, most businesses will simply not want to tie up capital in this way even if the money were available. Lastly, where the premises form part of a building, the same issue relating to the effective enforcement of both positive and negative covenants applies as discussed above.

The willingness of businesses to rent property creates a market for landlords to supply that need. In fact, commercial property forms an important part of the investment portfolios of institutions such as insurance companies, pension funds and the like. It has given rise to the development of what is often referred to as the 'institutional lease'. The landlord will seek to pass the day-to-day operational cost for occupying the property to the tenants, leaving the rent as pure profit in the hands of the landlord.

Historically, leases for periods of five to 21 years were common, but in recent years the trend has been towards shorter terms, and now periods of between five and 15 years are more usual. Whilst it is possible for a capital sum to be payable (both on the grant of the lease and any subsequent assignment of it), this is less usual than is the case for the grant or assignment of a long residential lease. Instead, the 'cost' to the tenant comes in the form of the payment of a market rent, much higher relatively than the rent which is payable under a long residential lease. Further, the rent is usually subject to review every few years under a term to this effect in the lease. A consequence of this is that leases of commercial property, whatever the length, usually contain detailed controls on the tenant's freedom to assign or otherwise deal with the property, as the landlord will be keen to ensure that any assignee, for example, is at least as able as the current tenant to meet the liabilities due under the lease.

The terms of commercial leases are often the subject of detailed negotiation between the parties on grant. In an attempt to improve the fairness of such negotiations, the Royal Institution of Charted Surveyors (RICS) has produced a professional statement ('Code for Leasing Business Premises', 1st edn). Whilst there have been previous versions of this Code, this is the first that has the status of a 'professional statement'. A professional statement is a professional standard for RICS members and breach of a professional standard would be relevant in disciplinary proceedings against a surveyor. However, the mandatory parts of the statement are fairly limited and confined to approaching negotiations constructively and ensuring that comprehensive written heads of terms are produced. The remainder of the document contains statements of good practice and is a useful tool to refer to in identifying what is a 'fair' position between landlord and tenant.

In terms of procedure, it is less usual for the parties to exchange contracts, and instead the transaction will often simply proceed straight to completion. This is because it is less usual to need to synchronise a chain of transactions than is the case in the residential context. Subject to this, the steps that make up the procedure for granting or assigning a commercial lease broadly follow those for the sale of freehold land. It should be noted, however, that for shorter terms, a prospective tenant or assignee may choose not to carry out some of the more usual steps, such as investigating title. This is a commercial decision for the client. The following chapters will work on the basis that the client does not wish to omit any of these steps.

34.4 KEY TERMINOLOGY – GRANT, ASSIGNMENT AND SUB-LETTING

It is important to understand the terminology in respect of dealings with leases. This is perhaps best explained by the diagram which follows:

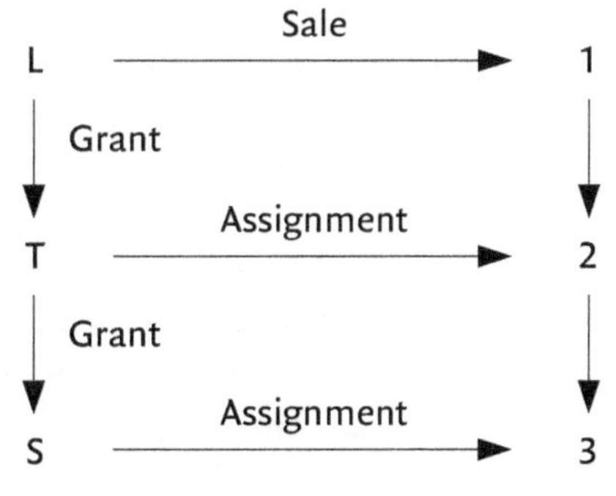

When a lease is brought into being, the transaction is known as a 'grant'. Thus, in the diagram, when the owner of the freehold (L) creates a lease in favour of the tenant (T), this is said to be the grant of that lease. This lease is the head-lease, because the only superior title above it is the freehold (also known as the freehold reversion). Just as the landlord is able to carve a lease out of their freehold, T can do the same out of their lease and so, in turn, when T grants a lease to S, this is called the grant of a sub-lease.

The effect of this is that there are now three legal estates in existence over the land: the freehold; the head-leasehold; and the sub-leasehold. Each of these estates can be bought and sold in its own right. Thus, L can transfer the freehold to 1, T can transfer the head-lease to 2, and S can transfer the sub-lease to 3. To distinguish between transfers of freeholds, on the one hand, and leaseholds on the other, it is usual to refer to the transfer of a leasehold as an 'assignment'.

It is important to distinguish between 'grant' and 'assignment' as they are distinct and separate types of transaction, as will be shown in **Chapters 35** and **36**. In particular, it is important to understand that the grant of a lease creates the lease for the first time (and the document giving effect to the transaction will be the lease itself), whilst an assignment transfers the remainder of such a lease once it has been created (and the document giving effect to the transaction will be a transfer or deed of assignment).

Two final points need to be made. First, when a tenant grants a sub-lease, the term of the sub-lease must be for a period that is shorter than the head-lease itself. If the tenant purports to grant a sub-lease for a term equal to or greater than the head-lease, this transaction will be treated instead as being an assignment of the tenant's lease. Secondly, in the example above, it has been assumed that there are no restrictions on either T's or S's freedom to dispose of their respective leasehold interests. In practice, it is common to find restrictions on a tenant's freedom to assign or sub-let. It is important to check the terms of any lease at an early stage of a transaction for any such restrictions.

34.5 CHARACTERISTICS AND TYPES OF LEASES, FORMALITIES AND REGISTRATION

34.5.1 Essential characteristics

A lease is an interest in land which grants exclusive possession of a property for a fixed period of time (*Street v Mountford* [1985] 2 All ER 289, HL). A crucial element of this is the grant of exclusive possession, that is, the right to exclude all others, including the landlord, from the property. If the person to whom the interest is granted does not have exclusive possession then it may be that they merely have a personal right to occupy, generally known as a licence. A licence does not create an interest in land as such and may be revoked at any time (or according to its terms). Whether a lease or a licence has been created depends on the intention of the parties in so far as it can be inferred from all the circumstances. The court will look at the substance of the agreement not the form and, for example, calling a document a 'licence' will not be conclusive in preventing it from being a lease.

A lease does not have to take effect in possession immediately and can be granted to take effect at some future time, provided it is within 21 years of its grant (LPA 1925, s 149(3)). The date when the term of the lease begins (ie, when the right to possession arises) is usually referred to as the commencement date. The commencement date can also be backdated to a date *before* the date of grant of the lease. This is sometimes done where a landlord grants a number of leases, eg of flats or offices, in the same building over a period of time and wishes the terms of all the leases to expire on the same day. All the commencement dates for the terms will be expressed to be the same, regardless of the date of grant of the individual leases.

34.5.2 Types of leases

Leases may be fixed term or periodic. Fixed-term leases are simply leases granted for a specific period of time (sometimes called the 'contractual term'). This term can be of any length, no matter how long or short, for example, one week or 99 years. Fixed-term leases automatically expire at the end of the term and at common law there is no need to serve any notice to determine them.

Periodic leases are leases granted for a period which will then renew from one period to the next, until determined by what is known as a 'notice to quit' (see **34.7**). The most common examples are yearly, quarterly, monthly and weekly periodic leases. Periodic leases may be granted expressly, but they can also arise by implication of law where an individual goes into occupation of a property and begins to rent on a regular basis. In such circumstances, the courts may be willing to imply that a periodic lease has arisen, the period of the tenancy reflecting the frequency with which rent is paid. Periodic leases can also arise by implication where the tenant holds over, with the landlord's consent, after the expiry of a fixed-term tenancy.

34.5.3 Formalities and registration

A lease may be legal or equitable.

34.5.3.1 Legal leases

A legal lease must be created by deed (LPA 1925, s 52(1) and Law of Property (Miscellaneous Provisions) Act 1989, s 1) unless it falls within s 54(2) of the LPA 1925. Section 54(2) provides that a lease which takes effect in possession for a term of years not exceeding three years (this includes a periodic tenancy) at the best rent reasonably obtainable without taking a fine may be made merely in writing, or even orally, and still be legal. A deed is always necessary to effect a legal assignment of a lease, even if the lease itself has been created informally under s 54(2).

Legal leases are prima facie binding on all comers; however, this position is modified by the LRA 2002 and depends on the length of the original term of the lease as follows:

(a) *Legal leases granted for a term of more than seven years.* Such leases must be registered with their own separate title number. The position then depends on whether or not the reversionary title is registered. If the reversion is registered, the grant of the lease amounts to a 'dealing' with the registered title and the lease must be registered with its own title, and in addition it must be noted on the reversionary title. If the reversionary title is unregistered, the grant triggers first registration of title to the lease but does not affect the title to the reversion, which will remain unregistered.

(b) *Legal leases for seven years or less.* If such a lease is granted out of a reversion with a registered title, it takes effect as an overriding interest under Sch 3 to the LRA 2002 whether or not the tenant is in actual occupation. No form of registration is required. If the reversionary title is unregistered, the lease is automatically binding and requires no form of registration.

34.5.3.2 Equitable leases

A lease which has not been created by deed and is not within s 54(2) of the LPA 1925 may take effect as an equitable lease (in effect as contract to create a lease), provided that it is for value and satisfies the requirements of the Law of Property (Miscellaneous Provisions) Act 1989, s 2 (ie it is in writing, incorporating all terms expressly agreed and signed by or on behalf of each party).

Equitable leases usually require some form of registration to make them binding on a purchaser of the reversion. If the reversionary title is unregistered, the lease must be registered as a Class C(iv) land charge against the name of the owner of the immediate reversion. If unregistered, it is void against a purchaser of the legal estate for money or money's worth. If the reversionary title is registered, the lease must be registered as a minor interest on the charges register of the reversionary title. If, however, the tenant is in actual occupation, the lease is an overriding interest under Sch 3 to the LRA 2002 and binding without registration.

34.6 LIABILITY ON COVENANTS IN LEASES

As has been seen, one of the major advantages of creating a lease relates to the enforcement of covenants between the parties. This section contains an outline of the underlying principles in this respect.

34.6.1 Leases granted on or after 1 January 1996

The Landlord and Tenant (Covenants) Act 1995 (LTCA 1995) applies to leases granted on or after 1 January 1996. Note that it is the date of the *grant* of the lease, not any subsequent assignment, that determines this.

The original parties to the lease have the benefit of the other's covenants and the burden of their own covenants while they remain as landlord and tenant. When the tenant lawfully assigns the lease they are automatically released from future liability under the lease covenants, unless they have agreed to enter into an 'authorised guarantee agreement' (AGA). The AGA is an agreement entered into by the outgoing tenant with their landlord in which the outgoing tenant guarantees the performance of the lease covenants by their immediate successor in title. A tenant is obliged to provide an AGA in the following circumstances only:

(a) In leases of commercial property, where the parties have agreed in the lease that an AGA is to be provided on assignment (see **36.5.3**). Note that it is not possible to agree such a condition in advance in a lease of residential property.

(b) If the landlord lawfully requires the provision of an AGA as a condition of giving consent to an assignment. This is explored in detail in **36.5.3**, but it is ultimately a decision for the courts as to whether a condition has been lawfully imposed in a particular case.

Note that the guarantee contained in the AGA extends to the performance of covenants by the immediate successor in title only, and will not extend to subsequent tenants. The outgoing tenant remains liable, however, for any breaches of covenant which were committed before the date of the assignment.

An assignee of a lease gets the benefit of the landlord's covenants when they take an assignment of the lease (LTCA 1995, s 3(2)(b)). The assignee is bound by all the tenant's covenants in the lease, except those expressly stated to be 'personal' to the original tenant (LTCA 1995, s 3(2)(a)). On a subsequent assignment, the assignee remains liable for any breaches committed before the date of the assignment but is released from liability for any future breaches, unless they too have been required to give an AGA to guarantee the performance of the lease covenants by their immediate successor.

Two final points should be noted about a tenant's liability. First, the automatic release provisions considered above do not apply if the assignment is in breach of a covenant in the lease, nor if it occurs by operation of the law (eg, on the death of the tenant where the lease passes to their personal representatives). Secondly, where a former tenant remains liable under an AGA, they should seek protection in the form of an indemnity covenant from the successor in title. This must be given expressly, as no indemnity is implied by statute.

As regards landlords, any subsequent assignee of the landlord's interest gets the benefit of the tenant's covenants when they take an assignment of the lease (LTCA 1995, s 3(3)(b)). Each landlord is not automatically released from their covenants when they sell the reversion, but can apply to the tenant for the time being to be released from future liability before or within four weeks of the date of the assignment of the reversion.

34.6.2 Leases granted before 1 January 1996

34.6.2.1 Liability of tenants

The LTCA 1995 generally does not apply to these leases.

The basic principle is that the original tenant remains bound by the covenants in the lease for the whole of the contractual term under the doctrine of privity of contract. This liability continues even after assignment, unless the landlord expressly agrees to release the original tenant. The significance of this is worth emphasising: unless released by the landlord, the original tenant is liable on all the express covenants in the lease for breaches committed at any time during the term of the lease, ie they are liable not only for breaches which they commit, but also for those committed by their successors in title.

In addition to the liability of the original tenant, any assignee will also be liable for breaches committed whilst ownership of the lease is vested in that assignee in respect of covenants which 'touch and concern' the land. In essence, covenants which 'touch and concern' are those which would be entered into between parties as landowners, rather than in their capacity as mere individuals. This is under the doctrine of privity of estate.

The original landlord, as original contracting party, has the benefit of the tenant's covenants by virtue of the principle of privity of contract. A landlord's successor in title takes the benefit of the tenant's covenants which have reference to the subject matter of the lease under s 141(1) of the LPA 1925.

Thus the landlord can potentially seek redress against either the original tenant or the assignee who committed the breach. Whilst the landlord cannot claim double compensation, this is nonetheless an advantage to the landlord as it gives a choice as to whom they can sue. This is particularly attractive if the assignee is in financial difficulties and so not worth suing. It should be noted that where the original landlord transfers the reversion, the right to sue passes to the transferee of that reversion (and any subsequent landlord for the time being), because on a transfer of the reversion all rights of action attached to the reversion pass to the transferee, including the right to sue for an existing breach of covenant (LPA 1925, s 141; and see *In re King (deceased); Robinson v Gray* [1963] Ch 459).

In the light of the above, an assignee of a lease will usually be required to indemnify their assignor in respect of any breach of covenant committed after the date of the assignment to them, regardless of whether they have parted with the lease. On the transfer of a registered lease, such an indemnity covenant is implied by Sch 12, para 20 to the LRA 2002 (preserving the effect of LRA 1925, s 24), whether or not value was given for the assignment. A similar indemnity provision is implied by s 77 of the LPA 1925 on the assignment of an unregistered lease, but only where value has been given for the assignment. Where, in unregistered land, there is to be no valuable consideration for the assignment, an express indemnity covenant will be required by the assignor. Standard Condition 4.6.4 and SCPC 7.6.5 require the transfer deed to contain an express indemnity covenant, except where one is implied by law.

One final point remains to be made. If the lease contains a requirement to obtain the landlord's consent before any assignment takes place, the landlord may, in appropriate circumstances, insist that any assignee enter into a direct contractual relationship with them to observe the tenant's covenants under the lease for the remainder of the term. This is usually contained in the same document in which the landlord gives their consent to the assignment, known as a licence to assign. This has the effect of imposing on any assignee the same liability under privity of contract as is faced by the original tenant.

34.6.2.2 Liability of landlords

The original landlord remains contractually bound to the original tenant throughout the term of the lease under the doctrine of privity of contract. If an original landlord is unable through their own act or default (eg, by transferring the reversion to a third party) to carry out an obligation imposed on them by the lease, the landlord may be liable in damages to the tenant. See, for example, *Eagon v Dent* [1965] 2 All ER 335, where a landlord sold the reversion to a third party and the original tenant, who failed in their attempt to exercise an unregistered option against the buyer of the reversion, recovered damages from the original landlord for breach of covenant.

In addition to the original landlord, any transferee of the reversion for the time being will also be liable in respect of breaches of covenant which touch and concern the land which are committed whilst the reversion is vested in them. Again, this is under the doctrine of privity of estate.

34.6.3 Default notices – liability of former tenants

As can be seen from the above, former tenants can remain liable for breaches of covenants by assignees; in the case of leases granted before 1 January 1996, under the doctrine of privity of contract, and for leases granted on or after that date, where the outgoing tenant has given an AGA. In order to afford some protection to former tenants in respect of arrears of fixed sums such as rent, s 17 of the LTCA 1995 provides that a landlord can pursue a former tenant only if they first serve what is known as a 'default notice' on the former tenant. This must be served within six months of the sum falling due. If the notice is not served, the landlord cannot pursue the former tenant. This protection applies to leases whether created before or after the LTCA 1995 came into force.

A former tenant who has been served with a s 17 notice and has made payment in full is entitled to call on the landlord to grant it an overriding lease (LTCA 1995, s 19(1)). An overriding lease is a concurrent lease of the premises demised by the first lease and makes the former tenant the immediate landlord of the defaulting tenant. It therefore gives the former tenant the right to forfeit the first lease to the defaulting tenant and/or exercise the landlord's other remedies for non-payment of rent.

34.6.4 Liability between head-landlord and sub-tenant

No privity of estate exists between a head-landlord and a sub-tenant, although a contractual relationship will exist between them if the sub-tenant has entered into direct covenants with the head-landlord (eg, where the head-landlord has insisted on this as a precondition to allowing the sub-letting). The sub-tenant will in any event be directly liable to the head-landlord on restrictive covenants in the head-lease of which the former had notice when they took the sub-lease. Irrespective of direct contractual liability, if the sub-tenant breaches a covenant in the head-lease, the head-landlord will have the right to forfeit the head-lease, and this will mean that the sub-lease which is derived out of the head-lease will also terminate.

34.7 DETERMINATION OF LEASES

At common law, leases can be determined in a number of ways which are considered below. Many types of leases, however, enjoy the benefit of statutory protections which allow them to be terminated only in prescribed ways which are not considered here. The most important examples of these rights in the commercial context are considered in **Chapter 40**.

34.7.1 Effluxion of time

In the case of fixed-term leases, when the contractual terms ends, the lease automatically determines by what is known as 'effluxion of time'. No notice is needed to do this.

34.7.2 Notice to quit

Periodic tenancies are determined by the appropriate period's notice to quit given by the landlord or tenant. At common law the notice period does not have to exclude the day of service and the day of expiry, in other words, 'clear' notice is not necessary. Careful attention must be paid, as notice periods are strictly enforced and the court will not grant equitable relief because of negligence or forgetfulness.

If the terms of the tenancy do not otherwise provide, the common law implies the following length of notice:

(a) *Yearly tenancies*. These are determined by at least half a year's notice expiring at the end of a completed year of the tenancy. Either the last day of the year of the tenancy (ie, the day before the anniversary of the commencement of the year) or the next following day may be specified in the notice as the expiry day. If the tenancy began on one of the usual quarter days 'half a year' means two quarters, otherwise it means 182 days, ie the odd half day is ignored.

(b) *Other periodic tenancies.* These are determined by one full period's notice (ie one quarter, month, etc) expiring at the end of a completed period of the tenancy. Thus, if a tenant has a monthly tenancy which starts on the first of each month and the landlord wants to serve a notice to quit on 14 August, the earliest date they can specify for expiry of the notice is 30 September, ie the notice must be at least one month long *and must expire at the end of a completed month.* If the landlord had wished to terminate the lease with effect at the end of August they would have had to serve notice *no later than* 1 August to expire on 31 August.

Any notice to quit premises occupied as a dwelling house must be given at least four weeks before it is to take effect, must be in writing and must contain certain prescribed information (Protection from Eviction Act 1977, s 5).

34.7.3 Surrender

Surrender occurs where the tenant yields up their lease to the immediate landlord who accepts the surrender. The lease is said to merge in the landlord's reversion and is extinguished. To be legal, surrender must be by deed (LPA 1925, s 52).

34.7.4 Merger

This occurs where the tenant acquires the immediate reversion on their lease (ie, acquires the landlord's estate in land). It can also occur where a third party acquires both the lease and the reversion. It is the converse of surrender. As with surrender, the lease automatically merges with the reversion and is extinguished unless the contrary intention appears.

34.7.5 Break clause

Some leases will contain an option to determine the lease part way through the contractual term. The terms of the break clause will need to be negotiated between the parties. They will need to agree on who can operate the break, at what point in the term it can be operated and how much notice must be given to exercise it. Sometimes the parties may agree that certain pre-conditions must be complied with if the break is to be exercised (for example, the lease may require that all rental payments are up to date when the tenant seeks to exercise the break). Case law indicates that the terms of a break clause must be strictly complied with if the exercise of it is to be valid (see, for example, *Avocet Industrial Estates LLP v Merol Ltd* [2011] EWHC 3422 (Ch)).

34.8 LANDLORD'S REMEDIES FOR BREACH OF COVENANT

34.8.1 For non-payment of rent

A landlord may consider the following remedies for non-payment of rent:

(a) Debt action. Under the Limitation Act 1980, an action to recover a debt, such as rent, must be commenced within six years of the sum falling due.

(b) Forfeiture (see **34.8.3**).

(c) Commercial rent arrears recovery procedure (CRAR) (see **34.8.4**).

(d) Collecting the rent from a sub-tenant. This is possible under s 81 of the Tribunals, Courts and Enforcement Act 2007. If CRAR is available to a landlord in respect of its immediate tenant (see **38.8.4**), the landlord may serve notice on any sub-tenant, setting out certain prescribed information including the amount of rent owing. The effect of the notice is, once 14 clear days have expired, to transfer to the landlord the right to collect the rent due under the sub-lease until the amount owing by the immediate tenant has been paid off.

(e) Bankruptcy and winding up. If the debt exceeds £5,000 in the case of an individual or £750 in the case of a company, a statutory demand can be served with a view to commencing bankruptcy or winding-up proceedings.
(f) Pursue former tenant(s). If former tenant(s) remain liable then the landlord can pursue them (but for limitations in respect of recovery of rent from such former tenants, see **34.6.3**).
(g) Pursue any guarantors of the tenant.

Restrictions on the landlord's ability to exercise forfeiture for non-payment of rent, exercise CRAR and present winding-up petitions were in force during the period of the Covid-19 pandemic. The Commercial Rent (Coronavirus) Act 2022 introduced a binding arbitration process to resolve claims for rent arrears that had accrued during periods of enforced closure (called 'protected rent debt'), supported by a voluntary code to encourage the parties to reach agreement.

34.8.2 For breach of other covenants

The following remedies are available to a landlord for breach of other covenants:

(a) Forfeiture (see **34.8.3**).
(b) Injunction. This is most appropriate for breach of a negative covenant such as a user covenant, or to prevent an anticipated breach of covenant such as an assignment in breach of covenant.
(c) Specific performance. This may be appropriate where the obligation to be enforced is sufficiently precise. It will not be ordered where performance or supervision is required over a period of time, or where damages are an adequate remedy.
(d) Damages. These are recoverable under normal contractual rules as laid down by *Hadley v Baxendale* (1854) 9 Exch 341. Special rules apply to the recovery of damages for the breach of a repairing covenant, which are considered at **34.8.5**.
(e) Pursue former tenant(s). If former tenant(s) remain liable then the landlord can pursue them.
(f) Pursue any guarantors of the tenant.

34.8.3 Forfeiture

This is a right to retake possession of the premises and so prematurely determine the lease. The right must generally be reserved expressly by the lease. The right is enforced in one of two ways: by court order, or by peaceable re-entry. Where premises are let as a dwelling, it is unlawful to enforce forfeiture otherwise than by court proceedings while any person is lawfully residing on any part of the premises (Protection from Eviction Act 1977, s 2). The ability to forfeit long residential tenancies is also severely restricted by the Commonhold and Leasehold Reform Act 2002. Further, whether the property is commercial or residential, it is an offence to use or threaten violence (Criminal Law Act 1977, s 6) to achieve re-entry where the landlord knew that there was someone on the premises opposed to the re-entry.

The landlord should also be aware that its right to forfeit may be waived, by carrying out any act demonstrating an intention to continue the relationship of landlord and tenant (for example, demanding or accepting rent from the tenant after the breach has arisen). Additionally, restrictions on forfeiture may exist where the tenant is subject to insolvency or bankruptcy proceedings or arrangements. The detail of such restrictions is beyond the scope of this book.

34.8.3.1 Forfeiture for non-payment of rent

Where the breach is a failure to pay rent, before attempting to forfeit the lease the landlord's solicitor should consider whether a formal demand for rent needs to be served on the tenant. Such a formal demand will be required unless the forfeiture clause dispenses with the need for it: most leases of commercial property will dispense with the need for a formal demand and the forfeiture clause should therefore be checked to ascertain the position. If no formal demand is required, the landlord can proceed to forfeit the lease either by peaceable re-entry or by court order. The tenant may claim relief against forfeiture and the court may grant relief on any terms it sees fit. See **Figure 34.1** below.

Figure 34.1 Forfeiture by landlord for breach of tenant's covenant in lease: non-payment of rent

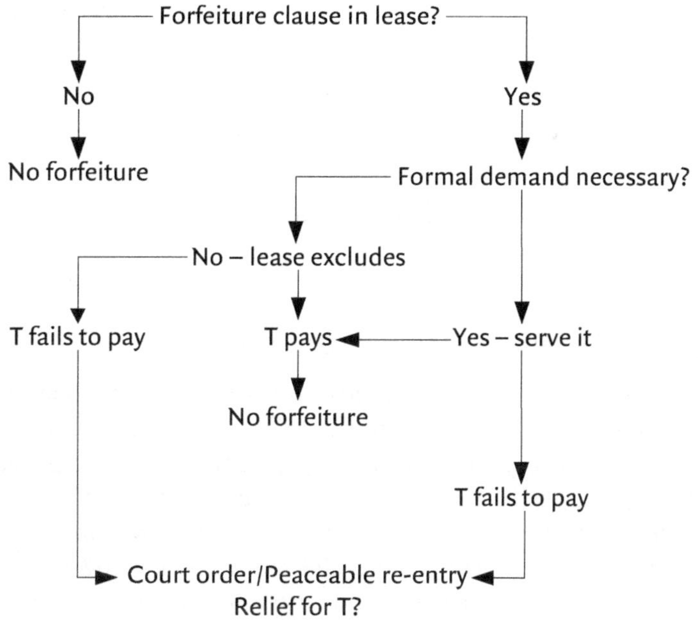

34.8.3.2 Forfeiture for breach of other covenants

Where the breach is something other than non-payment of rent, the landlord must first serve a notice on the tenant under s 146 of the LPA 1925, which:

(a) specifies the breach;

(b) requires it to be remedied if capable of remedy; and

(c) requires compensation if desired.

The tenant must be allowed a reasonable time within which to remedy the breach, and if they do so there can be no forfeiture and the landlord's costs are not recoverable unless the lease provides otherwise (which it generally does). If the tenant does not remedy the breach, the landlord may forfeit the lease by applying to the court for a possession order.

The tenant may apply to the court for relief against forfeiture and the court may grant such relief as it thinks fit (LPA 1925, s 146).

Note that additional requirements may apply where the landlord is seeking to forfeit for breach of a repairing covenant (see **34.8.5**). See **Figure 34.2** below.

Note further that the law is unclear as to whether a s 146 notice needs to be served for non-payment of sums such as service charge and insurance rent, where those sums are reserved as rent in the lease (see the contradictory Court of Appeal judgments in *Freeholders of 69 Marina, St Leonards-on-Sea v Oram and another* [2011] EWCA Civ 1258 and *Escalus Properties v Robinson, Escalus Properties v Dennis, Escalus Properties v Cooper-Smith and another, Sinclair Gardens Investments (Kensington) Ltd v Walsh* [1996] QB 231).

Figure 34.2 Forfeiture by landlord for breach of tenant's covenant in lease: non-rent covenant

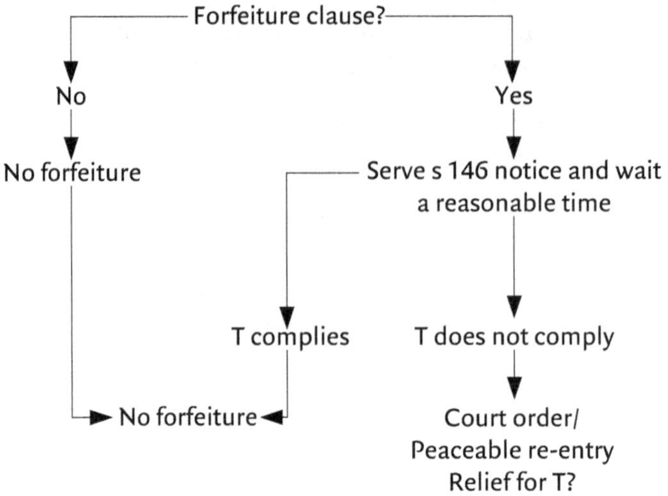

34.8.4 Commercial rent arrears recovery procedure

The common law remedy of distress or distraint allowed a landlord to enter the premises of a tenant and seize goods equal to the value of unpaid rent, generally without a court order or even notice to the tenant. The remedy was much criticised by tenants and legal commentators alike, who suggested it was in breach of the Human Rights Act 1998. The Tribunals, Courts and Enforcement Act 2007 (TCEA 2007) set out provisions for the abolition of distress and its replacement with a new commercial rent arrears recovery (CRAR) procedure. After a long delay, these provisions finally come into force on 6 April 2014.

Under the CRAR procedure, landlords will still have the power to enter the premises and remove and sell goods owned by the defaulting tenant, but subject to the following restrictions:

(a) CRAR applies to leases of commercial premises only. If any part of the premises is let or occupied as a dwelling (except where that occurs in breach of a term of the lease), CRAR is not available. It also cannot be used where the lease is oral.

(b) CRAR is only available in relation to 'pure' rent arrears (ie rent paid for possession and use of the premises), and at least 7 days' rent must be outstanding. Arrears of other payments (such as service charge and insurance rent) will not be recoverable using the CRAR procedure even if they are reserved as rent in the lease.

(c) The landlord will be required to serve an enforcement notice on the defaulting tenant, giving the tenant at least 7 days' clear notice (excluding Sundays and bank holidays) of its intention to enter the premises. On the expiry of that notice, only an enforcement agent will be able to enter the premises to remove goods. Part 2 of the Taking Control of Goods Regulations 2013 ('the Regulations') sets out the information that the enforcement notice must contain and how it must be given. A landlord may apply to court for an order that the notice period be shortened if it is likely that goods will be moved to avoid removal by the enforcement agent. Under s 78 of the TCEA 2007, a tenant who receives an enforcement notice may apply to the court for an order that the notice be set aside, or that no further steps be taken under the CRAR procedure without a further court order.

(d) Certain goods are exempt from CRAR and cannot be seized. These are set out in reg 4 of the Regulations and include items or equipment up to the value of £1,350 necessary for the tenant's business (such as computers, telephones and vehicles).

(e) The enforcement agent must give the tenant at least 7 days' clear notice of any sale of the seized goods (unless the goods would become unsaleable or substantially reduced in value as a result of the delay). The seized goods must be sold at a public auction.

(f) Any provision in a lease (or other contract) that purports to allow seizure of goods (outside of the CRAR procedure) for non-payment of rent will be void.

The Regulations also contain provisions dealing with the times at which goods can be seized, the manner of entry to the premises and the manner in which the goods can be secured and sold.

34.8.5 Additional rules for breach of a tenant's repairing covenant

34.8.5.1 Forfeiture

If a lease was originally granted for a term of seven years or more and has at least three years unexpired, the provisions of the Leasehold Property (Repairs) Act 1938 (LP(R)A 1938) apply. These provide that when a landlord serves a notice under s 146 of the LPA 1925 prior to forfeiture, it must include a statement of the tenant's right to serve a counter-notice within 28 days. If the tenant does so, the landlord may proceed with the claim (ie forfeiture) only if they get the leave of the court. Such leave will be granted only in specified circumstances, eg that the value of the reversion has been substantially diminished. See **Figure 34.3** following.

Figure 34.3 Forfeiture by landlord for breach of tenant's covenant in lease: repair covenant

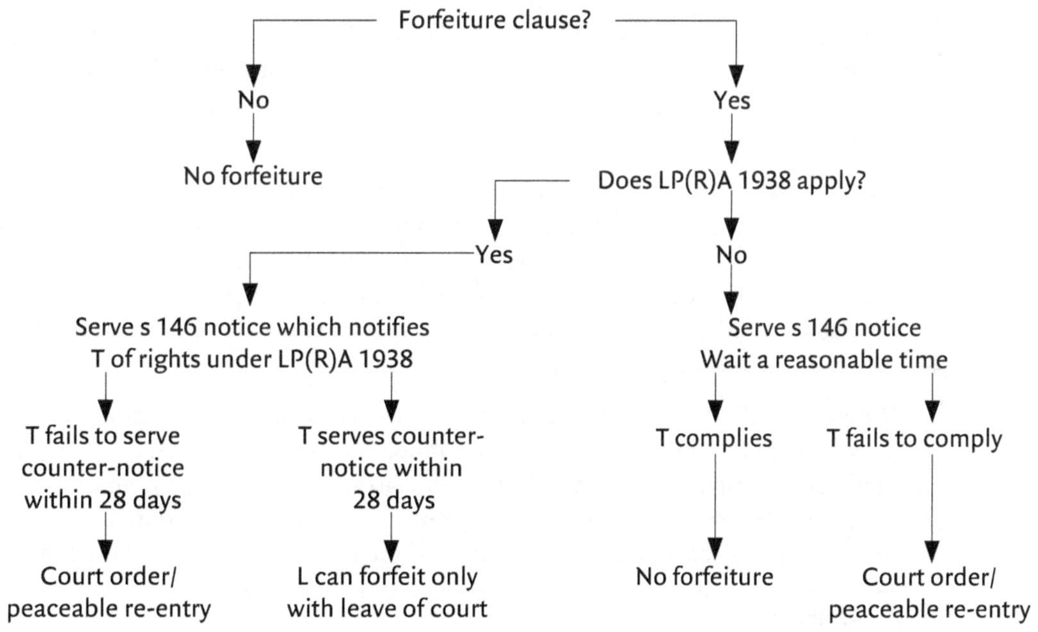

34.8.5.2 Damages

Under s 18 of the LTA 1927, damages for the breach of a tenant's repairing covenant are capped at the reduction in the value of the landlord's reversion caused by the breach. If the term lease has a significant time to run, the reduction in the value of the landlord's interest may be slight and may be considerably lower than the cost of doing the repairs. As a result it is not often worthwhile pursuing a damages claim during the lease term.

In addition, if the provisions of the LP(R)A 1938 (see **34.8.5.1**) apply to the lease, the landlord must serve a s 146 notice on the tenant (even though the landlord is not seeking to forfeit), and the notice must again include a statement of the tenant's right to serve a counter-notice within 28 days. If the tenant serves such notice, as with forfeiture, the landlord can proceed with their claim only with the leave of the court. If the provisions of the LP(R)A 1938 do not apply, there is no requirement to serve a s 146 notice in order to claim damages.

It should be noted that claims for damages for breach of repair on the expiry of the lease term ('terminal dilapidations') are subject to further statutory and common law provisions. These are beyond the scope of this book and a specialist text should be consulted for further detail.

34.8.5.3 Self-help

The limitations considered above can be circumvented if the lease contains a properly drafted 'self-help' clause. Such a clause allows the landlord to enter the premises and carry out repairs if the tenant has failed to comply with its obligations. The lease clause will then provide that the tenant should pay to the landlord the landlord's costs incurred in effecting the repairs. The case of *Jervis v Harris* [1996] Ch 195 confirmed that these costs are recoverable as a debt (although it is best to make this clear in the lease), not damages. The breach by the tenant that the landlord will be pursuing will be the tenant's failure to pay a debt due under the lease, not the tenant's failure to repair. Accordingly, the limitations and procedures imposed under LP(R)A 1938 and s 18 of the LTA 1927 can be avoided.

34.9 COMMONHOLD

In 2002 the Government introduced a new form of land ownership called 'commonhold', which was designed to overcome some of the disadvantages of leases in dispositions of units in interdependent premises, for example flats, office blocks and shopping centres. Each unit is held freehold, and the common parts are held by a Commonhold Association, which will be responsible for repairs, etc to the common parts. The Commonhold Association is a private limited company of which the unit owners will be members. A Commonhold Community Statement sets out the obligations of each unit holder, including the obligation to pay a service charge. These obligations, whether positive or negative, are binding on successors in title.

As each flat or other unit is held freehold, the problem of leases being a wasting asset is avoided. Also, the fact that a company owned by the tenants owns the common parts may avoid the problem that can sometimes arise in blocks of flats, of landlords charging excessive service charges. Commonhold is available both for new developments and for existing developments. The conversion of existing blocks is possible, however, only at the request of the landlord and with the consent of all the tenants.

Notwithstanding these potential advantages, since its introduction, commonhold has not proved popular and very few commonhold schemes have been registered. One of the drawbacks is that the Commonhold Association cannot forfeit a unit where the owner is in breach of the provisions of the Commonhold Community Statement, making it difficult to recover service charges. In consequence, some lenders will not lend on commonhold units.

SUMMARY

- Where a property forms part of a larger building, it is more likely to be let on a lease than sold freehold. The use of leases makes it easier to split repair and maintenance liabilities between the various owners in a way that will be enforceable against their successors in title.
- Most commercial properties are occupied under leases. This is because the occupier can choose the length of the term and spread the occupation costs over the term, rather than pay a large capital sum up front.
- A lease is *granted* when a landlord first creates the lease in favour of a tenant. The lease is *assigned* when the tenant transfers the lease to another tenant. A tenant may also dispose of all or part of the property by creating a *sub-lease*, rather than assigning their own lease.
- Most leases are legal (rather than equitable) and for a fixed term (rather than periodic).
- A legal lease for more than seven years must be registered with its own separate title.

- A tenant continues to be bound by the covenants in the lease even after the lease has been assigned to another tenant if the lease was granted before 1 January 1996, or (in the case of commercial leases only) if it was granted after that date and they entered into an AGA with the landlord at the time of the assignment. Otherwise, a tenant is released from liability once the assignment has taken place.
- A landlord has a number of remedies against a tenant who is in breach of the lease, but the nature of the remedies available and the procedures that must be followed will vary according to the type of covenant that has been breached.

CHAPTER 35

THE GRANT OF A LEASE

LEARNING OUTCOMES

After reading this chapter you will be able to:

- outline the steps involved in granting a long residential lease or a lease of commercial property
- understand why it is important for a tenant of a lease granted for more than seven years to be able to investigate the landlord's title
- arrange for the lease and counterpart to be executed and handed over by the relevant parties at completion
- calculate the advance rent payable by the tenant on completion
- deal with the payment of SDLT and (if necessary) register the lease following completion.

35.1 INTRODUCTION

This chapter considers the procedure for the grant of a lease. This will differ depending on whether the lease being granted is a short or residential letting or a commercial property lease.

35.1.1 Short residential lettings

The procedure set out in this chapter would not usually apply to the grant of a short residential tenancy. This is because the grant of such a tenancy is usually relatively informal: it often consists of the landlord taking references and presenting the tenancy to the tenant for signature on a 'take it or leave it' basis.

Short residential lettings are governed by statute (in England by the Housing Act 1988 and in Wales by the Renting Homes (Wales) Act 2016), the detail of which is outside the scope of the book.

Landlords of such tenancies should, however, be aware of the application of the Immigration Act 2014 (IA 2014) to certain residential leases of under seven years. This requires the landlord to check the status of prospective tenants to ascertain whether they have the right to occupy the premises and to ensure that the right to occupy does not lapse. The detail of the IA

2014 is outside the scope of this book. Landlords should also be aware of the Tenant Fees Act 2019 which bans most letting fees and caps tenancy deposits paid by tenants in the private rented sector in England on or after 1 June 2019.

35.1.2 The grant of a long residential lease

The conveyancing procedure employed in this type of transaction is similar to that used on a freehold sale and purchase. This chapter deals only with those matters where the procedure for the grant of a lease differs from that used in a freehold transaction.

The landlord grants the lease to the tenant on terms stipulated by the landlord. The draft lease will be annexed to the draft contract and is then open to negotiation with the tenant. The Protocol is expressed to apply to both freehold and leasehold transactions.

35.1.3 The grant of a lease of commercial property

The procedure on the grant of a commercial lease will follow a similar pattern to the above. However, it is less usual for a contract to be drawn up. Instead, the parties will agree the terms of the lease and then proceed directly to grant. As this is a commercial situation, the terms of the lease are often the subject of detailed negotiation between the prospective landlord and tenant.

Where a commercial lease is for a comparatively short term, a prospective tenant may choose not to carry out some of the more usual steps, such as investigating title. This is a commercial decision for the client. This chapter will work on the basis that the client does not wish to omit any of these steps.

35.2 TAKING INSTRUCTIONS FROM THE LANDLORD

Much of the information required by the landlord's solicitor from their client will be similar to that required from the seller in the case of a freehold transaction, which is discussed in **Chapter 8**. In addition, instructions need to be obtained from the client (and advice given to them) relating to such matters as the length of the term to be granted, the rent to be charged to the tenant, who is to be responsible for the repair and insurance of the property, and various other matters which will need to be dealt with in the lease itself. These matters are considered in **Chapter 37**.

Before drafting the lease, the landlord's solicitor should investigate their own client's title. This needs to be done for a number of reasons. First, to ensure that the client is entitled to grant the lease and to anticipate any problems with the title, such as covenants which prevent the use proposed under the lease. In addition, the landlord's solicitor will need to investigate title in order to be able to draft the contract (if there is one). Investigation is done in exactly the same way as if the solicitor was acting for a seller in a freehold transaction (see **Chapters 15** and **16**).

Particular consideration needs to be given to any mortgage over the property. Where the property is subject to an existing mortgage, the mortgage will frequently contain a provision which prohibits or restricts the borrower/landlord's ability to grant a lease of the property. In such a case, the lender must be contacted and its permission to grant the lease obtained before the matter proceeds.

35.3 DRAFTING THE LEASE

The landlord's solicitor will draft the lease. This will then be sent to the prospective tenant's solicitor for negotiation and approval. Some of the most usual terms to be included in a lease are examined in **Chapter 37**.

35.4 DRAFTING THE CONTRACT

Where a contract for the grant of the lease is to be entered into, this will also need to be drafted. It is drafted by the landlord's solicitor in the same way that the seller's solicitor will draft the contract in the case of the sale of a freehold. The particulars of sale must state that the property is leasehold and give details of the term to be vested in the tenant. Incumbrances affecting the freehold title must be disclosed (as these will affect the tenant in the same way as they would affect a buyer of the freehold) and the contract should provide for an indemnity to be given in the lease in respect of future breaches of any covenants affecting the title. In other respects, the contract will be similar to that prepared on a freehold transaction.

Except where the lease is to be for a term not exceeding three years, taking effect in possession and with no premium payable for its grant, the contract for the lease must satisfy s 2 of the Law of Property (Miscellaneous Provisions) Act 1989.

Standard Condition 8.2 (SCPC 11.2.3) provides for the lease to be in the form annexed to the draft contract, and for the landlord to engross the lease and supply the tenant with the engrossment at least five working days before the completion date.

35.5 DEDUCING TITLE

35.5.1 Leases

Ideally, a tenant will want the landlord to deduce title to its freehold interest. This is particularly important where a premium is to be paid for the grant of the lease, where the property is being offered as security for a loan or where a tenant is paying a significant rent for the premises. The absence of the freehold title will usually prevent the tenant and their successors from obtaining an absolute leasehold title on the subsequent registration of the lease unless the freehold is already registered.

At common law, the tenant is not entitled to call for deduction of the freehold title on the grant of a lease (LPA 1925, s 44(2)). This rule has been disapplied to grants of leases for more than seven years by Sch 11 to the LRA 2002. Further, where the lease will exceed seven years, SC 8.2.4 (SCPC 11.2.4) requires the landlord to deduce such title as would enable the tenant to obtain registration with an absolute title at Land Registry. The intending tenant will thus be able to insist on the deduction of the freehold title, and so should obtain registration with absolute leasehold title.

35.5.2 Sub-leases

At common law, in the case of the grant of a sub-lease out of an unregistered head-lease, the sub-tenant is entitled to call for the head-lease out of which the sub-lease is to be derived and all subsequent assignments under which the lease has been held for the last 15 years. However, s 44 of the LPA 1925 provides that the sub-tenant is not entitled to call for production of the freehold title.

This rule is again unsatisfactory where a premium is to be paid on the grant, where the sub-lease is to be used as security or where the tenant is paying a significant amount by way of rent. However, this rule has also been disapplied by Sch 11 to the LRA 2002 in respect of the grant of a sub-lease for more than seven years. The prospective tenant will thus be able to insist on the production of title to the head-lease and the freehold. Standard Condition 8.2.4 (SCPC 11.2.4) also applies to the grant of a sub-lease.

This requirement to provide details of the freehold title, whether under SC 8.2.4 (SCPC 11.2.4) or the LRA 2002, may cause problems to a head-tenant wanting to grant the sub-lease, when they did not call for the deduction of the freehold title when they took the head-lease. The head-tenant may not be able to comply, and so will need to exclude this requirement by a special condition in the contract.

The Sch 11 amendments to s 44 will also apply if the title to the head-lease is registered with its own title. If the head-lease is registered with absolute title, there will be no need to see the title to the freehold.

In any event, if the title to the reversion is registered, the Open Register rules will always allow the prospective tenant to inspect that reversion.

35.6 THE PRE-CONTRACT PACKAGE

35.6.1 General principles

As a matter of general principle, the landlord's solicitor should provide the tenant's solicitor with at least the following documents:

(a) draft contract (if applicable);
(b) draft lease;
(c) evidence of the freehold title;
(d) copies of any relevant planning consents; and
(e) evidence of the lender's consent to the grant of the lease (where relevant).

Where the Protocol is used, the landlord's solicitor will adopt the terms of that scheme in the same way as would be the case for the sale of freehold land. This will include providing the tenant's solicitor with a PIF and an F&C as part of the pre-contract package.

In addition to the above, in the case of the grant of a flat lease where there is going to be a management company providing the services, the company will need incorporating and share certificates (if relevant) and company documents will need to be prepared before the completion of the sale of the first flat. Details of the company should be included in the pre-contract package.

35.6.2 Energy Performance Certificates and Minimum Energy Efficiency Standards

From 1 October 2008, subject to certain limited exceptions (for example temporary buildings which are intended to be used for no more than two years), EPCs are required whenever a building is constructed, sold or rented out. The general rule is that an EPC is valid for 10 years unless a new EPC is issued to replace it. Energy Performance Certificates are discussed further at **8.1**. From April 2018, landlords of certain domestic or non-domestic buildings will not be able to grant new tenancies (or renew existing ones) unless the building being let has an EPC rating of at least E (see **8.1.3**).

35.7 ACTING FOR THE TENANT

The information required by the tenant's solicitor from their client will be similar to that required in a freehold purchase transaction (see **Chapter 8**).

35.7.1 The draft contract and draft lease

Where the parties are to enter into a contract before grant, the terms of the contract must be agreed before exchange, as is the case in the context of the sale of freehold land. The contract will normally require the tenant to accept the draft lease in the form annexed to the contract (see, eg, SC 8.2.3 or SCPC 11.2.3), and therefore the terms of the lease must also be settled so that the agreed version can be annexed to the contract ready for exchange. If the parties intend to proceed straight to the grant of the lease (as is often the case with leases of commercial property), the terms of the lease need to be agreed prior to grant.

In either case, even where the lease appears to contain 'usual' clauses appropriate to the particular transaction in hand, the document must be carefully examined by the tenant's solicitor to ensure that it contains provisions which are adequate to protect their client's interests and no onerous clauses.

The particular points to look out for when checking the draft lease are considered in **Chapter 37**.

35.7.2 Searches

The tenant's solicitor will want to undertake the same searches and enquiries (both before and after exchange) as if the tenant were buying the freehold (see **Chapters 17** and **28**). As with a freehold transaction, some of these searches may be undertaken by the landlord's solicitor and their results supplied to the tenant's solicitor as part of the pre-contract package.

As has been discussed, where a lease is for a shorter term, it is less usual for searches and enquiries to be made, since the low risk attached to these lettings does not justify the expense of making the searches.

35.7.3 Lender's requirements

Where the tenant is acquiring the lease with the aid of a mortgage, the tenant's lender's requirements, contained in the instructions given to the solicitors acting for the lender, must be observed.

The *Lenders' Handbook* requires compliance with the following conditions:

(a) the consent of the landlord's lender has been obtained to the transaction (where relevant);

(b) the length of the term to be granted provides adequate security for the loan (terms of less than 60 years are often unacceptable for mortgage purposes in the case of residential leases);

(c) the lease contains adequate insurance provisions relating both to the premises themselves and (where relevant) to common parts of the building, and the insurance provisions coincide with the lender's own requirements for insurance;

(d) title to the freehold reversion is deduced, enabling the lease itself to be registered with an absolute title at Land Registry;

(e) the lease contains proper repairing covenants in respect both of the property itself and (where relevant) the common parts of the building;

(f) in the case of residential leases, that there is no provision for forfeiture on the insolvency of the tenant.

35.7.4 Advising the client

The tenant's obligations under the lease, which are often complex and extensive, should be explained clearly to them. In particular, the tenant should be warned of the danger of losing the lease through forfeiture for breach of covenant.

35.8 ENGROSSMENT AND EXECUTION OF THE LEASE

The lease is normally prepared in two identical parts, the lease and counterpart. The lease is executed by the landlord and the counterpart by the tenant. On completion, these are exchanged so that each party has a copy of the lease signed by the other in case of subsequent dispute.

As with the transfer deed in the case of the sale of freehold land, a top copy (or engrossment) of the lease and counterpart will need to be made and it is these that the parties will sign. Standard Condition 8.2.5 (SCPC 11.2.5) provides that it is for the landlord's solicitor to prepare the engrossments. If the landlord requires the tenant to pay a fee for the preparation of the engrossment, this must be dealt with by special condition in the contract. The landlord will sign the lease itself in readiness for completion, and the counterpart should be sent to the tenant's solicitor at least five working days before contractual completion date (SC 8.2.5 and

SCPC 11.2.5) for execution by the tenant. The requirements for execution of a deed are dealt with in **27.4**.

35.9 APPORTIONMENT OF RENT

Most leases provide that rent is payable in advance, not in arrears. Unless completion takes place on a day when rent under the lease falls due, a proportionate amount of rent calculated from the date of completion until the next rent payment day will be payable by the tenant on completion. The apportionment should be shown on the completion statement supplied by the landlord. Neither set of standard conditions provides for the apportionment of rent on completion of the grant of a lease, therefore an express special condition is required to deal with this matter, unless, as is often the case, it is dealt with in the lease itself.

35.10 COMPLETION

On completion, in addition to or in substitution for the matters relevant to a freehold transaction, the landlord will receive:

(a) the counterpart lease executed by the tenant;

(b) any premium payable for the grant (less any deposit paid on exchange of contracts);

(c) an apportioned sum representing rent payable in advance under the lease (see **35.9**).

The landlord should give to the tenant:

(a) the lease executed by them;

(b) if not already done, properly marked or certified copies of the freehold title deeds (unregistered land only);

(c) where relevant and if not already done, a certified copy of the consent of the landlord's lender to the transaction.

In the case of a flat lease where a management company is to provide the services, the tenant's share certificate in the company (or an undertaking to provide it) will be handed over on completion. Frequently, however, the company will be limited by guarantee, not shares, so the flat buyer will have been required to become a member of the company, but there will be no share certificate to hand over.

35.11 AFTER COMPLETION

35.11.1 Registration

35.11.1.1 Short leases

A legal lease for seven years or less is not capable of being registered with its own title at Land Registry but will take effect as an overriding interest under the LRA 2002, whether or not the tenant is in actual occupation of the land. It is possible voluntarily to note leases of over three years in length.

In unregistered land, a legal lease is binding on all subsequent owners of the land, irrespective of notice.

35.11.1.2 Registrable leases

The grant of a lease for a term which exceeds seven years is registrable in its own right after completion, irrespective of whether the freehold title is itself registered. It will be registered with its own separate title and title number, and will also be noted against the landlord's title (see **35.11.2**).

35.11.2 The tenant

35.11.2.1 Stamp duty land tax

A land transaction return must be submitted to HMRC on the grant of a lease in the usual way. In the case of the grant of a lease, SDLT is potentially chargeable both on any capital sum being paid (referred to on the grant of a lease as a 'premium') and on the amount of the rent. In terms of SDLT on any rental element, a complex formula is used to identify the Net Present Value ('NPV') of the rent, and SDLT is then calculated using this figure. Calculating the NPV consists of working out how much rent is payable in total over the term of the lease and then discounting rental payments to be made in future years by 3.5% per annum.

Given the complexity of calculating SDLT on the grant of a lease, an online calculator is provided on HMRC's website, but the following is a summary of the position:

(a) In the case of *residential property*, the SDLT payable on any premium is calculated on the same basis as for the consideration on the sale of freehold land (see **6.3.2**). As regards rent, SDLT is charged at 1% on any element of the NPV that exceeds £125,000. It will be comparatively unusual for SDLT to be due on the rent in respect of a residential lease. By way of example, in the case of a 99-year lease, the annual rent would have to be around £4,500, which is rare.

(b) In the case of *non-residential property*, the SDLT payable on any premium is calculated on the same basis as for the consideration on the sale of freehold land (see **6.3.2.2**). As regards rent, SDLT is chargeable on the NPV as follows:

Net present value of rent	SDLT rate
£0 to £150,000	Zero
The portion from £150,001 to £5,000,000	1%
The portion above £5,000,000	2%

35.11.2.2 Registration of the lease

Where applicable, the lease must be registered at Land Registry within the relevant priority period or, on first registration, within two months of completion of the grant of the lease. If the freehold is unregistered, the tenant's application is for first registration. If the freehold is itself registered, the tenant's application is for registration of a dealing. Where the landlord's title is registered, the lease will be noted against the reversionary title.

35.11.2.3 Notice to landlord

Where the tenant is, as usual, obliged by the lease to give notice of dealings to the landlord, this covenant may (depending on its wording) include the obligation to give notice of a mortgage created by the tenant. In any event, para 5.13.13 of the *Lender's Handbook* requires notice of a mortgage to be served on the landlord and the management company (if any). Notice should be given by sending two copies of the notice, together with a cheque for the appropriate fee, to the landlord's solicitor or other person named in the covenant. The landlord should be asked to sign one copy of the notice and to return it to the tenant, so that the receipted notice may be kept with the tenant's title deeds as evidence of compliance with this requirement.

35.11.3 The landlord

After completion, the landlord may receive notice in duplicate from the tenant, in accordance with the tenant's covenant in the lease, of the tenant's mortgage of the property. One copy of the notice should be placed with the landlord's title deeds, the other should be receipted on behalf of the landlord and returned to the tenant's solicitor.

SUMMARY

- The steps involved in granting a long residential lease or a lease of commercial property are very similar to those involved in buying a freehold property.
- The landlord's solicitor must check whether the landlord's mortgage permits the grant of a lease.
- Where the lease is for more than seven years, the tenant is entitled to insist on the seller deducing the freehold (or superior leasehold) title. If the landlord does not do so, the tenant will be unable to obtain absolute leasehold title on the registration of their lease.
- Where the landlord's title is registered, the tenant will always be able to deduce the landlord's title.
- The landlord's solicitor will also have to draft the lease. Where the parties intend to enter into a contract, the terms of the lease are settled before exchange so that the agreed form of lease may be attached to the contract.
- The tenant's solicitor will have to report to the client (and any lender) on the agreed terms of the lease.
- The lease is prepared in two identical parts. The *lease* is executed by the landlord and given to the tenant; the *counterpart* is executed by the tenant and given to the landlord.
- On completion, the tenant will pay the rent due in advance for the period from the completion date to the next rent payment day under the lease.
- In all cases, a land transaction return must be submitted to HMRC following completion. Stamp duty land tax is payable on any premium paid for the grant of the lease and on the rent reserved by the lease.
- A lease for over seven years must be registered with its own separate title, regardless of whether the landlord's title is registered. A lease for seven years or less but more than three years may be noted voluntarily on the landlord's registered title. A lease for three years or less cannot be noted on the landlord's registered title.
- The landlord should be given notice if the tenant has taken the lease with the aid of a mortgage.

CHAPTER 36

The Assignment of a Lease

LEARNING OUTCOMES

After reading this chapter you will be able to:

- outline the steps involved in assigning a long residential lease or a lease of commercial property
- check whether the landlord's consent is required for the assignment and, if so, advise on the obligations of the seller/tenant and the rights of the landlord in relation to the obtaining of that consent
- advise on the terms of the contract that govern the time by which the landlord's consent must be obtained
- on behalf of a seller tenant, modify the implied covenants for title to preserve the principle of *caveat emptor* and obtain an indemnity from the buyer against the seller's continuing liability for breach of the tenant's covenants in the lease after the assignment has taken place
- apportion the rent and other outgoings at completion
- if necessary, deal with the payment of SDLT and register the assignment of the lease following completion.

36.1 INTRODUCTION

An assignment is the transfer of an existing lease by the tenant (the 'assignor' or 'seller') to a third party (the 'assignee' or 'buyer'). It will arise chiefly in the following two contexts:

(a) *Residential.* Assignment of short-term residential lettings is usually prohibited in the lease. The procedure considered in this chapter would not therefore apply to such transactions. Instead, in the residential context, assignment will take place in the case of a long lease of a house or flat, which, as has been seen, will have a capital value which translates into a purchase price on the market. The house or flat will be sold by a seller to a buyer for this price in the same way as a freehold property is also sold for its price.

(b) *Commercial.* Leases of commercial premises are usually capable of assignment. In the commercial context, however, as the tenant will be paying the market rent for the property, the lease is unlikely to have any capital value. In such a case, therefore, no 'purchase price' will be paid by the assignee to the assignor on the assignment (or if, unusually, one is payable, it will usually be for a comparatively small sum). Assignment is usually only allowed subject to the fulfilment of specified conditions, the detail of which will be considered later in this chapter.

For the sake of clarity, in the remainder of this chapter, the term 'seller' is used to denote the assignor and 'buyer' to denote the assignee, whether or not any consideration is actually being paid on the assignment.

It is important to understand the precise nature of the transaction into which the seller and buyer are entering. In the same way that a seller of freehold land is selling the freehold that they own, in the case of an assignment of a lease, the seller is selling their lease (or however much of the term granted by it now remains). The buyer will be acquiring that unexpired term together with the benefits, but subject to the burdens, that go with that lease. The terms of the lease are not open to negotiation by the buyer, because the lease is already in existence and the buyer must take it or leave it as it stands. The only way in which the buyer can obtain an alteration to the lease terms is by negotiating a deed of variation of the lease with the landlord.

The procedure on an assignment is similar to that used in a sale and purchase of freehold land. This chapter deals only with those areas which differ from a freehold transaction.

36.2 PRE-CONTRACT MATTERS: THE SELLER'S SOLICITOR

On taking instructions, the information required by the seller's solicitor will be similar to that needed in a freehold transaction (see **Chapter 8**), with the addition of details of the lease to be sold.

The seller's solicitor should investigate title in the same way as for the sale of a freehold. The superior freehold title should be checked as part of this process, as it should be remembered that any covenants or easements affecting the freehold will also bind the leasehold interest. Any potential problems should be identified and all relevant incumbrances will need to be disclosed in the contract.

Investigation of title should include checking the terms of the lease being assigned to anticipate any problems that may arise with the lease itself. Of particular importance is the question of whether the landlord's consent to the transaction will be required (see **37.3.13**). The length of the residue of the term should also be checked. Where the buyer is buying with the aid of a mortgage (as will usually be the case with the assignment of a long residential lease), their lender will usually require that a minimum stated length of the term remains unexpired at the date of acquisition of the buyer's interest in order to provide adequate security for the loan. A lease which has only a short length of its original term left to run may, unless the term is extended, be difficult to sell. Certain tenants may have the right to insist on an extension, but this is beyond the scope of this book.

Once title has been investigated, the seller's solicitor should be in a position to draft the contract for submission to the buyer's solicitor for amendment or approval.

36.3 THE PRE-CONTRACT PACKAGE

36.3.1 General principles

As a matter of general principle, the seller's solicitor should provide the buyer's solicitor with at least the following documents:

(a) draft contract;

(b) copy lease;

(c) evidence of title (see **36.6**);

(d) any licence permitting assignment to the current and previous tenants;

(e) the insurance policy relating to the property and receipt for the last premium due;

(f) receipts for the last payments of rent and service charge on the property; and
(g) where there is a management company providing services, details of that company.

Where the Protocol is used, the seller's solicitor will adopt the terms of that scheme in the same way as would be the case for the sale of freehold land. This will include providing the buyer with a PIF and an F&C as part of the pre-contract package.

36.3.2 Energy Performance Certificates

As from 1 October 2008, subject to certain limited exceptions (for example temporary buildings which are intended to be used for no more than two years), EPCs are required whenever a building is constructed, sold or rented out. They are therefore required in most commercial and residential sales, including assignments. The general rule is that an EPC is valid for 10 years unless a new EPC is issued to replace it. Energy Performance Certificates are discussed further at **8.1**.

36.4 PRE-CONTRACT MATTERS: THE BUYER'S SOLICITOR

The steps carried out by the buyer's solicitor on assignment of lease are, like those undertaken by the seller's solicitor, similar to those taken in the case of the sale of freehold land. The buyer's solicitor will need to investigate title and consider the terms of the draft contract supplied to them. The seller's solicitor will have supplied a copy of the lease, and the buyer's solicitor should check this carefully and identify and, if necessary, deal with any problems revealed. They should advise their client about their responsibility under the various covenants in the lease. The terms of the lease should be checked to ensure that they will be acceptable to the buyer's lender (see **Chapter 37**).

The buyer's solicitor should make the same searches, and for the same reasons, as on a purchase of a freehold (see **Chapter 17**). It may be the case, in the context of a commercial lease where the lease has only a short period left unexpired, that the buyer may choose not to carry out some or all searches, as the risk does not justify the cost involved.

36.5 LANDLORD'S CONSENT

36.5.1 General

Commercial leases usually provide for the landlord's consent to be obtained before any assignment can take place. The need for the landlord's consent is not usual in long residential leases, except, perhaps, in the last few years of the term, or in the case of high-value properties. In both cases, where consent is required, this must be obtained and will, in all likelihood, need both the seller's and the buyer's involvement in order to obtain it. Where the landlord's consent is required, it is usually embodied in a formal licence (so consent to assign would be embodied in a 'licence to assign').

Covenants controlling the tenant's freedom to assign usually also contain controls on other forms of dealing (or 'alienation') such as sub-letting or charging the property. This chapter concentrates on controls on assignment.

36.5.2 References

Where the lease requires the seller to obtain the landlord's consent to the assignment, the landlord will want to take up references on the prospective buyer to ensure that they are a solvent and trustworthy individual. The buyer should be asked to supply their solicitor with the names and addresses of potential referees so that this information may be passed on to the landlord's solicitor via the seller's solicitor as quickly as possible, in order to avoid any delay. References are commonly required from all or some of the following sources:

(a) a current landlord;
(b) the buyer's bankers;

(c) the buyer's employer;
(d) a professional person such as an accountant or solicitor;
(e) a person or company with whom the buyer regularly trades; and
(f) three years' audited accounts in the case of a company or self-employed person.

36.5.3 Surety

The landlord may also require the buyer to provide a surety (guarantor) to the lease as a condition of the grant of their consent. Further, on the assignment of a commercial lease, the landlord may require the seller to enter into an AGA to guarantee the performance of the tenant's covenants by the buyer (see **34.6**). The landlord may have inserted the need for an AGA in the lease as a pre-condition to giving consent (see **36.5.5**). In this case, the landlord can always insist on the seller entering into the AGA whether or not it is reasonable. In the absence of the provision in the lease, the landlord can insist on the AGA only if it is reasonable to do so.

Note that if the tenant had provided a surety when it took the lease, that surety cannot be required to guarantee the obligations of the incoming assignee in an AGA (*Good Harvest Partnership LLP v Centaur Services Ltd* [2010] WLR (D) 48). However, the tenant's surety may lawfully be required to guarantee the tenant's obligations in the AGA (*K/S Victoria Street v House of Fraser (Stores Management) Ltd* [2011] EWCA Civ 904). In other words, whilst a landlord cannot ask the outgoing tenant's surety to guarantee the assignee directly, the same result may be achieved by requiring the surety to act as a guarantor of the outgoing tenant's guarantee within the AGA.

36.5.4 Types of covenant – absolute covenants

If the covenant against alienation in the lease is absolute (eg, 'the tenant shall not assign or part with possession of the property'), any assignment (or other dealing depending on the wording of the restriction), although effective, will be a breach of covenant by the tenant and may lead to forfeiture of the lease. An absolute covenant is not subject to any statutory restrictions on its operation, except those imposed by the Equality Act 2010.

Where an absolute covenant exists, the tenant may ask the landlord's permission to grant a variation of the lease to permit assignment, but there is no obligation on the landlord to give consent, nor to give reasons for refusal. Absolute bars on assignment are never acceptable in long-term residential leases and would not be acceptable to a prospective lender. The landlord may waive the covenant and give consent to this transaction, but there is no guarantee that they would consent to any other disposition and so a buyer runs the risk that the lease would be unsaleable.

36.5.5 Types of covenant – qualified covenants

A qualified covenant permits the tenant to assign (or part with possession, as the case may be), provided that the seller tenant obtains the prior consent of the landlord to the dealing. Section 19 of the Landlord and Tenant Act 1927 adds to the covenant the non-excludable proviso that consent must not be withheld unreasonably by the landlord. If the landlord does refuse consent, the prospective buyer is unlikely to wish to proceed with the transaction, because they run the risk of the lease being forfeited against them.

The Landlord and Tenant Act 1988 provides that the landlord must, having been served with a written request for consent, give consent within a reasonable time unless it is reasonable to withhold consent. The landlord must serve written notice of their decision on the tenant within a reasonable time, stating what conditions (if any) are attached to the consent or, if consent is refused, stating the reasons for withholding the consent. Breach of the landlord's duty under the 1988 Act is actionable in tort as a breach of statutory duty, giving a remedy to the tenant in damages.

Tenants' solicitors should be aware, however, that the obligations under the 1988 Act will not be triggered unless the written application for consent has been correctly served on the landlord. In *EON UK plc v Gilesports Ltd* [2012] EWHC 2172 (Ch), the landlord's statutory duties under the 1988 Act were not triggered by an application for consent to assign made by the tenant via email. The lease contained requirements for service of notices on the landlord that did not allow for service by email. It was held irrelevant that the landlord had in fact received the application. In *No 1 West India Quay (Residential) Ltd v East Tower Apartments Ltd* [2016] EWHC 2438 (Ch), the High Court held that a tenant's request to assign a long residential underlease was not validly served as it had been sent to an address provided by the landlord in the sales pack, rather than to the landlord's registered office as specified in the notices clause in the lease. Tenants' solicitors must therefore ensure that they check and comply with the lease requirements for service of notices.

In leases of commercial property granted on or after 1 January 1996 the lease may provide for the circumstances in which the landlord would withhold consent to an assignment and any conditions subject to which such consent will be granted (Landlord and Tenant (Covenants) Act 1995). A landlord will not be withholding consent unreasonably if they insist on compliance with these conditions, so both buyer and seller should check them carefully and ensure that they can be complied with. See further **Chapter 37** as to the kind of conditions commonly imposed.

In an old commercial lease (ie, granted prior to 1 January 1996) it is common to find a requirement for the buyer to enter into a direct covenant with the landlord to comply with the covenants in the lease. This should be explained to the client, as it will mean that the buyer will remain liable on the covenants in the lease even after a subsequent disposition by them.

36.5.6 Demanding a premium for consent

Unless (unusually) the lease specifically allows the landlord to charge a premium for giving consent, the landlord may not require a premium to be paid by the tenant as a condition of the grant of consent.

36.5.7 Undertaking for landlord's costs

The landlord is entitled to ask the tenant to pay the landlord's solicitor's reasonable charges in connection with the preparation of the deed of consent (licence to assign). In *No 1 West India Quay (Residential) Ltd v East Tower Apartments Ltd* [2016] EWHC 2438 (Ch), the landlord of a long residential underlease was held to have unreasonably withheld consent because it had insisted on an undertaking for an unreasonable sum of £1,250 plus VAT. However, the landlord was entitled to costs of £350 plus VAT as specified in the lease, even though the tenant was free to assign without the consent. On the assignment of a commercial lease, it is usual for the landlord's solicitors to require an undertaking from the seller's solicitors for the payment of the costs, although it is not clear whether it is reasonable to insist on such an undertaking. The seller's solicitor should first seek their client's authority to give the undertaking, the undertaking should be limited to the reasonable costs incurred, and a cap on such costs could also be sought.

36.5.8 Standard Conditions of Sale

Standard Condition 8.3 requires the seller to apply for the landlord's consent at their own expense and to use all reasonable efforts to obtain such consent, the buyer providing all information and references reasonably required. Unless in breach of these obligations, either party may rescind the contract by notice if the consent has not been given three working days before completion date, or if, by that time, consent has been given subject to a condition to which the buyer reasonably objects. Although the existence of SC 8.3 allows contracts to be exchanged before the landlord's consent is obtained, it still gives rise to uncertainty as to whether the transaction is to proceed, as this will depend upon the consent being forthcoming.

In a transaction where timing of completion is important (eg, in the context of a residential transaction where there is often a dependent sale and purchase), it is safest not to exchange until the landlord's consent has been obtained. Otherwise this transaction may fall through when the landlord refuses consent, whereas the dependent transaction would still be binding.

36.5.9 Standard Commercial Property Conditions

The SCPC contain much more comprehensive provisions dealing with the situation where consent is needed from a landlord or superior landlord to an assignment or sub-letting. Standard Commercial Property Condition 11.3.3 requires the seller to enter into an AGA, if it is lawfully required. Standard Commercial Property Condition 11.3.5 further provides that if the landlord's consent has not been obtained by the completion date, completion is postponed until five working days after the seller notifies the buyer that consent has been given. The contract may not be rescinded until six months have passed since the original completion date (SCPC 11.3.6). Again, if timing of completion is important, it is safest not to exchange until the landlord's consent has been obtained.

36.5.10 Protocol for Applications for Consent to Assign or Sublet

Disputes over applications for landlord's consent to assign or sub-let are common and, in September 2014, Falcon Chambers and Hogan Lovells published a Protocol for Applications for Consent to Assign or Sublet (the Alienation Protocol) for use in commercial property transactions. The Protocol is free to use and available at www.propertyprotocols.co.uk. It is designed to improve communication between landlord and tenant, establish a workable timetable, avoid arguments over the information and documents that should form part of the application and, if a dispute arises, guide the parties towards alternative dispute resolution rather than the court.

36.6 TITLE

36.6.1 Lease registered with absolute title

Both sets of standard conditions (SC 4.1.1; SCPC 7.1.2) require the seller to provide the buyer with official copies of the register and title plan in the usual way. A copy of the lease must also be provided, and the buyer is then to be treated as entering into the contract knowing and fully accepting the lease terms (SC 8.1.2; SCPC 11.1.2). In any event, due to the Open Registry rules, the buyer can always inspect the seller's title. Since the title to the lease is guaranteed by Land Registry there is no need for the buyer to investigate the title to the freehold or superior leases.

36.6.2 Lease registered with good leasehold title

Both sets of standard conditions require the seller to provide the buyer with official copies of the register and title plan in the usual way. A copy of the lease must also be provided, and the buyer is then to be treated as entering into the contract knowing and fully accepting the lease terms. Registration with a good leasehold title provides no guarantee of the soundness of the title to the freehold reversion and thus, although not entitled under the general law to do so, the buyer should insist on deduction of the superior title. The provision for deduction of the reversionary title must be dealt with by special condition in the contract, because neither set of standard conditions deals with this point.

Without deduction of the reversionary title the lease may be unacceptable to the buyer and/or their lender (see para 5.6.2 of the *Lenders' Handbook* in **Appendix** 7). The reversionary title will be deduced by the appropriate method applicable to unregistered land (see **14.5**). The registers of title at Land Registry are open to public inspection, so that a buyer could make a search and obtain details of the reversionary title (assuming it is registered) if the seller was unable or unwilling to deduce it.

36.6.3 Unregistered lease

Under the general law contained in s 44 of the LPA 1925, the buyer is entitled to call for the lease or sub-lease which they are buying and all assignments under which that lease or sub-lease has been held during the last 15 years, but is not entitled to call for evidence of any superior title. Without deduction of the superior title, unless the reversion is already registered with absolute title, the buyer, on registration of the lease at Land Registry following completion, would obtain only a good leasehold title, which may be unacceptable to them and/or to the lender. Unless the contract contains a special condition requiring the seller to deduce the reversionary title, the buyer has no right under either the general law or the standard conditions to call for evidence of the reversionary title. Where title is deduced, the buyer will want to see deduction of the freehold title from a good root of title which was at least 15 years old at the date of the grant of the lease (see **14.5**).

36.7 THE TRANSFER DEED

In order to transfer legal title to an estate in land, it is necessary to do so by deed (LPA 1925, s 52(1)). This applies to the assignment of a lease as much as it does to the sale of a freehold. To distinguish between the two types of transaction, in the case of the assignment of a lease, the transfer deed is sometimes called a 'deed of assignment', but this document has the same effect and function as any other transfer deed.

In the case of the assignment of an existing registered lease, irrespective of how long it has left to run, the form prescribed under the Land Registration Rules 2003 (SI 2003/1417) for the transfer of a lease is the same as for the transfer of a freehold, namely a Form TR1. In the case of unregistered land, the assignment of a lease exceeding seven years in length will lead to compulsory first registration, and so Land Registry Form TR1 will normally be used. An alternative in this case is to use a deed of assignment similar in format to a conveyance of unregistered land. The deed of assignment format will always be used in the case of the assignment of a lease for seven years or less, as the assignment of such a lease will not trigger first registration.

It follows that, in most cases, Form TR1 will be used to transfer title. The drafting of the transfer deed was considered in **Chapter 27**, and the same points apply equally in the context of the assignment of a lease, but the following additional points should be noted.

36.7.1 Covenants for title

If a seller is in breach of a repairing covenant in the lease, the lack of repair could involve them in liability to the buyer after completion under the covenants for title which will be implied in the transfer deed (see **18.8.3**). This is because, where the seller sells with full or limited title guarantee, the covenants for title include a promise that the seller has complied with the tenant's covenants in the lease, including repair. However, the principle of *caveat emptor* (see **12.2**) makes it the buyer's responsibility to satisfy themselves as to the physical state of the property, and the seller should not be expected to make any promises in this respect.

Clearly, therefore, there is a conflict here between the promise implied by the covenants for title and *caveat emptor*. It is resolved by modifying the covenants for title to bring them into line with *caveat emptor* (see SC 3.2.2 and 4.6.3, and SCPC 4.2.2 and 7.6.4) by excluding references to repair.

This type of contractual condition must be reflected by an express modification of the implied covenants for title in the transfer deed itself. A suggested form of wording is as follows:

> The covenants set out in section 4 of the Law of Property (Miscellaneous Provisions) Act 1994 will not extend to any breach of the tenant's covenants in the lease relating to the physical state of the property.

Box 9 of Form TR1 contains space to insert this wording which could, alternatively, be inserted in box 11 (additional provisions).

36.7.2 Indemnity

In relation to the assignment of leases granted before 1 January 1996, an indemnity covenant from the buyer to the seller is implied except where, in unregistered land, value is not given by the buyer for the transaction (LPA 1925, s 77). In such a case, an express indemnity covenant will be inserted if required by the contract (see SC 4.6.4 and SCPC 7.6.5).

In relation to the assignment of leases granted on or after 1 January 1996, the seller will usually automatically be released for future liability on the assignment and so will not require indemnity. If, however, the seller is to remain liable (eg, under the terms of an AGA), an express indemnity covenant between the buyer and the seller should be included in the transfer deed. Again, SC 4.6.4 and SCPC 7.6.5 entitle the seller to insert an indemnity in such circumstances.

36.8 PREPARING FOR COMPLETION

36.8.1 The transfer deed

The transfer deed will be prepared by the buyer's solicitor. The form and contents of this document are discussed in **36.7**.

36.8.2 Pre-completion searches

36.8.2.1 Company search

The circumstances in which company searches should be carried out are set out at **28.8** and apply equally to leasehold transactions.

36.8.2.2 Title searches

Registered lease

An official search of the registers of the leasehold title should be carried out to check for any new entries and to gain a priority period within which to register the transfer (see **28.5**).

If the lease is registered with good leasehold title, additional searches against the freehold should be undertaken as follows:

(a) If the freehold title is registered, an official search against the freehold should be carried out to check for any new entries on the freehold that might affect the leasehold title.

(b) If the freehold is unregistered (and has been deduced to the buyer), a land charges department search against the estate owners of the unregistered freehold should be obtained. Again, this is to check for any incumbrances on the freehold that might also affect the leasehold interest.

Unregistered lease

A land charges search against the names of the estate owners of the leasehold title should be made (see **28.6**). If the freehold title has been deduced, additional searches will be necessary as follows:

(a) If the freehold title is also unregistered, the estate owners of the freehold title should be included in the land charges search application.

(b) If the freehold is registered, then an official search of the registered freehold should be undertaken to check for any new entries on the freehold that may affect the leasehold.

36.8.3 Landlord's consent

The landlord's solicitor will supply the engrossment (or 'top copy') of the licence, which must be by deed if it is to contain covenants. Where the buyer is to give direct covenants to the landlord, the licence is usually drawn up in two parts, the landlord executing the original licence which will be given to the seller on completion for onwards transmission to the buyer, the buyer executing the counterpart which will be given to the landlord on completion.

36.8.4 Apportionments

The seller will usually have paid rent in advance. Unless completion takes place on a day when rent and other outgoings become due under the lease, it will be necessary for these sums to be apportioned on completion, so that the buyer reimburses the seller for the period from completion until the next rent day. The seller should supply the buyer with a completion statement which shows the amounts due and explains how they have been calculated. Copies of the receipts or demands on which the apportionments are based should be supplied by the seller to the buyer with the completion statement, so that the buyer can check the apportioned sums. In many cases, it will not be possible to make an exact apportionment of outgoings such as service charges, since the figures required in order to make this calculation will not be available. In such a case, a provisional apportionment of the sum should be made on a 'best estimate' basis, in accordance with SC 6.3.5 (SCPC 9.3.5).

36.9 COMPLETION

The procedure on completion follows closely that in a freehold transaction (see **Chapter 30**). The buyer will pay the seller the balance of the purchase price (where one is to be paid) and any other sums due, including any apportionment as considered in **36.8.4** above.

36.9.1 Documents to be handed over by the seller

The seller will hand to the buyer such of the following documents as are relevant to the transaction in hand:

(a) the lease/sub-lease;

(b) the transfer deed (TR1 or deed of assignment, as appropriate);

(c) the landlord's licence to assign;

(d) marked abstract or other evidence of superior titles in accordance with the contract (lease not registered or not registered with absolute title);

(e) evidence of discharge of the seller's mortgage;

(f) copies of duplicate notices served by the seller and their predecessors on the landlord in accordance with a covenant in the lease requiring the landlord to be notified of any dispositions;

(g) insurance policy (or copy if insurance is effected by the landlord) and receipt (or copy) relating to the last premium due;

(h) receipts for rent and other outgoings (see **36.9.3**); and

(i) share certificate/stock transfer form for management company.

36.9.2 Items to be handed over by the buyer

The buyer should hand to the seller such of the following items as are appropriate to the transaction:

(a) money due in accordance with the completion statement;

(b) duly executed counterpart licence to assign; and

(c) a release of deposit.

36.9.3 Rent receipts

Section 45(2) of the LPA 1925 provides that, on production of the receipt for the last rent due under the lease or sub-lease which they are buying, a buyer must assume, unless the contrary appears, that the rent has been paid and the covenants performed under that and all superior leases. The buyer's solicitor should inspect the receipts on completion and also, where appropriate, receipts for payment of other apportioned outgoings. Standard Condition 6.6 (SCPC 9.6) requires a buyer to assume that the correct person gave the receipt.

36.10 AFTER COMPLETION

36.10.1 Stamp duty land tax

On the grant of a lease, SDLT is potentially payable both on any premium and on the rent. The position is different in the case of an assignment. In this case, SDLT is payable only on any purchase price charged by the seller, and is due at the same rates as for the sale of freehold land (see **6.3.2**). The same procedure for payment is also followed (see **31.7**). No SLDT will be charged on the rent.

36.10.2 Notice of assignment

Where, following completion, notice has to be given to a landlord of an assignment or mortgage, such notice should be given in duplicate accompanied by the appropriate fee set out in the lease. The *Lenders' Handbook* requires notice of a mortgage to be given to the landlord whether or not this is required by the lease. An example of such a notice is set out at **36.10.6**. The recipient of the notice should be asked to sign one copy of the notice in acknowledgement of its receipt, and to return the receipted copy to the sender. The receipted copy will then be kept with the title deeds as evidence of compliance with this requirement.

36.10.3 Registered lease

Where the lease is already registered at Land Registry, an application for registration of the transfer to the buyer should be made within the priority period given by the buyer's pre-completion search. This is irrespective of the length of time left on the lease: once registered, the lease continues to be registered until it expires.

36.10.4 Unregistered lease

An unregistered lease or sub-lease which, at the date of the transfer to the buyer, still has over seven years unexpired will need to be registered at Land Registry within two months of the assignment or will be void in respect of the legal estate. An application for registration with absolute title can be made where the buyer can produce to the Registry satisfactory evidence relating to the superior title(s). In other cases, only good leasehold title can be obtained (see **4.3.5.4**). An application for first registration of title should therefore be made within this time limit. If the title to the reversion is already registered, the lease will be noted against the superior title. In other cases, the buyer may consider lodging a caution against first registration against the freehold title, in order to protect their interests against a subsequent buyer of the reversion.

If the lease has seven years or less unexpired, it is incapable of registration with separate title, but will take effect as an overriding interest against a superior title which is itself registered.

36.10.5 Outstanding apportioned sums

As soon as the figures are available, the parties' solicitors should make an adjustment of the provisional apportionments which were made on completion. By SC 6.3.5 (SCPC 9.3.5), payment must be made within 10 working days of notification by one party to the other of the adjusted figures.

36.10.6 Example Notice of Assignment

Notice of Assignment

To: Jackson Properties Ltd,
15 Mount Street,
Weyford,
Blankshire ('the Landlord')

TAKE NOTICE that by an assignment dated the 5th day of July 2025 made between (1) JAMES BLISS ('the Seller') and (2) GRAHAM MARTIN WENTWORTH and SARAH JANE WENTWORTH ('the Buyer') the property known as 25, Mackintosh Way, Marshfield, Greatshire comprised in a lease dated 10th August 2020 and made between (1) the Landlord and (2) Mark John Green and Susan Margaret Green was assigned by the Seller to the Buyer for all the unexpired residue of the term

Dated 12 July 2025

Lytham and Co,
40 St Bede's Road,
Marshfield,
Greatshire

Solicitors for the Buyer

WE ACKNOWLEDGE receipt of a duplicate of this notice with a fee of £35 plus VAT this [ ] day of [ ] 2025

Signed Solicitors for the Landlord

SUMMARY

- The steps involved in assigning a long residential lease or a lease of commercial property are very similar to those involved in buying a freehold property.
- Since the lease is already in existence, the terms of the lease are not negotiable.
- The buyer's solicitor will have to report to the client (and any lender) on the terms of the lease.
- The seller's solicitor must check whether the landlord's consent is required for an assignment of the lease. Consent will usually be required in commercial leases, but not in long residential leases. Assignment is not usually permitted at all in short residential leases.
- Most commercial leases contain a fully qualified covenant against alienation, ie the landlord's consent must be obtained but will not be unreasonably withheld. Leases granted on or after 1 January 1996 ('new' leases) are likely to contain detailed requirements that must be met before the landlord's consent will be given.
- If the timing of completion is important, it is safest not to exchange until the landlord's consent has been obtained. However, both sets of standard conditions provide mechanisms for obtaining consent between exchange and completion, and for rescinding the contract if consent is not obtained by a certain date. The timescale for obtaining consent is much shorter in the SCs than in the SCPCs.
- In the transfer deed, the seller's solicitor should modify the implied covenants for title so that the seller is not implying that the repair and decoration covenants in the lease have been performed.
- The seller's solicitor should also ensure that the transfer contains an indemnity from the buyer where the seller is to remain liable for breach of the tenant's covenants in the lease after the assignment has taken place.

- Stamp duty land tax is payable on the purchase price (if any), but not on the rent reserved by the lease.
- The assignment of a registered lease must be registered at Land Registry. The assignment of an unregistered lease which has over seven years unexpired at the date of the assignment will trigger first registration.
- Notice of the assignment must be given to the landlord.

CHAPTER 37

DRAFTING LEASES

LEARNING OUTCOMES

After reading this chapter you will be able to:

- appreciate the wide range of issues addressed in a long residential or commercial lease
- incorporate the clauses prescribed by Land Registry for registrable leases granted on or after 19 June 2006
- explain the structure and contents of a typical lease
- ensure that a tenant of part of a building is granted all the rights over the remainder of the building necessary for the use and enjoyment of the premises
- ensure that the lease makes effective arrangements for insuring the building
- draft appropriate covenants controlling the way in which the tenant can alter, change use and/or dispose of the premises
- understand the difference between absolute, qualified and fully qualified covenants and the various statutory provisions that affect the process of obtaining the landlord's consent
- ensure that the lease makes effective arrangements for repairing the building
- protect a landlord client against breach of the tenant's covenants by including a forfeiture clause in the lease
- consider whether a scheme for the mutual enforcement of covenants between tenants is necessary and, if so, what legal means could be used to implement such a scheme.

37.1 WHY USE A LEASE?

The basic legal and practical considerations behind granting a lease of property rather than selling the freehold have already been discussed in **Chapter 34**, and should be borne in mind as a fundamental background to the issue of drafting leases.

37.2 DRAFTING AND APPROVING LEASES

37.2.1 Why are precedent leases so long?

In the case of a short-term residential lease, the lease may be only a few pages long and is usually presented to the tenant on a 'take it or leave it' basis. In the case of long residential leases and leases of commercial premises, the lease will usually be considerably longer, possibly running to over 100 pages. This is because the lease needs to govern the relationship between the parties for the duration of the term, and therefore needs to anticipate what could happen to the property throughout that period. Crucial issues such as repair and the provision of services need to be addressed. Further, in the case of commercial leases at least, there will often be complex provisions allowing for the rent to be reviewed on a periodic basis. Lastly, if the lease is of premises which form part of a larger development, the lease needs to deal with rights of access, and precisely to define what is and is not being let to the tenant.

The following are the matters to which particular attention should be paid:

(a) the description of the premises to be let;
(b) the easements to be granted and reserved;
(c) the arrangements for repair, maintenance and other services;
(d) the provisions for payment of the service charge (if any);
(e) the insurance arrangements;
(f) the restrictions on the use to which the premises may be put;
(g) any restrictions on assignment and sub-letting;
(h) any restrictions on the making of alterations and improvements;
(i) enforcement of covenants; and
(j) the provisions for rent and rent review.

Some of these matters will be of more significance to a commercial tenant (eg user) and others of more relevance in the case of a flat (eg the management scheme), but all must be considered in turn.

In recent years, the drive to cut carbon emissions has led to various 'green' initiatives being considered by both landlords and tenants of commercial premises (see, for example, the Better Buildings Partnership 'Toolkit'). This has led to the emergence of 'green leases', which impose obligations on the parties aimed at reducing energy consumption and improving sustainability.

37.2.2 Drafting a lease – landlord's solicitor

The draft lease is produced by the landlord's solicitor. Many firms will have their own precedents, or will rely on a set of published precedents, both of which are likely to be available in a word-processable form.

Although a precedent in its original form will be a useful starting point, it must be noted that it cannot necessarily be used just as it stands. It will be necessary to check the content carefully to ensure that it meets the needs and instructions of the landlord client. Further, just because a precedent appears in a well-known and respected published series does not automatically mean that it is free from errors or inconsistencies. Recent legislation or case law developments may not yet have been addressed. Often, it will be necessary to combine parts of one precedent with clauses from another in order to meet instructions, and where this happens, it is important to ensure that defined terms from the different documents are used consistently (eg, when taking a clause referring to 'lessee' from one document into another where the word 'tenant' is used).

Whilst the landlord's solicitor needs to protect the interests of their client, it is important to bear in mind the need not to draft the lease so strongly in the landlord's favour that it will be unacceptable to a prospective tenant. Harsh terms can also have a negative effect on rent review (see **39.4.2.5**).

37.2.3 Land Registry prescribed clauses leases

The LRA 2002 empowered Land Registry to prescribe a form of lease which would have to be used in all cases where the lease was registrable. This was necessary to facilitate the registration of the lease and also because of the proposed introduction of electronic conveyancing. After consultation, Land Registry decided against a prescribed form of lease as such. However, the Land Registration (Amendment) (No 2) Rules 2005 (SI 2005/1982) provide that certain leases must contain prescribed clauses.

Use of the prescribed clauses is compulsory for leases that are dated on or after 19 June 2006, which are granted out of registered land and are compulsorily registrable. These leases will be known as 'prescribed clauses leases'.

A lease will not, however, be a prescribed clauses lease if it arises out of a variation of a lease which is a deemed surrender and re-grant, or if it is granted in a form expressly required by any of the following:

(a) an agreement entered into before 19 June 2006;
(b) a court order;
(c) an enactment; and
(d) a necessary consent or licence for the grant of the lease given before 19 June 2006.

If an applicant claims that a lease is not a prescribed clauses lease due to one of these exceptions, a conveyancer's certificate or other evidence must be supplied with the application for registration.

The wording required in a prescribed clauses lease must appear at the beginning of the lease, or immediately after any front cover sheet and/or front contents page. Sch 1A was inserted into the Land Registration Rules 2003 (SI 2003/1417), which sets out the required wording and gives instructions as to how the prescribed clauses must be completed. Land Registry Practice Guide 64 gives detailed guidance on use of the clauses. This and other guidance may be accessed at <www.landreg.gov.uk>.

37.2.4 Approving the draft lease – tenant's solicitor

Upon receipt of the draft lease, the solicitor acting for the tenant must consider and, if necessary, amend it, in order to protect their client's interests. This will include checking that the document is clear, consistent and up-to-date. As when acting for a landlord, particular care should be taken over the matters identified in **37.2.1**, although a tenant's perspective will inevitably be different from that of the landlord. As an example, a landlord may be keen to restrict the tenant's freedom to dispose of the property, whilst a tenant may be keen to preserve greater freedom in this respect. Especially in the context of commercial leases, much will depend on the bargaining power of the parties. The RICS Code for Leasing Business Premises, 1st edn, contains useful guidance in this regard (see **34.3.2**).

Lastly, it should be noted that when approving a draft lease, the solicitor acting for the tenant should bear in mind that the tenant may want to assign the lease in the future. Although the original tenant may not have an issue with a particular provision, if it is likely to be unattractive to future assignees, it should be resisted.

37.3 THE CONTENTS OF THE LEASE

37.3.1 Commencement

The lease starts with the words 'This lease', followed by the date of its grant (this will be the date of completion of the transaction and is inserted on actual completion), and the names and addresses of the parties. Where the lease is created out of a registered title, the document will carry the usual Land Registry heading (county and district, landlord's title number, brief description of the property, and date) at the top of its first page.

37.3.2 Payment of premium and receipt

Where the landlord is to grant a long lease of residential premises, they will usually charge a capital sum, or premium, for its grant. This is broadly equivalent to the price which a buyer pays on purchase of freehold premises, and consideration and receipt clauses, which have the same effect as those included in a freehold transfer deed, are included in the lease. In addition to the premium, the tenant's consideration for the grant also comprises the payment of rent and the promise to perform various obligations under the lease (covenants), and these are mentioned as being part of the consideration (eg, 'IN CONSIDERATION of the sum of two hundred and forty thousand pounds (receipt of which the Landlord acknowledges) and of the rent reserved and of the covenants by the Tenant contained in this lease ...').

37.3.3 Operative words

The operative words in the lease were traditionally 'The Landlord hereby demises', but in more modern leases the Landlord 'grants', or 'lets' or 'leases' instead.

37.3.4 Title guarantee

The landlord may give the tenant the benefit of full or limited title guarantee covenants in the same way as on a transfer of freehold land (see **18.8.3**). The appropriate words 'with full title guarantee' or 'with limited title guarantee', together with any express modifications of the covenants, will be included in the document after the operative words.

37.3.5 Term

The length (term) of the lease, including its starting date, must be set out. Care should be taken with the commencement date of the term as often other matters are tied to it. For example, rent review is usually to occur on specified anniversaries of the commencement date. It is not unusual to find that the date specified is before the actual signature of the lease. So a lease entered into on 1 January 2014 might be stated to commence on 1 October 2013. This is common in lettings of offices and flats where the landlord wants all of the leases in the block to come to an end on the same day. When specifying a commencement date, it should be made clear whether or not the date specified is to be included in the term. So if a lease is stated to run for five years from 1 November 2014, it will, in fact, commence on 2 November and so expire at midnight on 1 November 2019. The use of the word 'from' excludes the day stated. If the 1st of November is meant to be included, this should be made clear by stating 'from and including'.

37.3.6 The parcels clause – the description of the premises to be let

37.3.6.1 Certainty

The precise extent of what is to be transferred must be stated clearly and exactly. This is always the case in any conveyancing document, but is particularly relevant in the case of offices and flats as the letting is likely to be of only part of a larger building. It must be possible to say with absolute precision what is and is not being let.

It is necessary to define precisely where one unit ends and another begins. Think of the wall which separates one office from another: where in that wall is the boundary between the two offices going to be? Similarly with the floor and ceiling which divide the premises to be let from those below and above it: where is the boundary going to be situated in the floor and ceiling? Often the tenants' repairing obligations are co-extensive with ownership, ie if a tenant owns a wall (or floor or ceiling) they have to repair it, so who owns what becomes especially important.

Often it will not be sensible to provide that the whole of a particular wall or floor belongs to one unit; the boundary will have to be somewhere within the wall or floor. Precisely where will depend upon the method of construction of the particular building. It will obviously be meaningless to talk of floor boards and wooden joists in a modern building constructed with concrete beams.

37.3.6.2 Top-floor and ground-floor units

Particular care should be taken with top-floor and ground-floor/basement lettings. In the case of a top-floor letting, is it intended to include the roof and the air space above it in the letting? If these are included, this will enable the tenant to extend upwards, which may not be the landlord's intention. The responsibility for repairing the roof may also be affected by such an inclusion. In the case of the ground floor or basement (if there is one), the same problems arise, but allowing a downwards rather than upwards extension.

37.3.6.3 Garage/car parking

Sometimes the letting of a unit (and particularly a flat) will also include a garage and/or car parking space.

Car parking may be underground or in the surrounding grounds. If a specific car parking space or garage is allocated, this should be included in the property let to the tenant. If the lease merely gives a right to park a car somewhere in a car park, this will be an easement. You should inform the client precisely which arrangement exists in each particular case. Numerous arguments can arise over car parking.

37.3.7 Easements to be granted

37.3.7.1 Access and services

As well as the precise definition of what is being let, it is important to look closely at the ancillary rights which benefit the property. In a letting of part, the tenant should be granted all necessary easements over the remainder of the block and the surrounding grounds. This not only involves rights of way – on foot over the entrance lobby, hallways, stairways and lifts inside the block, and by car and on foot from the street and over the surrounding grounds – but also easements for the various essential services to reach the office or flat. These may include water, gas, electricity, drains and telephone, depending upon the circumstances. In an office building the tenant may need the right to run computer cabling through other parts of the building. Do not forget either that the flat tenant will want to watch television. The arrangements for access to a suitable aerial or similar facilities should be checked. Is a communal aerial to be provided – and if so, a right to run a cable to it? And can the tenant install their own satellite dish, or is there to be a communal one? Or is there an easement allowing each tenant to fix their own aerial?

37.3.7.2 Access for repair, etc

An easement just to use pipes and cables is not enough on its own. Rights of access are necessary in order to inspect and to repair and replace them as required. You should check that these are granted as well.

37.3.7.3 New rights

In a lease that will run for some years, it is also sensible to make provision for the possible need to install new cables and facilities in addition to those already there on the grant of the lease. Technology makes great advances very quickly and it would be unfortunate if a lease did not allow the installation of some major new development into the block.

37.3.7.4 Use of toilets, etc

In office blocks (particularly older ones) it is sometimes the case that each office does not have its own separate toilet facilities. There are communal toilets located elsewhere in the block. In this kind of situation, it will be necessary for easements to be granted for the use of these facilities. The cost of maintaining and cleaning them will then be included in the service charge.

37.3.7.5 Rubbish

The question of disposal of rubbish will also have to be addressed. When acting for the landlord, it will be necessary to find out whether there is to be a communal bin or whether each unit is to have its own, and if so, where. Rights will have to be given for the use of communal facilities or for the placing of individual bins.

37.3.8 Easements to be reserved

As well as the benefit of easements over the rest of the block, you must also ensure that corresponding reservations are made in favour of the landlord and the other tenants in the block. Remember that one tenant's grant of an easement will be the next-door tenant's reservation. Each unit let will have to be made subject to rights similar to those granted to it. Each lease should therefore expressly reserve such rights. If it does not, it is likely that the rights granted will not have been reserved over the rest of the block and thus could be ineffective.

37.3.9 Rent and rent review

37.3.9.1 Flat leases

In the case of a flat lease, the annual rent will be comparatively low. After all, the tenant will have paid a large premium to 'buy' the flat and therefore cannot be expected to pay a large rent as well. So you will find that the rent will perhaps be in the region of £200 per year. The lease should make it clear what the rent payment date is and whether the rent is to be paid in advance or in arrears. Often, the rent is payable half-yearly rather than in one lump sum.

It is usual in a long lease to find some provision dealing with increases in rent. A rent fixed at the start of a 99-year term will very rapidly have its value eroded by inflation. If you are acting for a landlord, you should take instructions on this. The landlord will probably want to be able to increase the rent in order to compensate for this. However, the dictates of the market must be borne in mind. Tenants (and their mortgagees) are not going to find a lease acceptable which gives a landlord an unfettered right to increase the rent. Remember that a substantial premium has already been paid and a tenant (or mortgagee) will wish to recoup this on a subsequent assignment. This will not be possible if the landlord has imposed a large increase in the rent.

So it is usual in a flat lease to find that the rent increases are agreed in advance and set out in the lease. You might, for example, find that the rent for the first 20 years of the term is (say) £200, and then for the next 20 years £300, and so on. When acting for a tenant you should check the rent provisions and explain these to the client, particularly the provisions for increase.

In recent years, some developers have inserted so called 'doubling ground rent' provisions into long leases of new build flats and houses. These provisions have led to some tenants being unable to sell or remortgage their homes, as the levels of ground rent in the later years of the term can be extremely high. A buyer should not proceed with the purchase of a flat lease containing such provisions unless a deed of variation can be negotiated with the landlord to remove the offending provisions.

There is an additional problem for residential properties with ground rent exceeding £250 per annum (or £1,000 for properties in Greater London). Such a tenancy can, in theory, fall within the scope of the Housing Act 1988, as it satisfies the definition of an assured shorthold tenancy. The unintended consequence of this is that a landlord can obtain possession of the property if the tenant is late in paying its rent under Ground 8. This ground is mandatory, and the court will have no discretion as to whether to grant relief or not to the tenant. As a result, a tenant of a long lease who has paid a considerable premium on the grant of the lease could in theory lose that lease for non-payment of the ground rent if the ground rent level brings it within the remit of the Housing Act 1988. Some lenders are therefore reluctant to lend on long residential leases where the ground rent exceeds (or could during the term of the lease exceed) £250 per annum (or £1,000 for properties in Greater London). The Renters Rights Bill 2024 contains a provision that would close this loophole by excluding leases of more than 7 years from the definition of an assured tenancy. At the time of writing this Bill is still before Parliament and is not yet law.

Since 20 June 2022, the Leasehold Reform (Ground Rent) Act 2022 ('the 2022 Act') has restricted ground rents on most newly created long leases of houses and flats to an annual rent of one peppercorn (a token of no financial value). A lease will be 'long' for these purposes if it exceeds 21 years. There are some new long residential leases that will not be protected (for example, long leases where no premium is paid; statutory lease extensions of houses and flats), but the 2022 Act should resolve issues associated with ground rent for most newly created long residential leases. It should be noted that the 2022 Act does not apply retrospectively and so problems will remain for those trying to sell or mortgage existing long residential leases with problematic ground rent provisions. The Government has consulted on proposals to restrict ground rents in existing leases, but no firm proposals or draft legislation have been produced at the time of writing.

37.3.9.2 VAT – residential leases

The grant of a residential lease is zero rated, so no special provisions are required to deal with the payment of VAT on the rent. However, where the tenant is to be liable for the landlord's legal and other costs, the lease should make clear that the tenant is to pay these plus VAT.

37.3.9.3 Commercial leases

As with flat leases, the lease should make clear what the rental payment dates are and whether the rent is payable in advance or in arrears – in advance is usual. In all types of commercial lease, the amount of the rent will be a prime consideration for both landlord and tenant. Often this will be negotiated separately by surveyors acting on behalf of the landlord and the tenant. The provisions for reviewing the rent to take account of inflation are, however, a legal matter, and will be the concern of the landlord's and the tenant's solicitors. These provisions are dealt with in detail in **Chapter 39**.

37.3.9.4 VAT – commercial leases

The grant of a commercial lease is an exempt supply, but subject to the landlord's right to opt to tax and charge VAT. See **6.2** as to the purpose of this option to tax. If the landlord decides to opt to tax, it is essential that they should be able to add the VAT onto the agreed amount of rent. The effect of s 89 of the VATA 1994 is that if the landlord opts to tax before the grant of the lease, VAT can only be added to the rent if the lease contains a provision permitting this (see **6.2**). In every lease, therefore, there should be such a provision.

37.3.10 Alterations and improvements

At common law, the tenant's ability to make alterations or improvements is somewhat unclear. It all depends upon the centuries-old doctrine of 'waste'. It is best, therefore, for these matters to be dealt with expressly in the lease.

A landlord will usually want to exercise some form of control over what can and cannot be done on their premises. Whilst some alterations may well increase the value of the premises and the reversion, some may not. The landlord will be concerned, particularly in comparatively short commercial leases, lest any alterations carried out by a particular tenant will decrease the letting value of the premises when the time comes to re-let. This will be less of a problem in a 99-year lease of a flat, for example, but alterations may still affect the value of the reversion. There are also safety aspects: tenants cannot be allowed to remove or interfere with structural walls and the like, otherwise the whole block might collapse.

37.3.10.1 Absolute prohibitions

In a short-term lease, the landlord may wish to prohibit all alterations and so will impose an absolute covenant. Alternatively, the landlord may impose an absolute prohibition on structural alterations. Prospective tenants should consider absolute prohibitions carefully. Are the premises, as they are now, definitely going to be adequate for the tenant's needs throughout the lease and any possible renewal? It is true to say that the landlord could still grant permission for a particular alteration despite the absolute prohibition, but of course they do not have to. Further, even if the landlord is happy to give permission, the landlord may be prevented from doing so if the premises are part of a multi-occupied building and the landlord has covenanted in the leases of the building that it will enforce the tenant's covenants at the request of another tenant in the building. It is common in long residential leases to find such a landlord's covenant (see **37.5**), and in *Duval v 11-13 Randolph Crescent Ltd* [2020] UKSC 18, the Supreme Court held that if a landlord licensed a tenant to carry out alterations despite an absolute prohibition, the landlord would be in breach of its obligation to enforce the lease covenants at the request of another tenant in the building. In those circumstances the landlord would need to seek the consent of the other tenants of the building to the works that were absolutely prohibited.

So, if the tenant agrees to an absolute covenant against alterations (or certain types of alteration), the tenant will be at the mercy of the landlord (and in a multi-occupied building, potentially the other tenants), unless it can rely on either of the following statutory exceptions:

(a) A tenant of business premises can use the provisions of s 3 of the Landlord and Tenant Act 1927 to enable it to carry out works, even where there is an absolute prohibition. Under s 3, if the tenant wants to carry out improvements, it can serve a notice on the landlord detailing its proposals. The landlord has three months within which to object, and if it does then the tenant has the right to apply to the court for authorisation to carry out the improvements. The court can authorise the improvements if they add to the letting value of the property, are reasonable, and are suitable to the character of the property and do not diminish the value of any other property of the landlord (or any superior landlord). The court has the power to modify the plans and specification and impose conditions as it thinks fit.

    Instead of objecting or consenting to the works, a landlord can offer to carry out the works itself in return for a reasonable increase in the rent (Landlord and Tenant Act 1927, s 3(1)). A tenant is under no obligation to accept an offer by the landlord to carry out the works, and may withdraw its notice. If it does so, the landlord then has no right to carry out the works and increase the rent. However, if the tenant rejects the landlord's offer, the court cannot give the tenant authority to do the works itself (*Norfolk Capital Group Ltd v Cadogan Estates Ltd* [2004] EWHC 384 (Ch)).

    If the landlord does not offer to carry out the works itself or object to the improvements within three months (or if the court authorises the work), then the tenant may lawfully carry them out, even if the lease prohibits the works.

(b) The Equality Act 2010 provides for a regime of implied consents in relation to 'reasonable adjustments' required to meet the needs of those with disabilities. A specialist text should be consulted for further detail.

37.3.10.2 Qualified prohibition

From the tenant's perspective, a qualified covenant against alterations is preferable to an absolute prohibition. This prohibits alterations without the landlord's prior consent. Under s 19(2) of the Landlord and Tenant Act 1927, a term is implied into a qualified covenant against making improvements that the landlord cannot unreasonably withhold consent. That term cannot be excluded. This provision will thus apply to a covenant against making alterations to the extent that the alteration in question amounts to an improvement. According to *Lambert v FW Woolworth & Co Ltd* [1938] Ch 883, whether an alteration amounts to an improvement for these purposes must be looked at purely from the point of view of the tenant. If the works in question will increase the value or usefulness of the premises to the tenant then they will constitute an improvement, even if they will result in the reduction in the value of the landlord's reversionary interest. In relation to improvements, therefore, the landlord will not be able to withhold consent unreasonably; in relation to other alterations, the landlord can be as awkward as they like.

Although the *Woolworth* case is beneficial to tenants, they would often prefer a fully qualified covenant, one that makes it clear on the face of it that the landlord cannot withhold consent unreasonably to an alteration, whether or not it amounts to an improvement.

37.3.10.3 Compensation

Part 1 of the Landlord and Tenant Act 1927 entitles a tenant of business premises to claim compensation for improvements at the end of the term that 'add to the letting value of the holding'. The tenant must have obtained prior authorisation to make the improvements by using the s 3 statutory procedure (see **37.3.10.1** at (a)), and it must claim within certain statutory time limits. In practice, these provisions are rarely relevant as most leases contain a tenant's covenant to remove all alterations and reinstate the premises at the end of the term.

37.3.11 Insurance

37.3.11.1 General

It is clearly important, from both a landlord's and a tenant's perspective, to ensure that adequate provisions are in place to insure the property against damage by fire, flood, etc. From a landlord's perspective, the building forms the physical basis of their investment, and so they will want it to be reinstated in the event of damage. Equally, the tenant will want the building to be reinstated so that they can continue to occupy the let premises as intended under the lease.

In the case of a letting of whole, the tenant could be made solely responsible for insurance. Alternatively, the landlord could take out the insurance and charge the tenant for the cost, which has the advantage of giving the landlord the comfort that insurance is actually in place.

In the case of lettings of part, the most commonly adopted approach is for the landlord or management company to insure the whole block, with the cost being passed on to the tenants through the service charge or as a separate insurance rent. Sometimes the insurance company to be used will be specified, but more usually the choice is left to the landlord. When acting for the landlord you should ensure that they can recover the premium through the service charge or by requiring payment of a separate insurance rent when drafting the lease.

Whether the letting is of whole or part, the following matters should always be checked from both the landlord's and the tenant's perspective:

(a) risks insured against;
(b) amount of cover;
(c) application of policy monies.

37.3.11.2 Risks covered

An obligation 'to insure' is not sufficient – to insure against what? The risks insured against should be stated expressly. There is often an inclusive list of the risks which the landlord must insure against, for example 'fire, storm, flood, etc'. The problem with this, though, is that the landlord may continue to insure against unlikely or expensive risks; and if new risks arise (eg, terrorist violence), these may not be covered. Accordingly, it is common for the list of risks to conclude with such other risks as the landlord may reasonably require or the tenant may reasonably request.

You should inspect the policy itself (and not just rely on the covenant) and ascertain what risks are covered. If an important risk is not covered, it would, in theory, be possible for an individual tenant to arrange extra cover for that risk or renegotiate the clause, but this would probably not be possible in practice.

37.3.11.3 Amount of cover

You must ensure that the property is insured to its full reinstatement value, otherwise if the property is totally destroyed there will not be enough money to pay for its rebuilding. Full reinstatement value will include:

(a) costs of demolition and site clearance;

(b) professional fees (eg, architects, surveyors, etc);

(c) an allowance for inflation.

A professional valuation of the reinstatement value should be obtained when the insurance is first placed and regularly thereafter. An annual index-linked increase of the reinstatement value is also recommended.

37.3.11.4 Application of policy monies

There should at the very least be a covenant by the landlord to use the proceeds to reinstate the premises. Ideally, a tenant would like this extended to include an obligation for the landlord to make good any shortfall in the proceeds out of their own pocket.

You should also check whether there is any provision to deal with the possibility of reinstatement being impossible. Should this provide for the monies to be retained by the landlord, whose building it is, or to be passed over to the tenants who have been paying the premiums? It is probably fairest for the proceeds to be shared between landlord and tenant proportionate to the values of their respective interests.

37.3.11.5 Rent suspension

In the absence of an express term to the contrary, rent will continue to be payable even if the property is rendered unusable, for example because of a fire. The tenant should therefore ensure that the lease provides for the payment of rent to be suspended during any period that the premises cannot be occupied following damage by an insured risk. The landlord will normally be happy to allow such rent suspension, as they can insure against loss of rent in such circumstances. However, usually such insurance is limited in duration (often to three years) and the landlord may attempt to limit the rent suspension accordingly.

37.3.11.6 Termination

Unless the lease states otherwise, if the building is totally destroyed, it will only be in exceptional circumstances that the doctrine of frustration will apply and the lease will be terminated (see *National Carriers Ltd v Panalpina (Northern) Ltd* [1981] AC 675). In consequence, the lease will often give the landlord the right to determine the lease on notice if reinstatement should prove impossible. The tenant should try to ensure that they have the same right. Additionally, if the right to suspend the payment of rent is limited, the tenant should ensure that if the premises have not been reinstated by the end of the rent suspension period, they can terminate the lease.

37.3.12 Permitted user

At common law, a tenant can use premises for whatever purposes they wish – subject, of course, to planning laws and any covenants on the superior title. This may well not be acceptable to the landlord who will want to be able to exercise some control as to the use to which the premises are put. The landlord will want this control both for financial and for estate management reasons.

When you are acting for a tenant, you should consider the user provisions carefully, to ensure that they are not going to cause your client any problems in their occupation of the unit, or if they should wish to assign the lease.

Both parties should also be aware of the impact of competition legislation on such provisions (see **16.9.5** and *Martin Retail Group Ltd v Crawley Borough Council* (24 December 2013, Central London County Court)).

37.3.12.1 Flats

In the case of a lease of a flat, the landlord will usually want to ensure that the block is used solely for residential purposes. This is to preserve the value of the reversion. If one or more flats start to be used for commercial purposes, this may well make the other flats in the block less desirable residences and so more difficult to dispose of. This possibility of non-residential use might influence potential tenants into declining to take the leases when the block is being first developed. Illegal and immoral use will also be prohibited.

So, both landlords and tenants will have the same concerns, and a covenant limiting the use to residential only will be acceptable to both. (Sometimes you will find that certain professional uses are permitted, eg, doctor, solicitor, presumably on the basis that this kind of use would not affect the value of the other flats adversely.)

37.3.12.2 Commercial leases

Use is much more of a problem in commercial leases. In lettings of shops, for example, the landlord may need to prevent competition with other premises belonging to them, or may wish to ensure a good mix of retail units to make the development attractive to the shopping public. This may cause problems for a tenant who cannot change from an unprofitable shop use to one more profitable.

In a letting of an office block both landlord and tenants will again have a common interest in ensuring that it is all used just for office purposes. Use for (say) a manufacturing purpose would not be acceptable to the other tenants. This would almost certainly cause noise and other forms of pollution which would adversely affect the other tenants. Tenants would leave, offices could not be re-let, and the landlord would thus suffer financially.

The parties need to agree upon the way in which the permitted use is to be defined in the lease. Whether you are acting for landlord or tenant, you should bear in mind that a user clause can have an effect on the rent when it comes to rent review. A very restrictive user clause will inevitably have the effect of reducing the rent that would otherwise be payable; a very wide user clause will tend to increase the rent.

One common way to define user is to make use of the categories set out in the Use Classes Order 1987 (see **7.1.4.2**). Thus, in the case of a hotel, user could be limited to use within Class C1. Alternatively, the landlord may decide not to use the Use Classes Order and instead restrict the use to a stated purpose, for example office use for marketing consultants. This may suit the present tenant in their current business, but inhibits any change (or expansion) of business and limits the class of persons who might be interested in taking an assignment. It is for this reason that such a clause would almost certainly result in a lower rent at review than a wider user clause based on the Use Classes Order. A possible compromise is to have a specific use but allow changes to other uses within the same use class as the permitted user, but only with the landlord's consent. Thus, a lease might permit use as a warehouse 'or such other use within Class B8 of the Use Classes Order 1987 as the landlord shall permit'. There is no implication that the landlord's consent cannot be unreasonably withheld, but s 19(3) of the Landlord and Tenant Act 1927 does provide that the landlord cannot charge a fine or an increased rent as a condition of giving consent, provided no structural alteration is involved. However, a tenant would clearly prefer the covenant to be fully qualified, ie provide that a change to another use may be made only with the landlord's prior consent, such consent not to be unreasonably withheld.

37.3.13 Assignment and sub-letting

At common law a tenant is free to dispose of their premises, whether by an outright assignment of the lease or by a sub-lease. However, a landlord may well want to exercise close control over who will be in occupation of their property.

37.3.13.1 Flat leases

In long-term flat leases you will recall that the tenant will have paid a substantial premium on the grant of the lease. They will not want their freedom to dispose of the lease, and so recoup this premium, to be substantially restricted. Moreover, the landlord must accept that the lease must be acceptable to any prospective mortgagee. The mortgagee will want to be able to sell in exercise of its power of sale without any limitations being imposed.

It is usual, therefore, in a long flat lease to find that assignment is permitted freely. There may, however, be restrictions on the assignment or sub-letting of part, and controls on assignment are sometimes imposed in respect of assignments in the final few years of the term.

Even where dealings are permitted freely, the landlord will obviously want to know the identity of the new tenants, and so you will find that there will be a covenant by the tenant to register any dealings with the landlord and pay a fee.

37.3.13.2 Commercial leases

Much stricter controls are usual in office and other commercial leases. Such leases are usually for a much shorter term at a much higher rent. The identity and status of the occupier is of much greater significance than in a long flat lease with a low ground rent. An unsatisfactory tenant could greatly damage the value of the landlord's reversion, either by not paying rent or by damaging the property which the landlord has then to try to re-let.

Most leases contain covenants prohibiting the tenant from either parting with possession or sharing occupation of the premises, or strictly controlling the way in which the tenant does this. Parting with possession is doing something that means the tenant will no longer have legal possession of the premises, so includes assignment and sub-letting, but goes wider to include, for example, letting a purchaser into the premises pending completion of an assignment. However, it does not include granting a licence to another, unless the licence confers exclusive possession (*Street v Mountford* [1985] AC 809). A covenant prohibiting the tenant from sharing occupation will prevent the tenant from granting licences, entering into concession arrangements with other retailers and even from sharing occupation with a group company member (although it is common for a lease to provide that sharing with group companies is permitted as an exception to the general prohibition on sharing possession).

It is common for a commercial lease to contain a prohibition on parting with possession and sharing occupation, but then to allow assignment, sub-letting and/or sharing with group companies in certain circumstances.

37.3.13.3 Absolute prohibition

An absolute prohibition on assignment, sub-letting, etc would probably not be acceptable to a tenant, except perhaps in a very short-term letting. Although the landlord could waive the covenant in any given case, the tenant would be completely at the landlord's mercy.

37.3.13.4 A qualified prohibition

A qualified covenant on assignment, sub-letting, etc prohibits alienation by the tenant without the landlord's consent. Sometimes the covenant will go further and state that the landlord's consent is not to be withheld unreasonably. This is known as a fully qualified covenant. Such a covenant gives a tenant considerable leeway when seeking licence to assign from the landlord.

Section 19(1)(a) of the Landlord and Tenant Act 1927 provides that, notwithstanding any contrary provision, a covenant not to assign, underlet, charge or part with possession of the demised premises or any part thereof without the landlord's licence or consent, is subject to a proviso that such licence or consent is not to be withheld unreasonably. In other words, a qualified covenant can be converted into a fully qualified covenant by the operation of s 19(1)(a). As a general rule, a landlord will be acting unreasonably unless their reasons for refusal relate to the status of the proposed assignee, or the use to which the assignee proposes to put the premises.

The Landlord and Tenant Act 1988 further strengthened the position of a tenant seeking consent to assign, sub-let, charge or part with possession. The Act applies where the lease contains a fully qualified covenant against alienation (whether the proviso that the landlord's consent is not to be withheld unreasonably is express or implied by statute). The Act still applies even if the fully qualified covenant is subject to s 19(1A) of the Landlord and Tenant Act 1927 referred to at **37.3.13.5** below. When the tenant has made written application for consent, the landlord owes a duty, within a reasonable time, to give consent, unless it is reasonable not to do so (the giving of consent subject to an unreasonable condition will be a breach of this duty). In addition, the landlord must serve on the tenant written notice of the decision whether or not to give consent, specifying in addition the conditions they are imposing, or the reasons why they are withholding consent. The burden of proving the reasonableness of any refusal or any conditions imposed is on the landlord.

37.3.13.5 Special rules for covenants against assigning commercial leases

Under s 19(1A) of the Landlord and Tenant Act 1927 (inserted by s 22 of the Landlord and Tenant (Covenants) Act 1995), special rules apply in relation to covenants against assigning contained in commercial leases granted on or after 1 January 1996. These rules enable the landlord and tenant to agree in advance (ie, in the covenant against assigning) specified circumstances in which the landlord may withhold consent to an assignment and specified conditions subject to which consent to assignment may be given.

If the landlord withholds consent because any of those specified circumstances exist, or imposes any of those specified conditions on the consent, they will not be taken to be acting unreasonably. Hence, by careful use of s 19(1A) in the drafting of the lease, the landlord can provide themselves with cast-iron reasonable grounds for withholding consent to an assignment.

The provisions permitted under s 19(1A) may be either of a factual nature (eg, whether the assignee is a company quoted on the London Stock Exchange), or discretionary (eg, whether in the landlord's opinion the assignee is capable of performing the tenant covenants of the lease). Where the provision involves an exercise of discretion, s 19(1A) requires either:

(a) that the provision states that discretion is to be exercised reasonably (eg, 'if in the landlord's reasonable opinion the assignee is capable of performing the tenant covenants of the lease'); or

(b) that the tenant is given an unrestricted right to have the exercise of the discretion reviewed by an independent third party whose identity is ascertainable from the provision (eg, 'if in the landlord's opinion the assignee is capable of performing the tenant covenants of the lease, but if the tenant disagrees with the landlord's opinion, the tenant may apply to an expert appointed in accordance with the terms of the lease for a second opinion').

37.3.13.6 Sub-lettings

The landlord will wish to control sub-letting as well as assignment. In some circumstances, a sub-tenant can become the direct tenant of the head landlord, and so again the landlord could be faced with an unsatisfactory tenant causing financial damage to their interests.

Sub-lettings of the whole of the premises are usually subject to the same kinds of restrictions as assignments. However, in the case of sub-lettings of part, the lease provisions are usually considerably stricter. Sub-letting of part is often subject to an absolute prohibition. A landlord who let premises to one tenant does not want to find some time in the future that they now have to deal with a multi-tenanted block.

Section 19(1)(a) of the Landlord and Tenant Act 1927 and the Landlord and Tenant Act 1988 apply to covenants against assignment, sub-letting or parting with possession. However, s 19(1A) of the Landlord and Tenant Act 1927 applies only to assignments.

A similar result to s 19(1A) can nevertheless be achieved by careful drafting of the alienation provisions, by imposing conditions precedent to the landlord giving consent. Thus, for example, a requirement that the tenant first offer to surrender the lease without any consideration before assignment was held not to contravene s 19(1)(a) (*Bocardo SA v S & M Hotels* [1980] 1 WLR 17). The position is different if the lease seeks to exclude the right of the court to decide whether the landlord is acting reasonably (*Re Smith's Lease* [1951] 1 TLR 254). This will be a matter for the court to decide, and so the position is less certain than is the case if s 19(1A) applies.

37.3.13.7 Charging or mortgaging

Most leases will contain restrictions on charging as the landlord will be concerned that, if the tenant defaults on the mortgage, the lender may take possession of the premises or exercise its power of sale.

37.3.14 Repair

It will be in both parties' interests to ensure the demised premises are kept in good repair. The landlord's capital value may be adversely affected and the tenant may not be able to use and occupy the premises effectively if the premises (or the building of which the premises form part) become dilapidated. Repairing obligations usually differ in extent, depending on whether the tenant has a lease of the whole of a building or a lease of part only.

37.3.14.1 Who does what?

Where the tenant has a lease of a whole building it is usual for all the repairing obligations to be imposed on them. Where the tenant has a lease of part of the landlord's building (eg, a floor in an office block or a flat in a block of flats), responsibility will usually be divided between landlord and tenant. The tenant will normally be responsible for the non-structural parts of the premises, and the landlord will assume responsibility for the structural parts of the building and the common areas.

While repairing obligations will be implied into short residential tenancies under the Housing Act 1985, this is not normally the case for longer residential leases or for leases of commercial property of any length. Therefore, it must be made certain that every part of the building is covered by a repairing obligation, and clear also as to whose responsibility it is to repair each and every part. There must be no grey areas where responsibility is unclear; no black holes where no one has responsibility, and no overlaps where two persons are apparently responsible and can then start squabbling as to who will actually have to do the work.

37.3.14.2 Obligations by third parties

You will sometimes find that obligations to repair are placed on someone other than the tenant's immediate landlord. This is particularly common in flat leases, when a management company is often used. Such flat management schemes are considered in more detail in **Chapter 38**. If enforcement is not possible under normal landlord and tenant or privity of contract grounds, you will need to ensure that there is some other way in which the tenant will be able to enforce those obligations, should the need arise (see **38.2.2**). Sometimes, repairing obligations are imposed on other tenants. In this case, you should check to see that there is a covenant from the landlord that the landlord will enforce them against the other tenants on request, or that the provisions of the Contracts (Rights of Third Parties) Act 1999 are complied with (see **37.5**).

37.3.14.3 Who pays?

The landlord will normally wish to ensure that all repairing costs are passed on to the tenant. This is easy if the tenant is responsible for the repair of the whole of the landlord's building, but trickier where responsibility for repairs is split between the parties in a lease of part. In the latter case, the lease will usually contain provisions enabling the landlord to pass on the costs in maintaining the structure and common parts to the tenants via a service charge. Service charge provisions are dealt with in detail in **Chapter 38**.

37.3.14.4 The extent of the obligation

As in any other covenant, the party responsible for the repairs can be obliged to do only what they have agreed to do. You should ensure, therefore, that the operative words of the clause are sufficient to cover all foreseeable repair activities (eg, 'to repair maintain cleanse paint decorate ...'). A covenant to 'repair' only would not oblige the covenantor to decorate, for example. And if a service charge was being paid by the tenants, if the landlord did in fact decorate, the tenants could not be obliged to pay for this where they had promised to pay for 'repairs' alone.

Is the repairing covenant intended to include renewal and/or improvement? Many arguments arise in practice over this simple point. Replacement of defective window frames, for example, is within the ambit of a covenant to 'repair', but what if the old frame is to be replaced with improved, double-glazed units? This is probably not a repair but an improvement, and so is not within the obligation imposed by a covenant to 'repair'. As above, if the landlord did install double-glazed units, the tenants would not be obliged to pay for them through the service charge where they had agreed to pay only for 'repairs'.

If the covenant does include improvements, is this acceptable to the tenants? Do the tenants not want the property improved? Bear in mind, though, that the tenants will be expected to pay for any work done through the service charge. There is a risk that the landlord/ management company could decide to carry out large-scale improvements, which the tenants do not want or need, all at the tenants' expense.

Consider a clause 'to improve and renew to the extent such renewals or improvements are necessary or desirable to keep the Building in good and substantial repair ...' as a fair compromise.

In the case of inherent defects in design or construction of the building, you should appreciate that remedying these will normally be within the obligations imposed by a repairing covenant.

Where the landlord is insuring the building, the tenant should ensure that they are not responsible for repairing damage arising as a result of insured risks.

37.3.14.5 Breaches of repairing obligations

When a landlord enters into a repairing covenant, there will be no breach unless and until they have notice (no matter from what source) of the lack of repair. Even though the landlord may reserve a right of entry to view the state of repair, they are under no obligation to do so, and you should advise the tenant to inform the landlord of any lack of repair as soon as it is known.

When acting for a landlord, you should include a tenant's covenant to notify the landlord of the need to repair. If the tenant fails to do this, they will also be in breach of covenant and liable to the landlord for damages (ie, any extra cost incurred by reason of the delay in reporting it).

However, if the part of the property in question is in the control of the landlord, for example the common parts, then the landlord's liability does not depend upon the landlord having received notice of the disrepair.

Due to restrictions on the remedies that may be available for the breach of a tenant's repairing covenant (see **34.8.5**), the landlord will usually require the lease to contain a right for them to enter and effect any repairs which have not been done by a tenant, and then recharge the cost to the tenant. Such a right is often referred to as 'self help' (see **34.8.5.3**).

37.3.14.6 Occupiers' liability

If the landlord is in occupation of the common parts, they will owe the common duty of care to visitors under the Occupiers' Liability Act 1957. You should look out for clauses which require the tenant to indemnify the landlord against any such claim made by the tenant's visitors.

37.4 FORFEITURE CLAUSE

A proviso for a re-entry or a forfeiture clause is an essential part of a fixed-term lease. It enables the landlord to terminate the lease because of the tenant's breach of covenant. An express forfeiture provision is essential; without such a clause a landlord would be unable to remove a tenant until the end of the fixed term, even though the tenant was not complying with the covenants in the lease. The clause should give the landlord the right to forfeit if the rent is a specified number of days in arrears (eg, 21 days) and for breach of any other covenant. However, despite the existence of the clause, a landlord will not be able to forfeit for covenants other than non-payment of rent unless they have previously served a notice on the tenant under s 146 of the LPA 1925.

A court order will be required if possession cannot be acquired peaceably, and is always necessary in the case of residential property. The Commonhold and Leasehold Reform Act 2002 introduced severe restrictions on a landlord's right to forfeit residential leases. No forfeiture is possible in the case of non-payment of sums of money not exceeding £350 unless the sum has been outstanding for more than three years. For all other breaches, the landlord cannot forfeit unless the tenant has either admitted the breach, or a court or the Leasehold Valuation Tribunal has determined that there is in fact a breach of covenant.

In addition to being able to forfeit for breaches of the lease, it is common to find in leases of commercial premises, that the landlord is entitled to forfeit the lease in the event of the tenant becoming insolvent. Given that the tenant will be paying an open market rent for the property, the landlord's concern is obvious: it is likely that the tenant will be unable to pay the rent on the next occasion it falls due, and the landlord may not want to have to wait until this date arrives to begin the process of forfeiting the lease. In the case of residential long leases, however, such a provision should be resisted. The tenant is likely to be paying a comparatively small sum in rent and so the landlord's concerns (above) do not apply. Furthermore, the lease will represent a valuable capital asset for the tenant which they (and their lender) will not want to lose, especially if in financial difficulties.

37.5 MUTUAL ENFORCEMENT OF COVENANTS

37.5.1 Why the need?

When checking the lease on behalf of a prospective tenant of a flat, you will need to ensure that there is some effective scheme for the enforcement of covenants between the tenants. When drafting the lease on behalf of a landlord, therefore, you should ensure that such a scheme is set up.

It is unlikely that this will be necessary with regard to payment of the service charge provisions as the landlord/management company will be able – and anxious – to recover this. But due to the close proximity of flat tenants, it is usual to find that the tenants are subject to a wide range of covenants controlling their use of the units. So there will be covenants against business use and against causing a nuisance to the neighbours, for example, by noise. If these are to be enforced, it will be a matter for the flat owners themselves, as they are the ones affected by any breach.

In theory the same concerns would exist for commercial lease tenants of part of an office building or a unit in a shopping centre. However, in practice, tenants of commercial premises often seem content to rely on the landlord to enforce against adjoining tenants, without procuring any obligation on them to do so. Such tenants are probably aware that a landlord of, for example, a shopping centre, needs to ensure that tenants comply with their lease covenants if they are to have a successful and fully-let centre. They are also aware that if enforcement action against an adjoining tenant is undertaken by them, or at their insistence, it will usually be at their cost. This is something they would generally rather avoid.

37.5.2 What to look for

If an ability mutually to enforce covenants is desirable, you should check the following:

(a) There should be a covenant by the landlord in the lease that they will impose the same covenants in all the flat leases.

(b) There should then be a covenant by the landlord to enforce all the covenants in the lease against another flat owner on the request of another tenant. This will, of course, be at the requesting tenant's expense. There is often a proviso that the landlord is obliged to commence proceedings only if counsel's advice is produced recommending such a course of action. The advantage of this kind of clause is that it will enable the enforcement of both negative and positive covenants.

Another method of enforcement is a scheme of development, in freehold land often referred to as a 'building scheme', which works in the same way in leasehold flats as well. This will enable any flat owner to sue any other directly, ie without the landlord's assistance. This works, though, only in relation to negative (restrictive) covenants, for example those restricting the use of the property. You should check to ensure that the basic requirements of such a scheme are present, ie that the lease contains statements that it is intended to impose the same covenants on all the flats and that it is the intention of the parties that they should be mutually enforceable.

A further possibility is to make use of the provisions of the Contracts (Rights of Third Parties) Act 1999. This allows someone who is not a party to a contract to sue on it, provided that it purports to confer a benefit on them. The third party must be expressly identified, either by name or as a member of a class, or as answering a particular description, but need not be in existence when the contract is entered into. Thus, if the covenant purports to benefit 'the Tenants for the time being of the other flats in the Building', this would allow both present and future tenants to enforce the covenant.

37.6 UNFAIR TERMS

Part 2 of the CRA 2015 applies to contracts made between a 'trader' and a 'consumer'. It is envisaged that this will catch leases between a builder or professional landlord and a private individual. The requirements of the CRA 2015 should therefore be borne in mind when drafting such a lease (see **18.9**).

SUMMARY

- Long residential and commercial leases are relatively complex documents because they attempt to deal with all the issues that might conceivably arise during the term.
- Registrable leases granted on or after 19 June 2006 must contain certain clauses prescribed by Land Registry.

- Most leases have a similar structure: parties, extent of the demised property, tenant's covenants, landlord's covenants and provisos.
- When the lease is of part of the building, the tenant must be granted easements so that they can have access to and use necessary facilities which are not demised to them.
- The lease should make it clear who is to insure the building, how the insurance premium is to be passed on to the tenant(s) and what is going to happen to the building and the rent payable under the lease if the building is damaged by an insured risk.
- A lease must also set out a regime for dealing with a tenant's desire, perhaps several times during the term, to alter and/or change the use of the premises and to dispose of them.
- The tenant's alterations, user and alienation covenants should be drafted in a way that strikes a fair balance between the tenant's need for flexibility and the landlord's need to protect their other tenants and the value of the reversionary interest in the building.
- A covenant may be absolute, qualified or fully qualified.
- In relation to assignment and subletting, s 19(1)(a) of the Landlord and Tenant Act 1927 turns a qualified covenant into a fully qualified covenant. Where it would be unreasonable not to give consent, the landlord is also under a statutory duty to give consent within a reasonable time.
- In relation to assignment only, leases made on or after 1 January 1996 may contain specified circumstances in which the landlord may withhold consent and specific conditions subject to which consent to assignment may be given.
- The lease must set out who is responsible for repairing each part of the building. The costs of repair are borne by the tenant(s). You should consider whether the repair obligations (to carry out and/or to pay) should include renewal and improvement.
- If acting for a landlord, you must ensure that the lease contains a forfeiture clause allowing the landlord to terminate the lease for non-payment of rent or other breaches of covenant. A commercial lease will permit forfeiture on the insolvency of the tenant but this would not be acceptable in a long residential lease.

CHAPTER 38

Flat Management Schemes and Service Charge Provisions

LEARNING OUTCOMES

After reading this chapter you will be able to:

- understand how responsibility for repair and maintenance of a building is divided between the landlord and the tenants in multi-let buildings where the tenants are tenants of part
- appreciate that the landlord of a residential building has different concerns from a landlord of a commercial building
- describe the different legal forms that a flat management scheme can take
- explain the arrangements for the provision of services by the landlord and reimbursement of costs by the tenants in a commercial lease.

38.1 INTRODUCTION

Where a tenant occupies part only of the landlord's building, it is common for the landlord (or someone appointed by them) to assume responsibility for the repair of the structure and common parts of the building (see **Chapter 37**). The landlord (or their appointed agent) may also agree to provide other services, for example cleaning and lighting of the common areas.

In the case of an office block or shopping centre, the landlord will commonly provide the services themselves, either directly or through the use of agents who will manage the block on their behalf. Because of the high rental income and investment value of the reversion, the landlord will have a close personal interest in the management of the building.

In the case of a block of flats, however, the landlord will very often want to rid themselves of the responsibility for providing the services – and also of the hassle of dealing with complaining tenants. In such situations, some form of management company will often be used. There needs to be a scheme in existence which allows the tenants to enforce the provision of services against the company, and enables the company to enforce payment of the service charge against the tenants.

38.2 FLAT MANAGEMENT SCHEMES

38.2.1 The parties' objectives

38.2.1.1 Landlord's objectives

The objective for the landlord is to avoid all responsibility for the maintenance of the block, yet provide a system of maintenance which will be acceptable to prospective tenants and their mortgagees. The landlord will also often require a system which preserves the rental income and investment value of the reversion to the block, and will ensure that the service charge contributions are recoverable from successors in title to the original tenant.

38.2.1.2 Tenant's objectives

The objective for the tenant is to be able to enforce the maintenance and repairing obligations both as against the landlord and against their successors in title. In the larger schemes, it is usual for a management company to take over the landlord's responsibilities, and special problems can then arise. If, as is often the case with flats, the repairs are to be undertaken by a management company specially set up for that purpose, consideration should be given as to the worth of such a covenant, and if necessary (and possible) a guarantee should be obtained from the landlord. The danger here is that the management company may become insolvent and thus unable to carry out its repairing obligations. A guarantee from the landlord will not be implied by the courts.

38.2.1.3 Mortgagee's objectives

It is usual for an institutional mortgagee to insist that there should be a satisfactory scheme for enforcing landlord's covenants, and that a copy of a management company's memorandum and articles of association, together with the tenant's share certificate, should be deposited with the title deeds (see **38.2.2.3**).

38.2.2 Types of flat management scheme

38.2.2.1 Direct management by landlord

Here, the landlord has responsibility for providing the services personally because of the covenant to do so. The landlord will recoup the cost through the service charge. The tenants will then covenant to pay the service charge. The obligations will then be enforceable by and against successors in title under normal landlord and tenant principles.

38.2.2.2 Management by agent

In this case, as above, the landlord is responsible for the repairs, etc, but they discharge that responsibility by employing agents ('managing agents') to take day-to-day charge of matters. As the ultimate responsibility is the landlord's and the service charge is payable to the landlord, enforceability is as in **38.2.2.1**.

38.2.2.3 Use of a management company

The use of a management company has great attractions for both landlords and tenants. The landlord fulfils their objectives; they are free from the responsibility of running the block. The scheme is normally that the management company will be owned and controlled by the flat owners themselves, and so the tenants have the bonus of being in control of the maintenance of the block. They will thus be able to ensure that the block is properly maintained and that the service charges are not excessive. Unless the management company is 'limited by guarantee' (and therefore does not have shares), the flat owners will own shares in the management company. Indeed, it will usually be a condition of purchase that the flat buyer becomes a shareholder in the management company. Usually, the company's constitution will also require that, on a sale of the property, the shares in the management company must also be transferred to the new owner.

However, the company has to be run. Someone will need to look after the accounts, make the necessary returns to Companies House, and arrange for the provision of the services and repairs themselves. Is there someone willing to take on this often thankless job? Is the person who is willing actually able to do the job? Many blocks of flats with tenants' management companies work very well; but some of the most badly maintained are run by tenants' companies, where agreement to undertake work, which some tenants do not think necessary, can never be found.

There are various alternative schemes which make use of a management company.

Transfer of freehold

Here, the landlord transfers the reversion to the management company. The management company then becomes the tenants' landlord, and the covenants are enforceable against and by it under normal landlord and tenant principles. This has the disadvantage to a landlord that they lose the investment in the ownership of the freehold reversion.

Concurrent lease

Here, having granted leases of the individual flats, the landlord then grants a concurrent lease of the reversion in the whole of the block to the management company. This concurrent lease takes effect at the same time as and subject to the leases of the individual flats. It thus has the effect of making the management company the flat owners' landlord for the duration of the concurrent lease. (This will usually be perhaps one or two days shorter in length than the flat leases themselves.) In this way, the repairing obligations and the obligation to pay the service charge are enforceable under normal landlord and tenant principles.

Variations

Management company joins in the flat leases

The landlord grants the leases of the flats in the usual way, but the management company joins in those leases to covenant to provide the services. The tenants then covenant to pay the service charge to the management company.

The covenants between the management company and tenants are not covenants between landlord and tenant, and so, on the face of it, are not enforceable by and against successors in title to the tenant and the management company. However, for 'new leases' (ie, those granted on or after 1 January 1996), s 12 of the Landlord and Tenant (Covenants) Act 1995 provides that a covenant in a lease with a management company in these circumstances will be enforceable in the same way as covenants between landlord and tenant. Use of this provision will avoid the need for the complications (and slight extra expense) of the concurrent lease. However, where the management company has no legal estate in the common parts then it is necessary to ensure that it is given adequate rights of access to the building in order to enable it to carry out the repair and maintenance obligations.

Service charge directed to be paid to management company

In this scheme, the landlord grants the leases of the flats and covenants with the tenants to provide the services in the usual way. The management company joins in the leases and the landlord directs payment of the service charge to it, in consideration of its agreeing to provide the services. The covenants are then enforceable between the landlord and the tenants in the normal way. But if the management company defaults, the landlord has to provide the services. This is not good for the landlord, but it is a worthwhile reassurance for the tenants.

38.2.2.4 Management by the tenants

The Commonhold and Leasehold Reform Act 2002 gives flat owners the opportunity to run their own block through a Right to Manage Company. This includes the provision of services and the giving of consents in relation to qualified covenants. The legislation is complex and outside the scope of this book, and a specialist text should be consulted for further detail.

The *Lenders' Handbook* (see **Appendix 7**) also sets out detailed requirements as to what management arrangements are acceptable for mortgage purposes.

38.3 SERVICE CHARGE PROVISIONS

38.3.1 Introduction

Whether services are provided directly by the landlord or via a management company, the cost of providing the services will be passed on to the tenants by means of a service charge. The total expenditure in a year will be divided up between the various tenants in the building in proportions set out in the lease. In addition to repairs, the service charge payments will also usually cover other matters such as the painting and decoration of the building, and the cleaning and maintenance of the hallways, stairs, lifts, gardens, car parks, toilets, etc.

Many of the problems which arise as between landlord and tenant stem from service charge disputes. Tenants frequently complain of work not being done to proper standards, or of costs being too high – or both! Particular care should therefore be taken in drafting or approving this clause.

38.3.2 Contents of the clause

38.3.2.1 General principle

Tenants are obliged to pay only for matters which have been agreed in the lease. When acting for the landlord, you should take care in drafting the lease to ensure that all necessary expenditure on the building can be recovered from the tenants. When acting for a prospective tenant, you should also check precisely what the tenant will be agreeing to pay for if they enter into the lease. You should further check carefully what services the landlord/management company is actually *obliged* to provide.

38.3.2.2 Obligatory and discretionary services

It is usual for the landlord to be obliged to provide the essential services, for example repairs, and then for the lease to provide that if the landlord supplies various ancillary facilities, for example an entry phone system in residential flats, or the employment of security guards in a commercial block, the tenants will be obliged to pay for them if the landlord actually does provide those facilities. You should ensure that there is an obligation to provide all essential services, ie not just repairs but also cleaning and maintenance of the common parts (see further **38.3.2.3** below). Also, you should check to see what optional items are included, and warn the client if there is a potential for considerable extra expense in respect of non-essential items which the landlord might decide to provide. The renewal and replacement of plant and equipment and improvements to the building can be particularly controversial areas. The tenant should be aware that if the landlord can recharge such items of cost via the service charge, they may end up funding a refurbishment programme for the landlord's building. This may occur when the tenant's term is nearing its end, leaving them with very little time to enjoy the results of the refurbishment. Tenants should also be aware that landlords may look to reduce energy consumption, in some cases as a result of Government schemes that make it financially advantageous for the largest consumers of electricity to cut their consumption. In consequence, landlords may seek to replace inefficient air conditioning, lighting and heating systems. Again, if the lease allows the landlord to pass on the costs of doing this to the tenant via the service charge, this can prove very expensive for the tenant.

38.3.2.3 Landlord's obligations

The landlord's obligations for essential services should include:

(a) repairs and decoration;

(b) insurance;

(c) any payments under a head lease;

(d) furnishing, cleaning and lighting the common parts;

(e) car park/garden and grounds maintenance; and

(f) maintenance of lifts.

38.3.2.4 Discretionary services

The optional items may include:

(a) establishing a reserve or sinking fund;
(b) renewals and replacements of plant and equipment;
(c) improvements;
(d) entry phone system;
(e) resident caretaker; and
(f) security staff/other enhanced security arrangements.

38.3.2.5 Other expenditure

The landlord will probably have to incur other items of expenditure in providing the services. If you act for the landlord, you should make sure that these are expressly made recoverable, for example:

(a) legal expenses and other professional fees;
(b) management charge; and
(d) costs of enforcing the obligations under the lease, for example to pay the rent and service charge.

Otherwise, the landlord would have to bear the cost of these personally. The tenant's solicitor should, of course, ensure that their client is happy to pay such sums.

38.3.3 Methods of apportioning the cost

There are various formulae which you will find used to apportion the cost amongst the various tenants. Which one is appropriate in any given situation will depend upon the full circumstances of each particular case. When drafting a lease you should discuss the formula to be chosen with the landlord and the landlord's surveyors at an early stage so that the appropriate formula can be included in the draft lease.

The following is a selection of those you are most likely to encounter.

38.3.3.1 Proportionate to rateable value

This is common in older developments, the principle being that larger premises (with larger rateable values) should pay a larger share than the smaller ones. With the ending of domestic rates, this method is no longer possible for new flat developments.

38.3.3.2 Proportionate to floor area

This is another way of ensuring that larger premises pay a higher proportion for services than smaller premises.

38.3.3.3 Equally between the tenants

This is only sensible in a building where all the premises are the same size and will make the same use of the services.

38.3.3.4 A 'fair proportion'

This allows variations to be made to take into account the fact that different premises may make different levels of use of the various services provided. It also allows changes to be made during the term of the lease to take into account different uses or circumstances, for example an extension of the building. Such a vague provision may, however, lead to disputes with tenants as to what is in fact 'fair'.

38.3.3.5 A stated proportion of each of the various expenses

This proportion will vary depending upon the situation and size of premises concerned. This may be the same proportion of *all* the expenses, or it may allow almost infinite flexibility to apportion different elements of the service charge costs in different proportions amongst the various tenants. For example, why should ground-floor tenants have to contribute towards the (often large) cost of maintaining the lift? When acting for the landlord, care should be taken when you are drafting the leases to ensure that all the different proportions to be paid by the various tenants add up to 100%!

38.3.3.6 Unlet units

Both landlords' and tenants' advisers should think carefully about what is to be done regarding the contributions due in respect of any premises which are unlet.

If no one is making up the contributions from unlet units, this could have serious implications. It is likely to be the case that the cost of providing the services will still be the same, even though one or more units are unlet. Most tenants expect that the landlord will make up these payments, and the lease should be amended to reflect this.

38.3.4 Reserve and sinking funds

38.3.4.1 Purpose and effect

Although normally the idea behind a service charge is that all expenditure incurred in one year will be covered by the payments made in that year, you will sometimes find that the landlord/ management company will set up a reserve or sinking fund to deal with unexpected expenditure which might arise during a year, or to cover anticipated major expenditure. For example, every few years the outside of the building will need painting, an expensive task. Similarly, eventually the lifts will need replacing – a very expensive item to be paid for out of one year's service charges.

A large increase in the amounts demanded by way of service charge in one year when compared with the previous year could pose serious financial difficulties for the tenants and, if some are unable or refuse to pay, for the landlord/management company itself and the other tenants. It is often thought sensible, therefore, to build up a fund by small contributions every year, so that this can be used in years of expected or unexpectedly high expenditure to even out the amount of the service charge contributions.

Apart from evening out the bills in this way, a sinking fund may also be seen to be fairer when changes in the identity of the tenants are considered. For example, someone buying a flat in the year in which the lift was going to be replaced would have to pay a very large service charge that year to pay for it, whereas the previous owners who had used (and worn out) the lift would have had to pay nothing towards its replacement.

38.3.4.2 Express provisions required

In order to recover contributions to such a fund, express provision is required in the lease. The lease should declare that the fund is to be held on trust. This is to protect the fund against being seized by the landlord's creditors should the landlord become insolvent.

38.3.4.3 When can the fund be used?

When drafting or approving a clause dealing with a reserve or sinking fund, careful thought needs to be given as to when recourse to the fund may or must be made by the landlord. You must appreciate that everything depends upon the wording of the lease itself.

The landlord will not wish to be too tied down or restricted by the terms of the lease. On the other hand, the tenant will want to limit the landlord's discretion.

Is there a danger that when a major item of expenditure falls due, the landlord simply charges it to that year's service charge in the normal way and does not make use of the sinking fund? Equally, is there a risk that the landlord uses the reserve fund for items of a recurring nature, for example cleaning bills, rather than for the unexpected items for which it is really intended? Perhaps a fair compromise is a provision obliging the landlord to charge at least 50% of the cost of stated major items to the fund, for example painting the exterior, replacing lifts, etc.

38.3.4.4 Unlet units

As with the service charge itself, there is again the problem of unlet units. Is the landlord required to make the contributions in respect of these? The terms of the lease should make it clear whether the landlord's obligation to make the service charge contributions in respect of unlet units includes the contributions to the sinking fund or not.

38.3.4.5 Assignments of the lease

A tenant assigning their lease may wish to be reimbursed by the assignee with the amount of the unexpended contributions to the fund. After all, the incoming tenant will reap the benefit of these in the shape of reduced service charge contributions in the future. This will be possible, however, only if the landlord is obliged by the lease to provide information about the size, etc of the fund. The landlord will probably not wish to agree to this because of the work involved in providing the information.

38.3.5 Certificate of amount due

38.3.5.1 Who is to prepare the certificate?

The lease should state who is to prepare the accounts and certify the amount due from each tenant. It is common for the draft lease to state that this certificate is conclusive. It would obviously be inconvenient for the landlord if such a certificate were to be open to challenge. Tenants should be warned that apparently, at common law, if you agree to such a clause then it will be conclusive on matters of law, ie as to the construction of the service charge clause, as well as matters of fact, ie the costs incurred.

In *Sara and Hossein Asset Holdings Ltd v Blacks Outdoor Retail Ltd* [2020] EWCA Civ 1521, the Court of Appeal stated that where a certificate is stated to be conclusive, it is conclusive as to the amount of the total cost and the sum payable by the tenant (ie the tenant could not suggest that certain costs did not fall within the scope of the recoverable costs). Such provisions should therefore be resisted by tenants, particularly those of commercial properties, who do not have the statutory protections afforded to residential tenants (see **38.4**).

38.3.5.2 Can an employee be used?

When acting for a tenant, you should check carefully who is to prepare this certificate. It should be someone independent of the landlord and not an employee of the landlord or an associated company.

If the landlord wishes an employee to be able to prepare the certificate, this must be clearly stated. However, if it is clearly stated then this will be binding upon the tenant. Would you be prepared to accept this on behalf of a client?

In any event, under s 21 of the Landlord and Tenant Act 1985, a residential tenant is entitled to request a written summary of the costs incurred. If the service charges are payable by more than four tenants then those costs must be certified by a qualified accountant, defined to exclude an employee of the landlord or the landlord's managing agents. From 1 October 2007 (30 November 2007 in Wales), landlords must send long residential leaseholders a summary of their rights and obligations relating to service charges. If this information is not provided, the tenant may withhold payment of the service charge.

38.3.6 Methods of recouping costs

38.3.6.1 Payments in advance essential

Provision for advance payments will be essential to ensure that the landlord has sufficient funds in hand to finance the necessary works. The method of calculating the amount of the advance payment must also be specified in the lease. You will find several alternatives in use in precedents.

(a) The previous year's expenditure. This is obviously not going to be practical in the first year of a new development; special provision should be made for the first year. In any event, however, it should be borne in mind that expenditure in the previous year might not accurately reflect the expected expenditure in the following year. For example, one year's accounts may include the cost of decoration which would not need to be repeated in the following year.

(b) A fixed sum. There is a danger, however, that this, if it cannot be changed by the terms of the lease, will rapidly become ineffective due to inflation.

(c) An estimate of probable expenditure. This is often the most sensible method, as expenditure can vary greatly from year to year due to non-recurring items of expenditure.

38.3.6.2 Payment/refund of balance

There must be provision for a final balance to be paid when the actual costs for the year are known. Any underpayment will then be payable as a lump sum.

What is to happen to any overpayment? Is this to be repaid to the tenant, or credited towards the next year's account? Usually, the landlord will require it to be credited to the next year's account.

38.4 STATUTORY PROVISIONS RELATING TO SERVICE CHARGES

38.4.1 Residential

It should be noted that various statutory restrictions apply to the recovery of service charges in certain residential tenancies. In particular, the Landlord and Tenant Act 1985 limits what a landlord can recover to those costs that are 'reasonable' and requires landlords to consult with and provide information to tenants in certain circumstances. Additional rights for flat owners are contained in the Commonhold and Leasehold Reform Act 2002. This provides a mechanism for flat owners to manage their own block (including the provision of services) through the use of a Right to Manage Company. The Leasehold and Freehold Reform Act 2024 contains provisions to extend the Right to Manage and increase the rights of residential leaseholders regarding service charges, insurance, administration charges and litigation costs. At the time of writing, these provisions require secondary legislation to bring them into effect and so are not yet law.

The Building Safety Act 2022 offers some very limited protection for leaseholders in respect of work required to remedy building safety defects (eg the removal of unsafe cladding). It does not prevent the recovery of the costs of such remediation works from leaseholders but does impose obligations on the landlord to ascertain if there are alternative sources of funding or recovery for those costs. The Act also establishes new legal duties for landlords and building owners of high rise residential buildings of 18 metres or at least seven storeys to keep their building safe. There will be a cost associated with some of these duties, which can be passed to leaseholders (with a lease of seven years or more) through a new Building Safety Charge.

The detail of these provisions is outside the scope of this book and a specialist text should be consulted for further information.

38.4.2 Code of Practice for commercial property service charges

There are no equivalent statutory restrictions on service charges for commercial property and, unfortunately, disputes between landlord and tenant are common. The Royal Institution of Chartered Surveyors (RICS) has published a professional statement entitled 'Service Charges in Commercial Property (1st edition)', which can be accessed via the RICS website. This statement includes certain mandatory provisions relating to commercial property service charges, designed to ensure service charges are operated fairly and transparently. However, the statement only binds RICS members and regulated firms involved in property management. The City of London Law Society has drawn up service charge lease provisions that comply with the provisions of the RICS statement. These can be accessed from its website and are a useful resource for solicitors when negotiating a lease of commercial property containing service charge provisions.

SUMMARY

- In multi-let buildings, it is not appropriate for the tenants to be responsible for carrying out the repair and maintenance of the structural and common parts of the building as these parts are not demised to them. However, the costs of such repair and maintenance will be borne by the tenants.
- A landlord of a residential building will often prefer to hand over responsibility for repair and maintenance of the structural and common parts of the building to a management company, rather than directly managing the building themselves or employing an agent to do it for them. Often, the shareholders and officers of the management company are the tenants themselves. Even where this is the case, residential tenants must have a way of enforcing the landlord's covenants for repair and maintenance against the management company and there are a number of different ways to achieve this.
- A landlord of a commercial building may manage the building directly or employ an agent or management company to do it.
- A lease of part will contain detailed provisions as to what services the landlord will provide, what proportion of the costs the tenant will pay as service charge, when the tenant will pay the service charge and how the tenant can satisfy themselves that appropriate services have been provided in a cost-efficient manner.

CHAPTER 39

Rent Review in Commercial Leases

LEARNING OUTCOMES

After reading this chapter you will be able to:

- consider whether the rent reserved by a commercial lease should be reviewed during the term and, if so, how often the review should take place
- advise on the types of rent review available and the suitability of each type for particular commercial circumstances
- in relation to an open market revaluation review, explain the concept of the hypothetical letting and the purpose of assumptions and disregards
- implement the procedure for an open market revaluation review.

39.1 THE NEED FOR REVIEW IN COMMERCIAL LEASES

If the lease is granted for anything longer than about five years, the parties will have to address their minds to the question of whether provision should be made in the lease for varying the annual rent at intervals during the term.

39.2 REGULARITY OF REVIEW IN COMMERCIAL LEASES

Reviews are commonly programmed to occur at three- or five-year intervals during the term. In, say, a modern 15-year 'institutional' letting, reviews will be programmed to occur at every fifth anniversary of the term.

It is suggested that computation of the review dates in the lease is best achieved by reference to anniversaries of the term commencement date. However, if this method is adopted, the tenant should check that the term commencement date has not been significantly backdated by the landlord, as this would have the effect of advancing the first review date (eg, if the term runs from 29 September 2011, but the lease is completed only on 1 November 2012, the fifth anniversary of the term is less than four years away). Instead of calculating the dates as anniversaries of the start of the term, some leases set out the exact review dates in the lease. This ought to be avoided, though, since it can create valuation problems at review if the rent review clause in the lease (with its specific review dates) is incorporated as a term of the hypothetical letting.

Landlords may attempt to insert a rent review date on the penultimate day of the term. At first sight this might seem illogical since the term is about to end, but of course the tenant is likely to enjoy a statutory continuation of their tenancy under s 24(1) of the Landlord and Tenant Act 1954, whereby the tenancy will continue beyond the expiry date at the rent then payable. Whilst the landlord may be able to apply to the court under s 24A of the Landlord and Tenant Act 1954 for an interim rent to be fixed (see **40.9**) during the continuation, some landlords prefer to implement a penultimate day contractual rent review. This is because a penultimate day rent review can secure a greater increase in rent than an interim rent application due to the method of assessment used in the latter (see **40.9**).

The tenant ought to resist a penultimate day rent review for the obvious reason that s 24A may be a better deal. However, the issue has become less significant as, since 2004, tenants, as well as landlords, have the ability to apply for an interim rent under the 1954 Act. This means that even if the lease contains a penultimate day review, the rent determined under it can, after one day, be replaced by the rent determined under an interim rent application made by the tenant. The penultimate day review will therefore only be of use to the landlord if the tenant fails to make an interim rent application.

39.3 TYPES OF RENT REVIEW CLAUSES

There are various ways in which rent may be varied during the term of a commercial lease.

39.3.1 Fixed increases

The lease might provide, for example, that in a lease for a 10-year term, the rent is set at £10,000 for the first three years of the term, £15,000 for the next three years, and £20,000 for the remainder of the term. This sort of clause would be very rare, since the parties to the lease would be placing their faith in the fixed increases proving to be realistic.

39.3.2 Index-linked clauses

Some of the early forms of rent review clauses required the rent to be periodically reassessed by linking the rent to an index recording supposed changes in the value of money. Indexes such as the General Index of Retail Prices can be used in order to revise the rent either at the review dates, or at every rent payment date. Reference should be made to one of the standard works on landlord and tenant law for information as to how such clauses work in practice.

39.3.3 Turnover rents

A turnover rent is one which is geared to the turnover of the tenant's business, and can therefore be considered by the landlord only where turnover is generated at the premises. A turnover rent would be impractical in the case of office or warehouse premises, but could be considered, for example, in the case of a shop. The tenant's rent (or at least a proportion of it) is worked out as a percentage of the turnover. If a turnover rent clause is to be used, thought will have to be given in the lease to the definition of the turnover of the business (eg, whether credit sales are to be included with cash sales as part of the turnover, or whether Internet sales are to be included). The impact of VAT should also be dealt with, ie whether the turnover is to be taken as excluding or including VAT. Other considerations include whether access will be given to the landlord to inspect the tenant's books, how turnover is to be apportioned if it is generated at the demised premises and other premises, and whether the tenant is to be obliged in the lease to continue trading from the premises in order to generate turnover. Reference should be made to one of the standard works on landlord and tenant law for further details of the operation of turnover rent clauses.

39.3.4 Open market revaluation review clauses

An open market revaluation (OMRV) review requires the rent to be revised in accordance with changes in the property market.

The most common form of rent review clause will provide that at every rent review date (eg, every fifth anniversary of the term) the parties should seek to agree upon a figure that equates to what is then the current open market rent for a letting of the tenant's premises. The aim of the exercise is to find out how much a tenant in the open market would be prepared to pay, in terms of rent per annum, if the tenant's premises were available to let in the open market of the relevant review date. This agreement is achieved either by some form of informal negotiated process between the landlord and the tenant, or, more rarely, by the service of notices and counter-notices which specify proposals and counter-proposals as to the revised rent. If agreement cannot be reached, the clause should provide for the appointment of an independent valuer who will determine the revised rent. The valuer will be directed by the review clause to take certain matters into account in conducting their valuation, and to disregard others, and they will call upon evidence of rental valuations of other comparable leasehold interests in the locality.

Often, such reviews operate on an 'upwards only' basis; in other words, on review, the rent will be the higher of the rent currently being paid or that determined on review. In this way, rent will never decrease and at worst (from the landlord's point of view) will remain static. Preferable for the tenant are provisions which allow for rent to decrease on review if the OMRV has fallen, which is sometimes referred to an 'upwards and downwards' rent review.

The remainder of this chapter will focus on the OMRV clause, as this is the most frequently encountered in practice.

39.4 OPEN MARKET REVALUATIONS

In conducting the valuation on review, it should be understood what the valuer is assessing. This will be not only the value of the physical premises and their geographical location, but also the length of the term for which the premises are let and the terms of the lease under which they are held, as these elements can have just as important an impact on the level of rent as the state and location of the premises.

Having established that it is not the premises but an interest in the premises which has to be valued at each review date, it must also be understood that it is not the tenant's own interest that will be valued but a hypothetical interest in the premises, as the premises are not actually being made available on the market as the current tenant is in occupation of the premises under the terms of their existing lease. Given the artificiality of this exercise, it is necessary to build in certain adjustments to the valuation exercise to prevent unfairness and uncertainty between the parties. For example, consider the position of the tenant who, in breach of their obligations under the lease, has allowed the premises to fall into disrepair, which has had the effect of reducing the OMRV of the premises. Is it fair that the landlord should suffer at rent review by having the rent depressed on account of the tenant's breach of covenant? Equally, from a tenant's perspective, consider the position of a tenant who, in the fourth year of the term, at their own expense, voluntarily made improvements to the premises which had the effect of increasing the OMRV of their interest in the premises. Is it fair that the tenant should suffer at rent review by having to pay an increased rent which reflects in part the rental value attributable to these improvements?

These are just two of the many problems inherent in a valuation of the tenant's actual interest. As a result of these difficulties and injustices connected with such a valuation, it is accepted that the valuer should be instructed by the rent review clause to ascertain the OMRV of a hypothetical interest in the premises. The valuer should be directed by the clause to calculate how much rent per annum a hypothetical willing tenant would be prepared to pay for a letting of the premises, with vacant possession, for a hypothetical term. The valuer is directed by the lease to make certain assumptions about the terms of the letting, and to disregard certain matters which might otherwise distort the OMRV, in order to overcome the difficulties and eradicate the injustices referred to above.

39.4.1 The aim of the exercise

The valuer will be directed by the lease to ascertain the open market rental value of a hypothetical letting of the premises at each review date. It is common (where time is not of the essence) for the revised rent actually to be agreed upon or determined at some point either before or after the review date, with the lease providing for the new rent to apply from the review date. However, the tenant should not allow the valuation date to be capable of variation; the tenant should ensure that the valuer is directed to find the open market rent for the premises at the review date. Any clause which purports to allow the valuation date to be fixed by the service of a notice by the landlord is to be resisted for the simple reason that, in a falling market, the landlord would serve their notice early to secure a higher rent, whilst in a rising market they would serve the notice late at a time when the market was at its peak, safe in the knowledge that the revised rent would be backdated and payable from the review date.

Different phrases are used by different clauses to define the rent to be ascertained. Some leases will require the valuer to find a 'reasonable rent' for a letting of the premises, or a 'fair rent', or a 'market rent', or a 'rack rent' or 'the open market rent'. The last clause is the one most commonly used in practice, and is therefore a phrase with which professional valuers are familiar. Other phrases are less common, and are open to adverse interpretations by valuers and the court.

Most tenants would want to avoid the use of the expression 'the best rent at which the premises might be let', since this might allow the valuer to consider the possibility of what is known as a special purchaser's bid. If, by chance, the market for a hypothetical letting of the premises contains a potential bidder who would be prepared to bid in excess of what would ordinarily be considered to be the market rent, the 'best' rent would be the rent which the special bidder would be prepared to pay. For example, if the premises which are the subject matter of the hypothetical letting are situated next to premises occupied by a business which is desperate to expand, the 'best' rent might be the rent which that business would be willing to pay.

39.4.2 The circumstances of the letting

To enable the valuer to do their job, the rent review clause must clearly indicate the circumstances in which a hypothetical letting of the premises is to be contemplated. For example, the valuer must be able to establish which premises are to be the subject matter of the letting, whether there is a market for such a letting, whether the premises would be available with or without vacant possession, and what the terms of the letting would be. It is common for the clause to require the valuer to find the open market rent of a letting of the tenant's vacant premises, for a specified duration, on the assumption that there is a market for the letting which will be granted without the payment or receipt of a premium, and subject only to the terms of the actual lease (except as to the amount of the annual rent).

39.4.2.1 The premises

Usually, the valuer is required to ascertain the rental value of a hypothetical letting of the premises actually demised by the tenant's lease. The draftsman should therefore ensure that the demised premises are clearly defined by the parcels clause in the lease (see **37.3.6**), and that they enjoy the benefit of all necessary rights and easements to enable them to be used for their permitted purpose.

A valuer uses comparables as evidence in their valuation of a letting of the premises. They draw upon evidence of rents currently being paid by tenants of comparable buildings, let in comparable circumstances, on comparable terms. If the actual premises demised to the tenant are unique or exceptional (eg, an over-sized warehouse), there may be no comparables in the area for the valuer to use. In that case, the lease ought to require the valuer to adopt a different approach to their valuation, perhaps by directing them to take account of rental values of other premises which would not ordinarily count as comparables. This in itself may lead to valuation problems as, for example, in *Dukeminster (Ebbgate House One) Ltd v Somerfield Properties Co Ltd* [1997] 40 EG 157.

39.4.2.2 The market

As the hypothetical letting is an artificial creation, and since leasehold valuations cannot be carried out in the abstract, an artificial market has to be created. If the rent review clause does not create a well-balanced hypothetical market in which the letting can be contemplated, it would be open for the tenant (in appropriate cases) to argue at review that no market exists for a letting of the tenant's premises, and that therefore an 'open market' rent for the premises would be merely nominal, or a peppercorn. An example of this might occur if the tenant was occupying premises which were now outdated to such an extent that they were impractical for modern use, or where the premises were so exceptional that only the tenant themselves would contemplate occupying them. Only the actual tenant would be in the hypothetical market for such premises, and even they might not be in the market if they could show that they have actively been trying to dispose of the lease. The market might truly be dead.

To create a market, the rent review clause usually requires the valuer to assume that the hypothetical letting is taking place in the open market and being granted by a 'willing landlord' to a 'willing tenant'. In *FR Evans (Leeds) Ltd v English Electric Co Ltd* (1977) 245 EG 657, it was held that where such phrases are used, it means that the valuer must assume that there are two hypothetical people who are prepared to enter into the arrangement, neither of whom is being forced to do so, and neither of whom is affected by any personal difficulties (eg, a landlord with cash-flow problems, or a tenant who has just lost their old premises) which would prejudice their position in open market negotiations. A willing landlord is an abstract person, but is someone who has the right to grant a lease of the premises; and a willing tenant, again an abstraction, is someone who is actively seeking premises to fulfil a need that these premises would fulfil. It is implicit in the use of these phrases that there is at least one willing tenant in the market, and that there is a rent upon which they will agree.

Even if the lease is silent as to whether there is assumed to be a willing tenant, the Court of Appeal has held in *Dennis & Robinson Ltd v Kiossos Establishment* [1987] 1 EGLR 133 that such a creature is in any case to be assumed, since a rent review clause which asks for an open market valuation by its nature requires there to be at least one willing tenant in the market. This means that for rent review purposes, where an open market valuation is required, there will always be someone in the hypothetical market who would be prepared to take a letting of the premises, and therefore the tenant cannot argue that the market is completely dead. However, quite how much a willing tenant would be willing to pay is for the valuer to decide. If the market is well and truly dead, the landlord's only protection is an upwards only rent review clause.

39.4.2.3 The consideration

Any consideration moving between the parties at the time of the grant is likely to have a bearing on the amount of rent to be paid by the tenant. Such movements are not uncommon in the open market. For example, a landlord may seek to induce a tenant to take the lease at a certain level of rent by offering them a reverse premium (ie, a sum of money payable by the landlord to the tenant to induce them to take the lease), without which the tenant might only be prepared to pay rent at a lower level. A rent-free period may be offered by a landlord, either as a straightforward inducement as above, or to compensate a tenant for the costs that will be incurred in fitting out the premises at the start of the term. Without the rent-free period, the tenant might only be prepared to pay a lower rent. If the tenant pays a premium to the landlord at the outset, this may be reflected in the tenant paying a rent lower than they would otherwise pay.

As far as the hypothetical letting is concerned, it is common for the rent review clause to assume that no consideration (in the form of a premium) will be moving between the parties on the grant of the hypothetical letting. As seen above, such payments can distort the amount of initial rent payable by a tenant. Therefore, to get the clearest indication of what the market rent for the letting would be, it ought to be assumed that no premium is to be paid on the grant of the hypothetical letting. Furthermore, the landlord may seek to include a provision which states that no inducement in the form of a rent-free period will be given to the hypothetical tenant on the grant of the hypothetical lease.

This is an attempt by the landlord to deprive the tenant of the effect of such concessions granted in the market place (thereby keeping the level of rent, on review, artificially high). The landlord is trying to achieve a headline rent rather than an effective rent. For example, if the tenant agrees to take a lease at £100,000 per annum for a term of five years, but is to receive a 12-month rent-free period, whilst the headline rent (the rent stated to be payable under the lease) remains at £100,000 per annum, the annual rent effectively payable (the 'effective' rent) is only £80,000. At review, therefore, the landlord would argue that the effect of disregarding any rent-free period which might be available in the open market, is that the new rent payable from review should be a headline rent not an effective rent. The tenant would argue that since the hypothetical tenant is not getting the benefit of a rent-free period, the revised rent should therefore be discounted to compensate the hypothetical tenant for a benefit they have not received. There have been several cases on the effect of these types of provisions.

The Court of Appeal in *Broadgate Square plc v Lehman Brothers Ltd* [1995] 01 EG 111, applying the purposive approach to the interpretation of the relevant clause, said that 'the court will lean against a construction which would require payment of rent upon an assumption that the tenant has received the benefit of a rent-free period, which he has not in fact received' (*per* Leggatt LJ). However, such an approach cannot be adopted in the face of clear, unambiguous language. According to Hoffmann LJ, 'if upon its true construction the clause deems the market rent to be whatever is the headline rent after a rent-free period granted ... the tenant cannot complain because in changed market conditions it is more onerous than anyone would have foreseen'. However, the presence of such a clause in the hypothetical letting may itself be an onerous provision which justifies a reduction in the OMRV (possibly to the extent that it negates the effect of the landlord's clever drafting).

39.4.2.4 Possession

As the valuer is assessing the rental value of the tenant's existing premises, are they to assume that the tenant is still there (in which case rent to be paid by a hypothetical bidder would be very low), or are they to assume that the tenant has vacated? Naturally, they must assume that the tenant has moved out, and therefore most rent review clauses of this type include an assumption that vacant possession is available for the hypothetical letting.

Care must be taken in making this assumption, because in certain cases it can give rise to problems:

(a) If the tenant has sub-let all or part of the premises, an assumption that vacant possession is to be available will mean that the effect on rent of the presence of the sub-tenant will have to be disregarded. If the sub-tenant occupies for valuable business purposes (eg, the premises in question are high street offices where the ground floor has been sub-let as a high-class shop), the presence of the sub-tenancy would ordinarily increase the rental value of the head leasehold interest since the head tenant would expect to receive lucrative sub-lease rents. The assumption of vacant possession would deny the landlord the opportunity to bring a valuable sub-letting into account at review. If the sub-tenancy was for residential purposes, yielding precious little in terms of sub-lease rents, the assumption of vacant possession would allow the landlord to have the sub-letting disregarded and, depending on the other terms of the hypothetical letting, enable the premises to be valued as a whole for the permitted business purpose.

(b) The assumption of vacant possession means that the tenant is deemed to have moved out of the premises and, as all vacating tenants would do, they are deemed to have removed and taken their fixtures with them. In respect of shop premises, this might mean that all of the shop fittings must be assumed to have been removed, leaving nothing remaining but a shell. (Of course, in reality, the premises are still fully fitted out, but for hypothetical valuation purposes, the tenant's fixtures are assumed to have gone.) If a hypothetical tenant were to bid in the open market for these premises then, depending upon market forces prevalent at the time, they might demand a rent-free period in order to compensate for the time it will take to carry out a notional fitting out of the premises (ie, to restore the fittings that have notionally been removed). Since the revised rent has to be a consistent figure payable throughout the period until the next review date, this notional rent-free period would have to be spread out during the review period, or possibly over the rest of the term, thereby reducing the general level of rent (eg, the valuer finds that the rent for the next five years should be £10,000 per annum, but that an incoming tenant would obtain a rent-free period of 12 months; by spreading the notional rent-free period over the five-year review period the rent would be £8,000 per annum). The landlord can counter this problem by including an assumption that, notwithstanding vacant possession, the premises are fully fitted out for occupation (see **39.4.3.1**).

39.4.2.5 The terms

The valuer, in ascertaining the OMRV of a leasehold interest, must look at all of the proposed terms of the lease. The more onerous the lease terms, the less attractive the lease becomes from a tenant's point of view, and therefore the lower the OMRV of the interest. If the rent review clause is silent, the hypothetical letting will be assumed to be granted upon the terms of the tenant's existing lease, since the court does not like to stray too far away from reality, and there is a general preference by the court to construe rent review clauses in such a way as to ensure that the tenant does not end up paying in terms of rent for something that they are not actually getting. Usually, however, the clause directs the valuer to assume that the letting is to be made upon the terms of the tenant's actual letting, as varied from time to time. The fact that the valuer must take account of variations means that it is imperative that, when conducting the review, the valuer checks the terms of all deeds of variation entered into, and all licences granted since the date of the lease, to see if the terms of the actual lease have been changed.

Each of the terms of the lease will be analysed by the valuer at review to see if they will have any effect on the rental value. If either party, with sufficient foresight, feels that a particular term will have a detrimental effect on the rental value (because the term is too wide, or too narrow, or too onerous), that party may seek to have the term excluded from the hypothetical letting, by use of an assumption or a disregard (see **39.4.3**).

The valuer will look closely at all of the terms of the lease, but in particular at the following.

The alienation covenant

If the alienation covenant in the actual lease is too restrictive (eg, by prohibiting all forms of alienation), its incorporation as a term of the hypothetical letting will lead to a decrease in the OMRV of that interest. Similarly, if the actual lease allows only the named tenant to occupy the premises (or only companies within the same group of companies as the tenant), this will have a negative impact on the OMRV. In these cases it will be advisable for the landlord to exclude the excessive restrictions on alienation from the terms of the hypothetical letting. The tenant might consider this to be unfair, and perhaps a compromise would be to widen the alienation covenant in the actual lease.

The user covenant

If the actual lease narrowly defines the permitted use of the premises and allows little or no scope for the tenant to alter that use, a tenant bidding for the lease in the open market is likely to reduce their rental bid to reflect the fact that they would be severely hindered should they wish to dispose of the premises during the term or change the nature of the business. According to *Plinth Property Investments Ltd v Mott, Hay & Anderson* [1979] 1 EGLR 17, the possibility of the landlord agreeing to waive a breach of covenant (eg, by allowing a wider use of the premises than the covenant already permits) has to be ignored. This principle is applicable not just to user covenants (although the *Plinth* case specifically concerned a user covenant) but to all covenants where the landlord is freely able to withhold consent to a change. It is not open to the landlord at review to disregard the detrimental effect on rent of a restrictive clause which has been incorporated into the hypothetical letting by saying that they are or might be prepared to waive the restriction. Further, a landlord cannot unilaterally vary the terms of the lease (see *C & A Pensions Trustees Ltd v British Vita Investments Ltd* (1984) 272 EG 63). If the landlord is intent on tightly restricting the tenant in the user clause in the actual lease, but wants to maximise the rental value of the hypothetical letting at review and is concerned that the incorporation of the restrictive clause into the hypothetical letting will harm the OMRV, they should draft the review clause so that the actual user covenant is to be disregarded and an alternative permitted use is to be assumed. Obviously, the tenant should strongly resist such an approach, since they would find themselves paying a rent from review assessed on the basis of a freedom that they do not in fact possess. Again, a compromise might be to widen the user covenant in the actual lease.

If the lease allows only the named tenant to use the premises for a named business (ie, a very restrictive user covenant), the landlord should try to have the user covenant disregarded at review. If the landlord fails to do so, the court might be prepared to step in to assist them, as in *Sterling Land Office Developments Ltd v Lloyds Bank plc* (1984) 271 EG 894, where a covenant not to use the premises other than as a branch of Lloyds Bank plc was incorporated into the hypothetical letting, but with the name and business left blank, to be completed when the name and business of the hypothetical tenant were known.

Rent and rent review

The review clause will state that the hypothetical letting is to be granted upon the same terms as the actual lease save as to the amount of rent. As the aim of the review exercise is to vary the amount of rent, it is clear that the rent initially reserved by the lease must not be incorporated into the hypothetical letting. However, the tenant must be alert to guard against any form of wording which has the effect of excluding from the hypothetical letting not only the amount of rent reserved, but also the rent review clause itself.

It is a commonly-held view that a tenant bidding for a medium- or long-term letting of premises in the open market, where the annual rent cannot be increased during the term, is likely to pay more than if the letting contained a rent review clause. The tenant would pay a rent in excess of the current market rent in return for a guarantee that the rent will not rise but would be fixed at the initial rent for the entire duration of the term. A long series of cases followed the decision in *National Westminster Bank plc v Arthur Young McClelland Moores & Co* [1985] 1 WLR 1123, where the provisions of a rent review clause were interpreted in such a way as to exclude from the hypothetical letting the rent review provisions. This alone led to the annual rent being increased from £800,000 to £1.209 million, instead of £1.003 million if the rent review clause had been incorporated. Courts today tend to shy away from interpreting a rent review clause in such a way as to exclude a provision for review from the hypothetical letting. In the absence of clear words directing the rent review clause to be disregarded, the court will give effect to the underlying purpose of the clause and will assume that the hypothetical letting contains provisions for the review of rent. However, the tenant must always check carefully that the review clause is not *expressly excluded* from the hypothetical letting, since the court would be bound to give effect to such clear words. Ideally, the hypothetical letting should be 'upon the terms of this lease, other than the amount of rent'.

The length of term

Whether the lease is for a short term or a long term will affect how much rent a tenant is prepared to pay. Whilst a landlord often needs to guarantee rental income by granting a long-term lease, in times of uncertain trading tenants often prefer short-term lettings in order to retain a degree of flexibility and to avoid long-term liability in the event of business failure. If a short-term letting is more attractive to tenants in the current market, it follows that a tenant would be prepared to bid more in terms of rent per annum for such a letting than if a longer term was proposed. On the other hand, other tenants with long-term business plans and a desire for stability and security would be prepared to increase their rental bid in return for a longer letting. The rent review clause must define the length of the hypothetical letting. The landlord will want to maximise the rental value of the hypothetical letting by specifying as the hypothetical term a length which is currently preferred in the market by prospective tenants of premises of the type in question. The landlord will have to ask their surveyor for advice in this regard, since the term to be adopted is purely a matter of valuation, which will differ from lease to lease.

When the valuer makes their valuation, they are allowed to take into account the prospect of the term being renewed under the Landlord and Tenant Act 1954 (see *Secretary of State for Employment v Pivot Properties Limited* (1980) 256 EG 1176). Obviously, the rent will turn out to be higher if there is a strong possibility of renewal. In the *Pivot* case, that possibility led to an uplift in the rent of £850,000 per annum.

39.4.3 Assumptions to be made

Several assumptions have already been considered in respect of the circumstances of the hypothetical letting. Certain other assumptions are also commonly made.

39.4.3.1 Premises fitted out and ready for occupation and use

An assumption is made that the premises are fully fitted out and ready for immediate occupation and use by the incoming tenant. An assumption of vacant possession necessarily leads to an assumption that the tenant has moved out and taken all their fixtures with them. The assumption that the premises are fully fitted out attempts to counter the deemed removal of fixtures by assuming that the hypothetical tenant would be able to move straight into the premises without asking for a rent-free period in which to carry out their notional fitting-out works. Hence the assumption removes any discount the tenant would claim at review in respect of the rent-free period that the hypothetical tenant might have claimed. The phrase 'fit for occupation' does not appear to go as far as 'fully fitted out', since the former assumption anticipates a stage where the premises are simply ready to be occupied for fitting-out purposes, in which case the hypothetical tenant might still demand a rent-free period (see *Pontsarn Investments Ltd v Kansallis-Osake-Pankki* [1992] 22 EG 103). Some solicitors prefer to deal with this problem in a different way by including an assumption that 'no reduction is to be made to take account of any rental concession which on a new letting with vacant possession might be granted to the incoming tenant for a period within which its fitting-out works would take place'.

39.4.3.2 Covenants performed

An assumption is made that the covenants have been performed. Most rent review clauses include an assumption that the tenant has complied with their covenants under the lease. In the absence of such a provision, a court is willing to imply one in any case, since it is a general principle that a party to a transaction should not be allowed to profit from its own wrongdoing (see *Family Management v Grey* (1979) 253 EG 369). This is particularly important when considering the tenant's repairing obligation. Clearly the hypothetical tenant can be expected to pay more in terms of rent if the premises are in good repair and, conversely, less if they are in a poor condition (for whatever reason). A tenant should not be allowed to argue in reduction of the rent at review that the premises are in a poor condition, if it is through their own default that the disrepair has come about – hence the reason for the assumption under consideration.

The landlord may try to include an assumption in respect of their own covenants (ie, that the landlord has performed their covenants). The tenant ought to resist this, especially where the landlord will be taking on significant obligations in the actual lease. For example, in a lease of part of the landlord's premises, the landlord may be entering into covenants to perform services, and to repair and maintain the structure, exterior and common parts of the building. If the landlord fails to perform their covenants, the likely result is that the rental value of an interest in the building will decrease, since the building will be less attractive to tenants in the market. Accordingly, the rent at review would be adjusted to reflect this. However, an assumption that the landlord has performed their covenants enables the landlord to have the review conducted on the basis that the building is fully in repair (without regard to their own default), which means that the tenant would be paying for something at review (ie, a lease of premises in a building which is in first-rate condition) that they do not in fact have. Such an assumption should be resisted by the tenant.

However, the landlord will not concede the tenant's argument easily. Landlords will argue that, without it, the valuer will assess the new rent at a lower level, even though immediately afterwards the tenant might bring proceedings against the landlord in respect of the landlord's breach of covenant, forcing the landlord to put the building into repair. Landlords will argue that it is unfair that the rent will be set at a low level for the entire review period on the basis of a temporary breach of covenant which the landlord might soon be required to remedy. The tenant's counter-argument is that a claim for breach of covenant is no substitute for a dilapidated building.

39.4.3.3 Recovery of VAT

If the landlord has opted to tax in respect of the premises, so that VAT is payable in addition to the rent, this will negatively affect a tenant who has an adverse VAT status. Organisations such as banks, building societies and insurance companies make exempt supplies in the course of their business, and therefore do not receive any output tax which can be set off against the input tax to be paid on the rent. These organisations have to bear the VAT on the rent as an overhead of the business. Arguably, such tenants in the market would reduce their bids in order to compensate for the VAT overhead that they will have to absorb. Some landlords counter this by including an assumption that the hypothetical tenant will be able to recover its VAT in full (thereby removing the need for the hypothetical tenant to ask for a discount on rent to cover the VAT overhead), or by ensuring that the hypothetical letting includes a covenant by the landlord not to opt to tax for VAT purposes. Tenants ought to try to resist such a provision, leaving the valuer to value the lease on the basis of the reality of the actual letting.

39.4.4 Matters to be disregarded

In order to be fair to the tenant, the landlord usually drafts the review clause so that certain matters are disregarded which would otherwise increase the OMRV of a letting of the premises.

39.4.4.1 Goodwill

A letting of premises will be more attractive in the open market if there is existing goodwill at the premises, in the shape of a regular flow of clients or customers, or the benefit of a good reputation. The letting would command a higher rent than could otherwise be expected, as tenants will be eager to obtain possession of the premises in order to take advantage of the goodwill. However, it is the tenant who generates such goodwill, and so it is only fair that any effect on rent of that goodwill ought to be disregarded at review.

39.4.4.2 Occupation

The fact that the tenant, their predecessors or their sub-tenants have been in occupation of the premises is usually disregarded. It is accepted that if the tenant was bidding for a letting of their own premises, they would bid more than most others in the market in order to avoid the expense of having to move to other premises. The rental effect of occupation should therefore be disregarded. In appropriate cases, where the tenant also occupies adjoining premises, their occupation of those premises should also be disregarded, to avoid the argument that the tenant would increase their bid for the demised premises to secure a letting of premises which are adjacent to their other premises.

If the rent review clause requires occupation by the tenant to be disregarded but makes no similar requirement as regards their goodwill (see **39.4.4.1** above), the valuer should nevertheless disregard the rental effect of the tenant's goodwill, since goodwill must necessarily be the product of the tenant's occupation (see *Prudential Assurance Co Ltd v Grand Metropolitan Estate Ltd* [1993] 32 EG 74).

39.4.4.3 Improvements

If the tenant improves the premises then they usually do so at their own expense, but the result will inevitably be that the rental value of an interest in the premises will increase. It is unfair for the landlord to ask that the rent be increased at review to reflect the increase in rental value brought about by the tenant's improvements. If improvements were to be taken into account, the tenant would be paying for their improvements twice over (once on making them, and once again when the revised rent becomes payable). The landlord usually drafts the rent review clause so that the effect on rent of most of the tenant's improvements is disregarded.

It does not follow, however, that all improvements should be disregarded. The tenant will want to make sure that the effect on rent of all improvements that have been voluntarily carried out either by them, or by their sub-tenants or predecessors in title is disregarded, whether they were carried out during the term, during some earlier lease or during a period of occupation before the grant of the lease (eg, during a pre-letting fitting-out period). The tenant will also want to have disregarded the effect on rent of improvements executed by the landlord but which were carried out at the tenant's expense. The landlord, however, will want to make sure that any improvements that the tenant was obliged to make are taken into account. These will include improvements the tenant was obliged to carry out under some other document, such as an agreement for lease, or by virtue of a statutory provision requiring the tenant to carry out work (eg, the installation of a fire escape and doors).

39.4.4.4 User, alienation and improvements

It is possible that for their own benefit the landlord might try to have disregarded some of the more restrictive covenants contained in the actual lease, such as user, alienation and improvements. This is unfair to the tenant, who ought to be advised to resist such a disregard.

39.5 THE MECHANICS OF THE COMMERCIAL RENT REVIEW

There are two principal ways in which the review process can be conducted:

(a) (the most commonly encountered method) by negotiations between the parties, but in default of agreement, by reference to an independent third party for determination (see **39.5.2**);

(b) (the less commonly encountered method, but still seen in some older leases) by the service of trigger notices and counter-notices in an attempt to agree the revised rent, but in default, by reference to a third party (see **39.5.3**).

Whichever method is to be adopted, the first consideration to be dealt with is whether time is to be of the essence in respect of any time limits contained in the clause, or in respect of the rent review dates.

39.5.1 Is time of the essence?

As a general rule, if time is of the essence of a particular clause, a party who fails to act by the time limit specified loses the right given by that clause. If time is of the essence of the whole rent review clause, the slightest delay will mean that the landlord will be denied the opportunity to increase the rent until the next review date (or, indeed, the tenant will be denied the opportunity to decrease the rent until the next review date if the clause permits downward reviews).

The House of Lords in *United Scientific Holdings Ltd v Burnley Borough Council* [1977] 2 All ER 62 held that, in the absence of any contrary indications in the express wording of the clause, or in the interrelation of the rent review clause with other clauses in the lease, there is a presumption that time is not of the essence of the clause, and that the review can still be implemented and pursued even though specific dates have passed (see, eg, *McDonald's Property Co Ltd v HSBC Bank plc* [2001] 36 EG 181). It follows from this decision that there are three situations where time will be of the essence either of the whole clause, or in respect of certain steps in the review procedure.

39.5.1.1 An express stipulation

Time will be of the essence in respect of all or any of the time limits in the review clause if the lease expressly says so.

39.5.1.2 Any other contrary indication

The phrase 'time is of the essence' may not have been used in the lease, but there are cases where other forms of wording used by the draftsman have been sufficient to indicate an intention to rebut the usual presumption. In *First Property Growth Partnership v Royal & Sun Alliance Services Ltd* [2002] 22 EG 140, the clause required the landlord to serve notice of intention to review upon the tenant 12 months before the relevant review date 'but not at any other time'. This was held to make time of the essence, and thus the landlord's notice served after the relevant review date was invalid. In *Starmark Enterprises Ltd v CPL Distribution Ltd* [2001] 32 EG 89 (CS), the lease provided for service of a trigger notice by the landlord specifying the amount of rent payable for the following period, but went on to provide that if the tenant failed to serve a counter-notice within one month the tenant would be 'deemed to have agreed to pay the increased rent specified in that notice'. The Court of Appeal held that time was of the essence; the 'deeming' provision was a sufficient contra-indication to rebut the usual presumption. Reference should be made to one of the standard works on landlord and tenant law for further consideration of the many cases dealing with this issue.

39.5.1.3 The interrelation of the review clause with other clauses in the lease

The usual way in which a clause might interrelate with the review clause in such a way as to make time of the essence is if the tenant is given an option to break the term on or shortly after each review date. The inference in such an interrelation is that if the tenant cannot afford to pay the revised rent, or, where the level of rent is not yet known, they fear the prospect of an increase, they are given an opportunity to terminate the lease by exercising the break clause. Since time is usually of the essence in respect of the exercise of a break clause, time may also be construed to be of the essence of the rent review clause. It does not matter that the review clause and the option are separate clauses in the lease; the court simply has to be able to infer a sufficient interrelation. Nor, apparently, does it matter that the option to break is mutual and linked to only one of several rent review dates (*Central Estates Ltd v Secretary of State for the Environment* [1997] 1 EGLR 239).

Unless a rigid timetable for conducting the review is required by either party, it is not often that time will be made of the essence, because of the fatal consequences arising from a delay. It might be advisable to state expressly that time is not of the essence. However, in most leases the timetable is so flexibly drafted that the parties do not feel the need to make express declaration that time is not of the essence, preferring instead to rely upon the usual presumption (but see *Barclays Bank plc v Savile Estates Ltd* [2002] 24 EG 152). If any time clauses are intended to be mandatory, the lease should clearly say so.

39.5.2 The negotiated revision

The negotiated approach to arriving at a revised rent usually provides for the new rent to be agreed between the parties at any time (whether before or after the relevant review date) but that if agreement has not been reached by the review date, either or both of the parties will be allowed by the clause to refer the matter to an independent third party to make a determination as to the new rent. If such an approach is adopted, the tenant should ensure that the rent review clause does not reserve the right to make the reference to the third party exclusively to the landlord. The tenant must ensure that they also have the ability to make the reference. Even though the rent review clause may permit upward only revisions, it may be in the tenant's interests to have a quick resolution of the review, particularly if they are anxious to assign the lease or sell the business. In exceptional cases (eg, *Royal Bank of Scotland plc v Jennings and Others* [1997] 19 EG 152) the court might be prepared to imply an obligation upon the landlord to refer a review to the third party to give business efficacy to the clause.

39.5.3 Trigger notices

The service of a trigger notice usually requires the parties to follow a rigid timetable for the service of notices. One party sets the review in motion by the service of a trigger notice, specifying their proposal for the revised rent, and the other party responds by the service of a counter-notice. A typical clause might provide for the landlord to implement the review by the service on the tenant of a trigger notice, between 12 and six months before the relevant review date, in which the landlord specifies a rent that they consider to be the current market rent for the premises. The tenant should be given the right to dispute the landlord's proposal by serving a counter-notice within, say, three months of the service of the trigger notice. The parties would then be required to negotiate; but in default of agreement within, say, three months of the service of the counter-notice, either or both parties may be given the right to make a reference to a third party for a determination. Time may be stated to be of the essence in respect of all or part of the timetable.

Great care must be taken with this more rigid style of approach, particularly if time is of the essence (see **39.5.1**). Problems can easily arise, as follows:

(a) There is no requirement for the landlord to be reasonable when specifying a proposal for the revised rent in a trigger notice (see *Amalgamated Estates Ltd v Joystretch Manufacturing Ltd* (1980) 257 EG 489). This is very dangerous for the tenant where time is of the essence in respect of the service of the tenant's counter-notice. If the tenant fails to respond within the time limit required by the lease, they will be bound by the rent specified in the landlord's notice. A well-advised tenant should avoid such a clause.

(b) There has been much litigation surrounding the question of whether a particular form of communication, often in the form of a letter between the parties' advisers, suffices as a notice for the purposes of the review clause. If a communication is to take effect as a notice, it ought to be clear and unequivocal, and must be worded in such a way as to make it clear to the recipient that the sender is purporting to take a formal step, or exercise some right under the review clause. Phrases such as 'subject to contract' and 'without prejudice', although not necessarily fatal to the notice, are to be avoided.

(c) For the same reasons stated in connection with negotiated reviews, the tenant must ensure that the review timetable allows them to implement the review and to refer the rent revision for determination by the third party. These rights must not be left exclusively with the landlord.

Unless there is some compelling reason to the contrary, the negotiated approach is to be preferred.

39.5.4 The third party

A surveyor usually acts as the independent third party. The lease will provide for the parties to agree upon a surveyor, failing which one or both of the parties will be allowed to make an application to the President of the Royal Institution of Chartered Surveyors (RICS) for the appointment of a surveyor to determine the revised rent. The RICS operates a procedure to deal efficiently with such applications, and will appoint a surveyor with knowledge and experience of similar lettings in the area. It is important that the lease makes it clear in which capacity the surveyor is to act: as an arbitrator between the parties, or as an expert. There are considerable differences between the two:

(a) An arbitrator seeks to resolve a dispute by some quasi-judicial process, whereas an expert imposes their own expert valuation on the parties.

(b) The arbitrator is bound by the procedure under the Arbitration Act 1996, which deals with hearings, submission of evidence and the calling of witnesses. An expert is not subject to such external controls, and is not bound to hear the evidence of the parties. Whilst an arbitrator decides on the basis of the evidence put before them, an expert simply uses their own skill and judgement.

(c) There is a limited right of appeal to the High Court on a point of law against an arbitrator's award, whereas an expert's decision is final and binding unless it appears that they failed to perform the task required of them.

(d) An arbitrator is immune from suit in negligence, whereas an expert is not.

Using an expert tends to be quicker and cheaper, and is, therefore, often provided for in lettings of conventional properties at modest rents. Where there is something unorthodox about the property, which might make it difficult to value, or where there is a good deal of money at stake in the outcome of the review, an arbitrator is to be preferred so that a fully-argued case can be put. Alternatively, the review clause could leave the capacity of the third party open, to be determined by the party who makes the reference at the time the reference is made.

39.6 THE LATE REVIEW

As indicated at **39.4.1**, it is common for the revised rent to remain unagreed by the review date. This may be because neither party has implemented the review process by the review date, or because negotiations have become protracted. Provided time is not of the essence, such delay is not a problem, as long as the lease contains provisions to deal with this possibility. Most review clauses therefore contain the following types of provisions:

(a) that the existing rent (the old rent) continues to be payable on account of the new rent until the new rent has been ascertained;

(b) that the new rent, once ascertained, becomes payable from, and is backdated to, the rent review date;

(c) that as soon as the new rent has been ascertained, the tenant is to pay to the landlord the amount by which the old rent paid on account of the new rent since the review date actually falls short of the new rent; and because the landlord has been denied the benefit of this shortfall pending the outcome of the review, the tenant is to pay it with interest calculated from the rent review date until the date of payment.

The tenant should check the operation of these provisions. If the rent review clause permits both upward and downward reviews, they should ensure that there is some equivalent provision for the landlord to pay any overpayment (with interest) to the tenant if the new rent turns out to be lower than the old rent (although in *Royal Bank of Scotland v Jennings* the court was prepared to imply such a term in any case). The tenant should also check that the rate of interest at which the shortfall is to be paid is not set at the usual interest rate under the lease (4% or 5% above base rate). The usual rate is intended to operate on the occasion of tenant default, whereas in the case of a late rent review, the fault may lie with a delaying landlord as much as with a delaying tenant. The interest rate should be set at base rate itself or, perhaps, 1% or 2% above base rate. Finally, the tenant should check that the review clause allows the tenant to instigate the review process, and to force negotiations or the third party reference, since the tenant might prefer a speedy settlement of the review as an alternative to facing a future lump sum payment of a shortfall with interest.

39.7 RECORDING THE REVIEW

It is good practice to attach memoranda of the revised rent to the lease and counterpart as evidence for all persons concerned with the lease of the agreement or determination. The rent review clause usually obliges both parties to sign and attach identical memoranda to their respective parts of the lease. It is usual for both parties to bear their own costs in this regard.

SUMMARY

- Rent review is most likely to apply to leases of commercial property for a term of longer than five years.
- Rent reviews usually take place every three to five years. A tenant should resist a penultimate day review.
- Although there are different types of rent review, the most common type is the upward only open market revaluation review. With this type of review, the rent can go up or stay the same, but it can never go down.
- In an OMRV, the valuer is instructed by the rent review clause in the lease to value a hypothetical interest in the premises demised by the lease as at the rent review date.
- Assumptions and disregards are instructions to the valuer as how to conduct this hypothetical valuation in a way that will produce a result that is as close to the real open market value of the premises as possible. Assumptions and disregards that artificially inflate the rent in favour of one or other of the parties should be avoided.
- In terms of the procedure for rent review, time is not usually of the essence, and in practice the reviewed rent is often agreed or determined after the relevant review date. The lease will provide that the tenant continues to pay rent at the old rate and, following agreement or determination of the new rent, pays any additional amount to the landlord together with interest to compensate the landlord for the delay.
- The use of trigger notices to implement and agree the review should be avoided, particularly where time is expressed (or could be deemed) to be of the essence.

CHAPTER 40

The Landlord and Tenant Act 1954, Part II

LEARNING OUTCOMES

After reading this chapter you will be able to:

- explain what security of tenure under the Landlord and Tenant Act 1954, Part II means and who will qualify for it
- explain how a landlord client who wants to let premises without conferring security of tenure can do so
- acting for a protected tenant, terminate the tenancy effectively if the tenant does not want to stay on, or if the tenant does want to stay on and renew their tenancy, take the appropriate steps to protect their right to do so
- acting for a landlord who wants a protected tenant to move out, take the appropriate steps to terminate the tenancy and oppose the tenant's right to a new tenancy
- acting for a protected sub-tenant, serve the relevant notice on the correct (or 'competent') landlord
- advise on the statutory grounds available to a landlord to oppose the grant of a new tenancy and on whether compensation is payable to an unsuccessful tenant
- where the tenant's application for a new lease is successful, explain the terms on which the new lease is likely to be granted.

40.1 INTRODUCTION

'Security of tenure' is a generic phrase given to statutory rights granted to tenants to protect their interest under their leases. This might include, amongst other things, the right to renew or extend an existing tenancy. The exact nature of the protection given depends on the type of tenancy. This chapter is concerned with the protection made available to tenants of business premises contained in the Landlord and Tenant Act 1954 ('the Act').

The Act gives security of tenure to tenants who occupy premises for business purposes. A business tenancy will not come to an end at the expiry of a fixed term, neither will a periodic tenancy be terminated by an ordinary notice to quit. Instead, the tenancy will continue after the contractual termination date until it is ended in one of the ways specified by the Act. When it is terminated under the Act, the tenant has the right to apply to the court for a new lease to be granted and the landlord can oppose this new lease only on the grounds laid down in the Act. Any such new tenancy will also be protected under the Act. If the tenant has to vacate the premises, they may be entitled to compensation.

Separate statutory regimes exist in respect of residential tenants, granting some residential tenants security of tenure. In addition, residential tenants may have other statutory rights (eg a right not to be evicted without a court order, or a right to acquire the freehold reversion to their tenancy). These rights vary from tenant to tenant, depending on the type of residential tenancy they have.

The law relating to the rights of residential tenants is both extensive and complicated and is outside the scope of this book. However, for a buyer of the reversion of a property let for residential purposes, an understanding of it is essential, and a specialist text should be consulted. A separate regime also exists in respect of agricultural tenancies, but again this is beyond the scope of this book.

40.2 WHEN DOES THE ACT APPLY?

Section 23(1) provides that:

> ... this Act applies to any tenancy where the property comprised in the tenancy is or includes premises which are occupied by the tenant and are so occupied for the purpose of a business carried on by him or for those and other purposes.

The various parts of this provision must be looked at separately.

40.2.1 There must be a 'tenancy'

In order for the Act to apply, the person claiming security of tenure must occupy under the terms of a 'tenancy' (ie a 'lease'). For the purposes of the Act, the definition of tenancy includes an agreement for a lease and an underlease. Security of tenure will not be available if the person seeking to claim such rights merely occupies under a licence.

Deciding whether a particular arrangement has given rise to a lease or a licence will be a question of fact in each case. In the light of case law, the basic position is that a lease will be held to have been granted if the occupier has been given exclusive possession of the property for a fixed period of time and is paying a rent (see **34.5** for more details). This is a test of substance and not form and so even if a document calls itself a licence, the courts may still hold that what the parties have created is a lease.

Certain tenancies are specifically excluded from the protection of the Act (see **40.2.4**).

40.2.2 The premises must be occupied by the tenant

Whether a tenant is in occupation is a question of fact. Occupation can be by the tenant personally, or through the medium of an agent or manager, or by a company owned by the tenant.

In the case of sub-lettings, if there is a sub-tenant in occupation of the whole of the premises originally let to the head-tenant, the head-tenant will not benefit from security of tenure as, by definition, they will not be in occupation. Instead, it will be the sub-tenant who will enjoy the benefit of these rights, provided the other qualifying conditions required by the Act are also satisfied. Equally, in the case of a sub-letting of part only of those premises, the head-tenant will be protected in relation to the part they still occupy for business purposes and the sub-tenant will be protected in respect of the part the sub-tenant occupies.

40.2.3 Occupied for business purposes

The tenant must be occupying for the purposes of a business carried on by them. 'Business' is widely defined and includes 'a trade, profession or employment and in the case of a 'body of persons' any activity carried on by them. 'Any activity' means just that; it need not be a business or commercial activity. So, running a tennis club or running a hospital have both amounted to a business use under the final part of this definition, when carried on by a body of persons.

The business user need not be the sole purpose of occupation. The Act will still apply as long as the business user is the main purpose and not merely incidental to a residential or other purpose. So a shop with a flat above will be within the Act; but if a residential tenant occasionally brings work home with them, this would not result in the tenancy coming within the Act.

A tenancy does not attract security of tenure where business use is in breach of a term of the tenancy, unless the landlord has consented to, or acquiesced in, the breach. Section 23 of the Act is amended by the Small Business, Enterprise and Employment Act 2015 (SBEEA 2015) to provide that, even if the landlord has agreed to the breach (or acquiesced in it), the tenant still does not obtain security of tenure under the Act where the business use is solely for the purposes of a 'home business' (meaning 'a business of a kind which might reasonably be carried on at home'). It is envisaged that there will be regulations that clarify the meaning of the term further, but the SBEEA 2015 already stipulates that a business is not to be treated as a 'home business' if it involves the supply of alcohol for consumption on the premises.

40.2.4 Excluded tenancies

Various tenancies are excluded from protection under the Act. Amongst others, this includes the following:

40.2.4.1 Tenancies at will

A tenancy at will is a tenancy that can be terminated by either the landlord or tenant at any time, and such tenancies have been held to be outside the protection of the Act (see *Wheeler v Mercer* [1957] AC 416, *Hagee (London) v A B Erikson and Others* [1976] QB 209). Such tenancies can arise both expressly and impliedly. A common example of when a tenancy at will can arise impliedly is where an individual is let into occupation before a formal tenancy is granted, pending the outcome of negotiations for the formal term.

40.2.4.2 Fixed-term tenancies not exceeding six months

These are excluded unless the tenancy contains any provision for renewing or extending the term beyond six months, or the tenant has been in occupation for a period exceeding 12 months.

40.2.4.3 'Contracted-out' tenancies

Although contracting out of the Act is generally forbidden, s 38A allows the parties to agree that security of tenure under the Act should not apply to a given tenancy. This is possible, however, only in the case of fixed-term lettings. It is not possible to contract out in respect of a periodic tenancy.

For leases granted prior to 1 June 2004, the approval of the court to contract out had to be obtained prior to the grant of the lease. In the case of such leases, it is therefore important to check whether the necessary court order was indeed obtained.

For leases granted on or after 1 June 2004, a court order is no longer required and, instead, a notice procedure has to be complied with. The detail of this is as follows:

(a) the procedure must be completed either before the lease is granted or, if earlier, before the tenant becomes contractually bound to take the lease;
(b) the landlord must give the tenant notice in a prescribed form which contains a 'health warning', warning the tenant of the fact that they are agreeing to a lease without security of tenure and advising them to obtain professional advice;
(c) the tenant must then make a declaration (again in a prescribed form) that they have received the notice and agree that the lease should be contracted out. If the tenant is given the notice less than 14 days before the grant of the lease (or, as the case may be, is given the notice less than 14 days before they become contractually bound to take the lease), the tenant's declaration must be made in the form of a statutory declaration before an independent solicitor;
(d) a reference to the service of the notice and the tenant's declaration must be contained or endorsed on the lease itself.

40.2.4.4 Residential tenancies including a 'home business'

A tenancy of a dwelling house let to individuals as a home that permits a 'home business' (see **40.2.3**) to be operated from the dwelling will be excluded from the protection of the Act. The tenancy must not permit any other kind of business, other than a 'home business' if the exclusion is to apply.

40.2.4.5 Certain types of business lease

Agricultural tenancies, mining tenancies, service tenancies and farm business leases are also excluded by s 43 of the Act. Other statutes exclude certain leases of railway property (Railways Act 1993), military establishments (Armed Forces Act 1996) and dockyards (Dockyard Services Act 1986) from the remit of the Act.

40.3 CONTINUATION TENANCIES

A business tenancy within the Act will not come to an end on the expiry of the fixed term, but will continue on the same terms by virtue of s 24. Although it will continue at the same rent, the landlord is able to apply to the court under s 24A for an interim rent to apply until a new tenancy is granted (see **40.9**).

40.4 TERMINATION UNDER THE ACT

A business tenancy can be terminated only in one of the ways laid down by the Act:

(a) by the service of a landlord's notice under s 25;
(b) by the service of a tenant's request for a new tenancy under s 26;
(c) forfeiture;
(d) surrender;
(e) in the case of a periodic tenancy, by the tenant giving the landlord a notice to quit;
(f) in the case of a fixed-term lease, by the tenant serving three months' written notice on the landlord under s 27. This cannot expire before the contractual expiry date;
(g) in the case of a fixed-term lease, by the tenant ceasing to be in occupation for business purposes at the end of the lease (see Landlord and Tenant Act 1954, s 27(1A)).

Note that a business lease can still be forfeited for breach of covenant in the usual way. Apart from forfeiture, the usual methods of termination are the s 25 notice (see **40.6**) and the s 26 request (see **40.7**).

40.5 THE COMPETENT LANDLORD

The Act provides that the conduct of the various procedures under it (such as, for example, serving a s 25 or s 26 notice) must be carried out between the tenant and the tenant's 'competent landlord'. In the case of a lease granted straight out of a freehold, the position is simple: the competent landlord will be the freeholder. The position is more complicated in the case of a sub-lease, and is best illustrated by a diagram and explanation:

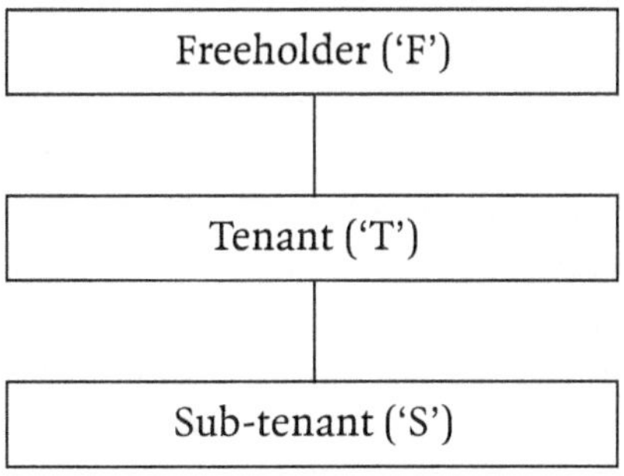

Under s 44 of the Act, a sub-tenant's competent landlord is defined as the person who has a superior tenancy which will not come to an end within 14 months or, if there is no such person, the freeholder.

Applying this to the diagram above, what this means is that if T does not enjoy security of tenure under the Act (say, for example, T has sub-let the whole of the premises to S and so is no longer in occupation for the purposes of the Act), whether T will be S's competent landlord is simply determined by how long T's lease has left to run. If the lease has more than 14 months left to run, T will be S's competent landlord, but if less than that, T will not be S's competent landlord and instead it will be F.

The position is different if T's lease does enjoy security of tenure. Say, for example, that T has sub-let only part of the premises to S and so remains in occupation of the remaining part. T's lease will still enjoy of tenure, although T's right to apply for a new tenancy will be restricted to the part T still occupies. If no steps have been taken to terminate T's lease, T will be S's competent landlord, and this is the case even if T's *contractual* term has 14 months or less to run: the operation of the Act means that this lease will automatically be continued when it ends. However, once a s 25 or s 26 notice to terminate T's lease has been served, T's lease will (as will be seen at **40.6** and **40.7**) terminate within 14 months, and so T will cease to be S's competent landlord and instead it will be F.

Mechanisms exist under the Act to allow the parties to determine who is the competent landlord at any given time.

40.6 THE SECTION 25 NOTICE

The usual way for a landlord to begin the process of terminating a lease is by serving notice on the tenant under s 25 of the Act.

40.6.1 The prescribed form

The notice must be in the prescribed form and must be given not less than 6 months, nor more than 12 months, prior to the date of termination specified in it. The date of termination specified cannot be before the contractual termination date of the lease but can be, and often is, after it. Apart from this, there is no requirement for the notice to expire on any particular day, as long as it is of the correct length.

The notice must also state whether or not the landlord will oppose an application by the tenant to the court for a new tenancy, and, if so, on which of the statutory grounds they will rely. The tenant has the right to apply for a new lease, but the landlord can oppose that application on one of seven grounds set out in s 30 of the Act (see **40.8**). The landlord is only able to rely on the grounds of opposition stated in their s 25 notice. However, commonly, the landlord will be willing to grant a new lease. The landlord will be ending the current lease so that a new tenancy can be granted on different terms, usually a higher rent. The landlord must indicate their proposals as to the terms of the new lease in the s 25 notice.

40.6.2 The application to the court

If the landlord has indicated in their s 25 notice that they will not oppose the grant of a new tenancy, the parties will now enter into negotiations for the grant of a new lease. But there is still a danger to the tenant. Unless the tenant applies to the court before the expiry of the s 25 notice, they will lose their rights under the Act. The application is usually made to the county court. This time limit can be extended by agreement between the parties – eg, where they are near to agreement on the terms of a new lease and wish to avoid the expense, etc of court proceedings. It is also possible for the landlord to make the application to the court for a new lease to be granted – eg, where the tenant is thought to be unreasonably dragging out the negotiations. Where the landlord is not opposing the grant of a new tenancy, it is unusual for applications to proceed to a hearing, the parties usually reaching agreement as to terms.

If the landlord has indicated that they will oppose the grant of a new tenancy, the tenant's only chance of obtaining a new lease is to apply to the court within the time limits stated above. As an alternative, the landlord can pre-empt this by applying for an order to terminate the lease on the grounds stated in their s 25 notice (but not if an application has already been made by the tenant asking for the lease to be renewed).

40.6.3 Summary of a tenant's options on receipt of a s 25 notice

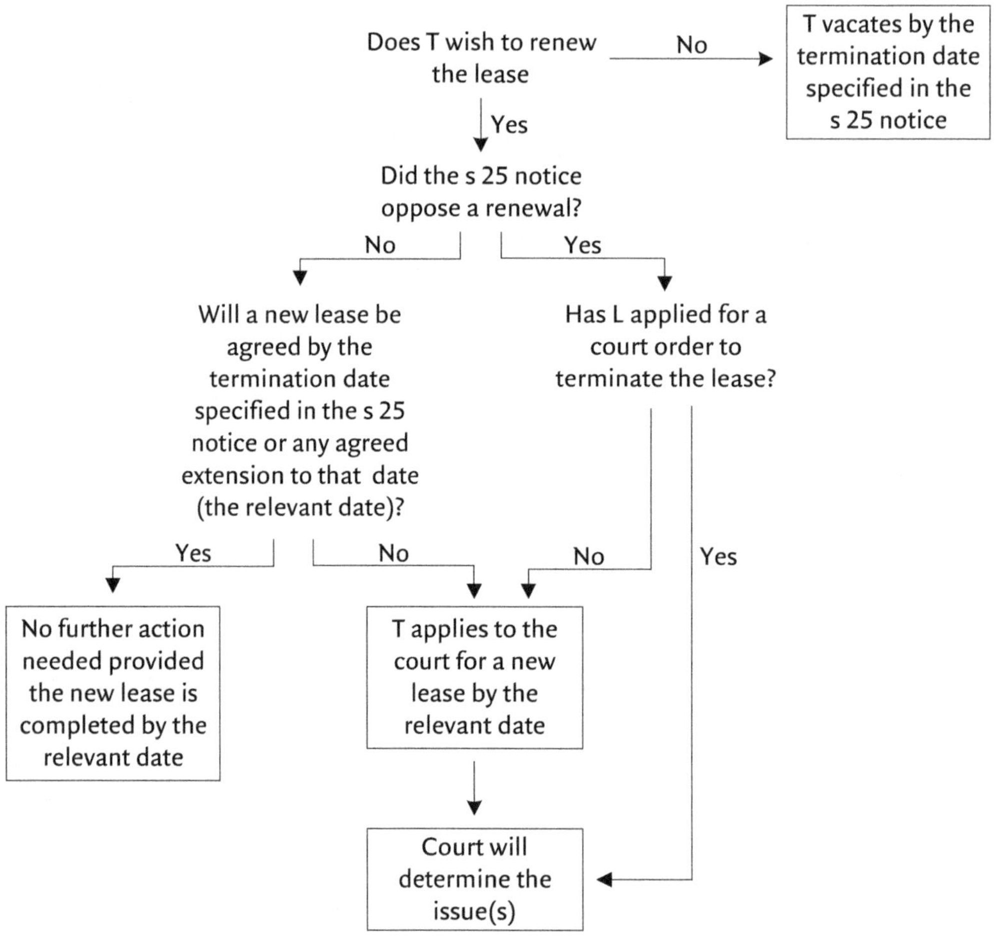

40.7 THE SECTION 26 REQUEST

Rather than wait for the landlord to serve a s 25 notice, the tenant can often take the initiative and serve a request for a new tenancy under s 26. However, this procedure is not available to periodic tenants, or those for a fixed term of one year or less. Although normally a tenant will be best advised not to serve a s 26 request (the sooner they get a new lease, the sooner the rent will go up), there are circumstances where this may be advisable. For example, if the tenant has plans to sell the lease, they might find it more marketable if they have already been granted a new fixed term. Equally, if the rent in the open market is less than that presently payable under the lease, they may want a new lease as soon as possible at a new, lower market rent.

40.7.1 The prescribed form

The s 26 notice must again be in a prescribed form and must be given not less than six months, or more than 12 months, prior to the start date stated in the notice: it must also state the proposed terms of the new tenancy.

40.7.2 The application to the court

If the landlord wishes to oppose the grant of a new tenancy, they must serve a counter-notice on the tenant within two months of the service of the tenant's s 26 request. The landlord must also state the s 30 ground(s) of opposition. If the landlord does this, the tenant must ensure that they apply to court for a new lease or they will lose their rights under the Act. The tenant must make this application prior to the commencement date of the new tenancy specified by them in the s 26 request (unless the landlord agrees an extension of this time limit). As an alternative, the landlord can pre-empt this by applying for an order to terminate the lease on the grounds stated in their counter-notice (but not if an application has already been made by the tenant asking for the lease to be renewed).

If the landlord does not wish to oppose the grant of a new tenancy, they need not serve a counter-notice. The parties will then negotiate the terms of the new lease. However, as with s 25 notices, the tenant must ensure that, if negotiations drag on, an application to court is made before the commencement date of the new tenancy specified by them in the s 26 request or lose their rights under the Act. Again, the parties can agree to extend this time limit and if negotiations are continuing satisfactorily, this is the most sensible method of proceeding.

40.7.3 Summary of a landlord's options on receipt of a s 26 notice

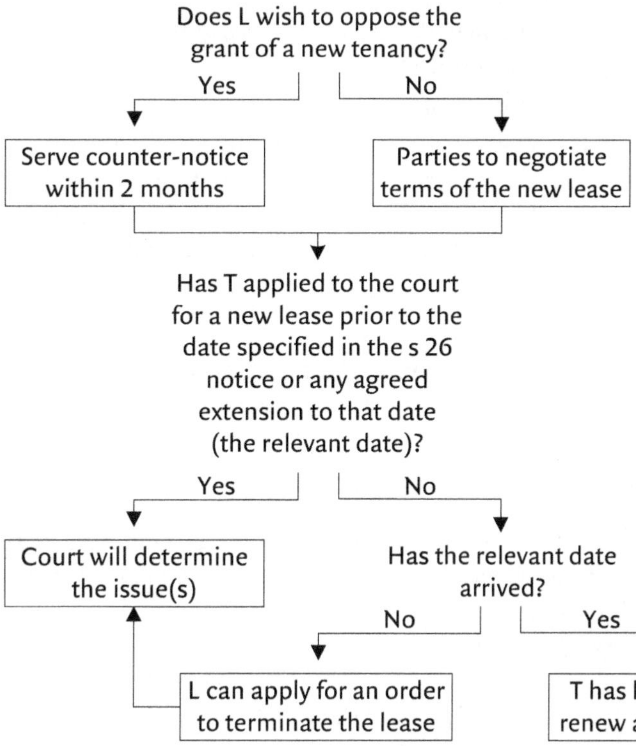

40.8 THE LANDLORD'S GROUNDS FOR OPPOSITION UNDER SECTION 30

When the landlord serves their s 25 notice, or their counter-notice to a tenant's s 26 request, if they wish to oppose the grant of a new lease they must specify the grounds of opposition. Section 30 sets out seven grounds of opposition. The landlord can rely only on the grounds stated in the notice or counter-notice; no later amendment is possible. The grounds are as follows.

Ground (a) *Tenant's failure to repair*

Ground (b) *Persistent delay in paying rent*

Ground (c) *Substantial breaches of other obligations*

All of these first three grounds are discretionary grounds. It is not sufficient for the landlord just to establish the ground; they also have to show that the tenant ought not to be granted a new tenancy in view of the facts giving rise to the ground.

Ground (d) *Alternative accommodation*

This must be suitable to the tenant's needs and on reasonable terms.

Ground (e) *Sub-letting of part where higher rent can be obtained by single letting of whole building*

This is little used, as the necessary requirements are seldom fulfilled. It applies only where the tenancy was created by the sub-letting of part of premises comprised in a superior tenancy and the head-landlord wishes to obtain possession so that they can let the whole as the combined rents from the sub-lettings are substantially less than can be obtained on a letting of the whole. Like grounds (a) to (c), this ground is also discretionary.

Ground (f) *The landlord intends to demolish or reconstruct and could not reasonably do so without obtaining possession*

This is the most frequently used ground. The landlord must show that, on the termination of the tenancy:

(a) they have a firm and settled intention to carry out the relevant work. This is a question of fact in each case, but the landlord's position will be strengthened if they can show, eg, that they have obtained the necessary planning permission and that their financial arrangements are in position; and
(b) they intend to demolish or reconstruct the premises (or a substantial part of them), or to carry out substantial works of construction on the holding or a part of it; and
(c) they cannot reasonably carry out the work without obtaining possession. This again is a question of fact, but the landlord will not succeed if the tenant will agree to terms which allow the landlord access to carry out the work, which can then be reasonably carried out without obtaining possession and without substantially interfering with the tenant's use.

As long as a landlord has a genuine intention, if it subsequently and honestly changes its mind after having obtained possession, the ground will be made out (*Fisher v Taylor's Furnishings* [1956] 2 QB 78).

Ground (g) *Landlord's intention to occupy the holding for their own business or as a residence*

This is also a frequently used ground: again the landlord must have a firm and settled intention, and the landlord must demonstrate at the date of the hearing that they have considered and taken practical steps to occupy the premises. The landlord must also have a reasonable prospect of achieving their intention, although they do not have to show that their business will be a success in that location. There is, however, an important restriction on the use of this ground. A landlord cannot rely on it if their interest was purchased or created within five years before the ending of the current tenancy. The object of this provision is to prevent a landlord buying the reversion cheaply within five years of the end of the lease and then acquiring vacant possession using this ground. It is important to note, however, that the ground will be available to a landlord who buys property with vacant possession, lets it and then seeks possession within five years of buying it. It may also be used by a competitor to drive out a business rival (*Humber Oil Terminals Trustee Ltd v Associated British Ports* [2011] EWHC 2043 (Ch)).

40.9 INTERIM RENT

Where a tenant has applied to the court for a new tenancy, the current tenancy will not end on the expiry of the s 25 notice or s 26 request. Instead it will be continued, at the same rent, until three months after the conclusion of the proceedings. It is possible, however, for either landlord or tenant to apply for an interim rent to apply pending the outcome of the proceedings.

The interim rent will normally be the rent payable under the new lease, as calculated according to the rules set out in **40.10.3**. However, this will not be the case if the landlord is opposing the grant of a new tenancy, if the terms of the new lease are substantially different from the old one or rental values have changed significantly in the period before the grant of the new lease. In these cases the interim rent will be set as the market rent for a yearly tenancy of the premises 'having regard' to the rent under the old lease. This formula will generally result in a lower rent being assessed than would otherwise be the case – hence the popularity with landlords of penultimate day rent reviews — see **39.2**.

40.10 THE TERMS OF THE NEW LEASE

40.10.1 The premises

The tenant is only entitled to a tenancy of the 'holding'. This means the property comprised in the current tenancy, but excluding any part not occupied by the tenant, ie those parts which the tenant has sub-let. However, the landlord (but not the tenant) has the right to insist that any new tenancy will be a tenancy of the whole of the originally demised premises, ie, including those parts sub-let.

40.10.2 Duration

This will be such as is reasonable in the circumstances but cannot exceed 15 years; it will normally be much less, for example, five or seven years.

40.10.3 The rent

This is the open market rent having regard to the other terms of the tenancy. But in assessing this, the court must disregard:

(a) the fact that the tenant and their predecessors have been in occupation;

(b) any goodwill attached to the holding;

(c) any effect on rent of any improvements voluntarily carried out by the tenant during the tenancy; and

(d) in the case of licensed premises, any addition in value due to the tenant's licence.

The court can insert a rent review clause in the lease, even though there was not one in the previous tenancy.

40.10.4 Other terms

In the absence of agreement, these will again be fixed by the court, which must have regard to the terms of the current tenancy and all other relevant circumstances. It is likely that the new terms will be much the same as the old. If a party wishes to change the current terms, the case of *City of London Real Property Co Ltd v O'May* [1983] 2 AC 726, establishes that it is for the party wanting a change to justify that change. The change must also be fair and reasonable.

40.10.5 Commencement of the new lease

Any new lease ordered by the court will not commence until three months after the proceedings are 'finally disposed of'. This is when the time limit for appeal has elapsed, ie, four weeks after the order. The new lease will thus commence three months and four weeks after the order.

If the tenant finds the terms of a new lease ordered by the court unacceptable (eg, as to rent), they may apply for the order to be revoked. Note that the landlord has no such right; if they are unhappy with the terms of the new lease, their only remedy is to appeal.

40.11 COMPENSATION FOR FAILURE TO OBTAIN A NEW LEASE

40.11.1 Availability

If the tenant does not obtain a new lease, they may be entitled to compensation. It is available only in the following circumstances:

(a) where the landlord's s 25 notice or counter-notice to a s 26 request specifies only one or more of grounds (e), (f) and (g) (see **40.8**); or

(b) where the landlord has specified one or more of grounds (e), (f) or (g) along with other grounds, and the court refuses to grant a new tenancy solely on one or more of grounds (e), (f) or (g), ie, the no-fault grounds (see **40.8**).

40.11.2 Amount

The amount of compensation will be equivalent to the rateable value of the holding, unless the tenant and their predecessors in the same business have been in occupation for at least 14 years, when it will be twice the rateable value.

40.11.3 Contracting out of compensation

Any agreement restricting or excluding the payment of compensation is void if the tenant or their predecessors in the same business have been in occupation for five years or more. This means that the clause commonly found in leases contracting out of the obligation to pay compensation will only be enforceable where the tenant has been in occupation for less than five years.

40.12 FUTURE DEVELOPMENTS

In November 2024, the Law Commission published the first of two consultations on the right to renew business tenancies under Part 2 of the Landlord and Tenant Act 1954. The consultation invited responses on whether the current contracting out model of security of tenure remains the right approach or whether one of three alternative models would be better suited to the current commercial leasehold market. The three alternative models are mandatory security of tenure, abolition of security of tenure and a contracting-in model. The consultation closed on 19 February 2025. The Law Commission will consider the responses and expects to publish a second consultation paper based on the responses received and the conclusions reached at a time to be confirmed.

SUMMARY

- Security of tenure under the Act means the right for the tenant to stay in the premises after the expiry of the contractual term and to apply for a new tenancy, which can only be denied on certain limited statutory grounds.
- To qualify for security of tenure under the Act, the tenant must have a tenancy and occupy the premises for business purposes under a lease that has not been excluded from protection ('TOBE').

- If the parties are agreed that the tenancy should not enjoy security of tenure, it is possible do this by granting a tenancy at will, a lease for six months or less or a contracted-out lease.
- A protected tenancy cannot be terminated other than by one of the ways laid down by the Act.
- A protected tenant who wants to terminate their lease *on* the contractual expiry date may do so by ceasing to occupy for business purposes by the end of the lease or serving a s 27 notice giving the landlord three months prior written notice. A tenant who wants to terminate their lease *after* the expiry of the contractual expiry date may only do so by serving a s 27 notice giving the landlord three months' notice or agreeing a voluntary surrender of the lease with the landlord.
- A protected tenant who wants to stay in the premises after the contractual expiry date and renew their tenancy may serve a s 26 request for a new tenancy on the landlord. They may also do nothing, continue to occupy the premises on the existing terms and wait for the landlord to take action.
- A landlord who is happy for the tenant to stay on may choose to do nothing and allow the tenancy to continue indefinitely. For greater certainty (or a higher rent), they may serve a s 25 notice terminating the tenancy on 6–12 months notice, but not opposing a renewal.
- A landlord who wants to terminate a protected tenancy may forfeit the lease (if they have grounds) or agree a voluntary surrender with the tenant. Otherwise, they must serve a s 25 notice on the tenant terminating the lease on or after the contractual expiry date and opposing the renewal of the tenancy on one of the statutory grounds. The s 25 notice must be given not less than 6 or more than 12 months before the date specified in the notice for termination of the tenancy.
- Where the protected tenancy is a sub-tenancy, the procedures laid down by the Act must be carried out between the sub-tenant and the competent landlord. This will be the next person in the chain above the sub-tenant with a lease which has at least 14 months to run or a freehold interest. In calculating the period of 14 months, you include a lease which has less than 14 months to run until the expiry of the contractual term but which will or could be continued under the Act for at least 14 months.
- A protected tenant who wishes to renew their tenancy should make an application to the court before the termination date stated in the s 25 notice or the date of commencement of the new tenancy stated in the s 26 request, unless this period is extended by agreement between the parties.
- A landlord who has been served with a s 26 request by the tenant and who opposes the renewal should serve a counter-notice on the tenant within two months of receiving the request and state the statutory grounds on which they will be relying.
- The landlord can only rely on the statutory grounds stated in their s 25 notice or their counter-notice to the s 26 request. They cannot add grounds later.
- Either party can apply to the court for interim rent, ie the rent payable while the renewal proceedings are continuing.
- The terms of the new lease are usually agreed between the parties, but if they are determined by the court, the renewal lease is likely to be on similar terms and conditions to the old lease.
- The landlord will have to pay compensation to the tenant if the new tenancy is refused, unless the reason for the refusal is that the landlord has established ground (a), (b) or (c) (where the tenant is at fault) or ground (d) (where alternative accommodation has been provided).

PART VIII

SALES OF PART AND NEW PROPERTIES

CHAPTER 41

SALES OF PART

LEARNING OUTCOMES

After reading this chapter you will be able to:

- ensure that the contract and the transfer contain an accurate description of the land being sold and the land being retained by the seller by reference to a plan
- explain why it is common practice to exclude any implied grant of rights and reservations that may otherwise have arisen on a sale of part
- consider what easements should be expressly granted for the benefit of the land being sold to the buyer over the land being retained by the seller
- consider what easements should be expressly reserved out of the land being sold for the benefit of the land being retained by the seller
- consider whether the parties should be imposing covenants on each other as to the future use of their respective parcels of land and, if so, advise on whether those covenants can be drafted so as to be binding on successors in title to the original parties
- draft a contract and a transfer for a sale of part.

41.1 INTRODUCTION

A sale of part is a more complex transaction than the sale of the whole of the seller's interest in a particular piece of land, and some additional matters must be considered. This chapter deals only with those matters which are exclusive to sales of part. Reference should also be made to **Chapter 18**, which deals with drafting the contract.

41.2 DESCRIBING THE LAND

The description of the land in the seller's existing register of title (or title deeds) must be adapted to provide a new, accurate description of the property which is being sold. It will be necessary to describe the land in the contract and the transfer by reference to a plan which shows clearly the extent of the land being sold and, where relevant, the extent of the land being retained by the seller. For more details on the use of plans, see **18.5.1**.

41.2.1 Retained land

It will usually be necessary to refer to the land which is to remain in the ownership of the seller after the sale (eg, in relation to easements and reservations). Such land must, therefore, be defined verbally in the contract and marked clearly on the plan attached to the contract and the transfer. Neither set of standard conditions contains an adequate definition of retained land.

41.2.2 Form CI

Where the sale comprises a plot on a building estate, the whole of which is registered at Land Registry, the seller will frequently have deposited a site plan at Land Registry and the official copies which are issued will give a certificate in Form CI in lieu of a title plan. This certificate states that the plot lies within the boundaries of the site plan deposited at the Registry but does not specifically identify the plot. It will also indicate whether any of the matters referred to in the charges register (eg, easements or covenants) affect that particular plot.

41.3 GRANTS AND RESERVATIONS OF EASEMENTS

On a sale of part of land, unless excluded, certain easements can be impliedly granted in favour of a *buyer*. This includes easements of necessity and common intention. In addition, s 62 of the LPA 1925 and the rule in *Wheeldon v Burrows* (1879) 12 Ch D 31 may give the buyer certain rights over the land retained by the seller for the benefit of the part sold. Section 62 of the LPA 1925 may operate to create easements over retained land where, at the time of sale, the two tenements are in separate occupation (although see *Wood and another v Waddington* [2015] EWCA Civ 538, in which the Court of Appeal said that there was no absolute rule that rights of way could not pass under s 62 if there was no prior separate occupation). The rule in *Wheeldon v Burrows* will impliedly grant as easements to the buyer all rights which are continuous and apparent and necessary to the reasonable enjoyment of the property sold, and actually in use at the time of the sale. So if, at the time of the sale, a drain from the land being sold passes through the retained land, the right to use this drain will be impliedly granted to the buyer as a legal easement. However, rights that do not already exist cannot be implied under *Wheeldon v Burrows*. So if the land being sold did not already have the benefit of the drain at the time of sale, a right to lay one would not be implied.

Thus, the rule in *Wheeldon v Burrows* will frequently not give the buyer all the easements they need. On the other hand, it may inadvertently give a buyer more than the seller intends to grant. It is, therefore, considered preferable to exclude the implied grant rules. This will be done in the transfer, but must be provided for by a special condition in the contract. Such a condition might be worded as follows:

> The transfer will contain a declaration that it will only operate to grant those easements expressly referred to and will not operate or be construed to imply the grant of any other easement.

The question of easements is then dealt with, again in the transfer as provided for in the contract, by granting specific easements tailored to suit the particular circumstances of the case. In such a case, the buyer should check very carefully to ensure that the property being bought will acquire all the easements necessary for its full use and enjoyment. The following may be relevant, depending upon the circumstances:

(a) a right of way to gain access to the property. Ensure that this is at all times, for all purposes, and allows access both on foot and by motor vehicles;

(b) a right for the usual services to reach the property – drains, water, gas, electricity, telephone, etc;

(c) a right of access to maintain all these;

(d) a right of light; and

(e) a right of support. Although there is a natural right for a piece of land to be supported by neighbouring land, there is no such right for the land to be supported where it has the extra weight of a building on it. This must be expressly granted. Although a right of support will normally be implied between terraced and semi-detached houses, if the implied grant rules are excluded, these will also need expressly granting.

If any rights are to be shared by the buyer and seller, for example use of drains or driveway, a covenant to maintain or contribute to the maintenance costs should also be imposed. Rights to enter to effect that maintenance (and make good any damage so caused) may be needed, as appropriate.

Remember that the seller can grant easements only over their own land; if the services, access, etc, are over someone else's land, the seller must either be passing on the benefit of rights already granted to them, or will have to negotiate with the owner of the land for a new deed of grant.

On the sale of, for example, a building plot, it is likely that the drains, etc will not be in existence at the time of the sale so that the easements for laying and using them will arise in the future. Thus you will be granting a future interest in land. Prior to 6 April 2010, the grant of a future interest had to comply with the rule against perpetuities. This basically required the new easement to come into existence within the perpetuity period of 21 years, although many draftsmen took advantage of the ability expressly to specify a longer perpetuity period and specified a period of 80 years (the maximum allowed under the Perpetuities and Accumulations Act 1964) within which the rights could arise. Since 6 April 2010, the rule against perpetuities has not applied to the grant of future easements, so it is merely a practical question of how long the seller wishes the arrangement to continue.

Where easements are being granted (or reserved in favour of the seller), the exact route of the right of way/drain, etc will need indicating clearly on the plan.

41.3.1 Reservations for the seller

Section 62 of the LPA 1925 and the rule in *Wheeldon v Burrows* operate only in the buyer's favour. There is no reciprocal section or case which entitles the *seller* to easements over the land being sold off (other than easements of necessity and common intention). For this reason it is important to consider what rights the seller will need to exercise over the land being sold (eg, passage of pipelines, drainage, etc) and to reserve these expressly in the transfer, as provided for in the contract.

41.3.2 Rights of light and air

Rights of light and air may pass to the buyer either under s 62 of the LPA 1925, or under the rule in *Wheeldon v Burrows*. If the buyer were to acquire rights of light and air, this might enable them at some future time to frustrate the seller's plans to build close to the boundary of the two properties. Thus the gain of rights of light and air by the buyer may be balanced by a consequent loss of amenity value to the seller's land. As the existence and extent of these rights may be difficult to ascertain, since they are not visible to the eye, it is usually considered particularly important to exclude the buyer's right to easements of light and air by an express condition in the contract which provides for the insertion of the exclusion in the transfer. The specimen clause given in **41.3** would exclude rights of light and air along with all other impliedly granted easements. If all implied grants are not to be excluded, then a condition in the following terms should be used:

> There is not included in the sale any easement of light or air which would or might interfere with or restrict the free use of the retained land for building or any other purpose. The transfer to the buyer must expressly exclude those rights.

Special condition 8 in the SCPCs provides the parties with an option either to attach a draft transfer or to set out appropriate express terms. There is no equivalent provision in the SCs, so a special condition will have to be drafted.

41.4 IMPOSITION OF NEW COVENANTS

On a sale of part, the seller will frequently wish to impose new covenants on the buyer for the protection of their retained land. All such new covenants will need to be stated expressly in the transfer and provided for in the contract; none will be implied. The seller should consider imposing some or all of the following, depending upon the circumstances of the case:

(a) restrictions on use, for example use as a single private dwelling house in the occupation of one family only;
(b) restrictions on building, for example no building without seller's consent; or seller to approve plans; or no building within (say) 10 metres of the boundary line;
(c) not to cause nuisance or annoyance to the seller and neighbouring owners;
(d) to erect and maintain boundary fence/wall; the materials, height, time limit for building, etc, must be specified; and
(e) to contribute to the maintenance of shared facilities, for example drains, rights of way.

In the case of restrictive covenants (ie, all of the above except (d) and (e), which are positive), care should be taken in the drafting to ensure that both the benefit and the burden will run to future owners of the land. The special condition in the contract should state that the covenants, when entered into in the transfer, will be 'given for every part of the Retained Land and that it is intended that the burden of the covenants will run with every part of the Property'.

The seller should be reminded that positive covenants will not be enforceable against the buyer's successors in title (although the existence of a chain of indemnity and the impact of the principle of mutual benefit and burden in *Halsall v Brizell* should be borne in mind – see **3.6.4.2**).

When acting for a buyer, you should ensure that the covenants being imposed are not too onerous.

41.5 CONSENT OF SELLER'S LENDER

Where the land to be sold consists of part of the land which is mortgaged to the seller's lender, the seller must obtain their lender's consent to the sale at the earliest possible opportunity. The lender should be asked whether the repayment of the whole or any part of the mortgage is required out of the proceeds of the sale of part and, if part, how much. Arrangements must be made for the lender to release the land being sold from the mortgage at or before completion. In registered land, the release will be effected by Form DS3 (accompanied by a plan to show the extent of the land being released). Alternatively, the release will be notified to the Registry electronically. In unregistered land, the lender will either give a deed of release, or it may prefer to be joined as a party to the conveyance in order both to release the land being sold and to give a receipt for the money being paid to it. An appropriate undertaking to discharge the mortgage should be obtained.

41.6 THE TRANSFER DEED

As will be clear from **41.3** and **41.4**, perhaps the major difference between a sale of whole and a sale of part is the need to provide for the imposition of new covenants and easements. These will actually be imposed in the transfer deed, but must be provided for in the contract. This can be done in one of two ways. First, the contract can specify the terms that the transfer deed should contain (see, for example, the wording to exclude implied grant of easements in **42.3**). Alternatively, a copy of the agreed transfer deed containing all the relevant provisions can be annexed to the contract, with a special condition stating that the form of the transfer deed shall be that annexed to the contract.

As regards the transfer deed itself, if title is registered, the transfer must be in the form of Land Registry Form TP1. This can also be used if the land being sold is unregistered, as the transaction will trigger the need for an application for first registration. Form TP1 is similar to Form TR1, used for a transfer of whole, but contains space for the new easements and covenants that may be required on a sale of part. All of the clauses referred to in the worked example of Form TR1 at **27.9** will be relevant to a sale of part, but the following will also be required, either in addition to or in substitution for the above.

41.6.1 Title number

The seller's existing title number is inserted in the document. A new title number for the part being sold will be allocated by Land Registry on registration of the transaction.

41.6.2 Description of land to be sold

A clear description of the land being sold must be included with reference to the plan annexed to the transfer. The land retained by the seller should be expressly defined and identified on the plan. The land should be described as 'part of title number LM12037' (or as appropriate). The description of the land given in the contract may be adequate for these purposes.

41.6.3 Easements and reservations

Where the contract made provision for the grant of easements to the buyer or reservations in favour of the seller, these contractual provisions must be implemented by insertion expressly into the transfer. The contract will usually provide for the exclusion of the implied grant of easements. A declaration to this effect must be inserted in the transfer to activate this requirement as follows:

> It is hereby declared that this transfer only operates to grant those easements expressly granted and will not operate or be construed to imply the grant of any other easement.

41.6.4 New restrictive covenants

New restrictive covenants are frequently provided for in a contract for the sale of part of land, and these must be expressly set out in the transfer. Except where the land sold forms part of a building scheme, covenants are enforceable against subsequent owners of that land only if they are for the benefit of land retained by the seller and the burden of them is annexed to the land sold. Express words should be included to give effect to these principles.

41.6.5 Schedules

Frequently, a short reference only to easements, covenants, etc is made in the body of the deed, the detail of such matters being set out in numbered schedules at the end of the document. Schedules should appear after the main body of the deed, but above the attestation clauses, to ensure that they are incorporated as part of the signed document and that there cannot be any argument about them having been added to it at a later stage.

41.6.6 Building estates

Where the land being sold forms a plot on a building estate, the draft transfer deed will often be prepared by the seller and attached to the draft contract, so that in this situation the buyer has no discretion over its form or contents (see **Chapter 42**).

41.7 COMPLETION AND POST-COMPLETION

41.7.1 Unregistered land

Where the land is presently unregistered, the seller will not be handing over their title deeds to the buyer on completion. The buyer should therefore verify the abstract or epitome against the original deeds and mark the abstract or epitome as examined against the original. The transaction will trigger first registration and so this procedure is necessary so that immediately after completion the buyer can produce proper evidence of the title to Land Registry with their application for first registration.

A note of any restrictive covenants imposed by the conveyance to the buyer (or a copy of that conveyance) should be retained by the seller, otherwise they will not have any evidence of those covenants when they come to sell their own land at a later stage. New restrictive covenants will automatically be entered on the register of the new title on first registration.

41.7.2 Registered land

Where the seller's title is already registered, it is not necessary to provide for an acknowledgement for production of the deeds, because the buyer will obtain their own title number on registration of the sale of part. New restrictive covenants imposed by the transfer of part will automatically be entered on the charges register of the new title on registration.

Application for the registration of the dealing on Form AP1 accompanied by such of the documents listed in **31.8.2** as are relevant to the transaction, must be made within the 30 working days protection period given by the pre-completion search. In the case of a sale of part, the search is submitted on Form OS2. This is essentially the same as Form OS1 used on the sale of whole, but reflects the nature of the transaction by identifying the property by its estate plan plot number (see **41.2.2**) or by a description and plan. Where the transfer imposes fresh restrictive covenants, a certified copy of it must also be supplied with Form AP1.

SUMMARY

- In a sale of part, the contract and the transfer should attach a plan showing the precise extent of the land being sold and the land being retained by the seller.
- Although certain rights may be impliedly granted to a *buyer* on a sale of part, it is common to exclude these and expressly grant the necessary rights to the buyer.
- Only very limited rights are impliedly reserved for the *seller* on a sale of part. Again, it is common to exclude these and expressly reserve any necessary rights.
- It may be appropriate for the parties to impose covenants on each other governing how each part of the land can be used following the sale. This is most commonly done by a seller who will be continuing to occupy the retained land. Only restrictive covenants are directly enforceable against successors in title to the original covenantor, and then only if the benefit of the covenant has been annexed to the retained land and the burden annexed to the land being sold.
- The new express easements will be created, and the new covenants will be imposed, in the transfer of the property. However, this must be agreed in the contract, either by special conditions setting out the easements and covenants to be contained in the transfer or by attaching the transfer containing the easements and covenants in the agreed form.

CHAPTER 42

NEW PROPERTIES

LEARNING OUTCOMES

After reading this chapter you will be able to:

- appreciate why a sale of a new property is more complex than the sale of an existing property
- ensure that a residential property has a home warranty and insurance policy in place
- check the arrangements for any new estate roads, drains and sewers to be adopted by the relevant authority
- appreciate that the sale of a new property may be a sale of part, and indeed one of one of multiple sales of part, so that the conveyancing procedure and documentation will be standardised accordingly.

42.1 INTRODUCTION

The sale of a new property is a more complex transaction than the sale of an existing house or building, and some matters additional to those relevant to a sale of an existing house or building must be considered. This chapter contains a summary of the matters which are exclusive to new and recently-built properties.

The main characteristics of this type of transaction which make it different from an ordinary sale and purchase are:

(a) it is a sale/purchase of a 'new property', eg a house or flat being constructed by the seller;

(b) it is often a 'sale of part'. The developer usually owns the whole site and is disposing of it in the form of building plots (or, in the case of a flat development, the developer owns the whole of the block and is disposing of the flats individually). Issues relating to sales of part are considered in **Chapter 41**;

(c) as the developer is disposing of a number of properties, they may adopt a slightly different conveyancing procedure from that normally encountered. All the usual steps will be taken, but not always by the same person as in a normal transaction, and sometimes in a different order. The developer adopts this different system for their own convenience (and to save expense) in dealing with a large number of sales simultaneously.

Note that although this chapter relates to new properties, you should bear the points dealt with in mind not just when buying directly from the developer, but also when buying 'second hand', ie buying a recently constructed house or flat.

42.2 NEW PROPERTY

42.2.1 Planning permission

Check whether planning permission has been granted. In particular, check whether any attached conditions have been or will be complied with. Bear in mind that the enforcement period for building works in breach of planning control is four years, so planning matters must be checked in the case of any purchase of a property within four years of its construction. For details of planning control, see **Chapter 7**.

42.2.2 Building regulations consent

Check that building regulations consent was granted.

The Building Regulations control the methods and materials to be used in the construction of a property to ensure that proper standards are maintained in all new properties. Thus, the lack of building regulations consent in a recently-constructed property may suggest that it may not have been constructed to the proper standards, and that it may be sensible to advise the client to point this out to their surveyor in order that a proper check on the structure of the property is made.

42.2.3 Structural guarantee

Some form of protection against defects in the design and construction of the structure of the new building should be offered. Without this a buyer may not be in a position to secure a mortgage. Although it may be possible to sue the builder for breach of express or implied development obligations in the contract, or under the Defective Premises Act 1972 (see *Harrison and Others v Shepherd Homes Ltd and Others* [2011] EWHC 1811 (TCC)), if any structural defects develop after purchase, the buyer may not be able to obtain compensation from the developer as they may no longer be in business; building companies have a very high failure rate. If the building work was supervised by, for example, an architect or a surveyor, a certificate to that effect may allow a claim to be brought against such person in the case of structural defects arising out of their negligent supervision, but the effectiveness of such action may well be dependent upon their having professional indemnity insurance.

42.2.3.1 Residential properties

In the residential context, new home warranty and insurance cover from an independent third party is essential, and will inevitably be a condition of any mortgage offer in relation to a new or recently-constructed house or flat. The NHBC 'Buildmark' scheme is the most widely used. It provides three types of protection:

(1) If the builder fails to complete the construction of the home, the NHBC will cover the cost of completing the work or refund the deposit to the buyer, as long as in either case the financial limit (usually 10% of the purchase price) is not exceeded.

(2) Once the home is completed, the developer agrees to be responsible to remedy all defects which occur within two years of purchase. In the case of default, the NHBC will itself step in, again to the extent of the financial limit, usually the purchase price.

(3) After the first two years, the NHBC provides an insurance-style guarantee that it will rectify damage resulting from a defect in construction, non-compliance with Building Regulations or contamination that requires remediation under Pt IIA of the Environmental Protection Act 1990 arising in the home during the next eight years, subject to a financial limit, usually the purchase price.

Thus a 10-year protection period is offered.

When buying a house (or flat) constructed within the previous 10 years, ensure that the property is covered by such a home warranty and insurance scheme. Although the balance of the NHBC cover is sometimes expressly assigned to a subsequent buyer, the NHBC has publicly stated that it will honour its obligations whether or not the benefit has been assigned. Statistically, most defects occur between 5 and 10 years after construction, emphasising the importance of obtaining home warranty and insurance cover even when not buying directly from the developer.

On the purchase of a new property, the contract with the developer should include a term that they are registered with the NHBC (and will continue to be so until completion) and that on exchange they will offer to enter into this 10-year home warranty and insurance scheme. Despite this contractual term as to membership, the buyer's solicitor should not exchange without checking that the builder is actually registered with the NHBC. This can be done online via the NHBC website. Alternatively, it would be in order to accept an undertaking from the builder's solicitor on exchange that the builder is registered with the NHBC. On exchange, a separate 'offer of cover' (Form BM 1) will be handed over. The acceptance of cover (Form BM 2) should be signed by the client and returned to the NHBC. There is also a comprehensive guidance booklet which the solicitor has to certify they have given to their client, ie, the buyer. Once the property is completed, the NHBC will undertake a final inspection and, if all is satisfactory, will issue a 'cover note'. This confirms that the NHBC will provide the 10-year insurance cover once the acceptance of cover form has been returned to the NHBC. The builder's solicitor should send the cover note to the buyer's solicitor as soon as it has been received from the builder client. Under the *Lenders' Handbook*, the solicitor acting for the lender is not able to submit the Certificate of Title to the lender (and thus request the mortgage advance) until this cover note has been received. In the case of flats, in addition to the 10-year notice in respect of the individual flat being bought, there will be a separate notice in relation to the common parts of the block.

Where the new property is to be bought with the aid of a mortgage loan, the *Lenders' Handbook* contains a requirement that a form of protection against construction defects is in existence.

Note that subsidence may not be covered by the home warranty and insurance scheme and so needs to be covered by the buyer's own buildings insurance.

42.2.3.2 Codes for Home Builders (Residential)

The Consumer Code for Home Builders (Consumer Code) is a voluntary code of practice for those involved in building residential properties, but is compulsory for builders and developers who are registered with certain home warranty and insurance providers, including NHBC. The Consumer Code is intended to provide additional consumer protection to individual home buyers who have reserved to buy a new or newly-converted home on or after 1 April 2010. The Consumer Code sets out what information must be provided to home buyers, and requires the home builder to monitor customer satisfaction.

There is an associated redress scheme for complaints about non-compliance with the Consumer Code arising and made within two years of completion of the purchase. Disputes are resolved using an adjudication process. Awards up to a maximum of £15,000 (inclusive of VAT) can be made, and home builders who are in serious breach of the Consumer Code could be removed from the registers of the home warranty and insurance provider of which they are a member. Further information can be obtained from www.consumercodeforhomebuilders.com.

The New Homes Quality Code (NHQ Code) was published in December 2021 by the New Homes Quality Board (NHQB). The NHQB has been requesting that builders and developers register with the NHQB since January 2021. Once builders and developers are 'activated', they are required to comply with the NHQ Code and the NHQB.

The NHQ Code contains detailed requirements about what must be included in reservation agreements and contracts and how pre-payments are to be protected. Registered developers and house builders are required to have an effective after-care service to address issues and 'snagging' items, and to offer a complaints service.

The NHQB regulates developer compliance with the NHQ Code. The New Homes Ombudsman Service (NHOS) reviews complaints from new homeowners to determine whether there has been non-compliance by the relevant developer with the NHQ Code. Further information can be obtained from www.nhqb.org.uk.

42.2.3.3 Commercial properties

A new commercial property development may be more complex than a residential one, and will typically involve more parties in the design and construction. Accordingly, there is no equivalent to the home warranty and insurance scheme for commercial properties. There are a number of different ways in which a buyer of a new commercial property can seek protection against structural defects, most of which rely on the creation of contractual obligations from the developer and their professional team to the buyer. For more details on these, you will need to refer to a specialist work on commercial property development (such as **Commercial Property**, ch 9).

42.2.4 Estate roads

The new estate roads (being, at present, unadopted private roads) are likely to be 'adopted' (ie, become publicly maintained) at some point in the future (but be aware that sometimes they might not be). As between the developer and the buyer, there should be a clause in the contract that the developer will be responsible for making up the roads to the local authority's standard and keeping them in that condition until they are adopted, at no extra cost to the buyer.

The roads are usually one of the last things a developer will complete when they are building an estate, and so there is a risk that if they do become insolvent they will not have completed them. In that situation, when the roads are adopted, the properties 'fronting' onto the road might incur road charges if the highway authority has to spend money to 'make up' the road to its standard. The local authority will divide the cost of making up the road between 'frontagers', ie the owners of the properties 'fronting' on to it. In this context, a building 'fronts' onto a road even if it is the back of the property which adjoins the road, and even if the property in question has no access onto the road. There is thus a danger that having paid for the roads as part of the price of the property, the buyer will have to pay for them all over again. Obviously, there would be a right of action against the developer, but this will be of little use if they are insolvent.

To protect the owners of such properties from these charges, check to see that a Highways Act 1980 Section 38 Agreement has been entered into by the developer with the highway authority. This is an agreement between the developer and the highway authority that the developer will be responsible for the roads. Obviously, on its own it suffers from the same defect as the similar agreement between the developer and buyer, ie if the developer becomes insolvent. This agreement must therefore be supported by a financial bond, issued by a bank or an insurance company, in a sufficient amount to cover against the developer defaulting on the Road Agreement. This, in effect, acts as an insurance policy against the developer defaulting, and is paid for by the developer. If the developer does default, the bank or insurance company will pay out under the bond; this thus avoids the risk of the 'frontagers' having to meet the cost of making up the road.

It can take several years for the roads on a new estate to be adopted, particularly if it is a large estate which takes years to be completed. Therefore, when buying a property 'second hand', always check the results of the enquiries of the local authority carefully to see whether the roads have been adopted, yet. If they have not, the existence of the agreement and bond will still be relevant.

In cases where there is no agreement and bond, a mortgage lender will usually protect itself against the property owner having to pay road charges by making a retention from the advance of the estimated cost of those charges. This retention will be released only when the roads are adopted, and may well cause the buyer financial problems on completion.

If an assessment to road charges is made by a local authority against a property, this will be registered as a local land charge. It is unlikely that any subsequent buyer would complete a purchase without this being discharged.

42.2.5 Drains and sewers

Similar problems can arise with regard to the new drains and sewers which will be necessary to serve the property. Check whether the ownership and maintenance of the drains has been or is to be transferred to the water authority. If the water authority were to adopt the drains without their having been constructed to the proper standards, there is a risk that the properties being served might incur charges. To protect the owners, ensure that a Water Industry Act 1991 Section 104 Agreement and Bond has been entered into. This works in a similar way to the Highways Act Agreement (see **42.2.4**).

42.3 SALE OF PART

42.3.1 Evidence of title

Evidence of title will be supplied as follows:

(a) *Unregistered title*: abstract/epitome of title in the usual form. However, as the original deeds, etc, will not be handed over on completion because the developer needs them to prove ownership of the remainder of the land, on completion the abstract/epitome, if not already marked, must be marked as a true copy of the original title documents.

(b) *Registered title*: official copies of the whole site, with title plan. With estate development, however, a Land Registry Form CI is often used instead of the title plan. This confirms that the plot being sold is within the developer's registered title, and indicates if any matters (eg, existing covenants in the charges register) affect that plot. The detail of this is considered at **41.2.2**.

42.3.2 Description of the property

Ensure that the contract contains a detailed description of the new property in the form of a verbal description and a professionally prepared plan.

42.3.3 Easements

Check that the contract provides for the grant to the buyer in the transfer of all necessary easements. These must include:

(a) a right of way over the estate roads until adopted;

(b) a right to use the drains and sewers;

(c) a right to use all the pipes and cables for all the other services, for example gas, electricity, water, telephone, etc;

(d) rights of access to maintain all of these.

42.3.4 Reservations

The contract should also provide for easements to be reserved in the transfer for the developer's retained land and the other buildings in the development, for example the right to run the services of water, gas and electricity across the buyer's property to the developer's adjoining land. The buyer should be told of the easements which will affect the property prior to exchange of contracts, although it is unlikely that the existence of such rights will restrict the client's proposed use of the property, if only because of the covenants that will be entered into restricting development (see **42.3.5** below). However, these easements will include a right of access onto the buyer's property for the purpose of inspection and maintenance of the various services, and the buyer must be made aware of this.

42.3.5 Covenants

New covenants will be created in the transfer of the property, some of a restrictive nature (eg, to use the property for residential purposes only) and some of a positive nature (eg, maintenance of boundary fences). Check that these are not too onerous and ensure that they are brought to the attention of the client. With residential properties there is frequently a covenant restricting the use of the property to that of a single private dwelling house, and other restrictions are common, for example prohibiting the parking of caravans or boats, or making any alterations without the developer's consent. All of these could pose problems for a buyer with special plans for the property, and should always be discussed with the client before contracts are exchanged. If the buyer and seller are businesses, it should also be ensured that any restrictive covenants affecting use are not prohibited by competition legislation (see **16.9.5**).

42.3.6 Existing mortgages

Check to see if the developer's title is mortgaged. If so, the lender's release is required for the sale. This release should be in Form DS3 for a registered title, or a Deed of Release if the title is unregistered. You should ensure that the appropriate document is available at completion, and that if there is a floating charge in favour of the developer's bank (to finance the development) a certificate of non-crystallisation will be handed over on completion.

42.4 CONVEYANCING PROCEDURES

42.4.1 Contract

The contract will be in the developer's standard form. Although this will normally incorporate one of the two sets of standard conditions, it may not be in familiar form. The developer is usually unwilling to accept amendments to this standard form contract. For administrative convenience the developer will want to ensure that every property in the development is sold on exactly the same terms.

In addition to dealing with the sale of the property, the contract may contain clauses dealing with the construction of the property, for example clauses requiring that the property is to be built in accordance with plans and specifications, time limits for building, clauses allowing for variations to original plans, etc.

42.4.2 Transfer

The draft transfer (and the engrossment of the transfer) is prepared by the developer (at the buyer's cost) in standard form, and is attached to and forms part of the contract. It will contain all of the new covenants and easements being imposed as a result of the sale. As with the contract, the developer will usually be unwilling to accept any amendments to this. The transfer deed will contain the detailed description of the property, easements and covenants.

42.4.3 Pre-contract package

42.4.3.1 General principles

The developer will need to provide the buyer with a bundle of information at the start of the transaction, just as in the case of the sale of the whole of an existing freehold property. In the context of a residential development, the developer will, at the start of the transaction, supply a package of information which is very similar to the Protocol package though in a different form. This will usually include copies of relevant planning permissions, building regulations consents, Highways Act and Water Industry agreements and bonds. In addition, the draft transfer will be included, as it is usually annexed to and forms part of the draft contract. Title will be deduced as stated above, but the standard PIF will not be used. However, similar information will be given on a printed sheet prepared specifically for that development.

42.4.3.2 Energy Performance Certificates

Energy Performance Certificates must be provided for all new buildings, whether commercial or residential (see **8.1**). Those carrying out the construction of the building are required to supply the EPC to the owner, who in turn, if they sell on, must supply it to any buyer of the building. The building control inspector will not issue a building regulation completion certificate for the property until the EPC has been supplied to the building owner.

If a property is being sold before construction is complete, the builder is obliged to provide the owner with a full EPC once the property is complete.

42.4.3.3 Disclosure of Incentives Form (residential properties)

In order to increase transparency as to the agreed price of new homes, UK Finance has introduced a requirement for a new 'Disclosure of Incentives Form' from the developer of any new-build, converted or renovated property. The Form requests information on all incentives and discounts offered by the developer, and is completed by the developer and supplied to the lender's solicitor by the developer's solicitor as part of the initial contract package. The lender's solicitor will then be required to report such information from this form as the relevant lender requests in Part 2 of the *Lenders' Handbook*.

42.4.4 Completion date

The completion date in the contract will not be a definite fixed date. This is because, when a property is in the course of construction, the developer cannot predict with certainty the precise date when it will be available for occupation. In such cases, the contract will usually provide for completion of the transaction to take place within a specified number of days after the developer certifies that the property is completed and ready for habitation.

This contractual provision could cause further problems for a buyer who has a contract for the sale of their present property. It may prove difficult to synchronise completion of both sale and purchase, as it is unlikely that the buyer's purchaser would be willing to agree to a similar condition in the sale contract. There are various practical solutions. The ideal is to wait until the house is completed before exchanging contracts and thus agreeing a fixed completion date. This is sometimes possible. In other cases, the developer will be able to give an indication as to when the property will be finished, for example 'about the last week in February'. Having taken the client's instructions and explained the problem to them, it would be possible to exchange on the dependent sale with a completion date of (say) 1 March. Thus if the house were to be completed as estimated, or a week later or even a week earlier, it would still be possible to complete both transactions in accordance with the terms of the respective contracts. The risks must be explained to the client, however, and if there is an exceptionally long delay in the completion of the new property, the danger of having to complete the sale and move into alternative accommodation must be discussed in full. You should ask the client to bear in mind also that in such a case there would be no question of claiming any compensation from the developer for the costs of this alternative accommodation.

It has to be said that although this uncertain completion date could potentially lead to all sorts of disasters, it does not normally do so in practice. Developers and their solicitors are fully aware of the problems involved and will usually do their best to assist purchasers.

SUMMARY

- A new property should have planning permission, an EPC, buildings regulation consent and some form of protection from defects in design and construction.

- Residential properties should normally be protected by a home warranty and insurance scheme, otherwise the property may be difficult to mortgage and sell within the first 10 years of construction.
- Often, the new estate roads will not have been adopted by the local authority by the time the buyer purchases the property. Similarly, the drains and sewers may not have been adopted by the water authority. If these facilities are to be adopted on completion of the development, you must check that arrangements are in place so that the buyer does not have to pay the charges of bringing these facilities up to adoption standard. There should be an agreement and bond between the developer and the relevant authority to protect the buyer if the developer becomes insolvent before the facilities are adopted.
- Where the transaction is a sale of part of the developer's land, easements and covenants may be appropriate and the points made in **Chapter 41** will apply.
- The conveyancing procedure is similar to the sale and purchase of an existing property, but where the developer is dealing with multiple sales they will issue a standard package of information and legal documentation which they will be very reluctant to vary or amend.

APPENDICES

Appendix 1

The Law Society Conveyancing Protocol

This protocol is known as the Law Society Conveyancing Protocol ('the Protocol').

The Protocol has been designed as the framework for the sale and purchase of a home for an owner occupier. It is assumed that both seller and buyer have lenders and that where a lender is involved it is also a client of the solicitor. It sets out a series of procedures that may be adapted for use in other types of land and property transfers. This Protocol is not intended for use in the purchase of new build homes.

The steps in the Protocol are not exhaustive and should not be regarded as a conveyancing 'checklist'. The transaction may not proceed in a fixed order, and many of the processes can take place simultaneously or be undertaken in a changed order. The use of the Protocol is intended to ensure that all clients are treated fairly and are protected when dealing with high value assets and liabilities. Processes that are open and transparent help make the experience more efficient and reduce wasted time and costs.

Protocol: general solicitor obligations in a conveyancing transaction

The key to reducing stress in a transaction is to manage the client's expectations; to do this you should be taking instructions on matters that could affect the chain (e.g. are parties separating, are they first time buyers, are their circumstances likely to change soon?). It is important to engage proactively with the client when getting your initial instructions. Clients may have been given unrealistic expectations by an estate agent or others about the conveyancing process or the timeframes and they may be unaware of the competing interests; you should engage with those expectations upfront and, where necessary, resetthem.

There are many uncertainties in any conveyancing transaction and you cannot be definitive at the beginning of the process. You need to manage your client's expectations at the start and throughout the transaction.

Solicitors are bound by professional obligations to their clients throughout the transaction. A solicitor is required to act in the best interests of each client and those obligations will take precedence over this Protocol.

The following obligations form part of the broader set of obligations of a solicitor and should be undertaken as a matter of course:

(a) To ensure that the transaction can proceed smoothly, you should ensure that all information is shared, subject to any confidentiality obligations that have not been waived.

(b) Ensure that you have managed and covered timing and other expectations and linked transactions such as chains appropriately.

(c) Consider any potential conflicts of interest during the whole transaction. These can arise when you are acting for more than one party: sellers, buyers and lenders.

(d) Ensure that you comply with duties to lenders.

(e) Act with courtesy and co-operate with third parties.

(f) Respond promptly particularly in relation to despatch and receipt of money, exchange of contracts andcompletion.

(g) Agree at an early stage how you will communicate with all others involved and respond promptly to communications.

(h) Ensure you always comply with regulatory and statutory requirements and SRA warnings.

(i) Ensure proper internal and external arrangements for file management have been communicated to your client in relation to holiday and sickness absence.

(j) Where you are acting for a lender as well as for either the buyer or the seller, the duties owed to the lender client are professional obligations and are subject to the lender client's specific instructions.

(k) Maintain high standards of courtesy and deal with others in a fair and honest manner.

(l) Use the most up-to-date version of the Code for Completion by Post, contract, forms and formulae and accompanying guidance published by the Law Society or such approved equivalent publications as may be notified by the Society through periodic updates made on its website at www.lawsociety.org.uk. Care should be taken to check the website regularly.

(m) Ensure you comply with the Money Laundering, Terrorist Financing and Transfer of Funds (Information on the Payer) Regulations 2017 and client identification requirements.

(n) Ensure that your publicity and costs information (including any website) meets the requirements of the SRA rules and codes of conduct and, to ensure transparency of costs and expenses, ensure you give an accurate estimate to your clients at the time of engagement and adjustments thereafter if relevant.

(o) Make a record of the advice given to seller, buyer and lender clients at all stages.

(p) Have regard to the risk management requirements of your professional indemnity insurer.

(q) Have a continuing awareness of potential cyber security issues.

Interpretation

This section helps with interpretation of the general obligations.

1 *Timetable for exchange and completion*

Every transaction is different, and the time it may take for each stage in the transaction will be different. Moreover, the timetable that will be expected by the parties at the outset may change and the order in which processes are undertaken may alter. There is no 'normal' transaction and you should communicate this to your clients who need to be made aware that timetables are often set by third parties and the original timetable is no more than a general indication.

2 *Transparency*

Recognise the value of making the process as transparent as possible. This is likely to assist your clients and help them to be better informed about the process.

3 *Lenders*

A lender may choose to instruct the conveyancer acting for the seller or the buyer to act on its behalf. Where the lender is a member of UK Finance, the provisions of the UK Finance Mortgage Lenders' Handbook ('Lenders' Handbook') will apply and should be followed (see www.cml.org.uk/lenders-handbook). Where a lender is a member of the Building Societies Association (BSA) it may choose to use the BSA Mortgage Instructions. In addition, lenders may have further and additional requirements that alter from time to time.

Lenders who are not members of UK Finance will have their own instructions and requirements which may differ from those in the Lenders' Handbook. Where you are instructed to act for those lenders or to transact through their separate representatives, you should consider the possible impact on timing. You should let those affected know.

If acting solely for the lender, the lender's conveyancer is expected to:

- follow such parts of the Protocol as apply to that retainer; and

- take all action as is necessary to enable both the buyer's conveyancer and the seller's conveyancer to comply with the timescales.

4 Practice points

Solicitors and all their conveyancing staff are expected to:

- consider and stay up to date with all relevant Law Society practice notes (see www.lawsociety.org.uk);
- attend regular training to ensure that they remain up to date with law, regulation and best practice.

5 Preferred practice

Use of this Protocol is considered preferred practice. It is only fully effective if both the seller's conveyancer and the buyer's conveyancer adopt it. However, if one party does not agree to adopt it, that does not prevent the use of the procedures by the other party.

Protocol framework

The Protocol sets out a framework for some of the work undertaken.

The seller of a property may be the buyer of another property and likewise the buyer may be the seller of another property. This chain of transactions may be extended by linked transactions. It may be necessary for exchange of contracts to take place simultaneously across the chain. The subsequent completions will usually need to coincide.

Where this occurs, there will be steps that are ascribed in the Protocol to the seller or buyer that the conveyancer will need to be taking at the same time in the mirror transaction in the chain that is linked. Those collateral steps are not set out in the Protocol but need to be considered and applied by conveyancers to ensure that the chain progresses smoothly.

Conveyancers may be instructed at different points in the buying and selling process and therefore the timings in this Protocol can only be indicative. Parties will enter the chain at different times and a chain can only progress as fast or as slow as the slowest member in it and/or the last person to join it.

Where a conveyancer is instructed solely on behalf of the lender and not jointly for both the lender and the borrower then the lender's conveyancer is expected to follow such parts of the Protocol as apply to the retainer and take all action as is necessary to enable both the buyer's conveyancer and the seller's conveyancer to comply with agreed timescales.

Every party will be progressing with their own agenda, which means that agreeing a realistic timetable and reaching final agreement on critical time limits and dates can be challenging. It is important to remember that moving dates or completion dates can only be set credibly and realistically when certain stages have been reached and certain initial requirements fulfilled.

Stage		**Steps**
A:	Instructions	1–9
B:	Pre-exchange – submitting a contract	10–19
C:	Prior to exchange of contracts	20–21
D:	Exchange of contracts	22–27
E:	Completion	28–32
F:	Post-completion	33–35

Stage A: Instructions

	Contact	Acting for the seller	Acting for the buyer	Contact
1	*Seller* *Agent*	**Client instruction** Obtain and confirm all instructions and establish the nature of the transaction. Obtain the agent's commission terms. Send to the seller the Property Information Form (TA6) and Fittings and Contents Form (TA10) (see paragraph (I) of general obligations for further guidance on the use of forms). **Linked transactions/chain of transactions** Check whether the seller has property to buy and whether an offer has been accepted and whether there is any linked transaction or chain of transactions. Remember that when you are acting for a seller, you may also be acting for that seller in his capacity as a buyer. **Occupiers** Ascertain the identity of all people aged 17 or over living in the property and consider whether their consent to the sale is required and whether they require independent advice. This may be relevant where they or anyone else may have made any financial contribution towards purchase of the property, mortgage payments, other outgoings or improvements.	**Client instruction** Obtain and confirm all instructions and establish the nature of the transaction. **Linked transactions/chain of transactions** Check whether the buyer has property to sell and whether an offer has been accepted and whether there is any linked transaction or chain of transactions. Remember that when you are acting for a buyer, you may also be acting for that buyer in their capacity as a seller. **Searches** Advise the buyer about obtaining searches. Consider which searches would be appropriate to obtain. If so instructed, instigate the searches. If there are two or more buyers, advise on the ways in which property can be owned.	*Buyer* *Agent*
2	*Seller*	**Regulatory requirements** Comply with all regulatory requirements (including Transparency Rules): (1) Provide an estimate of fees and disbursements. (2) Provide client care/retainer information and other information required by regulators. (3) Provide your terms and conditions. (4) Make clients aware of fraud risks and the methods for avoiding them. (5) Consider whether other tax advice may be relevant.	**Regulatory requirements** Comply with all regulatory requirements (including Transparency Rules): (1) Provide an estimate of fees and disbursements. (2) Quantify and explain non-optional disbursements: (a) HM Land Registry fees; (b) stamp duty land tax (SDLT), land transaction tax (LTT) including higher rate SDLT/LTT and multiple dwellings relief. If you cannot do so, refer the client to your tax department, a tax solicitor or accountant and/or advise your client to take specialist tax advice. (3) Explain other disbursements and give estimates, e.g. environmental report.	*Buyer*

	Contact	Acting for the seller	Acting for the buyer	Contact
			(4) Provide client care/retainer information and other information required by regulators. (5) Provide your terms and conditions. (6) Make clients aware of fraud risks and the methods for avoiding them. (7) Consider whether other tax advice may be relevant.	
3		**Client identity and verification** Take steps to satisfy yourself and to satisfy any third-party obligation as to the identity of your clients and continue to keep this under review. You should be aware that the buyer's conveyancer will expect you to comply with the undertakings in the Law Society Code for Completion by Post and if you are not able or willing to comply this should be communicated to the buyer's conveyancer at the earliest stage possible. **Authority to instruct** Consider which, if any, documents may need to be signed by an attorney and check whether powers of attorney are available. If your client is acting as trustee/ executor consider what documents might need to be signed. Take steps taken to satisfy yourself as to the identity of any signatory to contract or transfer so as to be able to satisfy HM Land Registry requirements upon registration. Obtain instructions for dealing with remittance of gross/net sale proceeds and details provided by the seller of UK bank account for remittance of proceeds. Obtain evidence that the bank account is properly constituted as an account conducted by the seller for a period of at least 12 months. Confirm that remittance will be made to that accountonly.	**Client identity and verification** Take steps to satisfy yourself and to satisfy any third-party obligation as to the identity of your clients and continue to keep this under review. Satisfy yourself that the seller's conveyancer will give the undertakings for completion in the Law Society Code for Completion by Post which means you do not need to raise further questions at this stage unless there are fraud indicators. **Power of attorney** Consider which, if any, documents may need to be signed by an attorney and check whether powers of attorney are available. Prepare or encourage the buyer to instruct someone to prepare any power that may be necessary.	

	Contact	Acting for the seller	Acting for the buyer	Contact
4	*Seller* *Agent* *Lender/ Broker*	**Mortgage redemption** Ask the seller how many mortgage accounts need to be redeemed and the approximate amounts outstanding on each account and monthly payment date. Obtain redemption figures and advise as to costs of obtaining redemption statements and any later updates and redemption charges. Check the mortgage or other loans and consider obtaining a statement of account to ascertain redemption penalties or negative equity. If it is apparent that there is negative equity, or for some other reason the seller will not be able to discharge the registered charges from the proceeds of sale, discuss what actions need to be taken. Advise the seller about continuing to make mortgage payments, ground rent and service charge payments that are due up to and including the completion date.	**Mortgage requirements** Check whether the buyer requires a mortgage offer in connection with any related purchase and, if so, whether: (a) a decision in principle has been obtained; (b) an application has been made; and (c) a mortgage offer has been issued. If a mortgage offer has been made, check that the special conditions can be satisfied. Suggest the buyer consults an independent surveyor for advice on different types of survey and home buyer reports.	*Buyer* *Agent* *Lender/ Broker*
		Restrictions Consider how to deal with any restrictions appearing on the register. **Lender representation** Tell the buyer's conveyancer whether you act for the seller's lender and if not, advise the buyer's conveyancer as to the identity of any solicitor who may be acting for the seller's lender. **Mortgage documentation** If you are not formally instructed by the seller's lender and you are not aware of any conveyancer who has been instructed to act for it, obtain relevant written authority from the seller to deal with the seller's existing lender. Obtain the title deeds, if any and/or ask the seller. In respect of any existing charges entered into by the seller, consider what evidence of discharge or undertakings for discharge are likely to be required by the conveyancers for the buyer's lender and the buyer.	**Lender representation** If you are not to be instructed by the prospective lender, find out who is and check their identity. Suggest the buyer obtains quotations for buildings insurance and advise that the terms of any policy taken out must be compliant with the lender's requirements (where applicable).	

	Contact	Acting for the seller	Acting for the buyer	Contact
5	*Seller*	**Written confirmation requirements** Ensure the seller has written confirmation of: (a) the name and status of the person who will carry out the work; (b) the name of the regulated individual supervising the work; (c) the complaints procedure; and (d) cancellation notice where applicable (referring to a cancellation notice if the client decided not to instruct the solicitor).	**Written confirmation requirements** Ensure the buyer has written confirmation of: (a) the name and status of the person who will carry out the work; (b) the name of the regulated individual supervising the work; (c) the complaints procedure; and (d) cancellation notice where applicable (referring to a cancellation notice if the client decided not to instruct the solicitor).	*Buyer*
6	*Seller*	**Costs, checks and payments on account** Agree costs estimated and terms for abortive charges. Carry out and record: (a) assessment of transaction risks; (b) potential conflicts; (c) capacity of client; (d) scope of authority to act, where there is more than one seller (issues of conflict between them are outside scope – affects remittance of proceeds of sale). **This obligation continues throughout the transaction.**	**Costs, checks and payments on account** Agree costs estimated and terms for abortive charges. Carry out and record: (a) assessment of transaction risk; (b) potential conflicts; (c) capacity of client; (d) scope of authority to act, where there is more than one buyer (issues of conflict between them are outside scope – affects remittance of proceeds of sale). **This obligation continues throughout the transaction.**	*Buyer*

	Contact	Acting for the seller	Acting for the buyer	Contact
7		**Title** If the title is registered, obtain: • up-to-date official copies of the register and title plan; • official copies of all filed documents; • an official copy of any registered lease; and • those documents on which the buyer can reasonably be expected to rely in order to deduce title (e.g. a certified copy of a grant of probate, a power of attorney). If the title is unregistered, obtain: • a land charges search against the seller and any other appropriate names; • an official search of the index map; • an epitome of title; • those documents on which the buyer can reasonably be expected to rely in order to deduce title (e.g. a certified copy of a grant of probate, a power of attorney). **Note:** check all plans on copied documents are complete and coloured accurately. **Defect in title** Consider and advise in relation to any apparent defect in title or missing items in title documents, e.g. missing lease or discrepancies in names or addresses. In some cases, indemnity insurance might be appropriate.	**Material information** Review the Memorandum of Sale and/or Property Particulars together with valid energy performance certificate. Explain the likely timescale of the transaction and discuss any factors that may affect it. Keep this under review throughout the transaction. Establish the funding requirements. **Potential lender requirements** When you know who the lender is, check the Lenders' Handbook, Part 2 for information about the lender's requirements. As required by the Lenders' Handbook, if you need to report a matter to the lender you must do so as soon as you become aware of it. You should tell the lender what he issue is, identify the relevant provision and provide a summary of the legal risks and your recommendations.	*Agent* *Lender*

	Contact	Acting for the seller	Acting for the buyer	Contact
8	*Seller* *Landlord* *Managing agent*	**Leasehold properties** (1) Obtain the lease or official copy of the lease and any deeds of variation. (2) Send to the seller a Leasehold Information Form (TA7) in addition to the Property Information Form (TA6) (see paragraph (I) of general obligations for further guidance on the use of forms) and obtain any documents that will be required, including a receipt for ground rent, service charge accounts and insurance details. (3) Obtain from the seller the contact details for the landlord and/or managing agent and obtain the cost of replies to enquiries in form LPE1 and obtain funds from the seller if required. (4) Consider the lease and advise as necessary concerning the residual lease term. (5) Consider timing of submission of LPE1 questions to the landlord/managing agent. (6) Consider whether any third parties will need to consent to the sale (e.g. landlord or management company).	**Leasehold properties** Ensure that the client is aware of the difference between freehold and leasehold ownership Check any lender requirements and report to lender as necessary. Each lender is different and has its own requirements in relation to leasehold properties. Consider the lease and advise the buyer as necessary as soon as you have the information concerning: (a) the residual lease term; (b) the amount of ground rent payable; (c) the method and timing of increases in the ground rent; (d) the amount of service charge payable. When you have the information provided by the managing agents in response to LPE1, particularly any potential or proposed works to the property which could lead to a substantial increase in the amount of service charge payable, report this to the buyer.	*Buyer* *Managing agent* *Landlord* *Lender*
9		**Continuing obligations** Review the costs estimate and revise if necessary, updating information regarding fees or disbursements including managing agent's fees. **Chain of transactions** Consider and advise in relation to any dependent purchase or sale. Advise the seller in relation to their potential tax liability or advise the seller to obtain tax advice as to the order of transactions, where related transactions may not be simultaneous, for SDLT or LTT impact.	**Continuing obligations** Review the costs estimate and revise if necessary, updating information regarding fees or disbursements. Consider the timeframe. If the property is leasehold, ensure that the buyer is aware that any enquiries may need to be answered by a third party and adjust the timeframe accordingly. **Chain of transactions** Consider and advise in relation to any dependent purchase or sale. Advise the buyer in relation to their potential tax liability or advise the buyer to obtain tax advice as to the order of transactions, where related transactions may not be simultaneous, for SDLT or LTT impact.	

Stage B: Pre-exchange – submitting a contract

The seller's conveyancer should generally carry out these steps within five days of confirmation of instructions and submit the draft contract upon receiving confirmation from the buyer's conveyancer that they are instructed.

If there is any delay, explain to the seller, the buyer's conveyancer and the estate agents. Following acceptance of an offer:

	Contact	Acting for the seller	Acting for the buyer	Contact
10	*Seller*	**Clients' instructions** Confirm the seller's instructions including checking whether any preliminary deposit or other direct payments have been offered or received. Advise seller not to accept any payment from the buyer. Confirm and update, where necessary, replies to enquiries if completed more than two months earlier.	**Clients' instructions** Confirm the buyer's instructions including checking whether any preliminary deposit or other direct payments have been offered or received. Advise buyer not to accept any payment from the seller or make any payments direct to the seller. Advise on liability for SDLT or LTT if you have not already done so. Explain the potential liability for higher rate SDLT/LTT and the circumstances in which this can be reclaimed or advise the buyer. Check availability of deposit. You should advise the buyer that there may be defects in the property which are not revealed by the valuation. You should also advise the borrower to obtain their own survey about the condition of the property. Advise the buyer to investigate the proposed buildings insurance. Where there are two or more people buying a property together, discuss the different types of co-ownership and whether a Declaration of Trust is required.	*Buyer* *Lender* *Surveyor*
		Chain The estate agent should ensure, so far as is possible, that the fullest information is made available as to the status of other transactions in the chain if not provided with the memorandum of sale.	**Chain** Ensure, so far as is possible, that the fullest information is made available as to the status of other transactions in the chain.	
11		**Conveyancer identification** Check the identity of the buyer's conveyancer. Follow the latest SRA and Law Society guidance.	**Conveyancer identification** Check the identity of the seller's conveyancer. Follow the latest SRA and Law Society guidance.	
12		**Confirmation of instructions** Provide the name of the seller, price and other terms agreed. State whether there is any related purchase(s) and extent of chain or any remortgage(s). Inform if seller requires mortgage or any other funding. Inform promptly of any changes. Confirm use of the Protocol and Law Society Code for Completion by Post and expected time required to prepare and submit pre-contract pack of documents.	**Confirmation of instructions** Provide the name of the buyer, price and other terms agreed. State whether there is any related sale(s) and extent of chain or any remortgage(s). Inform if buyer requires mortgage or any other funding. Inform promptly of any changes. Confirm use of the Protocol and Law Society Code for Completion by Post. Check details of client bank account.	

	Contact	Acting for the seller	Acting for the buyer	Contact
		Provide the seller with the information received from the buyer's conveyancer about any related sale by the buyer and any other transactions in the chain and details of the buyer's funding arrangements and mortgage if not previously supplied.	Provide the buyer with the information received from the seller's conveyancer about any related purchase by the seller and any other transactions in the chain.	
13		**Communication** **If you intend to email the contract bundle, please tell the buyer's conveyancer that you intend to do so.** **Delivery of contract bundle by email is acceptable but each document should be a separately identifiable attachment or uploaded individually.** **Contract bundle** If there is likely to be a delay in submitting a contract bundle, inform the seller, the buyer's conveyancer and the estate agents. So far as possible send the whole package at once. Prepare and submit to the buyer's conveyancer a contract bundle, which includes: (1) The draft contract: (a) incorporating the latest edition of theStandard Conditions of Sale; and (b) only with such additional clauses as are absolutely necessary for the purposes of the transaction; and (c) if appropriate FME1 in relation to service or maintenance charges with accompanying documentation. (2) If the title is registered: (a) up-to-date official copies of the register and title plan; (b) official copies of all filed documents; and (c) those documents on which the buyer can reasonably be expected to rely in order to deduce title (e.g. a certified copy of a grant of probate, a power of attorney, etc.)		

	Contact	Acting for the seller	Acting for the buyer	Contact
		At the time of submitting the contract bundle, entries in the register of title should be less than six months old. If any information needs to be updated (change of name, death of proprietor) the register should be updated. (3) If the title is unregistered: (a) a land charges search against the seller and any other appropriate names; (b) an official search of the index map; (c) an epitome of title; (d) those documents on which the buyer can reasonably be expected to rely in order to deduce title (e.g. a certified copy of a grant of probate, a power of attorney, etc.). **Note**: check all plans on copied documents are accurately coloured. (4) Property Information Form (TA6) with supporting documentation. **Note:** copies of competent person certificates are not always required if the existence of the certificate is clear as mentioned in the result of enquiries and noted on the relevant website (such as FENSA). (5) Fittings and Contents Form (TA10). (6) Required consents (e.g. under restrictive covenants or restrictions). (7) In relation to leasehold property: (a) Leasehold Information Form (TA7); (b) LPE1 in relation to service charge and ground rent with accompanying documentation; (c) official copies of the freehold and intermediate titles; (d) a copy of the seller's share certificate for any landlord/ management company where appropriate (e) draft of any required deed of covenant.		

	Contact	Acting for the seller	Acting for the buyer	Contact
		Confirm you will complete using the Law Society Code for Completion by Post if you have not already done so. (See paragraph (l) of general obligations for further guidance on the use of forms.) Consider including a draft transfer. Inform the estate agent and the seller when the contract bundle has been submitted. **If any document is unavailable or awaited, submit the contract bundle with an explanation as to when it is likely to be supplied.**		
14			**Receipt of contract bundle** Notify the buyer that the contract bundle has been received. Notify the seller's conveyancer if expecting to be instructed by the lender or communicate the identity of any other conveyancer instructed by the lender when known. **Search requirements** If you are not going to make such searches as are required on receipt of the draft contract, notify the seller's conveyancer and provide an indication as to why there may be a delay in submitting searches and when it is likely that they will be submitted.	*Buyer*
15	*Agent* *Seller*	**Additional enquiries** Obtain the seller's responses to additional enquiries. Explain that if inappropriate enquiries have been raised, answers need not be given. Respond to the additional enquiries from the buyer's conveyancer. You do not have to answer inappropriate enquiries. The seller should not be required to supply more information than is available in the documents. Inform the seller and the estate agent of any matters likely to delay exchange of contracts.	**Additional enquiries** **Raise only specific additional enquiries** required to clarify issues arising out of the documents submitted, or which are relevant to the title, existing or planned use, nature or location of the property or which the buyer has expressly requested. **Do not raise any additional enquiries** about the state and condition of the building unless arising out of your conveyancing search results, your buyer's own enquiries, inspection or their surveyor's report. **Indiscriminate use of 'standard' additional enquiries may constitute a breach of this Protocol. If such enquiries are submitted, they are not required to be dealt with by the seller/seller's conveyancer.** The seller's conveyancer does not need to obtain the seller's answers to any enquiry seeking opinion rather than fact.	

	Contact	Acting for the seller	Acting for the buyer	Contact
16	Seller	**Fittings and contents** Take instructions and agree any apportionment of the purchase price in respect of fittings and contents.	**Fittings and contents** Take instructions and agree any apportionment of the purchase price in respect of fittings and contents. Advise the buyer as to the impact of an apportionment of the purchase price for fittings and contents on any mortgage offer and SDLT/LTT.	Buyer
17			**Report to buyer** Report to the buyer on the documentation received and the results of investigations made. **Check title against lender's requirements.** **Draft SDLT/LTT form and signature of documentation** Prepare (from tax advice received if necessary) a draft online SDLT or LTT return. Consider timing and arrange for signature of any transfer, mortgage deed and SDLT or LTT return. Can be carried out later – see the Lenders' Handbook or the BSA Mortgage Instructions.	
18			**Mortgage instructions** Consider the mortgage instructions from the lender or the lender's conveyancer. Check the mortgage offer conditions with the buyer and if all approved obtain the buyer's signature to the mortgage deed. Consider the instructions from lenders in the Lenders' Handbook or the BSA Mortgage Instructions. If you have reported an issue to the lender, check you have the lender's further written instructions before exchange of contracts because the lender may withdraw or change the mortgage offer.	Buyer Lender
19	Seller	**Contract** Deal with any amendments to the contract after taking instructions if necessary. Reply to the Completion Information and Undertakings form (TA13) (see paragraph (l) of general obligations for further guidance on the use of forms). **Beware how you submit your bank details. It is good practice not to submit bank details by email.**	**Contract** Approve and return to the seller's conveyancer the draft contract (including the buyer's full name and address) and any necessary amendments. Submit a draft transfer deed and Completion Information and Undertakings form (TA13) (see paragraph (l) of general obligations for further guidance on the use of forms).	Buyer

Stage C: Prior to exchange of contracts

	Contact	Acting for the seller	Acting for the buyer	Contact
20	*Seller*	**Signing of contracts/transfer** Report to the seller with the contract for signature (including occupier if relevant) and arrange for the contract to be signed. Propose and agree deposit requirements, taking account of any deposit already paid. Agree the completion date. Ensure the seller is aware of the obligation to give vacant possession by the latest time in the contract (especially if the property is occupied or tenanted). Ask the buyer's conveyancer to check the date with others in the buyer's chain to see if it is agreed.	**Signing of contracts/transfer** Report to the buyer on the purchase documentation and send the contract for signature. Arrange for the contract to be signed and for the buyer to transfer the deposit, preferably electronically. Take instructions on the deposit. Agree arrangements for the amount and holding of the deposit where it is to be sent by or held by a third party. Take account of any deposit paid under any reservation or pre-contract agreement. Agree the completion date and time. Ensure that the buyer is aware of the binding nature of the commitment. Check the proposed date with the buyer and the buyer's chain to see if it is agreed. Tell the seller's conveyancer. Consider the terms on which the deposit is to be held and by whom. Advise the buyer of potential consequences of default if, for example, the deposit is held to order, is less than 10%, or is not held as stakeholder.	*Buyer*
21	*Seller* *Managing Agent/ Freeholder*	**Apportionments** Advise the seller about any apportionments that may be requested in addition to completion monies. Obtain the relevant receipts.	**Apportionments** Remind the buyer about the availability of balance of completion monies. Advise as to the date cleared monies are required for completion and any relevant apportionments. Check that the buyer has investigated the availability and cost of buildings insurance, so it is ready to be put in place on exchange or as required by the contract.	*Buyer*

Stage D: Exchange of contracts

	Contact	Acting for the seller	Acting for the buyer	Contact
22	*Seller*	**Exchange of contracts** Use the appropriate Law Society formula for exchange of contracts. Notify seller and seller's agent that exchange has taken place immediately after exchange of contracts.	**Exchange of contracts** Use the appropriate Law Society formula for exchange of contracts. Notify buyer that exchange has taken place immediately after exchange of contracts.	*Buyer*
23		**Completion information and undertakings** Complete TA13 if not already supplied (see paragraph (I) of general obligations for further guidance on the use of forms).	**Completion information and undertakings** Check replies to TA13 (see paragraph (I) of general obligations for further guidance on the use of forms).	

	Contact	Acting for the seller	Acting for the buyer	Contact
24		**Transfer** Provide the buyer's conveyancer with a copy of the transfer executed by the seller, to be delivered on completion.	**Transfer** Check execution of the copy transfer supplied. Consider whether the transfer requires execution by the buyer and whether a duplicate should be signed by the buyer in advance of completion.	
25			**Pre-completion searches** Submit pre-completion searches.	
26	*Lender*	**Redemption figures** Obtain up-to-date redemption figures.		
27			**Certificate of title** Send the certificate of title and/or requisition for funds to the lender (or the lender's conveyancer, if separately represented) promptly.	*Lender*

Stage E: Completion

	Contact	Acting for the seller	Acting for the buyer	Contact
28	*Seller* *Agent*	**Completion procedure** To manage expectations, explain to clients that there are two parts to completion: (a) legal completion: involving the transfer of funds and receipt by the seller's conveyancer; and (b) practical completion: checking the property has vacant possession and is empty, and arrangements for collection of keys by the buyer. Explain that these rarely happen simultaneously and that you will let them, or the estate agent, know when the keys can be handed over. This should be no later than the time stated in the contract. On the day before completion, or as early as reasonably possible on the day of completion, consider whether there is likely to be any delay. If there is, notify the buyer's conveyancer and thereafter agree how communication will be handled during the day until completion has taken place.	**Completion procedure** To manage expectations, explain to clients that there are two parts to completion: (a) legal completion: involving the transfer of funds and receipt by the seller's conveyancer; and (b) practical completion: checking the property has vacant possession and is empty, and arrangements for collection of keys by the buyer. Explain that these rarely happen simultaneously and that you will let them know when completion monies are transferred, and they will need to liaise with the estate agent or the seller as regards the release of keys. On the day before completion, or as early as reasonably possible on the day of completion, consider whether there is likely to be any delay. If there is, notify the seller's conveyancer and thereafter agree how communication will be handled during the day until completion has taken place.	*Buyer* *Lender*

	Contact	Acting for the seller	Acting for the buyer	Contact
29		**Completion by post** Comply with the Law Society Code for Completion by Post without variation unless there has been prior agreement to vary. General exclusions of liability for obligations within the code will be viewed as a breach of this Protocol in addition to any other consequences.	**Completion by post** Comply with the Law Society Code for Completion by Post without variation unless there has been prior agreement to vary. General exclusions of liability for obligations within the code will be viewed as a breach of this Protocol in addition to any other consequences.	
30	*Seller Agent*	**Completion monies and method of completion** On receipt of completion monies, complete the transaction in accordance with the Law Society Code for Completion by Post. This must take place by the latest time stated in the contract. Inform the buyer's conveyancer immediately if this is not possible. Report completion to the seller and proceed with any related purchase. On completion notify the estate agent and/or any other key holder and authorise release of the keys. Date the transfer deed Send the transfer and any title deeds to the buyer's conveyancer. Send sufficient monies to any lender in accordance with any undertakings.	**Completion monies and method of completion** Inform the seller's conveyancer of the commitment of funds to the banking system or instructions given to the bank in accordance with the code. Report completion of the purchase and the mortgage to the buyer. Date and complete the mortgage deed.	*Buyer Agent*
31	*Agent* *Seller*	**Payment of estate agent fees** Pay the estate agent's or property seller's commission, if so authorised.		
32	*Seller*	**Outstanding balance of sale proceeds** Account to the seller for any balance of the sale proceeds. Check funds are only being sent to the account details supplied at the beginning of the transaction.		

Stage F: Post-completion

	Contact	Acting for the seller	Acting for the buyer	Constact
33	*Lender*	**Discharge of undertaking** Provide the buyer with sealed Form DS1 (and ID forms where applicable) as soon as it is received and obtain related discharge of undertaking or confirmation as to lodging of END1 by lender if so notified.	**Application to HM Land Registry** Lodge the appropriate SDLT or LTT form with HMRC or the Welsh Revenue Authority as applicable and pay any SDLT/LTT due. Upon receipt of the transfer, lodge your application for registration at HM Land Registry within the priority period of the official search. To reduce the incidence of requisitions being raised by HM Land Registry, check the contents of the application very carefully: ensure that all necessary documents are dated, properly executed and attached and that any name discrepancies between deeds and the register are resolved or explained. Lodge Form DS1 when received (if applicable).	*Lender* *HMRC or Welsh Revenue Authority* *HM Land Registry*
34			**Registration** When registration (whether subject to 'early completion' or not) has been effected: (1) Check the titleinformation document carefully, including the address for service. (2) Supply a copy of the title information document to the buyer and remind the buyer to keep the address for service up to date. Advise the client of the existence of the HM Land Registry Property Alert service. (3) Ask the buyer to check the contents of the title information document. (4) Advise the buyer (and any lender) of completion of registration. (5) Deal with any other documents, e.g. mortgage loan agreements, planning permissions, indemnity policies, etc. in accordance with the lender's instructions.	*Lender* *Buyer*
35	*Seller*	**File closure** Close file after checking and confirm custody of sale contract and sale documents. Return to the client any original documents save for documents which it has been agreed should be retained.	**File closure** Check accounts balance, that addresses are updated, and ledger archived. Return to the client any original documents save for documents which it has been agreed should be retained.	*Buyer*

* Please provide any feedback in relation to the Protocol to property@lawsociety.org.uk

Appendix 2

Standard Conditions of Sale (Fifth Edition–2018 Revision)

(National Conditions of Sale 25th Edition, Law Society's Conditions of Sale 2011)

1. GENERAL

1.1 Definitions

1.1.1 In these conditions:

(a) 'accrued interest' means:

(i) if money has been placed on deposit or in a building society share account, the interest actually earned

(ii) otherwise, the interest which might reasonably have been earned by depositing the money at interest on seven days' notice of withdrawal with a clearing bank less, in either case, any proper charges for handling the money

(b) 'clearing bank' means a bank admitted by the Bank of England as a direct participant in its CHAPS system

(c) 'completion date' has the meaning given in condition 6.1.1

(d) 'contents price' means any separate amount payable for contents included in the contract

(e) 'contract rate' means the Law Society's interest rate from time to time in force

(f) 'conveyancer' means a solicitor, barrister, duly certified notary public, licensed conveyancer or recognised body under sections 9 or 23 of the Administration of Justice Act 1985

(g) 'lease' includes sub-lease, tenancy and agreement for a lease or sub-lease

(h) 'mortgage' means a mortgage or charge securing the repayment of money

(i) 'notice to complete' means a notice requiring completion of the contract in accordance with condition 6.8

(j) 'public requirement' means any notice, order or proposal given or made (whether before or after the date of the contract) by a body acting on statutory authority

(k) 'requisition' includes objection

(l) 'transfer includes conveyance and assignment

(m) 'working day' means any day from Monday to Friday (inclusive) which is not Christmas Day, Good Friday or a statutory Bank Holiday.

1.1.2 In these conditions the terms 'absolute title' and 'official copies' have the special meanings given to them by the Land Registration Act 2002.

1.1.3 A party is ready, able and willing to complete:

(a) if he could be, but for the default of the other party, and

(b) in the case of the seller, even though the property remains subject to a mortgage, if the amount to be paid on completion enables the property to be transferred freed of all mortgages (except any to which the sale is expressly subject).

1.1.4 These conditions apply except as varied or excluded by the contract.

1.2 Joint parties

If there is more than one seller or more than one buyer, the obligations which they undertake can be enforced against them all jointly or against each individually.

1.3 Notices and documents

1.3.1 A notice required or authorised by the contract must be in writing.

1.3.2 Giving a notice or delivering a document to a party's conveyancer has the same effect as giving or delivering it to that party.

1.3.3 Where delivery of the original document is not essential, a notice or document is validly given or sent if it is sent:

(a) by fax, or

(b) by e-mail to an e-mail address for the intended recipient given in the contract

1.3.4 Subject to conditions 1.3.5 to 1.3.7, a notice is given and a document is delivered when it is received.

1.3.5 (a) A notice or document sent through a document exchange is received when it is available for collection.

(b) A notice or document which is received after 4.00pm on a working day, or on a day which is not a working day, is to be treated as having been received on the next working day.

(c) An automated response to a notice or document sent by e-mail that the intended recipient is out of the office is to be treated as proof that the notice or document was not received.

1.3.6 Condition 1.3.7 applies unless there is proof:

(a) that a notice or document has not been received, or

(b) of when it was received.

1.3.7 A notice or document sent by the following means is treated as having been received as follows:

(a)	by first-class post:	before 4.00pm on the second working day after posting
(b)	by second-class post:	before 4.00pm on the third working day after posting
(c)	through a document exchange:	before 4.00pm on the first working day after the day on which it would normally be available for collection by the addressee
(d)	by fax:	one hour after despatch
(e)	by e-mail:	before 4.00pm on the first working day after despatch.

1.4 VAT

1.4.1 The purchase price and the contents price are inclusive of any value added tax.

1.4.2 All other sums made payable by the contract are exclusive of any value added tax and where a supply is made which is chargeable to value added tax, the recipient of the supply is to pay the supplier (in addition to any other amounts payable under the contract) a sum equal to the value added tax chargeable on that supply.

1.5 Assignment and sub-sales

1.5.1 The buyer is not entitled to transfer the benefit of the contract

1.5.2 The seller cannot be required to transfer the property in parts or to any person other than the buyer.

1.6 Third party rights

Unless otherwise expressly stated nothing in this contract will create rights pursuant to the Contracts (Rights of Third Parties) Act 1999 in favour of anyone other than the parties to the contract.

2. FORMATION

2.1 Date

2.1.1 If the parties intend to make a contract by exchanging duplicate copies by post or through a document exchange, the contract is made when the last copy is posted or deposited at the document exchange.

2.1.2 If the parties' conveyancers agree to treat exchange as taking place before duplicate copies are actually exchanged, the contract is made as so agreed.

2.2 Deposit

2.2.1 The buyer is to pay or send a deposit of 10 per cent of the purchase price no later than the date of the contract.

2.2.2 If a cheque tendered in payment of all or part of the deposit is dishonoured when first presented, the seller may, within seven working days of being notified that the cheque has been dishonoured, give notice to the buyer that the contract is discharged by the buyer's breach.

2.2.3 Conditions 2.2.4 to 2.2.6 do not apply on a sale by auction.

2.2.4 The deposit is to be paid:

(a) by electronic means from an account held in the name of a conveyancer at a clearing bank to an account in the name of the seller's conveyancer or (in a case where condition 2.2.5 applies) a conveyancer nominated by him and maintained at a clearing bank or

(b) to the seller's conveyancer or (in a case where condition 2.2.5 applies) a conveyancer nominated by him by cheque drawn on a solicitor's or licensed conveyancer's client account

2.2.5 If before completion date the seller agrees to buy another property in England and Wales for his residence, he may use all or any part of the deposit as a deposit in that transaction to be held on terms to the same effect as this condition and condition 2.2.6.

2.2.6 Any deposit or part of a deposit not being used in accordance with condition 2.2.5 is to be held by the seller's conveyancer as stakeholder on terms that on completion it is paid to the seller with accrued interest.

2.3 Auctions

2.3.1 On a sale by auction the following conditions apply to the property and, if it is sold in lots, to each lot.

2.3.2 The sale is subject to a reserve price.

2.3.3 The seller, or a person on his behalf, may bid up to the reserve price.

2.3.4 The auctioneer may refuse any bid.

2.3.5 If there is a dispute about a bid, the auctioneer may resolve the dispute or restart the auction at the last undisputed bid.

2.3.6 The deposit is to be paid to the auctioneer as agent for the seller.

3. MATTERS AFFECTING THE PROPERTY

3.1 Freedom from incumbrances

3.1.1 The seller is selling the property free from incumbrances, other than those mentioned In condition 3.1.2.

3.1.2 The incumbrances subject to which the property is sold are:

(a) those specified in the contract
(b) those discoverable by inspection of the property before the date of the contract.
(c) those the seller does not and could not reasonably know about
(d) those, other than mortgages, which the buyer knows about
(e) entries made before the date of the contract in any public register except those maintained by the Land Registry or its Land Charges Department or by Companies House
(f) public requirements.

3.1.3 After the contract is made, the seller is to give the buyer written details without delay of any new public requirement and of anything in writing which he learns about concerning a matter covered by condition 3.1.2.

3.1.4 The buyer is to bear the cost of complying with any outstanding public requirement and is to indemnify the seller against any liability resulting from a public requirement.

3.2 Physical state

3.2.1 The buyer accepts the property in the physical state it is in at the date of the contract unless the seller is building or converting it.

3.2.2 A leasehold property is sold subject to any subsisting breach of a condition or tenant's obligation relating to the physical state of the property which renders the lease liable to forfeiture.

3.2.3 A sub-lease is granted subject to any subsisting breach of a condition or tenant's obligation relating to the physical state of the property which renders the seller's own lease liable to forfeiture.

3.3 Leases affecting the property

3.3.1 The following provisions apply if any part of the property is sold subject to a lease.

3.3.2 (a) The seller having provided the buyer with full details of each lease or copies of the documents embodying the lease terms, the buyer is treated as entering into the contract knowing and fully accepting those terms.
(b) The seller is to inform the buyer without delay if the lease ends or if the seller learns of any application by the tenant in connection with the lease; the seller is then to act as the buyer reasonably directs, and the buyer is to indemnify him against all consequent loss and expense.
(c) Except with the buyer's consent, the seller is not to agree to any proposal to change the lease terms nor to take any step to end the lease.
(d) The seller is to inform the buyer without delay of any change to the lease terms which may be proposed or agreed.
(e) The buyer is to indemnify the seller against all claims arising from the lease after actual completion; this includes claims which are unenforceable against a buyer for want of registration.
(f) The seller takes no responsibility for what rent is lawfully recoverable, nor for whether or how any legislation affects the lease.
(g) If the let land is not wholly within the property, the seller may apportion the rent.

4. TITLE AND TRANSFER

4.1 Proof of title

4.1.1 Without cost to the buyer, the seller is to provide the buyer with proof of the title to the property and of his ability to transfer it, or to procure its transfer.

4.1.2 Where the property has a registered title the proof is to include official copies of the items referred to in rules 134(1)(a) and (b) and 135(1)(a) of the Land Registration Rules 2003, so far as they are not to be discharged or overridden at or before completion.

4.1.3 Where the property has an unregistered title, the proof is to include:

(a) an abstract of title or an epitome of title with photocopies of the documents, and

(b) production of every document or an abstract, epitome or copy of it with an original marking by a conveyancer either against the original or an examined abstract or an examined copy.

4.2 Requisitions

4.2.1 The buyer may not raise requisitions:

(a) on any title shown by the seller before the contract was made

(b) in relation to the matters covered by condition 3.1.2.

4.2.2 Notwithstanding condition 4.2.1, the buyer may, within six working days of a matter coming to his attention after the contract was made, raise written requisitions on that matter. In that event, steps 3 and 4 in condition 4.3.1 apply.

4.2.3 On the expiry of the relevant time limit under condition 4.2.2 or condition 4.3.1, the buyer loses his right to raise requisitions or to make observations.

4.3 Timetable

4.3.1 Subject to condition 4.2 and to the extent that the seller did not take the steps described in condition 4.1.1 before the contract was made, the following are the steps for deducing and investigating the title to the property to be taken within the following time limits:

Step		**Time Limit**
1.	The seller is to comply with condition 4.1.1	Immediately after making the contract
2.	The buyer may raise written requisitions	Six working days after either the date of the contract or the date of delivery of the seller's evidence of title on which the requisitions are raised, whichever is the later
3.	The seller is to reply in writing to any requisitions raised	Four working days after receiving the requisitions
4.	The buyer may make written observations on the seller's replies	Three working days after receiving the replies

The time limit on the buyer's right to raise requisitions applies even where the seller supplies incomplete evidence of his title, but the buyer may, within six working days from delivery of any further evidence, raise further requisitions resulting from that evidence.

4.3.2 The parties are to take the following steps to prepare and agree the transfer of the property within the following time limits:

Step		**Time Limit**
A.	The buyer is to send the seller a draft transfer	At least twelve working days before completion date
B.	The seller is to approve or revise that draft and either return it or retain it for use as the actual transfer	Four working days after delivery of the draft transfer

Step		Time Limit
C.	If the draft is returned the buyer is to send an engrossment to the seller	At least five working days before completion date

4.3.3 Periods of time under conditions 4.3.1 and 4.3.2 may run concurrently.

4.3.4 If the period between the date of the contract and completion date is less than 15 working days, the time limits in conditions 4.2.2, 4.3.1 and 4.3.2 are to be reduced by the same proportion as that period bears to the period of 15 working days. Fractions of a working day are to be rounded down except that the time limit to perform any step is not to be less than one working day.

4.4 Defining the property

The seller need not:

(a) prove the exact boundaries of the property

(b) prove who owns fences, ditches, hedges or walls

(c) separately identify parts of the property with different titles

further than he may be able to do from information in his possession.

4.5 Rents and rentcharges

The fact that a rent or rentcharge, whether payable or receivable by the owner of the property, has been, or will on completion be, informally apportioned is not to be regarded as a defect in title.

4.6 Transfer

4.6.1 The buyer does not prejudice his right to raise requisitions, or to require replies to any raised, by taking any steps in relation to preparing or agreeing the transfer.

4.6.2 Subject to condition 4.6.3, the seller is to transfer the property with full title guarantee.

4.6.3 The transfer is to have effect as if the disposition is expressly made subject to all matters covered by condition 3.1.2 and, if the property is leasehold, is to contain a statement that the covenants set out in section 4 of the Law of Property (Miscellaneous Provisions) Act 1994 will not extend to any breach of the tenant's covenants in the lease relating to the physical state of the property.

4.6.4 If after completion the seller will remain bound by any obligation affecting the property which was disclosed to the buyer before the contract was made, but the law does not imply any covenant by the buyer to indemnify the seller against liability for future breaches of it:

(a) the buyer is to covenant in the transfer to indemnify the seller against liability for any future breach of the obligation and to perform it from then on, and

(b) if required by the seller, the buyer is to execute and deliver to the seller on completion a duplicate transfer prepared by the buyer.

4.6.5 The seller is to arrange at his expense that, in relation to every document of title which the buyer does not receive on completion, the buyer is to have the benefit of:

(a) a written acknowledgement of his right to its production, and

(b) a written undertaking for its safe custody (except while it is held by a mortgagee or by someone in a fiduciary capacity).

4.7 Membership of company

Where the seller is, or is required to be, a member of a company that has an interest in the property or has management responsibilities for the property or the surrounding areas, the seller is, without cost to the buyer, to provide such documents on completion as will enable the buyer to become a member of that company.

5. RISK, INSURANCE AND OCCUPATION PENDING COMPLETION

5.1.1 The property is at the risk of the buyer from the date of the contract

5.1.2 The seller is under no obligation to the buyer to insure the property unless:

(a) the contract provides that a policy effected by or for the seller and insuring the property or any part of it against liability for loss or damage is to continue in force, or

(b) the property or any part of it is let on terms under which the seller (whether as landlord or as tenant) is obliged to insure against loss or damage.

5.1.3 If the seller is obliged to insure the property under condition 5.1.2, the seller is to: -

(a) do everything necessary to maintain the policy

(b) permit the buyer to inspect the policy or evidence of its terms

(c) if before completion the property suffers loss or damage:

(i) pay to the buyer on completion the amount of the policy monies which the seller has received, so far as not applied in repairing or reinstating the property, and

(ii) if no final payment has then been received, assign to the buyer, at the buyer's expense, all rights to claim under the policy in such form as the buyer reasonably requires and pending execution of the assignment hold any policy monies received in trust for the buyer

(d) cancel the policy on completion.

5.1.4 Where the property is leasehold and the property, or any building containing it, is insured by a reversioner or other third party, the seller is to use reasonable efforts to ensure that the insurance is maintained until completion and if, before completion, the property or building suffers loss or damage the seller is to assign to the buyer on completion, at the buyer's expense, such rights as the seller may have in the policy monies, in such form as the buyer reasonably requires.

5.1.5 If payment under a policy effected by or for the buyer is reduced, because the property is covered against loss or damage by an insurance policy effected by or on behalf of the seller, then, unless the seller is obliged to insure the property under condition 5.1.2, the purchase price is to be abated by the amount of that reduction.

5.1.6 Section 47 of the Law of Property Act 1925 does not apply.

5.2 Occupation by buyer

5.2.1 If the buyer is not already lawfully in the property, and the seller agrees to let him into occupation, the buyer occupies on the following terms.

5.2.2 The buyer is a licensee and not a tenant. The terms of the licence are that the buyer:

(a) cannot transfer it

(b) may permit members of his household to occupy the property

(c) is to pay or indemnity the seller against all outgoings and other expenses in respect of the property

(d) is to pay the seller a fee calculated at the contract rate on a sum equal to the purchase price (less any deposit paid) for the period of the licence

(e) is entitled to any rents and profits from any part of the property which he does not occupy

(f) is to keep the property in as good a state of repair as it was in when he went into occupation (except for fair wear and tear) and is not to alter it

(g) if the property is leasehold, is not to do anything which puts the seller in breach of his obligations in the lease, and

(h) is to quit the property when the licence ends.

5.2.3 The buyer is not in occupation for the purposes of this condition if he merely exercises rights of access given solely to do work agreed by the seller.

5.2.4 The buyer's licence ends on the earliest of: completion date, rescission of the contract or when five working days' notice given by one party to the other takes effect.

5.2.5 If the buyer is in occupation of the property after his licence has come to an end and the contract is subsequently completed he is to pay the seller compensation for his continued occupation calculated at the same rate as the fee mentioned in condition 5.2.2(d).

5.2.6 The buyers right to raise requisitions is unaffected.

6. COMPLETION

6.1 Date

6.1.1 Completion date is twenty working days after the date of the contract but time is not of the essence of the contract unless a notice to complete has been served.

6.1.2 If the money due on completion is received after 2.00pm, completion is to be treated, for the purposes only of conditions 6.3 and 7.2, as taking place on the next working day as a result of the buyer's default.

6.1.3 Condition 6.1.2 does not apply and the seller is treated as in default if:

(a) the sale is with vacant possession of the property or any part of it, and

(b) the buyer is ready, able and willing to complete but does not pay the money due on completion until after 2.00pm because the seller has not vacated the property or that part by that time.

6.2 Arrangements and place

6.2.1 The buyer's conveyancer and the seller's conveyancer are to co-operate in agreeing arrangements for completing the contract.

6.2.2 Completion is to take place in England and Wales, either at the seller's conveyancer's office or at some other place which the seller reasonably specifies.

6.3 Apportionments

6.3.1 On evidence of proper payment being made, income and outgoings of the property are to be apportioned between the parties so far as the change of ownership on completion will affect entitlement to receive or liability to pay them.

6.3.2 If the whole property is sold with vacant possession or the seller exercises his option in condition 7.2.4, apportionment is to be made with effect from the date of actual completion; otherwise, it is to be made from completion date.

6.3.3 In apportioning any sum, it is to be assumed that the seller owns the property until the end of the day from which apportionment is made and that the sum accrues from day to day at the rate at which it is payable on that day.

6.3.4 For the purpose of apportioning income and outgoings, it is to be assumed that they accrue at an equal daily rate throughout the year.

6.3.5 When a sum to be apportioned is not known or easily ascertainable at completion, a provisional apportionment is to be made according to the best estimate available. As soon as the amount is known, a final apportionment is to be made and notified to the other party. Any resulting balance is to be paid no more than ten working days later, and if not then paid the balance is to bear interest at the contract rate from then until payment.

6.3.6 Compensation payable under condition 5.2.5 is not to be apportioned.

6.4 Amount payable

The amount payable by the buyer on completion is the purchase price and the contents price (less any deposit already paid to the seller or his agent) adjusted to take account of:

(a) apportionments made under condition 6.3

(b) any compensation to be paid or allowed under condition 7.2

(c) any sum payable under condition 5.1.3.

6.5 Title deeds

6.5.1 As soon as the buyer has complied with all his obligations under this contract on completion the seller must hand over the documents of title.

6.5.2 Condition 6.5.1 does not apply to any documents of title relating to land being retained by the seller after completion.

6.6 Rent receipts

The buyer is to assume that whoever gave any receipt for a payment of rent or service charge which the seller produces was the person or the agent of the person then entitled to that rent or service charge.

6.7 Means of payment

The buyer is to pay the money due on completion by a direct transfer of cleared funds from an account held in the name of a conveyancer at a clearing bank and, if appropriate, an unconditional release of a deposit held by a stakeholder.

6.8 Notice to complete

6.8.1 At any time after the time applicable under condition 6.1.2 on completion date, a party who is ready, able and willing to complete may give the other a notice to complete.

6.8.2 The parties are to complete the contract within ten working days of giving a notice to complete, excluding the day on which the notice is given. For this purpose, time is of the essence of the contract.

6.8.3 On receipt of a notice to complete:

(a) if the buyer paid no deposit, he is forthwith to pay a deposit of 10 per cent

(b) if the buyer paid a deposit of less than 10 per cent, he is forthwith to pay a further deposit equal to the balance of that 10 per cent.

7. REMEDIES

7.1 Errors and omissions

7.1.1 If any plan or statement in the contract, or in the negotiations leading to it, is or was misleading or inaccurate due to an error or omission by the seller, the remedies available to the buyer are as follows.

(a) When there is a material difference between the description or value of the property, or of any of the contents included in the contract, as represented and as it is, the buyer is entitled to damages.

(b) An error or omission only entitles the buyer to rescind the contract:

(i) where it results from fraud or recklessness, or

(ii) where he would be obliged, to his prejudice, to accept property differing substantially (in quantity, quality or tenure) from what the error or omission had led him to expect.

7.1.2 If either party rescinds the contract:

(a) unless the rescission is a result of the buyer's breach of contract the deposit is to be repaid to the buyer with accrued interest

(b) the buyer is to return any documents he received from the seller and is to cancel any registration of the contract.

7.2 Late completion

7.2.1 If there is default by either or both of the parties in performing their obligations under the contract and completion is delayed, the party whose total period of default is the greater is to pay compensation to the other party.

7.2.2 Compensation is calculated at the contract rate on an amount equal to the purchase price, less (where the buyer is the paying party) any deposit paid, for the period by which the paying party's default exceeds that of the receiving party, or, if shorter, the period between completion date and actual completion.

7.2.3 Any claim for loss resulting from delayed completion is to be reduced by any compensation paid under this contract.

7.2.4 Where the buyer holds the property as tenant of the seller and completion is delayed, the seller may give notice to the buyer, before the date of actual completion, that he intends to take the net income from the property until completion. If he does so, he cannot claim compensation under condition 7.2.1 as well.

7.3 After completion

Completion does not cancel liability to perform any outstanding obligation under this contract.

7.4 Buyers failure to comply with notice to complete

7.4.1 If the buyer fails to complete in accordance with a notice to complete, the following terms apply.

7.4.2 The seller may rescind the contract, and if he does so:

(a) he may:

(i) forfeit and keep any deposit and accrued interest

(ii) resell the property and any contents included in the contract

(iii) claim damages

(b) the buyer is to return any documents he received from the seller and is to cancel any registration of the contract.

7.4.3 The seller retains his other rights and remedies.

7.5 Seller's failure to comply with notice to complete

7.5.1 If the seller fails to complete in accordance with a notice to complete, the following terms apply.

7.5.2 The buyer may rescind the contract, and if he does so:

(a) the deposit is to be repaid to the buyer with accrued interest

(b) the buyer is to return any documents he received from the seller and is, at the seller's expense, to cancel any registration of the contract.

7.5.3 The buyer retains his other rights and remedies.

8. LEASEHOLD PROPERTY

8.1 Existing leases

8.1.1 The following provisions apply to a sale of leasehold land.

8.1.2 The seller having provided the buyer with copies of the documents embodying the lease terms, the buyer is treated as entering into the contract knowing and fully accepting those terms.

8.2 New leases

8.2.1 The following provisions apply to a contract to grant a new lease.

8.2.2 The conditions apply so that:
'seller' means the proposed landlord
'buyer' means the proposed tenant
'purchase price' means the premium to be paid on the grant of a lease.

8.2.3 The lease is to be in the form of the draft attached to the contract.

8.2.4 If the term of the new lease will exceed seven years, the seller is to deduce a title which will enable the buyer to register the lease at the Land Registry with an absolute title.

8.2.5 The seller is to engross the lease and a counterpart of it and is to send the counterpart to the buyer at least five working days before completion date.

8.2.6 The buyer is to execute the counterpart and deliver it to the seller on completion.

8.3 Consent

8.3.1 (a) The following provisions apply if a consent to let, assign or sub-let is required to complete the contract
(b) In this condition 'consent' means consent in the form which satisfies the requirement to obtain it.

8.3.2 (a) The seller is to apply for the consent at his expense, and to use all reasonable efforts to obtain it
(b) The buyer is to provide all information and references reasonably required.

8.3.3 Unless he is in breach of his obligation under condition 8.3.2, either party may rescind the contract by notice to the other party if three working days before completion date (or before a later date on which the parties have agreed to complete the contract):
(a) the consent has not been given, or
(b) the consent has been given subject to a condition to which a party reasonably objects. In that case, neither party is to be treated as in breach of contract and condition 7.1.2 applies.

9. CONTENTS

9.1 The following provisions apply to any contents which are included in the contract, whether or not a separate price is to be paid for them.

9.2 The contract takes effect as a contract for sale of goods.

9.3 The buyer takes the contents in the physical state they are in at the date of the contract.

9.4 Ownership of the contents passes to the buyer on actual completion.

Appendix 3

Standard Commercial Property Conditions (Third Edition–2018 Revision)

PART 1

1. GENERAL

1.1 Definitions

1.1.1 In these conditions:

(a) "accrued interest" means:

(i) if money has been placed on deposit or in a building society share account, the interest actually earned

(ii) otherwise, the interest which might reasonably have been earned by depositing the money at interest on seven days' notice of withdrawal with a clearing bank

less, in either case, any proper charges for handling the money

(b) "apportionment day" has the meaning given in condition 9.3.2

(c) "clearing bank" means a bank admitted by the Bank of England as a direct participant in its CHAPS system

(d) "completion date" has the meaning given in condition 9.1.1

(e) "contract rate" means the Law Society's interest rate from time to time in force

(f) "conveyancer" has the meaning given by rule 217A of the Land Registration Rules 2003

(g) "lease" includes sub-lease, tenancy and agreement for a lease or sub-lease

(h) "mortgage" means a mortgage or charge securing the performance of any obligation (whether or not for the payment of money)

(i) "notice to complete" means a notice requiring completion of the contract in accordance with condition 9.8

(j) "option to tax" means an option to tax any land having effect under Part 1 of Schedule 10 to the Value Added Tax Act 1994 and references to exercising the option to tax include electing to waive exemption under previous legislation and option in this context includes such an election

(k) "post" includes postal services provided by a postal operator and "postal services" has the meaning given to it by section 27(1)(a) and (c) of the Postal Services Act 2011 and "postal operator" has the meaning given by section 27(3) and (4) of that Act

(l) "public requirement" means any notice, order or proposal given or made (whether before or after the date of the contract) by a body acting on statutory authority

(m) "requisition" includes objection

(n) "transfer" includes conveyance and assignment

(o) "VAT" means value added tax

(p) "working day" means any day from Monday to Friday (inclusive) which is not Christmas Day, Good Friday or a statutory Bank Holiday.

1.1.2 In these conditions the terms "absolute title" and "official copies" have the special meanings given to them by the Land Registration Act 20A2.

1.1.3 A party is ready, able and willing to complete:

(a) if it would be, but for the default of the other party, and

(b) in the case of the seller, even though the property remains subject to a mortgage, if the amount to be paid on completion enables the property to be transferred freed of all mortgages (except those to which the sale is expressly subject).

1.1.4 (a) The conditions in Part 1 apply subject to any variations or exclusions in the contract.

(b) A condition in Part 2 only applies if expressly incorporated into the contract.

1.2 Joint parties

If there is more than one seller or more than one buyer, the obligations which they undertake can be enforced against them all jointly or against each individually.

1.3 Notices and documents

1.3.1 A notice required or authorised by the contract is to be in writing.

1.3.2 Giving a notice or delivering a document to a party's conveyancer has the same effect as giving or delivering it to that party.

1.3.3 Where delivery of the original document is not essential, a notice or document is validly given or sent if it is sent by:

(a) fax to a fax number for the intended recipient expressly given in the contract for that purpose, or

(b) e-mail to an e-mail address for the intended recipient expressly given in the contract for that purpose.

1.3.4 Subject to conditions 1.3.5 to 1.3.7, a notice is given and a document delivered when it is received.

1.3.5 (a) A notice or document sent through the document exchange is received when it is available for collection.

(b) A notice or document which is received after 4.00 p.m. on a working day, or on a day which is not a working day, is to be treated as having been received on the next working day.

(c) An automated response to a notice or document sent by e-mail that the intended recipient is out of the office is to be treated as proof that the notice or document was not received.

1.3.6 Condition 1.3.7 applies unless there is proof:

(a) that a notice or document has not been received, or

(b) of the actual time of receipt.

1.3.7 A notice or document sent by the following means is treated as having been received as follows:

(a) by first class post:	before 4.00 pm on the second working day after posting
(b) by second class post:	before 4.00 pm on the third working day after posting
(c) through a document exchange:	before 4.00 pm on the first working day after the day on which it would normally be available for collection by the addressee
(d) by fax:	one hour after despatch
(e) by e-mail:	one hour after despatch

1.3.8 In condition 1.3.7, "first class post" means a postal service which seeks to deliver posted items no later than the next working day in all or the majority of cases.

1.4 Assignment and sub-sales

1.4.1 The buyer is not entitled to transfer the benefit of the contract.

1.4.2 The seller cannot be required to transfer the property in parts or to any person other than the buyer.

1.5 Third party rights

Nothing in this contract creates rights under the Contracts (Rights of Third Parties) Act 1999 intended to be enforceable by third parties.

2. VAT STANDARD RATED SUPPLY

2.1 The seller warrants that the sale of the property will constitute a supply chargeable to VAT at the standard rate.

2.2 The buyer is to pay to the seller on completion an additional amount equal to the VAT in exchange for a VAT invoice from the seller.

3. FORMATION

3.1 Date

3.1.1 If the parties intend to make a contract by exchanging duplicate copies by post or through a document exchange, the contract is made when the last copy is posted or deposited at the document exchange.

3.1.2 If the parties' conveyancers agree to treat exchange as taking place before duplicate copies are actually exchanged, the contract is made as so agreed.

3.2 Deposit

3.2.1 Unless otherwise agreed, the buyer is to pay a deposit of 10 per cent of the purchase price no later than the date of the contract. Where the agreed deposit is less than 10 per cent of the purchase price, condition 9.8.3 applies.

3.2.2 Except on a sale by auction the deposit is to be paid by electronic means from an account held in the name of a conveyancer at a clearing bank to an account in the name of the seller's conveyancer and is to be held by the seller's conveyancer as stakeholder on terms that on completion it is to be paid to the seller with accrued interest.

3.3 Auctions

3.3.1 On a sale by auction the following conditions apply to the property and, if it is sold in lots, to each lot.

3.3.2 The sale is subject to a reserve price.

3.3.3 The seller, or a person on its behalf, may bid up to the reserve price.

3.3.4 The auctioneer may refuse any bid.

3.3.5 If there is a dispute about a bid, the auctioneer may resolve the dispute or restart the auction at the last undisputed bid.

3.3.6 The auctioneer is to hold the deposit as agent for the seller.

3.3.7 If any cheque tendered in payment of all or part of the deposit is dishonoured when first presented, the seller may, within seven working days of being notified that the cheque has been dishonoured, give notice to the buyer that the contract is discharged by the buyer's breach.

4. MATTERS AFFECTING THE PROPERTY

4.1 Freedom from incumbrances

4.1.1 The seller is selling the property free from incumbrances, other than those mentioned in condition 4.1.2

4.1.2 The incumbrances subject to which the property is sold are:

(a) those specified in the contract

(b) those discoverable by inspection of the property before the date of the contract

(c) those the seller does not and could not reasonably know about

(d) matters, other than mortgages, disclosed or which would have been disclosed by the searches and enquiries which a prudent buyer would have made before entering into the contract

(e) public requirements.

4.1.3 After the contract is made, the seller is to give the buyer written details without delay of any new public requirement and of anything in writing which it learns about concerning a matter covered by condition 4.1.2.

4.1.4 The buyer is to bear the cost of complying with any outstanding public requirement and is to indemnify the seller against any liability resulting from a public requirement.

4.2 Physical state

4.2.1 The buyer accepts the property in the physical state it is in at the date of the contract unless the seller is building or converting it.

4.2.2 A leasehold property is sold subject to any subsisting breach of a condition or tenant's obligation relating to the physical state of the property which renders the lease liable to forfeiture.

4.2.3 A sub-lease is granted subject to any subsisting breach of a condition or tenant's obligation relating to the physical state of the property which renders the seller's own lease liable to forfeiture.

5. LEASES AFFECTING THE PROPERTY

5.1 General

5.1.1 This condition applies if any part of the property is sold subject to a lease.

5.1.2 The seller having provided the buyer with full details of each lease or copies of documents embodying the lease terms, the buyer is treated as entering into the contract knowing and fully accepting those terms.

5.1.3 The seller is not to serve a notice to end the lease nor to accept a surrender.

5.1.4 The seller is to inform the buyer without delay if the lease ends.

5.1.5 The buyer is to indemnify the seller against all claims arising from the lease after actual completion; this includes claims which are unenforceable against a buyer for want of registration.

5.1.6 If the property does not include all the land let, the seller may apportion the rent and, if the lease is a new tenancy, the buyer may require the seller to apply under section 10 of the Landlord and Tenant (Covenants) Act 1 995 for the apportionment to bind the tenant.

5.2 Property management

5.2.1 The seller is promptly to give the buyer full particulars of:

(a) any court or arbitration proceedings in connection with the lease, and
(b) any application for a licence, consent or approval under the lease.

5.2.2 Conditions 5.2.3 to 5.2.8 do not apply to a rent review process to which condition 6.1 applies or any negotiations or proceedings to which condition 6.2 applies.

5.2.3 Subject to condition 5.2.4, the seller is to conduct the proceedings in accordance with written directions given by the buyer from time to time (for which the seller is to apply), unless to do so might place the seller in breach of an obligation to the tenant or a statutory duty.

5.2.4 If the seller applies for directions from the buyer in relation to a proposed step in the proceedings and the buyer does not give such directions within 10 working days, the seller may take or refrain from taking that step as it thinks fit.

5.2.5 The buyer is to indemnify the seller against all loss and expense resulting from the seller's conduct of the proceedings in accordance with the buyer's directions.

5.2.6 Unless the buyer gives written consent, the seller is not to:
(a) grant or formally withhold any licence, consent or approval under the lease, or
(b) serve any notice or take any action (other than action in court or arbitration proceedings) as landlord under the lease.

5.2.7 When the seller applies for the buyer's consent under condition 5.2.6:
(a) the buyer is not to withhold its consent or attach conditions to the consent where to do so might place the seller in breach of an obligation to the tenant or a statutory duty
(b) the seller may proceed as if the buyer has consented when:
(i) in accordance with paragraph (a), the buyer is not entitled to withhold its consent, or
(ii) the buyer does not refuse its consent within 10 working days.

5.2.8 If the buyer withholds or attaches conditions to its consent, the buyer is to indemnify the seller against all loss and expense resulting from such withholding or attachment of conditions.

5.2.9 In all other respects, the seller is to manage the property in accordance with the principles of good estate management until completion.

5.3 Continuing liability

At the request and cost of the seller, the buyer is to support any application by the seller to be released from the landlord covenants in a lease to which the property is sold subject.

6. RENT REVIEWS AND PENDING LEASE RENEWALS

6.1 Rent reviews

6.1.1 Subject to condition 6.1.3, this condition 6.1 applies if:
(a) the rent reserved by a lease of all or part of the property is to be reviewed
(b) the seller is either the landlord or the tenant
(c) the rent review process starts before actual completion, and
(d) no reviewed rent has been agreed or determined at the date of the contract.

6.1.2 The seller is to conduct the rent review process until actual completion, after which the buyer is to conduct it.

6.1.3 Conditions 6.1.4 and 6.1.5 cease to apply on actual completion if the reviewed rent will only be payable in respect of a period after that date or if the rent review date precedes the completion date by more than two years.

6.1.4 In the course of the rent review process, the seller and the buyer are each to:

(a) act promptly with a view to achieving the best result obtainable
(b) consult with and have regard to the views of the other
(c) provide the other with copies of all material correspondence and papers
(d) ensure that its representations take account of matters put forward by the other, and
(e) keep the other informed of progress.

6.1.5 Neither the seller nor the buyer is to agree a rent figure unless it has been approved in writing by the other (such approval not to be unreasonably withheld).

6.1.6 The seller and the buyer are each to bear their own costs of the rent review process.

6.1.7 Unless the rent review date precedes the apportionment day, the buyer is to pay the costs of a third party appointed to determine the rent.

6.1.8 Where the rent review date precedes the apportionment day, those costs are to be divided as follows:

(a) the seller is to pay the proportion that the number of days from the rent review date to the apportionment day bears to the number of days from that rent review date until either the following rent review date or, if none, the expiry of the term, and
(b) the buyer is to pay the balance.

6.2 Pending lease renewals

6.2.1 This condition 6.2 applies if:

(a) the tenancy created by a lease of all or part of the property is continuing under Part II of the Landlord and Tenant Act 1954 at the date of the contract or at actual completion
(b) the seller is the competent landlord, and
(c) any of the following have been neither agreed nor determined at the date of the contract: an interim rent, the termination of the tenancy or the terms of a new tenancy.

6.2.2 Until actual completion the seller is to conduct any negotiations or proceedings relating to the matters mentioned in condition 6.2.1(c), after which the buyer is to conduct those negotiations or proceedings and is to apply without delay to be substituted for the seller as a party in any such proceedings.

6.2.3 In the course of those negotiations or proceedings, the buyer and the seller are each to act as described in condition 6.1.4(a) to (e).

6.2.4 Neither the seller nor the buyer is to agree an interim rent or any of the terms of the new tenancy without the written approval of the other (such approval not to be unreasonably withheld).

6.2.5 As from actual completion conditions 6.2.3 and 6.2.4 apply only to negotiations or proceedings relating to or affecting the amount of any rent (including any interim rent) payable from a date before actual completion.

6.2.6 The seller and the buyer are each to bear their own costs of the negotiations or proceedings.

7. TITLE AND TRANSFER

7.1 Proof of title

7.1.1 Without cost to the buyer, the seller is to provide the buyer with proof of the title to the property and of the seller's ability to transfer it or to procure its transfer.

7.1.2 Where the property has a registered title the proof is to include official copies of the items referred to in rules 134(1)(a) and (b) and 135(1)(a) of the Land Registration Rules 2003, so far as they are not to be discharged or overridden at or before completion.

7.1.3 Where the property has an unregistered title, the proof is to include:

(a) an abstract of title or an epitome of title with photocopies of the documents, and

(b) production of every document or an abstract, epitome or copy of it with an original marking by a conveyancer either against the original or an examined abstract or an examined copy.

7.2 Requisitions

7.2.1 The buyer may not raise requisitions:

(a) on any title shown by the seller taking the steps described in condition 7.1.1 before the contract was made

(b) in relation to the matters covered by condition 4.1.2.

7.2.2 Notwithstanding condition 7.2.1, the buyer may, within six working days of a matter coming to its attention after the contract was made, raise written requisitions on that matter. In that event steps 3 and 4 in condition 7.3.1 apply.

7.2.3 On the expiry of the relevant time limit under condition 7.2.2 or condition 7.3.1, the buyer loses its right to raise requisitions or to make observations.

7.3 Timetable

7.3.1 Subject to condition 7.2 and to the extent that the seller did not take the steps described in condition 7.1.1 before the contract was made, the following are the steps for deducing and investigating the title to the property to be taken within the following time limits:

Step		**Time limit**
1.	The seller is to comply with condition 7.1.1	Immediately after making the contract
2.	The buyer may raise written requisitions	Six working days after either the date of the contract or the date of delivery of the seller's evidence of title on which the requisitions are raised whichever is the later
3.	The seller is to reply in writing to any requisitions raised	Four working days after receiving the requisitions
4.	The buyer may make written observations on the seller's replies	Three working days after receiving the replies

The time limit on the buyer's right to raise requisitions applies even where the seller supplies incomplete evidence of its title, but the buyer may, within six working days from delivery of any further evidence, raise further requisitions resulting from that evidence.

7.3.2 The parties are to take the following steps to prepare and agree the transfer of the property within the following time limits:

Step		**Time limit**
A.	The buyer is to send the seller a draft transfer	At least twelve working days before completion date
B.	The seller is to approve or revise that draft and either return it or retain it for use as the actual transfer	Four working days after delivery of the draft transfer
C.	If the draft is returned the buyer is to send an engrossment to the seller	At least five working days before completion date

7.3.3 Periods of time under conditions 7.3.1 and 7.3.2 may run concurrently.

7.3.4 If the period between the date of the contract and completion date is less than 15 working days, the time limits in conditions 7.2.2, 7.3.1 and 7.3.2 are to be reduced by the same proportion as that period bears to the period of 15 working days. Fractions of a working day are to be rounded down except that the time limit to perform any step is not to be less than one working day.

7.4 Defining the property

7.4.1 The seller need not:

(a) prove the exact boundaries of the property

(b) prove who owns fences, ditches, hedges or walls

(c) separately identify parts of the property with different titles further than it may be able to do from information in its possession.

7.4.2 The buyer may, if to do so is reasonable, require the seller to make or obtain, pay for and hand over a statutory declaration about facts relevant to the matters mentioned in condition 7.4.1. The form of the declaration is to be approved by the buyer (such approval not to be unreasonably withheld).

7.5 Rents and rentcharges

The fact that a rent or rentcharge, whether payable or receivable by the owner of the property, has been, or will on completion be, informally apportioned is not to be regarded as a defect in title.

7.6 Transfer

7.6.1 The buyer does not prejudice its right to raise requisitions, or to require replies to any raised, by taking steps in relation to the preparation or agreement of the transfer.

7.6.2 Subject to conditions 7.6.3 and 7.6.4, the seller is to transfer the property with full title guarantee.

7.6.3 The transfer is to have effect as if the disposition is expressly made subject to all matters covered by condition 4.1.2.

7.6.4 If the property is leasehold, the transfer is to contain a statement that the covenants set out in section 4 of the Law of Property (Miscellaneous Provisions) Act 1994 will not extend to any breach of the tenant's covenants in the lease relating to the physical state of the property.

7.6.5 If after completion the seller will remain bound by any obligation affecting the property which was disclosed to the buyer before the contract was made, but the law does not imply any covenant by the buyer to indemnify the seller against liability for future breaches of it:

(a) the buyer is to covenant in the transfer to indemnify the seller against liability for any future breach of the obligation and to perform it from then on, and

(b) if required by the seller, the buyer is to execute and deliver to the seller on completion a duplicate transfer prepared by the buyer.

7.6.6 Where the seller's title to the property is not registered at Land Registry, the seller is to arrange at its expense that, in relation to every document of title which the buyer does not receive on completion, the buyer is to have the benefit of:

(a) a written acknowledgement of the buyer's right to its production, and

(b) a written undertaking for its safe custody (except while it is held by a mortgagee or by someone in a fiduciary capacity).

8. RISK AND INSURANCE

8.1 Risk

The property is at the risk of the buyer from the date of the contract.

8.2 Responsibility for insuring

8.2.1 Conditions 8.2.2 and 8.2.3 apply if:

(a) the contract provides that the policy effected by or for the seller and insuring the property or any part of it against loss or damage is to continue in force after the exchange of contracts, or

(b) the property or any part of it is let on terms under which the seller (whether as landlord or as tenant) is obliged to insure against loss or damage.

8.2.2 The seller is to:

(a) do everything required to continue to maintain the policy, including the prompt payment of any premium which falls due

(b) increase the amount or extent of the cover as requested by the buyer if the insurers agree and the buyer pays the additional premium

(c) permit the buyer to inspect the policy, or evidence of its terms, at any time

(d) if the policy does not cover a contractual purchaser's interest in the property, extend the cover accordingly at the buyer's request and expense, if the insurers agree, for the period until completion

(e) pay to the buyer, immediately on receipt, any part of an additional premium which the buyer paid and which is returned by the insurers

(f) if before completion the property suffers loss or damage:

(i) pay to the buyer on completion the amount of policy monies which the seller has received, so far as not applied in repairing or reinstating the property, and

(ii) if no final payment has then been received, assign to the buyer, at the buyer's expense, all rights to claim under the policy in such form as the buyer reasonably requires and pending execution of the assignment, hold any policy monies received in trust for the buyer

(g) on completion:

(i) cancel the insurance policy

(ii) apply for a refund of the premium and pay the buyer, immediately on receipt, any amount received which relates to a part of the premium which was paid or reimbursed by a tenant or third party. The buyer is to hold the money paid subject to the rights of that tenant or third party.

8.2.3 The buyer is to pay the seller a proportionate part of the premium which the seller paid in respect of the period from the date when the contract is made to the date of actual completion, except so far as the seller is entitled to recover it from a tenant.

8.2.4 Unless condition 8.2.2 or 8.2.5 applies:

(a) the seller is under no obligation to the buyer to insure the property

(b) if payment under a policy effected by or for the buyer is reduced, because the property is covered against loss or damage by an insurance policy effected by or for the seller, the purchase price is to be abated by the amount of that reduction.

8.2.5 Where the property is leasehold and the property, or any building containing it, is insured by a reversioner or other third party

(a) the seller is to use reasonable efforts to ensure that the insurance is maintained until completion

(b) if, before completion, the property or building suffers loss or damage the seller is to assign to the buyer on completion, at the buyer's expense, such rights as the seller may have in the policy monies, in such form as the buyer reasonably requires.

8.2.6 Section 47 of the Law of Property Act 1925 does not apply.

8.2.7 If the policy does not extend cover to a contractual purchaser's loss of rent from the property following completion, the seller has no responsibility lo arrange for it to do so.

9. COMPLETION

9.1 Date

9.1.1 Completion date is twenty working days after the date of the contract but time is not of the essence of the contract unless a notice to complete has been served.

9.1.2 If the money due on completion is received after 2.00p.m., completion is to be treated, for the purposes only of conditions 9.3 and 1 0.3, as taking place on the next working day as a result of the buyer's default.

9.1.3 Condition 9.1.2 does not apply and the seller is treated as in default if:

(a) the sale is with vacant possession of the property or part of it, and

(b) the buyer is ready, able and willing to complete but does not pay the money due on completion until after 2.00 p.m. because the seller has not vacated the property or that part by that time.

9.2 Arrangements and place

9.2.1 The buyer's conveyancer and the seller's conveyancer are to co-operate in agreeing arrangements for completing the contract.

9.2.2 Completion is to take place in England and Wales, either at the seller's conveyancer's office or at some other place which the seller reasonably specifies.

9.3 Apportionments

9.3.1 Subject to condition 9.3.6 income and outgoings of the property are to be apportioned between the parties so far as the change of ownership on completion will affect entitlement to receive or liability to pay them.

9.3.2 The day from which the apportionment is to be made ('apportionment day') is:

(a) if the whole property is sold with vacant possession or the seller exercises its option in condition 10.3.4, the date of actual completion, or

(b) otherwise, completion date.

9.3.3 In apportioning any sum, it is to be assumed that the buyer owns the property from the beginning of the day on which the apportionment is to be made.

9.3.4 A sum to be apportioned is to be treated as:

(a) payable for the period which it covers, except that if it is an instalment of an annual sum the buyer is to be attributed with an amount equal to 1/365th of the annual sum for each day from and including the apportionment day to the end of the instalment period

(b) accruing:

(i) from day to day, and

(ii) at the rate applicable from time to time.

9.3.5 When a sum to be apportioned, or the rate at which it is to be treated as accruing, is not known or easily ascertainable:

(a) at completion, a provisional apportionment is to be made according to the best estimate available

(b) if the sum to be provisionally apportioned is rent or service charge subject to review, final determination or adjustment, the provisional apportionment is to be made according to the amount payable on account

(c) as soon as the amount is known, a final apportionment is to be made and notified to the other party

(d) subject to condition 9.3.8, any resulting balance is to be paid no more than ten working days later, and if not then paid, so much of the balance as is from time to time unpaid is to bear interest at the contract rate from then until payment.

9.3.6 Where a lease of the property requires the tenant to reimburse the landlord for expenditure on goods or services, on completion:

(a) the buyer is to pay the seller the amount of any expenditure already incurred by the seller but not yet due from the tenant and in respect of which the seller provides the buyer with the information and vouchers required for its recovery from the tenant, and

(b) the seller is to credit the buyer with payments already recovered from the tenant but not yet incurred by the seller.

9.3.7 Condition 9.3.8 has effect if any part of the property is sold subject to a lease and Case 1 or Case 2 below applies:

(a) Case 1 is that:

(i) on completion any rent or other sum payable under the lease is due but not paid,

(ii) the contract does not provide that the buyer is to assign to the seller the right to collect any arrears due to the seller under the terms of the contract, and

(iii) the seller is not entitled to recover any arrears from the tenant

(b) Case 2 is that:

(i) a reviewed rent or interim rent is agreed or determined after actual completion as a result either of a review to which condition 6.1 applies or of negotiations or proceedings to which condition 6.2 applies, and

(ii) an additional sum then becomes payable or an allowance becomes due in respect of a period before the apportionment day.

9.3.8 (a) The buyer is to seek to collect all sums due from the tenant in the circumstances referred to in condition 9.3.7 in the ordinary course of management, but need not take legal proceedings or exercise the commercial rent arrears recovery (CRAR) procedure.

(b) A payment made on account of those sums is to be apportioned between the parties in the ratio of the amounts owed to each, notwithstanding that the tenant exercises its right to appropriate the payment in some other manner.

(c) Any part of a payment on account received by one party but due to the other is to be paid no more than ten working days after the receipt of cash or cleared funds and, if not then paid, the sum is to bear interest at the contract rate until payment.

(d) Any allowance due to the tenant is to be apportioned between the parties in the ratio of the amounts owed by each of them.

9.4 Amount payable

The amount payable by the buyer on completion is the purchase price (less any deposit already paid to the seller or its agent) adjusted to take account of:

(a) apportionments made under condition 9.3

(b) any compensation to be paid or allowed under condition 10.3

(c) any sum payable under condition 8.2.2 or 8.2.3.

9.5 Title deeds

9.5.1 As soon as the buyer has complied with all its obligations under this contract on completion the seller is to hand over the documents of title.

9.5.2 Condition 9.5.1 does not apply to any documents of title relating to land being retained by the seller after completion.

9.6 Rent receipts

The buyer is to assume that whoever gave any receipt for a payment of rent or service charge which the seller produces was the person or the agent of the person then entitled to that rent or service charge.

9.7 Means of payment

The buyer is to pay the money due on completion by electronic means in same day cleared funds from an account held in the name of a conveyancer at a clearing bank to an account in the name of the seller's conveyancer and, if appropriate, by an unconditional release of a deposit held by a stakeholder.

9.8 Notice to complete

9.8.1 At any time after the time applicable under condition 9.1.2 on completion date, a party who is ready, able and willing to complete may give the other a notice to complete.

9.8.2 The parties are to complete the contract within ten working days of giving a notice to complete, excluding the day on which the notice is given. For this purpose, time is of the essence of the contract.

9.8.3 On receipt of a notice to complete:

(a) if the buyer paid no deposit, it is without delay to pay a deposit of 10 per cent of the purchase price

(b) if the buyer paid a deposit of less than 10 per cent of the purchase price, it is without delay to pay a further deposit equal to the balance of that 10 per cent.

10. REMEDIES

10.1 Errors and omissions

If any plan or statement in the contract, or in the negotiations leading to it, is or was misleading or inaccurate due to an error or omission by the seller, the remedies available to the buyer are as follows:

(a) when there is a material difference between the description or value of the property, or any of the contents included in the contract, as represented and as it is, the buyer is entitled to damages

(b) an error or omission only entitles the buyer to rescind the contract:

(i) where it results from fraud or recklessness, or

(ii) where the buyer would be obliged, to its prejudice, to accept property differing substantially (in quantity, quality or tenure) from what the error or omission had led it to expect.

10.2 Rescission

If either party rescinds the contract:

(a) unless the rescission is a result of the buyer's breach of contract the deposit is to be repaid to the buyer with accrued interest

(b) the buyer is to return any documents it received from the seller and is to cancel any registration of the contract

(c) the seller's duty to pay any returned premium under condition 8.2.2(e) (whenever received) is not affected.

10.3 Late completion

10.3.1 If the buyer defaults in performing its obligations under the contract and completion is delayed, the buyer is to pay compensation to the seller.

10.3.2 Compensation is calculated at the contract rate on an amount equal to the purchase price (less any deposit paid) for the period between completion date and actual completion, but ignoring any period during which the seller was in default.

10.3.3 Any claim by the seller for loss resulting from delayed completion is to be reduced by any compensation paid under this contract.

10.3.4 Where the sale is not with vacant possession of the whole property and completion is delayed, the seller may give notice to the buyer, before the date of actual completion, that it will take the net income from the property until completion as well as compensation under condition 10.3.1.

10.4 After completion

Completion does not cancel liability to perform any outstanding obligation under the contract.

10.5 Buyer's failure to comply with notice to complete

10.5.1 If the buyer fails to complete in accordance with a notice to complete, the following terms apply.

10.5.2 The seller may rescind the contract, and if it does so:

(a) it may

(i) forfeit and keep any deposit and accrued interest

(ii) resell the property and any contents included in the contract

(iii) claim damages

(b) the buyer is to return any documents it received from the seller and is to cancel any registration of the contract.

10.5.3 The seller retains its other rights and remedies.

10.6 Seller's failure to comply with notice to complete

10.6.1 If the seller fails to complete in accordance with a notice to complete, the following terms apply.

10.6.2 The buyer may rescind the contract, and if it does so:

(a) the deposit is to be repaid to the buyer with accrued interest

(b) the buyer is to return any documents it received from the seller and is, at the seller's expense, to cancel any registration of the contract.

10.6.3 The buyer retains its other rights and remedies.

11. LEASEHOLD PROPERTY

11.1 Existing leases

11.1.1 The following provisions apply to a sale of leasehold land.

11.1.2 The seller having provided the buyer with copies of the documents embodying the lease terms, the buyer is treated as entering into the contract knowing and fully accepting those terms.

11.2 New leases

11.2.1 The following provisions apply to a contract to grant a new lease.

11.2.2 The conditions apply so that:

(a) "seller" means the proposed landlord

(b) "buyer" means the proposed tenant

(c) "purchase price" means the premium to be paid on the grant of a lease.

11.2.3 The lease is to be in the form of the draft attached to the contract.

11.2.4 If the term of the new lease will exceed seven years, the seller is to deduce a title which will enable the buyer to register the lease at Land Registry with an absolute title.

11.2.5 The seller is to engross the lease and a counterpart of it and is to send the counterpart to the buyer at least five working days before completion date.

11.2.6 The buyer is to execute the counterpart and deliver it to the seller on completion.

11.3 Consents

11.3.1 (a) The following provisions apply if a consent to let, assign or sub-let is required to complete the contract

(b) In this condition "consent" means consent in the form which satisfies the requirement to obtain it.

11.3.2 (a) The seller is to:

(i) apply for the consent at its expense, and to use all reasonable efforts to obtain it

(ii) give the buyer without delay a copy of all correspondence with a reversioner (whether or not immediate) in relation to obtaining the consent

(iii) give the buyer notice without delay on obtaining the consent

(b) The buyer is to comply with all reasonable requirements, including requirements for the provision of information and references.

11.3.3 Where the consent of a reversioner (whether or not immediate) is required to an assignment or sub-letting, then so far as the reversioner lawfully imposes such a condition:

(a) the buyer is to:

(i) covenant directly with the reversioner to perform and observe the tenant's covenants and the conditions in the seller's lease or (in the case of a sub-letting by the seller) in the new sub-lease

(ii) use reasonable endeavours to provide guarantees of the performance and observance of the tenant's covenants and the conditions in the seller's lease or (in the case of a sub-letting by the seller) in the new sub-lease

(iii) execute or procure the execution of the licence

(b) the seller, in the case of an assignment, is to enter into an authorised guarantee agreement.

11.3.4 Neither party may object to a reversioner's consent given subject to a condition.

(a) which under section 19(1A) of the Landlord and Tenant Act 1927 is not regarded as unreasonable, and

(b) which is lawfully imposed under an express term of the lease.

11.3.5 If any required consent has not been obtained by the original completion date:

(a) the time for completion is to be postponed until five working days after the seller gives written notice to the buyer that the consent has been given or a court has declared that consent has been unreasonably withheld

(b) the postponed date is to be treated as the completion date.

11.3.6 At any time after six months from the original completion date, either party may rescind the contract by notice to the other, if:

(a) consent has still not been given, and

(b) no declaration has been obtained from the court that consent has been unreasonably withheld.

11.3.7 If the contract is rescinded under condition 11.3.6 the seller is to remain liable for any breach of condition 11.3.2(a) or 11.3.3(b) and the buyer is to remain liable for any breach of condition 11.3.2(b) or 11.3.3(a) but condition 10.2 is to apply as if neither party is in breach of contract.

11.3.8 A party in breach of its obligations under condition 11.3.2 or 11.3.3 cannot rescind under condition 11.3.6 for so long as its breach is a cause of the consent being withheld.

12. CONTENTS

12.1 The following provisions apply to any contents which are included in the contract, whether or not a separate price is to be paid for them.

12.2 The contract takes effect as a contract for the sale of goods.

12.3 The buyer takes the contents in the physical state they are in at the date of the contract.

12.4 Ownership of the contents passes to the buyer on actual completion but they are at the buyer's risk from the contract date.

PART 2*

A. VAT

A1 Not a taxable supply

A1.1 Condition 2 does not apply.

A1.2 The seller:

(a) warrants that the sale of the property does not constitute a supply that is taxable for VAT purposes

(b) agrees not to exercise the option to tax in relation to the property, and

(c) cannot require the buyer to pay any amount in respect of any liability to VAT arising in respect of the sale of the property, unless condition A1.3 applies.

A1.3 If, solely as a result of a change in law made and coming into effect between the date of the contract and completion, the sale of the property will constitute a supply chargeable to VAT, the buyer is to pay to the seller on completion an additional amount equal to that VAT in exchange for a VAT invoice from the seller.

A1.4 The buyer is to pay to the seller on completion an additional amount equal to any VAT charged on the supply of any contents included in the sale in exchange for a VAT invoice from the seller.

A2 Transfer of a going concern

A2.1 Condition 2 does not apply

A2.2 In this condition "TOGC" means a transfer of a business as a going concern treated as neither a supply of goods nor a supply of services by virtue of article 5 of the Value Added Tax (Special Provisions) Order 1995.

A2.3 The seller warrants that it is using the property for the business of letting to produce rental income.

A2.4 The buyer is to comply with the conditions to be met by a transferee under article 5(1) and 5(2) for the sale to constitute a TOGC.

A2.5 The buyer is, on or before the earlier of:

(a) completion date, and

(b) the earliest date on which a supply of the property could be treated as made by the seller under this contract if the sale does not constitute a TOGC, to notify the seller that paragraph (2B) of article 5 of the Value Added Tax (Special Provisions) Order 1995 does not apply to the buyer.

A2.6 The parties are to treat the sale as a TOGC at completion if the buyer provides written evidence to the seller before completion that it is a taxable person and that it has exercised an option to tax in relation to the property and has given a written notification of the exercise of such option in conformity with article 5(2A) and has given the notification referred to in condition A2.5.

A2.7 The buyer may not revoke its option to tax in relation to the property at any time.

A2.8 If the parties treat the sale at completion as a TOGC but it is later determined that the sale was not a TOGC, then within five working days of that determination the buyer is to pay to the seller:

(a) an amount equal to the VAT chargeable in respect of the supply of the property, in exchange for a VAT invoice from the seller, and

(b) except where the sale is not a TOGC because of an act or omission of the seller, an amount equal to any interest or penalty for which the seller is liable to account to HM Revenue and Customs in respect of or by reference to that VAT.

A2.9 If the seller obtains the consent of HM Revenue and Customs to retain its VAT records relating to the property, it is to make them available to the buyer for inspection and copying at reasonable times on reasonable request during the six years following completion.

B. CAPITAL ALLOWANCES

B1 In this condition "the Act" means the Capital Allowances Act 2001.

B2 To enable the buyer to make and substantiate claims under the Act in respect of the property, the seller is to use its reasonable endeavours to provide, or to procure that its agents provide:

(a) copies of all relevant information in its possession or that of its agents, and

(b) whatever co-operation and assistance the buyer may reasonably require.

B3 If the seller has claimed capital allowances under Chapter 14 of the Act in respect of expenditure on plant and machinery that is a fixture:

(a) the seller is to take such steps and provide such information and written statements as the buyer may reasonably require to enable the buyer to meet the requirements of section 187A and section 187B of the Act

(b) the buyer is to use the information provided only for the stated purpose

(c) the buyer may not without the consent of the seller disclose the information which the seller expressly provides on a confidential basis

(d) on completion, the seller and the buyer are jointly to make an election under section 198 of the Act which is consistent with the apportionment in the Special Conditions

(e) the seller and the buyer are each promptly to submit the amount fixed by that election to HM Revenue and Customs for the purposes of their respective capital allowance computations

(f) the seller is to bring into account the disposal value of the fixtures fixed by the election in its tax return for the chargeable period in which completion takes place.

B4 If the seller is not entitled to claim allowances under Chapter 14 of the Act in respect of expenditure on plant and machinery that is a fixture but the buyer wishes to make such a claim:

(a) the seller is to use its reasonable endeavours to trace information about the historic expenditure from a predecessor in title of the seller by whom the expenditure was most recently incurred to enable the buyer to claim any available allowance in respect of the historic expenditure and to assist the buyer to do so

(b) the buyer is to indemnify the seller for the reasonable professional costs it properly incurs in complying with its obligations under (a).

C. REVERSIONARY INTERESTS IN FLATS

C1 No tenants' rights of first refusal

C1.1 In this condition, sections refer to sections of the Landlord and Tenant Act 1987 and expressions have the special meanings given to them in that Act.

C1.2 The seller warrants that:

(a) it gave the notice required by section 5

(b) no acceptance notice was served on the landlord or no person was nominated for the purposes of section 6 during the protected period, and

(c) that period ended less than 12 months before the date of the contract.

C2 Tenants' rights of first refusal in auction sales

C2.1 In this condition, sections refer to sections of the Landlord and Tenant Act 1987 and expressions have the special meanings given to them in that Act.

C2.2 The seller warrants that:

(a) it gave the notice required by section 5B, and

(b) it has given the buyer a copy of:

(i) any acceptance notice served on the landlord

(ii) any nomination of a person duly nominated for the purposes of section 6 and

(iii) any notice served on the landlord electing that section 8B shall apply.

C2.3 The following additional provisions shall apply:

(a) condition 9.1.1 applies as if "thirty working days" were substituted for "twenty working days"

(b) the seller is to send a copy of the contract to the nominated person as required by section 8B(3), and

(c) if the nominated person serves notice under section 8B(a):

(i) the seller is to give the buyer a copy of the notice, and

(ii) condition 10.2 is to apply as if the contract had been rescinded.

---

*The conditions in Part 2 do not apply unless expressly incorporated. See condition 1.1.4(b).

Appendix 4

The Law Society's Formulae for Exchanging Contracts by Telephone, Fax or Telex

Introduction

It is essential that an agreed memorandum of the details and of any variations of the formula used should be made at the time and retained in the file. This would be very important if any question on the exchange were raised subsequently. Agreed variations should also be confirmed in writing. The serious risks of exchanging contracts without a deposit, unless the full implications are explained to and accepted by the seller client, are demonstrated in *Morris v Duke-Cohan & Co* (1975) 119 SJ 826.

As those persons involved in the exchange will bind their firms to the undertakings in the formula used, solicitors should carefully consider who is to be authorised to exchange contracts by telephone, fax or telex and should ensure that the use of the procedure is restricted to them. Since professional undertakings form the basis of the formulae, they are only recommended for use between firms of solicitors and licensed conveyancers.

Law Society telephone/telex exchange – formula A (1986)

(For use where one solicitor holds both signed parts of the contract.)

A completion date of   is agreed.

The solicitor holding both parts of the contract confirms that he or she holds the part signed by his or her client(s), which is identical to the part he or she is also holding signed by the other solicitor's client(s) and will forthwith insert the agreed completion date in each part.

Solicitors mutually agree that exchange shall take place from that moment and the solicitor holding both parts confirms that, as of that moment, he or she holds the part signed by his or her client(s) to the order of the other. He or she undertakes that day by first-class post, or where the other solicitor is a member of a document exchange (as to which the inclusion of a reference thereto in the solicitor's letterhead shall be conclusive evidence) by delivery to that or any other affiliated exchange, or by hand delivery direct to that solicitor's office, to send his or her signed part of the contract to the other solicitor, together, where he or she is the purchaser's solicitor, with a banker's draft or a solicitor's client account cheque for the deposit amounting to £........

Note

1. A memorandum should be prepared, after use of the formula, recording:
   (a) date and time of exchange;
   (b) the formula used and exact wording of agreed variations;
   (c) the completion date;
   (d) the (balance) deposit to be paid;
   (e) the identities of those involved in any conversation.

Law Society telephone/telex exchange – formula B (1986)

(For use where each solicitor holds his or her own client's signed part of the contract.)

A completion date of   is agreed. Each solicitor confirms to the other that he or she holds a part contract in the agreed form signed by the client(s) and will forthwith insert the agreed completion date.

Each solicitor undertakes to the other thenceforth to hold the signed part of the contract to the other's order, so that contracts are exchanged at that moment. Each solicitor further undertakes that day by first-class post, or, where the other solicitor is a member of a document exchange (as to which the inclusion of a reference thereto in the solicitor's letterhead shall be conclusive evidence) by delivery to that or any other affiliated exchange, or by hand delivery direct to that solicitor's office, to send his or her signed part of the contract to the other together, in the case of a purchaser's solicitor, with a banker's draft or a solicitor's client account cheque for the deposit amounting to £........

Notes

1. A memorandum should be prepared, after use of the formula, recording:
   (a) date and time of exchange;
   (b) the formula used and exact wording of agreed variations;
   (c) the completion date;
   (d) the (balance) deposit to be paid; and
   (e) the identities of those involved in any conversation.
2. Those who are going to effect the exchange must first confirm the details in order to ensure that both parts are identical. This means in particular, that if either part of the contract has been amended since it was originally prepared, the solicitor who holds a part contract with the amendments must disclose them, so that it can be confirmed that the other part is similarly amended.

9 July 1986, revised January 1996

Law Society telephone/fax/telex exchange – formula C (1989)

Part I

The following is agreed:
Final time for exchange: pm
Completion date:
Deposit to be paid to:

Each solicitor confirms that he or she holds a part of the contract in the agreed form signed by his or her client, or, if there is more than one client, by all of them. Each solicitor undertakes to the other that:

(a) he or she will continue to hold that part of the contract until the final time for exchange on the date the formula is used, and

(b) if the vendor's solicitor so notifies the purchaser's solicitor by fax, telephone or telex (whichever was previously agreed) by that time, they will both comply with part II of the formula.

The purchaser's solicitor further undertakes that either he or she or some other named person in his or her office will be available up to the final time for exchange to activate part II of the formula on receipt of the telephone call, fax or telex from the vendor's solicitors.

Part II

Each solicitor undertakes to the other henceforth to hold the part of the contract in his or her possession to the other's order, so that contracts are exchanged at that moment, and to despatch it to the other on that day. The purchaser's solicitor further undertakes to the vendor's solicitor to despatch on that day, or to arrange for the despatch on that day of, a banker's draft or a solicitor's client account cheque for the full deposit specified in the agreed form of contract (divided as the vendor's solicitor may have specified) to the vendor's solicitor and/or to some other solicitor whom the vendor's solicitor nominates, to be held on formula C terms.

'To despatch' means to send by first-class post, or, where the other solicitor is a member of a document exchange (as to which the inclusion of a reference thereto in the solicitor's letterhead is to be conclusive evidence) by delivery to that or any other affiliated exchange, or by hand delivery direct to the recipient solicitor's office. 'Formula C terms' means that the deposit is held as stakeholder, or as agent for the vendor with authority to part with it only for the purpose of passing it to another solicitor as deposit in a related property purchase transaction on these terms.

Notes

1. Two memoranda will be required when using Formula C. One needs to record the use of Part I, and a second needs to record the request of the vendor's solicitor to the purchaser's solicitor to activate Part II.
2. The first memorandum should record:
   (a) the date and time when it was agreed to use Formula C;
   (b) the exact wording of any agreed variations;
   (c) the final time, later that day, for exchange;
   (d) the completion date;
   (e) the name of the solicitor to whom the deposit was to be paid, or details of amounts and names if it was to be split; and
   (f) the identities of those involved in any conversation.
3. Formula C assumes the payment of a full contractual deposit (normally 10%).
4. The contract term relating to the deposit must allow it to be passed on, with payment direct from payer to ultimate recipient, in the way in which the formula contemplates. The deposit must ultimately be held by a solicitor as stakeholder. Whilst some variation in the formula can be agreed this is a term of the formula which must not be varied, unless all the solicitors involved in the chain have agreed.
5. If a buyer proposes to use a deposit guarantee policy, Formula C will need substantial adaptation.
6. It is essential prior to agreeing Part I of Formula C that those effecting the exchange ensure that both parts of the contract are identical.
7. Using Formula C involves a solicitor in giving a number of professional undertakings. These must be performed precisely. Any failure will be a serious breach of professional discipline. One of the undertakings may be to arrange that someone over whom the solicitor has no control will do something (ie to arrange for someone else to despatch the cheque or banker's draft in payment of the deposit). An undertaking is still binding even if it is to do something outside the solicitor's control.
8. Solicitors do not as a matter of law have an automatic authority to exchange contracts on a Formula C basis, and should always ensure that they have the client's express authority to use Formula C. A suggested form of authority is set out below. It should be adapted to cover any special circumstances:

I/We . . . . understand that my/our sale and purchase of . . . . are both part of a chain of linked property transactions, in which all parties want the security of contracts which become binding on the same day.

I/We agree that you should make arrangements with the other solicitors or licensed conveyancers involved to achieve this.

I/We understand that this involves each property-buyer offering, early on one day, to exchange contracts whenever, later that day, the seller so requests, and that the buyer's offer is on the basis that it cannot be withdrawn or varied during that day.

I/We agree that when I/we authorise you to exchange contracts, you may agree to exchange contracts on the above basis and give any necessary undertakings to the other parties involved in the chain and that my/our authority to you cannot be revoked throughout the day on which the offer to exchange contracts is made.

15 March 1989, revised January 1996

Appendix 5

The Law Society's Code for Completion by Post (2019)

Warning: Use of this code embodies professional undertakings.

Introduction and scope

This code provides a voluntary procedure for postal completion for either residential or commercial transactions. It may also be used by licensed conveyancers. Solicitors adopting this code must be satisfied that its adoption will not be contrary to the interests of their client. When adopted, this code applies without variation unless otherwise agreed.

This code is intended to provide a fair balance of obligation between seller's and buyer's solicitors and to facilitate professional co-operation for the benefit of clients.

Procedure

General

1. To adopt this code, both solicitors must agree, preferably in writing, to use it to complete a specific transaction, except that the use or adoption of the Law Society Conveyancing Protocol automatically implies use of this code unless otherwise stated in writing by either solicitor.
2. In this code:
   (i) all references to the "Seller" are references to the person or persons who will at the point of completion be entitled to convey the legal and/or equitable title to the property and
   (ii) all references to the "Seller's Solicitor" are to the solicitor purporting to act for the party named as the seller in respect of the contract or purported contract that the buyer has entered into in order to acquire the property.
3. If the Seller's Solicitor has to withdraw from using this code, the buyer's solicitor should be notified of this not later than 4pm on the working day immediately before the completion date. If the Seller's Solicitor's authority to receive the monies is withdrawn later the buyer's solicitor must be notified immediately.
4. In complying with the terms of this code:
   (i) The Seller's Solicitor acts on completion as the buyer's solicitor's agent without fee or disbursement, but this obligation does not require the Seller's Solicitor to investigate or take responsibility for any breach of the seller's contractual obligations and is expressly limited to completion pursuant to paragraphs 11 to 13; and
   (ii) Where the Seller's Solicitor receives and/or holds the money received for completion, the Seller's Solicitor receives and/holds that money on trust for the person or persons who provided it, to be either
      (a) paid away only in respect of a completion in which the Seller executes and delivers a valid conveyance or transfer; or

(b) repaid to the person who remitted it, if completion does not take place.

Before completion

5. The buyer's solicitor will use reasonable endeavours to ensure that enough funds are collected from the buyer and any mortgage lender in good time to transmit to the Seller's Solicitor on or before the completion date.
6. The Seller's Solicitor should provide to the buyer's solicitor replies to completion information, and undertakings in the Law Society's standard form, at least five working days before the completion date unless replies have been provided to such other form requesting completion information as may have been submitted by the buyer's solicitor.
7. The Seller's Solicitor will specify in writing to the buyer's solicitor the mortgages, charges or other financial incumbrances secured on the property which on or before completion are to be redeemed or discharged to the extent that they relate to the property, and by what method.
8. The Seller's Solicitor **undertakes**:
   (i) to have the Seller's authority to receive the purchase money on completion; and
   (ii) on completion, to have the authority of the proprietor of each mortgage, charge or other financial incumbrance which was specified under paragraph 7 but has not then been redeemed or discharged, to receive the sum intended to repay it;

   BUT if the Seller's Solicitor does not have all the necessary authorities then:
   (iii) to advise the buyer's solicitor no later than 4pm on the working day immediately before the completion date of the absence of those authorities or immediately if any is withdrawn later; and
   (iv) not to complete without the buyer's solicitor's instructions.
9. The buyer's solicitor may send the Seller's Solicitor instructions as to any other matters required by the buyer's solicitor which may include:
   (i) documents to be examined and marked;
   (ii) memoranda to be endorsed;
   (iii) undertakings to be given;
   (iv) deeds or other documents including transfers and any relevant undertakings and authorities relating to rents, deposits, keys, to be sent to the buyer's solicitor following completion;
   (v) consents, certificates or other authorities that may be required to deal with any restrictions on any Land Registry title to the property;
   (vi) executed Stock Transfer Forms relating to shares in any companies directly related to the conveyancing transaction.
10. The buyer's solicitor will remit to the Seller's Solicitor the sum required to complete, as notified in writing on the Seller's Solicitor's completion statement or otherwise in accordance with the contract, including any compensation payable for late completion by reference to the 'contract rate' if either the Standard Conditions of Sale or the Standard Commercial Property Conditions are utilised, or, in default of notification, as shown by the contract. If the funds are remitted by transfer between banks, immediately upon becoming aware of their receipt, the Seller's Solicitor will report to the buyer's solicitor that the funds have been received.

Completion

11. The Seller's Solicitor will complete upon becoming aware of the receipt of the sum specified in paragraph 10, or a lesser sum should the buyer's solicitor and Seller's Solicitor so agree, unless
    (i) the buyer's solicitor has notified the Seller's Solicitor that the funds are to be held to the buyer's solicitor's order; or
    (ii) it has previously been agreed that completion is to take place at a later time.

Any agreement or notification under this paragraph should if possible be made or confirmed in writing.

12. When completing, the Seller's Solicitor **undertakes**:
   (i) to comply with any agreed completion arrangements and any reasonable instructions given under paragraph 9;
   (ii) to redeem or obtain discharges for every mortgage, charge or other financial incumbrance specified under paragraph 7 so far as it relates to the property which has not already been redeemed or discharged;
   (iii) that the proprietor of each mortgage, charge or other financial incumbrance specified under paragraph 7 has been identified by the Seller's Solicitor to the extent necessary for the purpose of the buyer's solicitor's application to HM Land Registry.

After completion

13. The Seller's Solicitor **undertakes**:
   (i) immediately completion has taken place, to hold to the buyer's solicitor's order every document specified under paragraph 9 and not to exercise a lien over any of them;
   (ii) as soon as possible after completion:
      (a) to confirm to the buyer's solicitor by telephone, fax or email the date and time at which completion has taken place;
      (b) to notify the Seller's estate agent or other keyholder that completion has taken place, and authorise them to make keys available to the buyer immediately;
   (iii) as soon as possible after completion and in any event by the end of the working day following completion, to send *written confirmation that completion has taken place, and*, at the risk of the buyer's solicitor, the items specified under paragraph 9 to the buyer's solicitor by first class post or document exchange;
   (iv) if the discharge of any mortgage, charge or other financial incumbrance specified under paragraph 7 takes place by electronic means, to notify the buyer's solicitor as soon as confirmation is received from the proprietor of the mortgage, charge or other financial incumbrance that the discharge has taken or is taking place.

Supplementary

14. The rights and obligations of the parties, under the contract or otherwise, are not affected by this code and in the event of a conflict between the contract and this code, the contract shall prevail.
15. When a licensed conveyancer adopts this code, references to a solicitor include that licensed conveyancer.
16. A dispute or difference arising between solicitors who adopt this code (whether or not subject to any variation) relating directly to its application is to be referred to a single arbitrator agreed between the solicitors. If they do not agree on the appointment within one month, the President of the Law Society may appoint the arbitrator at the request of one of the solicitors.

Notes to this code

1. The 2019 version of this code will apply to transactions where this code is adopted after the first day of May 2019.

2. The object of this code is to provide solicitors with a convenient means for completion on an agency basis when a representative of the buyer's solicitor is not attending at the office of the seller's solicitor.
3. As with the Law Society's formulae for exchange of contracts, this code embodies professional undertakings and is only recommended for adoption between solicitors and licensed conveyancers.
4. Paragraph 4(i) of this code provides that the Seller's solicitor will act as agents for the buyer's solicitors without fee or disbursements. The convenience of not having to make a specific appointment on the date of completion for the buyer's solicitor to attend to complete personally will offset the agency work that the Seller's Solicitor has to do in completing under this code. Most solicitors will from time to time act for both sellers and buyers. If a Seller's Solicitor does consider that charges and/or disbursements are necessary in a particular case, this would represent a variation in this code and should be agreed in writing before exchange of contracts.
5. Paragraph 4(ii) of this code makes explicit the effect of the decisions in *Twinsectra Ltd* v. *Yardley* [2002] UKHL 12, *Lloyds TSB Bank plc* v. *Markandan & Uddin (a firm)* [2012] EWCA Civ 65 and *P&P Property Ltd* v. *Owen White & Catlin LLP and Dreamvar (UK) Ltd* v. *Mishcon de Reya (a firm)* [2018] EWCA Civ 1082, that the Seller's Solicitor holds any purchase money received on trust for the person or persons who provided it and is under a fiduciary duty not to deal with that money other than in accordance with the terms of this code.
6. In view of the decision in *P&P Property Ltd v. Owen White & Catlin LLP and Dreamvar (UK) Ltd v. Mishcon de Reya (a firm)* [2018] EWCA Civ 1082, paragraph 8(i) of this code constitutes an undertaking that the Seller's Solicitor has authority from the true owner of the title to the property named in the contract to receive the purchase money, and that such person is at the point of completion entitled to convey such title as the contract states will be conferred. This case law is also reflected in the definition of "Seller" used throughout this code.
7. In view of the decision in *Edward Wong Finance Company Ltd v. Johnson, Stokes and Master* [1984] AC 296, paragraph 8(ii) of this code requires the Seller's Solicitor to undertake on completion to have the authority of the proprietor of every mortgage or charge to be redeemed to receive the sum needed to repay such charge. Such an undertaking remains an indispensable component of residential conveyancing. While the Seller's Solicitor will often not be specifically instructed by the Seller's mortgagee, the course of dealings between the solicitor and mortgagee in relation to the monies required to redeem the mortgage should at the very least evidence implicit authority from the mortgagee to the solicitor to receive the sum required to repay the charge (if, for example, the mortgagee has given its bank details to the solicitor for transmission of the redemption funds).

   On the basis of those dealings (and in the absence of any contrary statements from the mortgagee), the Seller's Solicitor should be in a position to give the undertaking to discharge (in the Law Society's recommended form, adapted where relevant for electronic discharges) and, for paper discharges (DS1, etc.), to undertake that they have identified the Seller's mortgagee to the extent necessary for the purpose of the buyer's solicitor's application to the Land Registry, on which the buyer's solicitor should be able to rely.

   The Seller's Solicitor should, if at all possible, receive an express confirmation from the Seller's mortgagee that the paper discharge, or an acknowledgment of discharge (for electronic discharges) will be supplied to them. If the Seller's mortgagee expressly prohibits the Seller's Solicitor from dealing with the redemption money, the Seller's Solicitor should notify the buyer's solicitor as soon as possible. The Seller's Solicitor and buyer's solicitor should consider whether in those circumstances they can adopt this code and, if so, the necessary variations.

8. In view of the decisions in *Angel Solicitors (a firm) v Jenkins O'Dowd & Barth (a firm)* [2009] EWHC 46 (Ch) and *Clark v Lucas Solicitors LLP* [2009] EWHC 1952 (Ch), the undertaking in paragraph 12(ii) of this code is to be taken, unless otherwise stated, as including confirmation that a satisfactory redemption statement has been obtained from the lender whose charge is to be redeemed.
9. Paragraph 14 of this code provides that nothing in this code overrides any rights and obligations of the parties under the contract or otherwise.
10. The Seller's Solicitor is to inform the buyer's solicitor of the mortgages or charges which will be redeemed or discharged (see paragraph 7 of this code). The information may be given in reply to completion information and undertakings (see paragraph 6 of this code). Such a reply may also amount to an undertaking.
11. Care must be taken if there is a sale and sub-sale. The sub-Seller's Solicitor may not hold the transfer nor be in a position to receive the funds required to discharge the Seller's mortgage on the property. Enquiries should be made to ascertain if the monies or some of the monies payable on completion should, with the authority of either the sub-Seller or the sub-Seller's Solicitor, be sent direct to the Seller's Solicitor and not to the sub-Seller's solicitor.
12. Care must also be taken if there is a simultaneous resale and completion. Enquiries should be made by the ultimate buyer's solicitor of the intermediate Seller's Solicitor as to the price being paid on that purchase. Having appointed the intermediate Seller's Solicitor as agent, the buyer's solicitor is fixed with the knowledge of an agent even without having personal knowledge.
13. For the purposes of paragraphs 10 and 13 of this code, as it will be in the best interests of the client to know as soon as possible that completion has taken place, it is assumed that procedures promptly to notify the arrival of monies will be in place.
14. Any variation of this code must be agreed in writing before completion.
15. These notes form part of this code and this code is to be construed by reference to them. These notes refer only to some of the points in this code that practitioners may wish to consider before agreeing to adopt it.

Appendix 6

Form of Undertaking to Discharge Building Society Mortgages Approved by The Law Society in Conveyancing Matters

In consideration of you today completing the purchase of........................

WE HEREBY UNDERTAKE forthwith to pay over to the..........................

Building Society the money required to redeem the mortgage/legal charge dated .... and to forward the receipted mortgage/legal charge to you as soon as it is received by us from the.......................... Building Society.

Appendix 7

UK Finance Mortgage Lenders' Handbook for England and Wales (last updated 1 July 2017)

1 GENERAL

Part 1 - Instructions and Guidance

Those lenders who instruct using the UK Finance Mortgage Lenders' Handbook certify that these instructions have been prepared to comply with the requirements of the Solicitors Regulation Authority (SRA's) Code of Conduct 2011 and the CLC Code of Conduct 2011.

1.1 The UK Finance Mortgage Lenders' Handbook is issued by UK Finance. Your instructions from an individual lender will indicate if you are being instructed in accordance with the Lenders' Handbook. If you are, the general provisions in part 1 and any lender specific requirements in part 2 must be followed.

1.2 References to 'we', 'us' and 'our' mean the lender from whom you receive instructions.

1.3 The Lenders' Handbook does not affect any responsibilities you have to us under the general law or any practice rule or guidance issued by your professional body from time to time.

1.4 The standard of care which we expect of you is that of a reasonably competent solicitor or licensed conveyancer acting on behalf of a mortgagee.

1.5 If you are regulated by the Solicitors Regulation Authority (SRA) the limitations contained in the SRA's Code of Conduct 2011 apply to the instructions contained in the Lenders' Handbook and any separate instructions.

1.6 You must also comply with any separate instructions you receive for an individual loan.

1.7 If the borrower and the mortgagor are not one and the same person, all references to 'borrower' shall include the mortgagor. Check part 2 to see if we lend in circumstances where the borrower and the mortgagor are not one and the same.

1.8 References to 'borrower' (and, if applicable, 'guarantor' or, expressly or impliedly, the mortgagor) are to each borrower (and guarantor or mortgagor) named in the mortgage instructions/offer (if sent to the conveyancer). This applies to references in the Lenders' Handbook and in the certificate of title.

1.9 References to 'mortgage offer' include any loan agreement, offer of mortgage or any other similar document.

1.10 If you are instructed in connection with any additional loan (including a further advance) then you should treat references to 'mortgage' and 'mortgage offer' as applying to such 'additional loan' and 'additional loan offer' respectively.

1.11 In any transaction during the lifetime of the mortgage when we instruct you, you must use our current standard documents in all cases and must not amend or generate them without our written consent. We will send you all the standard documents necessary to enable you to comply with our instructions, but please let us know if you need any other documents and we will send these to you. Check part 2 to see who you should contact. If you consider that any of the documentation is inappropriate to the particular facts of a transaction, you should write to us (see part 2) with full details and any suggested amendments.

1.12 In order to act on our behalf your firm must be a member of our conveyancing panel. You must also comply with any terms and conditions of your panel appointment.

1.12.1 Our instructions are personal to the firm to whom they are addressed and must be dealt with solely by that firm. You must not sub-contract or assign our instructions to another firm or body, nor may you accept instructions to act for us from another body, unless we confirm in writing otherwise.

1.13 If you or a member of your immediate family (that is to say, a spouse, civil partner, co-habitee, parent, sibling, child, step-parent, step-child, grandparent, grandchild, parent-in-law, or child-in-law) is the borrower and you are the sole practitioner, you must not act for us.

1.14 Your firm or company must not act for us if the partner or fee earner dealing with the transaction or a member of his immediate family is the seller, unless we say your firm may act (see part 2) and a separate fee earner of no less standing or a partner within the firm acts for us.

1.15 Your firm or company must not act for us if the partner or fee earner dealing with the transaction or a member of his immediate family is the borrower, unless we say your firm may act (see part 2) and a separate fee earner of no less standing or a partner within the firm acts for us.

1.16 If there is any conflict of interest, you must not act for us and must return our instructions.

1.17 Nothing in these instructions lessens your duties to the borrower. This does not apply if acting in accordance with Part 3 - Separate Representation Standard Instructions.

1.18 In addition to these definitions any reference to any regulation, legislation or legislative provision shall be construed as a reference to that regulation, legislation or legislative provision as amended, re-enacted or extended at the relevant time.

2. COMMUNICATING WITH THE LENDER

2.1 All communication between you and us should be in writing quoting the mortgage account or roll number, the surname and initials of the borrower and the property address. You should keep copies of all written communication on your file as evidence of notification and authorisation. If you use PC fax or e-mail, you should retain a copy in readable form.

2.2 If you require deeds or information from us in respect of a borrower or a property then you must first of all have the borrower's authority for such a request. If there is more than one borrower, you must have the authority of all the borrowers. This does not apply if acting in accordance with Part 3 - Separate Representation Standard Instructions.

2.3 If you need to report a matter to us, you must do so as soon as you become aware of it so as to avoid any delay. If you do not believe that a matter is adequately provided for in the Handbook, you should

- identify the relevant Handbook provision and the extent to which the issue is not covered by it.
- provide a concise summary of the legal risks.
- provide your recommendation on how we should protect our interest.

After reporting a matter you should not complete the mortgage until you have received our further written instructions. We recommend that you report such matters before exchange of contracts because we may have to withdraw or change the mortgage offer.

3. SAFEGUARDS

3.1 Safeguards for solicitors

3.1.1 This sub-section relates to solicitors and those working in practices regulated by the Solicitors Regulation Authority only.

3.1.2 You must follow the rules and guidance of your professional body relating to money laundering and comply with the current money laundering regulations and the Proceeds of Crime Act 2002 to the extent that they apply and you must follow other relevant guidance, for example, the Law Society of England and Wales mortgage fraud practice note; the Council for Licensed Conveyancers' Acting for Lenders and Prevention of Mortgage Fraud Code and Guidance, and take account of relevant regulatory warning notices.

3.1.3 If you are not familiar with the seller's regulated legal representatives (as defined by the Legal Services Act 2007 Schedule 4 and Schedule 2 paragraph 5), you must verify that they are currently on record with the Solicitors Regulation Authority, Council for Licensed Conveyancers or other legal regulatory body as practising at the address they have provided to you. Check part 2 to see whether we require you to notify us of the name and address of the regulated legal representatives (as defined above) acting for the seller.

3.1.4 If the seller does not have legal representation you should check part 2 to see whether or not we need to be notified so that a decision can be made as to whether or not we are prepared to proceed.

3.1.5 Unless you personally know the signatory of a document, you must ask the signatory to provide evidence of identity, which you must carefully check. You should check the signatory's identity against one of the documents from list A or two of the documents in list B:

List A

- a valid full passport; or
- a valid H M Forces identity card with the signatory's photograph; or
- a valid UK Photo-card driving licence; or
- any other document listed in the additional list A in part 2.

List B

- a cheque guarantee card, credit card (bearing the Mastercard or Visa logo) American Express or Diners Club card, debit or multi-function card (bearing the Switch or Delta logo) issued in the United Kingdom with an original account statement less than three months old; or
- a firearm and shot gun certificate; or
- a receipted utility bill less than three months old; or
- a council tax bill less than three months old; or
- a council rent book showing the rent paid for the last three months; or
- a mortgage statement from another lender for the mortgage accounting year just ended; or
- any other document listed in the additional list B in part 2.

3.1.6 You should check that any document you use to verify a signatory's identity appears to be authentic and current, signed in the relevant place. You should take a copy of it and keep the copy on your file. You should also check that the signatory's signature on any document being used to verify identity matches the signatory's signature on the document we require the signatory to sign and that the address shown on any document used to verify identity is that of the signatory.

3.2 Safeguards for licensed conveyancers

3.2.1 This sub-section applies to licensed conveyancers practices only.

3.2.2 You must follow the professional guidance of the Council for Licensed Conveyancers relating to money laundering and comply with the current money laundering regulations and the Proceeds of Crime Act 2002 to the extent that they apply and you must follow all other relevant guidance issued by the Council for Licensed Conveyancers.

3.2.3 If you are not familiar with the seller's regulated legal representatives (as defined by the Legal Services Act 2007 Schedule 4 and Schedule 2 paragraph 5), you must verify that they are currently on record with the Law Society or Council for Licensed Conveyancers or other legal regulatory body as practising at the address they have provided to you. Check part 2 to see whether we require you to notify us of the name and address of the regulated legal representatives (as defined above) acting for the seller.

3.2.4 If the seller does not have legal representation you should check part 2 to see whether or not we need to be notified so that a decision can be made as to whether or not we are prepared to proceed.

3.2.5 Unless you personally know the signatory of a document, you must ask the signatory to provide evidence of identity, which you must carefully check. You must satisfy yourself that the person signing the document is the borrower, mortgagor or guarantor (as appropriate). If you have any concerns about the identity of the signatory you should notify us immediately.

3.2.6 You should check that any document you use to verify a signatory's identity appears to be authentic and current, signed in the relevant place. You should take a copy of it and keep the copy on your file. You should also check that the signatory's signature on any document being used to verify identity matches the signatory's signature on the document we require the signatory to sign and that the address shown on any document used to verify identity is that of the signatory.

4. VALUATION OF THE PROPERTY

4.1 Check part 2 to see whether we send you a copy of the valuation report or if you must get it from the borrower. If you get a copy of the valuation report from the borrower, we do not expect you to check the content of that report matches the information we hold. For the avoidance of doubt, regardless of where the report is obtained from, you must carry out the checks detailed in sections 4.2 and 4.3.

4.2 You must take reasonable steps to verify that there are no discrepancies between the description of the property as valued and the title and other documents which a reasonably competent conveyancer should obtain, and, if there are, you must tell us immediately.

4.3 You should take reasonable steps to verify that the assumptions stated by the valuer about the title (for example, its tenure, easements, boundaries and restrictions on its use) in the valuation and as stated in the mortgage offer are correct. If they are not, please let us know as soon as possible (see part 2) as it will be necessary for us to check with the valuer whether the valuation needs to be revised. We are not expecting you to assume the role of valuer. We are simply trying to ensure that the valuer has valued the property based on correct information.

4.4 We recommend that you should advise the borrower that there may be defects in the property which are not revealed by the inspection carried out by our valuer and there may be omissions or inaccuracies in the report which do not matter to us but which would matter to the borrower. We recommend that, if we send a copy of a valuation report that we have obtained, you should also advise the borrower that the borrower should not rely on the report in deciding whether to proceed with the purchase and that he obtains his own more detailed report on the condition and value of the property, based on a fuller inspection, to enable him to decide whether the property is suitable for his purposes.

4.5 Where the mortgage offer states that a final inspection is needed, you must ask for the final inspection at least 10 working days before the advance is required. Failure to do so may cause delay in the issue of the advance. Your certificate of title must be sent to us in the usual way.

5. TITLE

5.1 Length of Ownership

5.1.1 Please report to us if the owner or registered proprietor has been registered for less than six months.

5.2 Seller Not The Owner or Registered Proprietor

5.2.1 Please report to us immediately if the person selling to the borrower is not the owner or registered proprietor unless the seller is:

- a personal representative of the registered proprietor; or
- an institutional mortgagee exercising its power of sale; or
- a receiver, trustee-in-bankruptcy or liquidator; or
- a developer or builder selling a property acquired under a part-exchange scheme; or
- a Registered Housing Provider (Housing Association) exercising a power of sale.

5.3 Conflict of Interest

5.3.1 If any matter comes to your attention which you should reasonably expect us to consider important in deciding whether or not to lend to the borrower (such as whether the borrower has given misleading information to us or the information which you might reasonably expect to have been given to us is no longer true) and you are unable to disclose that information to us because of a conflict of interest, you must cease to act for us and return our instructions stating that you consider a conflict of interest has arisen. This does not apply if acting in accordance with Part 3 - Separate Representation Standard Instructions.

5.4 Searches and Reports

5.4.1 In carrying out your investigation, you must ensure that all usual and necessary searches and enquiries have been carried out. You must report any adverse entry to us but we do not want to be sent the search itself. We must be named as the applicant in the Land Registry search.

5.4.2 In addition, you must ensure that any other searches which may be appropriate to the particular property, taking into account its locality and other features are carried out.

5.4.3 All searches except where there is a priority period must not be more than six months old at completion.

5.4.4 You must advise us of any contaminated land entries revealed in the local authority search. Check part 2 to see if we want to receive environmental or contaminated land reports (as opposed to contaminated land entries revealed in the local authority search). If we do not, you do not need to make these enquiries on our behalf.

5.4.5 Check part 2 to see if we accept personal searches.

5.4.6 Check part 2 to see if we accept search insurance.

5.4.7 If we accept personal searches or search insurance you must ensure that:-

- a suitably qualified search agent carries out the personal search and has indemnity insurance that adequately protects us; or
- the search insurance policy adequately protects us.

5.4.8 You are satisfied that you will be able to certify that the title is good and marketable unless stated otherwise in our specific requirements listed in part 2.

5.5 Planning and Building Regulations

5.5.1 You must by making appropriate searches and enquiries take all reasonable steps (including any further enquiries to clarify any issues which may arise) to ensure:

- the property has the benefit of any necessary planning consents (including listed building consent) and building regulation approval for its construction and any subsequent change to the property and its current use; and
- there is no evidence of any breach of the conditions of that or any other consent or certificate affecting the property; and
- that no matter is revealed which would preclude the property from being used as a residential property or that the property may be the subject of enforcement action.

If there is evidence of such a breach or matter but in your professional judgment there is no reasonable prospect of enforcement action and, following reasonable enquiries, you are satisfied that the title is good and marketable and you can provide an unqualified certificate of title, we will not insist on indemnity insurance and you may proceed.

5.5.2 If there is such evidence and all outstanding conditions will not be satisfied by completion, where you are not able to provide an unqualified certificate of title, you should report this to us in accordance with 2.3.

5.5.3 Check part 2 to see if copies of planning permissions, building regulations and other consents or certificates should be sent to us.

5.5.4 If the property will be subject to any enforceable restrictions, for example under an agreement (such as an agreement under section 106 of the Town and Country Planning Act 1990) or in a planning permission, which, at the time of completion, might reasonably be expected materially to affect its value or its future marketability, you should report this to us (see part 2).

5.5.5 If different from 1.11, contact point if the property is subject to restrictions which may affect its value or marketability.

5.6 Good and Marketable Title

5.6.1 The title to the property must be good and marketable free of any restrictions, covenants, easements, charges or encumbrances which, at the time of completion, might reasonably be expected to materially adversely affect the value of the property or its future marketability (but excluding any matters covered by indemnity insurance) and which may be accepted by us for mortgage purposes. Our requirements in respect of indemnity insurance are set out in section 9. If, based on your professional judgment, you are able to provide an unqualified certificate of title, we will not require indemnity insurance. You must also take reasonable steps to ensure that, on completion, the property will be vested in the borrower.

5.6.2 Good leasehold title will be acceptable if:

- a marked abstract of the freehold and any intermediate leasehold title for the statutory period of 15 years before the grant of the lease is provided; or
- you are prepared to certify that the title is good and marketable when sending your certificate of title (because, for example, the landlord's title is generally accepted in the district where the property is situated); or
- you arrange indemnity insurance. Our requirements in respect of indemnity insurance are set out in section 9.

5.6.3 A title based on adverse possession or possessory title will be acceptable if the seller is or on completion the borrower will be registered at the Land Registry as registered proprietor of a possessory title. In the case of lost title deeds, the statutory declaration must explain the loss satisfactorily;

5.6.4 We will also require indemnity insurance where there are buildings on the part in question or where the land is essential for access or services;

5.6.5 We may not need indemnity insurance in cases where such title affects land on which no buildings are erected or which is not essential for access or services. In such cases, you must send a plan of the whole of the land to be mortgaged to us identifying the area of land having possessory title. We will refer the matter to our valuer so that an assessment can be made of the proposed security. We will then notify you of any additional requirements or if a revised mortgage offer is to be made.

5.7 Flying Freeholds and Freehold Flats

5.7.1 If any part of the property comprises or is affected by a flying freehold or the property is a freehold flat, check part 2 to see if we will accept it as security.

5.7.2 If we are prepared to accept a title falling within 5.7.1:

- the property must have all necessary rights of support, protection, and entry for repair as well as a scheme of enforceable covenants that are also such that subsequent buyers are required to enter into covenants in identical form; and
- you must be able to certify that the title is good and marketable; and
- in the case of flying freeholds, you must send us a plan of the property clearly showing the part affected by the flying freehold.

If our requirements in the first bullet under 5.7.2 are not satisfied, indemnity must be in place at completion (see section 9).

5.8 Other Freehold Arrangements

5.8.1 Unless we indicate to the contrary (see part 2), we have no objection to a security which comprises a building converted into not more than four flats where the borrower occupies one of those flats and the borrower or another flat owner also owns the freehold of the building and the other flats are subject to long leases.

5.8.2 If the borrower occupying one of the flats also owns the freehold, we will require our security to be:

- the freehold of the whole building subject to the long leases of the other flats; and
- any leasehold interest the borrower will have in the flat the borrower is to occupy.

5.8.3 If another flat owner owns the freehold of the building, the borrower must have a leasehold interest in the flat the borrower is to occupy and our security must be the borrower's leasehold interest in such flat.

5.8.4 The leases of all the flats should contain appropriate covenants by the tenant of each flat to contribute towards the repair, maintenance and insurance of the building. The leases should also grant and reserve all necessary rights and easements. They should not contain any unduly onerous obligations on the landlord.

5.8.5 Where the security will comprise:

- one of a block of not more than four leasehold flats and the borrower will also own the freehold jointly with one or more of the other flat owners in the building; or
- one of two leasehold flats in a building where the borrower also owns the freehold reversion of the other flat and the other leaseholder owns the freehold reversion in the borrower's flat; check part 2 to see if we will accept it as security and if so, what our requirements will be.

5.9 Commonhold

5.9.1 If any part of the property comprises of commonhold, check part 2 to see if we will accept it as security.

5.9.2 If we are prepared to accept a title falling within 5.9.1, you must:

- ensure that the commonhold association has obtained insurance for the common parts which complies with our requirements (see 6.14);
- obtain a commonhold unit information certificate and ensure that all of the commonhold assessment in respect of the property has been paid up to the date of completion;
- ensure that the commonhold community statement does not include any material restrictions on occupation or use (see 5.6 and 5.10);
- ensure that the commonhold community statement provides that in the event of a voluntary termination of the commonhold the termination statement provides that the unit holders will ensure that any mortgage secured on their unit is repaid on termination;

- make a company search to verify that the commonhold association is in existence and remains registered, and that there is no registered indication that it is to be wound up; and
- within 14 days of completion, send the notice of transfer of a commonhold unit and notice of the mortgage to the commonhold association.

5.10 Restrictions on Use and Occupation

5.10.1 You must check whether there are any material restrictions on the occupation of the property as a private residence or as specified by us (for example, because of the occupier's employment, age or income), or any material restrictions on its use. If there are any restrictions, you must report details to us (see part 2). We may accept a restriction, particularly if this relates to sheltered housing or to first-time buyers.

5.11 Restrictive Covenants

5.11.1 You must enquire whether the property has been built, altered or is currently used in breach of a restrictive covenant. We rely on you to check that the covenant is not enforceable. If you are unable to provide an unqualified certificate of title as a result of the risk of enforceability you must ensure (subject to paragraph 5.11.2) that indemnity insurance is in place at completion of our mortgage (see section 9).

5.11.2 If there is evidence of a breach and, following reasonable enquiries, you are satisfied that the title is good and marketable; you can provide an unqualified certificate of title and the breach has continued for more than 20 years without challenge, then we will not insist on indemnity insurance.

5.12 First Legal Charge

5.12.1 On completion, we require a fully enforceable first charge by way of legal mortgage over the property executed by all owners of the legal estate. All existing charges must be redeemed on or before completion, unless we agree that an existing charge may be postponed to rank after our mortgage. Our standard deed or form of postponement must be used.

5.13 Balance of Purchase Price

5.13.1 You must ask the borrower how the balance of the purchase price is being provided. If you become aware that the borrower is not providing the balance of the purchase price from his own funds and/or is proposing to give a second charge over the property, you must report this to us if the borrower agrees (see part 2), failing which you must return our instructions and explain that you are unable to continue to act for us as there is a conflict of interest. You should also have regard to 6.3.1 with regard to any implications on the purchase price.

5.14 Leasehold Property

5.14.1 Our requirements on the unexpired term of a lease offered as security are set out in part 2.

5.14.2 There must be no provision for forfeiture on the insolvency of the tenant or any superior tenant.

5.14.3 The only situations where we will accept a restriction on the mortgage or assignment (whether by a tenant or a mortgagee) of the lease is where the person whose consent needs to be obtained cannot unreasonably withhold giving consent. The necessary consent for the particular transaction must be obtained before completion. If the lease requires consent to an assignment or mortgage to be obtained, you must obtain these on or before completion (this is particularly important if the lease is a shared ownership lease). You must not complete without them.

5.14.4 You must take reasonable steps to check that:

- there are satisfactory legal rights, particularly for access, services, support, shelter and protection; and

- there are also adequate covenants and arrangements in respect of the following matters, buildings insurance, maintenance and repair of the structure, foundations, main walls, roof, common parts, common services and grounds (the 'common services').

5.14.5 You should ensure that responsibility for the insurance, maintenance and repair of the common services is that of:

- the landlord; or
- one or more of the tenants in the building of which the property forms part; or
- the management company - see sub-section 5.15.

5.14.6 Where the responsibility for the insurance, maintenance and repair of the common services is that of one or more of the tenants the lease must contain adequate provisions for the enforcement of these obligations by the landlord or management company at the request of the tenant.

5.14.7 In the absence of a provision in the lease that all leases of other flats in the block are in, or will be granted in, substantially similar form, you should take reasonable steps to check that the leases of the other flats are in similar form. If you are unable to do so, you should effect indemnity insurance (see section 9). This is not essential if the landlord is responsible for the maintenance and repair of the main structure.

5.14.8 We do not require enforceability covenants mutual or otherwise for other tenant covenants.

5.14.9 We have no objection to a lease which contains provision for a periodic increase of the ground rent provided that the amount of the increased ground rent is fixed or can be readily established and is reasonable. If you consider any increase in the ground rent may materially affect the value of the property, you must report this to us (see part 2).

5.14.10 You should enquire whether the landlord or managing agent foresees any significant increase in the level of the service charge in the reasonably foreseeable future and, if there is, you must report to us (see part 2).

5.14.11 If the terms of the lease are unsatisfactory, you must obtain a suitable deed of variation to remedy the defect. We may accept indemnity insurance (see section 9). See part 2 for our requirements.

5.14.12 You must obtain on completion a clear receipt or other appropriate written confirmation for the last payment of ground rent and service charge from the landlord or managing agents on behalf of the landlord. Check part 2 to see if it must be sent to us after completion. If confirmation of payment from the landlord cannot be obtained, we are prepared to proceed provided that you are satisfied that the absence of the landlord is common practice in the district where the property is situated, the seller confirms there are no breaches of the terms of the lease, you are satisfied that our security will not be prejudiced by the absence of such a receipt and you provide us with a clear certificate of title.

5.14.13 Notice of the mortgage must be served on the landlord and any management company immediately following completion, whether or not the lease requires it. Please ensure that you can provide either suitable evidence of the service of notice on the landlord or management company or a receipt of notice. Check part 2 to see if a receipted copy of the notice or evidence of service must be sent to us after completion.

5.14.14 We will accept leases which require the property to be sold on the open market if re-building or reinstatement is frustrated provided the insurance proceeds and the proceeds of sale are shared between the landlord and tenant in proportion to their respective interests.

5.14.15 You must report to us (see part 2) if it becomes apparent that the landlord is either absent or insolvent. If we are to lend, we may require indemnity insurance (see section 9). See part 2 for our requirements.

5.14.16 You must check a certified or official copy of the original lease. In the case of a registered lease where the original lease is now lost, or destroyed by Land Registry, we are prepared to proceed provided you have checked an official copy of the lease from the Land Registry.

5.15 Management Company

5.15.1 In paragraphs 5.15.1 to 5.15.2 the following meanings shall apply:

- 'management company' means the company formed to carry out the maintenance and repair of the common parts;
- 'common parts' means the structure, main walls, roof, foundations, services, grounds and any other common areas serving the building or estate of which the property forms part.

If a management company is required to maintain or repair the common parts, the management company should have a legal right to enter the property; if the management company's right to so enter does not arise from a leasehold interest, then the tenants of the building should also be the members of the management company. If this is not the case, there should be a covenant by the landlord to carry out the obligations of the management company should it fail to do so. For leases granted before 1 September 2000, if the lease does not satisfy the requirements of paragraph 5.15.1 but you are nevertheless satisfied that the existing arrangements affecting the management company and the maintenance and repair of the common parts and you are able to provide a clear certificate of title, then we will rely on your professional judgement.

5.15.2 You should make a company search and verify that the company is in existence and registered at Companies House. You should also obtain the management company's last three years' published accounts (or the accounts from inception if the company has only been formed in the past three years). Any apparent problems with the company should be reported to us (see part 2). If the borrower is required to be a shareholder in the management company, check part 2 to see if you must arrange for the share certificate, a blank stock transfer form executed by the borrower and a copy of the memorandum and articles of association to be sent to us after completion (unless we tell you not to). If the management company is limited by guarantee, the borrower (or at least one of them if two or more) must become a member on or before completion.

5.16 Insolvency Considerations

5.16.1 You must obtain a clear bankruptcy search against each borrower (and each mortgagor or guarantor, if any) providing us with protection at the date of completion of the mortgage. You must fully investigate any entries revealed by your bankruptcy search against the borrower (or mortgagor or guarantor) to ensure that they do not relate to them.

5.16.2 Where an entry is revealed against the name of the borrower (or the mortgagor or guarantor):

- you must certify that the entry does not relate to the borrower (or the mortgagor or guarantor) if you are able to do so from your own knowledge or enquiries; or
- if, after obtaining office copy entries or making other enquiries of the Official Receiver, you are unable to certify that the entry does not relate to the borrower (or the mortgagor or guarantor) you must report this to us (see part 2). We may as a consequence need to withdraw our mortgage offer.

5.16.3 If you are aware that the title to the property is subject to a deed of gift or a transaction at an apparent undervalue completed within five years of the proposed mortgage then you must be satisfied that we will acquire our interest in good faith and will be protected under the provisions of the Insolvency (No 2) Act 1994 against our security being set aside. If you are unable to give an unqualified certificate of title, you must arrange indemnity insurance (see section 9).

5.16.4 You must also obtain clear bankruptcy searches against all parties to any deed of gift or transaction at an apparent undervalue.

5.17 Powers of Attorney

5.17.1 If any document is being executed under power of attorney, you must ensure that the power of attorney is, on its face, properly drawn up, that it appears to be properly executed by the donor and that the attorney knows of no reason why such power of attorney will not be subsisting at completion.

5.17.2 Where there are joint borrowers the power should comply with section 25 of the Trustee Act 1925, as amended by section 7 of the Trustee Delegation Act 1999, or with section 1 of the Trustee Delegation Act 1999 with the attorney making an appropriate statement under section 2 of the 1999 Act.

5.17.3 In the case of joint borrowers, neither borrower may appoint the other as their attorney.

5.17.4 A power of attorney must not be used in connection with a regulated loan under the Consumer Credit Act 1974.

5.17.5 Check part 2 to see if:

- the original or a certified copy of the power of attorney must be sent to us after completion; and
- where the power of attorney is a general power of attorney and was completed more than 12 months before the completion of our mortgage, whether you must send us a statutory declaration confirming that it has not been revoked.

5.18 The Guarantee

5.18.1 Whilst we recommend that a borrower should try to obtain a full title guarantee from the seller, we do not insist on this. We, however, require the borrower to give us a full title guarantee in the mortgage deed. The mortgage deed must not be amended.

5.19 Affordable Housing: Shared Ownership and Shared Equity

5.19.1 Housing associations, other social landlords and developers sometimes provide schemes under which the borrower will not have 100% ownership of the property and a third party will also own a share or will be a taking a charge over the title. In these cases you must check with us to see if we will lend and what our requirements are unless we have already provided these (see part 2).

5.20 Energy Technologies Installed on Residential Properties

5.20.1 Where a property is subject to a registered lease of roof space for solar PV panels we require you to check that the lease meets the UK Finance minimum requirements. Where you consider it does not, check part 2 to see whether you must report this to us and for details of any additional requirements.

5.20.2 If, after completion, the borrower informs you of an intention to enter into a lease of roof space relating to energy technologies, you should advise the borrower that they, or the energy technology provider on their behalf, will need to seek consent from us.

5.20.3 UK Finance has issued a set of minimum requirements where a provider/homeowner is seeking lender consent for a lease of roof space for solar PV panels. See part 2 for our additional requirements relating to these leases.

5.20.4 Check part 2 to see whether we require you to disclose the details of any existing Green Deal Plan(s) on a property.

6. THE PROPERTY

6.1 Mortgage Offer and Title Documents

6.1.1 The loan to the borrower will not be made until all relevant conditions of the mortgage offer which need to be satisfied before completion have been complied with and we have received your certificate of title.

6.1.2 You must check your instructions and ensure that there are no discrepancies between them and the title documents and other matters revealed by your investigations.

6.1.3 You should tell us (see part 2) as soon as possible if you have been told that the borrower has decided not to take up the mortgage offer.

6.2 Boundaries

6.2.1 These must be clearly defined by reference to a suitable plan or description. They must also accord with the information given in the valuation report, if this is provided to you. You should check with the borrower that the plan or the description accords with the borrower's understanding of the extent of the property to be mortgaged to us. You must report to us (see part 2), if there are any discrepancies.

6.3 Purchase Price

6.3.1 The purchase price for the property must be the same as set out in our instructions. If it is not, you must tell us (unless we say differently in part 2).

6.4 Incentives

6.4.1 You must obtain a completed copy of the UK Finance Disclosure of Incentives Form for any property that is yet to be occupied for the first time, or for the first time in its current form, for example, because of a renovation or conversion. You should only report incentives to the lender as instructed below.

6.4.2 You will not be able to send a completed Certificate of Title to the lender unless you have received the UK Finance Disclosure of Incentives Form. When you send a completed Certificate of Title you are confirming you are in receipt of a completed UK Finance Disclosure of Incentives Form from the developer/seller's conveyancer which complies with your instructions.

6.4.3 This does not override your duty to the lender via the instructions provided elsewhere in the Lenders' Handbook.

6.4.4 You must tell us (unless we say differently in part 2) if the contract provides for or you become aware of any arrangement in which there is:

- a cashback to the buyer; or
- part of the price is being satisfied by a non-cash incentive to the buyer or
- any indirect incentive (cash or non cash) or rental guarantee.

Any such arrangement may lead to the mortgage offer being withdrawn or amended.

6.4.5 You must report to us (see part 2) if you will not have control over the payment of all of the purchase money (for example, if it is proposed that the borrower pays money to the seller direct) other than a deposit held by an estate agent or a reservation fee of not more than £1,000 paid to a builder or developer.

6.5 Vacant Possession

6.5.1 Unless otherwise stated in your instructions, it is a term of the loan that vacant possession is obtained. The contract must provide for this. If you doubt that vacant possession will be given, you must not part with the advance and should report the position to us (see part 2).

6.6 Properties Let at Completion

6.6.1 Unless it is clear from the mortgage offer that the property is let or is to be let at completion then you must check with us whether we lend on 'buy-to-let' properties and that the mortgage is for that purpose (see part 2).

6.6.2 Where the property, or part of it, is already let, or is to be let at completion, then the letting must comply with the details set out in the mortgage offer or any consent to let we issue. If the letting does not comply, or no such details are mentioned, you must report the position to us (see part 2).

6.6.3 Check part 2 for whether counterparts or certified copies of all tenancy agreements and leases in respect of existing tenancies must be sent to us after completion.

6.6.4 Where the property falls within the definition of a house in multiple occupation under the Housing Act 2004 see part 2 as to whether we will accept this as security and if so what our requirements are.

6.7 New Properties - Building Standards Indemnity Schemes

6.7.1 If the property has been built or converted within the past ten years, or is to be occupied for the first time, you must ensure that it was built or converted under a scheme acceptable to us (see part 2 for the list of schemes acceptable to us and our requirements).

6.7.2 Where the cover under a scheme referred to in clause 6.7.1 is not yet in place before you send us the certificate of title, you must obtain a copy of a new home warranty provider's cover note from the developer. The cover note must confirm that the property has received a satisfactory final inspection and that the new home warranty will be in place on or before legal completion. This does not apply to self-build schemes. Check part 2 to see what new home warranty documentation should be sent to us after completion.

6.7.3 We do not insist that notice of assignment of the benefit of the new home warranty agreement be given to the builder in the case of a second and subsequent purchase(s) during the period of the insurance cover. Check part 2 to see if any assignments of building standards indemnity schemes which are available should be sent to us after completion.

6.7.4 Where the property does not have the benefit of a scheme under 6.7.1 and has been built or converted within the past 6 years check part 2 to see if we will proceed and, if so, whether you must satisfy yourself that the building work is being monitored (or where the work is completed was monitored) by a professional consultant. If we do accept monitoring you should ensure that the professional consultant has provided the lender's Professional Consultant's Certificate which forms an appendix to this Handbook or such other form as we may provide. The professional consultant should also confirm to you that he has appropriate experience in the design or monitoring of the construction or conversion of residential buildings and has one or more of the following qualifications:

- fellow or member of the Royal Institution of Chartered Surveyors (FRICS or MRICS); or
- fellow or member of the Institution of Structural Engineers (F.I.Struct.E or M.I.Struct.E); or
- fellow or member of the Chartered Institute of Building (FCIOB or MCIOB); or
- fellow or member of the Architecture and Surveying Institute (FASI or MASI); or
- fellow or member of the Chartered Association of Building Engineers (C.Build E MCABE and C.Build E FCABE); or
- member of the Chartered Institute of Architectural Technologists (formally British Institute of Architectural Technologists) (MCIAT); or
- architect registered with the Architects Registration Board (ARB). An architect must be registered with the Architects Registration Board, even if also a member of another institution, for example the Royal Institute of British Architects (RIBA); or
- fellow or member of the Institution of Civil Engineers (FICE or MICE).

6.7.5 At the time he issues his certificate of practical completion, the consultant must have professional indemnity insurance in force for each claim for the greater of either:

- the value of the property once completed; or
- £250,000 if employed directly by the borrower or, in any other case, £500,000. If we require a collateral warranty from any professional adviser, this will be stated specifically in the mortgage instructions.

6.7.6 Check part 2 to see if the consultant's certificate must be sent to us after completion.

6.8 Roads and Sewers

6.8.1 If the roads or sewers immediately serving the property are not adopted or maintained at public expense, there must be an agreement and bond in existence or you must report to us (see part 2 for who you should report to).

6.8.2 If there is any such agreement, it should be secured by bond or deposit as required by the appropriate authority to cover the cost of making up the roads and sewers to adoptable standards, maintaining them thereafter and procuring adoption.

6.8.3 If there is an arrangement between the developer and the lender whereby the lender will not require a retention, you must obtain confirmation from the developer that the arrangement is still in force.

6.8.4 Where roads and sewers are not adopted or to be adopted but are maintained by local residents or a management company this is acceptable providing that in your reasonable opinion appropriate arrangements for maintenance repairs and costs are in place.

6.9 Easements

6.9.1 You must take all reasonable steps to check that the property has the benefit of all easements necessary for its full use and enjoyment. All such rights must be enforceable by the borrower and the borrower's successors in title. If they are not check part 2 for our requirements.

6.9.2 If the borrower owns adjoining land over which the borrower requires access to the property or in respect of which services are provided to the property, this land must also be mortgaged to us unless all relevant easements are granted in the title of the land to be mortgaged to us and those rights are and remain enforceable in accordance with section 6.9.1.

6.10 Release of Retentions

6.10.1 If we make a retention from an advance (for example, for repairs, improvements or road works) we are not obliged to release that retention, or any part of it, if the borrower is in breach of any of his obligations under the mortgage, or if a condition attached to the retention has not been met or if the loan has been repaid in full. You should, therefore not give an unqualified undertaking to pay the retention to a third party.

6.10.2 Check part 2 to see who we will release the retention to.

6.11 Neighborhood Changes

6.11.1 The local search or the enquiries of the seller's conveyancer should not reveal that the property is in an area scheduled for redevelopment or in any way affected by road proposals. If it is please report to us (see part 2).

6.12 Rights of Pre-emption and Restriction on Resale

6.12.1 You must ensure that there are no rights of pre-emption, restrictions on resale, options or similar arrangements in existence at completion which will affect our security. If there are, please report this to us (see part 2).

6.13 Improvements and Repair Grants

6.13.1 Where the property is subject to an improvement or repair grant which will not be discharged or waived on completion, check part 2 to see whether you must report the matter to us.

6.14 Insurance

6.14.1 You must make reasonable enquiries to satisfy yourself that buildings insurance has been arranged for the property from no later than completion.

You should remind the borrower that they:

- Must have buildings insurance in accordance with the requirements of the mortgage contract no later than completion, and
- Must maintain such buildings insurance throughout the mortgage term.

7. OTHER OCCUPIERS

7.1 Rights or interests of persons who are not a party to the mortgage and who are or will be in occupation of the property may affect our rights under the mortgage, for example as overriding interests.

7.2 If your instructions state the name of a person who is to live at the property, you should ask the borrower before completing the mortgage that the information given by us in our mortgage instructions or mortgage offer about occupants is correct and nobody else is to live at the property.

7.3 Unless we state otherwise (see part 2), you must obtain a signed deed or form of consent from all occupants aged 17 or over of whom you are aware who are not a party to the mortgage before completion of the mortgage. If you are acting in accordance with part 3 - Separate Representation Standard Instructions you should refer to section 7 ('Other occupiers') of part 3.

7.4 We recognise that in some cases the information given to us or you by a borrower may be incorrect or misleading. If you have any reason to doubt the accuracy of any information disclosed, you should report it to us (see part 2) provided the borrower agrees; if the borrower does not agree, you should return our instructions.

8. CIRCUMSTANCES REQUIRING INDEPENDENT LEGAL ADVICE

8.1 Unless we otherwise state (see part 2), you must not advise:

- any borrower who does not personally benefit from the loan; or
- any guarantor; or
- anyone intending to occupy the property who is to execute a consent to the mortgage and you must arrange for them to seek independent legal advice.

If you are acting in accordance with part 3 - Separate Representation Standard Instructions you should refer to section 8 (Circumstances Requiring Independent Legal Advice) of part 3.

8.2 If we do allow you to advise any of these people, you must only do so after recommending in the absence of any other person interested in the transaction that such person obtains independent legal advice. Any advice that you give any of these people must also be given in the absence of any other person interested in the transaction. You should be particularly careful if the matrimonial home or family home is being charged to secure a business debt. Any consent should be signed by the person concerned. A power of attorney is not acceptable.

9. INDEMNITY INSURANCE

9.1 You must effect an indemnity insurance policy whenever the Lenders' Handbook identifies that this is an acceptable or required course to us to ensure that the property has a good and marketable title at completion. This paragraph does not relate to mortgage indemnity insurance. The draft policy should not be sent to us unless we ask for it. Check part 2 to see if the policy must be sent to us after completion.

9.2 Where indemnity insurance is effected:

- you must approve the terms of the policy on our behalf; and
- the limit of indemnity must meet our requirements (see part 2); and
- the policy must be effected without cost to us; and
- you must disclose to the insurer all relevant information which you have obtained; and
- the policy must not contain conditions which you know would make it void or prejudice our interests; and
- you must provide a copy of the policy to the borrower and explain to the borrower why the policy was effected and that a further policy may be required if there is further lending against the security of the property; and

- you must explain to the borrower that the borrower will need to comply with any conditions of the policy and that the borrower should notify us of any notice or potential claim in respect of the policy; and
- the policy should always be for our benefit and, if possible, for the benefit of the borrower and any subsequent owner or mortgagee. If the borrower will not be covered by the policy, you must advise the borrower of this.

10. THE LOAN AND CERTIFICATE OF TITLE

10.1 You should not submit your certificate of title unless it is unqualified or we have authorised you in writing to proceed notwithstanding any issues you have raised with us.

10.2 We shall treat the submission by you of the certificate of title as confirmation that the borrower has chosen to proceed with our mortgage offer and as a request for us to release the mortgage advance to you. Check part 2 to see if the mortgage advance will be paid electronically or by cheque and the minimum number of days notice we require.

10.3 See part 2 for any standard deductions which may be made from the mortgage advance.

10.4 You are only authorised to release the loan when you hold sufficient funds to complete the purchase of the property and pay all stamp duty land tax and registration fees to perfect the security as a first legal mortgage or, if you do not have them, you accept responsibility to pay them yourself. This does not apply if acting in accordance with Part 3 - Separate Representation Standard Instructions.

10.5 Before releasing the loan when the borrower is purchasing the property you must either hold a properly completed and executed stamp duty land tax form or you must hold an appropriate authority from the borrower allowing you to file the necessary stamp duty land tax return(s) on completion.

10.6 You must ensure that all stamp duty land tax returns are completed and submitted to allow registration of the charge to take place in the priority period afforded by the search.

10.7 You must hold the loan on trust for us until completion. If completion is delayed, you must return it to us when and how we tell you (see part 2).

10.8 You should note that although your certificate of title will be addressed to us, we may at some time transfer our interest in the mortgage. In those circumstances, our successors in title to the mortgage and persons deriving title under or through the mortgage will also rely on your certificate.

10.9 If, after you have requested the mortgage advance, completion is delayed you must contact us immediately after you are aware of the delay and you must inform us of the new date for completion (see part 2).

10.10 See part 2 for details of how long you can hold the mortgage advance before returning it to us. If completion is delayed for longer than that period, you must return the mortgage advance to us. If you do not, we reserve the right to require you to pay interest on the amount of the mortgage advance (see part 2).

10.11 If the mortgage advance is not returned within the period set out in part 2, we will assume that the mortgage has been completed, and we will charge the borrower interest under the mortgage.

11. THE DOCUMENTATION

11.1 The Mortgage

11.1.1 The mortgage incorporates our current mortgage conditions and, where applicable, loan conditions. If the mortgage conditions booklet is supplied to you with your instructions you must give it to the borrower before completion of the mortgage.

11.1.2 You should explain to each borrower (and any other person signing or executing a document) his responsibilities and liabilities under the documents referred to in paragraph 11.1.1 and any documents he is required to sign.

11.2 Signing and Witnessing of Documents

11.2.1 Except where we specify otherwise in our individual instructions, the signature of a document that needs to be witnessed must be witnessed by an independent person. The witness's signature must clearly record the witnessing of the signing of the document by the individual concerned, and the name and address of the witness must appear in legible form. All documents required at completion must be dated with the date of completion of the loan.

12. INSTALMENT MORTGAGES AND MORTGAGE ADVANCES RELEASED IN INSTALMENTS

12.1 Introduction

12.1.2 The borrower is expected to pay for as much work as possible from his own resources before applying to us for the first instalment. However, we may, if required, consider advancing a nominal sum on receipt of the certificate of title to enable the mortgage to be completed so long as the legal estate in the property is vested in the borrower.

12.1.3 The borrower is responsible for our valuer's fees for interim valuations as well as the first and final valuations.

12.2 Applications for Part of the Advance

12.2.1 As in the case of a normal mortgage account, funds for instalment mortgages may be sent to you. However, instalments (apart from the first which will be sent to you to enable you to complete the mortgage) can be sent directly to the borrower on request. We may make further payments and advances without reference to you.

12.3 Requests for Intermediate Funds

12.3.1 To allow time for a valuation to be carried out, your request should be sent to us (see part 2) at least 10 days before the funds are required.

12.4 Building Contract as Security

12.4.1 We will not lend on the security of a building contract unless we tell you to the contrary. As a result the mortgage must not be completed and no part of the advance released until the title to the legal estate in the property has been vested by the borrower.

13. MORTGAGE INDEMNITY INSURANCE OR HIGHER LENDING CHARGE

13.1 You are reminded to tell the borrower that we (and not the borrower) are the insured under any mortgage indemnity or similar form of insurance policy and that the insurer will have a subrogated right to claim against the borrower if it pays us under the policy. Different lenders call the various schemes of this type by different names. They may not involve an insurance policy.

14. AFTER COMPLETION

14.1 Registration

14.1.1 You must register our mortgage as a first legal charge at the Land Registry.

14.1.2 Where the borrower or mortgagor is a company an application to register the charge must be lodged at Companies House within the required time period.

14.1.3 Our mortgage conditions and mortgage deed have been deposited at the Land Registry and it is therefore unnecessary to submit a copy of the mortgage conditions on an application for registration.

14.1.4 Where the loan is to be made in instalments or there is any deferred interest retention or stage release, check part 2 to see whether you must apply to Land Registry on form CH2 for entry of a notice on the register that we are under an obligation to make further advances. If the mortgage deed states that it secures further advances, and that the lender is under an obligation to make them, there is no need to submit a form CH2 provided the mortgage deed also states that application is made to the Registrar for a note to be entered on the register to that effect and the mortgage deed bears a Land Registry MD reference at its foot.

14.1.5 The application for registration must be received by the Land Registry during the priority period afforded by the subsisting Land Registry or Land Charges search at the time of completion. Please check part 2 to see if we require the original mortgage deed and/or any other original title documents to be returned to us. You may use any available Land Registry process for registration including electronic registration. You should retain any original documents until you are satisfied that the registration is completed. You are not otherwise required by us to retain any original documents.

14.2 Title Deeds

14.2.1 All title deeds, official copies of the register (where these are issued by the Land Registry after registration), searches, enquiries, consents, requisitions and documents relating to the property in your possession must be held to our order pending completion of the retainer and you must not create or exercise any lien over them. Check part 2 for our requirements on what you should do with these documents following registration. If registration at the Land Registry has not been completed within three months from completion you must advise us in writing with a copy of any correspondence with the Land Registry explaining the delay.

14.2.2 You must only send us documents we tell you to (see part 2). You should obtain the borrower's instructions concerning the retention of documents we tell you not to send us.

14.3 Your Mortgage File

14.3.1 For evidential purposes you must keep your file for at least six years from the date of the mortgage before destroying it. You should retain on file those documents as specified in these instructions, and/or our individual instructions, and any other documents which a reasonably competent solicitor/conveyancer would keep. Microfiching, data imaging or material held electronically constitutes suitable compliance with this requirement. It is the practice of some fraudsters to demand the conveyancing file on completion in order to destroy evidence that may later be used against them. It is important to retain these documents to protect our interests.

14.3.2 Where you are processing personal data (as defined in the Data Protection Act 1998) on our behalf, you must;

- take such security measures as are required to enable you to comply with obligations equivalent to those imposed on us by the seventh data protection principle in the 1998 Act; and
- process such personal data only in accordance with our instructions. In addition, you must allow us to conduct such reasonable audit of your information security measures as we require to ensure your compliance with your obligations in this paragraph.

14.3.3 Subject to any right of lien or any overriding duty of confidentiality, you should treat documents comprising your file as if they are jointly owned by the borrower and us and you should not part with them without the consent of both parties. You should on request supply certified copies of documents on the file or a certified copy of the microfiche to either the borrower or us, and may make a reasonable charge for copying and certification. This does not apply if acting in accordance with Part 3 - Separate Representation Standard Instructions.

15. LEGAL COSTS

15.1 Your charges and disbursements are payable by the borrower and should be collected from the borrower on or before completion. You must not allow non-payment of fees or disbursements to delay the payment of stamp duty land tax, the lodging of any stamp duty land tax return and registration of documents.

16. TRANSACTIONS DURING THE LIFE OF THE MORTGAGE

16.1 Request for Title Documents

16.1.1 All requests for title documents should be made in writing and sent to us (see part 2). In making such a request you must have the consent of all of the borrowers to apply for the title documents.

16.2 Further Advances

16.2.1 Our mortgage secures further advances. Consequently, when a further advance is required for alterations or improvements to the property we will not normally instruct a member of our conveyancing panel but if you are instructed the appropriate provisions of this Handbook will apply.

16.3 Transfers of Equity

16.3.1 You must approve the transfer (which should be in the Land Registry's standard form) and, if we require, the deed of covenant on our behalf. Check part 2 to see if we have standard forms of transfer and deed of covenant.

16.3.2 When drafting or approving a transfer, you should bear in mind that:

- although the transfer should state that it is subject to the mortgage (identified by date and parties), it need give no details of the terms of the mortgage;
- the transfer need not state the amount of the mortgage debt. If it does, the figure should include both principal and interest at the date of completion, which you must check (see part 2 for where to obtain this);
- there should be no statement that all interest has been paid to date.

16.3.3 You must ensure that every person who will be a borrower after the transfer covenants with us to pay the money secured by the mortgage, except in the case of:

- an original party to the mortgage (unless the mortgage conditions are being varied); or
- a person who has previously covenanted to that effect.

16.3.4 Any such covenant will either be in the transfer or in a separate deed of covenant. In a transfer, the wording of the covenant should be as follows, or as close as circumstances permit: 'The new borrower agrees to pay the lender all the money due under the mortgage and will keep to all the terms of the mortgage.' If it is in the transfer, you must place a certified copy of the transfer with the deeds (unless we tell you not to in part 2).

16.3.5 If we have agreed to release a borrower or a guarantor and our standard transfer form (if any) includes no appropriate clause, you must add a simple form of release. The release clause should be as follows, or as close as circumstances permit: 'The lender releases ... from [his/her/their] obligations under the mortgage.' You should check whether a guarantor who is to be released was a party to the mortgage or to a separate guarantee.

16.3.6 You must obtain the consent of every guarantor of whom you are aware to the release of a borrower or, as the case may be, any other guarantor.

16.3.7 You must only submit the transfer to us for execution if it releases a party. All other parties must execute the transfer before it is sent to us. See part 2 for where the transfer should be sent for sealing. Part 2 also gives our approved form of attestation clause.

16.4 Properties to be let after Completion (other than 'Buy-to-Let')

16.4.1 If prior to completion of the retainer, the Borrower informs you of an intention to let the property you should advise the borrower that any letting of the property is prohibited without our prior consent. If the borrower wishes to let the property after completion then an application for consent should be made to us by the borrower (see part 2).

16.4.2 Check part 2 to see whether it is necessary to send to us a copy of the proposed tenancy when making the application.

16.4.3 If the application for our consent is approved and we instruct you to act for us, you must approve the form of tenancy agreement on our behalf in accordance with our instructions.

16.5 Deeds of Variation etc

16.5.1 If we consent to any proposal for a deed of variation, rectification, easement or option agreement, we will rely on you to approve the documents on our behalf.

16.5.2 Our consent will usually be forthcoming provided that you first of all confirm in writing to us (see part 2) that our security will not be adversely affected in any way by entering into the deed. If you are able to provide this confirmation then we will not normally need to see a draft of the deed. If you cannot provide confirmation and we need to consider the matter in detail then an additional administration fee is likely to be charged.

16.5.3 Whether we are a party to the deed or give a separate deed or form of consent is a matter for your discretion. It should be sent to us (see part 2) for sealing or signing with a brief explanation of the reason for the document and its effect together with your confirmation that it will not adversely affect our security.

16.6 Deeds of Postponement or Substitution

16.6.1 If we agree to enter into an arrangement with other lenders concerning the order of priority of their mortgages, you will be supplied with our standard form of deed or form of postponement or substitution. We will normally not agree to any amendments to the form. In no cases will we postpone our first charge over the property.

17. REDEMPTION

17.1 Redemption Statement

17.1.1 When requesting a redemption statement (see part 2) you should quote the expected repayment date and whether you are acting for the borrower or have the borrower's authority to request the redemption statement in addition to the information mentioned in paragraph 2.1. You should request this at least five working days before the expected redemption date. You must quote all the borrower's mortgage account or roll numbers of which you are aware when requesting the repayment figure. You must only request a redemption statement if you are acting for the borrower or have the borrower's written authority to request a redemption statement.

17.1.2 To guard against fraud please ensure that if payment is made by cheque then the redemption cheque is made payable to us and you quote the mortgage account number or roll number and name of the borrower.

17.2 Discharge

17.2.1 On the day of completion you should send the discharge and your remittance for the repayment to us (see part 2). Check part 2 to see if we discharge via a DS 1 form or direct notification to the Land Registry.

Appendix 8

City of London Law Society Land Law Committee Protocol for Discharging Mortgages of Commercial Property

1. INTRODUCTION

This proposed protocol has been prepared by a sub-group of the City of London Law Society Land Law Committee ("the Committee"), incorporating input from the Association of Property Lenders and the CLLS Financial Law Committee.

The Committee is aware that there are a number of different procedures in the City for dealing with the discharge of mortgages of commercial property and it is concerned that an undue amount of time can be spent in negotiating completion mechanics suitable for a transaction that is acceptable to the various parties. Unlike residential conveyancing, there is no Law Society endorsed code for completion that relates to commercial property.

Unlike the Law Society's Code for Completion by Post, which envisages that the Code will be adopted wholesale by solicitors, this protocol is intended to be a guide as to steps and procedures that solicitors (and their clients) might adopt and which the Committee regards as being appropriate and fair to all parties. It is for the parties to any transaction to decide on a case by case basis whether to apply the protocol, whether at all or with such variations as they might agree.

This protocol sets out procedure which the Committee considers appropriate in the most common situations, and also addresses an alternative scenario that reflects particular commercial circumstances and where the first procedure is not applicable.

Although principally designed for commercial transactions, the protocol may also be appropriate for high value residential transactions; although consideration should be given to the protocol's interaction with the Law Society's conveyancing quality scheme and the handbooks of the Council of Mortgage Lenders and Building Societies Association.

2. SCENARIO ONE - THE STANDARD TRANSACTION

This section describes a standard form of transaction which this protocol is designed to address. Where transactions have different features, then all or part of this protocol may be helpful.

The standard transaction is as follows:

- There is a property owned by the seller. Title to the property is registered at the Land Registry and is subject to a registered first legal mortgage in favour of the seller's bank. There are no other registered charges.
- It is proposed that the property will be sold to the buyer. On completion of the sale, the mortgage in favour of the seller's bank will be discharged out of the sale proceeds.
- The buyer is borrowing from the buyer's bank to assist with the purchase and, on completion, a new mortgage is to be granted to the buyer's bank.
- All four parties (the seller, the seller's bank, the buyer and the buyer's bank) are represented by different firms of solicitors. (The procedure is easily adapted if the seller's bank does not instruct separate solicitors.)
- The sale contract requires the purchase price (or the balance of the purchase price if a deposit has been paid) to be paid to the seller's solicitors on completion.

The key issues this protocol will seek to address include:

- the transfer of the completion monies between the various parties;

- the release of title deeds including all occupational lease documentation and other appropriate documentation relating to the property from the seller to the buyer;
- the completion (electronically or in paper form) of a discharge and the manner of its release to the buyer or the Land Registry as appropriate;
- suggested forms of undertaking that might be appropriate between the different firms of solicitors.

In addition, the protocol takes into account the following features:

- It is usual for the buyer and the buyer's bank to require the seller's bank's DS1 (the Land Registry form to discharge a mortgage) to be available on completion or to be signed in advance and delivered legally on completion with the original to follow shortly afterwards.
- The seller's bank will not want to release control of the DS1 until it knows that the redemption monies are in a solicitors' client account and it (or its solicitors) has the benefit of an unequivocal undertaking to pay the monies to the seller's bank shortly after completion and within a specified time frame to enable the mortgage to be fully discharged.

It is recognised that from the point of view of any particular organisation (whether property owner/investor or financier) they are likely to appear at different times on different sides of the standard transaction. The Committee considers that it is not appropriate for any organisation to insist on something when it is on one side of the transaction that it would not accept on the other side – nor should its solicitors.

Finally, the standard transaction assumes that the seller's bank will produce a paper discharge (in form DS1) and if appropriate a deed of release which will release chattels, contracts, warranties and other assets which are part of the sale but not released by a DS1. These documents will be collectively referred to as the DS1. Electronic discharges are addressed separately below.

3. PRIOR TO EXCHANGE OF CONTRACTS

- The seller and the buyer should agree the extent to which the protocol will be used.
- The contract will require the seller to provide an executed DS1 on completion, and evidence of authority of the signatories if appropriate (before agreeing this, the seller will need to check the seller's bank's requirements).
- The seller and the buyer must agree the timing of completion. Completion at 2pm should give the seller's solicitors time to send monies on to the seller/seller's bank after completion and to achieve same day funds, but this may depend on whether the seller's bank insists on having the money at an earlier time, for example, to unwind interest rate hedging arrangements. It may be that the seller's bank requires completion earlier in the day, and the seller's solicitors may want to check this before exchange, but the Committee regards 2.00pm as the usual contractual requirement.

Appendix 1 contains suggested drafting for inclusion in the contract.

4. BEFORE COMPLETION

- The DS1 shall be signed by the seller's bank and left undated and sent to the seller's solicitors or seller's bank's solicitors (held to the seller's bank's solicitors' order) with appropriate evidence of authority on the part of the seller's bank's signatories to sign (see paragraph 8 below).
- The seller's bank's redemption statement is to be provided to the seller and agreed, setting out what sum is required to complete on a particular day and whether there is a time cut off. If money is required early in the day because, for example, a swap needs to be unwound, it is not unusual for an extra day's interest to be added to the redemption monies to allow completion to take place after the cut-off time. Ideally the statement

should include a daily rate. If appropriate, there may be a rebate to the seller after completion. It is recognised that the seller's bank may not be able to provide the statement until the morning of completion.

- Completion monies will be transferred to the seller's solicitors (held to the buyer's solicitors' order). This scenario assumes that all of the monies are transferred to the seller's solicitors and then dispersed by them after completion.
- The seller's solicitors have before completion undertaken to the seller's bank's solicitors or the seller's bank to transfer the agreed redemption figure to the seller's bank immediately after completion (or by a specified time if appropriate).
- The seller's solicitors have before completion undertaken to the buyer's solicitors to hold the completion monies to the buyer's solicitors' order.

Appendix 2 contains suggested forms of undertaking for the seller's solicitors to give to the seller's bank or seller's bank's solicitors and to the buyer's solicitors.

5. COMPLETION TELEPHONE CALL

(This assumes completion by telephone. The same steps could be carried out at a meeting or at a combination of the two.)

- The solicitors for all parties will be on the same call.
- The parties agree that once the steps have started all of the steps will be completed.
- The seller's bank's solicitors unconditionally release the DS1 and title deeds. (Reference to "title deeds" includes other documents relating to the property that are kept with the deeds.)
- The buyer's solicitors unconditionally release funds to the seller's solicitors.
- The DS1, TR1 (transfer) and other transaction documents are completed in the usual way.
- The new mortgage is completed.
- The seller's solicitors undertake to send the completed DS1/TR1/title deeds to the buyer's solicitors. This could be a verbal undertaking made on the call, or a written undertaking issued in advance and effective from completion.
- The buyer's solicitors undertake to send the completed TR1 (etc.) to the seller's solicitors. The buyer's solicitors issue any agreed undertaking to the buyer's bank's solicitors.

6. AFTER COMPLETION

- The seller's solicitors comply with their undertaking to send the redemption money to the seller's bank.
- The seller's solicitors comply with their undertaking to send the completion documents to the buyer's solicitors.
- The buyer's solicitors comply with their undertakings to the seller's solicitors and the buyer's bank's solicitors.

7. SCENARIO TWO

Scenario One envisages that the completion monies will all be collected together by the buyer's solicitors and transferred to the seller's solicitors before completion and then dispersed by the seller's solicitors after completion. Although this is the preferred position, it is sometimes not achievable, and the main reasons for this are either that the seller's bank insists on having completion monies in its own solicitors' client account before completion can take place, or, alternatively, that there is a concern as to whether the money will arrive with the seller's bank early enough for their internal redemption to take place. It is recognised that it may be an absolute requirement of the seller's bank that the money is with their own solicitors at the point of completion.

Scenario Two envisages split transfers with monies being held by the seller's solicitors and the seller's bank's solicitors.

This scenario is an alternative. The main reason for preferring Scenario One to Scenario Two is that Scenario Two requires information about the seller's banking arrangements, that may be sensitive, to be divulged to third parties.

Paragraphs 3 – 6 above are repeated but with the following changes:

- The seller's solicitors' completion statement requires the completion monies due on completion to be split so that part is sent to the seller's solicitors and part to the seller's bank's solicitors. Both sets of solicitors will undertake to hold the money to the buyer's solicitors' order.
- In this scenario, the DS1 will be held by the seller's bank's solicitors.
- At completion, the seller's bank's solicitors undertake to send the completed DS1 to the buyer's solicitors after completion (and a copy to the seller's solicitors).
- The buyer's solicitors unconditionally release funds to the seller's solicitors or to the seller's bank's solicitors.
- The monies due to the seller's bank will be sent not by the seller's solicitors but by the seller's bank's solicitors.
- After completion, the seller's bank's solicitors comply with their undertaking to send the completed DS1 to the buyer's solicitors (and a copy to the seller's solicitors).

Scenario Two does not work if the seller's bank is not instructing separate solicitors. Scenario One, however, is easily adapted to this circumstance.

The contract provision in Appendix 1 and the completion undertakings in Appendix 2 will need to be adapted for Scenario Two.

There are also occasional circumstances where the seller's bank may want to insist that the money (or that part of it required to discharge the mortgage) is held by the seller's bank itself at the point of completion. The Committee does not regard this as being a preferred approach and consider that it should only be necessary in very unusual circumstances. If this is agreed by the buyer and the buyer's bank then alternative arrangements will need to be made.

8. PROPER EXECUTION OF DS1

The Committee regards it as being the responsibility of the seller's bank to provide a DS1 that is either executed in a form that gives automatic protection to a purchaser (i.e. under Section 44 of the Companies Act 2006), or the executed DS1 is accompanied by evidence of an appropriate facility letter or other arrangement with the Land Registry or an up to date and properly executed power of attorney or a legal opinion (particularly in the case of an overseas bank) or other appropriate evidence that will be acceptable to the Land Registry to enable the DS1 to be registered. This should be made available at the same time that the DS1 is signed and handed over on or before completion.

If the seller's bank is not separately represented by a firm of solicitors, then the parties will need to consider what the seller will be required to provide to enable the buyer's solicitors to register the DS1 at the Land Registry. The seller's solicitors and the buyer's solicitors will need to agree what is to be provided.

Any requirements of the buyer in this respect should be reflected in the contract and should be reviewed where appropriate with the seller's bank and its solicitors in the light of the seller's bank's signing arrangements and requirements for redemptions generally.

9. ELECTRONIC DISCHARGES

There are a small number of lenders who use electronic discharges (EDs). E-DS1s are generally not used on commercial property transactions. By the nature of an electronic discharge, there will be no physical DS1 handed over on completion, nor is it considered appropriate for the seller's bank's solicitors to give an undertaking relating to the discharge of the mortgage (as would be the case with residential conveyancing). In this case, it should be explained to the buyer and the buyer's solicitors that there is a risk that the electronic discharge will not be issued after completion and appropriate confirmation should be obtained directly from the seller's bank (given by somebody with appropriate authority) that the seller's bank will arrange for the electronic discharge to be issued to the Land Registry promptly following completion.

It is noted that even when there is an electronic discharge of the mortgage, it may still be necessary for there to be a deed of release, (as highlighted in the final paragraph of paragraph 2) and this should be dealt with as per Scenario One or Two as appropriate.

10. PROFESSIONAL INDEMNITY INSURANCE

Although by no means standard, it is not uncommon for a firm of solicitors that will be holding a large sum of money on completion to be asked to confirm whether it has appropriate professional indemnity insurance at a level to cover the amount. The Committee has no view on whether this should be regarded as normal practice and regards it as a matter between the parties and their solicitors.

11. PROCEEDS SHORTFALL

In the current market, it is not unusual for the sales proceeds of a property to be less than the amount required to discharge the mortgage. It is the view of the Committee that it is appropriate for the seller to be asked to confirm whether the sale proceeds will be sufficient to discharge the mortgage. If they are not (or if confirmation is not given) it will be appropriate for the buyer's solicitors to request confirmation before exchange of contracts that the seller's bank has approved both the terms of the sale contract and the completion mechanics referred to and that completion may occur and its mortgage will be discharged (even though the sale proceeds may be insufficient to discharge the mortgage). Committee members have had recent experience of difficulty at completion where a mortgagee, that is not being repaid in full and has not been fully consulted on the details of the transaction, creates particular difficulties when it comes to completion mechanics.

January 2014

APPENDIX 1

DRAFT CONTRACT PROVISION

1. DISCHARGE OF CHARGES

1.1 This clause [ ] applies where a charge over the Property is to be discharged on completion and the person with the benefit of that charge (the "Lender") is to execute the Discharge.

1.2 On completion the Seller shall supply to the Buyer's Solicitors an executed Discharge.

1.3 If the charge is registered at the Land Registry:

1.3.1 Where the Lender is represented by a conveyancer (which in this clause [ ] has the meaning set out in Rule 217A Land Registration Rules 2003), the Seller shall procure that, on or before the Completion Date, the Seller's Solicitors provide the Buyer's Solicitors with written details of the name, address and reference of the conveyancer acting on behalf of the Lender or written confirmation that the Seller's Solicitors are acting as the Lender's conveyancer; and

[1.3.2 Where the Lender is not represented by a conveyancer (as defined above), the Seller shall procure that at the same time as the Seller sends the executed Discharge to the Buyer's Solicitors, the Seller also sends to the Buyer's Solicitors a duly completed Form DS2 signed by [either] [the Seller's Solicitors] [or] [the Lender], to enable the Buyer's Solicitors to register the Discharge at HM Land Registry.]

["Discharge" means the DS1/DS3/deed of release as appropriate]

N.B.1 In clause 1.2, the parties should consider whether it is appropriate to include a requirement that evidence of proper execution (as referred to in paragraph 8) is provided. Similarly clause 1.3.2 may not be appropriate in every case.

N.B.2 This drafting does not apply to electronic discharges.

N.B.3 If a DS3 will be delivered on completion then 1.3.2 should be amended either to require the Seller to deliver a duly completed Form AP1 (rather than a DS2) to allow its registration or for it to provide sufficient information for the Buyer's Solicitors to be able to confirm the identity of the unrepresented Lender.

APPENDIX 2

DRAFT COMPLETION UNDERTAKINGS

1. UNDERTAKING GIVEN BY SELLER'S SOLICITORS TO SELLER'S BANK (OR SELLER'S BANK'S SOLICITORS)

This Undertaking relates to the sale of [ ] (the "Property") and the discharge of the registered charge over the Property (together the "Transaction"). [We confirm that you have authorised us to collect the Redemption Monies (defined below) on completion of the sale on your behalf.] We confirm that [we are holding] [on receipt we will hold] the signed DS1 [and deed of release (together] (the "DS1") [and the title deeds, as per Schedule 1] to your order. This is on the basis that we can complete the DS1 and hand it over unconditionally to the [buyer or the buyer's solicitors] [with the title deeds] on completion of the Transaction, but subject to the undertaking set out below.

We undertake as follows.

(i) We will not complete the Transaction unless we are holding in our client account at [bank] a sufficient sum to pay the amount (the "Redemption Monies") set out in the redemption statement in Schedule 2 (the "Redemption Statement").

(ii) Following completion of the Transaction we will [by the time specified in the Redemption Statement] [by [pm] on [date] give instructions to [bank] to transfer the Redemption Monies to your[1] account as set out in the Redemption Statement.

SCHEDULE 1 – Title Deeds

SCHEDULE 2 – Redemption Statement

2. UNDERTAKING GIVEN BY THE SELLER'S SOLICITORS TO THE BUYER'S SOLICITORS AND (IF APPROPRIATE) THE BUYER'S BANK'S SOLICITORS.

This Undertaking relates to the sale of [ ] (the "Property") and the discharge of the registered charge over the Property (together the "Transaction").

(i) We confirm that we are holding the Release Documents as set out in Schedule 1 signed by [ ] (the "Bank") and the Transaction Documents as set out in Schedule 2 signed by the seller and the title deeds listed in Schedule 3.

(ii) On receipt from the buyer's solicitors of the amount (the "Completion Amount") set out in the Completion Statement in Schedule 4 we will hold the Completion Amount strictly to the order of the buyer's solicitors until completion of the Transaction.

[Alternative to number (ii)]

On receipt from the buyer's solicitors of the sum of £[ ] [the first tranche] and from the buyer's bank's solicitors of the sum of £[ ] [the second tranche], together in aggregate the Completion Amount as set out in the Completion Statement in Schedule 4, we will hold the first tranche strictly to the order of the buyer's solicitors and the second tranche strictly to the order of the buyer's bank's solicitors until completion of the Transaction.

---

[1]This will need amending if the account is not that of the recipient of the undertaking.

(iii) Unless the Transaction has already completed, we will on your instructions return [the Completion Amount to the buyer's solicitors] [the first tranche to the buyer's solicitors and the second tranche to the buyer's bank's solicitors] as soon as possible within banking hours on that day or as soon as practicable thereafter.

[(iv) We confirm that we have the authority of the seller [and the Bank] to receive the Completion Amount on completion.]

(v) We confirm that the Completion Amount (together if appropriate with other monies we already hold in our client account) is sufficient to redeem the existing charge in favour of the Bank (as advised by the [Bank]) and that we are authorised by the Bank to complete the Release Documents on completion of the Transaction.

(vi) Following completion of the Transaction we shall send to the [buyer's solicitors/buyer's bank's solicitors] the Release Documents and the Transaction Documents by courier or DX. Where documents are sent by courier we shall not be responsible for any delay or failure to deliver by the courier provided that the courier instructed is a reputable and responsible company. Where documents are sent by DX we shall not be responsible for any failure in the DX system provided that we deliver them to the[DX depot].

[(vii) *If the discharge is electronic* We will notify the buyer's solicitors and the buyer's bank's solicitors as soon as confirmation is received from the Bank that the discharge has taken or is taking place.]

SCHEDULE 1 – Release Documents

SCHEDULE 2 – Transaction Documents

SCHEDULE 3 – Title Deeds

SCHEDULE 4 – Completion Statement

N.B. If the discharge is electronic, in addition to the inclusion of paragraph (vii), amendment will need to be made in relation to the reference to "Release Documents" in the undertaking.

Index